Professor Mabry's basic theme is that labor market phenomena can best be understood through economic analysis. He reasons that students must come to grips with basic economic principles in order to comprehend labor market subjects that are essentially economic in character. This premise does not however deny the contributions to our understanding of labor market phenomena made by allied disciplines such as history, psychology and other social sciences. In applying this modern approach to his new text, he concentrates on explaining how and why institutions and individuals operate and events occur in the labor market.

The wide range of standard topics treated includes collective bargaining, labor legislation, discrimination, and wages and fringe benefits. Much of the text's originality and distinction lies in the fact that along with an in-depth analysis of each topic, all pertinent literature in the area is reviewed, thus exposing the reader to a broad sampling of current research in labor and manpower economics.

Coverage of the following relevant topics is also unique in a text of this level:

- Analysis of wage-price stabilization programs
- An integrated macro model of the labor market
- Extensive analysis of wage differentials
- The economics of health in the human resources approach
- Recent developments in the Phillips curve approach to inflation and unemployment
- Using macro models in manpower planning

Economics of Manpower
and the Labor Market

Economics of Manpower and the Labor Market

BEVARS D. MABRY
Bowling Green State University

INTEXT EDUCATIONAL PUBLISHERS

New York and London

Library of Congress Cataloging in Publication Data
Mabry, Bevars DuPre, 1928-
    Economics of manpower and the labor market.
    Bibliography: p.
    1. Labor supply. 2. Labor economics.
I. Title.
HD5706.M14   331.1'1   73-4217

ISBN 0-7002-2438-6

Intext Educational Publishers
257 Park Avenue South
New York, New York 10010

Text design by Paula Wiener

To My Most Treasured Human Resources—
Mary Jeanne, Michael, and Maria

Contents

Part II. Evolution of Labor Market Analysis

Part III. The Micro Theory of the Labor Market

Preface

The latest textbooks in labor economics have in common a basic premise—that economic phenomena in the labor market can best be understood through economic analysis. This premise does not deny that such phenomena have demographic and geographical dimensions, historical and anthropological roots, sociological and psychological manifestations, and ethical and legal implications. Furthermore, it readily acknowledges that these allied disciplines can enrich our perspective of the phenomena. Yet, if the student is to comprehend that which is essentially economic in character, he must come to grips with the economic principles which condition the phenomena. This new approach emphasizes to a lesser degree the itemization, history, and description of the various events and institutions in the labor market. Instead, it concentrates more on explaining how and why events of given magnitudes occur and how and why institutions operate. I have employed this approach in the preparation of this textbook.

Labor market analysis can be used to develop consistent answers to job market problems to which students have been or soon will be exposed. In many cases, these problems can only be understood through such analysis. Instructors will find here many topics that are customarily treated in courses in labor and manpower economics, and some which are not. The Index and Table of Contents will reveal numerous references to unions, bargaining, labor force participation, employment, unemployment, labor legislation, etc. The book's originality and distinction lies, I trust, not in the kind of topics presented, but in the method by which they are treated. Not only has an in-depth analysis been undertaken, but the literature pertinent to important topics has been reviewed in order to expose students to a sample of the type of scientific research that is continuing in the field of labor and manpower economics. Inevitably, I suppose, this collection of topics and references will fail to correspond completely with the choices of some instructors. I hope, of course, that my omissions and slights are sufficiently few so that the instructor may easily remedy them through supplemental assignments. I have tried to keep in mind that no book can cover everything, and especially that contemporary American students demand that their professors expose them to more material than that covered by their textbook.

Sufficient material has been included to occupy a class for a full semester. However, I would be very much surprised if an instructor chose to cover all of the contents. He is, of course, free to pursue chapters and topics of greatest interest and relevance to himself and his class. Some, for example, may choose to delete those chapters (4 and 5) on the development of labor market analysis. Others may wish to emphasize the principles of bargaining (Chapter 13) or manpower planning (Chapter 23), while still others may wish only to sample the analysis of discrimination (Chapter 17) or the macro fundamentals of wages and employment (Chapter 18). Perhaps only in advanced classes will the instructor wish to hold his students responsible for the more rigorous material in appendixes and footnotes.

Although the ideas for this text have been germinating for some fifteen years, it was not until 1967, while I was a Visiting Professor at Thammasat University in Bangkok, Thailand under the auspices of the Rockefeller Foundation, that I began writing. Upon my return to Bowling Green State University, progress proceeded slowly until early 1971 because administrative responsibilities preempted my time and attention. I am grateful to Bowling Green University for providing released time in the winter quarter of 1971 to update, revise, and expand the manuscript; and I remain indebted to Thammasat University and the Rockefeller Foundation for their continued support during a second visiting professorship in Bangkok in late 1971 and 1972 during which the manuscript was completed. I have discussed portions of the book with Professors Lawrence Stifel and William McCleary of Thammasat University and the Rockefeller Foundation; Paul B. Trescott of Southern Methodist University; and Neal Browne, Frank Zahn, Thomas Hall, and J. David Reed of Bowling Green State University. Their counsel and advice have been most helpful. Also, I have benefited from the reviews of Peter S. Barth and Ernst W. Stromsderfer, whose suggestions have, I feel, led to significant improvement in the text. Mrs. Tanomjit Phanchet Kompor, a former graduate assistant, collected much of the original data used in the chapter on manpower planning and deserves my appreciation for her dedicated efforts. Among the many typists who have from time to time struggled over revisions of the manuscript, my greatest indebtedness goes to Mrs. Stanley Reynolds and Miss Suphaporn Kanchanaranya, who have unselfishly assisted me in meeting deadlines. I, of course, accept responsibility for errors, omissions, and the presentation of ideas contained herein.

I also gratefully acknowledge the permission to quote from the published material of the following journals, publishers, and copyright holders: W. B. Saunders and Company, Columbia University Press, St. Martins Press, The Conference Board, Regional Science Association, *The Economic Journal*, *Industrial Relations*, *Industrial and Labor Relations Review*, *Journal of Political Economy*, and *Western Economic Journal*.

Part I

INTRODUCTION

1

An Introduction to Labor Markets

A market is defined as an arrangement under which buyers and sellers are brought together for purposes of entering into an exchange. The arrangement may take place in a specific setting, such as at a farmers' market in an urban center for the purchase and sale of produce. The arrangement may also encompass a network of localities and facilities, such as exist for the purchase and sale of financial securities in an organized stock exchange, with its linkages to brokers, dealers, and agents across the country. A labor market is, therefore, an arrangement whereby buyers and sellers of human energies, skills, and time are brought together. In exchange for human services, wages and/or salaries are paid, and these remunerations may be either in money or in commodities or services. The rise of the labor market has paralleled the rise in the use of paid labor.

Labor markets may be viewed in terms of various dimensions. Ordinarily, we are concerned with a labor market at a point or within a given interval of time. At the most elemental level we can consider the labor market of the firm. The firm possesses a structure of jobs for which it requires labor. The source from which it draws its labor may be considered the firm's labor market. In recent years, the process by which workers are allocated among jobs within the firm has been identified as "an internal labor market." There is also a geographical dimension to labor markets. We may be concerned with the demand for and supply of labor of all the contiguous firms in a locality. Our local labor market may be either urban or rural. Ordinarily, the geographical size of an identifiable labor market is determined by the access of participants to the market. Hence, when the geographical area is expanded to include a region, a state, or even the

3

country as a whole, it should be obvious that for a large number of participants access may be only a potential, and that such an enlargement of the concept of a labor market implies some mobility of participants. Labor markets may be delineated by occupations, and we may thereby refer to the market for engineers or teachers or physicians. Other partitions of the concept of a labor market are possible. We may partition the labor market by groups and refer to the "teen-age market" or the "market for female labor." Obviously, the number of combinations in which buyers and sellers of labor can be classified is large, but no matter how we arrange them, our various classifications of labor markets will be interconnected.

Institutional Changes in the Labor Market

Various institutional and environmental forces influence the scope and nature of labor markets. These forces have changed over the years and correspondingly have altered the nature of labor markets in the United States. In this section, we shall briefly examine some of the changes that have occurred.

Environmental Changes

In an agrarian society where farms are family owned and operated, and where most of the means of subsistence are home produced, labor markets utilizing paid labor are almost nonexistent. There is little or no opportunity for labor services to be bought or sold. The abundance of cheap land in the early years of this country perpetuated the agrarian system and kept the labor market small. Labor markets did exist in cities of the United States, but they were relatively small—little more than towns—and isolated from one another. Moreover, the existence of the frontier provided a "safety valve" which permitted escape from dependence upon the labor market if working conditions became oppressive. Thus, the frontier helped to preserve the agrarian character of the labor force. As Turner has written,[1]

> "Whenever social conditions tended to crystallize in the East, whenever capital tended to press upon labor or political restraints to impede the freedom of the mass, there was this gate to the free conditions of the frontier. . . . Men would not accept inferior wages, and a permanent position of social subordination, when this promised land of freedom and equality was theirs for the asking."

[1] Frederick Jackson Turner, *The Frontier in American History* (New York: Holt, Rinehart and Winston, Inc., 1920), p. 259.

The frontier was not officially declared closed until 1890, and it was not until 1920 that the urban population exceeded the rural population.

Because land transportation was inefficient and slow, early cities were almost always located along navigable rivers, at their mouth or at junctions with others, or along the sea coast. The accessibility of the hinterland, on which cities depended for their raw materials and food, determined the size of cities and the extent of their labor markets. The revolutionary transportation development that transformed the size of cities and enlarged labor markets from local to regional or national ones was the advent of the railroad. Not only was physical mobility of labor enhanced, but the competition of the products produced by them became regional or national in scope.

Government land policy was instrumental in shaping the character of the labor market. Anxious to fill the country with people, Homestead Acts provided cheap land to facilitate the westward movement. Land grants to railroad companies facilitated the extension of railroads across the country. The tolerance of the Federal government of slavery until the Civil War not only perpetuated the plantation system, but established in the minds of Americans a class system based on color that continues to generate labor market problems to this day.

Manufacturing developed slowly in the United States. In 1810 the largest factory in the country was worth less than $250,000, and it has been estimated that manufacturing output did not exceed $200 million.[2] The 1849 Census of Manufacturing revealed that output was only about $1 billion. By 1899 it had increased to $11 billion and in 1939 to almost $57 billion. Hence, as a source of employment and of urban growth, manufacturing increased slowly, accelerating after the Civil War. It was then that America's great cities began to rise.

Immigration policies were liberal until 1920. In the 100-year period prior to this, some 36 million persons immigrated to this country, although it is estimated that 30% returned to their homeland. The majority were adult males, and only about 15% were skilled.[3] These immigrants first settled in urban centers, although many later moved westward. As unskilled laborers, they helped to build the canals, the roads, and the railroads of the country, and later found employment in the mushrooming factories. The closing of the door in 1920 to immigrants deprived these factories of an important supply of cheap labor.

[2] Herman F. Krooss, *American Economic Development* (Englewood Cliffs: Prentice-Hall, Inc., 1955), p. 304.
[3] *Ibid.*, p. 89.

Concentration in Labor Markets

Industrial concentration became prevalent after the Civil War, although the seeds of the movement were planted when states legitimatized the corporate charter in the 1830s and 1840s as a means of raising capital. The trust device as a means of concentrating economic control was first used in the late 19th century, followed by holding companies and mergers. Of course, they were eventually regulated by antitrust legislation, but in the interim these concentrations of economic power came to control the employment destinies of sizable proportions of American laborers. In manufacturing, about one-fourth of workers were employed in establishments with $1 million or more of capital; in 1939, the percentage was 55. The largest 200 corporations, only a minute fraction of 1% of all corporations, today employ about one out of every eight workers in the United States. Such large buyers of labor were able to dominate the wage bargain and to exercise great control over the terms under which labor was purchased.

Attempts to form combinations of workers as a means to influence the terms under which labor was sold can be traced back to 1778 when, in New York City, journeymen printers pursued joint action to secure an increase in wages. Because the supply of labor could more easily be controlled through apprenticeship programs, early attempts to form labor organizations succeeded only among the skilled trades. Most of these organizations were local in their sphere of influence, although in 1834 a short-lived effort to establish a national labor federation in the National Trades' Union took place. National labor organizations developed after the 1850s when railroads had contributed to the establishment of national markets. Trade unions became aware that they could maintain and protect labor standards against the competition of lower-paid labor only by organizing on a wider geographical front. Attempts to organize the less skilled workers continued throughout the 19th century and into the 20th century, but except for isolated industries such as coal mining, these efforts were unsuccessful on a permanent basis. The lack of success was attributed to a number of factors; the "individualism" of the American public, continued by agrarianism; the lack of class consciousness, conditioned by the ready availability of land; an unfavorable, even hostile, legal and judicial environment; the prevalence of a plentiful supply of cheap immigrant labor; and the ability of large businesses to use their power to win economic contests with industrial unions. In 1886 the American Federation of Labor was established, which promoted the organization of national craft unions.

Not until the Great Depression, when immigration portals had been closed and the frontier had long since disappeared, did public sentiment become sufficiently favorable to permit legislation to be enacted sympathetic to the organization of nonskilled labor. Such organization did proceed with increasing rapidity in the late 1930s and in the 1940s, and today labor unions of both the skilled and unskilled are important organizations in establishing the terms under which labor is sold. Although subsequent legislation has modified the power of organized labor, much as the antitrust laws have affected the power of large-scale businesses, labor unions remain the single most important institution in the labor market, with, perhaps, the exception of the Federal government. In recent years, again as the result of a combination of favorable market conditions and permissive legislation, professional employees and public servants have joined unions in large numbers.

Protective Labor Legislation

By specifying who may participate in the labor market and under what terms, labor legislation has altered the market structure. Legislation to protect children was first enacted in 1848 in Pennsylvania, where the minimum age for workers in commercial firms was set at 12 years. Other states followed this example. Legislation was enacted for Federal employees in 1840 and 1868 regulating the length of the workday, but early efforts of states to establish such regulations were ruled unconstitutional by the U.S. Supreme Court. Later, efforts of states were directed to enacting maximum hours legislation to apply to women and children to prevent their exploitation. Moreover, age restrictions for minors were imposed in hazardous occupations, and conveniences for women employees were specified. Federal attempts to regulate child labor in 1916 and 1919 were declared unconstitutional, and a proposed constitutional amendment in 1924 failed because it was ratified by an insufficient number of states. Similarly, early minimum wage legislation was rejected as being unconstitutional. However, by the middle of the 1930s, the Supreme Court had come to accept the social desirability of protecting women and children in employment, and legislation limiting their hours of work, the conditions under which work could be performed, including age limitations, and the minimum wage to be paid to them, had been enacted in numerous states. Hours of work and minimum wages were regulated in interstate commerce in 1938 by the Federal Fair Labor Standards Act, and in 1949 this act was amended to prohibit the shipment in interstate commerce of goods on which illegal child labor, as defined by the Act, had been used in production.

Related to child labor laws are compulsory school attendance statutes which exist in most states. Both the Federal government and states have enacted legislation establishing minimum safety standards in business establishments. Wage payment laws that establish obligatory procedures in the form and method of disbursing wages are common, also, to most states.

These statutes alter the labor market by excluding large numbers of potential participants. Except for family employment or in very limited endeavors, the labor of children under age 14 has been generally abolished. For years, women were prohibited in many states from working at night, and hence their eligibility for jobs with these hours of work was nullified. However, it should be noted that enforcement of such state laws was never stringent and recent Federal legislation defining equal employment rights for women probably preempts much of this state legislation. Minimum wage laws and hours legislation establish legal limits to the terms of exchange of labor, and conditions of employment are regulated by other protective legislation. Employers who cannot provide these minimum standards can legally be excluded from the labor market, whereas low productivity workers may not be employed if the employer's judgment is that they are not worth the expense of hiring them.

Education

In 1910, less than 60% of the population age 5 to 20 years were attending school, and only one-half of those age 16 and less than 10% of those age 20 were in school. By 1969, about 90% of all persons between ages 5 and 20 were enrolled in school, and 90% of those of age 16 and 27% of those of age 20 were still in school. Median years of schooling for all races of persons 25 years and older had increased to 12.1 years in 1969 from 8.4 years in 1940. For whites in the age group 20–24 years, the median years of schooling in 1969 was 12.7 years; for nonwhites it was 12.2 years. In 1940, the corresponding median years of schooling were 8.7 and 5.8 years. Such dramatic changes in the proportion of young people attending school affects the labor market in two ways. First, it removes large numbers from full-time participation in the labor market and, hence, tends to lengthen the lag in time from changes in the birth rate to changes in the rate of growth of the labor force. Second, it leads to an upgrading in the quality and trainability of the labor force. This in turn tends to increase hiring standards, which will adversely affect the employment opportunities of those persons whose educational attainments are below the standards.

Female Participation

A combination of factors has led to an increase in the proportion of women who participate in the labor market (Chart 1.1). First, differences in educational attainments between males and females have disappeared over the years, upgrading the employability of females. Second, changes in birth control technology have not only reduced the average number of children that women now have, but have permitted more rational family planning. For most women, child-bearing ends by age 35. Third, advancing

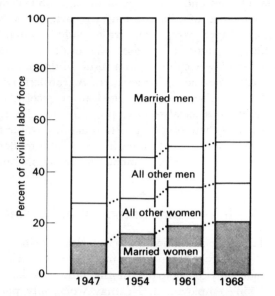

CHART 1.1. Married women represent a growing proportion of the labor force. Source: U.S. Department of Labor. *Manpower Report of the President, 1969*, p. 54.

technology in home production has reduced the amount of time and drudgery associated with homemaking, and has provided women with more time and energy for use in other activities. Fourth, changes in job content and the availability of part-time jobs have increased employment opportunities for women. Nevertheless, a smaller proportion of women participate in the labor market in the United States than in some other industrial countries—for example, in Japan, U.S.S.R., or Sweden.

Population Changes

As the death rate has declined and life expectancy has increased, more older workers are found in the labor market. Concurrently, along with the decline in the birth rate, the average age of the labor force has increased. This has implications on the number of inexperienced workers entering the labor market, the mobility of the labor force, and its trainability. Moreover, the urbanization of society has altered family patterns and labor force participation. In rural economies, work activity, of some type, of most members of the family of school age or above is common. Opportunities for family employment, however, are more limited in urban societies. The weakening of family ties and of a sense of familial obligations to the aged has been a consequence of urbanization. In part, this is a result of an increased number of aged parents relative to children; that is, the burden of caring for the aged, more numerous as a result of the declining death rate, is shared among fewer children, as a result of the smaller size of urban families. The burden has therefore increased. A transference of this private obligation to a social one, since the aged must receive care, has been manifested in the various social security programs for the aged. The labor market consequence of these programs is to make it possible for the aged to withdraw from the labor force at an earlier age. The tendency appears to be moving toward an earlier retirement age for more and more older workers.

The Importance of the Labor Market

The sellers of labor are identified as being either primary or secondary members of the labor force. A person is a member of the primary labor force if he (or she) normally participates in the labor market; that is, he is employed or seeking employment. He may work only part of the time, although most participants prefer full-time employment because they or their families depend upon employment for their livelihood. Members of the secondary labor force are those whose commitment to the labor market is marginal. If job opportunities develop at unusually attractive wages, a secondary worker may be drawn into the labor force. Others may withdraw if they feel that suitable job opportunities are scarce or if other roles assume primary importance. The teen-ager who gives up employment to return to school belongs to the secondary labor force, as does the housewife who enters the job market only because her husband has been temporarily disabled and cannot work.

Persons who are engaged in the labor market as sellers of labor are called labor force participants. Labor force participation rates measure the percentage of persons in any given population, however defined, that are in the labor force. Hence, there are labor force participation rates for males, females, Whites, nonwhites, teen-agers, the aged, etc. Ordinarily, labor force participation rates are higher for groups whose constituents are normally in the primary labor force; participation rates are lower for groups whose members are in the secondary labor force.

For most persons, participation in the labor market is their most important economic activity. It is the primary source of their income which determines their level of living. Their choice of job and occupation influences their self-image, their life expectancy, their economic security, where they will reside, their friends, and perhaps even their choice of a mate and the number of children they will have. In no other single activity, except perhaps sleeping, will they spend as much of their lives as they will in their jobs.

As important as the labor market is to their economic well-being, few participants really understand the phenomena they are experiencing. They possess even less understanding of the general principles by which the labor market functions. We cannot blame them for this, because they have not had the opportunity to acquire the perspective and the analytical tools that would permit them to interpret their experiences. Without training in economic analysis, how could they be expected to answer such questions as the following?

1. What types of manpower problems are capable of being studied through labor market analysis? How can labor market analysis contribute to a solution of these problems?

2. How has our understanding of the functioning of the labor market evolved? How are concepts of the labor market related to other economic ideas?

3. What determines the worth of occupations? Why are wages in some jobs higher than in others? How does the market adjust to wage differences? What are the economic considerations that influence an employer in the selection and remuneration of his employees?

4. How can the concept of capital formation be used to comprehend the development of human resources? What does a youth need to know to choose and plan rationally for a career?

5. What motivates people to enter or leave the labor force? How else might they use their time?

6. How do unions affect employment opportunities and benefits? Do they really increase wages, and if so, through what process?

7. Does it make any difference in terms of wages in what industry or region a person is employed? If so, why do wages differ among these labor markets? What forces, if any, are at work to eliminate such differences?

8. Is a man worth more than a woman in the market? Is a White worker more valuable than a Black one? Is a younger person more desirable than an older worker? Why might the market make such judgments as these?

9. How do minimum wages affect employment opportunities? Why do unions support minimum wages? Do minimum wages help the poor or the disadvantaged?

10. Why do workers change jobs? How can fringe benefits lower costs?

How important are such benefits in the total compensation picture?
11. Are our tools of analysis the same for analyzing household and firm phenomena of the labor market as those used in explaining phenomena on a national level? In the aggregate, what kind of changes occur in the structure of the labor market? Who are affected, and at what times and to what degree?
12. Why do prices and unemployment change? Is there any relationship between their changes? What can the government do to modify price and unemployment changes?
13. How are indices of wages, prices, and unemployment related to other economic phenomena? Should the government consider these relationships in formulating policies, and if so, how?
14. Why do skills become obsolete? Who bears the brunt of unemployment, and why? What type of manpower policies are necessary to remedy labor market imperfections? How successful have past manpower policies been?
15. Is it possible to estimate manpower needs before they arise and to develop plans to meet these needs? What are the consequences of labor market imbalances on national economic objectives? How are manpower needs related to economic growth?

These are complex questions indeed. If most participants had had the benefit of university training in economics and of a course such as the one in which this text is used, they would have acquired the capacity to handle such questions. In fact, it would not at all be inappropriate for your professor to examine you at the end of the term on these very questions.

The Changing Composition of the Labor Force

Definitional Changes

The labor force that your grandfather entered was different from the one that his son entered or the one that you will enter. As late as 1930, workers who were 10 years of age were counted as gainfully employed, although at that time fewer than 6% of children of ages 10 to 15 were at work. In 1940 a formal definition of the labor force was adopted and it excluded persons under 14; in 1967, persons under 16 were excluded. Ordinarily, to be in the labor force one must be employed or actively looking for employment. Prior to 1967, it was sufficient to be counted as in the labor force if one were unemployed, but not looking for work only because it was believed that no job was available. Since 1967, such an unemployed person is excluded from the definition. One may be employed but not at work if he is temporarily ill, on vacation, on strike, or absent from his job because of bad weather. One is also unemployed if he is on temporary layoff, has a job but begins work within the next thirty days, or has sought no employment in the preceding four weeks. (See Chart 1.2.)

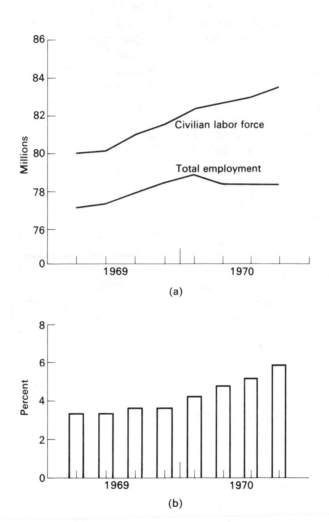

(a)

(b)

CHART 1.2. Employment did not keep pace with labor force growth during 1970, so the unemployment rate rose sharply. (a) Labor force and employment (quarterly data, seasonally adjusted). (b) Unemployment rate.

Source: Department of Labor. *Manpower Report of the President, 1971*, p. 18.

Age

The age composition of the labor force depends upon such varied institutional conditions as school attendance, pension programs, prior birth rates, and reductions in death rates. In 1941, about 21.5% of the labor force was composed of persons age 16 to 24. In 1960, this percentage was only 17.6, reflecting the lower birth rate of the 1930s, the period of the Great Depression. In 1970 the percentage had risen to 23.2, where it will remain until about 1980. However, by 1985 the percentage in this age category is expected to fall to 20.8, again reflecting the decline in the birth rate experienced in the late 1960s. However, Black and other races have a higher percentage of their labor force in the 16–24 age category, reflecting in part a higher birth rate and in part a lower rate of attendance in higher educational institutions. The percentage of the labor force in 1940, age 65 and over, was about 4%. In 1960 it had risen to 4.7%, but fell to 3.7% in 1970 and will continue to decline to 3.2% by 1985 as more and more are able to retire with social security benefits. (See Chart 1.3.)

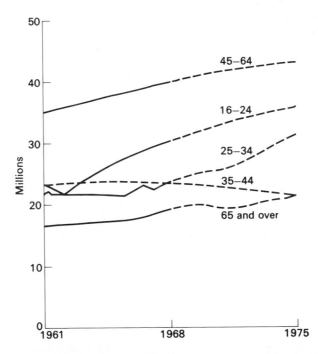

CHART 1.3. Population is declining in 35–44-year age group, rising in other groups.

Source: U.S. Department of Labor, based on data from the U.S. Department of Commerce. *Manpower Report of the President, 1969,* p. 51.

Sex and Race

Females are more active in the labor force than formerly. In 1930 less than 22% of the labor force was made up of women. By 1960, females had increased to about 32% of the labor force and in 1970 to 36.7%, where their percentage is expected to stabilize until 1985. The primary explanation for this seems to be the greater labor force participation of married women. In 1947, about 51% of all single women participated in the labor force, but only 20% of wives with husbands, and 37% of married women without husbands so participated. However, in 1970, although 53% of single women were labor force participants, representing only a small change, about 40% of married women in both categories participated in the labor force. Many of them have part-time jobs.

The racial composition of the labor force has also changed, with nonwhites becoming a larger percentage. From 10.6% of the labor force in 1940, nonwhites made up 11.1% in 1970 and are expected to comprise 12.5% in 1985.

Occupational Changes

Occupations have been grouped into four broad classifications: (1) white collar, (2) blue collar, (3) service, and (4) farm workers. The most pronounced changes in these categories are found among white-collar occupations and farm workers. From 1958 to 1970, the former increased as a percent of employment from 42.6 to 48.3, while the latter decreased over the same period from 8.5 to 4.0%. Blue-collar occupations have also slightly declined as a percent of total employment, 37.0 to 35.3, whereas service occupations have registered only a slight increase, from 11.9 to 12.4%. (See Tables 1.1 and 1.2.)

Women have always had a majority of their sex employed in white-collar occupations, and the majority is becoming greater as they appear to be shifting from other employment to this category. A greater proportion of men also is moving into white-collar occupations, where about 41% of all men were employed in 1970. In fact, since 1958, the percentage of men in all three nonfarm occupations has increased, although very slightly in blue-collar and service employment, whereas their percentage in farm employment has declined from 10.4 in 1958 to 5.3 in 1970.

The most marked change in the occupational distribution of Blacks and other races has been the increase in the proportion in white-collar employment. Between 1958 and 1970, the percentage of nonwhites in this occupational category increased from 13.8 to 17.9. The proportion in blue-collar employment also increased slightly, from 40.7 to 42.2%, whereas the proportions in service occupations and on farms declined. Thus, there appears to be a distinct trend in occupational upgrading among nonwhites.

TABLE 1.1
EMPLOYMENT BY OCCUPATION GROUP, 1960, 1968, AND PROJECTED 1980 REQUIREMENTS

(Numbers in thousands)

Occupation Group	Actual				Projected 1980[a] Requirements	
	1960		*1968*			
	Number	*Percent Distri- bution*	*Number*	*Percent Distri- bution*	*Number*	*Percent Distri- bution*
Total employment	65,778	100.0	75,920	100.0	95,100	100.0
Professional and technical workers	7,469	11.4	10,325	13.6	15,500	16.3
Managers, officials, and proprietors	7,067	10.7	7,776	10.2	9,500	10.0
Clerical workers	9,762	14.8	12,803	16.9	17,300	18.2
Sales workers	4,224	6.4	4,647	6.1	6,000	6.3
Craftsmen and foremen	8,554	13.0	10,015	13.2	12,200	12.8
Operatives	11,950	18.2	13,955	18.4	15,400	16.2
Service workers	8,023	12.2	9,381	12.4	13,100	13.8
Nonfarm laborers	3,553	5.4	3,555	4.7	3,500	3.7
Farmers and farm laborers	5,176	7.9	3,464	4.6	2,600	2.7

[a] These projections assume 3% unemployment and a services economy in 1980, as described in *The U.S. Economy in 1980* (Washington: Department of Labor, Bureau of Labor Statistics, 1970), Bulletin 1673.
Source: *Manpower Report of the President, April 1971*, p. 297.

Projected employment by occupational group for 1980 is presented in Table 1.1. The absolute decline in agricultural employment and the relative decline in employment in goods-producing industries, compared with the relative increase in employment in service-producing industries, is shown in Table 1.2. These data are consistent with the trends noted in the preceding discussion.

The Nature of Labor Market Analysis

An automobile mechanic needs to know how the parts of an automobile fit together before he can repair it. A physician needs to understand how the human body functions in order to be able to diagnose its infirmities, and if he is a specialist, he has an in-depth knowledge of the manner in which a subsystem of the body performs, its biochemical composition and its response to chemical prescriptions, and its interaction with other subsystems. Similarly,

the same interval of time each will have a magnitude, and our set of observations will cover a range of magnitudes for each variable. Next, pair the observations at consistent time intervals and plot them on a graph. We will obtain a familiar scatter diagram consisting of a number of dots, where each dot represents a magnitude of y and a magnitude of x, at a moment of time. Next, imagine that there exists a straight line passing through the scattering of dots such that the line minimizes the total vertical distances from each dot to the straight line. The line must pass through the dot representing the means (average value of the observations) of x and y. If the dots are indeed scattered, and if the distances between dots above the line and the line are treated as positive deviations, and the distances between dots below the line and the line are treated as negative deviations, it will be true that the arithmetic sum of the deviations will total zero, and the average of this arithmetic sum will also total zero. In order to avoid this problem, we first square the deviations so that all become positive, and then sum the squared deviations. The square of each deviation is called a variance; hence, the sum of all squared deviations measures the total variance. The line of best fit, logically, must be the line that has the lowest sum of squared deviations, and hence the lowest total variance. The line can be represented in equation form as follows:

$$y = a + bx$$

where y is treated as the dependent variable explained by the independent variable x; a and b are constants. Variations in the magnitude of x may explain much or little of the variations in y. If much is explained, the total variance of the dots will be relatively small. The equation states that as x varies by one unit, y will vary by b units. If x has zero value, y will have a value of a. The parameter a is treated as a fixed summation of all the other events (or independent variables) that can influence the magnitude of y, where these other events are treated as fixed in magnitude. Hence, even if x has no value, the value of y is still influenced, by an amount equal to a, by fixed quantities of other variables. The equation is a linear regression equation.

Now, let us assume that we have observed a given magnitude of x. Without actually knowing the true associated value of y, the equation allows us to estimate this value. If variations in x truly explain most or all of the variations in y, then our estimated value of y should be very close to its actual value. There are various measures which permit us to conclude that the equation does or does not establish a relationship between y and x, and that variations in x do or do not explain much about the variations in y.

First, it is possible that x has no relationship with y, that changes in x have no effect on changes in y. If this were so, the value of b should equal zero. It is possible that the true value of b does equal zero, but in the process of observation, random errors have occurred and resulted in a calculation of b different from zero. What we wish to know is whether or not it is reasonable to assume that the true value of b is different from zero. Given our calculation of the value of b, how probable is it that we have obtained a nonzero value of b when its true value is zero? If we find that the chances of getting the nonzero value of b when its true value is zero is, say, only one in twenty, or one in one hundred, we can be confident that there is high probability that x and y *are* related.

A computation of the standard error of estimate of b, S_b, lets us determine the range in which most of the estimates of the value of b fall. Approximately 95% of the estimates of b will lie within two standard errors of b. For example, if b is 25 and the standard error of b is 2, then 95% of the estimates of b will fall between the values of 21 and 29, values which obviously are significantly different from zero. Similarly, about 99% of the estimates of b will lie within three standard errors of estimates of b. Let us take another example. Let our estimate of b now equal 5, while the standard error of estimate remains at 2. If we wish to be confident that only one time out of twenty will the true value of b equal zero when the estimated value of b is nonzero, we can accept a b value of 5 as being significantly different from zero. However, if we wish to be even more confident and consider the probability that only one time out of one hundred are we willing to make a mistake in assuming a nonzero value of b when its true value is zero, then we cannot accept a value of b equal to 5 as being significantly different from zero. Our test then is to discover if the following relationship is satisfied:

$$b - tS_b > 0, \qquad b > tS_b, \qquad b/S_b > t$$

If the ratio of b to S_b exceeds t, we are reasonably satisfied that our estimate of b is nonzero and that a true relationship exists between x and y. The more confident we wish to be of this relationship the greater must be our value of t.

Similarly, we may wish to know whether there is any influence of nonspecified variables, fixed in amount, on y. Does our estimate of a depart significantly from zero? To answer this, we need to know the standard error of estimate of a, i.e., S_a. Normally, in a regression equation the custom is to put in parentheses, below the value of the a and b parameters, the value of their standard errors. With such a procedure, it is easy for another person to interpret whether or not the parameter estimates are or are not significantly different from zero. Consider the following two examples:

$$y = 30 + 10x \qquad\qquad (1.1)$$
$$(8) \quad\ (6)$$

We can see that $S_a = 8$ and $S_b = 6$, so that $a/S_a = 3.75 > 2$ and $b/S_b = 1.67 < 2$. Consequently, at a one-in-twenty (0.05) level of confidence, we accept that the value of a is truly nonzero, but we do not accept that the value of b is truly nonzero.

$$y = 1.86 + 0.75x \tag{1.2}$$
$$(0.98) \quad (0.15)$$

In this example, $S_a = 0.98$ and $S_b = 0.15$; $a/S_a = 1.89 < 2$ and $b/S_b = 5 > 2$. We do not accept that the true value of a is nonzero, but we do accept that the true value of b is nonzero.

Our regression equation (line) can also be used to measure the proportion of the variations in y that are explained by the variations in x. As we have seen, the equation tells us that by allowing x to change by one unit, y will change by b units. If, in actuality, we find that when x changes by one unit, y changes by more or less than b units, then some other event must have influenced the change in y. Part of the actual change in y has been explained by the change in x; part of the actual change in y has not been explained by x. Treating the variations in terms of squared deviations (variance) we get the following measure:

$$R^2_{yx} = \frac{\text{explained variance}}{\text{total variance}}$$

$$= \frac{\text{explained variance}}{\text{explained variance} + \text{unexplained variance}}$$

$$r_{yx} = \sqrt{R^2_{yx}}$$

R^2_{yx} is called the coefficient of determination; r is the correlation coefficient. By taking the square root of R^2 to obtain r, we reverse the process of squaring the deviations. Although r is a better measure of the proportion of deviations of y that are explained by deviations of x, the R^2 is the measure most frequently reported. This is owing in part to the statistical properties of R^2. Either measure, however, can be used as an estimate of how completely the independent variable explains the dependent variable. As r approaches 1, more and more of the deviations in y are explained by x. As r approaches zero, fewer and fewer of y's deviations are explained. If r equals zero, we say that x has no explanatory power on y; whatever happens to x will not influence y. If the true value of b is zero, then r also will be zero. If the true value of b is negative, r also will be negative, which means that x has a negative influence on y.

Instead of using one independent variable to explain variations in y, we may use several. When more than one independent variable is used, our equation will no longer represent a line but rather a plane. Our equation will, therefore, define a plane of best fit to a scatter of dots (observations) in n dimensions. The value of n depends upon the number of variables in the equation. When y can be influenced by a number of independent variables, the trick is to select from this set those variables which exert the greatest influence on y. We can have standard errors of estimate for each parametric coefficient b_i of the independent variables x_i. These standard errors are used just as in the linear equation to evaluate the relationship between the independent variable and y. Similarly, there are R^2 and r that measure the proportion of explained variance and deviation of y to the total. It is possible that we may select some variables which have no influence on y, or at least appear to have no influence. Consider an equation with three independent variables, x_1, x_2, x_3,

$$y = a + b_1 x_1 + b_2 x_2 + b_3 x_3$$

Suppose we find that $b_1 = 8$, $b_2 = 3$, and $S_{b_1} = 2$, $S_{b_2} = 1.8$. May we conclude that there is no relationship between x_2 and y? Not necessarily. It may be that if we were to compute the relationship between x_1 and x_2, we might find that their correlation coefficient is 0.98, or 98% of the deviations in x_1 are explained by the deviations in x_2. Now it is obvious that x_1 is related to y; x_1 does explain some of the variation in y. But since most of the variation in x_1 is explained by the variation in x_2, adding x_2 to our equation does not appreciably improve the relationship between y and the x_i's. Hence, b_2 may have a value insignificantly different from zero. We could drop x_2 and not lose much in the explanation of y. Similarly, we could drop x_1 but retain x_2 and probably not lose much by way of explaining y. Alternatively, it may be that by retaining both x_1 and x_2, we improve somewhat our explanation of y. By examining only the b_i value and their respective standard errors of estimate, we may be led to exclude one of the variables as having no relationship to y, and in so doing we may lose some explanatory power. We need to know, therefore, whether or not there is any relationship among our independent variables, such as the one described between x_1 and x_2. That is, we need to know if any of our independent variables are intercorrelated and to what extent. Unfortunately, this information is not always provided. The student is reminded, therefore, to interpret with caution those b_i values which appear to be nonsignificantly different from zero.

Another interesting possibility occurs when all the b_i values are significantly different from zero, yet only a small part of the variance in the dependent variable is explained by the variance in the independent variables. Consider the following:

$$Y = 20.0 + 3.0x_1 + 2.5x_2 + 1.8x_3 + 3.4x_4$$
$$ (3.7) \quad (0.8) \quad (0.6) \quad (0.3) \quad (0.9)$$

$$R^2 = 0.16$$

In this illustration, there is less than one chance out of one hundred that the b_i values are truly zero, given their estimated values. Thus, at a confidence level of (0.01) we may say that all the x_i's are significantly related to the y variable. Yet, less than one-fifth of the variance is explained by these independent variables. Obviously, there are other important events which influence the dependent variable that have not been included in the equation. In fact, it is possible that y is influenced by so many events that no one single event can explain very much of the variance in y.

In many of the chapters to follow, we shall report on studies which have used regression equations to identify and measure relationships between economic variables. With this introduction, the student should be equipped to interpret the meaning of these equations.

Discussion Questions

1. Define the labor market for the following type of employers: an automobile electronic parts manufacturer; a retail clothing store; a university; the National Labor Relations Board; a commercial farm; a hospital.
2. Explain how the development of the automobile has altered the nature of the labor market. What parallels exist with respect to the size of the labor market during the automotive era and that of the railroad?
3. Suppose that immigration restrictions had not been imposed in the 1920s. How would this have affected the contemporary labor market?
4. Until 1940, the Bureau of the Census measured "the gainfully employed" rather than the "labor force." Why? Would the former be a more appropriate measure of participants in the job market of an underdeveloped country? Explain.
5. Explain the effect of the Civil Rights Act on the labor market. Of Equal Wage Laws. Of school integration.
6. How can employment and unemployment both increase at the same time? Which is a better measure of economic activity? Why?
7. The birth rate during the 1960s has declined, the median age of marriage is lower, and the proportion of the population in the most active childbearing ages has increased. Is this paradoxical? Explain. What does this imply about the labor force in the 1980s?
8. "It may be all right in theory, but it will never work in practice." Evaluate critically this often repeated phrase.

2

Manpower Problems and the Labor Market

Humans possess a bundle of aptitudes and inherent abilities which can be and are developed through educational and training programs to perform multitudinous tasks. In varying degrees, the source of training may be informal and provided by the family, as it essentially is in underdeveloped countries, in which the bulk of the population are agriculturally employed, or it may be formal and provided by institutions such as the school or the firm. In modern societies using advanced technology, the training provided by the family perhaps has more psychological than economic importance, since vocational training has tended to become the province of formal institutions. Normally, the child receives love, nurture, and aspirational and motivational reinforcement and direction within the family, whereas the school system provides the child with the basic requirements of communicative and computational skills. Both groups participate in developing the social skills of cooperation within prescribed rules. At some point a collective but joint decision is made by the child, the parents, and the educational system that sufficient intellectual skills have been acquired, along with a sufficient level of social and physical maturation, to enable the child to cope with the economic realities of life. At this time the person enters the labor market searching for some economic institution that is willing to purchase the use of his acquired skills. If the purchasing institution deems that the offered bundle of skills, aptitudes, and ability is sufficient to be successfully transformed into a productive unit of human inputs through further specialized training and supervision, the person is then employed.

The point at which the child stops his formal education depends on many variables: his aspirations, his intellectual abilities, his family's ability and willingness to offer financial support. The extent of training which he receives upon employment also is subject to many variables: his previous level of education, his aptitudes and abilities, the job for which he is hired, and the kind of firm in which he is employed.

Additional skills are developed in the work environment. Some of these skills also are social, such as learning to work with others, to accept responsibility for material and the welfare of others, to follow directions, and to make decisions. Other skills relate to techniques of physical movement, of manipulation of materials, of timing of actions, and of following sequences of motions. To the extent that the acquisition of these skills enhances the bundle of abilities possessed by the individual and desired by other firms, the number of employers to whom he may sell his services is enlarged. Consequently, his work experience also affects his employability should he, for some reason, seek to change jobs.

In any interval of time, new participants are entering the labor force whereas others, already in the labor force, are in the process of changing jobs. The number entering the labor force depends, among other variables, upon the educational structure, the level of economic development, and the birth rate of some fifteen to twenty years earlier. The number changing jobs depends upon the current level of aggregate demand, the pace and nature of technological change, the changing nature of consumer demand, and the perception of employed individuals of the chances of improving their economic position via a change. These active seekers of employment are offering a wide spectrum of abilities, aptitudes, skills, and experience, and *they represent the flow of manpower into the labor market*. The capabilities of humans to perform tasks, then, is the meaning of the term *manpower*. These capabilities are inputs into production—a resource—and collectively constitute the human resources of a society.

On the other hand, the firms and institutions utilize a wide variety of human capabilities to perform the myriad of tasks required in a modern, technologically sophisticated economy. As the economy expands, more tasks must be performed and more human resources are required. As the economy develops and technology advances, the mix of needed skills undergoes change. New skills are required, some existing skills are no longer utilized or are utilized less, and the importance of others is modified. The introduction of new products and changing consumer tastes result in the expansion of some industries while others concurrently decline. The consequence of these changes is an altered pattern in the demand for human resources. Growing industries expand their use of those skills unique to their production processes; declining industries reduce the use of those skills relevant to their processes. The abilities of workers displaced in the latter are not necessarily those which are sought by the former industries. Expansion of industries does not necessarily occur in the same geographical regions where industries decline. As a result, there can develop a spatial unevenness in the demand for and supply of manpower.

There appears to be, therefore, a positive relationship between the dynamic nature of an economy and the mix as well as the magnitude of human resources which are called for by this dynamism. At the same time, independent forces are bringing human capabilities at different levels and in different magnitudes into the market at rates of flow which need not coincide with the changing manpower requirements of industry. The push and pull of market forces accommodate to some extent whatever imbalances materialize, as we shall see in later chapters. The existence of market imperfections, however, impairs the effectiveness and speed of this accommodation. The existence and persistence of imbalances at different levels in manpower demand and supply define the nature of manpower problems. Imbalance between the actual and potential level of skill development constitutes a manpower problem at the level of the individual. Inequality between the number of persons with given levels of education and skill seeking employment and the number of available jobs utilizing that level of skill or education is another aspect of the manpower problem. An excess supply or demand for manpower on a regional or national basis is a similar problem, but of different dimensions. Solutions to these problems require a removal of these imbalances, a matching of supply and demand. In this chapter, we shall examine specific forms of manpower imbalances and shall discuss their origins.

Manpower Policies at the Microlevel

The manpower problem of the individual enterprise is essentially one of getting and keeping personnel with qualifications sufficient to perform the set of integrated and coordinated tasks that make up the activities of the firm.[1] Logically, the firm has organized a set of jobs which, when performed coincidentally and/or sequentially, permit the production of output. This organization is reflected in the job structure of the establishment. In turn this structure requires a staff of personnel. Determining the qualifications of personnel needed to man these jobs is one of the first steps in assembling the work force of the firm. Once these qualifications have been determined, the

---

[1] An interesting perception of the firm as a special kind of labor market is described in Peter B. Doeringer and Michael J. Piore, *Internal Labor Markets and Manpower Analysis* (Lexington, Mass.: D. C. Heath and Company, 1971).

necessary labor force must be recruited and selection among applicants via a screening process is then carried out. Although those who are selected possess general aptitudes, education, skills, and experience which are potentially capable of being successfully utilized in the performance of job tasks, additional training is usually necessary to adapt these basic traits to the specific requirements of each job within the structure. Since the selection and training procedures involve fixed or sunk costs, the firm is interested in minimizing these costs by employing those persons most responsive to training and who are likely to remain in the firm. In addition, consistent with its cost minimization goals, the firm seeks to encourage the full application of the energies and skills of its personnel to the set of work tasks which are to be performed. Therefore, the firm is concerned with establishing policies to motivate and retain its labor force. Finally, the firm must establish policies and procedures that can enable its job structure and matching manpower to adapt to the changes that are imposed upon it by shifting market demand and advancing technology.

The processes by which these manpower policies are implemented within the context of the firm are briefly described in this section.[2] The various phases of the personnel program can be identified by the terms (1) job analysis, (2) recruitment, (3) selection, (4) training, and (5) commitment.

Job Analysis

The initial step in manpower planning within the firm is a systematic identification and description of the job structure. The *job description* is just that. It identifies and defines the duties, relationships, and requirements of each job. It is the result of a careful gathering of facts and, ideally, the job description should be revised periodically as the job itself undergoes change. The *job specification* is derived from the job description and identifies or specifies the particular qualifications or traits required on each job, including aptitudes, intelligence, educational levels, age, height, weight, experience. From the job specifications related groups of jobs can be identified, called job families. Somewhat related are the *manning tables* which outline the distribution of workers among jobs and the relationship of jobs throughout the establishment. These tools permit the personnel department to plan for manpower expansion or contraction, and for replacement. Sales forecasts can be converted into production schedules, which call for a given magnitude of jobs to be manned. If more jobs are to be filled than there are available

---

[2] A more detailed description of these procedures can be found in almost any text on Personnel Management. Two references among many excellent ones are: Paul Pigors and Charles Myers, *Personnel Administration*, 6th ed. (New York: McGraw-Hill, 1969); Dale Yoder, *Personnel Management and Industrial Relations*, 6th ed. (Englewood Cliffs, N.J.: Prentice-Hall, 1970).

personnel, or if replacements are required, the job specifications inform the department of the type of labor to recruit. If jobs are fewer than available personnel, layoffs may be required. Through job families and *manning tables*, the personnel department can determine what readjustments of employees among jobs are possible or feasible, given the various customary and contractual constraints under which the firm must operate.

Recruitment

Job requisitions for new positions or for replacement of old ones are forwarded to the hiring office from the various departments as the need arises (see Table 2.1). The department may seek to fill these requisitions either from internal sources or from external sources. Vacancies in positions at higher levels in the job hierarchy may be filled by advancements from within the firm through a process of upgrading. Since this procedure may initiate a chain reaction of advancements throughout the hierarchy, the eventual outside recruitment may occur for a position near the bottom of

TABLE 2.1

JOB OPENINGS RESULTING FROM CHANGE IN EMPLOYMENT
AND DEATHS AND RETIREMENTS, BY MAJOR OCCUPATION
GROUP, 1965 TO 1975

(Thousands)

		Openings[a]	
Major Occupation Group	Total	Due to Employment Change	Due to Deaths and Retirements
Total	38,780	16,525	22,255
Professional and technical workers	6,513	4,020	2,493
Managers, officials, and proprietors	3,921	1,860	2,061
Clerical workers	7,835	3,430	4,405
Sales workers	2,533	1,085	1,448
Craftsmen and foremen	3,967	2,180	1,787
Operatives	4,563	1,610	2,953
Service workers, including private household	7,892	3,260	4,632
Nonfarm laborers	546	−155	701
Farmers and farm managers, laborers, and foremen	1,010	−765	1,775

[a] Detail may not add to totals due to rounding.

Source: *Manpower Report of the President, 1969*, p. 67.

the job structure, requiring skills dissimilar from those of the original requisition. If this pattern is followed, jobs for which outside recruitment is most frequent are termed "entry jobs."[3] Labor is obtained from a variety of sources: unions, the plant employment office (the gate), employment offices (public or private), personnel contacts of employees, the newspaper want ads, or visitations to schools and colleges. Primary sources vary, depending upon the type of labor being sought (manual or white collar), the state of the economy, or the region of the country.[4] From these sources, a list of applicants is compiled.

Selection

The selection procedure is designed to eliminate from the list of applicants those who are least qualified for the position.[5] It involves a series of progressive steps, each of which is designed to reveal or identify particular traits of the applicant that are either acceptable or undesirable. Hence, a screening procedure is performed which leaves a residue of the most preferred or the least undesirable candidates (depending upon the tightness of the labor market). The application form as an initial step can reveal such traits as illiteracy and can provide references for verifying listed qualifications; the personal interview can reveal characteristics or personality, sex, age, superficial physical conditions, race, or rudimentary verification of claimed attributes. Tests can be administered to measure and determine aptitudes, intelligence, levels of competency, personality, and other pertinent traits. The medical examination can reveal physical competency to perform the job, but because of costs this screening device is usually one of the last to be given. A final interview with the requisitioning supervisor normally completes the screening process. If the applicant is not eliminated in one of these steps, employment usually is offered.

Training

The ideal situation for management would be to employ only those applicants whose skill and experience identically match those required by the job vacancy. The employment procedures are in fact designed to approach this ideal as nearly as possible in order to produce recruits for whom only a minimum amount of training is required. The tightness of the local labor market tends to determine how closely this ideal can be

[3] The probability that this pattern may follow is strengthened in tight labor markets. It is a feature of "internal labor markets." See Doeringer and Piore, *op. cit.*, Chapters 3 and 5.

[4] See F. T. Malm, "Recruiting Patterns and the Functioning of Labor Markets," *Industrial and Labor Relations Review*, Vol. 7, No. 4 (July 1954), pp. 507–525.

[5] Doeringer and Piore describe this procedure as one in which "type I (rejecting a qualified applicant) and type II (accepting an unqualified one) errors" are balanced. *Op. cit.*, pp. 103–106.

approached. When unemployment is high and employers have a wide choice among applicants, high standards are often established, much in excess of minimum job requirements. In extremely tight markets, standards tend to be lowered and less-qualified applicants are accepted.[6] Cost considerations, of course, are behind this desire to minimize training. The amount of training provided the beginning worker, of course, varies also with the level of the entry job in the job hierarchy. Training may consist of only a few procedures designed to introduce the worker to the job, with decreasing supervisory attention given to the worker as proficiency develops. These induction procedures may involve simply a recitation of company rules, of the location of materials and facilities, of lines of direction and control, and an introduction to the work site. Usually, training is more involved. Most training takes place on the job under the supervision of the foreman or an experienced fellow worker. The trainee produces while he learns. When his output increases to some predetermined normal level and it appears that he can sustain this level, the worker is said to be trained.[7] When training takes place on special equipment under simulated production conditions in a separate location, it is called vestibule training. This form of training is useful in beginning plant operations, where large-scale expansion occurs, or where refresher courses to upgrade or transform skills are necessary. The training cockpit for airline pilots in which various types of emergencies can be simulated is a good example of a program designed to keep sharp those skills which may be little used but are an integral part of the job. Apprenticeship programs are, in fact, an extended combination of vestibule and on-the-job training. Programmed instruction has also been used to teach basic skills in machine operation, where learning proceeds as bits of information are presented to the trainee; his comprehension is immediately tested and correct responses are immediately reinforced. The uses of programmed

[6] Seymour Wolfbein describes the willingness of employers to accept high-school dropouts as labor shortages developed, whereas before such shortages the minimum educational standard was the high school diploma. *Employment, Unemployment, and Public Policy* (New York: Random House, 1965), p. 172. The reluctance of employers to lower hiring standards, because of the cost implications of the long-term employment commitments to less-qualified employees, is described by Doeringer and Piore, *op. cit.*, p. 105.

[7] The length of time devoted to training varies. Under apprenticeship programs, the period may extend over several years. The period of time allocated for training also depends upon the employer's estimate of the group undergoing training. If he feels that under normal training procedures, the group will still have below-par productivity, the program may be extended. This attitude explained the longer than usual, or necessary, period of training provided by employers to Indian trainees, where their wages during training were partially subsidized by the Federal government. See Loren C. Scott, "The Economic Effectiveness of On-the-Job-Training: The Experience of the Bureau of Indian Affairs in Oklahoma," *Industrial and Labor Relations Review*, Vol. 23, No. 2 (January 1970), pp. 220–236.

learning in industry are at present limited, but the technique is promising, particularly where training involves the development of concepts which can be broken down into component parts and which can be presented in building-block fashion, often through the use of visual aid equipment. Not only is the learning process simplified and expedited, but it also may require fewer man-hours of instruction.

Commitment

Since recruitment, selection, and training involve costs, the employer is anxious to minimize them by keeping turnover as low as possible. He also seeks to encourage the full utilization of the skill and energy potential of his labor force in order to minimize unit labor costs. Hence, a motivational system must be designed to accomplish these twin objectives. The primary element in this system, of course, is the method of payment. When pay is related through some formula to output per unit of time, it is called an incentive system. Where output is subject to the control of the worker, where it can be measured in units, and where some normal output per interval of time can be established through standardized work routines, then the ingredients are present for establishing an incentive system. It may be instituted on an individual or group basis. Normally, allowances are made for interruptions in the flow of work beyond the control of the worker. If these ingredients are not present, then a rate of pay per time unit may be established, where the unit of time may be an hour, a week, a month, or in rare cases a year.

Although adequate pay appears to be a necessary condition for retaining intact the firm's labor force, it is not a sufficient condition. Therefore, various motivational supplements have been adopted to reduce turnover. Seniority, or longevity within a plant (or department therein), bestows rights and privileges which are lost if the worker terminates his employment. Pension plans also tend to tie the labor force to the employer. Supplemental unemployment benefits enable the worker to sustain his economic dependence upon the firm, even in periods of reduced work and layoffs.

The firm seeks to control the functioning of employees not only through the provisions of financial rewards—the carrot—but it also can enforce sanctions—the stick—when performance falls outside tolerated limits. Reprimands, suspensions, transfers, nonpromotion, and in extreme cases dismissal are instruments of discipline whereby the employer seeks to correct through punitive means undesired employee behavior. On the other hand, the employer can establish, perhaps jointly with a union, a grievance procedure, by means of which a worker may appeal actions of the employer relative to the motivational system that he believes are unjust or inappropriate. These procedures and others may be interpreted as efforts of the employer to maintain a more permanent and cooperative relationship between the firm and its employees. They are designed to commit the worker to the establishment; thereby, mutual interests are promoted through joint cooperation. In turn, through the various fringe programs which the employer undertakes to provide security to his labor force, the firm establishes commitments to the welfare of its employees.

Adaptation to Change

Manpower requirements of firms are subject to change from at least two sources. Changes in product demand may alter the needs for personnel, although sales forecasts to some extent may mitigate disruptions in the firm's labor force. Forecasts of temporary demand expansion may be met, not by additions to the labor force, but by inventory depletion, by the scheduling of overtime, or by subcontracting for supplementary help. Such measures may involve less cost than those incurred in recruiting and training workers. If there is seasonal expansion in demand, the employer may rely upon transient workers or upon those only marginally in the labor force—the secondary labor force—for whom only minimum training is economically feasible. Temporary reductions in demand may be met by inventory accumulation, by a reduced work week,[8] by nonreplacement of normal attrition, and ultimately by layoffs. If reductions in demand are more permanent, as they tend to be in declining industries, layoffs also become permanent. When workers are permanently severed, they are compelled to enter the labor market. If the firm has laid off substantial numbers at one time and is an oligopsonistic buyer of labor, the impact on the local labor market may be substantial.[9] The employer may attempt to ease the transition process by trying to assist workers in locating other jobs, or through internal transfer and resettlement in other labor markets, but these efforts are not, in such circumstances, apt to be very fruitful. A permanent expansion in demand, on the other hand, will require an increase in the firm's labor force, and recruitment and training costs will be increased.

Technological change can also compel alterations in the manpower structure of a firm. Often, sufficient lead time is given for management to forecast the extent of manpower adjustments and to establish policies with which to deal with the change. (The advent of the Boeing 747 airplane is a case in point, where new maintenance programs and in-flight and airport passenger service facilities required major changes in the number of personnel and the nature of their duties.) Technological change seems to be a fact of

[8] For a study of the relationship between the number of hours worked and employment in different periods of the business cycle, see Hazel M. Willacy, "Changes in Factory Workweek as an Economic Indicator," *Monthly Labor Review*, Vol. 93, No. 10 (October 1970), pp. 25–31.
[9] Such a situation is described by J. J. Palen and F. J. Fahey, "Unemployment and Reemployment Success: An Analysis of the Studebaker Shutdown," *Industrial and Labor Relations Review*, Vol. 21, No. 2 (January 1968), pp. 234–250.

life, inevitable and continuing. It can be imposed upon a firm because of market pressures, but it also evolves internally, both on a planned basis as management searches for cost-reducing opportunities and on an ad hoc basis as shortcuts are discovered or as operational necessities require inventive adaptations.[10] New techniques may either be labor neutral, labor using, or labor saving, although the labor-saving type seems to predominate. All may require readjustments in the labor force, but the last type is a source of labor redundancy within the firm. Different skills are utilized in the new techniques. In some cases, old skills may be made obsolete or the over-all level of skills is reduced; in other cases, new skills of a higher order are required. Where redundancy occurs, firms may attempt to absorb displaced labor through internal transfers, either at the point of the technological innovation or elsewhere within the plant or company. If workers are redeployed, some retraining is inevitable. Where new skills are required the firm must make a decision whether it will cost less to retrain old workers or to recruit and train new workers. The age of old workers, their level of skill, the existence of termination pay, and the social conscience (reinforced, perhaps, by contractual and legal obligations) of employers all influence the decision of whether to retrain and transfer, or to recruit and train workers.[11] The older the worker, the greater the divergence between the existing skill of the worker and the new skills required, and the fewer the contractual obligations of the employer, then the more costly it may be to the employer to retrain and retain the existing employee.

Causes of Structural Imbalances

Although imbalances between the demand and supply for manpower may have numerous causes, only five major sources will be identified. They are: (1) wage–productivity imbalances, (2) the deficiencies of disadvantaged groups, (3) the impact of age, (4) technological changes, and (5) geographical immobility and skill obsolescence. These are interrelated, although they are treated separately here.

Wage–Productivity Imbalances

By establishing a floor under wages, it has been argued, the minimum wage law and labor unions effectively exclude segments of the noninstitutional population with very low productivity from labor force

---

[10] Some of these sources of technological change are discussed by Doeringer and Piore, *Internal Labor Markets and Manpower Analysis*, pp. 119–132.

[11] The manpower implications of technological change are discussed at length in L. C. Hunter, G. L. Reid, and D. Boddy, *Labour Problems of Technological Change* (London: George Allen and Unwin, Ltd., 1970). See especially Chapters 1, 4, 7, 10, 12, and 13.

participation. Employers, prevented from paying less than the floor, simply refuse to offer employment to these submarginal workers whose revenue contribution to the firm is thought to be less than their cost. To be sure, some workers are absorbed into the limited number of jobs excluded from coverage of minimum wage laws or unions; others enter the casual labor force and accept employment on a day-to-day basis. In every large city there are certain street corners where casual workers congregate and offer their services at less than the minimum wage on a "handyman" basis. However, such jobs are limited, and many persons merely withdraw from the labor force. Since 1967, the number of discouraged workers, of which about two-thirds are probably submarginal, has been estimated from the Current Population Survey. In 1967 and 1968, there were about 700,000 who believed searching for a job was futile; this number fell to 600,000 in 1969.[12] Inflation can, of course, raise the value of the comparatively low output of these submarginal workers; if union or minimum wage law adjustments lag sufficiently behind price increases, in time employers may find it profitable to hire them. Historically, a compelling argument for the minimum wage has been that it would eliminate poverty caused by sub-standard wages.[13] However, poverty is a relative concept, depending in part on the size of the family. The minimum wage to a breadwinner which would lift his family out of poverty, assuming employment at 40 hours a week for 50 weeks a year, was estimated in 1969 as follows.[14]

Family Size	Required Hourly Wage, $
3	1.39
4	1.78
5	2.09
6	2.35
7	2.89

[12] Paul O. Flain and Paul M. Schwab, "Employment and Unemployment in 1969," *Monthly Labor Review* (February 1970), Vol. 93, No. 2, p. 53.

[13] This point has been cited by Gordon Bloom and Herbert Northrup since 1950 through six editions of their *Economics of Labor Relations*. See the 6th ed. (Homewood: Richard D. Irwin, Inc., 1969), p. 452. Also see T. G. Moore "The Effect of Minimum Wages on Teenage Unemployment Rates." *Journal of Political Economy* (July–August 1971), Vol. 79, pp. 899–900.

[14] Report of the President's Commission on Income Maintenance Programs, *Poverty Amid Plenty: The American Paradox* (Washington: U.S. Government Printing Office, November 1969), p. 94.

Not only must the minimum wage be higher than the current $1.60 for workers with families of 4 or more, but "simply passing a law to regulate wages will not provide the necessary demand for low-skilled labor sufficient to guarantee forty hours of work per week all year long to all workers."[15]

The Disadvantaged Worker

Those segments of the population who are believed by employers to have low productivity may be called the disadvantaged. These persons ordinarily have substandard educational attainments, are unskilled, have low labor-force commitments, have evidence of employment instability, or are believed to be more expensive to train. Members of this group are most adversely affected by the minimum wage laws. They include the school dropouts, the teen-ager, members of minority groups, including especially the nonwhites, and women who are heads of households. Those who leave school before completion of a high school education are frequently considered to be employment risks because they may either be "quitters" or difficult to train. In either case, a firm's investment in them for training is risky. Being less preferred, they are the last to be hired. Unemployment rates for youths age 16 to 19 have remained above 10% since 1954 (see Table 2.2). Their lack of employment experience and a disproportionate number who are looking for their first job together cause unemployment rates to be high among this group. Women and Blacks, in this as in other age groups, have higher unemployment rates than men and Whites, respectively. Job openings for women are more restricted as, perhaps, are their opportunities for search. The service industries provide the largest source of employment for women—and for teen-agers, as well (see Chart 2.1). The weaker degree of labor force commitment, together with a greater incidence of absenteeism, also probably accounts for a greater reluctance of employers to hire women. Blacks are handicapped in securing jobs because of the greater difficulties they experience in job search, a lower level of educational attainment, and a higher proportion of teen-agers and women in the labor force.[16] Indians have even lower educational attainments and are more restricted in their opportunities for job search. There seems to exist a feeling that Indians are less productive and are less easy to train than are other racial groups—although Scott's evidence contradicts this[17]—and that their labor-force commitment is weaker.

These traits either require that the disadvantaged receive relatively more training or suggest that the firm will be less apt to reap the benefits

---

[15] *Ibid.*, p. 94.
[16] *Ibid.*, p. 49.
[17] L. C. Scott, *The Economic Effectiveness of On-the-Job-Training*, pp. 224–236.

TABLE 2.2

UNEMPLOYMENT RATES FOR PERSONS 16 YEARS AND OVER AND FOR TEEN-AGERS, AND PERCENT OF ADULT MEN NOT IN LABOR FORCE, IN METROPOLITAN AREAS,[a] BY COLOR, 1970

	Unemployment Rate				Percent Not in Labor Force			
	Persons 16 Years and Over		Teen-agers, 16 to 19 Years		Men, 25 to 44 Years		Men, 45 to 64 Years	
Place of Residence	White	Black and Other Races	White	Black and Other Races	White	Black and Other Races	White	Black and Other Races
Central cities	4.9	8.3	14.3	31.8	4.2	6.6	10.3	15.2
Suburbs	4.5	7.4	14.0	26.6	2.2	5.8	8.5	14.2
Poverty areas[b]	6.3	9.5	16.3	35.8	6.3	9.4	17.3	18.6

[a] Data for central cities and suburbs apply to all standard metropolitan statistical areas; those for poverty areas, only to SMSA's with 250,000 population or more.

[b] Poverty areas were derived by ranking all census tracts in SMSA's of 250,000 or more population on the basis of 1960 data on five poverty-linked characteristics. The tracts in the lowest quartile form the poverty areas. About 85% of the residents of these poverty areas live in their SMSA's central cities; the other 15% are in the suburbs.

Source: *Manpower Report of the President, 1971,* p. 87.

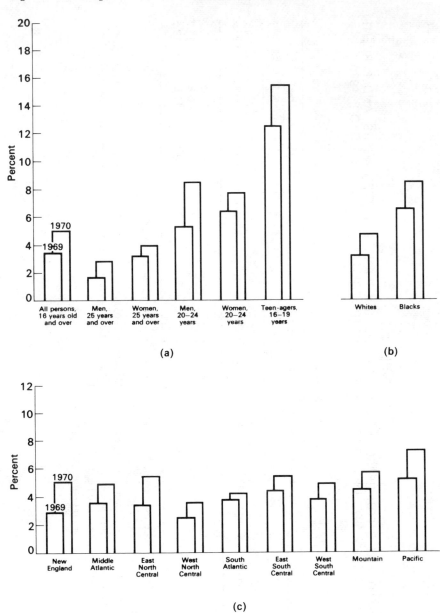

CHART 2.1. Unemployment rates vary among labor force groups and among geographic areas. Unemployment rates (a) by age and sex, (b) by race, and (c) by area.

Source: Department of Labor. *Manpower Report of the President, 1971,* p. 20.

from the training imparted to them. As a result, the disadvantaged tend to be shunted into jobs for which only a minimum amount of training is necessary. These low-skill jobs, however, are a declining proportion of total employment. In 1960 nonfarm laborers comprised 5.5% of the employed labor force; in 1975, the percentage is expected to be only 4.2. Farm employment accounted for 8.1% of the total in 1960, but will only account for 3.9% in 1975.[18] Unless proportions of the disadvantaged can be reduced concurrently through removal of the traits or the prejudices which place them under exceptional handicaps in obtaining employment, their search for jobs will meet with increasing frustrations and become increasingly unsuccessful. The supply of manpower with low skills will greatly exceed the job vacancies suitable for them.

The Older Worker

This group includes those members of the labor force who are 45 years of age and older. Although members of this group are less apt to become unemployed, when they do lose their jobs the period of unemployment is apt to persist longer. In some respects, unemployed members of this group possess many of the traits of the disadvantaged. Although they have had sustained work experience, their average educational attainments are usually less than those of the teen-age labor force. Although their labor-force commitment is high, they are entering an age group which is more susceptible to fatigue, illness, and disability. Hence, absenteeism may be expected to be higher than among other groups. Although many are skilled, some of their skills may be in declining demand in the locality in which they live, and there is less willingness among them to move to other areas. Although many have had stable work records, the willingness of employers to retrain them varies inversely with their remaining expected work life. Employers' attitudes about their capacity to absorb retraining may be as prejudiced as they sometimes are towards minority racial groups. "You can't teach an old dog new tricks."

Because of these traits, workers over 45 who become unemployed experience more difficulty in finding new employment. This conclusion was confirmed by the reemployment experience of workers displaced by the Studebaker shutdown. It was found that age "has a stronger relationship with employment success than the socioeconomic status characteristics of income, education, and occupation."[19] Whereas age, through seniority, had been an asset while employed, after displacement it became a distinct

---

[18] *Manpower Report of the President, 1967*, p. 274.
[19] Palen and Fahey, "Unemployment Success: An Analysis of the Studebaker Shutdown," p. 237.

liability. The burden of job displacement owing to declining demand or technological change falls, as a consequence of their traits, disproportionately upon the older workers. The magnitude of the problems attending changes in demand and technology is related to the number and percentage of older workers in the labor force. That older workers as a proportion of the total labor force have increased is implied in the trend of persons over 65 as a percentage of the population. This latter group in 1930 amounted to about 9% of the population, but in 1966, they constituted 17.1%. In the decade of the sixties, the labor force comprising persons between the ages of 45 and 65 increased by about five million, a 17% increase, but owing to declining immigration and birth rates before and during the Great Depression, the increase in the decade of the seventies will total only about 1.7 million. A Senate Special Committee on the Aging reported in November 1971 that more than one million persons past age 45 were unemployed, an increase of 67% over the past decade. There appears to be an increasing tendency to ease older workers between the ages of 60 and 64 from the work force. The consequence of prolonged unemployment or underemployment is a reduction in the size of their retirement income. No wonder that the likelihood of being poor is more than twice as great for older persons than it is for younger ones.

Technological Change

It has often been asserted that the pace of technological change is quickening. This assertion is due primarily to two phenomena, (1) the vast expenditures on research and development, which during the late sixties exceeded $20 billion annually, and (2) the reduction in the length of time between a discovery and its commercial or industrial implementation.[20] The manpower consequences of this change are that not only are some advanced skills made obsolete, but many unskilled and semiskilled jobs are eliminated. The labor-saving nature of major technological innovations can have serious impact on the available supply of jobs in a community. Although significant changes in the structure of skill requirements may occur, the reduction in the total number of jobs depends upon (1) the cost-saving nature of the innovations, (2) the transmission of lower costs into prices, (3) the elasticity of demand, and (4) the growth in demand. Compensation for substantial labor-saving innovations may occur if product

---

[20] This length of time has declined from 37 years in the pre-World War I period to 24 years in the interwar period, to 14 years in the post-World War II period. See National Commission on Technology, Automation and Economic Progress, "Technology and the American Economy," in John A. Delehanty, *Manpower Problems and Policies* (Scranton: International Textbook Co., 1970), pp. 152–154.

demand is highly elastic and growing, so that even with the innovations the total supply of jobs may increase. Where demand has low elasticity and/or is not increasing, technological unemployment in the local labor market may be serious. The introduction of the automated steel rolling mill generated vast amounts of unemployment in steel-producing communities, and the mechanization of coal mining in the face of declining demand wiped out hundreds of thousands of jobs in the coal mining communities of Appalachia. In England it is estimated that technological changes displace up to one million workers yearly.[21]

It was noted above that many firms plan systematically the introduction of new processes and arrange to retrain workers for the requirements of the processes. Workers may thereby be reabsorbed into the plant. Others are offered the opportunity to transfer, perhaps to plants in other regions. However, often the consequence is to narrow the range of skill variations, so that tasks are more simplified.[22] As a result, both very highly skilled and unskilled jobs may be eliminated. If workers in these jobs cannot be reabsorbed by the company, they must seek jobs elsewhere. During their employment search, they also face the problem of sustaining their level of living. The shorter the period of search, the easier the second problem is made.

If unemployment from technological change is substantial, a significant imbalance may develop in the community between the supply of jobs and the number of those seeking jobs. The greater is this imbalance, the more difficult is the reemployment of the displaced workers and the greater will tend to be their period of search. The existence and dissemination of job vacancy information through a centralized employment exchange can reduce the trial and error nature of the employment search and thereby reduce its duration. Wolfbein reports, for example, that the Swedish employment service has a telephone-answering service whereby information on job vacancies can rapidly be transmitted to job seekers.[23] The willingness of the unemployed to change localities also affects the length of time for reemployment. Obviously, the distribution of traits of the displaced workers will determine how quickly a large proportion of them can find new jobs. If a substantial number is over 45 or if their educational level is relatively low, or if a substantial number is Black or Mexican-American, the correction of the labor market imbalance may take longer. Similarly, the availability of facilities to assist workers in acquiring new skills and their

---

[21] Hunter, Reid, and Boddy, *Labour Problems of Technological Change*, p. 330.
[22] James Bright has written, " . . . there was more evidence that automation had reduced the skill requirements of the operating work force, and occasionally of the entire factory force, including the maintenance organization." "The Relationship of Increasing Automation to Skill Requirements," in Delehanty, *Manpower Problems and Policies*, p. 175.
[23] *Employment, Unemployment, and Public Policy*, p. 131.

willingness to avail themselves of these facilities can improve their prospects for reemployment.

The quickening pace of technological change means that more and more displacement can be expected. The maintenance of a level of aggregate demand sufficient to provide an adequate supply of job vacancies is a necessary prerequisite for the reabsorption of the redundant employees, but it is not a sufficient one. Workers must be informed of the job vacancies, retrained to meet the job requirements, and relocated to the job sites. In addition, they must be sustained in the process. Unless market arrangements and facilities are developed to accomplish these objectives, the level of frictional unemployment may be expected to increase, carrying with it the built-in tendencies for inflationary pressures accompanying expansion in aggregate demand.

Immobility and Changes in the Supply of Jobs

Although data reveal that the labor force in the United States is highly mobile, there are subgroups whose mobility patterns—the proportion changing localities in a given period of time—are substantially lower than the national average. Generally, these subgroups are found among the disadvantaged. Movement from one location to another costs money, both in transportation outlays for people and possessions, and also for living expenses in the new location until employment is found. Consequently, those persons whose savings are meagre or nonexistent and who are without adequate sources of credit in fact cannot *afford* to move. It is among the disadvantaged that funds are most apt to be lacking. Women who are heads of households, with dependent children, are often out of the labor force where child-care facilities are absent. Moreover, if these women are receiving welfare payments to care for children they may be deterred from moving to locations where job vacancies and child-care centers both are present; in moving they may lose their eligibility for such welfare payments. Residence requirements normally must be satisfied by recipients of such aid. Although large numbers of Blacks have migrated from the South to cities in the North and West, they still are less mobile than Whites, partly because of lack of funds, low skills, and ignorance of job vacancies. The immobility patterns of Indians are even more pronounced. Until recently, a majority of those who left the reservation for urban employment returned home. The alien environment of the city proved to be too formidable an obstacle. Only when social services are provided in these urban centers and a community of Indians has developed to ease the transition have America's most oppressed minority been able to relocate successfully.

These subgroups all contain a disproportionately large number of persons who have low levels of educational attainments. The tendency of employers to hire them only as a last resort increases the risks of job search in a strange location and the costs incurred by moving. In addition, those with substandard educational achievements are likely to be the ones who are most ignorant of job openings. Hence, low education imposes a double barrier to movement. These impediments are also faced by older workers (see Table 2.3), but other factors also exist which tend to lessen their willingness to change their place of residence. The difficulty of leaving friends and acquaintances or the unwillingness of children to change schools reflect social pressures against change. There are significant and unique costs also involved. A separated older worker may dream of reemployment with his old employer, with a chance of regaining his lost seniority and accrued pension rights. He may be reluctant to undertake a subsidized retraining program, for the income received from his redundant skills may

TABLE 2.3

EDUCATIONAL ATTAINMENT OF PERSONS 25 YEARS AND OVER, BY COLOR AND RESIDENCE, MARCH 1970

	Percent of Population with—			
	8 Years of School or Less		*12 Years of School or More*	
Age and Residence	*White*	*Black*	*White*	*Black*
Total	26.1	43.0	57.4	33.7
Metropolitan areas	22.1	36.0	61.5	38.8
Nonmetropolitan areas	33.2	60.9	50.0	20.6
Nonfarm	31.7	59.1	51.2	21.6
Farm	43.1	74.5	42.0	11.9
25 to 44 years	11.8	22.4	71.6	47.9
Metropolitan areas	9.4	18.0	74.7	52.2
Nonmetropolitan areas	16.5	36.3	65.9	34.2
Nonfarm	15.9	34.3	66.2	35.3
Farm	21.8	54.1	62.3	23.7
45 years and over	36.8	63.1	46.6	19.9
Metropolitan areas	32.1	55.7	51.2	24.2
Nonmetropolitan areas	44.9	78.9	38.7	10.5
Nonfarm	43.4	77.9	40.0	11.3
Farm	53.5	86.4	31.9	4.6

Source: Department of Commerce, Bureau of the Census. *Manpower Report of the President, 1971*, p. 132.

have been significantly greater than the income which he could earn in a newly learned skill. Even though the probability of being able to practice again his superfluous occupation may be remote, the older worker may gamble on such a possibility. Finally, to move may require him to dispose of home and property at a substantial capital loss, especially if unemployment in his locality has been severe and has glutted the used-housing market.

It is the less-binding family and social ties, lower costs of subsistence, and a greater willingness of employers to accept younger persons in jobs requiring training, together with perhaps a zest for adventure, that explains the greater mobility of the teen-ager.

Technological change and major changes in product demand can greatly reduce the employment opportunities in a given locality or region. This is particularly true when industries so affected are concentrated in a few localities or regions. Examples of decimated regions are numerous. The change in the use of fuel from coal to petroleum and natural gas, together with the mechanization of the mines, reduced drastically the employment of miners in most of the Appalachian Mountain states. The rapid improvement in agricultural technology, including farm mechanization, development of higher-yielding varieties of crops, irrigation, pesticides, and fertilizers vastly reduced the number of farmers that were required to feed the nation. The shift in transportation facilities curtailed employment opportunities in many small railroad junction towns, as diesel engines, automatic switching equipment, motor vehicles, and a marvelous network of highways, not to mention the speed of jet airplane travel, came into being. The automotive society has also brought about the decay of urban transportation, so that those who lack the means to acquire and/or operate an automobile can become marooned in a ghetto island of the central city. An inability to travel about a city not only limits the ability to search for a job, but it also constrains the area for which daily accessible employment is possible. With the movement of industry out of the central city into the suburbs, employment possibilities become even more limited to the disadvantaged group contained in the ghetto.

Changes in national priorities can also bring about vast incidences of unemployment in specific localities or regions (see Chart 2.2). Of course, when general demobilization occurs after a war, the whole country is affected. However, the recent abandonment of the supersonic jet project resulted in unemployment for thousands of workers, many highly skilled, in the Seattle–Tacoma area. Similarly, the deemphasis of the space program wiped out the jobs of hordes of highly trained professional engineers and scientists in Houston, Cape Kennedy, and other space centers in the country, while creating a glut of mathematicians, physicists, and engineers in their respective labor markets. The scaling down of foreign aid brought

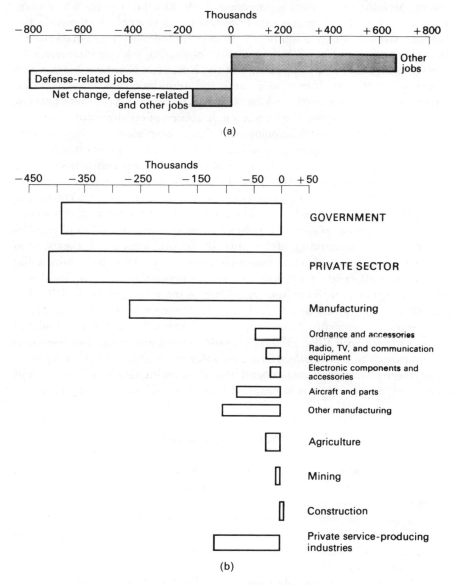

CHART 2.2. Defense cutbacks more than offset expansion of employment in the rest of the economy in 1970 with defense-related job losses concentrated in government and manufacturing. (a) Change in numbers of jobs, 1969 to 1970. (b) Change in number of defense-related jobs [attributable to Federal purchases of goods and services for defense (includes Armed Forces)], 1969 to 1970.

Source: Department of Labor. *Manpower Report of the President, 1971*, p. 155.

many specialists in overseas assignments back into the country where their numbers added to the excess supply of trained personnel. A change in the comparative advantage of industries can deprive them of foreign markets and bring them face to face with the necessity of sharing the domestic one with foreign competitors. The appearance of the European Common Market and Japanese steel and automobiles, and the inundation of foreign textile products, have threatened the jobs of many in communities where firms in these industries comprise the largest single source of employment.

To the extent that unemployment from these sources arises in communities containing large proportions of labor force members with low mobility, regional labor market imbalances can develop and persist. These imbalances call for remedial policies, the effectiveness of which can influence the level of structural unemployment, the rate of inflation, and the degree of deprivation experienced by those who simply are unable to find a job.

It is, of course, possible for policies to be formulated and implemented without any understanding of the cause of the problems which they seek to remedy or without any clear comprehension of the process by which the policies will effectuate a solution. Few would argue that this is an ideal way to proceed, however. Some understanding of the principles by which labor markets operate would be a logical prerequisite to understanding the nature of manpower problems. Moreover, it would seem that policies formulated in accordance with these principles would be more relevant and successful in attacking those problems. Hence, in order to be able to evaluate existing manpower policies or to recommend new ones, an inquiry into the scope and nature of labor markets is in order. It is to this task that we now turn.

Discussion Questions

1. Compare and contrast the nature of parental influence on someone you know who has "dropped out" of school and the influence to which you have been subject.
2. Manpower problems are a result of change. Discuss.
3. The Industrial Relations department and the union are the two principal agencies concerned with manpower problems at the level of the firm. Discuss.
4. What are the relative advantages and disadvantages of promoting from within in order to fill job vacancies?
5. Suppose a menial job vacancy exists which at most requires a seventh grade education. Two applicants seek the job; each are the same age, sex, and size, possess the same aptitudes and intelligence, and each needs

the job to the same degree. What other criteria may the employer use in selecting between the two and why?

6. If the disadvantaged members of the labor force, actual or potential, are those with low productivity, why isn't it a simple matter to remedy their state by merely increasing their productivity? Why are not older members of the labor force disadvantaged unless they become unemployed?

7. If technological change produces wide-scale unemployment, isn't it the more rational policy to control its rate of introduction? Discuss.

8. Since the labor force of the United States, relative to other countries, is highly mobile, are not manpower problems primarily of a short-run nature? Discuss.

3

Manpower Problems and Policies in America

Introduction

Unemployment is the principal symptom of a manpower imbalance in the economy. It appears in two broad forms: (1) deficient demand and (2) structural unemployment. Deficient demand produces unemployment because the economy is growing at a rate insufficient to absorb the growing labor force. In the decade of the 1960s, the labor force grew at an average annual rate of 1.76%. Output per man-hour over the decade grew slightly less than 3% per year. Consequently, in order to absorb the growing labor force with no change in unemployment, real gross national product during the decade would have had to increase by an annual average of about 4.75%. Actually, the rate of increase was slightly greater than this as the unemployment rate declined from 5.5% of the labor force in 1960 to 3.5% in 1969. The labor force in 1970 totaled 85.9 million and is expected to reach 100.7 million persons in 1980. In the decade of the seventies, the labor force will grow at an annual rate of about 1.65%, requiring a continued rate of growth in GNP of over 4%. The United States has had little success in the post-World War II period in sustaining an annual rate of growth of GNP of over 4% for more than a few years.

In 1970, the unemployment rate increased to 4.9% and in 1971 to almost 6%. Part of the increase in unemployment resulted from adjustments associated with winding down the Vietnam War; part was owing to monetary–fiscal policies designed to control inflation. In any event, in the first two years of the decade of the seventies, manpower imbalances owing to deficient demand were apparent.

51

Major shifts in aggregate demand, such as those associated with moving into or out of a war, can be associated with some manpower imbalances as the structure of production is modified. These imbalances may be only temporary, provided sufficient aggregate demand can be maintained. In the months after the close of World War II, unemployment rose temporarily as returning veterans were reabsorbed into the educational system or into the labor force, and as women abandoned the factories to resume their roles as wives and mothers; unemployment, however, quickly fell to less than 4%, where it remained until 1949. Similarly, after the Korean War, unemployment in 1954 rose above 5%, but then fell to around 4% for the next three years. The transition from the Vietnam War has proven to be more difficult, since maintaining aggregate demand also implied a validation of strong inflationary pressures and a deteriorating balance-of-payments deficit. The imposition of a tight monetary policy throughout 1970 and ultimately the establishment in August 1971 of a wage–price freeze, followed by wage–price control in November, mitigated somewhat the inflationary pressures.[1] Sufficient public projects with high social priority—education, health, housing, ecological improvements, etc.—were contemplated such that, if they were all implemented by 1975, over 101 million jobs could be generated. This figure will exceed by some 10 million the estimated size of the labor force.[2]

Although in earlier chapters the question of whether structural unemployment could persist in the face of sufficient aggregate demand has been discussed, it has by no means been resolved. There is a belief that the rate of frictional unemployment has trended upward in the United States since 1945. Reduction of unemployment to the frictional floor conceivably could occur, if the pace of reduction were not too rapid, without the development of significant inflationary pressures. After World War II it was felt that this frictional rate was about 3.0 to 3.5%. The experience of the midfifties suggested that the rate had risen to about 4.0 or 4.5%, and the unemployment rates of the early 1960s and early 1970s are cited as evidence that the frictional rate may have increased to about 5%. To reinforce this argument, the increase in inflation in the late 1960s, as the unemployment rate declined below 4.0% and approached 3.5%, is cited. The increase in the frictional

[1] *Manpower Report of the President, March 1965*, p. 46. In 1968, the Council of Economic Advisers had estimated that up to $3 billion might have to be expended on social programs to supplement private demand in order to facilitate the manpower adjustment. *Economic Report of the President, February 1968*, pp. 89–91.

[2] Leonard A. Lecht, *Manpower Requirements for National Objectives in the 1970's*, U.S. Department of Labor, Manpower Administration, 1968. Reprinted in John A. Delehanty (ed.), *Manpower Problems and Policies* (Scranton: International Textbook Co., 1970), p. 111.

floor is a result, it is argued, of structural changes in the economy which make adjustments in the labor market more difficult. Therefore, even in the face of sufficient aggregate demand—i.e., real aggregate demand that is growing at the same pace as the natural increase in the labor force— structural unemployment exists and is reflected in persistent manpower imbalances among particular segments of the labor force, in various industrial sectors, and in different regions of the country.

It is to a consideration of policies designed to remedy these manpower imbalances that we now turn.

Manpower Policies in America

Comprehensive and systematic manpower programs in the United States are of comparatively recent vintage, beginning early in the decade of the 1960s. The relatively high level of unemployment, persisting since late 1957, focused attention upon structural causes and led to a number of remedial programs. Concern about unemployment waned somewhat in the full-employment years of the late 1960s, although programs to lower the excessively high unemployment rates among the disadvantaged were continued. The recurrence of rates in the early 1970s comparable to those of the early 1960s again shifted government interest back to programs to restore people to jobs. Four basic kinds of programs will be considered in the following pages: (1) regional (area) development; (2) training; (3) last-resort employment; and (4) job information. The manpower legislation of the 1960s cuts across all four of these programs, although the major enactments emphasize to different degrees one or more types.

Regional Development

There is a long history of programs to develop the resources of particular regions of the country. The Homestead Acts and the land grants to the railroads of the 19th century were designed to develop the West by providing self-employment opportunities to potential farmers and by encouraging the extension of transportation and industry. Similarly, land grants to colleges beginning in 1862 were offered to promote agricultural and technical training. The Tennessee Valley Authority Act of 1933 was designed to promote the regional growth of the depressed area drained by the Tennessee and Cumberland Rivers by a multifaceted development of resources. Individual states, particularly in the South, after World War II sought to provide jobs for their inhabitants by attracting industry through tax concession grants, low-cost leases of plants, and development of plant sites in

which water, gas, sewage, and electricity installations were provided either
at no or low costs.

The Area Redevelopment Act of 1961 sought to improve the economic
conditions of depressed regions, so identified if they possessed excessively
high unemployment rates (see Chart 3.1). A region is depressed if, in three
of the last four years, its unemployment rate (UR) has been 50% greater
than the national average; or, in two of the last three years, its UR has been
75% greater than the national average; or, in one of the two preceding
years, its UR has been twice the national average.[3] All these criteria are

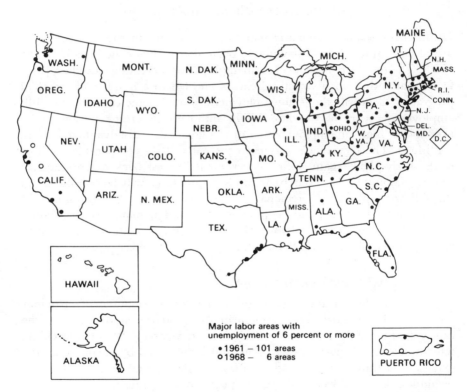

CHART 3.1. Number of depressed areas dropped sharply from 1961 to 1968.

Source: U.S. Department of Labor. *Manpower Report of the President, 1969*, p. 47.

[3] These rates are determined by the Bureau of Employment Security. For a criticism of the
BES procedures and a proposal for an improved one based upon the covered unemployment
rate, see John H. Lindauer, "Effects of Selected Methods to Improve Unemployment
Rates Used to Identify Depressed Areas," *Industrial and Labor Relations Review* (April 1967),
Vol. 20, No. 3, pp. 433–440.

subject to a minimum UR of 6%. The number of such areas declined from about 1300 in 1965 to 850 in 1968, of which about 275 had rates two or more times the national average. The program was revised in 1965 by the Economic Development Act and the Appalachian Regional Development Act. In addition, regional commissions have been established to oversee programs in Appalachia, the Ozarks, the Upper Great Lakes, and the four-corner area of Colorado, Utah, New Mexico, and Arizona.

Depressed regions have become so partly because their dominant industry has declined and partly because the capital base, including human capital, is inadequate.[4] The principal means used to promote jobs for the unemployed in these areas is to encourage industry to relocate and expand into them. A variety of incentives is provided. Federal grants have been extended to improve the capital infrastructure, such as the building of roads and other public works. Low-interest loans have been available to businesses seeking to develop plants in these regions, and technical assistance has been made available. The designation of a region as a depressed one qualifies industries located therein to preferential consideration in their bids on government contracts. These firms need not be the lowest bidder. Some retraining programs for unemployed workers were established, but emphasis was not placed on this form of development. Training was made available to those unemployed persons whose chances of employment in local jobs upon completion of the program were judged to be reasonable. The programs provided for up to 16 weeks of training and for allowances equal to the state's average weekly unemployment compensation. Since the employment prospects of the disadvantaged were not favorable, few were included in ARA programs.[5] Because of the opposition of politicians who feared the loss of constituencies, the proposed relocation of unemployed persons from depressed areas to other more prosperous regions was not made a part of ARA. Thus, the program sought primarily to remedy the physical capital deficiencies of the depressed regions, with little attention given to increasing the human capital base.

In 1962 the Trade Expansion Act did provide for relocation services for persons whose unemployment was substantially caused by import liberalization policies. Moving and transportation costs were to be paid to workers finding jobs in other regions and a cash allowance equivalent to 250% of the average weekly wage was given to the displaced worker. However, until 1970

[4] It has been argued that ghettos of central cities meet all the requirements of depressed regions defined under the Area Redevelopment Act. See the President's Commission on Income Maintenance Program, *Background Papers* (Washington, November 1969), p. 385.
[5] For a description and analysis of a retraining program under ARA, see Richard J. Solie, "Employment Effects of Retraining the Unemployed," *Industrial and Labor Relations Review* (January 1968), Vol. 21, No. 2, pp. 21–25.

few if any workers qualified for relocation allowances.[6] (More liberal were the retraining provisions of the TEA, which permitted up to 78 weeks of training and paid the trainee 65% of his average weekly wage.) In earlier years, between 1935 and 1946, attempts had been made to resettle sub-marginal farmers onto better lands under the Resettlement Administration and its successor, the Farm Security Administration. However, the latter's successor, the Farm Home Administration, abandoned these efforts of resettlement and instead sought to assist the farmer to improve the size and productivity of his farm through low-interest loans.

Under MDTA, 61 pilot programs up to 1969 provided assistance in relocating some 14,000 unemployed or underemployed workers, and experimental programs have been continued through 1971. Some of the projects served only workers whose reemployment potential was high; others served disadvantaged workers. All programs provided (1) job information, (2) moving expenses, and (3) counseling to assist adjustment to an urban environment. The costs amounted to an average of $850 per family, and the projects sought to provide solutions to the kind of operating problems that would be faced if the program were expanded on a much larger scale. So far, it has been discovered that a period of trial and error is necessary to work out relocating procedures and that large support organizations are necessary in both emigrating and immigrating areas. Preliminary visits to the area of relocation of migrants are also desirable.

The area redevelopment programs have been subjected to a number of criticisms.[7] The imprecise definition of a depressed area and the changing composition have made administration difficult. An insufficient amount of resources were appropriated to service the large number of areas that met the definition, and as a result efforts were spread thinly among them. Firms that responded to the incentives of the program often located only a small portion of their facilities in the region. Many of these firms were low paying and had low productivity and, although they provided jobs, they did not upgrade the skills of the workers nor did they provide much employment security. The training programs were not directed at the hard-core unem-ployed, who were the least mobile of the unemployed. Hence, the jobs that

---

[6] The provision of relocation allowances has been called the best method of relieving labor surpluses. Under the Economic Opportunity Act of 1964, demonstration projects were established, and it was found that the younger workers were the most willing to be relocated; older workers were reluctant to move, and rural workers tended to return home after relocation. See Edward C. and Karen S. Koziara, "Development of Relocation Allowances as Manpower Policy," *Industrial and Labor Relations Review* (October 1966), Vol. 20, No. 1, pp. 66–75. In 1970, for the first time under TEA some 16,000 workers were certified as eligible for direct assistance and the program was expanded in 1971.

[7] President's Commission on Income Maintenance Programs, *Background Papers*, p. 385.

were provided may have gone to persons who would have had an advantage in obtaining employment even without the program. The reduction in the number of depressed areas in the second half of the 1960s suggests that deficient demand rather than structural unemployment had qualified these regions under the Act, but it was the latter type of unemployment that the Act sought to remedy.

The commitment of the United States to regional development has been much less than that of the United Kingdom. Although unemployment rates since 1945 have been normally below 2%, pockets of substantial unemployment did and do exist in Britain. To correct these heavy incidences of unemployment, Britain has emphasized programs that bring jobs to workers.[8] Under the Local Employment Acts of 1960 and 1963, the Board of Trade allotted the construction of new plants by issuing industrial development certificates. These certificates prevented industry from locating in overcrowded centers. In addition, the Board of Trade also built and leased new plant facilities in areas of high unemployment, and it provided loans and grants for the purchase of plant and equipment in these areas. In 1964 the Industrial Training Act was passed which provided training allowances for new industries locating in depressed areas. Although emphasis is placed upon training provided by private employers, over 50 Government Training Centers existed in 1970 to provide trainees with six-month courses in new or higher level skills. In addition, tax rebates and investment allowances are provided to industries locating in depressed regions. Emphasis has been placed upon providing guidance and counseling to young people to assist them in their vocational choices, and an efficient national employment exchange is in operation. Planning for technological displacement of workers has permitted firms to mitigate much unemployment, and lump-sum separation payments are required under the Redundancy Act for displaced workers. Finally, resettlement payments are provided to workers willing to transfer from depressed areas. Although unemployment rose to one million persons in the U.K. in late 1971, a rate of 5%, this was a result of deficient demand.

Training

The Manpower Development and Training Act (MDTA) was passed in 1962 to provide training for those structurally unemployed owing to the relocation of industry and for technologically displaced workers. Revisions of

[8] See OECD, *Manpower Policy in the United Kingdom*, Paris, 1970; L. Hunter, G. Reid, D. Boddy, *Labour Problems of Technological Change* (London: George Allen and Unwin, Ltd., 1970); and William H. Miernyk, "Experience Under the British Local Employment Acts of 1960 and 1963," *Industrial and Labor Relations Review* (October 1966), Vol. 20, No. 1, pp. 30–49.

the Act in 1963 and 1965 extended the training benefits to the disadvantaged. Also designed to assist the disadvantaged, the Economic Opportunity Act of 1964 provided training and direct employment opportunities to the unemployed. There are three basic types of training provided by the two Acts; institutional, on the job (OJT), and the Job Corps.[9] Another related training program is that associated with vocational education (see Table 3.1).

Institutional Training

Institutional training is provided in a classroom setting. Skills are taught which ordinarily can be mastered in one year: auto mechanics, welding, nurses' aid, etc. In addition, general training applicable to a variety of skills is offered. Disadvantaged youths are taught how to conduct themselves in an employment interview, how to dress, and in some cases, how to speak. Trainees receive a living allowance, which accounted for about 60% of the average cost of $2000 per trainee. Although the program is more expensive than on-the-job training, it appears to have paid benefits greater than the cost. It has reportedly attracted trainees who were the "cream of the crop" among the disadvantaged, not too old or too uneducated; about one-half were from families with annual incomes of less than $3000.

On-the-Job Training

On-the-job training is a shorter program and has fewer of the disadvantaged enrolled in it. It contains about one-half of all those in training programs, and it is a program in which training is carried out by employers. Trainees are referred to cooperating employers by the Employment Service and those selected for training by employers are subsidized by MDTA. The average subsidy per trainee has been about $500. The lower cost is explained by the fact that trainees receive salaries and that part of the cost is borne by the employer. The subsidy is used to persuade the employer to lower hiring standards. Because of the lower cost, OJT has been favored by the MDTA and Congress. Another advantage is the increased relevance of the program to future employment, a motivational factor of some importance in encouraging completion of the program. In order to increase the chances of success of OJT, some programs have devised a "buddy system" whereby an experienced worker not only coaches a trainee in job techniques but also provides moral support. The purpose is to prevent alienation or rejection of

[9] Descriptions of these programs can be found in the President's Commission on Income Maintenance, *Background Papers, Poverty Amid Plenty* (Washington, November, 1969). Sar A. Levitan, "Manpower Aspects of the Economic Opportunity Act," and Earl D. Main, "A Nationwide Evaluation of MDTA Institutional Job Training," both in John A. Delehanty, *Manpower Problems and Policy* (Scranton: Intext Publishing Co., 1970), pp. 364–389.

TABLE 3.1
FIRST-TIME ENROLLMENTS[a] IN FEDERALLY ASSISTED WORK AND TRAINING PROGRAMS, FISCAL YEARS 1964 AND 1969–1972
(Thousands)

Program	1964	1969	1970	1971 (esti-mated)	1972 (esti-mated)
Total	278	1,745	1,819	2,027	2,194
Institutional training under the MDTA	69	135	130	130 ⎫	
JOBS (federally financed) and other on-the-job training[b]	9	136	178	226 ⎪	
Neighborhood Youth Corps:				⎪	
In school and summer		430	436	411 ⎪	
Out of school		74	46	64 ⎬ 1,205[c]	
Operation Mainstream		11	13	12 ⎪	
Public Service Careers[d]		4	4	39 ⎪	
Concentrated Employment Program		127	112	113 ⎪	
Job Corps		53	43	45 ⎭	
Work Incentive Program		81	93	125	187
Veterans programs	([e])	59	83	115	120
Vocational Rehabilitation	179	368	411	442	385
Other programs[f]	21	267	271	304	297

[a] Generally larger than the number of training or work opportunities programmed because turnover or short-term training results in more than one individual in a given enrollment opportunity. Persons served by more than one program are counted only once.

[b] Includes the MDTA-OJT program which ended with fiscal 1970 and the JOBS-Optional Program which began with fiscal 1971.

[c] Relates to the President's request in the 1972 budget for special revenue sharing for manpower training. No enrollments for categorical programs are estimated since, under the manpower reform proposal, States and local communities would be given the opportunity to determine how funds would be used.

[d] Enrollees in the Supplemental Training and Employment Program (STEP) segment of PSC are not included since they have previously been enrolled in one of the other manpower programs.

[e] Included with "other programs."

[f] Includes a wide variety of programs, some quite small—for example, Foster Grandparents and vocational training for Indians by the Department of the Interior. Data for some programs are estimated.

Note: Detail may not add to totals because of rounding.

Source: Office of Management and Budget, "Special Analyses, Budget of the United States Government, Fiscal Year 1972," p. 138 (with a few minor revisions in 1970 data for programs administered by the Department of Labor). *Manpower Report of the President, 1971*, p. 37.

minority group trainees by the work force. If the trainee successfully completes the program, a bonus is paid to the "buddy."

An important subsidiary of OJT is the program sponsored by the National Alliance of Businessmen in 1968 called Job Opportunities in the Business Sector (JOBS). The goal of JOBS was to provide 500,000 jobs for the hard-core unemployed in the three-year period ending in 1971. Subsidies were provided to businessmen to offset training costs, and it was estimated that the cost per trainee amounted to $3000. This figure is higher than OJT because a less qualified trainee is accepted. When unemployment began to increase in 1970, many participating employers discontinued or curtailed the program, since reductions in their labor force made training unnecessary to fill their employment needs. Hence, in 1971 the JOBS program appeared to fall short of its goal. There are also numerous individual projects funded by MDTA which have specific training objectives.[10]

Job Corps

This is a residential program for disadvantaged youths aged 14 to 21. Originally it was to be restricted to men, who were ideally thought to be the principal breadwinners. In 1966, however, women were admitted to the program. By 1967 over one-half of the enrollees were Blacks. It is a multipurpose undertaking designed to provide remedial education, guidance and counseling, job skills, work experience, and conservation services. In 1968 about 100,000 men were enrolled in 109 centers at an average cost of almost $7000 per trainee. Some Job Corp Centers are located in urban areas; others are located in Conservation Centers where about 40% of the work is in conservation. In the urban centers, greater stress is placed on work-oriented vocational training, with educational training in math and reading. For every nine months spent in the Job Corps, the reading level has been raised by 1.5 years and the math level by 1.8 years. The employment record of those completing the program is good, and morale of participants has been high. The younger the enrollee, the greater has been the likelihood of his dropping out of this program. In 1969, over one-half of the Job Corps Centers were closed and 30 new centers, to concentrate on training and job placement instead of conservation, were planned for inner city sites.

---

[10] One such project is described by David B. Lipskey, John E. Drotning, Myron D. Fottler, "Some Correlates of Trainee Success in a Coupled On-the-Job Training Program," *Quarterly Review of Economics and Business* (Summer 1971), Vol. 11, No. 2, pp. 41–62. "Coupled OJT" combines OJT with classroom training. This project provided 44 weeks of training, with 12 hours per week devoted to tutoring the trainee in order to bring him up to the level of an 8th grade education. The employee received his regular wage during the tutoring; the employer provided space for the classroom and was reimbursed for the costs he incurred. The program was designed primarily for Blacks.

In 1970 two new types of centers were opened: (1) residential manpower centers, and (2) residential support centers. These centers are located near the homes of enrollees in order to reduce the dropout rate. The manpower centers offer training both to residents and nonresidents, whereas in support centers additional guidance and counseling services are offered to residential youths with special problems. Training resources in the localities supplement the services of both types of centers.

Other Training Programs

For persons completing OJT who were still unable to find jobs but who could benefit from additional training, a new program was established in 1970. Called STEP (Supplemental Training and Employment Program), the program may be repeated if after a 13-week program has been completed, participants are still unable to find jobs. STEP is a part of the Public Service Careers program.

The Public Service Careers program (PSC), also started in 1970, also includes the New Careers program, a program to provide on-the-job training in human service occupations where a manpower shortage exists, such as in health, welfare, and education. Other PSC programs place workers in regular jobs in Federal, state, and local government agencies. Training and supportive services are provided to enrollees. The program is designed to assist the disadvantaged in obtaining work experience.

The Concentrated Employment Program has been designed to provide jobs and training for workers in urban slums and rural areas of poverty. However, in 1971 this program in 80 local centers was operating at a reduced level although it had been redesigned in 1969. Additional experimental training programs have been undertaken to assist drug offenders and prison inmates in learning marketable skills. Inmate training occurs at state and local levels, and some success has been achieved. Results so far have been discouraging with drug offenders.

Vocational Education and Rehabilitation

The Vocational Education Acts of 1963 and 1965 sought to modernize this form of education in which most enrollees were in agricultural and home economics programs. Although these programs still contain a majority of the students, the proportion is diminishing. Federal funds were appropriated to support the development of area vocational schools, teacher training, and vocational guidance on a matching basis with state funds. In the late 1960s, one of every four secondary students was enrolled in a vocational education program. The recent trend seems to be to develop postsecondary sub-professional training. The 1968 amendments to the Act authorized studies

on manpower needs at the national, regional, state, and local levels in order
to orient vocational education in proper directions.

Vocational rehabilitation programs, long successful in finding jobs for
the physically handicapped (Chart 3.2), but not necessarily for socially or
economically disadvantaged workers, were broadened in 1965 to include
those handicapped by behavioral disorders. Emphasis has been and remains
centered on guidance and counseling rather than training. Training is
frequently subsidized for enrollment in existing educational institutions.
Much of the training is for clerical or service occupations. Grants have been
made available for expanded research, for training of rehabilitation
personnel, and for expansion of coverage of the program. In the past, heavy
case loads and the pressure to report results led to an avoidance of
difficult cases. Increased federal funding and standards are designed to
remedy this defect and to expand the number of handicapped persons
eligible to receive assistance under the state-administered programs. State
residence requirements are being abolished for eligibility, and racial
discrimination has been prohibited. It is estimated that 4.5 million persons
could benefit from vocational rehabilitation.

Evaluation

Training programs appear to be worthwhile in terms of benefits
provided in relationship to costs; however, most authors of cost–benefit
studies appropriately qualify their conclusions. Graduates of the programs
appear to be helped in securing employment; yet, whether or not the jobs
are necessarily better paying than earlier ones is not clear. Unquestionably
the employment growth accompanying the vigorous economic expansion
beginning in 1964 obscured the results of the programs. The fact that
trainees were able to find jobs upon completion of the program may have
been owing as much or more to the economic situation than to the program.
The administrators of the programs have been under pressure to show
results in order to qualify for refunding; therefore, the programs have been
accused of favoring the enrollment of those trainees who were most likely to
find jobs, even without the training. Consequently, questions have been
raised as to whether those who most need assistance in acquiring job skills
have been the benefactors of the programs. Congress appears to have been
quick to experiment with new programs without giving old ones a chance
to mature and benefit from earlier mistakes. Preliminary research into the
problems of the disadvantaged, the forms of training which they can absorb,
and the methods by which they can be taught appear to have been absent
(see Table 3.2).

Nevertheless, these programs have affected large numbers of trainees.
Almost 1.6 million persons were enrolled in MDTA and the Job Corps

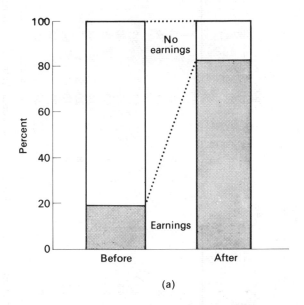

(a)

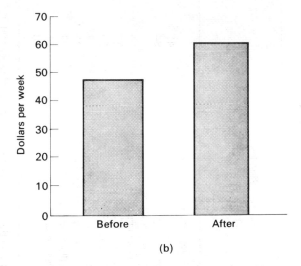

(b)

CHART 3.2. (a) Rehabilitation quadrupled proportion of handicapped people with earnings, and (b) increased median pay by almost one-third.

Source: U.S. Department of Labor, based on data from the U.S. Department of Health, Education, and Welfare. *Manpower Report of the President, 1969*, p. 115.

TABLE 3.2
CHARACTERISTICS OF ENROLLEES IN FEDERALLY ASSISTED WORK AND TRAINING PROGRAMS, FISCAL YEAR 1970

Percent of Total Enrollees

Program	Women	Black[a]	Age		Years of School Completed		On Public Assistance[b]
			Under 22 Years	45 Years and Over	8 or Less	9 to 11	
Manpower Development and Training Act:							
Institutional training	41	36	37	9	15	38	13
On-the-job training	34	30	35	11	17	36	6
Neighborhood Youth Corps:							
In school and summer	50	42	100		17	82	32
Out of school	52	44	98		32	66	33
Operation Mainstream	29	25	4	51	52	28	18
New Careers	77	63	21	7	13	42	32
Concentrated Employment Program	42	67	41	8	20	45	12
JOBS (federally financed)	32	72	47	4	15	50	16
Work Incentive Program	71	43	23	6	24	44	100
Job Corps	26	61	100		37	56	31

[a] Substantially all the remaining enrollees were white except in Operation Mainstream, JOBS, and Job Corps. In these programs, 10 to 12% were American Indians, Eskimos, or Orientals.

[b] The definition of "public assistance" used in these figures varies somewhat among programs (e.g., it may or may not include receipt of food stamps and "in kind" benefits). In the NYC program, it may relate to enrollees' families as well as enrollees themselves.

Source: *Manpower Report of the President, 1971*, p. 39.

between 1962 and 1970. Of this number, less than one million completed the programs. It has been estimated that about 175,000 persons out of almost one million served by State and Vocational Rehabilitation Agencies were rehabilitated in 1967.[11] These are large numbers, especially in a full-employment economy. It suggests the magnitude of training programs that will be needed in the future if structural unemployment continues to expand.

Last Resort Employment Programs

A number of programs under the Economic Opportunity Act have been termed "make work" projects. They are (1) the Neighborhood Youth Corps, (2) Operation Mainstream, and (3) the Work Incentive Program. They have been called "last resort" programs because most participants would not otherwise have been employed. The "make work" term refers to the sometimes trivial nature of the tasks assigned to the enrollees.

Neighborhood Youth Corps

The Neighborhood Youth Corps[12] (Table 3.3) attracted almost three million young people up to 1970. It consists of two basic programs. One is an in-school program offering temporary employment during the school year and ten weeks of employment in the summer. The other is designed to accommodate young people who have dropped out of school. The in-school component offers ten hours of employment weekly at hourly rates of $1.25, mostly in public agencies. Girls perform clerical tasks or serve as library assistants; boys do custodial, maintenance, or conservation work. The program has been called an income supplement program whose main accomplishment is to keep in school potential dropouts. The summer program has been called a form of antiriot insurance. Although some work experience has been provided, few skills with a market value are learned. The out-of-school program also provides work experience. Its principal value appears to be the counseling service which it provides. Many are encouraged to return to school. The average enrollment is for about 14 weeks. Both programs show a positive relationship between participation and subsequent successful employment; however, this may be owing to the fact that participants enter the labor market, particularly in the in-school programs, later than they otherwise would. Hence, they are somewhat more mature. Ninety percent or more of the cost of the programs may be

[11] President's Commission on Income Maintenance Programs, *Background Papers*, pp. 313, 314; *Poverty Amid Plenty*, pp. 101, 102.
[12] *Background Papers*, pp. 389–391.

TABLE 3.3

CHARACTERISTICS OF YOUTH ENROLLED IN NEIGHBORHOOD YOUTH CORPS PROJECTS, BY SCHOOL STATUS, SEPTEMBER 1965–AUGUST 1970

Characteristic	In School[a]					Out of School				
	September 1969–August 1970	September 1968–August 1969	September 1967–August 1968	September 1966–August 1967	September 1965–August 1966	September 1969–August 1970	September 1968–August 1969	September 1967–August 1968	September 1966–August 1967	September 1965–August 1966
Percent living in public housing	13.5	17.5	16.5	14.4	11.8	16.7	17.2	14.9	14.0	14.2
Percent with family on public assistance	32.3	30.3	28.2	27.3	26.0	33.0	32.0	28.1	26.4	27.5
Percent contributing to family support before NYC	46.1	37.4	37.9	37.3	37.5	56.5	59.6	59.0	56.7	52.0
Percent who ever had a paying job	56.8	36.8	38.3	43.8	41.5	58.4	66.5	66.6	65.3	61.9
Hours worked per week on last paying job:										
1 to 15 hours	17.8	30.0	35.1	32.0	36.7	9.9	9.2	12.1	10.6	11.1
16 to 40 hours	78.0	66.2	59.0	59.4	53.2	77.0	78.3	74.2	70.5	69.4
More than 40 hours	4.6	4.8	5.8	7.7	10.1	13.1	12.5	13.7	18.9	19.5

[a] Includes 1,493,000 youth enrolled in summer projects since the beginning of the program in January 1965.

Source: *Manpower Report of the President, 1971*, p. 309.

subsidized by EOA, and up to 10% by the cooperating public agency, although in practice the share of the local sponsor may be as low as 1%.[13]

Operation Mainstream[14]

Operation Mainstream (Table 3.4) is similar to the Neighborhood Youth Corps, except that it is directed at the hard-core adult, rural unemployed. The average age of participants is about 45. It too utilizes participants in conservation and public projects. By reintegrating the long-term unemployed into the labor force, it seeks to encourage movement to better jobs.

Work Experience and Training[15]

Work experience and training projects have been sponsored by the Health, Education, and Welfare Department and, like Mainstream, seek to improve the employment opportunities of the rural adult. Participants in the Work Incentive Program (WIN) are welfare recipients for whom jobs, usually menial, are offered with the goal of encouraging them to acquire means of self-support. Since the jobs are low paying and of uncertain duration, there is little incentive for welfare recipients to accept them. Where welfare payments are reduced when income is earned, there is even less incentive to "work for nothing." At present, WIN is expanding rapidly and rivals NYC in size. About 71% of enrollees in WIN are women; about 43% are Blacks.

Evaluation

The rationale behind the "last resort" employment projects is that in their absence, relief or welfare payments must be provided. It is argued that, for youths, the alternatives would be the costs of controlling increased unrest or delinquency. How much better it would be, the argument goes, for the country to receive some output in return for these payments. Not only does the society benefit by receiving marginal services, but the participants also gain self-respect and work experience. If the work provided truly is trivial, one wonders just how much self-respect and work experience is provided. However, except for the NYC, most of the programs have not been on a large scale (see Table 3.5).

Although economic expansion concealed somewhat the effects of manpower programs after the U.S. involvement in the Vietnam War, there

---

[13] See Gerald G. Somers and Ernest W. Stromsdorfer, *A Cost-Effectiveness Analysis of the In-School and Summer NYC*, Department of Economics, University of Wisconsin, Madison, 1969.
[14] For a brief criticism of this program, see Sar Levitan, "Manpower Aspects of the Economic Opportunity Act," pp. 365–374.
[15] *Ibid.*, pp. 365, 370–371.

TABLE 3.4
CHARACTERISTICS OF PERSONS ENROLLED IN OPERATION MAINSTREAM, FISCAL YEAR 1970

(Percent distribution)

Characteristic	Enrollees	Characteristic	Enrollees
Total: Number (thousands)	12.5	Marital status:	
Percent	100.0	Single	21.9
		Married	53.4
Sex:		Widowed, divorced, separated	24.7
Male	70.8		
Female	29.2	Estimated annual family income: Median	$1,718
		Percent	100.0
Age: Median	44.9		
Percent	100.0	Below $1,000	69.7
Under 19 years	2.0	$1,000—$1,999	18.9
19 to 21 years	1.7	$2,000—$2,999	7.3
22 to 34 years	29.1	$3,000—$3,999	2.9
35 to 44 years	16.7	$4,000—$4,999	1.3
45 years and over	50.6	$5,000 and over	
		Head of household:	
Race:		Enrollee	64.5
White	61.6	Father	18.0
Black	24.6	Mother	6.7
Other	13.8	Other	10.7
Spanish surname	12.2	Percent with children	40.6
		Percent living in public housing	10.1
Years of school completed: Median	8.9	Percent with family on public assistance	18.4
Percent	100.0	Percent contributing to family support before enrollment	81.7
Under 8 years	29.7	Percent who ever had a paying job	93.6
8 years	21.9		
9 to 11 years	28.1		
12 years	18.6		
Over 12 years	1.7		

Source: *Manpower Report of the President, 1971,* p. 309.

68

TABLE 3.5
UNEMPLOYMENT BY AGE, SEX, AND RACE, 1969

Age, Sex, and Race	Number (thousands)	Percentage distribution	Rate (percent)[a]
Total unemployment	2,831	100	3.5
Teenagers 16–19 years of age	853	30	12.2
Males	441	16	11.4
White	343	12	10.1
Black and other races	97	3	21.3
Females	412	15	13.3
White	317	11	11.5
Black and other races	95	3	27.7
Adults 20–44 years of age	1,370	48	3.2
Males	630	22	2.4
White	509	18	2.1
Black and other races	122	4	4.2
Females	740	26	4.7
White	571	20	4.2
Black and other races	168	6	7.2
Adults 45 years of age and over	608	21	2.0
Males	332	12	1.7
White	285	10	1.6
Black and other races	47	2	2.8
Females	276	10	2.4
White	235	8	2.3
Black and other races	41	1	3.3

[a] Number of unemployed in each group as percent of labor force in that group.

Note.—Detail will not necessarily add to totals because of rounding.

Source: Department of Labor, Bureau of Labor Statistics. *Economic Report of the President, 1970*, p. 152.

is some evidence that unemployment rates were reduced. The primary impact was to reduce unemployment rates for young persons, ages 16–21, by 2.5%. Over-all unemployment rates were affected as follows:[16]

Year	Reduction in UR (%)
1965	0.15
1966	0.3
1967	0.4

[16] M. S. Cohen, "The Direct Effect of Federal Manpower Programs in Reducing Unemployment," *Journal of Human Resources*, Vol. 4, No. 4 (Fall, 1969).

The Neighborhood Youth Corps accounted for about two-thirds of the 1967 reduction.

Providing Job Information

There are two dimensions to successful job placement. One involves guidance and counseling of preentrants into the labor force and of unemployed members in order to determine the types of occupations and jobs for which they are best suited.[17] This requires aptitude testing and testing of educational levels of achievement in order to know the type and extent of training or remedial education most beneficial to those being counseled. The growth of manpower programs has logically led to increased demand for and utilization of these services. The second aspect requires a knowledge of job availability and of applicants seeking employment, together with a procedure whereby prospective employees can be directed into the appropriate job vacancies. Not only must the state of the current labor market be determined, but rational manpower planning requires a detailed knowledge of the changing occupational structure and job content. Forecasting structure and content requires a knowledge of their past determinants and how these determinants, when undergoing change, have altered the content and frequency of jobs. Estimation of the dimensions and geography of these determinants then permits estimates of the changing nature of the job structure at some predetermined time.[18] From these estimates, desirable mobility patterns and training needs can be ascertained. The performance of these two dimensions to job placement requires labor market information, and the agency responsible for assembling and utilizing this information in most countries has been the employment exchange service.

The original United States Employment Service was established in World War I to recruit workers to meet the vast expansion of wartime industry. It was disbanded at the end of the war, and efforts to revive it were unsuccessful until the early 1930s, when massive unemployment made the need for a labor market information service painfully obvious. In 1933 the Wagner–Peyser bill established the United States Employment Service (USES), a coordinating agency for state employment offices. Thus, a joint federal–state program was established under which the federal government

[17] "Guidance and Counseling are central to the whole educational and training process in terms of adjustment and orientation to the work environment." S. Wolfbein, *Employment, Unemployment, and Public Policy* (New York: Random House, 1965), p. 136.

[18] "Given the structure and nature of the capital stock, technology, product and factor markets affecting use of resources, and the levels of education and training, the various types of jobs which will exist are substantially determined." James G. Scoville, *The Job Content of the U.S. Economy, 1940–1970* (New York: McGraw-Hill Book Company, 1969), p. 11.

paid all administrative expenses and matched funds provided by participating states for the programs of the state employment offices. Under the Social Security Act of 1935, a system of unemployment insurance compensation (UI) was established whereby states were encouraged to adopt UI programs through rebates of 90% from a 3% payroll tax on the first $3000 of annual income of covered employees. The state unemployment compensation offices, which received and processed claims, were combined with the state employment offices. In addition to their other duties the ES offices were given the responsibility of determining if work eligibility criteria of claimants had been satisfied. Moreover, during periods of heavy unemployment ES personnel have been utilized by the UI offices to process claims, to the neglect of the job placement duties of the ES personnel. As a result of the subordination of ES services to those of the UI, it has colloquially become known as the "unemployment office." The remainder of the 3% payroll tax not rebated to the states has been used for administrative expenses of the UI and ES offices. During World War II, the state employment offices were federalized and placed under the War Manpower Commission, with the responsibility of providing an efficient national employment exchange, which it proceeded to do. The success of this wartime experience of an integrated, coordinated, creative national employment exchange, together with the deficiencies of the pre- and post-World War II combined UI and ES services, has led to repeated recommendations for the establishment of a separate nationwide federal service. Apparently, however, it will require a major manpower crisis for this to occur.[19]

The state employment services have been beset with many problems. They have been accused of being passive agents in locating jobs for applicants, so much so that many applicants have come to regard the job placement services of ES as being valueless.[20] Little effort had been devoted to actively seeking new positions for applicants or encouraging employers to list openings with them. Priorities for the placement of applicants appear to have been lacking, even when national policy is designed to accommodate particular groups. Although the number of recorded placements has long dominated the criteria for the funding of ES and for promotion of personnel, no clear-cut goals concerning the nature and permanence of placements have been established. In fact, a system was devised that emphasized placements

[19] Pilot projects in 1962 in 55 major urban centers involved a physical separation of UI and ES services and centers, resulting in a substantial improvement in nonfarm placements. The President's Commission on Income Maintenance Programs, *Background Papers*, p. 375. Opposition to separation has come from the state UI bureaus, private employment agencies, and surprisingly from the AFL–CIO.

[20] F. F. Foltman, *White and Blue Collars in a Mill Shutdown* (Ithaca: School of Industrial and Labor Relations, Cornell University, 1968), pp. 72–73.

in nonpermanent, low-skilled jobs because such placements required less processing time per applicant. Such placements were preferred because of insufficient personnel to provide fully all the services for which ES was responsible. The deficiency in personnel resulted from a budget smaller in 1960 than in 1948. On the one hand, ES has been faced with declining funds; on the other, under the federal manpower programs it has been assigned increasing responsibilities in testing and placing trainees and disadvantaged persons in the programs. Because the state ES offices were oriented more toward servicing the needs of the combined UI–ES offices, the ES perhaps has not been as responsive or as creative in servicing the needs of the federal programs as the administrators of the latter would prefer.

The Job Bank

In response to increasing pressure, in 1969 the USES was renamed the U.S. Training and Employment Service and placed in the Office of Manpower Administration. The local employment security offices have been designated "manpower service centers"; however, they are still connected with the UI program. Since many of the testing services were ill-suited to measure aptitude and educational achievement levels of the disadvantaged, new tests have been devised. More extensive testing and counseling services are offered to secondary students before they finish school in order to assist them in preparing for tomorrow's job market. In 1970 a computerized job bank service to match persons with jobs was established in major U.S. cities (see Table 3.6). In 1971 it was extended to over 100 large cities with plans to extend job information services across state lines. Larger Congressional appropriations have been made available to the centers, and proposals to increase the payroll tax base from $3000 to $6000 have been proffered in order to provide more funds for the centers. Proposals giving high priority to an increase in the quality and quantity of ES personnel have also been made. Yet implementation of proposals to improve ES has only partially occurred.[21] Until this is done, the United States will lack a national employment exchange service as efficient as other industrial countries possess or as it enjoyed during World War II. The establishment of job banks in large urban markets is a desirable step. Such a service will

---

[21] An Employment Service Task Force, chaired by George Schultz, in 1964 unanimously recommended the following: (1) Identification of the appropriate role and mission of the ES. (2) Further separation of the administration of the ES from that of UI. (3) Improving relations with other groups in the labor market. (4) Improving the quality and compensation of ES personnel, principally at the State and local levels. (5) Improving interarea recruitment procedures with the aid of modern information technology. (6) Improving the quality of management in the Service and strengthening its finances. The President's Commission on Income Maintenance, *Background Papers*, p. 377.

be of particular value to Blacks and other minority groups whose source of job information has been found to be inferior to that of Whites.[22] The USTES is their primary institutionalized source of information, and in the past the pressure to register a high incidence of placements when faced with a limited budget caused the Employment Service to channel Black applicants into low-skill, casual jobs. Little testing, counseling, or other employment services were provided and the jobs to which they were referred came to be identified as "Negro jobs." Job information is particularly scarce for Blacks migrating between geographical regions, and as a consequence the unemployment rates among migrating Blacks is higher than the norm. Hopefully, the job banks will remedy this information gap.

One of the other programs under OEA, the Community Action Program, has been commended for some of its innovations in developing jobs for disadvantaged persons. The CAP is a federally funded, community sponsored program designed to organize services for the poor. Through "outreach" it seeks to locate the unemployed poor, and then to enlist the aid of employers in the community to provide immediate jobs to the disadvantaged. It has been so successful and innovative in its job develop-ment procedures that the USES has patterned some of its job recruitment policies after CAP procedures. CAP also has established local training programs at the subprofessional level, often based upon surveys to determine the type of jobs in which trainees could best be placed.

Conclusion

The United States experimented with a wide variety of manpower pro-grams during the 1960s. It is this diversity, however, which is the source of much of the criticism of the nation's policy to correct manpower im-balances. There has been no systematic, coordinated program to attack the sources of structural unemployment; rather, Congress has capriciously favored one approach and then another. The programs have been accused of being implemented without knowledge of what the problems actually were or whether the proposed remedies reached the source of the problems. Inadequate funding and dispersed administrative responsibility almost assured that less than optimal results would be achieved. In order to produce quick and visible results, unemployed persons were assisted who least required it, while the hard-core and disadvantaged remained outside the programs. In fact, appraisal of the programs is difficult because the diverse agencies responsible for administration also disperse the sources of data upon

---

[22] M. Lurie and E. Rayack. "Racial Differences in Migration and Job Search: A Case Study," *Southern Economic Journal*, Vol. 33, No. 1 (July 1966).

TABLE 3.6
SELECTED EMPLOYMENT SERVICE ACTIVITIES, FISCAL YEARS 1969–1970

(Thousands)

State	Total Nonagricultural Placements				Nonagricultural Job Openings		New Applications				Initial Counselling Interviews			
	All Applicants		Disadvantaged				All Applicants		Disadvantaged		All Applicants		Disadvantaged	
	FY 1970	FY 1969	FY 1970	FY 1969	FY 1970	FY 1969	FY 1970	FY 1969	FY 1970	FY 1969	FY 1970	FY 1969	FY 1970	FY 1969
United States	4,604	5,524	964	972	6,736	7,903	9,957	9,963	1,640	1,680	1,083	1,145	459	469
Alabama	84	93	20	18	121	131	213	208	49	45	17	19	8	7
Alaska	14	16	2	3	18	20	27	21	3	3	2	2	1	1
Arizona	76	85	13	13	99	111	111	119	19	20	7	7	4	4
Arkansas	82	101	34	43	94	113	132	146	38	52	11	14	7	10
California	395	482	54	63	719	832	926	1,192	158	134	70	91	33	37
Colorado	86	94	6	6	112	119	146	128	12	10	14	14	5	3
Connecticut	50	64	11	11	85	97	190	160	21	21	19	17	9	7
Delaware	5	6	(a)	1	10	11	18	18	2	2	2	2	(a)	1
District of Columbia	39	43	26	27	74	75	93	104	60	75	8	7	6	5
Florida	163	184	32	28	254	274	220	219	43	36	21	24	11	11
Georgia	105	138	27	19	160	204	213	196	41	35	19	18	11	11
Guam	1	(a)	—	—	11	9	2	2	—	—	(a)	(a)	—	—
Hawaii	11	11	1	1	24	26	44	37	4	3	3	3	1	1
Idaho	29	33	1	2	39	43	55	52	3	2	5	5	2	1
Illinois	151	182	21	27	226	251	431	385	86	89	63	67	30	32
Indiana	104	124	18	23	145	176	269	247	18	23	18	23	7	10
Iowa	55	69	6	7	77	92	91	87	6	7	8	9	3	3
Kansas	52	63	7	10	75	90	106	98	8	10	12	13	4	4
Kentucky	52	61	13	15	67	80	163	151	32	31	21	20	11	10
Louisiana	65	93	25	27	79	108	153	146	39	37	15	12	8	7
Maine	16	16	1	1	28	28	39	37	2	2	6	7	2	2

Maryland	58	67	14	16	110	124	169	162	32	44	21	23	7	11
Massachusetts	107	121	49	42	143	163	281	250	94	65	34	30	28	19
Michigan	164	202	19	20	203	246	511	432	49	56	46	51	20	22
Minnesota	82	104	6	8	106	136	188	191	13	19	14	16	4	4
Mississippi	87	87	21	22	105	105	153	150	37	41	28	28	11	4
Missouri	93	107	20	25	141	153	232	231	31	39	23	26	7	10
Montana	32	33	2	2	39	42	59	55	4	4	9	9	2	9
Nebraska	41	48	2	4	54	61	61	62	4	5	8	9	2	2
Nevada	29	29	2	1	40	40	45	39	3	3	3	5	1	2
New Hampshire	13	14	(a)	(a)	28	29	44	38	1	1	8	8	(a)	1
New Jersey	115	135	20	18	180	209	342	327	38	41	43	45	17	19
New Mexico	32	34	15	13	40	41	64	63	15	18	8	10	5	6
New York	557	639	129	81	778	972	761	734	143	124	108	107	35	31
North Carolina	89	102	14	14	153	170	244	236	31	31	24	28	7	10
North Dakota	22	23	3	3	31	32	36	33	4	3	3	3	1	1
Ohio	164	216	30	30	257	314	411	478	59	93	34	36	14	13
Oklahoma	138	153	44	35	166	181	154	145	26	29	18	19	8	11
Oregon	56	66	12	11	91	97	128	144	8	12	16	15	6	6
Pennsylvania	224	276	19	23	327	369	498	517	51	54	78	87	27	31
Puerto Rico	32	64	14	24	44	76	137	180	72	77	11	11	9	7
Rhode Island	20	23	1	1	33	37	54	46	2	2	8	9	3	2
South Carolina	54	61	13	12	80	92	123	120	24	26	9	11	4	4
South Dakota	22	25	5	4	33	38	36	33	6	5	5	4	4	2
Tennessee	93	106	15	14	126	145	178	181	34	32	19	20	10	11
Texas	368	476	125	143	493	615	692	659	123	125	75	75	31	33
Utah	31	35	7	11	41	50	62	68	6	5	9	10	3	4
Vermont	9	11	1	1	19	21	17	19	2	2	3	3	1	1
Virginia	92	104	17	18	130	148	197	192	29	31	27	29	6	9
Virgin Islands	3	2	—	—	7	8	7	5	—	—	1	(a)	—	—
Washington	47	99	9	14	70	130	159	163	16	16	7	7	4	4
West Virginia	26	24	7	5	31	29	85	81	20	18	16	16	7	7
Wisconsin	53	66	8	9	95	118	170	161	17	20	20	17	7	6
Wyoming	15	16	2	2	21	23	17	17	2	2	2	2	1	1

[a] Less than 500.

Source: *Manpower Report of the President, 1971*, p. 313.

which evaluation can proceed. Moreover, the changing and short-lived nature of Congressional policy has prevented administrators from benefiting from their mistakes.

Establishing an independent and adequately funded national employment service would be a step in the right direction toward a sound manpower policy.[23] Presumably, because structural causes of unemployment are not expected to diminish, the provision of permanent subsidized vocational institutions would be a necessary service of the national organization. Such an organization might also be given responsibility and means to assist or encourage industry to move to chronic areas of unemployment, and simultaneously to subsidize the movement of the hard-core unemployed to areas of labor shortages, with interim arrangements for sufficient training to enable them to compete for jobs. Moreover, national educational policy perhaps should be directed toward providing individuals with the type of education which can best serve their abilities and aptitudes. An expansion of vocational education at the secondary level may be expected as a result of such a policy. Not only must this policy provide a meaningful educational curriculum, but remedial services must be provided to assist those students who have ceased to learn and are merely awaiting the day when they can withdraw legally from school. Preventive unemployment may be just as valuable and as economical as preventive medicine.

Discussion Questions

1. What are the manpower problems associated with a rise in the level of frictional unemployment?
2. What are the problems encountered in moving industry into depressed regions? In moving labor out of depressed regions? Does either policy attack the source of regional unemployment?
3. (a) Does England have any advantages over the United States in assisting in the relocation of industry? In providing retraining for workers whose skills become obsolete as a result of technological innovations?
   (b) What are the advantages of institutional training over on-the-job training?
4. (a) Why might businessmen be more willing to cooperate in training programs for the disadvantaged when the labor market is tight than when it is loose?
   (b) The Job Corps has been described as a multi-purpose training program. Discuss.

[23] This recommendation has also been made by Richard A. Lester, *Manpower Planning in a Free Society* (Princeton: Princeton University Press, 1966), see Chapters 3 and 4.

5. (a) Vocational rehabilitation has essentially the same objective as any other manpower training program. Discuss.
   (b) Why are day care centers a necessary correlate of the WIN program? Appraise the rationale on which WIN is based?
6. (a) What are the obstacles to establishing a centralized, coordinated national employment exchange?
   (b) Why have state unemployment insurance compensation agencies subordinated ES functions to their own?
7. "Unless concurrent policies to maintain aggregate demand are implemented, manpower programs are not likely to be successful." Discuss.
8. (a) What effects are manpower programs likely to have on the Phillips curve?
   (b) Discuss the need for manpower programs in a society with perfect equality in educational opportunities.

Part II

EVOLUTION OF LABOR MARKET ANALYSIS

4

Early Conceptions of the
Labor Market

Introduction

The current level of understanding of the forces at work in the labor market, and how these forces interact, has evolved over a 700-year period. When markets were small and relatively simple, the small volume of exchanges did not require more than an intuitive understanding of the market processes. Indeed, until almost the 19th century, labor markets as we know them today did not exist in the Western world. Since most of the population was rural, labor was usually familial or manorial and as such did not receive a money wage. Even in urban centers, labor in most of the shops came from family sources. Some artisans did employ apprentices, but custom and tradition governed the employment contract, and in many respects the master–servant relationship resembled an extended family. Man's awareness of impersonal market forces at work developed in bits and pieces, usually in response to some development which custom and tradition could not accommodate. As markets developed and became more complex, man's thought more and more came to focus upon the principles by which a market functions.

In this chapter, the development of premodern thinking concerning the principles governing the purchase and sale of labor are presented. It will be seen that even a rudimentary classification of these forces into elements of supply and demand did not occur until the industrial revolution, at which time the rise of the factory system witnessed the rapid development of the labor market. For almost a century after supply and demand were identified as price or wage determinants, there was no clear understanding of the

81

forces which determined the demand or supply of labor. Almost in building-block fashion, a succession of economic thinkers added to the insights of their predecessors and contemporaries as they groped their way to the modern theory of how wages and employment are determined in labor markets. The contributions of thinkers from the early Christian era until the industrial revolution are presented in the next section. In the section after that, the views of writers who have come to be known as the Classical School—the predecessors of modern economic science—are presented with their interpretation of how the market imparts value to objects or services exchanged therein. In the third following section, the development of the classical theory of labor demand is discussed, and in the next section, the components of their theory of labor supply are examined. An outline showing the period in which each contributor lived is presented here in order to provide the reader with a time perspective for the material presented in this chapter and in Chapter 5.

Outline of Contributors to Labor Market Theory, by School of Thought and Period

I. Scholastics:
      (A) St. Thomas Aquinas   (1225–1274)

II. Mercantilists:
      (A) Gerard de Malynes   (1586–1641)
      (B) Sir William Petty   (1623–1687)
      (C) Richard Cantillon   (1680–1734)

III. Physiocrats:
      (A) François Quesnay   (1694–1774)

IV. Classical:
      (A) Adam Smith   (1723–1790)
      (B) Thomas Malthus   (1766–1834)
      (C) J. B. Say   (1767–1832)
      (D) David Ricardo   (1772–1823)
      (E) John Stuart Mill   (1806–1873)
      (F) John E. Cairnes   (1823–1875)
      (G) Johann Heinrich Von Thunen   (1783–1850)
      (H) Karl Marx   (1818–1883)

V. Marginalists:
      (A) English
             1. William Stanley Jevons   (1835–1882)
             2. Alfred Marshall   (1842–1924)
             3. J. A. Hobson   (1858–1940)
             4. Philip Wicksteed   (1844–1927)

(B) Austrians
    1. Carl Menger   (1840–1921)
    2. Friedrich von Wieser   (1851–1926)
    3. Eugene von Bohm-Bawerk   (1851–1971)
(C) Other Europeans
    1. Leon Walras   (1834–1910)
    2. Enrico Baronne   (1859–1924)
    3. Knut Wicksell   (1851–1926)
(D) Americans
    1. Henry George   (1839–1897)
    2. John Bates Clark   (1847–1938)

Preclassical Wage Theory

The Scholastics

Much of the literature of economic relevance prior to the time of Columbus was that of learned monks and priests of the Roman Catholic Church—the Scholastics—who were concerned primarily with moral questions—what ought to be—and not with how something was determined. This was true in relation to their concepts of the "just price," of which the "just wage" is a variation. The just price, as Schumpeter argues, was nothing more than the competitive price,[1] and from this he concludes that St. Thomas Aquinas was the first to discover the 19th-century Law of Cost.

> " . . . if we identify the just price of a good with its competitive common value . . . and if we further equate that just price to the cost of the good . . . , then we have . . . stated the law of cost not only as a normative but also as an analytic proposition."

In a sense, the just price was a prevailing price and in that same sense, the just wage was the prevailing market wage for each type of labor. This is hardly an analytical conclusion, however, for it simply states that the just wage was *whatever wage happens to exist in the market* without analyzing those factors that influence that wage. Since it is more difficult to determine the

---

[1] "If the just price were something else than the normal competitive price, practices other than fraud would be more important. . . . For if there exists a competitive market price, individual deviations from it are hardly possible except through fraudulent representations about the quantity and quality of the goods." Joseph A. Schumpeter, *History of Economic Analysis* (New York: Oxford University Press, 1954), p. 93 n.

cost of producing labor as distinct from a commodity, the concept of the just wage became a normative one. The just wage is the cost of replenishing labor, which means that the wage at a minimum ought to be sufficient to maintain that worker at that class level to which society had relegated him. This approximates the classical economist's concept of the subsistence wage. Therefore, at a minimum the just wage "ought to be," and in fact will be in the long run through the operation of the market, at least a socially determined subsistence wage. We may credit the Scholastics with having an insight into this basic proposition, but we cannot say that they clearly understood or expressed it.

It is also held that the early Scholastics developed an early argument for the labor theory of value. Since the cost of labor was almost the only cost of making an object, and since a person is entitled by natural law to the fruit of his labors, the value of an article is in essence the value of the labor used in making it. Furthermore, since interest was condemned as unjust and unnatural—money is barren—the contributions of capital, the other major element in cost, could not be regarded as significant. Just profits were simply wages paid to the entrepreneur. Although it may be argued that the sum of these costs implies a labor theory of value, it was not formally stated, nor does it appear that such a conclusion was actually reached by the Scholastics.

Mercantilism

In this age of the 20th century in which nationalism is flourishing and the economic development of emerging nations takes the spotlight, it is appropriate to reflect briefly upon the economic doctrines of the mercantilist. The Commercial Revolution, which accompanied and spurred the emerging nations of Europe—particularly England—from the 15th to the 18th century, gave rise to a group of writers who espoused a series of policies designed to promote and strengthen the wealth and power of the realm. These policies were concerned not only with producing a change in the structure of the economy, from agriculture and the self-sufficiency of the manor to that of trade and industry, but they also sought to bring about major changes in other social institutions, including the pattern of relationships with dependent societies, colonies, and rival competing nations. It must be acknowledged that these pamphleteers were guided more by the principle of expediency than by logic in the policies which they espoused. Indeed, their understanding of economic phenomena was rudimentary and quite often simply fallacious, and the doctrines which they propounded were based upon what they hoped to achieve and were a defense of what they were already doing rather than upon analytically or empirically derived conclusions. Their policies designed to achieve a favorable balance of trade, their confusion over the qualities of gold and wealth, the concept of the relationship of colonies to the mother country, their appeals to the King for monopoly favor, and the creation of the giant trading monopolies in India and Canada are all well known to the student of English history. The fact that many of these policies were successful in spite of being based upon fallacious assumptions suggests that they were appropriate, but for the wrong reasons. [2]

The mercantilist concept of the motivations of man were somewhat contradictory when applied to the entrepreneur and to members of the working class. This concept led the mercantilist to favor logically inconsistent policies for these two classes. Entrepreneurs were viewed as rational, self-seeking individuals who, if left to their own devices, would make the best use of their talents and the resources at their command. Private enterprise was generally favored, for it was felt that the prospect of great rewards stimulated the entrepreneurial class to greater effort. Not so for the working class, however. [3] It was generally held, particularly in the early days of mercantilism, that the standard of living of the lower class was more or less invariant, and that if wages were to rise, the supply of labor offered by the working class would be reduced. Thus, a low-wage policy was called for in order to extract the maximum amount of labor from the lower classes. [4]

Although the mercantilists had at best a fuzzy concept of the workings of the price system, they were aware that the cost of goods depended to a great extent upon the price of labor and they did recognize that if the country was to secure a favorable balance of trade through expansion of its exports, it was desirable that export goods be low in price relative to those of other countries. This in turn called for a low-wage policy. The low-wage policy, as we have seen, was also consistent with their concept of the requirements for a plentiful supply of labor, although they viewed low wages as a cause and not an effect. However, in order to have low wages, food prices also would have to be low, and this meant that agricultural production was important as an indirect means of promoting trade, industry, and commerce. [5] They also recognized that policies to augment the labor force

[2] See Chapter 23 of J. M. Keynes, *The General Theory of Employment, Interest, and Money* (New York: Harcourt, Brace, and Co., 1936).

[3] There was a general belief that education would make the working classes dissatisfied with their lot, create social disorder, and deplete the ranks of the lower class.

[4] Towards the end of the mercantilist period, a growing awareness developed among writers (Petty, Cantillon, and others) that higher wages were positively related to the amount, the efficiency, and advancement of skill of workers, and therefore to the supply of a high-quality labor force. A similar enlightenment began to develop regarding the desirability of education of the lower classes.

[5] Agricultural output also was recognized as an important source of raw materials which, if domestically produced, would not have to be imported, and which would contribute to a favorable trade balance.

would tend to depress wages, which suggests that intuitively they may have had some awareness of the supply and demand determinants of price.

It was desirable to augment the labor force, not only to depress wages, but also to increase output. Having no concept of the principle of diminishing returns and regarding output per worker as being fixed, it followed that greater national output could be achieved by a growing labor force. The mercantilists' low regard for the landed gentry can be viewed as one means of encouraging the demise of the feudal system which tied the major part of the labor force to the land. Not that agriculture was unproductive, but since trade, industry, and commerce were so much more productive, output could be augmented by a transfer of labor resources to the latter uses. Consistent with the desire to expand the labor force, emigration was opposed, while immigration was encouraged, particularly among those who possessed skills. Policies which put to work such dependents as women, children, and the poor were implemented in order to expand the labor force, and work was regarded as a primary virtue which should be taught at an early age. Although a lower mortality rate was desired in order to increase population, there was no overt awareness in a Malthusian sense that a higher wage would reduce mortality by raising living standards (which were regarded as fixed) and the health of the population. Hence, the subsistence-wage theory cannot be said to have influenced wage policy in this era. Policies to reduce the level of unemployment were consistent with the desire to expand national output, for if the unemployed or the least productively employed could be channeled into occupations that produced export goods, the wealth and power of the nation could be favorably affected. Labor-saving inventions and innovations were encouraged (via the origin of the patent monopoly) as a means to increase output and to conserve the labor force, although sporadic but dramatic displays of worker opposition to these innovations were manifested from time to time.

In summary, then, it can be said that the mercantilist had no theory which explained the determination of wages or prices other than a rudimentary cost-of-production theory. Given the fixed pattern of living of the working class, desirable wage policy was one which yielded the lowest wage consistent with this standard of living. This policy would produce an abundant, docile, and hard-working labor force, which was consistent with maximum national output, low prices, and a favorable balance of trade.

The Physiocrats

The Physiocrats were among the first to use abstract economic reasoning. The *Tableau Economique* of Quesnay was a rudimentary model of the economy showing the circular flow of economic activity and the distribution of its product. The attention given by the Physiocrats to income (product) distribution was unique and represents the first attempt to explain the process by which various sectors shared in the product of industry. The Physiocrats were also the first to use the concept of capital as a series of advances to the productive process; fixed capital was described as either *avances primitives* (buildings and tools), or *avances fonciéres* (improvements to the land), and variable capital was identified as *avances annuelles*, which included among other things the wages of labor. Thus, we see the beginning of the concept of the wages fund, although it was not highly developed. The Physiocrats also introduced the concept of productive and unproductive labor, the distinction lying in whether or not labor produced a net addition to income over and above their wage. The Physiocrats also recognized a relationship between the increase in per capita income and the growth of population, and their fear that the strong propensity of the population to grow might endanger the growth of per capita income laid the groundwork for the classical school's subsistence wage theory. Although the Physiocrats recognized the influence of competition on prices, which would tend to force the value of nonagricultural output down to the sum of the wages paid to workers and management, they offered no explicit explanation of the process by which these wages are determined. The manner in which income is and should be distributed was described, but how or why distributive shares came to be what they were was not explained.

Classical Value Theory

If the discipline of economics began with Adam Smith, then we can say that speculation about the causes of wages and prices also began with him. In the following pages, we shall examine the ideas of Smith and his followers who dominated economic thinking in the hundred years after the appearance of Smith's *Wealth of Nations*. More than is commonly realized, the ideas of Thomas Malthus, David Ricardo, Karl Marx, and John Stuart Mill still influence the mode of economic thought.

Value and Labor

The belief that labor (man) is the origin and source of all value is not as ridiculous as it appears at first glance. Certainly, as a concept, "value" requires a human judgment in the context of human thought. Meaning is transmitted to the concept by human behavior.[6] Furthermore, since an

---

[6] This is the essence of the late 19th century Austrian school's argument that value is subjectively determined. However, in this sense the human or labor concept of value applies to the demand side, and it may be interpreted as a labor command theory, as propounded by Adam Smith. The usual representation of theory is concerned with the supply side—the amount of labor embodied or contained within a product or service—as first presented by David Ricardo.

abstract primitive society was imagined in which the ratio of resources to population was so large, the early classical economists could regard all resources other than labor as free goods. Only labor had value because in this primitive society it was the only scarce resource. Hence, the tangible products created by labor reflected in value only the amount of labor which was required to produce those products, and products tended to exchange in the ratio of the labor embodied in them. At the other extreme John M. Keynes has argued that in a superadvanced society where capital is so abundant that it may be regarded almost as a free good (yielding a zero rate of return), the value of goods and services may be regarded as determined by the labor embodied therein. It followed from this primitive conception of an economy that tangible products—including land which had been cleared and improved by the expenditure of labor—were combined with labor to produce other goods and services: the resulting products would tend to be exchanged in terms of the ratios of the sums of the direct and indirect labor (capital and land) contained therein. For example, if a unit of cloth had four hours of labor embodied in producing it while a bushel of wheat required only three hours of direct and indirect labor, then the price of wheat in terms of cloth would be $\frac{3}{4}$ ($\frac{3}{4}$ unit of cloth for 1 bushel of wheat). If it is assumed that production techniques are known and that the best technique will be generally adopted, then the proportions of direct and indirect labor are also determined and fixed, which determines and fixes the exchange ratio. Finally, although it was recognized that not all labor is of homogeneous productivity, nevertheless, a standard unit of labor of average productivity can be defined, and more productive labor can be expressed as multiples of the standard unit. Thus, the value of a good or service is determined by the wage paid to a standard unit of labor multiplied by the number of standard units used in producing the good or service.[7]

This is essentially the labor theory of value as developed by Ricardo, and which was taken over and developed to its logical conclusion by Karl Marx. Since the amount of labor included in a product is technologically determined in the final analysis, the remaining variable to be explained in determining exchange value is that which determines the wage rate. As we shall see, Marx developed a bargain (exploitation) theory of wages, whereas Ricardo explored both long-run and short-run determinants of the wage

---

[7] Let P_I be the price or value of good I and P_{II} be the price or value of good II. Let $L_1 =$ amount of standard labor in good I and $L_2 =$ amount of standard labor in good II and w is the wage. Then $P_I = wL_1$ and $P_{II} = wL_2$, so that $P_I/P_{II} = wL_1/wL_2 = L_1/L_2$. In two societies (or two countries) where equal quantities of standard labor are embodied in any good of each society, the exchange rate between the two goods of these countries is determined by the ratio of the wage rates prevailing in the society. Consequently, it is apparent that the wage rate influences the terms of trade between any two countries.

rate, but in general his thinking was dominated by the Malthusian population principle and the prevailing views concerning the character and
motivation of the labor class.

Before leaving the labor theory of value, however, we should acknowledge a fundamental qualification which Ricardo introduced into this theory
about the influence of the structure of capital and of the period of production
on exchange value. Production takes time and wages must be advanced, at
least initially, before the product is sold in order to permit labor to acquire
a stock of goods (called wage-goods) on which they may subsist during the
production period. These wages, or in real terms the stock of goods which
they command, make up the variable or circulating capital required by a
firm. Since the ratio of fixed capital (embodied labor) to labor is technologically determined and invariant in the absence of a technological change,[8]
the ratio of fixed to circulating capital is determined. However, the life of
the fixed capital was not regarded as of long duration, and in any event, the
ratio of fixed to circulating capital was regarded as quite small. Consequently, no great damage was done by treating all of capital as circulating
capital. In any event, capital must earn a rate of return,[9] and if the rate
of return is greater than zero, then goods cannot exchange in direct relationship to the amount of labor embodied within them unless each has the same
production period. To see this, let us assume that the rate of return is
represented by r and the production period by n_i for good i. Therefore, with
P_i as the price of good i and L_i the amount of labor used in producing
good i, and w as wages,

$$P_1 = w(1 + r)^{n_1}L_1 \qquad P_2 = w(1 + r)^{n_2}L_2$$

$$\frac{P_1}{P_2} = \frac{L_1(1 + r)^{n_1}}{L_2(1 + r)^{n_2}}$$

If the production period n_1 does not differ greatly from n_2, say if both
are one year or less, and if the ratio of fixed to variable capital is always
small, then the labor theory of value gives a good approximation to exchange
value. Also, if capital does not require or deserve a positive rate of return,
the labor theory of value is true. In Ricardo's time, most production periods
were of short duration and the ratio of fixed to circulating capital was in
most cases quite small. Thus, we can excuse Ricardo for ignoring variations
in these conditions. In Marx's time, however, the ratio of fixed to circulating
capital was no longer insignificantly small, and production periods varied

[8] Which was infrequent in Ricardo's time.
[9] Called profits by Ricardo. Why capital should earn interest was not a question which
concerned Ricardo. He may have regarded it as an opportunity cost or as a payment
necessary to induce waiting—of postponing consumption.

significantly. Marx was certainly aware of this. How then could Marx defend the labor theory of value? Since Ricardo left him with no usable theory of interest and Ricardo never really sought to explain why capital must earn a positive rate of return,[10] Marx argued and concluded that capital required and deserved no positive rate of return. Hence, the exchange value of any two goods was equal to the ratio of their embodied labor. This bit of economic nonsense has, as a result, long plagued the doctrinaire communist countries which, adhering to Marx, had no rational allocative mechanism for planning the use of capital.

Adam Smith's labor theory of value more appropriately can be called a "labor command" theory of value,[11] and in some ways can be regarded as a forerunner of the Austrian school's theory of subjective value. If the embodied labor theory of value can be properly regarded as a supply determinant of value, then the labor command theory can be regarded as a demand determinant. Smith thought that men regarded work as unpleasant, and yielding disutility. Thus, the value of a good or service is equal to the pain or discomfort which would otherwise have been incurred if that good or service were not available. Presumably, a purchaser of the good or service would be willing to offer in exchange an amount of his own labor measured in a money wage or in the goods which his labor produced up to that which he would willingly expend in providing the good or service himself. Thus, the value of a good is the labor which it commands in exchange. Labor used in producing a good or service is valued in relation to the value of the goods which that labor produces (a derived value) and which in turn commands the equivalent of additional labor. A man is richer or poorer the more labor in exchange his own labor commands, and in the same sense so is a nation. Viewed in this context, Smith's emphasis upon the division of labor as a method of increasing the productivity of labor is the foundation for his assertion that the division of labor determines the *wealth of a nation*.

The Classical Theory of Labor Demand

Although the classical economists recognized that wages are determined by forces of supply and demand, just as is any price, it is fair to say that their primary interest lay in explaining those forces in the market which determined the supply of labor. The demand for labor, in general, was considered to be inelastic and relatively unchanging. Furthermore, wage analysis was

[10] Indeed, since Ricardo regarded the rate of return to capital as profits and since he predicted the ultimate disappearance of profits, i.e., they go to zero, it may be said that Ricardo had no long-run theory of interest.

[11] This is only one of the several theories of value suggested by Smith.

usually expressed in macroeconomic terms rather than in microeconomic terms. There was some attempt to identify causes of interindustry and interoccupation wage variations, but primarily the classical economists sought to explain the long-run determinants of the general wage level.

Demand

Smith and Ricardo both believed that in earlier economies, a favorable ratio of resources to labor produced an agricultural surplus which was used to exchange for goods and services produced by nonagricultural labor. This surplus could also originate from technical improvements in agriculture, which, perhaps, were stimulated by the rising prices of these nonagricultural products. In any event, the existence of such a surplus not only permitted but encouraged labor to diversify and to specialize in various occupations. Specialization was encouraged by the enhanced productivity and exchange value of one's labor, and it was made possible by the development of a fund of agricultural products to sustain the nonagricultural labor while it was otherwise engaged. This fund of consumer goods advanced and purchased by wages in real terms was identified as *wage-goods* and has come to be known as the wages fund. As the surplus is accumulated, the amount of labor which can be supported by the fund grows and the demand for labor correspondingly expands. The surplus is expressed in terms of profits, and the higher the profits, the greater is the growth of the wages fund and the greater is the demand for labor.[12] The wages fund then becomes a source of capital which is invested essentially in advancing to labor their wages during the period of production.[13] In some respects, the recognition by the classical economists that it was the size of the wages fund (investment) which determined the state of aggregate demand (for labor) predates the argument of Keynes along this same line. However, the classicists regarded investment in a much more restricted sense than did Keynes. The wages fund consisted essentially of a stock of agricultural products and its investment was restricted primarily to variable, or circulating, capital.

As long as the wages fund grew more rapidly than the labor force, real wages could advance. It was generally held that the food portion of the wages fund was fixed in the short run, since, once the harvest was in, the stock of food was determined for that growing season, and that it was exhausted from one growing season to another. Thus, growth in the wages fund occurred at discrete annual intervals.

[12] A modern theory of the wages fund is to be found in John Fei, and Gustav Ranis, *Development of the Labor Surplus Economy* (Homewood, Illinois: Richard D. Irwin, Inc., 1964).

[13] As Mark Blaug has observed, the concept of the wages fund marks the beginning of sound thinking in a theory of capital. *Economic Theory in Retrospect* (Homewood Illinois: Richard D. Irwin, Inc., 1962), p. 168.

There were real constraints on the growth of the wages fund, however. Ricardo showed, through the principle of diminishing marginal returns, that as an increasing population and labor force were applied to the fixed quantity of land, in the absence of technological advance, then output would increase by less and less until eventually the surplus would be eliminated, profits would decline, and accumulation would cease. This prediction was not a part of Smith's conceptual framework, and Smith believed that the growth of the demand for labor, and wages, might increase uninterruptedly.

Smith foresaw a possible limit to the expansion of the demand for labor if wages rose to such an extent that they encroached upon the profits of capital. If profits declined because of high wages, accumulation might cease and the demand for labor might stagnate. Of course, Smith had no well-developed concept of diminishing returns, although there is some evidence that he was not unaware of it. Consequently, although he acknowledged that profits might disappear as a result of high wages, the parallel with Ricardo is superficial only. They reach the same conclusion of a stagnant rate of accumulation by different analyses. Ricardo attributed the decline in profits to the high rents received by landowners, which increased as the margin of cultivation was extended to poorer grades of land. If employers shared their surplus with labor in the form of high wages, this did not eliminate the surplus; it was merely transferred to labor. However, the surplus, no matter how it was shared, must eventually decline as rent takes up a greater share of a product growing at a declining rate. Smith did not consider that wages might contain an element of transferred surplus, and he did not, as did Ricardo, regard the declining rate of profits as inevitable.

Malthus tended to agree with Smith about the cause of a rise in wages. He agreed with Ricardo that if diminishing returns occurred in agriculture and if population grew, food prices would rise. If real wages were constant, this would require a higher money wage. (This will be explained later.) If real wages rose, then money wages would rise more. Malthus expected real wages to rise under capital accumulation as owners of capital entered the labor market in order to employ labor for the purpose of producing other goods, from which they expected to earn a surplus. The effect of the wage rate on the labor force, however, becomes the crucial determinant as to whether wages will remain high and whether there will continue to be sufficient aggregate demand to purchase the output from which the employers expected to earn the surplus. If there is not sufficient aggregate demand, the profit rate will fall, and even though a capital–wages fund exists, at low profit rates it may not be utilized to employ labor.

John Stuart Mill later expanded upon this idea of Malthus, which the latter disputed with Ricardo in a now famous dialogue. Mill recognized that the decision on how to use the surplus (profits) together with the proceeds from the sale of the products financed by the wages fund was optional. It could be used to reconstitute and/or to enlarge the wages fund, it could be spent on consumption, or it could be spent on fixed capital, which perhaps might be labor saving. Mill concluded that demand for labor, therefore, does not necessarily vary in a fixed relationship with the wages fund or the demand for commodities. It all depends on how the demand is constructed. Later, Mill refuted the wages-fund doctrine by recognizing that the fund did not constitute a fixed amount. It could be augmented or decreased at intervals less than that of the agricultural cycle, and it consisted of a wide variety of goods. It could be increased or decreased by diversion of consumption goods into and out of the fund, and the periods of production and the levels of production were sufficiently flexible so as to accommodate a wide range of employment. Consequently, employment was not tied directly to a previously produced stock of goods. In the sense that both acknowledged that the wages fund was neither fixed nor predetermined at the beginning of a production period, and indeed that production periods were indistinguishable, Marx and Mill were in agreement concerning the validity of the wages-fund concept.

Nevertheless, the wages-fund doctrine has had surprising resiliency. In modern development economics, there is an awareness that industrial development requires a transfer of resources from the agricultural to the nonagricultural sector, and to facilitate this transfer, arrangements must be made to redistribute surplus food and raw materials from the former sector into the latter sector. If the level of aggregate output is expanding and the employed labor force is growing, the incremental part of this labor force must receive advances until its output is marketed. In this sense, the wages-fund concept, viewed as a form of investment to make possible a growing economy, still survives.

Seeds of Marginal Analysis

The ingredients for a marginal productivity theory of the demand for labor were present in Ricardo's development of the principle of diminishing returns, which he used to explain the phenomenon of rent. A number of influences prevented Ricardo from seeing the obvious, however. As we shall see, Ricardo accepted the Malthusian population doctrine almost without question and, given his concept of human nature, he considered that the trend of wages therefore was predetermined. In other words, the implications of this set of beliefs were of such a nature as to remove the determinants of wages from the field of inquiry. Given wages, his inquiry turned to the origin and nature of rent. Ricardo recognized that, because the labor–land ratio had a tendency to increase, resulting in an enhancement of the average and marginal productivity of land, the value of land in real terms was thereby increased. It should have been obvious to him that the converse, the declining value of marginal increments of labor to fixed amounts of land, necessarily followed. It was not obvious because he was not looking for an explanation of how wages were determined; he already had an explanation consistent with his conceptual scheme.

Ricardo held to a subsistence-wage theory and a residual-profit (interest) theory. Since he thought he knew the answer to how wages and profits were determined, he was inhibited from using his statement of the principle of diminishing returns as a general analytical tool in explaining factor prices. If we wish to be charitable, we might say that a marginal productivity theory of wages is implied in Ricardian analysis. Given the perfect elasticity of the labor supply at the subsistence wage, any marginal product in excess of this real wage will call forth an augmented supply of labor, as a result of population growth, until the marginal product of labor declines to the level of the subsistence wage. Ricardo may or may not have reasoned thus. We simply do not know.

It can also be argued that Ricardo's theory of wages fitted nicely into his policy proposals concerning taxation and free trade.[14] Because of these influences, the mainstream of economic thought had to wait three-score years before marginal productivity theory came into its own.

Bargaining Power

Smith, Mill, and Marx all recognized that the actual level of wages was influenced by the relative bargaining powers of employers and labor. Smith believed that employers always had greater bargaining power than workers. Employers had greater staying ability in an economic contest because of their superior resources; workers' meager savings were quickly used up, hence workers could not withhold their labor for more than a few days. Employers, being fewer, also could better organize themselves. Collusive agreements not to raise wages were common among employers, Smith observed. Finally, the law tended to favor the employer. Mill felt that unions might be able to counter the collusive efforts of employers to depress wages and favored them on this ground. Marx, of course, developed a well-

[14] Ricardo was able to argue that free trade relieved population pressure, lowered the price of food, and encouraged specialization, which in turn increased productivity, encouraged economic growth by maintaining the rate of profits, and kept money wages low but provided for increasing real wages. In the absence of free trade, rents would rise, profits would fall, and real wages and economic growth would stagnate. The villains were the landlords, and their policy of protectionism should be abandoned. Furthermore, landowners should bear the burden of taxation.

reasoned theory of exploitation which was based upon the superior bargaining strength of the employer class.

Marx, using the classicists' reasoning, acknowledged that workers were paid a wage sufficient to reproduce their labor—the subsistence wage. Workers were exploited, however, because they were compelled to work more hours than was necessary to produce a product equal in value to their wage. If eight hours of labor were necessary to produce a product equal in value to the wage of each worker, the employer could benefit if he could require his labor force to work twelve hours per day. The worth of the product, consistent with the labor theory of value, was equivalent to its embodied labor, and the surplus was expropriated by the employer. The working class was unable to share in this surplus because it possessed greatly inferior bargaining power. The working class was propertyless. Hence, it could not sustain itself by withholding its labor over an interval of time in order to force higher wages from the employer. The members of the working class could not become self-employed because they possessed no capital with which to acquire the means of production.

A reserve army of the unemployed, periodically augmented by bankrupted former capitalists who were forced out of business by the ruthless competitive practices of their rivals, kept wages depressed by their competition with the employed. As control of industry became more and more centralized into fewer and fewer hands, bargaining power tended to become more and more unequal. Labor unions could at best but stem the tide; they could not through their own strength prevent the growing misery of the working class. Intermittent cycles of capital expansion might temporarily raise demand and increase wages, but the continued expropriation of surplus value inevitably produced a condition of deficient demand— insufficient purchasing power of the consuming proletariat to equal the value of the products placed on the market. The deficient demand led to redundancy in an expanded labor force, and the unemployed became more numerous than in the last depression.

Alfred Marshall later identified additional features of the labor market which work to labor's disadvantage in bargaining for the sale of their services. Ordinarily, labor does not have access to a capital market which will permit them to acquire the tools needed to become self-employed or to educate their young. This inability to upgrade the quality of the skills of their offspring tends to perpetuate the privileges of class which results in partitioning of the labor force into noncompeting groups. Marshall observed that only parents would be willing to invest large amounts of capital in the training and education of their young in order to enable them to rise out of the class into which they were born. Employers could not be expected to invest the necessary funds in the training of labor, since the worker owns himself, and the benefits of training do not necessarily accrue to the one bearing the costs. Since working class parents ordinarily do not have the capital to expend, their children remain uneducated, and the class system is perpetuated. Somewhat related to the absence of a capital market for the working class is the meager savings—reserve funds—of the working class, which deprives them of the ability to hold out for better terms. Combined with the perishability of the labor resource, the economic loss accompanying a strike is accentuated. Labor not sold today cannot be sold at a later date. In cooperation with time and if not used, labor vanishes as time elapses. Thus, there is an urgency in the sale of labor which is not present in the sale of material resources.

Labor is at a bargaining disadvantage also because the vendor of labor cannot be separated from his services. Once the worker accepts a contract for the purchasing of his services, he also accepts the conditions of work which constitute the environment in which labor is performed. If these conditions are sufficiently adverse, there may be an irreversible deterioration in the quality and efficiency of labor, such as occurred in the sweated trades. This inseparability also limits the mobility of labor. Alternative employment opportunities cannot be sought or knowledge of them acquired if the worker cannot leave his post. Thus, it is difficult for labor to improve the terms of employment once he enters into an employment relationship. Skilled workers fare somewhat better than unskilled workers, but if a deficiency of demand develops, the inelasticity of the supply of skilled services tends to depress wage rates even in those trades. Of course, the contrary is true when demand for skilled services expands.

The Classical Theory of Labor Supply

If the wages-fund doctrine represented the aggregate demand theory of wages, then the aggregate supply theory of wages was represented by the subsistence-wage theory. The subsistence-wage theory received its strongest support from the Malthusian population principle, which seemed more or less to prove the assertions of this long-run wage doctrine. Earlier writers on economic problems, including Adam Smith, had hinted at this doctrine, but its use as a datum in the classicists' analysis of income distribution, economic growth, and problems of employment depended upon the more or less concurrent development of the principle of diminishing returns, a technological condition, and the population principle, a merger of technological conditions with biological propensities of human nature. Furthermore, when combined with the implications of a declining rate of growth of the wages fund, in its most extreme form it was propounded as an "iron law of wages."

The relationships among these determinants are explained in the following pages.

Malthusian Population Doctrine

Because land is fixed in supply, as population grows and as labor is applied to land in increasing amounts, the growth in food production is finite. At best it can increase only arithmetically, and more likely the rate of increase will diminish. Diminishing returns can be postponed through technological progress, but in Malthus' time the rate of technological progress was slow and Malthus had little experience upon which he could draw to lead himself to expect any significant change in the rate of technological advance. Yet, population has a tendency to increase geometrically. Adam Smith believed that population would double every 25 years under favorable conditions. The conclusion was inescapable. Population has a tendency to grow more rapidly than food production; hence population eventually must press upon the means of subsistence.

Malthus observed that in practice population had not increased rapidly in the centuries preceding the Europe of his day. This was owing to the positive and preventive checks operating on the population. Positive checks acted upon the death rate by increasing it. If population grew too fast and pressed upon the limits of subsistence, diseases of epidemic proportions—plagues—would decimate the famished and undernourished population. Infant mortality, the number of stillborn, and the premature termination of pregnancies all would increase. War would further limit the population as countries sought to augment their food-producing lands by the attachment of others. Intensive cultivation of the land would deplete its fertility, producing famine and, if possible, mass emigration.

Preventive checks operated to reduce the birth rate. Social institutional arrangements would develop to postpone the age of marriage and thus to reduce the effective fertility period within which women are exposed to pregnancy. Other social arrangements would come about which promoted celibacy and/or moral continence. Young men and women might enter religious organizations within which nonmarriage was considered to be an honorable condition of membership. Husbands and wives might forgo their marital sexual privileges in order to limit the number of their offspring. More likely, however, since it was more consistent with human nature, celibacy and moral continence would not be practiced. Vice would provide an outlet for the sex drive, and in this the Reverend Malthus included not only extramarital relations but also the practice of birth control between husband and wife.

The positive checks were the stronger for they were biological conditions. Voluntary family limitation was not possible, either because of the state of technology relating to birth control, or because of the general ignorance of those techniques which did exist and their implications to the reproductive process, or because the passions of the mass of the population were too strong for their limited willpower. The working of the positive check tended to maintain a high death rate and consequently a relatively stable population. Given the stable population, its age distribution tended to remain unchanged, and so also did the size of the labor force.

The Subsistence Wage Theory

Out of this milieu of thought developed the subsistence-wage theory. The subsistence wage is one which enables the working population to obtain the minimum necessities required to maintain a stationary population. It is a wage which just enables a family to rear its young so that entrants into the family's labor force proceed at a rate which is equal to those exiting from the labor force because of illness, old age, or death. A wage higher than this permits the family to keep more children alive until they reach a productive age than would be possible under the subsistence wage, and a lower wage results in a greater toll among young children. Since the subsistence wage produced a constant labor force in size, it was often referred to as the "natural" wage.

The subsistence wage was not necessarily in real terms a fixed amount. In the abstract sense, there existed a biological minimum wage, below which life could not be sustained or reproduced. If actual wages persisted at levels below this biological minimum, in the long run the labor force would disappear. But as the labor supply contracted (and increasing marginal returns occurred), wages would tend to rise because of the increasing scarcity of labor. The subsistence wage represented a floor below which long-run wages in actuality could not fall. There was not uniform agreement among the classical economists concerning the tendency of actual wages in the long run to stabilize at this biologically determined minimum wage. Custom and tradition also influenced people's concept of what goods are necessary to sustain life. (Wouldn't Americans regard an automobile as a necessity?) If market wages persisted at levels higher than the natural rate or even drifted upward, people might become accustomed to higher levels of living and regard the minimum socially permissible standard to be substantially in excess of the biological subsistence wage. As a minimum standard of living, the subsistence wage could be pulled upward by a rising market wage. Adam Smith regarded as very probable a market wage which would continue to exceed the subsistence wage. Malthus and Ricardo acknowledged the possibility of this occurrence, and Ricardo even acknowledged the possibility that the natural wage would drift upward, but neither attached much importance to these tendencies.

This can be illustrated by Figure 4.1. Total product (TP) rises at a decreasing rate and eventually flattens out. However, as employment grows, rent rises, so that net total product (TP − Rent = NP) flattens out more rapidly, and the distance between TP and NP gets larger and larger as we move to the right. If the subsistence wage always prevails, the total wage—representing the wages fund—is a straight line through the origin with

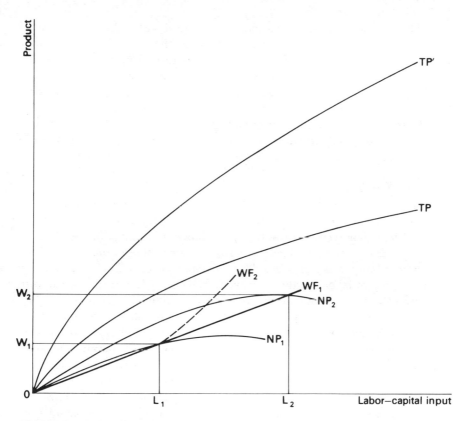

FIGURE 4.1. A subsistence-wage model under constant and rising living standards.

slope equal to the subsistence wage. However, if the NP exceeds the wage bill, profits or a surplus exists and the wages fund can be augmented, but it is obvious that beyond $0L_1$, given WF_1 and NP_1, the wage bill and employment cannot rise. Up to L_1, wages may even exceed the subsistence wage, but this is a temporary phenomenon. If technological progress shifts TP and NP upward, say to TP′ or to NP_2, two possibilities emerge. Either employment will expand to $0L_2$ at the subsistence wage, or the subsistence wage might drift upward as the workers' standard of living rises through custom and habits developed while wages were rising. This implies that the wage bill and the wages fund increase at an increasing rate rather than at a constant rate. Nevertheless, for this increasing rate to be sustained, TP and NP must continuously shift upward so that they always cut the accelerating WF at points successively to the right. Otherwise, the Malthusian population law would be violated.

The market rate may exceed the natural rate. As we indicated earlier, if the wages fund grows more rapidly than the size of the labor force, then competitive bidding of capitalists will pull up the wage. If the rate of growth of the wages fund continues to exceed the rate of growth of the labor force, market wages can continue to rise. However, in the classical scheme this was not possible because, given diminishing returns, the surplus which feeds the wages fund ultimately increases the size of the labor force to such an extent that wages return to the subsistence level. A simple ratio illustrates this: wages fund/labor force = wage.

Labor Supply Elasticity

Adam Smith, Malthus, and others recognized the interrelationship of the amount of wages and the supply of labor. Smith believed that the demand for labor regulates the supply of labor. (An index of the demand for labor is the wage rate.) The classicists all agreed that in the long run the higher population which is induced by the higher wage will assure a perfectly elastic supply of labor. In the short run, however, Malthus disagreed with Smith and Ricardo about the degree of elasticity of the labor force. Both Smith and Ricardo believed that higher wages in the short run would bring new entrants into the labor force and that the supply of labor in terms of effort was wage-elastic. Malthus argued to the contrary. Because of man's "incorrigible laziness," Malthus believed that an individual's labor supply curve was backward sloping. Less labor would be offered at higher wages. Also, in the short run, new entrants would not automatically increase the size of the labor force. In the long run, population adjustments would swell the labor force, but this involved a lag of from ten to twenty years. Malthus and Ricardo carried on quite a discourse over the question of whether the labor force adjusted instantaneously or with a lag to an increase in the wage rate. Malthus argued that if a growth in the labor force occurred in the short run in response to a wage increase, then in ten to twenty years, when the enlarged family entered the labor force, a surplus of labor would develop and wages would fall.

The prediction of the inevitable return to the subsistence wage led many social commentators, particularly Thomas Carlyle, to label the new discipline of economics as the "dismal science." The inescapability of this result caused others to call it the "iron law of wages." Wages above the subsistence rate stimulate population expansion and a perfectly elastic supply of labor. The principle of diminishing returns assures that the wages fund cannot grow more rapidly than population and thus postpone or prevent the inevitable subsistence wage from occurring. Two escapes from the dilemma—technological progress or voluntary family limitation—were improbable if not impossible. The subsistence wage might drift upward through custom and habit, but in so doing it would limit the expansion of employment, given a wages fund fixed in the short run, i.e., from one production period to another.

Sources of Wage Differentials

The classical economists also sought to explain conditions in the supply of labor which would permit either variations in wages, since not all workers earned just the subsistence wage, or variations in the level of employment. As we have seen, Adam Smith and others regarded work as generating disutility. Different occupations generate different degrees of disutility. If wages are paid to reimburse the worker for the unpleasantness of the job, then wages must vary as the desirability of the job varies. Smith believed that competition among workers for jobs results in equality in the net advantages among jobs, including wages, and not necessarily equality in the wage rate itself. Differences in wages are, therefore, a result of differences in such attributes as (1) the pleasantness of the job, (2) the skill required to perform the job, (3) the regularity of employment, (4) the responsibilities contained in the job, and (5) the probability of earning superior rewards.

Wages will be high or low, depending upon whether the environment in which the work is performed is clean or dirty, dangerous or safe, quiet or noisy. Presumably, unpleasant occupations will require higher wages to attract persons into them. The fact that many dirty occupations such as those of ditch digger, garbage collector, or street sweeper receive, on the contrary, very low wages has led some writers to attribute an error to Smith's reasoning. However, as Smith pointed out, it is net advantages which are equalized. Because these jobs require very low skill, they attract workers who could receive no wage in other occupations since they are not qualified for them. The relative abundance of nonskilled workers has assured that wages in these undesirable occupations will not have to be high in order to obtain sufficient labor. Only where occupations have similar attributes with respect to skill, responsibility, regularity of employment, and probability of success, but differ in the desirability of the work environment, will wages be high or low in conformance with pleasant or unpleasant working conditions.

Wages will differ with skill requirements. In one sense, the greater the skill, the less effort per time unit is required in completing a task, and therefore a skilled worker saves his employer a greater amount of labor disutility within any large block of time. Thus, the skilled worker commands a higher wage which is equal to the disutility that society avoids by employing that worker. In another sense, the skilled worker produces a more valuable product and therefore is in greater demand. His skills take time to learn, and higher wages on the supply side are required to motivate a worker to take the time to learn those skills (an embryonic form of the concept of human capital). Smith implicitly was aware of the interaction of supply and demand in determining wages.

Jobs which offer more regular employment have a larger supply of labor upon which to draw, because these jobs are in greater demand by workers. They are more desirable because they provide a worker with a regular flow of income and, therefore, provide more security to the worker. The greater sense of security relieves tensions and anxieties, and therefore produces more utility. Because the disutilities of such jobs are less (utilities are greater), assuring a greater supply of labor for these occupations, wages are therefore lower. The converse is true for jobs which entail greater degrees of responsibility. Tensions are greater for the worker and the jobs are correspondingly less pleasant. Therefore, higher wages are necessary to attract those persons who are capable of assuming these tensions and fulfilling the responsibilities.

Smith observed that in occupations where the probability of earning very large wages is high, beginning wages are often very low relative to the education and training required. Attracted by the prospect of receiving future high incomes, the number of applicants for these jobs is high, which in turn depresses the beginning wage rate. Smith was the first to introduce probability into economic analysis, and in this he was generations ahead of other economists. Smith recognized that every occupation has different risks associated with it in terms of the likelihood of earning high wages, and that this risk factor is incorporated into the judgments of workers concerning the desirability of a job. Smith developed an explanation of wage differentials that preceded by over one hundred years the analogous theory that the rate of profit varies with the degree of risk associated with an endeavor.

Labor Market Imperfections

Smith observed that of all commodities, labor was one of the most difficult to transport. Expanding upon this recognition of the spatial immobility of labor, J. E. Cairnes introduced the concept of noncompeting groups to denote groups of workers or firms whose members were obstructed from moving into other groups. Cairnes divided the labor force into four layers—unskilled, artisans, highly skilled, and professional. This concept was further developed by John Stuart Mill to explain the existence of wage and profit differentials among localities, occupations, and industries. If participants in the labor market have knowledge of differentials and freedom to act upon such knowledge, competition among them ordinarily leads to elimination of the differentials. This occurs through adjustments in supply as resources move from lower paying to higher paying sectors. If mobility is restricted, however, differentials can persist. Mobility can be restricted if either knowledge or the freedom to act upon such knowledge is restrained. Occupational differentials, for example, can persist if labor markets for these occupations are structured so as to limit access to them.

Mill identified some of the causes for the persistence of these distinct and ordered labor markets. In the main, occupational levels follow economic and social class lines. Nepotism is one factor which opens or closes doors to favored occupations. Equally important is the education and training required for different levels of occupations. Workers from the lower class and their children find it difficult to rise from unskilled, low paying jobs, because this class normally is poorly educated, which is in part owing to their parents' inability to finance better education for their offspring. Workers in the skilled trades often limit apprenticeships to close relatives. Professional members of the labor force require extensive education, and only the wealthy can afford such education for their children. Occasionally, as Adam Smith observed,[15] some mobility between groups does occur, but Mill regarded this as the exception rather than the rule. Heredity determines the social class into which a person is born, and social class determines the grade of labor which is offered by members of that class.

Wages and Employment

Variations in the level of employment depended in part upon the relative rates of growth of the wages fund and the labor force, which respectively determined the supply of and demand for labor. Given the size of the wages fund, the level of employment varied inversely with the wage rate. A rise in the wage rate would permit a wages fund of given size to employ fewer workers.

Smith, Ricardo, and Mill believed that the persistence of high wages tended to depress the profit rate, and the latter two economists recognized the existence of a feedback effect of the profit rate on the size of wages

[15] "The drive of ambition causes the poor man's son to study to distinguish himself in some laborious profession. With the most unrelenting ambition he labours night and day to acquire talents superior to all his competitors. He endeavors next to bring those talents into public view, and with equal assiduity solicits every opportunity of employment." *The Wealth of Nations*, E. Cannan, ed. (New York: Modern Library, Random House, 1937), p. 260.

disbursed from the wages fund. This feedback effect was related to the role of capital goods in influencing wages. Wages and profits competed for shares in the distribution of income. Ricardo acknowledged that high wages may induce entrepreneurs to seek the development of labor-saving capital innovations and that these innovations may produce short-run technological unemployment. John Ramsay McCullock, the founder of the wages-fund doctrine, went so far as to advocate government assistance to workers displaced by machinery, particularly if their reabsorption into the labor force was prolonged. Both Ricardo and Mill regarded the ratio of fixed to circulating capital to be technologically determined and constant, although they recognized that a labor-saving innovation would alter this ratio. Mill developed an argument which showed that displaced labor would ultimately be reabsorbed into the labor force. The innovation would lower labor cost and price. Even though the lower wage bill, and perhaps a lower wage rate if the resulting unemployment depressed the wage rate, would reduce aggregate demand—a point earlier recognized by Malthus—the lower price would stimulate larger sales. If the affected industry itself did not expand sales, the competition of labor for jobs in other industries would lead to lower prices in those industries, which in turn would increase sales. Ultimately, labor would be reabsorbed. Consequently, technological unemployment would be a short-run phenomenon. To the extent that high wages lead to labor-saving innovations, conditions are created which tend to protect the profit rate from the competition of wages.

Von Thunen

Johann Heinrich Von Thunen (1783–1850) was one of the most original thinkers in economics and deserves to be ranked with Ricardo in terms of his insights into economic phenomena. Although contemporary with Ricardo's, Von Thunen's ideas were developed independently and unfortunately did not enter the mainstream of economic thought until late in the 19th century.[16] He was at least as rigorous a thinker as Ricardo if not more so. He was a model builder, using first a simple abstract model and then introducing complications to make the model more nearly approach the real world. He made use of calculus to determine the maximum output and in this respect his analytical tools were superior to those of Ricardo's. He had a well-developed statement of the principle of diminishing returns,[17]

[16] The first volume of *Der Isolerte Staat* appeared in 1826, the first part of the second in 1850, and the latter part of the second and the third volume were published in 1863. The full title of his work is "The Isolated State in Relation to Agricultural and Political Economy, of Investigations Concerning the Influence Which Grain Prices, the Richness of the Soil and Taxes Exert Upon Tillage."

[17] "Incremental units of capital added to a fixed quantity of labor on marginal land result in decreasing product per unit" (*Ibid.*, p. 101 of the 3rd edition).

and he applied the marginal productivity theory in determining the return to labor and capital.[18] In addition to stating the marginal principle as applied to maximizing behavior,[19] he made other pioneering contributions to location theory and to taxation theory. In addition he developed a differential rent theory based upon the location of land relative to markets, although he recognized that differential fertility could also generate rent along the lines developed by Ricardo.

Von Thunen was concerned not only with what determined wages but also with the ethical question of what wages ought to be. His wage theory, of course, is based upon marginal productivity, but wages so determined can be lower than the total income received by workers who have invested capital.

Assume that on a marginal (no rent) farm the wages bill (fund) is W, the A is the subsistence wage bill, and P is the value of the output.[20] (Von Thunen expressed all prices in terms of grain.) In a stationary state with a fixed labor supply (and population), with no-rent (free) land in existence, and in a given production period, we can treat P and A as constants. The wages bill W can be treated as circulating capital, and $(P - W)/A$ is the rate of return (profit or interest) on capital. If W is greater than A, workers can save and they can accumulate capital. Thus, the income from savings (capital) is $[(P - W)/W](W - A)$. In order to yield a high rate of return on capital it is desirable that W be small, but in order to have substantial savings for investment, it is desirable for W to be large. To maximize income from savings, it is necessary to define an optimum W. Differentiating $[(P - W)/W](W - A)$ with respect to W and setting the derivative equal to zero, we find that

$$W = \sqrt{AP}$$

which is the optimum wage bill for maximizing the income from capital. Von Thunen called this the natural wage and believed he had discovered an important principle. He reasoned that since this was the natural wage, this is what wages ought to be. If product P exceeds A, the subsistence wage, then W will be in excess of the subsistence wage.

[18] "The return upon all of capital is determined by the last bit of capital utilized" (*Ibid.*, p. 99), and "The last laborer employed receives the product that he contributes; this product determines the wage for all laborers of equal skill" (*Ibid.*, p. 100).
[19] In essence, he states that total product is a maximum only if each resource is added to the point where the product of the marginal unit is equal to its cost. At this point, resources are apportioned equimarginally.
[20] For a slightly different treatment, see Joseph Schumpeter, *History of Economic Analysis* (New York: Oxford University Press, 1954), p. 467 or Mark Blaug, *Economic Theory in Retrospect*, pp. 295–296.

The solution, however, reduces to an absurdity, given the way the problem is formulated. Since marginal no-rent land is being utilized, P must equal the sum of wages and the income from capital; i.e.,

$$P = W + \left(\frac{P - W}{W}\right)(W - A).$$

This is possible only if $W = A = P$, in which case there would be no savings and no income from savings. Wages would be equal to the subsistence wage, and Von Thunen's "natural" wage, consequently, would be no different from Ricardo's natural wage.[21]

In spite of this erroneous formulation of the "natural" wage, as Schumpeter has stated, Von Thunen remains the true discoverer of the marginal productivity theory.[22]

Summary

In this chapter, the development of man's thinking concerning the nature and causes of wages in the labor market has been traced. It was shown that in early Christian thought, wages were considered to be just if they provided a worker with a level of living consistent with his established status in

---

[21] One might just as well argue that a self-employed worker on marginal land, using only his own labor, may wish to maximize his total income which is equal to his wage plus the income from savings. The rate of return on capital is $(P - W)/W$ but the maximum amount of savings is $P - A$ rather than $W - A$. Solving, we set

$$\frac{d}{dW}\left[W + \left(\frac{P - W}{W}\right)(P - A)\right] = \frac{d}{dW}\left(W + \frac{P^2}{W} - \frac{AP}{W} - P + A\right) = 1 - \frac{P^2}{W^2} + \frac{AP}{W^2}$$

$$= 0;$$

$$W^2 = P^2 - AP$$

$$W = \sqrt{P^2 - AP} = \sqrt{P^2(1 - A/P)} = P\sqrt{1 - A/P}$$

In this case, as long as A is less than P, then W will be less than P. It is possible for the wage to be less than the subsistence wage $(W < A)$, but this eventually would reduce the total labor supply and permit labor to be employed on more productive land, thus raising wages so that $W > A$. Of course, neither one of these solutions is formally correct. The P is not a constant because it depends on L, the labor supply, which in turn depends on W, the wage rate. The subsistence wage A, even if known, may not be a constant, varying with the size and age distribution of the family, not to mention the culture.

[22] *History of Economic Analysis*, p. 839. Mountifort Longfield (1802–1884) in his *Lectures on Political Economy* (1833) had earlier presented a theory of distribution based upon the marginal productivity theory. Both profits and wages were explained in terms of the contribution of the last element of capital or labor to the total product in the production process. However, there are some flaws in the details of his argument. See Schumpeter, *Ibid.*, pp. 464–465.

society. As such, it was more of a prevailing wage than a subsistence one. Indeed, the subsistence theory of wages dominated mercantilist thought and it was believed in this period that labor supply was negatively related to wages above the subsistence level. Later the subsistence wage received additional affirmation from the Malthusian population doctrine and, coupled with the classical theory of economic development, became known as the "iron law of wages." The supply curve of labor was viewed as being perfectly elastic, although Malthus and Ricardo disputed whether this was true in the short run as well as in the long run. The demand for labor was treated as being determined by aggregate forces—the wages fund—and the magnitude of the wages fund coupled with the subsistence wage determined the level of employment.

Although the development of rent theory suggested the modern theory of wages and distribution, the classicists failed to expand upon the principle of diminishing returns contained in rent theory or to apply it to other factors of production. One might excuse this oversight by acknowledging that the political question of the day centered upon the application of trade tariffs to agricultural imports, and rent theory along with international trade theory was developed to show that tariffs were not desirable. There was less concern about the nature and origin of wages, and profit (interest) was regarded as a residual.

Marx, of course, developed a concept of the labor market in which propertyless workers were exploited by being paid a wage less than their contribution to the value of the product they produced. Marx accepted the labor theory of value, which is the simplest form of a cost-of-production theory of value. The absence of the power to withhold their labor from the market, a consequence of being propertyless, prevented employees from securing better terms from the wage bargain. It has been claimed that the modern theory of wage determination has developed as a retort to the ethical implications contained in Marx's analysis. Although Von Thunen "discovered" the marginal productivity theory, it was ignored by the mainstream of economic thought. It will be shown in Chapter 5 how this modern theory has developed and survived a number of conceptual attacks, but first a simplified treatment is provided early in Chapter 5 to assist the student in understanding the later, more technical discussion.

Discussion Questions

1. Why would not an understanding of market processes be as important in a barter economy as in a money exchange economy? Is Adam Smith's oft-quoted dictum, "The division of labor is limited by the extent of the market," relevant here?

2. In a Catholic parish in Ohio in 1938, the average wage and living and car allowance totaled about $200 a month for a priest pastor. In 1970, this same total was less than $300. Considering the rise in the cost of living and the relative economic position of a pastor in 1938, what should a "just wage" have been for a priest in 1970? Considering the actual remuneration received by the priest profession in 1970, what economic prediction might one make about the number of entrants into this occupation?

3. Today, modern industrial nations seek to secure a balance among wages, productivity, and prices in order to prevent an unfavorable balance of payments. Are there any parallels between these and the objectives of the mercantilists?

4. It has been argued that the labor theory of value is essential to the critique of capitalism given by Karl Marx. Does this theory of value have any relevance today?

5. To what extent is the Malthusian population doctrine meaningful today? Is the "iron law of wages" applicable in underdeveloped countries?

6. In a much publicized work, John Fei and Gustav Ranis have argued that in poorer economies where labor is unemployed or underemployed (and therefore in surplus), economic development requires the expropriation of the surplus agricultural output which can then be used to finance development. In what way is this argument related to the wages-fund doctrine?

7. Is the modern concept of the minimum wage the same as the crude "subsistence wage theory"? . . . the "modified subsistence wage theory"?

8. In a labor market where job knowledge is universally and freely available and where costs of mobility are negligible, all wages will tend to be equal. Discuss.

9. If technology and the capital–labor ratio remain relatively constant over a long period, what would you expect to be the trend of real wages in that period? Explain.

5

The Marginal Productivity Theory
and Its Evolution

The marginal productivity theory is essentially a statement concerning the price which a purchaser of a factor of production tends to offer, given certain conditions. It explains a central tendency behind input prices. Under competition purchasers of production inputs (factors) will be compelled by the market and by the maximizing goal to pay the owners of the coefficients a price equal to the value of the marginal product. If the input price exceeds the value of the marginal product, the purchaser will incur losses and he will reduce the use of the input, which according to the principle of diminishing marginal returns, will raise its marginal product and the value thereof. If the price of the input is less than the value of the marginal product, the purchaser can increase profits by utilizing a greater quantity of the input. As he does so, the marginal product declines. The marginal productivity theory, therefore, is a behavioral principle, whereas the marginal product expressed in terms of diminishing marginal returns is a technological principle. To understand the development of the marginal productivity theory, it is helpful to trace the origin of the concept of the marginal product as it has evolved from the development of the principle of diminishing returns.

In order for the student to appreciate the stages of development of the marginal productivity principle, it is desirable that he have some initial familiarity with the principle.[1] In the next few pages, a summary of the

---

[1] As we shall see, one prominent economist, Hobson, did question the relevancy of the marginal productivity principle used by Alfred Marshall, but the criticism was not valid. See below.

principle will be developed, and in a later section its evolution will be treated more rigorously in order to bring out its various properties.

The Production Function

The production function can be defined as a mathematical statement of the relationship between the inputs of resources and the output of product. A production function is perhaps most appropriate to the concept of the firm, although industry production functions and aggregate production functions for the national economy have been developed. The process by which quantities of inputs are combined to yield varying quantities of output is technologically determined and in this sense it involves a physical relationship. However, the description of this relationship can be summarized in equation form which can be obtained from empirical studies of the productive process. Some processes are more amenable to a reduction to equation form than others. For example, the production function for a particular product in the petrochemical industry can be stated with more mathematical precision, and this is true for manufacturing in general, than can a production function for a retail establishment. By this it is meant that the equation which describes the technical relation is a line of best fit (in the simplest case) with smaller deviations of observed data about the regression line.

The production function describes all possible variations in inputs which yield any given output. As output varies, input quantities may vary widely. The function is changed whenever the technology underlying the process changes, for this permits new combinations of existing inputs or it introduces new kinds of inputs into the production process. In the former case, a change in technology may permit the same quantity of inputs to produce a greater quantity of output, or the same quantity of inputs to produce a product with superior qualities, which in some cases may so alter the nature of the output as to cause it to be identified as a new product. In the latter case, a new kind of input may substitute for all or part of an old type, although the nature of the product need not be changed. Whenever a new product is developed, this implies that someone has developed a new set of relationships among the inputs so that the properties of the input are transmitted into characteristics peculiar to the product which distinguishes it from all other products. Thus, whenever relationships among inputs are altered so that new products or new quantities of existing products are formed, a new mathematical statement is required if the process is to be described in precise quantitative form. Of course, you and I know that not all production processes are reduced to mathematical statements, and indeed the small businessman would be surprised to discover that anyone would suggest expressing the production process in his firm by means of an equation or set of equations. Yet, there is often a wide diversity between that which is practiced and that which is possible. If pressed for details, almost every businessman could reduce the operating needs of his firm into quantitative terms, although the reduction might eventually appear in a very complicated expression. A manufacturer, for example, must have some idea of the number of man-hours of labor required for producing various quantities of a product, given the types and quantities of raw materials that he utilizes and the type, location, and size of the physical plant and equipment that are present in the firm.

The production functions that we shall use will be quite simple. We are not so much interested in any specific production function as we are in the fact that the production function exists. Often, the expression will be given in the form $Q = f(X_1, X_2, \ldots, X_n)$ which means that Q, the quantity of product, is a function of, or depends upon, the amounts of the inputs $X_1, X_2, \ldots, X_n$. The inputs are coefficients in the production function and may be referred to as *coefficients of production*. Since a multiplicative relationship is normally involved—a multiple of the inputs yields a multiple, but not necessarily the same multiple, of output—the inputs are also referred to as *factors* of production, after the algebraic process known as factoring common elements from an equation.

Production functions may appear in a variety of forms. If inputs are combined in fixed proportions, an example of a simple production function involving three factors might be

$$aX_1 + bX_2 + cX_3 = Q \tag{5.1}$$

The factors X_1, X_2, X_3 must be combined in the proportions $a:b:c$, respectively, in order for the equation to hold. Production functions may also be homogeneous of varying degrees. A homogeneous function is defined as follows. The function $Q = f(X_1, X_2, \ldots, X_n)$ is homogeneous of degree r if $f(\lambda X_1, \lambda X_2, \ldots, \lambda X_n) = \lambda^r Q$. A linear homogeneous production is of degree one, and Equation (5.1) is a special case, for

$$a(\lambda X_1) + b(\lambda X_2) + c(\lambda X_3) = \lambda(aX_1 + bX_2 + cX_3) = \lambda(Q).$$

Another example of a linear homogeneous production function is

$$Q = 100\ X_1^{0.5}X_2^{0.5}, \qquad \text{since} \quad 100\ (\lambda X_1)^{0.5}(\lambda X_2)^{0.5}$$
$$= 100\ \lambda^{0.5}\lambda^{0.5}X_1^{0.5}X_2^{0.5} = 100\ \lambda X_1^{0.5}X_2^{0.5} = \lambda(Q) \tag{5.2}$$

A homogeneous production function of degree two is illustrated by $Q = BX_1X_2 + CX_2X_3 + DX_1X_3$. Can you show that

$$B(\lambda X_1)(\lambda X_2) + C(\lambda X_2)(\lambda X_3) + D(\lambda X_1)(\lambda X_3) = \lambda^2 Q? \tag{5.3}$$

How would you represent a homogeneous function of zero degree?

A function is nonhomogeneous if the above definition does not hold. The following function is not homogeneous:

$$Q = 100 + aX_1X_2 + \frac{bX_1}{X_3} + \frac{cX_2X_3}{X_1}.$$

Can you prove that it is not homogeneous?

A homogeneous production function of degree one states that a proportionate change in all the factors yields a change in output of equal proportion. If all factor inputs are doubled, then output will exactly double. If all factor inputs are halved, then output will be reduced by one-half. For homogeneous production functions of degree greater than one, an increase of a given proportion in all inputs will increase output by a greater proportion. For example, if a function is homogeneous of degree two, a doubling of factor inputs will quadruple output. Similarly, for homogeneous production functions of degree less than one, a change in all inputs of a given proportion yields a change in output of smaller proportion. If inputs are doubled, when a production function is of degree zero, what is the change in output?

Production functions reflect a return to scale principle. Homogeneous production functions of degree more than one are characterized by increasing returns to scale. As the size of the firm grows, output grows in greater proportion. Homogeneous functions of degree less than one yield decreasing returns to scale. As the size of the firm changes, output changes in smaller proportions. Linear homogeneous production functions reflect constant returns to scale. It is possible for nonhomogeneous functions to yield increasing returns to scale as a relatively small-scale firm grows in size; at some intermediate size the firm can be subject to constant returns to scale, and as the firm grows beyond the intermediate range, it experiences decreasing returns to scale. Thus, nonhomogeneous production functions may incorporate all three types of returns to scale. Some economists have argued that this input–output pattern is most typical.[2]

Inputs have the characteristic of being complementary with and substitutable for one another. If the coefficients of production are fixed, such as when one and only one man per machine is possible, then no substitution among inputs is possible. If output is to be varied, then the number of machines and men must be varied in like manner.[3] The inputs are comple-

---

[2] Among these economists are Marshall, Walras, Wicksell, and Viner. See George J. Stigler, *Production and Distribution Theories* (New York: The Macmillan Co., 1946), Chapter 12.

[3] Stigler unequivocally argues that in the long run factor inputs are variable, but that in the short run some fixidity occurs. However, he acknowledges that the existence of some fixed factors of production in the short run does not imply fixed coefficients of production. See his "Production and Distribution in the Short Run," *Journal of Political Economy*, Vol. 47 (June 1939), pp. 305–327.

mentary, but perfectly so. In such a situation, the inputs in combination may be regarded as a complete factor input unit. Complementary factors may be said to cooperate with one another, to assist each other in the production process. The usual case is not fixed complementary coefficients, however, but substitutable complementary inputs. One or more laborers may work with one or more machines with a varying quantity of raw materials within a given period of time. More workers may replace some machines and/or some quantities of raw material with no change in output. Many combinations of inputs may exist which all yield identically the same amount of product. As more of factor A and less of factor B is used, output remaining unchanged, we say that A is substituted for B. A small plot of land can be cultivated intensively with the application of much fertilizer and much labor to yield 1000 bushels of corn, or a much larger parcel of land can be cultivated with less labor or less fertilizer to yield the same size crop. Land becomes a substitute for labor or fertilizer and vice versa.

The period of production in which all factors can be varied or substituted for one another has been defined as the "long run"; the "short run" is defined as the period for which some factors are variable while others are fixed; and as an extreme case, the "immediate period" identifies the interval in which all inputs are fixed. In the long run, the variation of all factors in equal proportion is possible and therefore only in the long run can returns to scale be observed. For the firm, the operating time period is the short run, for most firms can vary output within limits by using more or less labor, more or less raw materials, more or less energy, etc., all in combination with a fixed supply of land, building, equipment, and managerial staff.

In the short run it is not possible to vary all inputs in equal proportions because by definition some kinds of inputs cannot be changed in amount. As variable quantities of nonfixed resources are utilized, the ratio of variable to fixed inputs is changed. The rearrangement of the inputs in their complementary, cooperative relationship permits changes in the output which are derived from the new combinations. The relationship between the changes in output and the changes in input ratios has been identified as the law of variable proportions. It has been stated as follows:

In a given state of the art, after a certain output has been reached, the application of further units of any variable factor to another fixed factor (or fixed combination of factors) will yield a percentage increase in output less than the percentage increase in the variable factor.[4] This law is illustrated in Table 5.1. (What type of production function is represented in this table?) A comparison of columns 4 and 6 reveals that the percentage increase in the variable factor is more than the percentage increase in output.

[4] See John M. Cassels, "On the Law of Variable Proportions," reprinted in *Readings in the Theory of Income Distribution*, ed. William Fellner and Bernard F. Haley (Philadelphia: The Blakiston Co., 1951), p. 106.

TABLE 5.1
FACTOR CHANGES SHOWING THE LAW OF DIMINISHING RETURNS

(1) F	(2) V	(3) F/V	(4) Percent Increase in V	(5) Q	(6) Percent Increase in Q	(7) Change in Q ΔQ	(8) MP = ΔQ/ΔV	(9) AP = Q/V
10	1	10	—	3142	—	—	—	3142
10	2	5	100	4392	40	1250	1250	2196
10	3	3.3	50	5297	21	905	905	1765
10	4	2.5	33	6005	13	708	708	1501
10	5	2	25	6571	9	566	566	1314
10	6	1.67	20	7026	7	455	455	1171
10	7	1.43	16.66	7387	5	361	361	1055
10	8	1.25	14	7664	4	277	277	958
10	9	1.11	12.5	7867	3	203	203	874
10	10	1.00	11.1	8000	1.67	133	133	800
10	11	0.91	10	8068	0.84	68	68	734
10	12	0.83	9.09	8074	0.0007	6	6	672
10	13	0.77	8.33	8021	-0.006	-53	-53	617
—	—	—	—	—	—	—	—	—
—	—	—	—	—	—	—	—	—
10	28	0.36	3.7	1053	—	-799	-799	37
10	29	0.34	3.6	209	—	-844	-844	8
10	30	0.33	3.4	-679	—	-888	-888	-22

Symbols: Q = quantity of product; F = quantity of fixed factor; V = quantity of variable factor; MP = marginal product; AP = average product; production function: $Q = 1000 \, (F^{0.5} V^{0.5} - 20 V^2)$.

The Law of Diminishing Returns

The fundamental principle underlying the law of variable proportions is the law of diminishing marginal returns. It may be stated as follows:

Beyond some finite level of output, with a fixed technology (a given production function) and a given quantity of another factor (or fixed combination of factors), the application of incremental units of any variable factor will cause output to increase by successively smaller increments.

As additional units of the variable factor are added (column 2), output increases (column 5), but the increase is successively smaller as seen in columns 7 and 8. The rate of increase of output with respect to the variable input decreases.[5] If output is plotted on the vertical axis and the variable input is plotted on the horizontal axis, as in Figure 5.1, it can be seen that the slope of the total product curve is the rate of change of output. Total output reaches a maximum, between the eleventh and twelfth addition of variable input, beyond which it declines. Thus, *total diminishing returns* develop with the twelfth input. Diminishing marginal returns as represented

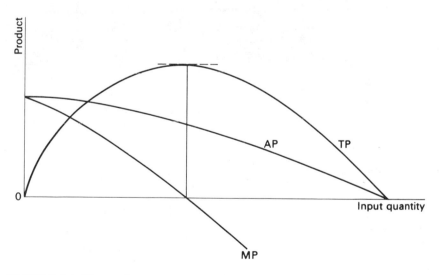

FIGURE 5.1. The total, average, and marginal product curves.

[5] This can be expressed in mathematical terms as follows: If $Q = f(F, V)$, then $\partial^2 Q / \partial V^2 < 0$ beyond the point of diminishing returns.

by the marginal product (incremental product per incremental unit)—column 8—set in with the first input. This is true also for diminishing average returns. Thus, there are three types of diminishing returns—total, average, and marginal. With a different production function, marginal and average diminishing returns need not begin with the first input. In fact, it is possible, given the technology and the amount of the cooperating fixed factors, for increasing returns to occur until a large amount of the variable input is used. A graph representing this different type of production function is shown in Figure 5.2.

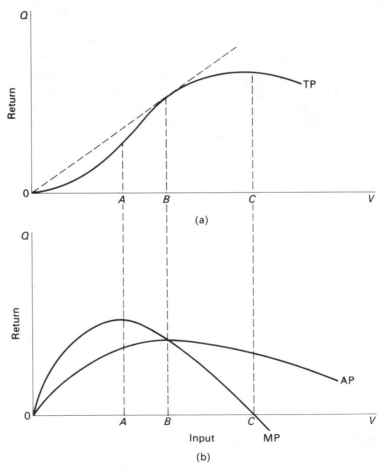

FIGURE 5.2. The relationship of average and marginal products (b) to total product (a).

Until 0*A* amount of the variable input *V* is used, increasing marginal returns occur. Diminishing marginal returns set in immediately beyond 0*A*. However, increasing average returns continue until 0*B* units are utilized, at which point average product equals marginal product, and beyond which diminishing average returns occur. Increasing total returns occur until 0*C* quantity of input is utilized, and beyond this amount total diminishing returns occur. However, a rational businessman would never knowingly or willingly operate with more variable inputs than 0*C*.[6] Why?

To see diminishing marginal returns as the fundamental principle underlying the other two diminishing returns and the law of variable proportions, let us examine columns 2 and 4 in Table 5.1. It is obvious from the nature of the increase of the variable unit in column 2 why the percentage increase in column 4 declines. The increment in *V* is uniform, but the base from which is computed the percentage becomes progressively larger.[7] In column 5, output is increasing but at a decreasing rate because of the principle of diminishing marginal returns. Therefore, in computing the percentage increase in output in column 6, not only is the denominator (output) getting larger, but the numerator, the change in output, is getting smaller. Therefore, the ratio of increased output to output must decline more rapidly than the ratio of the increment in *V* to *V*.

It should be obvious why diminishing marginal returns ultimately produce diminishing total returns. If the marginal product is the slope of the total product curve, as it is, then as marginal product goes to zero (incremental output decreases from some positive amount), the upward slope of the total product must become more flat until it is parallel to the *V* axis at the point where MP = 0. At this point, the total-product curve is perfectly flat. However, if even more units of the variable input are added, diminishing marginal returns continue and now the marginal product becomes negative. Therefore, as marginal product goes from a positive value through zero to a negative value, total product correspondingly increases to a maximum and then declines.[8]

The relationship between marginal and average returns is not quite so obvious. If the student will reflect upon his computation of a bowling score,

---

[6] For a discussion of the irrational region, "stage III," see O. P. Tangri, "Omissions in the Treatment of the Law of Variable Proportions," *American Economic Review*, June 1966, pp. 484–489.

[7] The formula for determining the percentage in column 4 is $[(V_n - V_{n-1})/V_n] \times 100$. If $V_n - V_{n-1}$ is a constant for all n's, then as V_n increases, the ratio declines.

[8] The mathematical expression for this is as follows: $Q = AF \cdot f(V)$; F, the fixed factor, and A are constants, and V is the independent variable. The Q is a maximum if

$$\frac{dQ}{dV} = \text{MP} = 0, \text{ and } \frac{d^2Q}{dV^2} = \frac{d(\text{MP})}{dV} < 0.$$

or the computation of a baseball player's batting average, the following principle should be intuitively apparent.

> "If the marginal value is greater than the average value, the average value is increased; if the marginal value is less than the average value, then the average value is decreased. If the marginal value equals the average value, then no change occurs in the average value."[9]

The principle is illustrated in Figure 5.2. To the left of 0B, the marginal product exceeds the average product and the latter rises. Beyond 0B, the marginal product is less than the average product, which then declines. At 0B, marginal and average products are equal.

If the marginal product did not decline, then the law of variable proportions need not be true nor would total or average diminishing returns necessarily occur. An appropriate question, therefore, is why must the marginal product ultimately decline. One explanation involves the co-operative nature of the fixed and variable inputs combined with the advantages of specialization. For two reasons it may be possible initially for increasing returns to be realized as variable inputs are added. On the one hand, the addition of labor, for example, can permit the division of labor and the advantages which accrue from specialization to develop. Motions are reduced, skill is enhanced, short cuts in the performance of tasks are discovered, precision is developed. As the division of labor continues and the fractionization of tasks is extended, surely the advantages of further specialization begin to diminish. On the other hand, the fixed factors of production may have properties which cannot be fully utilized with relatively small quantities of labor. As more labor is added and specialization allows labor to attune itself to these unique properties, the capabilities of fixed factors become more fully utilized. This continues until an optimum utilization occurs. In effect, the efficiency with which the factors cooperatively combine is enhanced. Taken together, specialization of the variable factors and increasingly efficient utilization of the fixed factors increase output, at first strongly and later with less strength.

---

[9] The rate of change of the average product is given by

$$\frac{d(\text{AP})}{dV} = \frac{d}{dV}\left(\frac{Q}{V}\right) = \frac{V dQ/dV - Q}{V^2}$$

Since dQ/dV is the marginal product, if $dQ/dV > Q/V$, then $V dQ/dV > Q$ and the slope of AP is positive. If $dQ/dV < Q/V$, then $V dQ/dV < Q$ and the slope of AP is negative. When AP is a maximum, its slope is zero, so $V dQ/dV - Q = 0$. This implies that $dQ/dV = \text{MP} = Q/V = \text{AP}$.

An opposing force is at work, however. From column 3 of Table 5.1 it is obvious that the ratio of the fixed factor to the variable factor declines as the latter increases. Since production results from the cooperation of the services, and since the variable factor has less and less of the fixed factor with which to cooperate as the former increases, it is to be expected that the average productivity of the variable input and the marginal productivity of the incremental input should be less with increasing quantities of the variable input. These two opposing forces, the one enhancing production and the other retarding it, operate with different strengths at different levels of intensive utilization of the fixed factors. When increasing returns initially occur, the forces enhancing production exceed in strength the force which reduces average and marginal product. Eventually, however, the disadvantages produced by the declining ratio of the fixed factor to the variable factor must come to dominate the advantages of specialization, and diminishing marginal returns become inevitable.

In the long run, all factors are variable. Yet if some factors increase or change more rapidly than others, the declining ratios must eventually yield diminishing returns in the face of an unchanging technology. The changes in total product can be determined by varying one input and then another, and by observing in each case the effect on total output. Thus, the marginal product for each factor at each level of utilization for all combinations of inputs can theoretically be computed if the production function is known. If the amount of one factor is increased relative to another, normally the marginal product of the other is increased. Thus, a set of marginal product curves exists for the variable factor, one curve for each given quantity of the cooperating inputs.

The Marginal Productivity Principle

The physical basis for the marginal productivity principle is the law of diminishing marginal returns, for it is the marginal product which ultimately must diminish. Most inputs and products are exchanged for money rather than for each other, so that we must convert the application of the principle into monetary terms. Therefore, we shall look at the market economy in which a firm operates and by means of the marginal productivity principle explain how the prices of inputs would be determined in a world which is perfectly competitive. The model of perfect competition in economics is analogous to the concept of a vacuum in physics. Neither exists in reality, but as a limiting concept it is extremely useful for analytical purposes.

A number of heroic assumptions are necessary to construct our hypothetical model. Given these assumptions and the correctness of our logic, the results which follow are valid. At present we are ignoring whether or not the results have any relevance whatsoever. Let us assume that a number of products are produced in an economy which has fixed resources and a fixed technology. Even though the total amount of resources is fixed, each firm producing a type of product can acquire varying quantities of resources by bidding them away from other firms. The owners of resources compete among themselves to sell the services of their resources and the purchasers of services compete among themselves for the services and also for the sale of their products. Consumers compete for the purchase of the products.

We assume that all participants are economically motivated—i.e., they are income and utility maximizers. Everyone sells to the highest bidder and tries to buy at the lowest prices, given the quality and quantity of the resource or product. Resources are highly mobile and move freely from one use to another. Entrepreneurs can move into one product or another with perfect ease. Entry into and exit from an industry, therefore, are perfect. Each type of factor is homogeneous—identical with every other unit within that type—and each product within an industry is homogeneous. Market knowledge is perfect. New technology can easily be acquired, prices are instantaneously reported, profit levels within firms and industries quickly become known. The number of firms in an industry is quite large and no one firm has a sufficiently large share of the market so that it can influence either the market price of its product or the market prices of the inputs which it purchases. Similarly, no one owner of an input controls sufficiently large quantities to influence the price of that type of input.

Perfect competition therefore requires the following conditions:

1. Active rivalry between buyers and sellers
2. Maximizing behavior
3. Homogeneous products per industry and inputs per factor type
4. Perfect product and factor market knowledge
5. Ease of entry into and exit from the market by product and factor type
6. So many small buyers and sellers of products and factors that no one buyer or seller can influence the price

Behavioral patterns among the factors and the products are expressed by conditions 1, 2, and 6. Uniformity and facility for making comparisons are contained in condition 3; mobility conditions are determined by conditions 4 and 5.

The firm, in selling its product in the market, is faced with a given price. Industry demand and supply determine this price and the firm is too small to influence the price. Since it is too small also to affect the price of the inputs, these factor prices also are given (exogenous) to it. However, as an industry expands or contracts, resources are reallocated and all prices can change as a result. Given the production function of a firm where it operates in the short run with a given quantity of fixed factors, the firm is faced with the decision of how much output to produce. Once this decision is made, the production function simultaneously determines how many variable inputs are to be utilized. Given the profit maximizing objective, output and input use are determined by the existing prices. Let us examine this process.

From Table 5.1 we can derive a schedule relating the variable input to the output. If the product price is taken to be 10¢, the revenue derived from selling the product can be computed. This is shown in Table 5.2. As the firm adds more units of the variable input, the additional output when sold increases total revenue. This increase in total revenue per new unit of variable input is defined as the value of the marginal (extra) product. As long as the value of the marginal product exceeds the extra cost (price) of the marginal variable input, total profit will increase. (The cumulative sum of the difference between VMP and MO is equal to the profit. Why?) When the price of the variable input is $70, profit is maximized by employing four variable units. If the price of the variable unit had risen to $90, the optimum quantity of the variable unit to use would be three; at a unit price of $45, the optimum quantity would be six. (The student should check the validity of these statements by completing the appropriate columns in Table 5.2 with the new factor price.)

An important principle is illustrated by the above discussion. It is as follows:

"A firm in perfect competition can increase profits by increasing the employment of an input if the value of its marginal product (VMP) exceeds its marginal outlay (MO), or by decreasing the employment of an input if its marginal value product (VMP) is less than its marginal outlay (MO). It follows, therefore, that profits are a maximum when the value of the marginal product of a factor equals its marginal outlay."[10]

---

[10] Mathematically speaking, profit is a maximum when the difference between total revenue product and total cost is a maximum. Given TRP = $P \times Q$; TC = TFC + TVC = $(P_f \cdot F) + (P_v \cdot V)$, then the maximization solution is given by taking the first derivative of the difference between these two magnitudes, setting it to equal to zero and solving; i.e.,

$$\frac{d}{dV}(\text{TRP} - \text{TC}) = \frac{d}{dV}[P \cdot Q - (P_f \cdot F + P_v \cdot V)] = P\frac{dQ}{dV} - P_v = 0;$$

$$P\frac{dQ}{dV} = P_V$$

dQ/dV is the marginal product of V and when multiplied by P yields the value of the marginal product. The P_V is a constant to the firm and therefore MO = d/dV (TC) = P_V.

TABLE 5.2
FACTORS AFFECTING REVENUE COSTS AND PROFITS

F	V	Q	MP	TRP	VMP	TFC	TVC	TC	MO	Profit	MR	MC
10	1	3142	1250	$314.20	$125.00	$300	$ 70	$ 370	$70	$ −70	$.010	$0.056
10	2	4392	905	439.20	90.50	300	140	440	70	−0.80	0.10	0.077
10	3	5297	708	529.70	70.80	300	210	510	70	19.70	0.10	0.099
10	4	6005	566	600.50	56.60	300	280	580	70	20.50	0.10	0.123
10	5	6571	455	657.10	45.50	300	350	650	70	7.10	0.10	0.153
10	6	7026	361	702.60	36.10	300	420	720	70	−17.40	0.10	0.193
10	7	7387	277	738.70	27.70	300	490	790	70	−52.30	0.10	0.252
10	8	7664	203	766.40	20.30	300	560	860	70	−93.60	0.10	0.344
10	9	7867	133	786.70	13.30	300	630	930	70	−143.30	0.10	0.526
10	10	8000		800.00		300	700	1000		−200.00		

Symbols:

F = fixed factor quantity
V = variable factor quantity
Q = output quantity
MP = marginal product
TRP = total revenue product = product price × output
VMP = value of marginal product = product price × output
TFC = total fixed cost = fixed factor price × F

TVC = total variable cost = variable factor price × V
TC = total cost = TVC + TFC
MO = marginal outlay of the variable input = $\Delta TC/\Delta V$
$Profit$ = TRP − TC
MR = marginal revenue of the product = $\Delta TRP/\Delta Q = P$
MC = marginal cost of the product = $\Delta TC/\Delta Q$

122

Since in the long run all factors are variable, it follows that profit maximization requires each factor to be employed until the VMP of each factor is equal to its respective marginal outlay. Since to each firm the price of each factor is given—that is, the firm can employ as much or as little of each factor without affecting its price—the supply of the factor to each firm is infinitely elastic. This means that factor price and marginal outlay are identical, because the extra cost of a marginal factor is simply its price. Thus, in the long run for N factors of production, optimum profit is achieved when the firm employs factors such that

$$P \cdot MP_1 = VMP_1 = P_1$$

$$P \cdot MP_2 = VMP_2 = P_2$$

$$\vdots \qquad \vdots \qquad \vdots$$

$$P \cdot MP_N = VMP_N = P_N$$

From this it follows that

$$P = \frac{P_1}{MP_1} = \frac{P_2}{MP_2} = \frac{P_3}{MP_3} = \cdots = \frac{P_N}{MP_N}$$

However, in perfect competition in the long run a firm's product price equals its marginal cost, so that P_i/MP_i also equals marginal cost.[11]

Let us now examine how the marginal productivity principle works among firms within an industry and between industries. Suppose a firm discovers a new and cheaper way to produce a given product so that more output can be produced with each given combination of inputs.[12] The marginal product of one or several inputs may be increased as a result. This simultaneously increases the respective VMP and decreases MC (why?), which induces, according to the profit-maximizing principle, an increase in the use of those inputs whose MP has risen, and an expansion in output. The corresponding fall in unit costs, given the fixed product price, raises the

---

[11] In perfect competition, the student will remember, a firm's product demand is perfectly elastic, since no matter how much or little of its product it sells, it cannot influence the industry market-determined price. Therefore, its price and marginal revenue are identical. Given this result, the general profit-maximizing principle in determining output quantity can be shown to be equivalent to the profit-maximizing principle for determining input quantity,

$$VMP_i = P_i \qquad P \cdot MP_i = P_i \qquad P = MR = P_i/MP_i = MC.$$

[12] In a subsequent chapter the nature of inventions will be discussed more fully.

profit of the entrepreneur and, since entrepreneurship is a factor of production, raises the return (price) of entrepreneurship in that firm. Because of perfect knowledge, this information quickly is disseminated throughout the economy and the new technology is rapidly copied. Because of the ease of entry and the mobility of factors, old firms adopt the new technology and/or new firms enter the industry. The industry expands and the industry demand for inputs increases as industry supply increases.

This expansion produces two simultaneous occurrences. As industry output expands, product price declines,[13] and as the industry demand for specific types of inputs increases, the prices of these inputs are bid up in order to induce them to move out of other industries. As inputs whose marginal products have been increased at each level of utilization, because of the new invention, are added relative to those inputs, the marginal products follow the law of diminishing returns and decline. Since, however, product price is declining, the VMP curve which initially has shifted upward now begins to shift once again to the left. Concurrently, the factor price is rising. For example, in Figure 5.3 whereas the initial increase in the VMP curve from VMP_1 to VMP_2 would have increased the use of a representative input from $0V_1$ to $0V_2$ in the absence of a product price and factor price change, other results are obtained if either one or both changes occur. If only the product price had declined, V_1V_3 more of the input would have been used. If only the factor price had changed from $0P_1$ to $0P_2$, then V_1V_4 more of the input would have been employed. However, if the tendency is for both prices to change, then V_1V_5 additional inputs are used.

Therefore, as firms and inputs enter the industry and adopt the new technology, the new, higher value of the marginal product for the affected inputs begins to decline in that industry. In other industries which are losing inputs, however, the respective marginal products are rising also. The principle of diminishing returns works in reverse as well. Firms in other industries must pay factors more in order to keep them. This process can be seen for a representative input used by a representative firm of each of two industries (Figure 5.4). In industry X (see Figure 5.4) the innovation shifts the VMP curve to VMP'_{I_A}. The scarcity of input I in industry X raises the price of the input from $0P_1$ to $0P_2$. The differential input price between industries X and Y attracts input I from Y and X and simultaneously, as industry X expands its output and product price falls, VMP begins to shift leftward from VMP'_{I_A}. Input price rises in industry Y as the industry competes to keep its inputs, but

[13] Although the individual firm cannot influence price, the industry as a whole can sell more only if it lowers price, for its demand obeys the "law of demand"; i.e., price and quantity vary inversely.

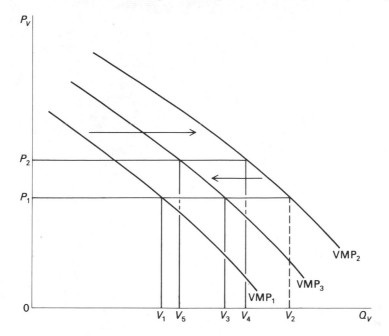

FIGURE 5.3. Effect of changes in the value of the marginal product curve on labor utilization.

falls from P_2 in industry X, and a new equilibrium input price exists at $0P_e$. Input in the amount of G_2G_1 has been taken from each firm in industry Y and F_1F_2 more of the input is used in each firm in industry X. The process of adjustment continues among all industries until the price differentials for homogeneous inputs are eliminated.

Perfect knowledge, ease of entry and exit, homogeneity by input type, and perfect mobility assure these results. Any change in demand for an input, demand for a product, productivity of an input, supply of a product or an input will produce a corresponding price change which will induce some factor mobility. Inputs will be reallocated among firms and industries, and product prices and input prices will adjust to a new equilibrium level.

The Evolution of the Marginal Productivity Theory

William Stanley Jevons (1835–1882)

Although Jevons is considered one of the founders of marginalism, and although he did have some insight into the marginal productivity theory, he

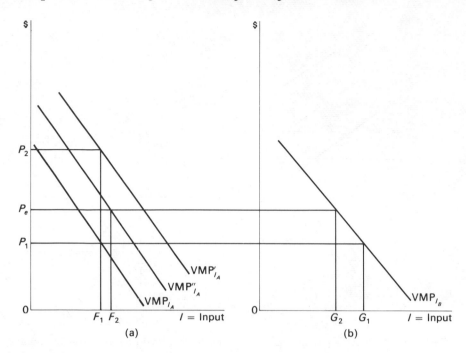

FIGURE 5.4. Interindustry factor adjustments to a disequilibrium situation:
(a) firm A, industry X; (b) firm B, industry Y.

did not apply it as a general theory of distribution. He did argue that interest is determined by the added output of a given amount of capital when the time over which the capital is utilized is increased by some marginal period. Thus, his marginal productivity theory is in terms of the length of the capital investment time period, and the rate of interest is the ratio of this marginal product to the total product, the latter representing the total amount of capital invested in the incremental time interval. On the other hand, his theory of wages is expressed in terms of pain and pleasure and is more a theory of labor supply than it is of labor demand. According to Jevons, the utility of the wage must equal the disutility of the labor at the margin in order to call forth a marginal increment of labor. Changes in the wage rate yield changes in the utility associated with labor and as a result cause changes in the amount of labor that an individual worker will offer. This concept of individual labor supply is still used in the literature today. Jevons expressed the value of the incremental product of an incremental unit of labor in terms of the utility of that product to consumers.

Thus, the Jevons demand for labor was equal to the imputed value (utility) of the marginal product. However, this formulation of the marginal productivity theory as applied to labor was less clear than that of his applications to capital.

The Austrians

The three most distinguished economists of the Austrian school were Carl Menger (1840–1921), Friedrich Von Wieser (1851–1926), and Eugen von Bohm-Bawerk (1851–1917). Menger was one of the pioneers, along with Jevons, Marshall, and Walras, in developing the theory of subjective value.[14] Menger originated the concept of "orders of goods" in which consumption goods are identified as goods of the first order. As the process of production is extended backward from consumption, intermediate goods become goods of higher order, the magnitude of the order depending upon their proximity to consumer goods, and the goods of the highest order would be the primary factors.

Menger conceived of goods being allocated on a priority basis. On the one hand there were human wants of varying intensity, and on the other hand there were goods capable of satisfying these wants. The most intense wants were satisfied first. The value of the last want (marginal) satisfied by any good determined the value of that good in all its uses. If quantities of a good used in satisfying a want are homogeneous, then the least valuable want which is satisfied measures the value of the marginal use.[15] From the value of the lower order good is derived (or imputed) the value of the higher order goods which produce the former.

Menger solved the problem of imputing value to a higher order good by introducing the concept of variable proportions. Menger recognized that a given quantity of any good of lower order can be produced from different combinations of goods of higher order,[16] and this includes those goods of lower order, such as chemicals, in which are combined fixed quantities of goods of higher order. (Stigler observes that the formulation of this principle

---

[14] See George J. Stigler, *Production and Distribution Theories* (New York: The Macmillan Co., 1946), p. 177 for a defense of Menger's claim to discovering the marginal utility theory of value.

[15] This is so because, being homogeneous, any good within a type could serve to satisfy that marginal use. No one good of a type is superior in the marginal use to another. If any one unit is removed, the marginal use goes unsatisfied.

[16] Joseph Schumpeter has argued that Menger's formulation of the principle of variable proportions foreshadowed the concept of equal product curves—isoquants. See *History of Economic Analysis*, p. 917n.

leads directly to the theory of marginal productivity, and without it no satisfactory solution to the problem of distribution was possible.)[17]

By reducing the quantity utilized of one input and observing its effect upon the quantity yielded of the lower order good, the value of the variable input can be determined. This value is proportional to the value of the lost utility which results from the reduced quantity of the lower order good. Although this is at best only a rudimentary statement of the marginal productivity principle, the essential ingredients for determining the value of a productive input are present. If inputs are combined in fixed proportions and if a unit of the combined inputs is withdrawn from producing one good for use in producing some other good, the value of the combined unit (which properly should be considered as a distinctive factor) is equal to the sum of the utility lost from the reduced supply of one good and the utility gained from the increased supply of the other good.[18]

Von Wieser followed Menger's classification of the orders of goods, although he did not accept Menger's formulation of the principle of variable proportions. Rather, he argued that higher order goods were combined in fixed proportions in the production of lower order goods. Imputation, although not by Menger's method, could still be used to determine the value of the higher order goods. Competition among consumers for the use of lower order goods fixed the value for these goods. If one consumer had an unsatisfied want of greater intensity than another consumer, he would bid for the good to satisfy that want. First order goods would therefore be produced and allocated consistent with the equal-marginal utility principle. On this basis, producers would compete for the use of higher order goods, and these inputs would be transferred from among alternative uses in the production of the lower order goods. No owner of a higher order good would accept less in one use than he could obtain from another use. No producer of a lower order good would pay more for the use of higher order goods than the marginal utility of the former. The marginal utility of any one lower order good was at least as great as the marginal utility of any other lower order good, given the resources which could be used to produce either one. Thus, Von Wieser formulated a complete statement of the principle of alternative costs.

By means of the alternative costs principle, the theory of imputation of joint inputs, and the marginal utility determination of the value of first order products, Von Wieser was able to show that the allocation of factors

---

[17] *Op. cit.*, p. 150. However, Menger did not explicitly derive the principle of diminishing marginal returns.

[18] In some respects, this predates Alfred Marshall's concept of the marginal net product, to be discussed later in this chapter.

and products, together with their prices, can be determined.[19] Von Wieser's primary contributions are, therefore, (1) his calling attention to the problems of allocation and (2) his development of the alternative cost doctrine, which is important in any theory of allocation.

It is true that in the short run in some firms, fixed coefficients of production are possible. If coefficients are fixed, they are nonsubstitutable for one another. A body of literature has recently developed in which the theory of production is examined for special types of factors, called "limitational and limitative."[20] A factor is limitational if an increase in its use is a necessary but not sufficient condition for an increase in output. In the case of a factor which is a perfect complement when used with other factors, output cannot be increased unless all inputs are increased equiproportionally. Hence, an increase in the perfect complement is necessary for output to increase, but no increase in output will occur if other inputs are not increased also. A limitative factor is one in which an increase in its use is both necessary and sufficient for output to increase. As long as the marginal product of any factor is positive, it is a limitative factor. Hence, the classification of factors as limitational or limitative is analogous to a classification of factor complementarity and substitutability within the economic range of production.

Bohm-Bawerk also used the method of fixed coefficients, although he was less rigid about it than Von Wieser, and he held that productive inputs derive their value from that of the final product. Specifically, the value of an input is equal to the marginal utility derived from its least economical

---

[19] If the value of a unit of the product is equal to the value of the inputs used in fixed proportions to produce the input, i.e.,

$$a_1x_1 + a_2x_2 + \cdots + a_nx_n = P_1,$$

$$\vdots \qquad \vdots \qquad \qquad \vdots \qquad \vdots$$

$$z_1x_1 + z_2x_2 + \cdots + z_nx_n = P_n$$

where $a_i \cdots z_i$ are constant quantities of inputs, not all zero, of value x_i, and P_i is the given value of good i, then a set of simultaneous equations exists by means of which the input values X_i can be determined. See Stigler, *op. cit.*, pp. 166–178. Stigler points out that the allocation problem cannot be solved unless the value of the final product is given, for this determines the value of the marginal product of inputs. In return, the VMP determines the economically feasible uses to which inputs can be put. The determination of the value of first order products, the allocation of first order products, the value of higher order goods and their allocation call for a general equilibrium solution in which all magnitudes are simultaneously determined. This solution was not visualized by the Austrians. See pp. 190–191.

[20] For summaries, see C. F. Ferguson, *The Neoclassical Theory of Production and Distribution* (Cambridge: University Press, 1969), pp. 8–11 and Chapters 2, 3; Sidney R. Finkel and Vincent J. Tarascio, *Wage and Employment Theory* (New York: Ronald Press, 1971), Chapters 4, 5.

use among alternative uses. Any user of the input must pay this value in order to obtain the input. In this sense, Bohm-Bawerk adopted Von Wieser's alternative cost principle. In the absence of competition among buyers of the input he acknowledged that the imputed value of an input might exceed the actual price paid to an input, and thus he foresaw the theory of exploitation which later was developed by Pigou and which was derived from the theory of imperfect competition. However, where competition existed, buyers would bid up the price of the input as they expanded the use of the input until the price was equal to the value of its derived marginal utility.

Following Jevons, Bohm-Bawerk recognized that the supply of labor and capital were somewhat variable. This distinguishes him from Menger and Von Wieser who assumed that aggregate quantities of higher order goods were fixed. Labor would vary if the marginal disutility of labor varied or if the marginal utility of the wage varied. Therefore, the disutility of labor was an ingredient in the derived utility of labor and, consequently, affected the value of labor. This influence, however, was not considered to be quantitatively important. Also, with Jevons, Bohm-Bawerk made use of the marginal productivity principle in determining the return to capital. The function of capital was to lengthen the period of production, and as the period was lengthened, output would increase. However, output would increase in less proportion than the increase in the period of production, and this involved a recognition of the principle of diminishing returns. The lengthening of the period of production required more capital, but it also resulted in greater output.[21] In effect, a marginal increment in capital led to a marginal time increment in the period of production, which in turn led to a marginal increment in product.

Bohm-Bawerk held that wages and interest are simultaneously determined. He assumed in the economy a given stock of capital and a given quantity of labor. Each capitalist has an equal amount of the available capital with which he could employ labor. Wages are paid continuously and uniformly throughout the period of production so that one-half of the total wage bill is invested during the period of production. Given the wage and the capital available to each producer, this determines the amount of labor which can be employed for each period of production which will maximize the return to his capital. Since capital is fixed, this occurs when total product less wages (profits) is a maximum. The interest rate is thereby determined. However, given the aggregate labor supply, the sum of the amount of labor actually utilized by all capitalists may be greater than, less than, or equal to this aggregate supply. If the sum is greater than the aggregate supply,

---

[21] Bohm-Bawerk did not explain why more roundabout production yielded greater output. He assumed it to be an empirical fact.

wages of labor will be bid up; fewer laborers will be used in each production period, but the production period must lengthen in order to match the wages; and the interest rate will fall as the marginal product from the incremental extension of the production period declines. If the sum of the amount of labor utilized is less than the aggregate supply, unemployed labor will bid wages down; more labor will be employed in each production period; the average production period will decrease; and interest will rise. Only when the aggregate labor supply and demand are equal will wages and interest be in equilibrium. The interesting conclusion from this is that the interest rate, which measures the marginal productivity of capital, is inversely related to the period of production and the wage rate.

The Americans

Although John Bates Clark (1847–1938) had a legitimate claim to be the American discoverer of the marginal productivity theory, he himself acknowledged his debt to his contemporary, Henry George (1839–1897). George had argued that wages were determined by the return to marginal (no rent) land and that wages at this point were equal to the product of labor on that land. If land is cultivated both extensively and intensively, this product could be considered as the marginal product of labor, since presumably an increment of labor would not be transferred to "free" land if a greater product could be obtained from the intensive use of this increment of labor on nonfree land. George, in essence, had taken the Ricardian rent doctrine and applied it to determine the return to labor. George, however, believed that the marginal product of labor could be determined only by observing labor's output on no-rent land.

The evidence seems to indicate that Clark discovered the marginal productivity principle some time during the 1870s, arriving at it by converting the Ricardian rent theory into a principle that was of general application in determining the return to all types of factors of production. He assumed a world of perfect competition with a given quantity of resources used in producing known kinds of products under given technology. Changes which were introduced into this world were allowed to yield an equilibrium in a time vacuum. Thus, in the absence of risk and with perfect knowledge, the entrepreneurial function reduces to a managerial one, and profits become the wages of management. Thus, management is looked upon as a higher form of labor. In the real world, a dynamic one with growth and change, entrepreneurship is distinctive from labor as a factor of production.[22]

All factors are assumed to be mobile, including land. Labor is assumed to be homogeneous. Land can be considered to be a special form of capital,

---

[22] His explanation of the determination of the supply of labor is similar to that of Jevons.

and a distinction is made between capital and capital goods. Capital is conceived of as a revolving fund, whereas capital goods are tangible productive items (plant and equipment) in which the fund takes specific form. As the capital goods release their services over time, by means of a depreciation reserve, the capital fund is replenished. Thus, the capital fund can be quantitatively fixed, but it can be expressed in a variety of types of capital goods which are capable of changes in form over time. This distinction between capital and the services which it relinquishes over time is carried over to the other factors of production. It is the services of labor and land which are used in the production process. In this sense, the services of all factors of production, including land, are variable. As more of one input is used with other inputs, the production process is rearranged to make use of their complementary properties

Because of the rearrangement of factors as more of one is used, diminishing marginal returns is assumed to be a universal phenomenon. As more of one factor is used in combination with a fixed quantity of another, total product increases at a diminishing rate because each one of the larger number of the variable factors now must work with less of the services of the fixed factor. The variable factor will be used until its return is equal to its marginal product and the marginal product is measured by the change in total product which results from a unit change in the variable factor. If the marginal product is in excess of the return to the variable input, managers will bid up the price of the input, and if the marginal product is less than the return, the owners of the input, as their services become unemployed, will bid down their prices. If marginal products of inputs among firms are unequal, mobility of the factors from firms yielding low marginal product to those yielding high marginal product, together with the competition of buyers and sellers of inputs, will equate the marginal products.

Clark also clearly saw that the marginal product paid to each factor would exhaust the total product. To be sure, this insight was owing to the two-variable model which he utilized. Assume in Figure 5.5 that the marginal product of the Lth unit of labor is $0W$ and that this is the wage. The total product is $0YNL$[23] and the total wage bill is $0WNL$. The residual WNY is the return to capital, assuming only capital and labor are utilized. In order for the exhaustion of product not to be a tautology, Clark had to show that the marginal product of capital times the amount of capital used also was equal to WNY. By analogous reasoning, he was able to show that the return to capital would equal its marginal product if capital were the variable input. However, his proof of the exhaustion of product is not

---

[23] If the $MP_L = d(TP)/dL$, then $\int_0^L MP_L dL = TP$, given a function represented by the graph in Figure 5.1.

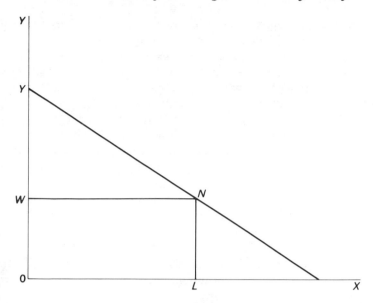

FIGURE 5.5. Clark's model of product exhaustion.

logically conclusive, although we must credit him with insight into the nature of the problem. His lack of understanding of the calculus and his imprecise concept of the production function prevented him from solving the product exhaustion problem. (See Appendix for the solution of this problem.)

Alfred Marshall (1842–1924)

Marshall first used the marginal productivity concept in his *Economics of Industry* (1879) written with his wife, Mary Paley Marshall. In this work and in the first two editions of his *Principles of Economics*, Marshall referred to the utility value of the marginal product, "the increment of satisfaction individual consumers experience from that increment of product."[24] In this respect his theory resembles that of Jevons and the Austrians. However, in the third edition of his *Principles* (1895), Marshall used the concept of the value of the marginal product, where value is expressed as the monetary measure of the marginal utilities of the marginal product.[25] Under perfect

[24] Schumpeter, *op. cit.*, pp. 941–942. If U is the utility function of X produced by the variable factor a, then the value of the marginal product (in utility) is $dU/dX \cdot dX/da$, or the marginal utility of the product (dU/dX) times the marginal product of the factor (dX/da).

[25] See Note 14, *Principles of Economics*, 8th Edition (London: Macmillan and Co., Ltd., 1961), p. 697. The value of the marginal product is taken to be ($dH/dB \cdot dB/da$), where dH/dB are the marginal receipts (price) from the marketing of the marginal increment of the product B produced by a marginal increment of the factor a, or (dB/da).

competition, this monetary measure is price. Elsewhere, Marshall expressed the value of the marginal product in real terms, such as when he showed the relationship between the output in sheep and input in shepherds. The marginal product was expressed in sheep, and the wage that was set equal to the value of the marginal product was also expressed in sheep.[26]

Although Marshall frequently states that a factor will be utilized up to the point where its marginal gains are equal to its marginal cost,[27] he argues that the marginal productivity principle is not a theory of distribution in and of itself; rather, it is only a part. Wages, interest, and rent are prices and as such are determined jointly by forces of supply and demand. Whereas the schedule of the value of the marginal product represents the demand schedule, the point at which it becomes unprofitable to hire a marginal factor depends upon the forces of supply. This is a representation of the famous "scissors" analysis developed by Marshall. Neither blade is sufficient to cut, both are necessary. The wage rate that an employer is compelled to pay is determined by the labor supply schedule; that which he is willing to pay is determined by the value of the marginal product schedule. Marshall held to Jevons's theory of labor supply in which the utility of the wage must be equal to the marginal disutility of work. At the margin, the monetary measure of the disutility of work must be equal to the monetary measure of the utility of the marginal product.[28]

Marshall also recognized that the amount of the marginal product depends upon other influences. The efficiency of a factor depends not only upon its own quantity and quality, but also upon the quantity and quality of its cooperating factors. These in turn depend upon the state of the art, i.e., the progress of technology. The value of the marginal product depends upon the market for the product, and this in turn is influenced by the whole pattern of interrelationships among complementary and substitutable products, upon their respective prices, upon consumer tastes, etc. Marshall was very much aware of the interdependency among economic variables. He used the method of analysis known as partial equilibrium in which the values of all variables other than the one in question are treated as constants (parameters), and results are measured from minute changes in that one variable. However, he repeatedly qualified his methodology by reminding the reader that the general equilibrium model, in which all variables are interrelated, cannot be neglected. It is in this sense, therefore, that one must

[26] *Ibid.*, p. 428n.

[27] See, for example, *Ibid.*, pp. 298–299, 337, 363, 428, 430, 433, 697.

[28] *Ibid.*, p. 696. If $a_1, a_2, \ldots, a_n$ are the factors, V is the monetary measure of the effort cost, H is the receipts from the product B, then

$$\frac{dV}{da_1} = \frac{dH}{dB} \cdot \frac{dB}{da_1} = \cdots = \frac{dH}{dB} \cdot \frac{dB}{da_n}$$

interpret his denial of the marginal productivity doctrine as being a theory of wages.[29]

Marshall's marginal productivity doctrine is a specific application of his more general principle of substitution. Producers are always trying to produce more products with the same outlay of money or to produce the same output with less outlay. Consumers are continuously trying to increase the total utility derived from the products they purchase with a given sum of money, or to obtain the same utility by expending a smaller sum of money. The inputs used to produce outputs vary in efficiency, depending upon how they are combined. Within broad limits, quantities of factors may be rearranged or varied when used in combination, and thus factors can substitute for each other. Similarly, consumers may alter consumption patterns by substituting one product for another. Maximizing behavior for both producers and consumers occurs by substituting that input or product whose marginal product (utility) per unit of money outlay is greater than the marginal product (utility) per unit of money outlay of any other input or product. Only when the ratios of marginal product (utility) to money outlay are in all cases equal is minimum cost or maximum utility obtained.[30]

[29] *Ibid.*, pp. 129–130. "The doctrine that the earnings of labor tend to be equal to the net product of his work, has by itself no real meaning; since in order to estimate net product, we have to take for granted all the expenses of production of the commodity on which he works, other than his own wages . . . the doctrine throws into clear light the action of one of the causes that govern wages."

[30] *Ibid.*, pp. 99, 335–338. A mathematical statement is given on p. 698. The V represents total outlay, H is total receipts, $B_1 \cdots B_n$ are substitute products; $X_1 \cdots X_n$, $Y_1 \cdots Y_n$, $Z_1 \cdots Z_n$ are types of factors of production. Then

$$\frac{dV}{dX_1} = \frac{dH}{dB_1} \cdot \frac{dB_1}{dX_1} = \frac{dH}{dB_2} \cdot \frac{dB_2}{dX_1} = \cdots = \frac{dH}{dB_n} \cdot \frac{dB_n}{dX_1}$$

$$\vdots \qquad\qquad\qquad \vdots$$

$$\frac{dV}{dX_n} = \frac{dH}{dB_1} \cdot \frac{dB_1}{dX_n} = \cdots \qquad = \frac{dH}{dB_n} \cdot \frac{dB_n}{dX_n}$$

$$\vdots \qquad\qquad\qquad \vdots$$

$$\frac{dV}{dY_1} = \frac{dH}{dB_1} \cdot \frac{dB_1}{dY_1} = \cdots \qquad = \frac{dH}{dB_n} \cdot \frac{dB_n}{dY_1}$$

$$\vdots \qquad\qquad\qquad \vdots$$

$$\frac{dV}{dZ_n} = \frac{dH}{dB_1} \cdot \frac{dB_1}{dZ_n} = \cdots \qquad = \frac{dH}{dB_n} \cdot \frac{dB_n}{dZ_n}$$

Now dV/dX_i, dV/dY_i, dV/dZ_i represent the prices of the respective types of factors, and dH/dB_i represents the price of the respective product and dB_i/dX_i, dB_i/dY_i, dB_i/dZ_i represent the marginal products of the respective inputs in producing the respective product. Thus, it can be shown that in equilibrium, for any two inputs k and j producing any product i, $MP_i/P_k = MP_j/P_j = P_i$.

Marshall recognized that workers differ in efficiency and that they can be classified into noncompeting groups. If we take the day's work of an unskilled laborer as a standard efficiency unit, workers of greater skill can be compared with this standard in terms of multiples of the standard. Similarly, the efficiency of other factors can be compared. If the efficiency per unit of any factor rises, so that the marginal product per dollar outlay on that factor rises, this leads to substitution of the factor for other factors. However, since the ratio of the augmented factor to others rises, and since factors are complementary in production, this also raises the marginal product of the other factors. Since factor prices tend to equal the value of the marginal product, a rise in the wage of one factor, resulting from a higher marginal-value product, leads by the principle of substitution to a higher wage (return) to other factors. Similarly, if one type of labor increases in supply and its wage falls as competition bids it down, then its substitution will tend to cause the wages of other types of factors to rise.[31]

Substitution is more possible in the long run. Marshall recognized that in the short run some factors are fixed and the principle of substitution is not generally applicable. It is in such a case that the value of the marginal product can be most easily determined for the nonfixed factor or factors. By varying the amount of input of a factor and measuring the resulting change in the output, one can determine the marginal product of the factor. Marshall called this the net product. The value of the net product would then be equal to the marginal product times price. Alternatively, it could be determined by subtracting the cost of the fixed inputs, and the resulting variation in net receipts as the variable input changed would measure the input's marginal contribution to revenue. In the short run, if two factors were used jointly, the marginal value product of one could be determined by subtracting the cost of the other from the marginal receipts. In principle, since any factor could be treated as either a fixed or variable input, this method of determining the value of the product could be generally used. In the long run if the return paid to a factor exceeded its marginal value product, less of the factor would be used, and vice versa.

This method has been criticized on two fronts. One criticism of the net-product method alleges that one cannot deduct the expenses of employing the cooperating factors to determine the value of the net product of another factor unless one knows the prices of the complementary factors or their marginal products. On the one hand, it is argued that we need to know the value of the marginal product of any complementary product in order to know its price, so we cannot deduct that which we are trying to determine. On the other hand, even if we did know the prices of cooperating factors

[31] *Ibid.*, p. 554.

used in fixed proportions (and, therefore, which cannot be substituted), we cannot deduct these expenses to determine the net value product of the factor in question. A combination of inputs used in fixed proportions should be treated as a single factor and no marginal product for an individual input exists.[32] If the marginal productivity of an input to a firm alone determines its price, the first objection would be true. Marshall's objection to the marginal productivity doctrine is meaningful here. In a competitive world it is the offer price of the input in the factor market and the value of the marginal product in alternative uses taken together which determine the price that a firm must pay for any input. Thus, to a firm, input prices are given. The decision to employ a marginal factor hinges on whether the net marginal product exceeds, is equal to, or is less than its price. Thus, Marshall's methodology is appropriate. The second part of the objection is valid if fixed proportions strictly hold, for the marginal product of a specific input cannot be distinguished. This is a straw man, however, for Marshall does not limit his methodology to this unique case.

The second basic objection was offered by J. A. Hobson, a contemporary of Marshall's. Hobson argued that the net product computed by Marshall's methodology overstated the true marginal product of the factor. Since inputs cooperate by exploiting one another's special properties, the reduction of any one input necessarily lowers the efficiency of its cooperating factors. Thus, a reduction in output which shows up when the input in question is reduced is caused partly by the loss of the efficiency contribution of that input and partly by the efficiency loss of its coefficients of production. Marshall replied that (1) marginal changes are very small changes indeed, and readjustments in the manner by which inputs are combined are possible for such minute changes so that any appreciable efficiency loss of cooperating factors is quickly arrested, (2) when input combinations are optimally derived in terms of efficiency, any slight change in input proportions diminishes that efficiency by an amount of the "second order of smalls," and (3) we may assume that minute changes are possible because in economics, as in physics, changes are continuous.[33] This reply of Marshall's is not completely satisfactory. As Stigler observes, Marshall's second point is the most crucial in his argument,[34] but this optimum combination is true only when all inputs can be substituted or varied, i.e., in the long run. In the short run, neither observation (2) nor observation (1) need be true. Changes in the prices of any one input, changes in technology, or destructive forces

---

[32] See Blaug, *op. cit.*, p. 413.

[33] *Op cit.*, p. 339. On another page, Marshall accused Hobson of confusing average productivity and marginal productivity, which implied that Hobson knew not "of what he spoke," p. 429n.

[34] *Op. cit.*, p. 355.

of nature may occur which upset the optimum combination (2) or which induce a nonminute change in any one factor (1). This possibility is admitted by Marshall. More fundamentally, there is also some question as to whether Marshall's second point is valid in a mathematical sense.[35]

Marshall thus held that the return to any factor of production tended to equal the value of its marginal product, and that the quantity employed of factors (which determined their respective marginal products), given technology, was dependent also upon supply conditions for factors. His scissors analysis, stressing both demand and supply, thus gave us one of the first complete theories of distribution. Going farther, Marshall also held that the sum of the returns to all factors utilized by a firm exhausted the total product of the firm, when the returns were equal to the respective marginal products. In other words, the return to *no* factor need be treated as a residual; marginal productivity theory, given supply, explained all factor prices and factor shares. The proof of this proposition, however, was developed by other economists.

Leon Walras (1834–1910)

Walras is a codiscoverer of the theory of subjective value—of marginal utility analysis. He had a well-developed concept of the alternative cost doctrine, recognizing that any price paid for a resource must be equal to the price which the resource can command in alternative uses. He made a useful distinction between the factors of production and the services which they release over time and in this sense preceded the distinction recognized by John B. Clark between capital and capital goods. However, there is some question concerning whether or not he *originated* a marginal productivity theory of distribution.[36] Walras apparently believed he had and he accused Wicksteed of failing to give him proper recognition in the latter's *Coordination of the Laws of Distribution* (1894). Walras claimed that Wicksteed's production function was in substance the same as one he had used earlier, differing only

---

[35] Let $Q = 10V^4$, then $dQ/dV = 40V^3$ and $d^2Q/dV^2 = 120V^2$. If V is 2, then: dV/dQ is 320 and d^2V/dQ^2 is 480. A derivative can also be interpreted as a ratio of two differentials. Let dQ be 0.000032, which is near zero. If $dV = 0.0000001$, which also is near zero, then $dQ/dV = 320$.

It is true that a differential of the second order (d^2Q) is of the second order of smalls, since we are letting the change in a quantity which is in magnitude itself near zero change by a near-zero magnitude. However, it is not true that a *derivative* of the second order is near zero (d^2Q/dV^2), and in particular the cross-partial derivative need not be near zero $(\partial^2Q/\partial L\,\partial K)$; e.g., the change in the marginal product of one factor, say, labor (dQ/dL), when another factor, capital, changes by a marginal amount $[(\partial/\partial K)(\partial Q/\partial L)]$.

[36] If one uses Schumpeter's concept of marginal productivity (see note 15 above), one can charitably attribute a marginal productivity theory to Walras. It has also been argued that an alternative cost theory implicitly contains the seeds of the marginal productivity theory. See Blaug, *op. cit.*, pp. 440–441.

in form. Therefore, he argued that his function implied the conclusions later derived explicitly by Wicksteed. Stigler flatly denies that Walras had a marginal productivity theory before the third edition of his *Elements* which appeared in 1896.[37] In the first two volumes of *Elements*, Walras did not specify the nature of his production function other than to assume that the coefficients of production were in fixed proportions. Although he recognized that factors possessed the property of variability, he did not expand on the implications of this property. Since he did not relate variation in output to variation in input, he did not identify specifically the marginal product. Nowhere, states Stigler, did Walras relate the price of the input to this marginal product. However, beginning with his 3rd edition, Walras did incorporate the marginal productivity theory into his general equilibrium model.

Summary

Although Jevons and the early Austrians were cofounders of marginal analysis, no marginal productivity theory of wages is implicit in their writings. The works of Bohm-Bawerk among the Austrians approach most closely the modern theory of distribution. In the United States, the first explicit statement of the marginal productivity principle was made by John Bates Clark, although he acknowledged an indebtedness to Henry George. One of the earliest and clearest statements of the marginal productivity principle was given by Alfred Marshall, who incorporated it into a supply-and-demand theory of wages. Marshall's methodology, however, was criticized because of his system of partial equilibrium analysis. Walras developed the first general equilibrium model, but because of the nature of the production function used in his early model, he cannot be credited with developing a consistent theory of distribution. This credit belongs to Wicksteed, Wicksell, and Baronne, whose contributions are noted in the appendix. Except for minor modifications, the marginal productivity theory remains the essential principle for explaining wages and employment in both micro and macro labor markets.

Appendix: The Euler Theorem Controversy[38]

It was Philip Wicksteed in England, Knut Wicksell in Sweden, and Enrico Baronne in Switzerland who contributed most to the solution of the product

---

[37] *Op. cit.*, p. 370. Schumpeter is more kind to Walras: "Moreover it is a misunderstanding to think that Walras claimed personal priority for the theory of marginal productivity as defined by himself," *op. cit.*, p. 1033n.

[38] Three references of particular interest on this controversy are Stigler, *Production and Distribution Theories*, Chapter 12; Blaug, *Economic Theory in Retrospect*, Chapter 11; Schumpeter, *History of Economic Analysis*, pp. 1032–1053.

exhaustion problem. If each factor is paid according to its marginal contribution to the value of the product and a surplus still remains, then one factor, the entrepreneur or the renter, receives the residual and that factor receives a share in excess of its marginal value product. If a shortage occurs, the factor receives a share less than its marginal value product. Obviously, the above statement contains a contradiction. If each factor receives *only* the value of its marginal product, the value of the *product* must be exhausted by the sum of the factor payments. If $X_1, X_2, \ldots, X_n$ represents the quantities of factors of production, $M_1, M_2, \ldots, M_n$ represents their respective marginal products, and Q represents the total output of the product, with the production function given by

$$Q = f(X_1, X_2, \ldots, X_n) \tag{5.4}$$

Then, the product exhaustion principle states that

$$X_1 M_1 + X_2 M_2 + \cdots + X_n M_n = Q \tag{5.5}$$

where $X_i M_i$ represents the total payment to each type of factor i.

Although Wicksteed was the first to state this principle clearly in his *Coordination of the Laws of Distribution* (1894), he was not aware that this represented a specific form of a general property of homogeneous functions which had been proven by the mathematician Leonhard Euler (1707–1783).[39] For linear homogeneous functions, Equation (5.5) is an identity.

---

[39] The general properties of a homogeneous production function $Q = f(X_1 X_2)$ of degree r are

(1) $Q = X_1^r g\left(\dfrac{X_2}{X_1}\right) = X_2^r h\left(\dfrac{X_1}{X_2}\right)$

(2) $\dfrac{\partial Q}{\partial X_1}, \dfrac{\partial Q}{\partial X_2}$ are homogeneous of degree $(r - 1)$

(3) $X_1 \dfrac{\partial Q}{\partial X_1} + X_2 \dfrac{\partial Q}{\partial X_2} = rQ$

(4) $X_1^2 \dfrac{\partial^2 Q}{\partial X_1^2} + 2X_1 X_2 \dfrac{\partial^2 Q}{\partial X_1 \partial X_2} + X^2 \dfrac{\partial^2 Q}{\partial X_2^2} = r(r - 1)Q$

See R. G. D. Allen, *Mathematical Analysis for Economists* (London: Macmillan Co., 1938), pp. 317–320. These properties can be generalized to include any number of factors. Property (1) is derived from the definition of homogeneous function by setting $\lambda = 1/X_1$ or $\lambda = 1/X_2$. Properties (2) and (3) are derived by differentiating property (1). Property (3), of course, is the property identified by A. W. Flux, where the partial derivatives represent the marginal products of the respective factors. Since a linear homogeneous production function is of degree one, property (3) applies directly to the product-exhaustion problem. It should be obvious that for homogeneous production functions of degree other than one, the product-exhaustion solution does not hold. This is the source of the controversy to be discussed in the following pages.

This was clearly brought out by A. W. Flux in his review of Wicksteed's *Coordination* in the *Economic Journal*. Not only did Flux identify the mathematical nature of the product exhaustion principle, but because he was a more able mathematician than Wicksteed, he was able to derive a more elegant proof that the residual return to a factor (specifically, to land) was equal to the marginal product of that factor.[40]

Wicksteed had assumed that variability of factors is possible within broad limits, and with free substitutability, no factor share could be a residual.[41] If (1) a factor received a return less than its marginal product or (2) the ratio of its marginal product to its cost exceeded the corresponding ratios of other factors, then that particular factor would be increased in case (1) and substituted for others in case (2). In both cases the marginal product would decline until variation in the factor no longer was economical. This free variability permitted inputs to be varied both proportionately and nonproportionately. The first gives rise to returns to scale and the second to diminishing marginal returns if the production function is of degree one or less.[42] Since Wicksteed assumed it was self-evident that a proportionate increase in inputs yielded a proportionate increase in output, the constant returns to scale implied by a linear homogeneous production function were present in his proof. Since his homogeneous production function was linear, diminishing marginal returns were also assured. The question of whether constant returns to scale were necessary, and if so, whether it was a reasonable assumption became the controversy of the day. Edgeworth in England and Pareto on the continent held to the view that it was not a reasonable assumption, but it remained for Wicksell and Baronne to show that it was not a necessary assumption. If constant returns to scale do not hold, the critics argued, then the product exhaustion theorem was not universally true, and the marginal productivity theory was not a general theory of factor returns. If the product exhaustion theory were not true, then one or

[40] For a restatement of this proof, see Stigler, *op. cit.*, pp. 328–329.

[41] Wicksteed's analysis assumed a fixed quantity of each type of factor, although wide variability among their alternative uses and in combination was possible. Wicksteed also was critical of the practice of classifying factors of production into land, labor, and capital. Rather, he felt that inputs were of such variety as to make the number of classifications based on homogeneity endless.

[42] In order for an economic (nonfree) factor to be used, its marginal product must be greater than zero. From property (3) in note 39, it can be seen that it is possible for some factors to be negative, and therefore not to be used, if the function is of degree less than one. If the function is of degree one or more, all factors can be positive and all may be used if supply conditions permit the price of the factor to be at least equal to its marginal product. In order for diminishing marginal returns to occur, the second partial derivative must be less than zero: $(\partial^2 Q/\partial X^2 < 0)$. From property (4), it can be seen that this is true if r is 1 or less, but it need not be true if r is greater than 1.

more factors could receive a residual so that its return might differ from its marginal product. Wicksteed later acknowledged the correctness of this criticism, although he continued to expound the theorem in his writings.[43]

The criticisms of Pareto and Edgeworth were directed towards (1) whether a production function was homogeneous, and (2) if so, whether it was linear.[44] The homogeneity question revolves about whether it is realistic to suppose on the one hand that all factors can be increased in any given proportion. Are not some processes such that some inputs are by their nature indivisible—railroads, entrepreneurs, refineries? Even if it is possible to increase all factors in the same proportion, does it necessarily follow that output will increase in that proportion raised to the order of the function? If neither of these is generally true, then the empirical relevance of the homogeneity assumption is restricted to those cases in which it is true.

Frank Knight and others have argued that if factors are perfectly divisible, then only linear homogeneous production functions are possible. It is the existence of indivisible productive coefficients which makes possible increasing returns to scale (homogeneous functions of degree greater than one). As some factors are increased proportionately, other fixed factors are used more efficiently. Similarly, decreasing returns to scale (functions of degree less than one) develop when certain fixed factors are intensively utilized by other variable ones beyond the point of optimum efficiency. Presumably, the production function in question is a partial one, which relates output only to the variable inputs. If all inputs are variable, it is argued, inputs will be substituted so that all are used with optimum efficiency relative to cost. When this optimum combination is reached, variation in the scale of inputs will retain this proportion. Pareto rejected the homogeneity

---

[43] Perhaps it was this criticism which led Wicksteed to develop in more complete form in his *Common Sense of Political Economy* (1910) the alternative cost doctrine. Like the Austrians, Wicksteed showed that, with a fixed supply of the various factors, competition would cause each factor to be employed in such a way that its marginal utility would be equated among its alternative uses. He very clearly showed that the cost of using a factor in one use, given its limited supply, was the utility foregone by not being able to use it elsewhere. Buyers would bid the resource away from competing uses if, in those uses, the factor was receiving less than the value of its marginal utility in alternative uses. The mobility of resources and the wish of owners to maximize their returns would assure that the cost in one use would be equal to its value in another. Wicksteed, of course, ignored the important qualification of factor immobility which severely limits the applicability of this doctrine. This qualification is of particular importance for labor. Wicksteed might be called the complete marginalist, for he expanded the equimarginal principle to all phases of human behavior. Illustrative is his famous example of the South American planter who is being attacked by the enemy and who, while praying to the Lord for deliverance, must at some point weigh the marginal utility of an extra few seconds of prayer against the marginal utility of taking up arms to defend himself (pp. 79–80, 1932 reprint).

[44] See Schumpeter, *op. cit.*, pp. 1039–1040.

postulate because of its limited empirical applicability; he rejected the linearity postulate partly because of the divisibility assumption and partly because he recognized that inputs were not only substitutes for one another, which is implied by the linearity assumption, but that they may be complementary with or even independent of one another.[45] Consequently, if the linear homogeneity function is not generally applicable, then the marginal productivity theory is not a general theory of distribution. These criticisms were not against the logic of the product-exhaustion theory, but against its relevance.

It remained for Baronne to show that the production function did not have to be homogeneous of degree one for the product-exhaustion theorem to be true, and for Wicksell to explain clearly the conditions under which the product-exhaustion theory is true. Baronne had corresponded with Walras in 1894 suggesting that the latter use variable coefficients which were substitutable rather than fixed coefficients. Also, Baronne published in 1896 in *Giornale degli Economisti* two articles on distribution theory using those suggestions offered to Walras. Baronne, in the tradition of Jevons, Bohm-Bawerk, and later Wicksell, made use of the concept of the production period and the discounted marginal productivity doctrine.[46]

Assume the production function $Q = f(X_1, \ldots, X_n)$ where X_i represents the quantity of the factor i.

M_T = marginal product of time.

$M_i = \partial Q / \partial X_i$, or the marginal product of i.

P_i = price of the factor i.

P = price of a unit Q.

r = the interest rate computed as simple interest.

With K being the capital required for production in a period t, then

$$K = at \sum_{i-1}^{n} X_i P_i \tag{5.6}$$

---

[45] Given $r = 1$ and diminishing marginal product $(\partial^2 Q / \partial X^2 i < 0)$, from note 39, property (4) implies that the cross partial of any two factors is positive. This means that an increment of factor 1 increases the marginal product of factor 2, or vice versa. However, in the case of perfect complementarity—fixed production coefficients—or perfect independence, $\partial^2 Q / \partial X_1 \, \partial X_2$ is zero.

[46] See Stigler, *op. cit.*, pp. 278–295 for a concise exposition of Wicksell's development of the discounted marginal productivity theory and its use in his theory of distribution. The following formulation of Baronne's theory is adapted from Stigler, *ibid.*, pp. 360–361.

where a is a constant less than 1 which is the fraction of the production period during which K is equivalently invested. Setting the discounted value of the marginal product equal to the factor price, we have

$$P \cdot M_i \left(1 + \frac{rt}{a}\right)^{-1} = P_i \qquad (5.7)$$

and

$$P \cdot M_T = \frac{rK}{t} \qquad (5.7a)$$

since $dK/dt = a\sum_{i=1}^{n} K_i P_i$ and $t(dK/dt) = K_i$. Therefore, $dK/dt = M_T = K/t$. The unit price of the capital used in the production period is $r(K/t)$.

The equilibrium condition in perfect competition is total revenue equals total cost, or

$$\text{TR} = P \cdot Q = \text{sum of factor costs} = \sum_{i=1}^{n} X_i P_i + rK \qquad (5.8)$$

From (5.7a), $rK = t \cdot P \cdot M_T$, and substituting for P_i,

$$PQ = \sum_{i=1}^{n} PX_i M_i \left(1 + \frac{rt}{a}\right)^{-1} + tM_T \cdot P \qquad (5.9)$$

or

$$Q = \sum_{i=1}^{n} X_i M_i \left(1 + \frac{rt}{a}\right)^{-1} + tM_T \qquad (5.9a)$$

which is Euler's theorem if the period of production is also considered to be a factor in production.

Baronne, therefore, made two important contributions to the product-exhaustion question. First, he showed that with a general production function, not necessarily linear, and under perfect competition, payments in real terms to factors on the basis of their marginal product would exhaust the product. Second, he showed that the product-exhaustion theory was consistent with long-run equilibrium under perfect competition. Walras incorporated these ideas into the 4th edition of his *Elements* (1900).[47]

Wicksell not only contributed to Baronne's concept of the discounted marginal productivity theory, but he also demonstrated how the nonlinear production function could satisfy the product exhaustion theory in equi-

---

[47] Schumpeter, *op. cit.*, p. 1035.

librium under perfect competition.[48] Wicksell believed that production functions usually demonstrate first increasing and then decreasing returns to scale, each at different ranges of output. Within the specific interval where increasing returns have ceased but before decreasing returns commence, constant returns to scale are present. Thus, all three returns to scale may exist in the production function.

If we think of increasing, constant, and decreasing returns as being represented in monetary terms by decreasing, constant, and increasing unit costs,[49] respectively, then we get the familiar U-shaped long-run unit-cost curve of the firm. Prices of inputs together with the production function determine the shape and position of the curve. Higher factor prices shift the cost curve upward, and either improvements in technology or lower factor prices shift the long-run cost curve downward. Even though the individual firm is unable to influence the prices of factors or of the product because of its small size relative to the industry, nevertheless, general movements in industry demand for inputs can cause an increase in their respective prices, and changes in the size of the industry as firms enter or leave can result in changes in product price. Competition will force each firm in the industry to adopt the optimum scale plant.

Wicksell was the first to describe this process by which the product-exhaustion condition is satisfied. Shortly thereafter in the 4th edition of his *Elements* (1900) Walras also specified the conditions under which product exhaustion holds. Under perfect competition and in the long run all factors will be paid according to their marginal productivities. However, this is an equilibrium condition and does not depend exclusively upon the production function. If the marginal productivity theory is to hold, at some point the production function must exhibit constant returns to scale, the firm must produce, buy, and sell in perfect markets, and the time reference must be of sufficient duration to permit substitution and variation among factor quantities. If, for example, the production function does not at any point yield constant returns to scale, then the marginal productivity theory will not guarantee that the sum of the marginal products of each factor will

[48] Wicksell first developed his discounted marginal productivity theory in 1893 in *Uber Wert, Kapital und Rente*, forgot about it, and rediscovered it in 1900 in his article, "On Marginal Productivity as the Basis for Economic Distribution." In this article he credits Wicksteed with discovering the theory, although his *Uber* (1893) appeared before Wicksteed's *Coordination* (1894). In his *Uber* and with a two-factor market consisting of labor and capital, he showed that wages are equal to the discounted value of labor's marginal product and that the return to capital, interest, is equal to the rate of discount. Taken together, total wages and total interest would exhaust the product.

[49] Although increasing, constant, and decreasing returns to scale are not synonymous with decreasing, constant, and increasing costs, no great error occurs in so regarding them. See Schumpeter, *op. cit.*, p. 1045n.

exhaust the product. This means that the share of some factor or factors is determined as a residual and not by marginal product. Similarly, if the production function exhibits only increasing returns to scale, then pure competition becomes an impossibility as firms become of larger and larger size relative to the market. Once we allow monopoly elements to characterize the market, we have no guarantee that all factors will receive a return equal to their contribution to total revenue.

In conclusion, it is apparent that the Euler theorem controversy is not just a controversy over the marginal productivity theory as a general theory of income distribution. In part it is a controversy over the nature of the production function as well. The controversy was resolved by showing under what production and market conditions the Euler theorem holds and by showing that the long-run equilibrium of perfect competition will satisfy these conditions if the production function at some point is tangent to one which is linear and homogeneous.

Discussion Questions

1. Find the degree of the following production functions if they are homogeneous where X, Y, Z are inputs and a, b, c, and d are constants.

   (a) $aX + bY + cZ = d$
   (b) $aX \cdot Y/Z + bY \cdot Z/X + cX \cdot Z/Y = Q$
   (c) $aX \cdot Y + bX^2 + cY^2 + dZ^2 = Q$
   (d) $aX \cdot Y + bZ + cX/Z + d = Q$

2. "The law of diminishing marginal returns is analogous to taking the partial derivative of a production function with respect to some input." Discuss.

3. Formulate your own definition of the principle of diminishing returns. If all inputs are variable in the long run, does the principle of diminishing marginal returns hold in this period? Explain.

4. Are there really three types of diminishing returns, or is there really only one type from which the other two are derived? Discuss.

5. Given the following production function: $Q = 100 \sqrt{K}\sqrt{L}$, where Q is output, K is capital input, and L is labor input, $P = \$10$.

   (a) Construct a short-run demand schedule for labor when $K = 9$; $K = 16$; $K = 25$. What conclusion follows from increasing K?
   (b) Assuming that the employer can hire as much labor as he wishes at any given wage, what is the maximum wage an employer would pay for 5 units of labor for each value of K? For 6 units of labor? For 10 units of labor?

6. It has been said that the development of marginal analysis represents the beginning of modern economic theory. Do you agree?

7. Show how changes in the demand for different kinds of labor are derived from changes in the demand for the following goods and services. Explain how these effects on labor are reflected in wages and employment.

(a) The demand for medical services.
(b) The demand for coal.
(c) The demand for automobiles.
(d) The demand for education.

8. "In an increasing proportion of productive processes, the amount of labor that can be used with capital equipment is rigidly fixed by technological specifications, and little substitution of either input for the other is possible." Discuss the validity and implications of this statement.

9. It has been said that the marginal productivity theory as an explanation of how income is distributed was developed to answer the ethical implications of Marx's theory of labor exploitation. Discuss.

10. Discuss Marshall's objection to the marginal productivity theory as a theory of wages.

11. Since its formulation, the marginal productivity theory of wages has been subject to numerous criticisms. Some critics have attacked the mathematical assumptions on which it is based; others have attacked its relevance to man's actual behavior; others have found fault with its predictive ability; some have questioned whether labor can be treated as a homogeneous input; while others deny that prices or wages are determined essentially by "maximizing principles." Nevertheless, the theory survives and persists. Why?

Part III

THE MICRO THEORY OF
THE LABOR MARKET

6

An Introduction to the Quality of Labor and Human Capital

The Meaning of Labor Supply

The price of labor is determined by forces of demand and supply in a labor market. Since we have to consider one or the other first, and since we have already dealt at length with one of the basic determinants of demand—marginal productivity—it is perhaps appropriate to devote our attention at this point to those forces affecting the supply of labor. In a subsequent chapter, we shall consider in greater detail the forces determining the demand for labor.

When reference is made to the market *labor supply*, this refers to the number of people who are at work, are seeking work, or would be seeking work if jobs at acceptable wages were believed to be available in the domain defined as the market. The concept of labor supply differs from that of the *labor force*. The labor force of the United States as analyzed in Table 6.1 is based upon a definition by the Bureau of the Census, and it is a narrower concept. Whereas the concept of labor supply includes potential sellers of labor with no clear restrictions on age or institutional affiliation, such is not the case in the definition of the labor force. Only persons 16 years of age or older who are members of the noninstitutional population and who are either employed or unemployed, but actively seeking employment, are counted in the latter definition. *Active* participation in the labor market of a restricted segment of the population is the essential criterion. A distinction is made between the *total labor force*, which includes the armed forces, and the *civilian labor force*, which does not. Because the magnitude of the labor force is determined by the number of persons actively in the labor market

TABLE 6.1
LABOR FORCE, EMPLOYMENT, AND UNEMPLOYMENT FOR
SELECTED YEARS
[Thousands of persons]

Item	1947	1960	April 1971
Total noninstitutional population	103,418	119,759	142,088
Not in labor force	42,477	47,617	56,308
Total labor force	60,941	72,142	86,665
Civilian labor force	59,350	69,628	83,783
Employed:	57,039	65,778	78,698
In nonagricultural industries	49,148	60,318	75,140
In agriculture	7,891	5,458	3,558
Unemployed	2,311	3,852	5,085
Unemployment rate (%)	3.9	5.5	6.1

Source: U.S. Department of Labor.

in a given interval of time, the specification of that time interval is important. Weekly, monthly, quarterly, and annual time intervals are used, although the basic unit is the week. Averages of the component weeks comprise the count for the other time units.

A person is *employed* if he has worked for wages for as little as one hour in a specified week, or if as a family member in a family enterprise, he has worked at least 15 hours in that week. He is considered employed if he has a job but has been temporarily absent because of illness, vacation, a labor dispute, or a variety of other similar, acceptable reasons. A person is considered to be *unemployed*, but in the labor force, if he has actively sought work in the past four weeks, is temporarily on layoff from his job, or is scheduled to begin a new job within 30 days of the survey date. Persons not in the labor force include those who are under 16, those over 16 but who are at school, at home, inmates of institutions, disabled by a long-term illness or injury, too old, retired, or persons who did not look for work because they believed no jobs were available. Many of the persons not counted as in the labor force are potential employees, and sometimes these have been called the *secondary labor force*. The *secondary labor force* is distinct from the *primary labor force* as defined by the Bureau of the Census, and includes those who are marginally attached to the labor market.

Members of the labor force are called *labor force participants*. A *labor force participation rate* is the ratio of the persons in a group who are in the labor force to the total population of the group. The total labor force participation rate is the ratio of the total labor force to the total noninstitutional population 16 years of age or older; the civilian labor force participation rate is the ratio of the civilian labor force to the civilian noninstitutional population age 16 years or older; the labor force participation rate of females of age 20–24 is the ratio of the number of women between the ages of 20 and 24 who are in the labor force to the total number of noninstitutional women age 20 through 24. Because people enter and/or leave the labor force at different times of the year, the size of the labor force and group labor force participation rates also vary throughout the year. This phenomenon also explains why the number of labor force participants during the year normally exceeds the annual average size of the labor force.

At any given time, the size of the labor force is obviously a function of the size of the population, but other influences upon its size are also important. Present and past demographic factors determine the rate of growth of the population and subsequently the size of the labor force. The relative birth and death rates not only determine the future magnitude of the labor force but also affect the present economic participation of women in the labor force. The percentage of the economically active population is influenced by such matters as the stage of economic development, the cultural role of women, the stage of the business cycle, or the institutional structure of the economy. All of these influence the labor force participation rate. In addition to the mere number of workers, the amount of labor forthcoming from a given population is also a function of the length of the work day and work year—the hours of work. As we shall see, the hours of work are determined in part by the institutional requirements, in part by the remuneration for work, and in part by the preference structure (tastes) of laborers.

There is also a qualitative dimension to the supply of labor. The efficiency with which a given number of workers can produce, who are employed for a given work-week, depends upon the health and stamina of the labor force and upon the degree and relative distribution of skills among the labor force. Stamina and health are influenced by nutrition, and disease prevention and treatment. An undernourished worker cannot work with the same intensity or as long as one who is adequately nourished. A laborer suffering from a debilitating disease such as malaria or tuberculosis in turn has his capacity for work impaired. Not only is stamina lessened, but morbidity increases absenteeism and impairs the performance reliability of a labor force. The dimensions of malnutrition and disease vary with the degree of economic development of a country, but in some underdeveloped countries the quality of the labor force is seriously affected by these problems.

The health and educational levels of a population influence also the learning capacity and therefore the trainability of the labor force. Given the native abilities, which in a large population should follow the pattern of a normal statistical distribution, and given the same basic level of educational attainments, any population should be equally capable of being trained. The actual degree of training and the type of training will be reflected in the occupational distribution of the labor force. Investment in health, education, and training of a labor force utilizes resources, and the product of these inputs is a labor force of a given quality. However, economists have questioned whether the allocation of resources designed to improve the caliber of the labor force should properly be considered as personal consumption or as capital formation. To the extent that quality increases the productivity of a labor force, it seems reasonable to regard the use of resources to develop that quality to be a form of capital investment. However, since resources devoted to nutrition, education, and training are often, if not typically, in the form of household expenditures, they are concealed under the heading of consumption.

In this and the following chapter, we shall examine the qualitative dimensions of a labor force. Later we shall examine the individual worker's decision on how to allocate his time among alternative activities, the result of which leads to an individual labor supply function. From there the determination of the size of the labor force will be considered together with an analysis of the labor supply function under a variety of labor market situations.

Health

The health of the population depends not only upon the prevention and cure of disease, but also upon the provision of adequate nutrition. Indeed, malnutrition and disease are closely related, for an undernourished person is particularly susceptible to contracting numerous diseases. For example, it has been found that malnutrition among children is sufficient to cause chronic diarrhea, and tuberculosis, pneumonia, and other infectious diseases are associated with poor nutrition.[1] The benefits from the improved health of a population are reflected in improved productivity of the labor force which results from a qualitative improvement in the character of the labor force and a quantitative improvement in the numbers actually in the labor force at any given time. The term most frequently used to describe the impairment of a worker's productivity on a job owing to ill health is *debility*. Illness can affect both physical and mental performance on a job. Not only

---

[1] "Infection and parasitic disease, ubiquitous in the tropics, are so closely associated with malnutrition that, in practice, it is difficult to disentangle the ill effects which each produces." George R. Allen, "The World Food Shortage: Nutritional Requirements and the Demand for Food" in *Food, One Tool in International Economic Development* (Ames: Iowa State University Press, 1962), p. 36.

can an illness affect the time in which a worker is capable of completing a task, but it can affect his motivation and his problem-solving ability in accomplishing a task. *Morbidity* is a term used to describe an absence from work caused by an illness. *Mortality* refers, of course, to death resulting from an illness. In the case of malaria, the relationship has been described as follows:

"Malaria is a parasitic disease . . . The parasites invade red blood cells and cause them to rupture synchronously, thus producing the attacks of chills, fever, and sweating associated with the disease. These attacks cause temporary disability and are sometimes fatal. Those victims who survive the febrile attacks are left in a weakened state because of the massive destruction of their blood cells, and hence are more susceptible to death or disability from other diseases. Their debilitation reduces work efficiency."[2]

Reduction of debility, therefore, represents a qualitative improvement in the labor force, reduction of morbidity produces both a qualitative and a quantitative increment to the labor force, and reduction in mortality has essentially a quantitative impact. It is, of course, more difficult to measure the qualitative changes in the labor force, but some attempts have been made to measure the effect of debility upon worker efficiency. For example, comparisons have been made of accomplishments of work groups before and after disease control and of differences in the piece-rate earnings between controlled work groups; in one group members had a debilitating disease while members of the other group were largely free of the disease.[3] The magnitude of the effect of debility, of course, will depend upon the incidence of the health impairment and its frequency of occurrence in occupations with different productivities. For example, it has been found that malaria primarily affects members of the labor force with low income and low productivity. This is so because it can be avoided by appropriate measures that are in part dependent upon a money expenditure (mosquito netting, antimalarial medicines, residences with adequate drainage and spraying) or through precautions based upon knowledge (education).[4] Members of the labor force with higher incomes and more education are better able to protect themselves from malaria.

[2] Robin Barlow, "The Economic Effects of Malaria Eradication," *American Economic Review* (May 1967), p. 131.
[3] See Selma J. Mushkin, "Health as an Investment," *Journal of Political Economy* (Supplement, October 1962), pp. 133, 142.
[4] Barlow, *op. cit.*, p. 133.

Nutrition directly affects labor productivity in terms of debility and indirectly through its effect upon disease. Adequate nutrition requires that a person receive the minimum necessary inputs of calories, minerals, vitamins, fats, and especially proteins. Galenson and Pyatt found that comparable increments in investment in different countries produced different yields in economic growth and, to explain this phenomenon, they analyzed qualitative differences in the labor forces of these countries. Diet was considered as one of the factors affecting economic growth. They concluded that the related factors of health and nutrition (caloric intake) among countries seemed best to explain their observed differences in economic growth.[5] The importance of food calories to the efficiency of a given labor force should be apparent, for there is a physical relationship between inputs of energy by man and its utilization. Total human energy requirements are made up of three components: (1) the energy utilization of the basal metabolism and this tends to be dependent upon weight, age, and sex; (2) the energy cost of physical activity and the duration of this activity; (3) the dynamic action of food itself. In a 165-pound man doing moderately heavy work the caloric expenditure of these components is of the magnitudes, respectively, of 1800 calories, 1500 calories, and 200 calories, so that over 90% of energy expenditure is consumed by the first two uses. Table 6.2 suggests the relationship between the energy expenditure and the nature of the activity.

TABLE 6.2
DAILY ENERGY REQUIREMENTS BY ACTIVITY AND BY SEX

Type of Activity	Total Calories		Calories per Kg of Body Weight
	Male	Female	
Sedentary, at rest	2000–2200	1600–1800	30–33
Sedentary, but manual work	2200–2700	1900–2000	34–37
Moderate work performed erect	2800–3000	2300–2500	38–42
Work developing muscular strength	3100–3500	2600–3000	43–50
Work requiring very strong muscles	4000–6000	—	55–70

Source: L. Jean Bogert. *Nutrition and Physical Fitness*, 7th Edition (Philadelphia: W. B. Saunders and Co., 1963), p. 62.

[5] Walter Galenson and George Pyatt, *The Quality of Labor and Economic Development in Certain Countries* (Geneva: International Labour Office, 1964). A similar conclusion was reached by Hector Correa and Gaylord Cummins, "Contribution of Nutrition to Economic Growth," *The American Journal of Clinical Nutrition*, Vol. 23, No. 5 (May 1970), pp. 560–565. They conclude, "The aggregate effect of nutrition on output may well have exceeded that of education."

A labor force whose members receive an inadequate supply of calories will be incapable of performing sustained heavy work. An undernourished worker is more subject to fatigue, and it has been found that overfatigue has in some cases been responsible for malnutrition through the adverse effect of fatigue on appetite. One noted economist has pointed out that extra food in some poor countries has the attribute of a "producer good" . . . clothing, housing, and perhaps medical services may be similar.[6]

Protein deficiency in some cases is more serious than caloric deficiency. Animal sources of protein are particularly important and in Asia in particular, these sources are scarce. Protein requirements vary with age, sex, and physical activity. The Food and Nutrition Board of the National Research Council recommends the daily amounts of protein, in grams, given in Table 6.3.[7] Protein deficiency can cause fatigue, reduce blood pressure, result in enzyme deficiency; it can lower resistance to disease, impair digestion, and impair waste elimination. Heavy work requires protein for

TABLE 6.3
DAILY PROTEIN REQUIREMENTS BY AGE AND SEX
[Grams]

| | *Children* | | | *Adults* | |
Age	Boys	Girls	Men	Women	
1–3	40	40	70	60	
4–6	50	50		Pregnancy 85	
7–9	60	60		Lactation 100	
10–12	70	70			
13–15	85	80			
16–20	100	75			

[6] Theodore W. Schultz, "Investment in Human Capital" in *The Goal of Economic Growth*, ed. Edmund S. Phelps (New York: W. W. Norton & Co., 1962), p. 113. See also the article by Harry Oshima, "Food Consumption, Nutrition, and Economic Development," *Economic Development and Cultural Change* (July 1967). In this article, Oshima questions the adequacy of caloric intakes in Asian countries for work purposes rather than health. The effect on productivity of inadequate nutrition has also been extensively discussed by Alan Berg and Robert Muscat, *Nutrition and Development: The View of the Planner*, Paper prepared for May 3–7, 1971, Meeting of the Secretary General's Panel to Formulate a United Nations Strategy Statement on the Protein Problem Confronting the Developing Countries.
[7] Adelle Davis, *Let's Eat Right to Keep Fit* (New York: Harcourt, Brace, & World, Inc., 1964), p. 31. The increase in labor productivity from use of supplemental sources of protein has been noted by J. L. Simon and D. M. Gardner, "World Food Needs and 'New Proteins,' " *Economic Development and Cultural Change* (July 1969), Vol. 17, No. 4, p. 524.

tissue building. Protein malnutrition in underdeveloped countries is a serious problem, for the basic source of food in many such countries is from starchy grains such as rice which, because of an increasing tendency to remove the hulls, has resulted in a loss of many valuable nutrients, especially protein. It is interesting that the length of life expectancy parallels the consumption of protein.

Protein is especially important to the human embryo and the new-born child in the building of brain tissue. In addition to retarding physical growth of the body, protein deficiencies have been found also to retard the development of headsize and brain weight, inhibiting mental development. This finding has led one economist to simulate the effects on the normal distribution of intelligence in a protein-deprived population, and one of the important consequences is the finding of a significant reduction in the proportion of population with I.Q.'s of over 110, that group from which most white-collar occupations are drawn.[8] A reduction in the source of high-level manpower potential from which engineers, scientists, managers, technicians, and professionals are drawn can have serious consequences on the development of a country.

The effect of vitamin deficiency is well known. Vitamin A deficiency impairs eyesight, lack of vitamin D produces rickets, lack of vitamin C causes scurvy. Less well known are the effects of the B-complex vitamin deficiencies. The B vitamins are sometimes called the blood-building, antistress, antifatigue, and antitoxic vitamins. An inadequacy of vitamins, proteins, and calories can impair the proficiency and efficiency of a worker, for an anemic, fatigued, or psychologically disturbed person cannot perform as energetically and imaginatively as an employee enjoying normal health, nor is he likely to sustain a consistently high level of performance.

There is another possible effect of poor nutrition upon the quality of the labor force. A pediatrician engaged in public health programs of the Rockefeller Foundation discussed with me the findings of a team of medical specialists on the effect of malnutrition upon the health of children in Colombia. Improper and insufficient diets among very young children can so weaken the body that the body may be unable to control the natural intestinal flora of the child, and the child may suffer from chronic, acute diarrhea. This diarrhea can so dehydrate the child that nerve cells, par-

---

[8] Pedro Belli, "The Economic Consequences of Malnutrition: The Dismal Science Revisited," *Economic Development and Cultural Change*, Vol. 20, No. 1 (October 1971), pp. 2–10. Another observer of the effects of nutritional deprivation on the mental development of Guatemalan children has made the suggestion "that an individual whose intersensory organization is retarded may require a longer training period, in order to acquire job skills, may be less adept at manipulating industrial equipment, and may be more accident prone." Victor E. Childers, "Infant Nutrition: Priority for Development?" *International Development Review* (June 1969), p. 14.

ticularly in the brain, can deteriorate, and mental retardation can result. Poor sanitation, of course, is also a causal factor as well as other socio-economic conditions in producing diarrhea and/or malnutrition. However, the ultimate result of poor nutrition may reduce the educability or train-ability of the child. If the child lives to adulthood and enters the labor force, the quality of his labor will consequently be impaired.

Reduction of morbidity through low-cost health programs can often be substantial. As a result of malaria control programs, absenteeism from work in many countries has been drastically reduced—from 35 to 4% in the Philippines—and fewer workers were required as a result.[9] Morbidity has been dramatically lowered also through health programs against schistoso-miasis, hookworm, trachoma, leprosy, tuberculosis, filariasis, and oncho-cerciasis. Productivity of the labor force has been enhanced not only by increasing the number of man-hours per year which each previously ill worker was able to generate, but also by reducing general malaise which accompanies a debilitating illness and which retards the pace of a worker's activity.

Gains also are realized in planning and coordinating the activities of a more stable labor force in an establishment, a difficult task indeed when morbidity can reduce the size of the labor force by one-third in critical operating periods. Where health programs lessen the incidence of childhood sicknesses, such as with pure water or sanitation programs or with school lunches, where children as captive audiences can be given one wholesome, well-balanced meal daily, the future quality of the labor force can be enhanced. This is so because the educability of the child is improved as school absenteeism is reduced; obviously a child, or a worker, cannot be trained if he cannot attend the place of training. Similarly, if life expectancy is increased, the period over which training is utilized is extended. Thus, for a given labor force of given skills, increased life expectancy can reduce the amount of training necessary to sustain that quantity of skill. Expressed another way, a given time–resource expenditure of training for a population with a constant labor force will augment the skill of that labor force if life expectancy is increased. Attrition because of premature death, disability, morbidity, and debility will be less, and therefore resources heretofore devoted to replacing that attrition can be diverted to improving the quality of the given labor force.

Attempts have been made to measure the benefits from improved health.[10] A health program may yield fruits other than those reflected in the

---

[9] Carl E. Taylor and Marie-Francoise Hall, "Health, Population, and Economic Develop-ment," *Science*, Vol. 157 (August 11 1967), p. 653. Similar results have been experienced through the control of other infectious diseases, such as yaws.

[10] See Mushkin, *op. cit.*, pp. 129–157. Much of the following discussion is based upon her excellent article.

labor force, such as when land—once inaccessible because of malaria—is opened up, but certainly its effect upon labor as a resource is of substantial importance. The benefits from a health program which prevents or cures disease can be approached in one of three ways. A health program can have consequences upon economic growth, both in the short run and in the long run. An attempt can be made to measure its influence upon economic growth, as was done by Robin Barlow in the case of Ceylon where a malaria eradication program was successfully undertaken. Short-run gains from increased worker productivity and augmentation of the labor force were found to be offset by adverse long-run demographic consequences. Increased female fertility and lower infant mortality combined together to increase the rate of population growth. The increased number of children diverted funds from high-productivity capital investments to increased educational expenditures or to low-yield housing investments. The larger families tended to reduce personal savings and ultimately capital formation.

Barlow concluded that for the first few years after the malaria eradication program had been completed, per capita income was higher than if no program had been undertaken. However, after ten years, per capita income was lower with the malaria control program than it would have been without the program. Ceylon, of course, is an underdeveloped country with a population and economic growth-rate problem. The Malthusian specter can be expected to be more appropriate to an economy such as this than to one in which demographic and economic growth patterns are much different. *Nevertheless, Barlow's article does remind one that health programs are not necessarily beneficial in the long run.* There is a real question as to whether an augmentation in the labor force adds very much if the added workers cannot find employment because of insufficient job creation accruing from economic growth, or if the increased numbers of people, saved from death or disability owing to a disease such as malaria, contract some other terminal disease because their resistance has been lowered through malnutrition.

A second method which has been used to measure the benefits from improved health is an estimation of the amount of loss avoided when a reduction in the potential labor force through premature death or disability is prevented. Resources are used to raise a child to become a productive worker. If that person is unable for some reason to enter the labor force, the family and the society incur an economic loss at least equivalent to the resources devoted to producing that potential worker at the time, say, he dies prematurely. The benefit of a health program, therefore, is at least equivalent to the resources which would have been lost if the child or adult had died. Calculations based upon this method, as Mushkin notes, have been used (1) to determine the amount of indemnity to which a survivor or dependent is entitled in accidental injury cases, (2) for purposes of determining the size of family allowances to be paid (similar to the negative income tax) in certain European countries, or (3) for purposes of determining the size of child welfare payments.

The third method for measuring the benefits from improved health is through computing the present value of the future product resulting from increased numbers of workers and from their improved productivity. The first step in this process is to estimate the gain in work time and to convert this gain into full-time equivalent workers. As an illustration of this method, Mushkin calculated the number of persons employed in 1960 who would not have survived to 1960 if the mortality rate of earlier years had been in effect. By this method, she estimated the additional persons in the labor force attributed to increased life expectancy.[11] To determine the gain in future work time of survivors at each age, work-life tables of the Bureau of Labor Statistics can be used to estimate the remaining years of work life at each age and for each sex. The next step is to estimate the value of this gain, and this may be accomplished either by estimating the incremental output attributed to these equivalent workers and then valuing this product at market prices, or alternatively by using earnings as a measure of labor's product. Of course, a frequency distribution of the incidence of the augmented work time and earnings among different occupational levels is necessary in order to ascertain the proper weighting to give to this valuation.

The Nature of Human Capital

To the extent that the quality of the labor force affects and is positively related to the productivity of the labor force, improvements in the quality of the labor force improve its productivity. A more productive worker is worth more to an employer who is not only willing to pay more for the services of such employees but under competition must pay higher wages to more productive workers. The enhanced productivity is inherent in the services of the worker himself. Two workers, each working with given amounts of complementary inputs, differ in the quality of their services if one consistently produces more than the other. Members of a homogeneous labor force, of course, may produce different quantities of output if each member has his services combined with different quantities of complementary inputs, but workers of the same quality working with identical amounts of, say, fixed capital goods must all produce the same. If they do not, this is

---

[11] Mushkin, *op. cit.*, p. 145. She found that in 1960, 235,000 more men and 75,000 more women were added to the labor force as if the 1950 mortality experience had continued. Corresponding increments based upon the 1900 mortality experience were 8,743,000 men and 4,467,000 women.

prima facie evidence that quality differs. Viewed in this sense, quality can be measured in terms of a productivity index.

If wages are related to productivity and productivity is related to quality, then superior workers will be paid more than inferior workers. Where income is the only motive for entering an occupation, differences in earnings in a perfect world therefore will reflect differences in quality. The present value of earning differentials can be measured in the same manner as any periodic income received over an interval of time. The income received in future periods is discounted by a rate of return per period. Thus, if y income were received in each of t periods for worker Y, and x income per period were received by worker X over the same t periods, where $y > x$ and r is the discount rate per period, then the present values of the future incomes of Y and X are given by the formula

$$V_y = \sum_{i=1}^{t} \frac{Y_i}{(1 + r)^i} \qquad\qquad (6.1\text{a})$$

$$V_x = \sum_{i=1}^{t} \frac{X_i}{(1 + r)^i} \qquad\qquad (6.1\text{b})$$

The difference between the present values of the income streams of the two workers,

$$D = V_y - V_x = \sum_{i=1}^{t} \frac{Y_i - X_i}{(1 + r)^i} \qquad\qquad (6.2)$$

tells us how much more Y is worth than X in income-earning ability. We have *capitalized* their future earnings. If Y and X were slaves and were placed upon the block to be sold, ignoring their maintenance cost, a buyer through competition would be forced to pay D more for Y than for X. Viewed differently, if Y and X did not differ in quality (productivity) but Y possessed capital, and X did not, which Y invested at r rate of interest for t periods, then the value of this capital would be equal to D, for the income of Y's labor alone would be equal to that of X's labor. Any differential income would be owing to the capital resources of Y. In this sense, it can be said that the differential quality of superior labor is equivalent to capital.

Income differences can arise from a number of sources. In any large population, differences in intelligence, aptitude, and length of life can be expected to be normally distributed about a mean. This would be a result of natural dispersion in a population subject to homogeneous environmental and developmental forces. To the extent that productivity is enhanced by higher intelligence or greater aptitudes (inherent ability) and to the extent that total lifetime earnings are increased by a longer work life,[12] the present value of the future income of workers will differ. Natural abilities can be sharpened, however, through education and training. Productivity will differ among workers of equal natural ability but who have received different levels of education or training. As we have shown in the previous section, productivity can be improved also, through improvements in the health of a worker. Improved health not only increases current productivity through enhanced stamina and reduced morbidity and debility, but it also increases life expectancy and years of work through lower mortality.

Moreover, workers of equal ability, training, stamina, and life expectancy may differ in productivity if they differ in motivation or emotional stability. Workers who have learned (been taught) that present efforts are related to future rewards, whose learning experiences have reinforced such behavior as diligence, perseverence, and patience, and as a result who have learned to recognize and establish realistic goals will experience greater motivation than workers who have not. The behavioral traits which are reflected in superior motivation are a product of family training, and to the extent that families differ in developing these traits among their children, children will develop, as they mature, different degrees of motivation and different capacities for productivity.

Workers whose ability, motivation, training, health, and work-life expectancy are equal may have different productivity and incomes if they are employed in occupations using different quantities, but of given quality, of complementary resources per worker. These income differences can be reduced if workers from low-paying occupations (or regions) move to the higher paying ones. A given spatial and occupational distribution of workers in a historically changing and dynamic society of diverse regions will be paralleled by a structure of wages influenced in part by the diversity of regions and in part by the cultural lags present in the society. Willingness to search for jobs, to change occupations, or to migrate (that is, to reallocate labor resources) can enhance the productivity of an unfavorably situated worker and hence his earnings. To the extent that the present value of his earnings is increased, he has acquired a capital equivalent.

Any condition which generates an increment in earnings or an increment in the present value of future earnings may be said to be of the form of a capital acquisition. In this sense, if an individual can create for himself a situation which reduces the duration or frequency of unemployment, for

---

[12] If t is the worklife of X and z is the worklife of Y, given that X and Y are of the same quality and earn the same income per period, it is obvious that

$$V_X = \sum_{i=1}^{t} \frac{X_i}{(1+r)^i} > V_Y = \sum_{i=1}^{z} \frac{Y_i}{(1+r)^i}, \qquad \text{if} \quad t > z.$$

example, he has developed something which possesses a capital value. Some of these capital-generating conditions are acquired through natural (nonself-induced) processes; others can be acquired only as a result of an expenditure of effort and/or other resources. We shall examine at length the implications of this concept of human capital and how this capital is acquired. At present, the student should recognize that human capital is a concept based upon (1) differential earnings which (2) have been capitalized over some relevant time interval. These differential earnings are realized because the productivity of labor has been increased either within a given period of time or through a lengthening of the active work life of the laborer.

Where resources are expended on human beings either on an individual or social basis in order to increase their productivity, and where this increased productivity continues over a finite interval of time, this process is akin to capital formation. The investment of resources, however, results in the creation of a nonmaterial form of capital inseparable from the human agent. For this reason, the now more productive human agent has been said to have acquired "human capital," the process is known as "investment in human capital," and the services resulting from this investment, like those of capital in general, are released in the productive process over time.

Recognition that investment in human capital occurs has been obscured by the fact that much of this resource allocation has been classified as consumption expenditures. Private expenditures on health and education and even those on migration are treated as household expenditures on final products, not to mention expenditures for reading materials, educational toys, home workshop tools, automobile driving lessons, adult classes, and the like.[13] More seriously, public expenditures on salaries for educators, health officials, and the like are classified in national income accounts of countries using the United Nations format as *"government consumption expenditures"* and not as *"government capital expenditures."*[14] The significance of this omission from public and private capital formation accounts is that gross capital formation is significantly understated, as is the rate of growth of national resources.

The services provided by government employees, who are paid the wages that constitute the bulk of government consumption expenditures, can be capitalized. If it is assumed, for example, that the magnitude of expenditures or the amount of government services is held constant or increases at a slower rate than that of population, such as in Asia, Latin America, or urban areas of the United States, per capita services must decline. Fewer

[13] See the comments by one of the pioneers of this concept, Theodore W. Schultz, "Investment in Human Capital," *American Economic Review* (March, 1961), pp. 1–3.

[14] A criticism of this practice is contained in my article, Mabry, "Government Consumption Expenditures and Economic Development: A Rose by Any Other Name," *Economic Journal of Thailand* (Fall, 1968), pp. 11–20.

children will be educated, or the average number of years of school attendance will decline, or the quality of education will decline. The shortage of physicians, already serious, will become more critical, and the general hygiene instruction of the public will deteriorate as public health officers become relatively more scarce and more overworked. Traffic congestion and air pollution will become more severe as the number of vehicles increases, since traffic policemen and pollution inspectors per 1000 automobiles become less numerous. Similarly, crime can be expected to increase as police protection is diluted. The postal service may become less efficient as the mail load increases, a backlog of mail deliveries will accumulate, more letters will be lost, longer queues will develop at postal stations. A smaller proportion of banks will be examined, relatively fewer factories will be inspected for compliance with safety legislation, more labor trouble will develop as industrial accidents increase. Investment will be discouraged and companies will become increasingly reluctant to move to areas where public services decline. If the private sector of the economy advances, and wage differentials widen between private and public employment, deterioration in the quality of the civil servants can be expected as the more qualified persons are attracted to positions in the private sector. If these and other conditions come about, it is unlikely that the rate of economic growth will be unaffected.

Government services may be considered also as complementary to capital projects. Schools must be manned by teachers, highways must be patrolled if traffic is to flow smoothly, waterworks and sewage systems must be operated and repaired, buildings must be protected from fires and vandalism, irrigation and power systems must be operated and maintained, disputes over the use of property must be adjudicated. As capital facilities expand, the complementary services, it is reasonable to assume, must expand at a rate sufficient to assure their optimum use. A corollary of this is that the marginal productivity of civil servants will increase, and if they receive no higher wages, civil servants become exploited, in the Joan Robinson sense, via government monopsony. If the former expands but the latter does not, the principle of diminishing returns assures us that the productivity of those capital goods will be impaired, and total output resulting from them will be less than it otherwise would be. Therefore, both from the standpoint of the stagnation of the human-capital infrastructure and from their necessarily complementary relationship to social capital, a constant level of government services (or a level which increases at less than some optimum) must impair the growth rate of the national product.

It is this differential in the growth rate over time which must be discounted in order to determine the present value of any given level of government services. Only in this sense can government services be evaluated in proper economic perspective as a form of social investment. It is only by means of relevant comparisons among present values and current costs of different projects that yield both current and future services, that a correct economic decision can be made concerning the allocation of government resources. The difficulties involved in obtaining relevant information to permit such an evaluation and comparison are undeniably great, particularly in the absence of well-defined social productivity functions. Yet, only in this sense is it meaningful to distinguish between the productivity of government capital expenditures and government "consumption expenditures." It is obviously fallacious to assume that the former are productive and the latter are not.

Schultz has argued that inclusion of human capital formation in the resource base may well explain why national income has had a tendency to increase more rapidly than the (recorded) resource base and why the ratio of capital to income has had a tendency to decline.[15] To indicate the significance of a labor force embodied with substantial amounts of human capital, he questions how productive a country like India would be if it suddenly were endowed with the physical capital stock of the United States while no change occurred in its supply of skills and educated labor force.[16] Consequently, it does not seem realistic to ignore the qualitative aspects of the labor force in considering labor supply. When we treat of the supply of labor, we must recognize the heterogeneity of the aggregate labor force and also recognize that this heterogeneity is a *product* of the allocation of resources for the improvement of the skills of man.

Earlier Concepts of Human Capital[17]

Adam Smith, J. B. Say, John Stuart Mill, Alfred Marshall, and Leon Walras were economists before the 20th century who regarded the development of human skill as being essentially of the same nature as that of capital formation. Marshall compared an educated man to an expensive machine. Nassau Senior, however, felt that the education of children by parents should be considered as a consumption expenditure, since the parents derive pride and a sense of accomplishment, not income, from their outlays upon their children's schooling.[18] All these economists believed that the wealth of a

[15] Schultz, *op. cit.*, p. 4. In fact, he argues that the latter may turn out to be an illusion.
[16] Theodore W. Schultz, "Reflections on Investment in Man," *Journal of Political Economy* (Supplement, October 1962), pp. 2–3.
[17] The following discussion draws heavily upon the article by B. F. Kiker, "The Historical Roots of the Concept of Human Capital," *Journal of Political Economy* (October, 1966), pp. 481–499. See also, Richard Blandy, "Marshall on Human Capital," *Journal of Political Economy* (December 1967), pp. 874–875, and Selma Mushkin, *op. cit.*, pp. 149–157.
[18] Marshall recognized that the different degrees of willingness of a family to expend resources on the development of a child constituted an imperfection in the capital market. The property rights to education accrue to the student and not to the parents.

nation was directly influenced by the stock of human skill in a country, and that an increase in the supply of trained abilities also would increase the national dividend (income).[19]

Two methods of estimating the stock of human capital have typically been used. One estimates the cost of producing—or what is put into—a human being (development cost) and the other computes the present value of future earnings. The two methods have also been combined. The cost-of-production method involves an estimate of the costs—medical, nursery layette, etc.—incurred up to birth together with the sum of annual costs on maintenance and education. If r is the annual rate of increase in costs from C_0 (the cost to birth), then C_n (the cost to age n) is, using compound interest, the following:

$$C_n = \sum_{j=0}^{n} C_0(1 + r)^j \tag{6.3}$$

This method, but in different form, was used by Ernest Engel in 1883 to measure the cost of producing a lower, middle, and upper class German male up to the age of 26.

The other method of capitalizing future earnings was used by Sir William Petty in his *Political Arithmetic*, as early as 1691, although Petty ignored maintenance cost as a deduction from gross earnings and did not correct for the finiteness of human life. However, his estimate was based upon the earnings of the total population, which can properly be treated as infinite in life, although net earnings of reproduction (subsistence) cost would have been more appropriate. Subsequent writers have not only allowed for maintenance costs, but have included probability estimates of an individual living to enter the labor force and/or continuing therein for n number of years.[20] A simplified formula for determining the capital value C_x of an individual is given as follows:[21]

$$C_x = \sum_{j=n}^{x} \frac{p \cdot V}{(1 + i)^j} - a \cdot R_x \tag{6.4}$$

[19] J. S. Nicholson in 1891 estimated the amount of "living capital" to be five times the amount of material capital. S. S. Huebner in 1914 estimated a similar ratio for the United States to be six or eight to one.

[20] Such as William Farr (1853) in an article in the *Journal of the Statistical Society*, and L. I. Dublin and A. J. Lotka, *The Money Value of a Man* (1930).

[21] V = value of future annual output; N = age of entering labor force; X = age at death (assuming no retirement); p = probability estimate weighted for life expectancy and employability; i = market rate of interest; a = annual maintenance (consumption) expenditure; R_x = value of \$1 annuity purchased at birth maturing at

$$n \text{ years} = \sum_{j=0}^{x} (1 + i)^j.$$

This equation merely states that the capital value is the *expected* present value of future earnings minus maintenance costs.

These measures of human capital were used for purposes other than those of estimating national wealth. Although Gary Becker, Theodore Schultz, and Jacob Mincer have recently completed significant research on the importance of education as a measure of human capital, J. R. Walsh in 1935 preceded them in an attempt to measure the capitalized value of the stock of education. Irving Fisher reported in 1909 on the billions of dollars which could be saved if diseases were prevented, and he showed how these savings could be treated as capital gains.[22]

Depending upon whether people are moving into or out of a country, that country will be gaining or losing human capital. Sir William Petty, Friedrich Kapp, and Charles Brace all made estimates of the gains and losses from migration. Ludwig Von Thunen and Thomas Farr both were aware that inequities occurred as a result of tax policies which treated expenditures for training and education as consumption rather than as investment outlays. Social justice, the implication ran, would be enhanced if policy were revised accordingly. Sir William Petty, and later John M. Clark in his *Social Control of Business*, attempted to measure the economic loss incurred by a nation from premature deaths attributable to war. All these studies emphasize one thing in common—society incurs an opportunity cost of the nature of a negative capital gain if it permits its human resources to go undeveloped by virtue of underinvestment in education or through an unwise tax policy, or to waste away because of migration, war, or preventable diseases and accidents.

Others have measured the asset value of human life to determine how much insurance an income recipient should carry.[23] Just as a firm insures its capital stock against unexpected, but predictable, loss, so might an individual. Others have used estimates of human value to determine compensation claims for premature deaths or for disability resulting in a reduction of earning power.[24] Industrial accident and personal injury claims are now with increasing frequency making use of such estimates.

[22] "Report on National Vitality: Its Wastes and Conservation," National Conservation Commission, *Bulletin of One Hundred on National Health*, No. 30 (Washington, 1909). Miles M. Dawson in 1904 showed how losses from preventable deaths could be estimated from actuarial tables.

[23] For example, S. S. Heubner (1914) and later E. A. Woods and C. B. Metzger made calculations comparing the asset value of human capital with the value of current life insurance: *America's Human Wealth: The Money Value of Human Life* (New York, 1927).

[24] Theodore Wittstein in 1867 developed a method of calculation combining the present value of future earnings with maintenance cost as a guide for estimating the size of compensation claims for industrial injuries and death. The work of Dublin and Lotka has been similarly used.

Implicit in the use of measures of human value is the idea that some people, because of their inherent or acquired abilities or because of their role in society or their age, are more productive than others. A rational measure of their worth must consider the proxy measure of their productivity —i.e., their earning power. Failure to distinguish between the productivity of individuals is as illogical as treating as equal the productivity of all machines.

Discussion Questions

1. It has been found that malnutrition in early childhood retards mental development. Discuss the impact of widespread malnutrition on the human resource base from which entrepreneurs, scientists, technicians, teachers, and other professionals are drawn, and indicate what implications can be drawn, if any, with respect to the country's rate of economic growth.
2. Suppose a country were to adopt a welfare policy whereby high-protein food would be distributed to the population.

    (a) What allocation decisions must be undertaken for optimal benefit from the food program?
    (b) Can such a program have an economic rationale? Explain.

3. Suppose a simple, inexpensive vaccine for cancer were developed. What would the human capital consequences be for such a discovery?
4. Compare the human capital implications of a population control program in a sparsely populated country such as Australia with that of a heavily populated country such as India.
5. How can the origin of the term "government consumption expenditures" be explained? Is it of the same nature as the term "capital consumption expenditures"?
6. In many states, the widow in a wrongful-death suit can collect remedial damages for the lost income of her deceased husband. Yet, it is more difficult for a surviving husband to collect remedial damages against the lost income of a deceased wife under similar causes of death. How can this apparent inconsistency be explained by human capital analysis?

7

The Acquisition of Human Capital

The Theory of Training

Human skills can be acquired through formal education and/or on-the-job training, and the allocation of resources to the acquisition of skill is, as we have seen from the discussion in Chapter 6, analogous to the investment process.[1] Under competition in the capital market, an investment is carried to the point where the present value of the yields is equal to the value of the current expenditures, i.e., discounted future returns equal current costs. The yields under consideration here refer to the value of the marginal product which is enhanced when a worker receives additional training or education. The costs involved are the cost of training, including the direct outlay on resources used in the training program and the indirect—or opportunity—cost of accepting a lower wage during the training program than would have been received if alternative employment had been chosen in which present wages are greater (but no greater in the future). This opportunity cost can also be expressed as the difference between the value productivity of the worker not receiving on-the-job training and that which he generates when receiving such training. (Presumably the former is greater, because the worker's time and energy are devoted primarily to current production.) Total output may be greater, also, because the time and energy of other workers need not be diverted to assist the one receiving the training. In the case of full-time, formal schooling, the value of the person's product is near zero, for no marketable work is ordinarily performed.

Training received by workers can be either general or specialized. General training imparts skills which can be used widely in the labor

[1] The basic theory has been developed by Gary Becker. See his *Human Capital*, (New York: Columbia University Press, 1964), Chapters II, III, for a more comprehensive discussion.

market; specialized training develops skills limited to one occupation, and in the extreme case, to one employer. Normally, skills acquired through formal education are general in nature, for they can be marketed to a wide variety of employers. On-the-job training may be either general or specific, and usually is both. For example, a clerk in a retail store must learn the type, location, and price of the merchandise dispensed by the store. Knowledge of the type of merchandise is a skill which can be marketed to retail shops of similar types, since presumably an employer prefers a worker with experience in the line to one with no experience. Knowledge of the location of the merchandise on the display shelves of the shop is completely specific. Similarly, secretarial skills are partly specific to a firm and partly general. Interestingly, Jacob Mincer has found that there has consistently been a strong positive relationship between the amount of formal education and the amount of on-the-job training that is devoted to an employee, as Table 7.1 indicates. This suggests that the more extensive is generalized formal training, the more extensive is the specialized on-the-job training that follows it. The ratio of on-the-job training to schooling is larger the higher the level of schooling for the years 1939, 1949, 1958.

TABLE 7.1
AGGREGATE ANNUAL INVESTMENT IN TRAINING AT SCHOOL AND ON THE JOB, UNITED STATES MALES, 1939, 1949, 1958, BY LEVEL OF SCHOOL[a]
(Current $ in billions)

Type of Training	1939			1949			1958		
	I	II	III	I	II	III	I	II	III
(A) School	1.1	1.8	0.9	3.8	3.4	2.1	8.7	8.4	4.5
(B) On-the-Job	1.0	1.4	0.6	4.3	3.8	0.9	8.7	3.8	1.0
Ratio B/A	0.91	0.78	0.67	1.13	1.12	0.43	1.0	0.45	0.22

[a] I = college, II = high school, III = elementary.
Source: Jacob Mincer: "On-the-Job Training: Costs, Returns, and Some Implications," *Journal of Political Economy*, (Supplement, October, 1962), p. 57.

The general procedure in acquiring skills is for the worker first to attend school in order to obtain a basic education for an occupation. This education can be extensive or rudimentary. The worker then acquires a job at which he receives additional training. The worker may or may not work while in school. Where compulsory school attendance laws are in effect, normally he will not work before a minimum age. If he attends school full-time after this minimum age, he forgoes income from work. During the training period, if he accepts a wage lower than that which he otherwise could have received, he incurs an opportunity cost in forgone wages. The total cost to the worker is his outlay on his education and the opportunity costs from wages forgone as a result of further education and/or training. These represent the capital investment in himself. Differential inherent ability may be evaluated in order to arrive at a total human capital stock of a worker. However, if abilities are distributed normally, superior ability in the aggregate may be negated by inferior ability.

The employer also experiences costs. Direct outlays are made on the training process in terms of instruction, materials, special equipment, and supervision. Indirect costs are incurred in wastage, spoilage, and under-utilization of equipment. Wages during the training period may exceed productivity. The employer plans to recapture these advances from enhanced future productivity of the worker, in which case, until costs are at least recovered, the worker will subsequently earn less than his marginal product. If the worker, on the other hand, bears the training costs, his wages during the training period will be less than the marginal product. In either event, ultimately the worker bears the cost of the training in the sense that these costs are recouped from his future productivity.

The general formula which depicts the relationships among productivity, wages, and costs to the employer of the worker with X work life is

$$M_P + M_T = W_P + W_T + T \tag{7.1}$$

where $\quad M_P = \displaystyle\sum_{m=1}^{X-J} \frac{M_m}{(1+i)^{J+m}} = \quad$ present value of marginal productivity in the posttraining period.

$\quad M_T = \displaystyle\sum_{n=1}^{J} \frac{M_n}{(1+i)^n} \quad = \quad$ present value of marginal productivity during the training period of J duration.

$\quad W_P = \displaystyle\sum_{m=1}^{X-J} \frac{W_m}{(1+i)^{J+m}} = \quad$ present value of actual wages in the posttraining period.

$\quad W_T = \displaystyle\sum_{n=1}^{J} \frac{W_n}{(1+i)^n} \quad = \quad$ present value of actual wages paid in the training period.

$\quad T = \displaystyle\sum_{n=1}^{J} \frac{T_n}{(1+i)^n} \quad = \quad$ present value of training costs during training period of J duration.

The interest rate is symbolized by i, and $n + m = X$, the work life. Thus, the sum of the present value of marginal product equals the sum of wages plus training costs. If the training period J is zero, T will be zero, and marginal productivity under competition will always equal the wage. If T is greater than zero, but wages equal marginal product in the training period, M_P will exceed W_P by T. If wages are less than marginal product in the training period by T, then M_P will equal W_P. Whatever the case, $M_P + M_T$ will exceed $W_P + W_T$ by T. In this sense, training costs are always ultimately assumed by the worker.

The preceding paragraph measures T, the investment of the employer in training, but it does not accurately measure the investment of the worker in his education and/or training. It is the latter which is most important from the social point of view, for it is the increment in his education and training which increases his productivity. The cost to him involves not only the direct (either present or future) cost of his education or training, but also the indirect costs of forgone earnings during the period of training. Forgone earnings are the difference in the wage he receives W and that which he could have received W' during the earning period.

$$\sum_{n=1}^{J} \frac{(W_n' - W_n)}{(1 + i)^n} = A \tag{7.2}$$

If while in school he receives no wages, the alternative cost is, in each period, the wage forgone $(A_n = W_n')$. Therefore, the total investment of the worker in his training is

$$A + T = K \tag{7.3}$$

In terms of total marginal product and total costs, the following relationship exists.

$$M_P + M_T = K + W_P \tag{7.4}$$

The present value of wages in the posttraining period will be less than the present value of marginal product by the amount of the present value of investment in training,[2] i.e., human capital. Marginal product must rise sufficiently to provide a return to the worker for his investment over and above the posttraining wage. This return may be in the form of wage differentials (supplements) if the worker bears fully the training and opportunity costs. The employer may receive all or part of K, depending upon the degree to which the employer underwrites the costs. Ordinarily, A will be in the form of a wage supplement unless the employer has borne

---

[2] If formal, full-time education is included in the training period, M_T is zero and A is W'. Posttraining marginal product must therefore cover A, T, and W_P. If the worker underwrites his own on-the-job training or has none, such as a beginning attorney, then $M_P = W_P$. The relationships in Equation (7.4) can be varied to cover numerous situations.

the opportunity cost by paying the worker the alternative wage. If the worker receives A, it is to the employer a part of his wage bill, but to the worker, it is differential income necessary to reward him for his human investment.

As Becker has noted, investment in human capital can explain the positive slope of the age–earning cross-sectional curve.[3] At young ages, investment in human capital is less and wages and wage supplements are less. Also, to the extent that workers bear the training costs, wages will be lower at younger ages when training normally is most frequent. However, at later ages these workers recapture more of their enhanced productivity in greater wage payments. The steepness of the earning curve therefore depends upon the degree of training costs underwritten by a worker. It is also influenced by the length of the training period. Training tends to be concentrated among the younger because the present value of net productivity $(M_P + M_T - T)$ is greater, since the enhanced productivity extends over a longer work life than it would if older workers received the training. Another important variable appears to be the ability of the person to learn. Among low-achievers, as indicated by their score on the Armed Forces Qualification Test, Hansen and others have found that it is what one learns in school, not length of schooling, that most influences earnings.[4]

The extent to which a worker assumes his training costs depends upon whether his training is general or specific. If his training is general and the employer underwrites the training, the employer may not be able to recoup these costs. When trained, the worker's marginal productivity will be greater also in other firms and other employers will bid for these services until the offered wage equals the larger productivity. Under competition, therefore, general training will be offered only if the worker assumes the training costs. However, if the enhanced skills are applicable only in the firm providing the training, the "finished" worker cannot demand higher wages from other employers than he could receive in the absence of the training. In such a situation, the employer may underwrite the training cost, pay the worker his opportunity costs, and collect his advance from the fruits of the augmented productivity. However, if the worker leaves before

---

[3] Becker, *op. cit.*, pp. 15–16. Kenneth J. Arrow argues that earnings increase for the most part with age because workers gain experience on the job. He argues that this learning does not involve an opportunity cost and is more or less automatic. See his "The Economic Implications of Learning by Doing," *Review of Economic Studies*, June 1962. Mary Jean Bowman, however, favors Becker's position. See her "Costing of Human Resource Development" in *The Economics of Education*, E. A. G. Robinson and J. E. Vaizey, eds. (New York: St. Martin's Press, 1966), pp. 421–450.

[4] W. H. Hansen, B. A. Weisbrod and W. J. Scanlon, "Schooling and Earnings of Low-Achievers," *American Economic Review*, Vol. 60, No. 3 (June 1970), pp. 409–418.

these costs are recovered, the employer loses at least part of his investment. It is, therefore, to the employer's benefit to share the returns from the augmented production with the worker in the form of wages higher than are paid in occupations using the nonspecific skills of the worker. This would make the training firm's position more remunerative than those of other firms and thereby reduce turnover in the former. In terms of Equation (7.4) if b is the share of human investment costs incurred by the employer, then $1 - b$ is the share borne by the worker. Net investment costs to the employer K_N are given by $(K - M_T)$, and therefore

$$M_P - bK_N = (1 - b)K_N + W_P \tag{7.5}$$

The right-hand term of (7.5) is the amount paid to the worker, and bK_N is the deduction from marginal product necessary to reimburse the employer for his advances.

Walter Y. Oi has argued that specific training converts labor into a quasi-fixed factor of production, and that this conversion contradicts the traditional treatment of labor as a variable factor.[5] Using his notation,

$$M^* + \Delta M^* = W^* + R \tag{7.6}$$

The expected present value of marginal productivity of labor M^* plus its increment from training ΔM^* is equal to the expected present value of the wage rate W^* plus employment costs R, which include hiring and training costs. The degree of fixity is indicated by the ratio

$$R/(W^* + R) \tag{7.7}$$

which relates employment costs to total labor costs. Changes in the market demand under competition are reflected in changes in the value of the marginal product. Employment of the quasi-fixed factor will not increase or decrease as demand increases or decreases in the short run, however, unless the expected value of the marginal product rises or falls by more than R. Employment costs are sunk costs, so the firm will not lay off workers even though their marginal value product falls to W (instead of remaining equal to $W + R$), and the firm will not add workers unless the expected marginal value product rises by more than R.

Empirically, Oi argues, this tendency to stabilize employment of quasi-fixed labor should be reflected in cyclical wage rates which fluctuate less as the degree of fixity of the factor rises, since fixed labor inputs tend to be complementary with capital goods and thus enjoy low demand elasticity. Relatively *larger* changes in wages are necessary to produce large

[5] "Labor as a Quasi-Fixed Factor," *Journal of Political Economy*, (December 1962), pp. 538–555.

changes in employment, but since fixity reduces employment changes, wage rates cannot fluctuate widely. Thus, the higher the wage the less the employment variability. To minimize employment costs, rational firms should take measures to reduce employment turnover through pension plans, bonuses, periodic cumulative premiums, etc. Thus, reduced turnover is also implied by quasi-fixed factors. Oi uses the wage rate as an index to the degree of fixity, based upon data obtained from the International Harvester Company. By observing patterns of wage and employment changes in selected high, middle, and low wage industries during the period 1928–1931, he concludes that this data supports the implications of his argument. He also cites unemployment data by age, sex, and color to show that unemployment rates are higher with groups who have less specific training—i.e., for the young and for non-Whites.

Jacob Mincer has criticized Oi's assumptions and methodology.[6] Mincer has found that wage rates correspond to total training; schooling (general) and on-the-job (part general and part specific); that on-the-job training varies with length of schooling, and that specific training is the smaller part of on-the-job training. Thus, the wage rate is not necessarily a good index of specific training. Methodologically, Mincer pointed out that Oi made no correction for the age factor in his analysis and that "larger proportions of younger people in an industry, or occupation, mean both more turnover and lower wages," which could bias the correlation results. Thus, a negative correlation between wages and turnover may be owing to cross-sectional age differences, rather than to degrees of specific training. Within each age group, however, a negative wage–turnover relation correlation coefficient might support Oi's hypothesis, but Oi did not analyze his data by this method.

Investment Theory and Human Capital[7]

The present value of the yield of an asset is given by

$$V = \sum_{t=1}^{n} \frac{R_t}{(1 + i)^t} \tag{7.8}$$

This equation states that the total present value V is equal to the yield in

---

[6] Jacob Mincer, "On-the-Job Training: Costs, Returns, and Some Implications," *Journal of Political Economy* (Supplement, October 1962), pp. 67–70. Mincer's criticism was directed to Oi's dissertation on which his later article was based.

[7] For a more comprehensive analysis, see Gary Becker, *Human Capital, op. cit.*, Chapter III, pp. 37–66. This section is based on Becker's analysis.

each period t discounted over n periods by the market rate of interest i to the present. To acquire the income-yielding asset, the owner incurs a cost. The rate of return which equates the cost of the capital good with the present value of its net yield is given by r. If the life of the capital was only one period, then $r = (R - C)/C$. Where the life of the capital good extends over a longer period, r can be found from the formula

$$C = \sum_{j=1}^{n} \frac{R_j}{(1 + r)^j} \tag{7.9}$$

It can be seen that the present value of future returns will exceed the cost of capital (i.e., $V > C$) if the return to capital is greater than the market rate of interest. Thus, if $r > i$, it is reasonable to acquire the asset, for no greater opportunity to earn a higher return exists, since the market rate of interest reflects *normal* returns under competition. Presumably, a rational person would make a similar evaluation concerning an investment to be made in human capital. He would compare the return to investment in human capital with that in the market, and invest in education and/or training if that return is higher.

If training occurs in one period—this is a reasonable assumption, for we can make a period as long or as short as we like—then if we subtract training costs from the first period earnings in that activity Y, net earnings in period 1 is given by Y. The opportunity cost of choosing occupation Y instead of occupation X is the forgone earnings in the initial period, or $X_1 - Y_1 = C$. However, the increased productivity from training raises the future earnings in occupation Y and produces a differential income supplement to Y. The present value of this supplement v is

$$v = \sum_{n=2}^{t} \frac{(Y_n - X_n)}{(1 + i)^n} \tag{7.10}$$

If we select a rate of return r on the total costs of training such that the present value of this differential return just equals the cost, we have the following relation

$$v = \sum_{n=2}^{t} \frac{(Y_n - X_n)}{(1 + r)^n} = C \tag{7.10a}$$

If the income stream were permanent and if the differential between the two occupations were a constant B, then $C = B/r$.

From Figure 7.1 we can see that v approaches C as n goes to infinity $(n \rightarrow \infty)$. However, since n is finite (work life is limited) an addition must

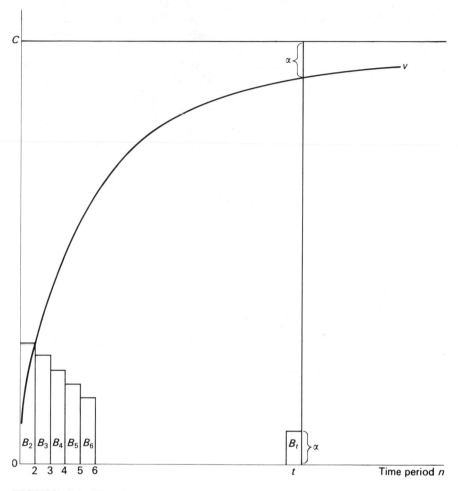

FIGURE 7.1. The time path of v. $C \equiv$ opportunity cost of occupation Y; $v = \sum_{n=2}^{t} B_n$; $B_n = (y_n - x_n)/(1 + i)^n$; $\alpha = B_t$.

be made to v to bring it to equality with C. This addition is the discounted value of B at the last work period t of the investor in human capital.

$$v + \frac{B}{(1 + r)^t} = C \qquad (7.11)$$

where $B/(1 + r)^t = \alpha$ in the figure. Therefore,

$$R = C = \frac{B}{r} - \frac{B}{(1 + r)^t} = \frac{B}{r}\left[1 - \frac{r}{(1 + r)^t}\right] \qquad (7.12)$$

Of course if the actual or expected rate of return r^* is greater than r, where $r = i$, then the investment in human capital is clearly preferable. If $r^* < i$, then the individual should choose an occupation in which no incremental training (schooling or on-the-job) is required.

We may look upon the earnings in X or Y as those earnings which are received by a worker of average ability, who can acquire the necessary training for Y occupation in the standard training period. If the individual possesses superior ability, the necessary period of training may be less than the standard, or vice versa. For example, college students of superior ability have been known to complete a baccalaureate program in less than four years, whereas students of inferior ability may take considerably longer. Consequently, costs of training may be correspondingly reduced or increased, and net earnings increased or reduced, as the case may be. The variation in net earnings can alter the differential in the present period C and in later periods B, and therefore, the rate of return to investment, r. This means that the rate of return to an investment in human capital of an individual in part depends upon that individual's inherent ability to acquire training.[8]

It is obvious that the above analysis is overly simplified. The differential earnings per period, for example, are not usually constant. Modifications in parameters are necessary to allow for risks, lack of knowledge, and even the probability of unemployment. Nevertheless, the essential relations have been developed, in this brief explanation, of the decision-making process for investment in human capital.

Empirical Studies on Human Capital

A substantial literature is developing which reports on studies made on matters relating to human capital.[9] We have earlier cited the studies of Jacob Mincer and Selma Mushkin. Theodore Schultz has estimated the stock of human capital in the United States and its annual rate of increase. These estimates are reproduced in Table 7.2 and the data for 1957 should be compared with the estimates of Jacob Mincer cited in Table 7.1. In Table 7.2, line 2 differs from line 3 primarily because of the exclusion of educated women who have elected not to participate in the labor force. Nevertheless, they represent a reservoir of human capital and, of course,

---

[8] However, B. A. Weisbrod and P. Karpoff have found that three-fourths of the differential in earnings between college and high school graduates was owing to the difference in educational attainment, and only one-fourth was owing to nonschooling variables, including ability. "Monetary Returns to College Education, Student Ability and College Quality," *Review of Economics and Statistics*, Vol. 50, No. 4, (November 1968), pp. 491–510.

[9] For a survey article on the literature, see Jacob Mincer, "The Distribution of Labor Incomes: A Survey with Special Reference to the Human Capital Approach," *Journal of Economic Literature*, Vol. 8, No. 1 (March 1970), pp. 1–26.

TABLE 7.2
STOCKS OF CAPITAL AND ANNUAL RATES OF INCREASE
BETWEEN 1929 AND 1957 IN THE UNITED STATES
IN 1956 DOLLARS

Human Capital	Billions of Dollars		Annual Rate of Growth (3)	% Rate Applied to 1957 (2) × (3) ($ billion)
	1929 (1)	1957 (2)		
1. Reproducible tangible wealth	727	1,270	2.01	25.5
2. Educational capital in population	317	848	3.57	30.3
3. Educational capital in labor force	173	535	4.09	21.9
4. On-the-job training of males in labor force	136 (For 1939)	347	5.36	18.6
5. Total of lines 3 and 4	309	882	—	40.5
6. Percent of lines (2 + 4) of 1.	62	94	—	—

Source: Theodore W. Schultz, "Reflections on Investment in Man,"
Journal of Political Economy, Vol. LXX, No. 5, Pt. 2 (Supplement, October 1962), p. 6.

provide nonpaid, nonschool educational services to their children. On-the-job training for males together with the educational stock of capital for the population, as a percent of reproducible tangible wealth, were 62% in 1929 and 94% in 1957. Human capital is becoming a relatively more important part of the nation's total capital stock.

A number of estimates have been made on rates of return from further education or training. Mincer has estimated from the annual income of medical specialists, residents, and general practitioners that the rate of return of specialized medical training beyond that of a general practitioner is 12.7% before taxes and 11.3% after taxes.[10] He has found that rates of return from apprenticeship training in the metal, printing, and building trades are, for operatives in the same industry, respectively in percentages, 16.4, 16.0, and 18.3. However, the operatives had different amounts of schooling and apprenticeship training. Since, during the period of training, investment in schooling or training is cumulative, and so correspondingly must enhance productivity—that is, an apprentice after 3 years of training has more investment than he had after 2 or 1 years of training and is correspondingly more productive—adjustments must be made in these rates of return to allow for this accumulated investment and for differential

[10] Jacob Mincer, "On-the-Job Training," *op. cit.*, p. 65.

apprenticeship of schooling periods. Assuming a 10% return on additional schooling or training, the above figures are adjusted to 9.5, 8.0, and 9.7%, respectively.[11] For schooling, Gary Becker has made estimates of the rates of return, unadjusted for ability, to college and high school education. These are given in Table 7.3. Ashenfelter and Mooney have found that rates of

TABLE 7.3
PRIVATE RATES OF RETURN TO COLLEGE AND HIGH SCHOOL EDUCATION FOR SELECTED YEARS SINCE 1939
(Percent)

Year	College Graduates	High School Graduates
1939	14.5	16
1949	13[+]	20
1956	12.4	25
1958	14.8	28
1961	Slightly higher than in 1958	

Source: Gary Becker, *Human Capital*, National Bureau of Economic Research (New York: Columbia University Press, 1964), p. 128.

return to graduate education in the United States range from 5 to 10%.[12] For 1950, Becker found that the rate of return to college education was 10% of private costs after taxes, but only 9% of total cost. The latter cost figure included estimates of opportunity costs (forgone wages).[13] The corresponding return for on-the-job training varied from 9 –12.7% for total costs and from 8.5–11.3% for private costs after taxes (see also Chart 7.1).

The author has computed rates of return to education in Thailand. Wages and educational data by occupational placement are collected by the Employment Exchange Bureau of the Department of Labour. Costs of education were estimated in two parts: (1) subsistence and schooling costs, and (2) forgone earnings. Following the procedure used by Harberger in India, component (1) was estimated to be equal to the average monthly wage of occupations having the minimum amount of education, up to four years.[14] This wage was multiplied by nine months, which is the length of

[11] *Ibid.*, p. 64.

[12] O. Ashenfelter and J. D. Mooney, "Some Evidence on Private Returns to Graduate Education," *Southern Economic Journal*, Vol. 35, No. 3 (January 1969).

[13] "Underinvestment in College Education?" *American Economic Review*, Vol. 48, No. 2 (May 1960), p. 347.

[14] A. C. Harberger, "Investment in Men vs. Investment in Machines: The Case of India," in *Education and Economic Development*, C. A. Anderson and M. J. Bowman, editors (Chicago: Aldine Publishing Co., 1965).

TABLE 7.4
EARNINGS AND WORK-LIFE EXPECTANCY, BY
EDUCATIONAL LEVEL, IN THAILAND

Mean Educational Level (Years)	Monthly Wage (Baht)	Annual Earnings (Baht)	Expected Age of Entry into Labor Force	Work-life Expectancy (Years)
18	2364	28,368	25	40
15	1545	18,540	22	43
12	922	11,064	19	46
9	604	7,248	16	49
6	403	4,836	15	50

the school year. The second type of costs consisted of forgone earnings in occupations requiring differential educational levels in three-year intervals from six years of schooling to 18 years. Pertinent information by level of education is summarized in Table 7.4.

Work-life expectancy to age 65 is based upon a life expectancy which extends beyond age 65. Annual earnings are computed by multiplying average monthly wages by twelve. To the extent that the degree of employment regularity varies directly with the level of education, rates of return

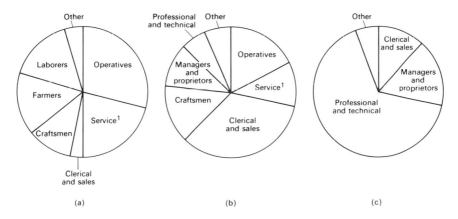

CHART 7.1. Occupational distribution of employed workers 18 years old and over with selected amounts of formal education, March 1970. (a) Less than 5 years of schooling. (b) High school graduates. (c) College graduates.

[1] Includes private household workers.

Source: William Deutermann, "Educational Attainment of Workers, March 1969 and 1970," *Monthly Labor Review*, Vol. 93, No. 10 (October 1970), p. 15.

are likely to be understated the higher the educational level. The rate of return r was estimated from the following formula:

$$(A + F)e^{sr} = C + \sum_{t=0}^{n} De^{-rt}$$

where A = type (1) component costs; F = type (2) component costs; s = incremental years of schooling beyond age 15; C = total compounded costs to age of entry into labor force; D = differential annual earnings by level of education; n = work-life expectancy. The rates of return to incremental levels of education in Thailand are presented in Table 7.5. Education yields greater returns in Thailand than in the United States, and it generally yields greater returns than Harberger found for India. Blaug has reported that in England three years of secondary education beyond the school-leaving age of fifteen yield private rates of return of 13% and six years of education beyond age fifteen, including the university, yield a private rate of return of 14%.[15]

The Value of Job Information

To the extent that information about available employment opportunities permits a worker to obtain a higher paying job, the acquisition of that information permits him to earn a differential return. Thus, labor market information and the discovery of the processes by which it can be

TABLE 7.5
RATES OF RETURN TO INCREMENTAL LEVELS OF EDUCATION

Educational Level Comparisons	Rates of Return r (%)
18 over 15	22.3
18 over 12	25.5
18 over 9	23.5
18 over 6	21.3
15 over 12	24.3
15 over 9	24.5
15 over 6	22.1
12 over 9	19.5
12 over 6	21.0
9 over 6	19.5

[15] Mark Blaug, "The Rate of Return on Investment in Education in Great Britain," *The Manchester School* (September 1965), pp. 205–261. Social rates of return are, respectively, 12.5 and 8%.

obtained constitutes a type of investment in knowledge, and since the knowledge is possessed by a human agent, this is a form of human capital. For example, it has been found that Blacks have a poorer source of job information than Whites both in terms of institutional contacts and informed contacts among friends, and this results in a poorer employment record and lower wages for them.[16] Studies in the economics of information have been made by George J. Stigler,[17] in which he estimates the gains and costs of additional search for job offers. He assumes that wage offers are normally distributed and that the standard deviation of wage offers σ_w is $\overline{W}/10$, where $\overline{W}$ is the average wage. The expected maximum value of a wage offer, W_N, of a worker in n searches is, therefore,

$$W_N = 0.65n^{0.37} \cdot \sigma_w + \overline{W} = (0.065n^{0.37} + 1)\overline{W}$$

By differentiating partially W_N with respect to n, and then fixing W, the formula for the marginal wage rate gain W_m can be derived from which this gain can be computed for different values of n.[18]

For an average annual salary (wage) of $10,000, W_m varies from about $100 for four searches to about $340 for 20 searches. The value of W_m is greater the larger is $\overline{W}$, and the present value of W_m is greater the longer the period of employment. One would, therefore, expect the dispersion of wages to be greater at lower wages and for shorter terms of employment. This would tend to be true since search for jobs offering higher income and/or longer employment is encouraged by the larger capitalized value of W_m. The greater is the amount of search for a particular job (and, therefore, the more perfect the labor market information for that job), the less likely is an applicant to accept wages below the average. McCall has described the process of search as one involving the application of shopping rules to employment seeking. Searchers are assumed to know the distribution of wages for their particular levels of skill and as job offers are made, the searcher accepts or rejects them on the basis of some critical reservation wage which he has adopted as a goal. Dropouts from the labor force are those who become discouraged by not receiving a job offer equal to or

---

[16] M. Lurie and E. Rayack, "Racial Differences in Migration and Job Search: A Case Study," *Southern Economic Journal*, Vol. 33, No. 1 (July 1966).

[17] In his "Economics of Information," *Journal of Political Economy*, Vol. 69 (June 1961), pp. 213–225, he shows that investment in information at the margin is limited by the costs of obtaining incremental information. As a result, he concludes that complete job information is never possessed by an applicant. Additional empirical results are reported in "Information in the Labor Market," *Journal of Political Economy* (Supplement, October 1962), pp. 94–105. A more recent analysis of search is given by Reuben Pronau, "Information and Frictional Unemployment," *American Economic Review*, Vol. LXI, No. 3 (June 1971), pp. 290–301.

[18] The formula for the marginal wage gain W_m is approximately

$$\frac{\partial W_N}{\partial n} = \overline{W}_m = \frac{0.025\overline{W}}{n^{0.67}}$$

above the critical wage.[19] Kasper has found that the asking wage is lowered as unemployment lengthens and, in fact, workers who successfully obtained reemployment had an average wage concession rate twice that of those still unemployed.[20] Age and sex affect prospective lengths of employment, and data in selected occupations are quoted by Stigler to show that wage dispersion increases with age (shorter employment life), and is greater for women than for men.

Stigler shows that information provides capital value for both workers and employer; for workers the capitalized differential earnings from higher wages constitutes this value, and might be as much as $100 billion for the entire labor force; for employers the capital value of information is determined by the savings realized from paying lower wages. (In effect, a more perfect labor market conceivably could increase the supply of labor to a high-wage-paying employer.) For example, because migration of workers varies positively with earning levels, but negatively with distance, Galloway has speculated that distance acts as a barrier, and as a source of imperfection, in the dissemination of job information.[21] Fabricant has found, however, that insofar as long-distance migrations are involved, social and informational cost are not related to physical distance.[22] However, it is difficult to see how, in the aggregate, some of the capitalized values can avoid offsetting one another. Some employers, presumably low-paying ones, benefit from an imperfect labor market; others from a more perfect labor market. The same is true for workers. One of the by-products of education is, of course, an increase in the skill of acquiring information. It is just possible that capitalizing the incremental earnings from incremental education and from incremental searches may involve double counting. Thus, an attitude of caution is perhaps advisable in capitalizing independently each source of differential earnings, because these sources may not be independent of one another.

Human Capital Formation as a Source of Growth

To the extent that national output is increased from a more efficient allocation of labor, social capital can be enhanced by a more perfect market in job knowledge, particularly if there are increasing returns to scale in producing this knowledge. Theodore Schultz, as noted earlier in this chapter, is one of the strongest advocates of the position that it is the growth in

[19] J. J. McCall, "Economics of Information and Job Search," *Quarterly Journal of Economics*, Vol. 84, No. 1 (February 1970).
[20] Herschel Kasper, "The Asking Price of Labor and the Duration of Unemployment," *Review of Economics and Statistics*, Vol. 49, No. 2 (May 1970).
[21] L. E. Galloway, "Industry Variations in Geographic Labor Mobility Patterns," *Journal of Human Resources*, Vol. 2, No. 4 (Fall 1967).
[22] R. A. Fabricant, "An Expectational Model of Migration," *Journal of Regional Science*, Vol. 10, No. 1 (April 1970), pp. 13–24.

human capital which explains the discrepancy in the United States growth rates between national outputs and tangible capital. The rates between 1919 and 1957 were, respectively, 3.1 and 1.8%.[23] Also, the discrepancy between output and tangible capital input growth rates appears to be widening, and this widening is not owing to an increasing growth rate of other physical inputs. Rather, the latter growth rates in weighted man-hours in the above period declined from 2.2 to 0.8% and changes in land growth rates, themselves already close to zero, were negligible. This discrepancy would suggest some mystical force at work. A substantial part of this discrepancy can be explained by the growth in the stock of nontangible, human capital. Annual investment in education at cost amounted to $180 billion in 1930 and to $535 billion in 1957, measured in 1956 dollars. The estimated return on this stock accounted for, perhaps, one-fifth of the growth in income in that period.[24]

Edward Denison has explored in depth the sources of growth in the United States in the past and the probable sources in the future.[25] He argues that an increase in the quality of the labor force through more education has tended to increase the growth rate of national output because (1) the labor force is such a large percentage of all factors of production (about 73%) and (2) the amount of the increase in education was very large (about 2% per year per worker). The effect of education on total national output and per employed worker output is summarized as follows.[26]

	Period		
Output and Education	*1909–1929*	*1929–1956*	*1960–1980*
I. National output			
A. Growth rate	2.82	2.93	3.33
B. Percent of growth rate owing			
to education	12	23	19
II. Output per employed worker			
A. Growth rate	1.22	1.60	1.62
B. Percent of growth rate owing			
to education	29	42	40

[23] Theodore W. Schultz: "Investment in Man: An Economist's View," in *Capital Accumulation and Economic Development*, Shanti S. Tangri and H. Peter Gray, editors (Boston: D. C. Heath & Co., 1967), p. 138.

[24] *Ibid.*

[25] *The Sources of Economic Growth in the United States and the Alternatives before Us*, Supplementary Paper No. 13, Committee for Economic Development, New York, January 1962. For a summary of this report and an extension to and comparison with selected other countries, see his "Measuring the Contribution of Education to Economic Growth" in *The Economics of Education*, E. A. G. Robinson and J. E. Vaizey, editors (New York: St. Martin's Press, 1966), pp. 202–260.

[26] *Ibid.*, p. 234.

The growth in education per employed worker was estimated to have increased national output much more than the increase in tangible capital per worker in the 1929–1957 period. The former accounted for an increase of 23% in the growth rate, whereas the latter accounted for only 5% of the growth rate.

With respect to the contribution of education to earnings, Denison compared the experience of England and Italy with that of the United States. He asked the following questions: "If, at every educational level, British (Italian) workers earned the same average income as American workers with the same amount of education, how much would average income differ because of the difference in the distributions by educational level?"[27] He found that earnings in 1957 in England would have been about 8% lower than in the United States, and in Italy about 44% lower.

Frederick Harbison addressed himself to a similar problem in measuring the influence of the development of human capital on economic growth.[28] Since the quality of the labor force appears to be a significant part of a country's resource endowment, a reasonable hypothesis is that economic development and the stock and growth of human capital go hand-in-hand. To demonstrate this relationship requires a measure of human resource development. Ideally, an index of human resource development would incorporate data on the following.

1. Number of teachers, engineers, scientists, physicians, and dentists per 10,000 population.
2. Pupil enrollment at (1) primary, (2) secondary, and (3) post-secondary levels as a percentage of the age groups 5–14, 15–19, and 20–24, respectively.

The index which he actually developed was a composite of only 2(2) and 2(3), however, with the latter weighted five times as much as the former in order to reflect the greater importance of higher education.[29] According to

---

[27] *Ibid.*, p. 247. For example, 47% of the labor force had the equivalent of a high school education in the United States; corresponding figures in England and Italy, respectively, were 7.3 and 5.7%. Corresponding percentages for completion of eight years of schooling are 83 (United States), 98 (England), 15 (Italy).

[28] "Quantitative Indicators of Human Resource Development," in *The Economics of Education*, Robinson and Vaizey, editors, *ibid.*, pp. 349–370. C. A. Myers was a collaborator of Harbison's in developing the index.

[29] *Ibid.*, pp. 353, 357, 358. Some economists would not agree with this degree of weighting. For example, Hla Myint points out the growing problem of graduate unemployment in Asian countries owing to the production of the wrong type of human capital. He also observed, "Certain changes which might widen the educational horizon of a people, and thus increase their longer-run productivity, might at the same time undermine the capacity of the social and institutional framework to mobilize resources," such as through the development of new consumer wants. "Investment in the Social Infrastructure," in *Capital Accumulation and Economic Development*, Tangri and Gray, editors, *op. cit.*, p. 132.

their index score, countries were classified into four stages of human resource development, and these stages of development for selected countries are presented in Table 7.6. Harbison found significant correlations between the index score and the per capita GNP, which he believes supports the reliability of the index. Because estimates of GNP are still quite crude in many under-developed countries, the index might well be a better indication of the level of economic and human resource development. My experience in Thailand suggests that the index is a better indication since the stated per capita income figure for that country significantly understates the relative well-being of the country. The same is also true for Japan.

Conclusion

Research into the causes and implications of human capital is still in the embryonic state. There is a fertile field for further investigations, however.

TABLE 7.6

LEVEL OF DEVELOPMENT, PER CAPITA GNP IN UNITED STATES DOLLARS, AND COMPOSITE INDEX OF SELECTED COUNTRIES (1958–1959)

Index	Country	GNP ($)	Index	Country	GNP ($)
Level I—Underdeveloped			Level III—Semiadvanced		
0.75	Ethiopia	55	33.0	Mexico	262
1.9	Afghanistan	50	35.1	Thailand	99
4.95	Nigeria	78	35.2	India	73
5.3	Haiti	105	40.0	South Africa	395
7.55	Sudan	60	47.7	Venezuela	648
			53.9	Hungary	490
Level II—Partially developed			56.8	Italy	516
10.7	Guatemala	189	66.5	Poland	475
19.5	China (mainland)	72	73.8	Norway	1130
20.9	Brazil	293			
23.65	Malaya	356	Level IV—Advanced		
25.2	Pakistan	70	79.2	Sweden	1380
27.2	Turkey	220	85.8	West Germany	927
30.2	Peru	179	92.9	U.S.S.R.	600
			101.6	Canada	1947
			111.4	Japan	306
			121.6	United Kingdom	1189
			137.7	Australia	1316
			261.3	United States	2577

Source: Frederick Harbison, "Quantitative Indicators of Human Resource Development," *The Economics of Education*, Editors, E. A. G. Robinson and J. E. Vaizey (New York: St. Martin's Press, 1966), pp. 359–369.

Becker has also suggested a number of important implications of the concept of human capital which, if true can explain a variety of phenomena which have long puzzled social scientists.[30] Problems requiring further study include the following:

1. Because marginal productivity is greater than the wage rate by the cost of training, changes in wage rates should result in less fluctuations in employment among specifically trained workers. Walter Oi, as we have noted, has studied this, but more work needs to be done.

2. Pension plans and long-term contracts may be more closely tied to specifically trained workers as an inducement to prevent turnover. In the past two decades, labor unions in the United States have increasingly been able to secure guaranteed annual wage contracts and pension plans for generally trained workers. This may be explained by the increased ability of a union to impose a fixed cost on employers through threats of work stoppages. This fixed cost may be analogous to the fixed cost incurred by a firm in offering specific training.

3. A discrepancy between a worker's marginal product and his wage has been treated in the literature of economics as exploitation, and suggests an imperfection in the buying side of the labor market. Becker argues that this is also normal in a competitive labor market where training costs are incurred by the competitive firm. However, to the extent that ease of entry or exit into an occupation is restricted by impediments to meeting training requirements, this by definition means that the market is imperfect. An imperfectly competitive market may be more normal than a competitive market.

4. Universities and businesses typically underwrite the cost of search for high-level personnel. Executives and university professors often have their moving expenses paid by their new employer when they change institutions. How prevalent is this practice? The theory of human capital would lead one to suspect that the employer's willingness to underwrite the cost of search and migration depends upon the length of the expected employment period of the worker. If these costs are substantial, fringe benefits and/or wages might be offered which would encourage the future immobility of the worker. Is this true?

5. The effect of market size on the incentive to invest in skills may be significant. Becker suggests that a larger market not only permits

[30] Gary Becker, "Investment in Human Capital: A Theoretical Analysis," *Journal of Political Economy*, Vol. 70, No. 5 (Supplement, October 1962), pp. 9–49.

greater specialization, but induces it because it extends the life of the specialty and thus increases its capital value. We need to know therefore the flow of causation and whether or not there is any correlation between the work life of an occupation and the size of the market.

6. Wage ratios, or relative wages, are more important for understanding the forces determining the demand for labor, because this ratio is equal to the ratio of marginal products at minimum cost output. Given the production function, output at minimum cost determines input use. However, absolute wage differences are more important for an understanding of labor supply, for the present value of a differential is the capital value of one skill compared to that of another. It is a difference in capital values which induces movement into and out of occupations.

   If the relative supply of higher skills has increased, as it has in the United States, wage ratios can be expected to narrow. This narrowing, Becker argues, has not been accompanied by a decline in the rate of return to skill, however. Technological progress has offset any such tendency for the rate of return to decline. Even though wage ratios may decline, wage differences need not do so. Thus, shifts in the supply of skill need not result in a lower rate of return to skill. Whether rates of return have or have not declined is, of course, an empirical question.

7. Capital market imperfections may affect investment in human capital differently than investments in tangible capital, since it is more costly to postpone the former than the latter. Costs of postponement are high at younger ages, because postponement shortens the pay-off period and raises the opportunity costs of forgone wages. For example, an investment in a professional education may be profitable at age 20, marginal at age 30, and unprofitable at age 40.

8. Economists have noted that high-wage countries tend to export relatively more labor-intensive commodities. This paradox can be explained if one recognizes that a labor force rich in human capital will have a comparative advantage in the production of labor-intensive goods where the necessary inputs of labor are of high quality.

9. Persons with greater ability would tend to invest more in themselves because the return would be greater. Earning differentials might therefore reflect not only differences in human investment but also differences in native ability. Even though inherent ability in a population may be normally distributed, the relatively greater

investment of super-able persons would tend to skew the income distribution to the right, so that persons with greater I.Q.'s would tend to earn proportionately more income.

Summary

Labor supply depends on quality and quantity. Past analysis of labor supply has focused on the quantity aspects. The quality of labor has been emphasized in these two chapters, and the quantity dimensions are considered in the next three chapters.

Labor quality is reflected in physical productivity.[31] Health and stamina determine the amount and kind of work that can be done. The degree of health and stamina is related to the extent of malnutrition—nutritional deficiency. Estimates of minimum forms of nutrients necessary to prevent malnutrition, such as calories, proteins, and vitamins, have been considered. Measures to improve labor productivity through health programs concerned with pure water and sanitation control, disease prevention, and health education have been presented. Such programs that neglect population control can be of only temporary benefit in improving productivity and income, however. The effect of malaria on labor productivity and the long-run impact of its eradication have been cited as an example. Measurements of improved health can be transmitted into increased productivity, and it is shown that the greater income from increased productivity can be capitalized.

Indeed, it has been demonstrated that the general procedure of capitalization—computing the present value of future income—can be applied to a wide variety of activities that increase the productivity and earning potential of human labor. Expenditures on these activities are therefore an investment in man, and the product of this investment is *human capital*. Attention is directed to the range of government services that ordinarily are not recognized as a form of capital formation. Although there has been a veritable explosion in the past 10 or 15 years in the number of studies applying cost–benefit analysis to investment in human resources, it is shown that the concept of human capital has been implicit in the writings of major economists over the past 200 years.

---

[31] In recent years there has been increased interest and attention given to the role of nutrition and health as a determinant of labor productivity. Therefore, it is surprising that William H. Nichols has not considered the role of malnutrition in the low labor productivity attributed to the best of Brazilian farm labor—only one-fourth, or less, of the labor productivity on cotton farms of the United States South and less than one-eighth of the average of all United States farms. "The Brazilian Food Supply: Problems and Prospects," *Economic Development and Cultural Change*, Vol. 19, No. 3 (April 1971), pp. 383–390.

In the present chapter, general and specific training are distinguished, and the general theory of training as an investment in human capital is presented. It has been found that the amount of education and job training are related positively, and that specific training converts labor into a quasi-fixed factor of production. Other forms of investment in human capital are job search, incremental education, and migration. Human capital formation is shown to be related to economic growth, and failure to count this type of capital formation can lead to errors in predicting the rate of growth and in explaining the causes of growth. Research in this developing area of study will undoubtedly continue, and suggested areas for further study have been explored.

Discussion Questions

1. Is there any justification for giving military personnel with specialized skills higher rank? Explain.
2. In order to attract an all-volunteer army, a military pay increase has been proposed. What considerations are necessary in establishing the size of the pay increase, given the military manpower requirements.
3. In earlier years, physicians upon retiring or upon moving to another location often "sold their practices." What was the economic rationale of this phenomenon? Today, why do some communities subsidize the practice of a local physician?
4. What economic explanation can be given for the rise in the practice of osteopathy?
5. It has been said that one of the implicit economic benefits of a college education is that it enables the graduate to complete his own income tax form. Explain.
6. Mincer has found that on-the-job training correlates positively with levels of education. Explain this phenomenon.
7. Social rates of return to education are likely to be lower than private rates of return. Explain.
8. A self-employed professional may have a higher capitalized value than a truck driver of the same age, even though their weekly incomes are the same. Explain.
9. A country with the same human and capital resource base as another may be wealthier because it has a more efficient national employment exchange. Explain.
10. What are the human capital implications of the narrowing educational differential between Whites and Blacks? Evaluate the economic value of the Civil Rights Act to minority groups.

8

The Supply of Labor
of the Individual

Introduction

The supply of labor in a market depends upon a variety of conditions: the amount of services, measured in time, offered by an individual in response to variations in wage rates; the number of individuals who offer such services; the size of the market and/or its linkage to other markets; and the interval of time within which offer and acceptance decisions are made. With respect to an employer of labor, his labor supply is related not only to the labor market within which he buys labor but also to his size in relation to that market. These interrelationships are explored in this and the following chapters. First we shall consider those influences which condition a worker to offer his services for wages. The number of hours which he devotes to work is dependent not only upon wages but also upon other activities which impose demands upon his time. Next we shall relate the labor-force participation rate to a number of variables which determine that portion of the labor force that is actively in the labor market. In conclusion, the concept of a labor market will be explored and its dimensions will be discussed. The size of a labor market is influenced by communication and transportation constraints, and these constraints may vary by occupation, employer, and region. It should be obvious as a result of this limited introduction that the supply of labor has several dimensions, and clarity requires a delineation of these facts when reference is made to the term "labor supply."

The Individual's Supply of Labor

In the derivation of the individual labor supply function, the worker is viewed as making a choice among activities in the allocation of his time. His preference function for income, which yields utility, and the set of activities in which he may engage, each of which yields utility, together with the wage rate and available work opportunities, determine his allocation of time. Traditionally, this approach has used a dichotomization of activities in terms of work (income generating) and leisure activities.[1] However, a clearer dichotomy exists if activities are identified as work or nonwork.

The Nature of Work and Income

Work is here defined as that set of activities by which a person principally earns his livelihood. Even this definition is not completely unambiguous. For some occupations shadow areas exist which are difficult to distinguish as work or nonwork. In these shadow areas, activities may be work related but nonmarketable, or they may be nonwork related but marketable. Whether or not the activities are marketed depends upon other considerations. A university professor who spends time in writing a textbook may be regarded as working, regardless of whether the manuscript can be sold.

It is customarily assumed that work involves disutility.[2] In Figure 8.1, work continues until the net utility NU from work (utility from work-derived income plus utility from work—$U_y + U_w$, where $U_w < 0$) is a maximum. At this point the marginal utility of income (dU_y/dw) just equals the negative value of the marginal utility of work (dU_w/dw). Any increment in work beyond W_0 yields greater marginal disutility in expended effort than it yields marginal utility from incremental income. Work need not involve disutility initially, however. Beyond some point, perhaps disutility is

---

[1] One of the earliest treatments is given by Lionel Robbins, "On Elasticity of Demand for Income in Terms of Effort," *Economica* (June 1930). For a mathematical presentation, see James M. Henderson and Richard E. Quandt, *Microeconomic Theory: A Mathematical Approach* (New York: McGraw-Hill, 1958), pp. 23–24. Extensive treatments are also found in L. N. Moses, "Income, Leisure, and Wage Pressure," *The Economic Journal* (June 1962), pp. 320–335; other articles dealing with the same subject are by Richard Perlman, "Observation on Overtime and Moonlighting," *The Southern Economic Journal* (October 1966), pp. 237–244, and by Jan Mossin and Martin Bronfenbrenner, "The Shorter Workweek and the Labor Supply," *The Southern Economic Journal* (January 1967), pp. 322–331. I presented a similar analysis of faculty moonlighting at the April 1963 meeting of the Midwest Economic Association in St. Louis.

[2] Jevons first made this assumption, and Alfred Marshall, Lionel Robbins and others have continued to use it. In one sense, all activities involve an opportunity cost and, hence, imputed disutility, but this is not the basis for this assumption.

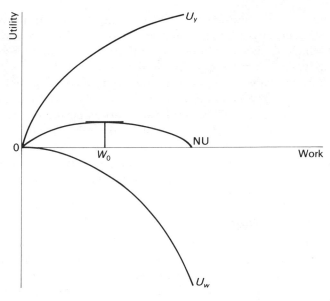

FIGURE 8.1. Deriving the net utility of work.

involved, but in all occupations and for all persons, the time and effort devoted to work need not extend beyond that point. This can be seen in Figure 8.2. At W_0', the utility from work is a maximum and wages or salaries paid for this work are up to this point a supplement to the utility

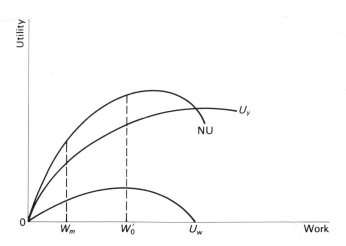

FIGURE 8.2. The net utility of work when work yields positive utility.

of work, and not a reimbursement for the disutility of work. If the maximum work period occurs at W_m, the person may not be permitted to work beyond a point at which his time and effort expenditures become burdensome.

Normally, current earnings are viewed as being positively related to the time or effort expended in work activities, but since many employment contracts are fixed for a period of a year or more, current earnings may be independent of effort or time.[3] Also if paid work opportunities are limited, no relationship may exist between income and work beyond the time for which work is remunerated. For example, a combination of a maximum workweek and limited job opportunities might exist which negate the opportunity for moonlighting and which produce an independent relationship between marginal work and income.

The Nature of Nonwork

Nonwork includes all activities other than work. The term most often used to describe nonwork activities is "leisure," and although this term will be used occasionally in the analysis to follow, it should be noted that the word almost defies definition in economic terms. Normally leisure is nonpaid, but not necessarily so. It may or may not be unproductive—for example, the hobbies of gardening or photography may be highly productive and highly remunerative. Certainly, S. de Grazia's definition, "Leisure is a state of being in which activity is performed for its own end," does not sufficiently distinguish among a wide variety of activities.[4] The motivation of a scholar's pursuit of knowledge has been so characterized. Most activities yield some amount of utility and they are engaged in to achieve those utilities. A leisure activity is no exception. A more meaningful definition might be as follows: "A leisure activity is one which yields relatively low net utility per unit of time expenditure and for which there are few or no opportunity costs in the use of that time." Time in this sense approximates the nature of a free good. However, the set of such activities does not necessarily exclude other activities, even work-related activities. When a university professor or a physician reads the literature of his discipline at his home in the evening, is this work or nonwork (leisure)?[5] A trichotomization

---

[3] Later, the assumption of independence between work earnings will be dropped, and an analysis will be offered which relates current effort with future earnings.

[4] *Of Time, Work and Leisure* (New York: The Twentieth Century Fund, 1962), p. 15.

[5] In a 1963 survey of 51 new faculty members at my university, it was found that the activity overwhelmingly regarded as most pleasant (94%) and for which too little time was available (78%) was "the reading of recent literature in one's discipline." See Bevars DuPre Mabry, "Faculty Attitudes toward Employment at a Midwestern University," *Journal of Human Relations*, XIV (Spring 1966), p. 203.

of activities into paid work, unpaid work, and "free time" has even been suggested.[6]

In more general terms, nonwork activities may or may not be marketable, although the individual usually chooses to sell only those activities in which he has a comparative advantage in the market and to perform those nonwork activities for which he has a comparative advantage in the home.[7] Nonwork activities can be divided into subcategories—those which he may choose to perform for himself and those which he has no choice but to perform for himself. Those set of activities which involve a choice may be performed by the individual himself or he may employ someone (a maid) or something (an automatic dishwasher) to perform them for him.[8] Child care, home repair, food preparation, and gardening are illustrations of the first category of nonwork activities. The second class of nonwork activities involves such matters as sleep, elimination of body wastes, child bearing, eating. The time and effort costs of these categories can be reduced by the complementary use of goods. Ordinarily, the time and effort spent on the first set of nonwork activities can be reduced or eliminated, but the time and effort cost of the second set can only be reduced.

The term "nonwork" will be used generally in the subsequent analysis. The reader is reminded that nonwork is used to refer to many types of activities, including but not restricted to those which yield "low utility per unit of time and low opportunity costs."

Income–Activity Preference Maps

A remunerated activity yields income per unit of time in which the activity is engaged. Time is a wasting resource, of course, and use of it for one activity precludes use of that moment or interval for another. Moreover, time necessarily must be consumed. Thus, an individual must use his time, and how he uses it determines the magnitude of the satisfactions which he derives. If he sells his services for a period of time, he derives income. He engages in a work activity, he acquires satisfactions of a different kind or of

[6] Jacob Mincer, "Labor Force Participation of Married Women," in *Aspects of Labor Economics* (Princeton: Princeton University Press, 1962).

[7] A comparative advantage for an activity exists for an individual if the ratio of its marginal utility to any other is greater for the individual than the ratio of the marginal utility for that activity to the corresponding one for any other individual.

[8] This he will do if the comparative advantage which he possesses in performing these activities is altered. For example, an increase in the relative earnings (wage) rate of work compared to nonwork activities may lead to an increase in the marketing of work (assuming the substitution effect exceeds the income effect). The increase in money income from the marginal work permits him to employ persons or goods to perform those nonwork-related activities for which the person now possesses a comparative disadvantage.

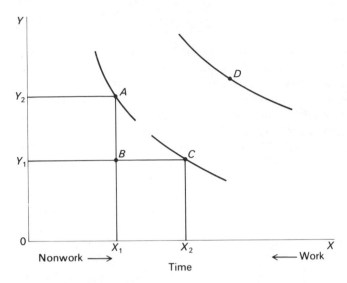

FIGURE 8.3. An income–nonwork indifference curve.

a different order. An individual, therefore, elects to allocate his time among a variety of activities, and presumably he is led to select one combination of activities, say A, over another, B, because A yields a greater sum of satisfactions than does B. Combinations of income-yielding activities and nonincome-yielding ones exist in an infinite variety, some of which are preferred to others, and among some, the individual is indifferent as to which combination is selected—that is, he is indifferent to combinations which give the individual equal satisfaction. Let us assume a number of conditions. First let us assume that a person makes a choice between earning income Y, or engaging in a nonwork activity X. The more time he spends in earning Y, the less time he has available for X. Given the time spent in X, he prefers more Y to less Y; or, alternatively, given Y, he prefers to spend more time in X than less time in X. In Figure 8.3, A is preferred to B, since Y_2 exceeds Y_1 when $0X_1$ amount of time is spent in nonwork. Similarly, C is preferred to B, for $0X_2$ exceeds $0X_1$ when $0Y_1$ income is received. However, we do not know whether A is preferred to C or vice versa. This depends upon the income–activity function (tastes) of the individual. However, we can say that point D is preferred to either points A, B, or C.

There exist other points which give the same satisfaction to the individual as A. If we connect these points by a line running through A, we have an income–activity indifference curve. Similarly, we can find points which give the same satisfaction as does point B and we can find an indifference curve running through *B*. In the same way, indifference curves can be found going through *C*, *D*, and in fact any other point on the area enclosed by Figure 8.3. The combination of income and the activity represented by a point gives the same satisfaction as any other combination represented by another point found on the same indifference curve. Normally, movement in a northeasterly direction indicates higher and higher levels of satisfaction. However, indifference curves cannot intersect. This amounts to the proposition: if *R* is preferred to *S* and *S* is preferred to *T*, then *T* can never be preferred to *R*. To see the contradiction which would be implied, allow two indifference curves to intersect, as in Figure 8.4. The individual is indifferent between *R* and *T* and between *T* and *S*. Therefore, he should be indifferent between *T* and *S*, but since *T* represents more income than *S*, both with the same quantity of *X*, then *T* must be preferred to *S*. Therefore, the intersection is a contradiction of our assumption.

The indifference curves normally are concave from above (convex from below). This implies that the slope of the indifference curve becomes steeper as it rises to the left and becomes flatter as it falls to the right. The slope of the indifference curve measures the marginal rate of substitution of nonwork activities *X* for income *Y*. As incremental units of time are devoted to the income-yielding activity, time devoted to nonwork activities must decrease correspondingly. However, as less and less time becomes available for nonwork activities, each decrement of such time involves a greater and

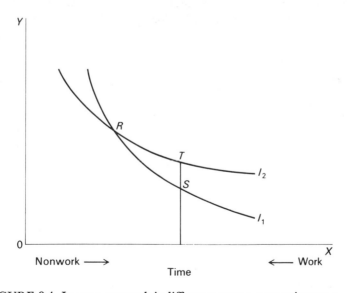

FIGURE 8.4. Income–nonwork indifference curves cannot intersect.

greater sacrifice as nonwork activities of increasing priority must be abandoned. To compensate for this increasing sacrifice of satisfaction, income must increase at an increasing rate, since the satisfaction from a given increase in income, as income becomes larger and larger, at best remains constant and very likely will diminish (i.e., diminishing marginal utility). Consequently, the slope of the indifference curve becomes greater as we move to the left along the curve and substitute income for nonwork time.[9] Similarly, as we move to the right, more time becomes available for nonwork activities of lower priority commodities, and greater and greater losses of satisfaction result from the lower income. Consequently, the marginal rate of substitution of X for Y becomes smaller. Proportionally more X must become available to compensate for the loss of satisfaction from a given decrease in Y.

It should be noted that the income–activity map does not represent achievable levels of satisfaction. It does, however, represent combinations to which a worker is indifferent or for which he has different orders of preference, *if the combinations are achievable*. In Figure 8.3, he might be prevented from achieving combination D, but if he could he would prefer D to A, B, or C.

The level of income which a worker earns depends upon the time he spends in an income-yielding activity and the time-rate of pay. In Figure 8.5, the straight line X_0Y_0 with slope α is the income line at a given rate of pay α. As hours of work increase—that is, as we move from right to left —income also increases. The individual can increase the satisfaction available to him by substituting hours of work for hours of nonwork as long as the rate of pay exceeds the marginal rate of substitution (MRS) of X for Y. If he were at point B, and he increased work by DB, he would lose ED in satisfaction from giving up time from nonwork. In other words, it would only take ED more income to compensate him for this loss of nonwork time. However, he gains DC more income, which carries him to a higher-level indifference curve. As long as α is greater than MRS_{xy}, then he will gain more satisfaction from the income derived from work than the satisfaction he will lose from nonwork. Similarly, if he is at point F, a reduction in income of FG can be compensated by an increase in nonwork of GH. However, if income is reduced by FG, then GJ amount of work time is released for nonwork, and the individual moves to a higher indifference

---

[9] If the level of satisfaction S is a function of income Y and nonwork activities X, i.e., $S = f(Y, X)$, then the marginal rate of substitution of X for Y is $-dY/dX = \text{MRS}_{xy}$. The total differential of S is $dS = fxdx + fydy$, where fx and fy are partial derivatives of S with respect to X and Y. The partial derivatives are also marginal satisfaction from increments in X or Y. Movement along the indifference curve involves no change in satisfaction, so $dS = 0$, and $-dY/dX = fx/fy$. The marginal rate of substitution of X for Y is equal to the ratio of the marginal satisfaction from X to the marginal satisfaction from Y.

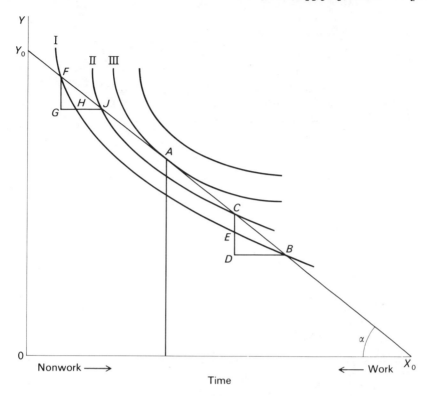

FIGURE 8.5. The income line and the income–nonwork indifference map;
$$\alpha = Y_0/X_0.$$

curve. Movement in either direction continues to point A, where the income line is tangent to indifference curve III. No higher indifference curve can be reached, given the rate of pay α. At A, $\alpha = \text{MRS}_{xy}$.[10]

---

[10] Since $\alpha = -Y/X$, then $Y = -\alpha X$ and $dY/dX = -\alpha$. Since $\text{MRS}_{xy} = -dY/dX$, and the slope of the income line is equal to the slope of the indifference curve at A, then $\text{MRS}_{xy} = \alpha$. Therefore, $\text{MRS}_{xy} = -fx/fy = \alpha = -dY/dX$. For this to be a maximum, the following conditions must hold, $d^2S_2/dX < 0$. Because $dY/dX = -\alpha$, therefore,

$$\frac{dS}{dX} = fx + fy \frac{dy}{dx} = fx - \alpha fy$$

$$\frac{d^2S_2}{dX} = \frac{d}{dx}(fx - \alpha fy) = \frac{\partial}{\partial X}(fx - \alpha fy) + \frac{\partial}{\partial Y}(fx - \alpha fy)\frac{dy}{dx}$$

$$= fxx - \alpha fxy + (fxy - \alpha fyy)(-\alpha) = fxx - 2\alpha fxy + \alpha^2 fyy < 0.$$

If diminishing marginal satisfaction occurs, fxx and fyy are always negative. If fxy is positive, the maximizing condition is therefore satisfied. Under our assumptions fxy is positive, because the marginal satisfaction is increased, given either X or Y if, respectively, either Y or X is increased, and vice versa. That is, the indifference curves are convex from below.

The Individual Labor Supply Curve

The individual's supply curve of labor can be derived from the income–activity map. As the wage rate increases, the income line rises to intersect the income axis at higher and higher levels of income, and in the process, each income line becomes tangent to higher and higher indifference curves. In Figure 8.6a, if each point of tangency is connected by a straight line, it

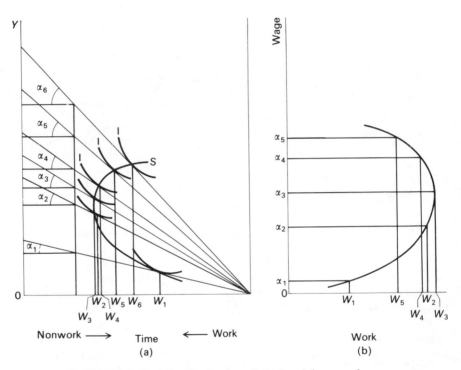

FIGURE 8.6. Deriving the backward sloping labor supply curve.

can be seen that the individual's offer curve of work for wages turns backwards at a given wage, and as wages rise above the specified wage, less and less work is offered. The individual's supply curve of labor is plotted in Figure 8.6b, using the corresponding wage rate and work time derived from Figure 8.6a. The fact that workers may prefer less work rather than more at higher wages was recognized at least as far back as the mercantilists, who advocated a low wage policy in order to induce workers to work longer hours.

That this is true can be intuitively seen. Workers seek income in order to spend it on goods and services. As wage rates rise, the same quantity of goods and services can be obtained with fewer work hours. Since the wage rate has risen, satisfactions which can be derived from an hour's worth of work have risen, and this motivates workers to substitute work hours for nonwork hours. This is the substitution effect from a wage gain. However, the enhanced income also increases the satisfactions derived from nonwork or leisure hours. Both newer types of goods and/or services and larger quantities of both can be consumed. These goods and services, therefore, tend to be complementary with nonwork activities and enhance the satisfactions attributable to these activities. New goods and larger quantities also may require more or less time in which they can be consumed. The ability to alter nonwork activities because of a larger income and the changed time dimensions within which these activities can occur together may tend to either increase or decrease the demand for time to devote to them.[11] This is the income effect from a higher wage rate. The income effect may tend to reduce or enlarge the hours offered for work. The total effect is the sum of the two and may be positive or negative. The total effect may be negative—that is, hours of work may be reduced as wages rise—if the income effect reduces hours of work more than the substitution effect increases hours of work.

The effects of a wage increase are shown in Figure 8.7. The initial wage is given by $0Y_1/0X$ and is subsequently raised to $0Y_2/0X$. Work hours increase from XA to XB if I_2 is the appropriate indifference curve, but decrease to XD if I_2 is the relevant indifference curve. If income is reduced by Y_1Y_2, by the imposition, say, of a fixed tax in order to compensate for the higher wage rate so that the worker receives the same amount of satisfaction as he received at the lower wage rate, the point of tangency would be at C', and the change in the wage rate alone would lead to a substitution of work for nonwork by CA number of hours. Since BA is the total effect of a noncompensated wage rate change, the income effect is given by BC. Both the income effect and the substitution effect are positive.

If I_2' is the appropriate indifference curve, to which the new income line is tangent, a compensating reduction in income which would leave the worker on his original indifference curve produces the same substitution

[11] Goods or services used in conjunction with a nonwork activity may either increase or reduce the time required for the activity. Automatic washing machines conserve time; high fidelity stereo sets may require more time. Typically, as time is conserved in one activity, new activities are developed to fill the time vacuum. Some are productive in an income-yielding sense; others consume time.

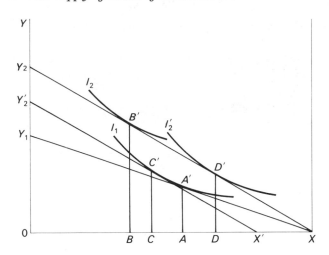

FIGURE 8.7. Income–substitution effects of a wage increase.

effect AC, but now the income effect is negative. The total effect is $AD = -DA$; therefore, the income effect is $CD = -DC$ and exceeds the substitution effect by DA. An individual who is offering fewer services at higher rates of pay—whose supply curve is backward sloping—values marginal time at the higher rates of pay more than he does marginal income; that is to say, his negative income effect exceeds his substitution effect.

Labor Force Participation

If a worker's preference for nonwork time is such that his marginal rate of substitution everywhere exceeds the wage rate, he will not enter the labor force at that wage. The slope of any indifference curve exceeds the slope of the income line so that no point of tangency is possible for hours of work greater than zero. The marginal satisfaction from nonwork activities is so great relative to the marginal satisfaction from income that it could take a very high wage to induce entry into the labor force. By way of illustration, a woman whose husband receives a high salary and who either has young children or is in the process of developing a family may have this type of preference function for work and nonwork. Similarly, an elderly person who has accumulated large savings may be ready for retirement and could be persuaded to continue in the labor force only if special considerations were made available to him.

Another possibility exists which limits the labor force participation of a prospective employee. It may be true that the rate of pay is sufficient to yield a point of tangency between the income line and an indifference curve, but this point of tangency may be for work which is less than the minimum period required by the employer. In Figure 8.8 the optimum work time is *AW*, but the minimum work time is *AM*. If no employer will use the person for *AW* number of hours, then the person may not enter the labor force. In recent years in the United States, part-time employment has increased, especially among women, non-Whites, and young people in school[12] (see Tables 8.1 and 8.2). If part-time work were not available, growth in the labor force would have been less. Of course, data on the unemployed do not include those persons who would be willing to work part time at a going

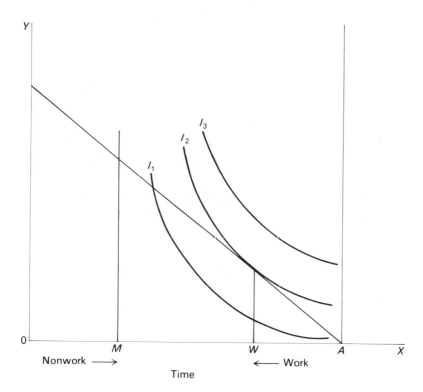

FIGURE 8.8. Labor force participation when the minimum work period exceeds the optimum.

[12] Between 1955 and 1965, part-time employment increased by almost 4 million, and by 1975 it is estimated to increase by another 3.5 million. One-fourth of all employed women work part time and over one-fifth of nonfarm workers work part time. See U.S. Department of Labor, *Population and Labor Force Projections for the United States*, 1960–1975, p. 2.

TABLE 8.1

PERSONS WITH WORK EXPERIENCE DURING THE YEAR, BY EXTENT OF EMPLOYMENT, 1950–1969

(Persons 14 years and over for 1950–1966, 16 years and over for 1966 forward)

| | | Number Who Worked during Year (Thousands) | | | | | | | | Percent Distribution | | | | | | | | |
| | | Full Time | | | | Part Time | | | | | Full Time | | | | Part Time | | | |
Year	Total	Total	50 to 52 Weeks	27 to 49 Weeks	1 to 26 Weeks	Total	50 to 52 Weeks	27 to 49 Weeks	1 to 26 Weeks	Total	Total	50 to 52 Weeks	27 to 49 Weeks	1 to 26 Weeks	Total	50 to 52 Weeks	27 to 49 Weeks	1 to 26 Weeks
Both Sexes																		
1950	68,876	58,181	38,375	11,795	8,013	10,695	3,322	2,214	5,162	100.0	84.5	55.7	17.1	11.6	15.5	4.8	3.2	7.5
1951	69,962	59,544	40,142	12,018	7,384	10,418	3,144	2,240	5,034	100.0	85.1	57.4	17.2	10.6	14.9	4.5	3.2	7.2
1952	70,512	60,294	40,486	12,374	7,434	10,218	3,092	2,294	4,832	100.0	85.5	57.4	17.5	10.5	14.5	4.4	3.3	6.9
1953	70,682	60,532	41,601	12,003	6,928	10,150	3,270	2,333	4,547	100.0	85.6	58.9	17.0	9.8	14.4	4.6	3.3	6.4
1954	71,797	60,059	40,080	12,025	7,954	11,738	3,701	2,663	5,374	100.0	83.7	55.8	16.7	11.1	16.3	5.2	3.7	7.5
1955	75,353	62,581	42,624	11,952	8,005	12,772	4,773	2,573	5,426	100.0	83.1	56.6	15.9	10.6	16.9	6.3	3.4	7.2
1956	75,852	62,437	42,778	11,791	7,868	13,415	4,760	2,693	5,962	100.0	82.3	56.4	15.5	10.4	17.7	6.3	3.6	7.9
1957	77,664	62,874	42,818	11,981	8,075	14,790	4,989	2,872	6,929	100.0	81.0	55.1	15.4	10.4	19.0	6.4	3.7	8.9
1958	77,117	61,676	41,329	11,546	8,799	15,441	5,402	3,025	7,014	100.0	80.0	53.6	15.0	11.4	20.0	7.0	3.9	9.1
1959	78,162	63,004	42,030	12,515	8,459	15,158	5,173	3,104	6,881	100.0	80.6	53.8	16.0	10.8	19.4	6.6	4.0	8.8
1960	80,618	64,153	43,265	12,132	8,756	16,465	5,307	3,290	7,868	100.0	79.6	53.7	15.0	10.9	20.4	6.6	4.1	9.8
1961	80,287	64,218	43,006	12,042	9,170	16,069	5,191	3,068	7,810	100.0	80.0	53.6	15.0	11.4	20.0	6.5	3.8	9.7
1962	82,057	65,327	44,079	12,102	9,146	16,730	5,130	3,368	8,232	100.0	79.6	53.7	14.7	11.1	20.4	6.3	4.1	10.0
1963	83,227	66,157	45,449	11,565	9,153	17,060	5,229	3,353	8,478	100.0	79.5	54.6	13.9	11.0	20.5	6.3	4.0	10.2
1964	85,124	67,825	46,846	11,691	9,288	17,299	5,268	3,374	8,657	100.0	79.6	55.0	13.7	10.9	20.3	6.2	4.0	10.2
1965	86,186	68,697	48,392	11,171	9,134	17,489	5,418	3,268	8,803	100.0	79.7	56.1	13.0	10.6	20.3	6.3	3.8	10.2
1966	88,553	70,449	50,081	10,654	9,714	18,104	4,854	3,587	8,663	100.0	79.6	56.6	12.0	11.0	20.4	6.6	4.0	9.8
1966	86,266	70,140	50,049	10,647	9,444	16,126	5,407	3,380	7,339	100.0	81.3	58.6	12.3	10.9	18.7	6.3	3.9	8.5
1967	88,179	71,909	51,705	10,702	9,502	16,270	5,641	3,430	7,199	100.0	81.5	58.6	12.1	10.8	18.5	6.4	3.9	8.2
1968	90,230	73,266	52,285	11,115	9,866	16,964	5,769	3,720	7,475	100.0	81.2	57.9	12.3	10.9	18.8	6.4	4.1	8.3
1969	92,477	74,153	52,796	11,381	9,976	18,324	6,282	4,112	7,930	100.0	80.2	57.1	12.3	10.8	19.8	6.8	4.4	8.6

Source: *Manpower Report of the President, 1971*, p. 251.

TABLE 8.2
LABOR FORCE STATUS OF MARRIED WOMEN WITH CHILDREN UNDER 18 YEARS AND NUMBER OF CHILDREN INVOLVED, MARCH 1967

(Numbers in thousands)

Item	Total	*Mother Was—*	
		In the Labor Force	*Not in the Labor Force*
Mothers with children under 18 years old: Number	24,495	8,655	15,840
Percent	100.0	35.3	64.7
Mothers with children under 6 years old: Number	13,120	3,481	9,639
Percent	100.0	26.5	73.5
Children under 18 years old: Number	59,659	19,455	40,204
Percent	100.0	32.6	67.4
Children under 6 years old: Number	20,407	5,074	15,333
Percent	100.0	24.9	75.1
Average number of children per family	2.44	2.25	2.54

Source: *Manpower Report of the President, 1971*, p. 55.

wage, but do not seek employment because of the lack of part-time work opportunities.

Changes in the satisfaction derived from marginal income or from marginal nonwork time can cause shifts in the preference map and can induce entry into the labor force. The development of labor-saving household appliances has reduced the time necessary to perform essential household tasks and undoubtedly has lowered the marginal satisfaction of nonwork time relative to work time. A family financial crisis, such as the loss of a breadwinner through death, illness, or unemployment, may raise the marginal satisfaction of income, since the income flow or wealth stock has been reduced, and this may motivate other members of the family to enter the labor force. In cyclical downswings when loss of earnings from unemployment of the breadwinner occur with more frequency, it has often been suggested that workers are added to the labor force (but not necessarily the employed labor force) as women and children seek to supplement or restore family income by searching for jobs. Others may withdraw from the labor force because of the scarcity of the kinds of jobs for which they are qualified or which they desire, and one of the conditions of desirability or qualification may be hours of work which are compatible with the person's schedule of high-satisfaction nonwork activities. Behavior of this latter group reflects discouragement. Taken together, the added worker and the discouraged worker hypotheses have been used to explain cyclical variations in labor-force participation rates.[13]

Taxation Effects

The effect of taxation on the amount of labor offered by an individual will vary with the nature of the tax and with the relative position of the individual's offer curve. Taxation may be by some constant amount, it may be proportional, or it may be progressive. A fixed or constant tax has the effect of shifting the income line downward from its intersection with the income axis by the amount of the tax. The new income line, $X'Y'_2$ in Figure 8.7, is parallel to the original income line, XY_2. The new income line intersects the time axis at a positive amount of work (instead of the previous zero amount of work). This correctly implies that the effect of the tax is to impose a burden on the taxpayer equivalent to having him work some given amount of time (XX' in Figure 8.7) at a zero wage rate. If the tax causes the point of tangency of the income line to shift from I_2 to I_1 in Figure 8.7, fewer hours of work—BC—will be offered. If, however, the shift occurs from I'_2 to I_1, more hours of work—DC—will be offered. A proportional tax has the effect of reducing the wage rate by the amount of the tax rate, and in Figure 8.7 the aftertax or net income line XY_1 can be seen to lie below the original income line XY_2. Both intersect the time axis at zero hours of work. If the wage–offer curve slopes up and to the left, that is, if I_2 is the original indifference curve to which the pretax income line was tangent, then the proportional tax will lower by BA the time offered for work. However, if the shift occurs from a point on the backward sloping wage–offer curve, work time will increase (by DA in Figure 8.7). It is clear that either

---

[13] These hypotheses have been tested by Thomas F. Dernburg and Kenneth T. Strand in "Hidden Unemployment, 1956–62: A Quantitative Analysis by Age and Sex," *The American Economic Review* (March 1966), pp. 71–95. Unemployment rates have increased because of the added workers, but decreased because of withdrawals owing to discouragement. The net effect depends on the relative magnitudes of each; Dernburg and Strand suggest that the withdrawal rate exceeds the addition rate. Labor force participation rates vary more for the very old and the very young, and for women. Jacob Mincer in his study of the labor force participation of married women in *Aspects of Labor Economics*, National Bureau of Economic Research (Princeton University Press, 1962). pp. 63–97, suggests that the family, rather than the individual, is the relevant entity which determines whether a person will seek longer hours of paid work or will choose to spend more time in nonpaid activities. Dr. Mincer finds that point-in-time cross-sectional studies do empirically support the backward-sloping labor supply curve. The monumental study by W. G. Bowen and T. Aldrich Finnegan, *The Economics of Labor Force Participation* (Princeton: Princeton University Press, 1969) in general confirms Mincer's earlier results.

a fixed or a proportional tax can increase or decrease the time spent at work of a worker, and this depends upon whether the effect of the tax moves him down along the backward sloping portion or back along the upward sloping portion of his offer curve.

A progressive tax ordinarily is imposed in steps, as in the structure of the United States income tax where the marginal tax rate rises at discrete marginal levels of income. If for illustrative purposes we assume that the marginal tax rate increases continuously instead of at discrete intervals, the income line can be seen to shift in Figure 8.9 from XY_1 to XY_2. The same

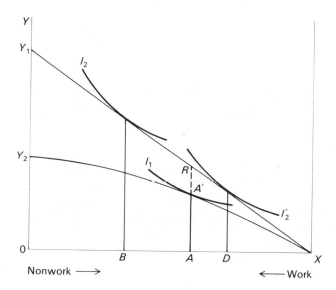

FIGURE 8.9. Effect of a progressive tax on work.

results occur with the progressive tax as with the other kinds of taxes. Whether or not more or less work is forthcoming depends upon the shape of the wage-offer curve and the relevant points of tangency of the pretax and posttax income lines.[14] It also depends upon the magnitude of the tax;

[14] In Figure 8.9, it can be shown that a fixed tax equal to RA gives an income tax with a point of tangency on an indifference curve to the left of A, since the slope of the income line Y_1X is greater than that of Y_2X and Y_1X is parallel to the income line net of the fixed tax. If the wage–offer curve is positively sloped, the equivalent fixed tax yields a smaller reduction in labor time than does the progressive tax; if the wage–offer curve is negatively sloped, the equivalent fixed tax causes a greater increase in the offered labor time. Similarly, it can be shown that an equivalent proportional tax at A' gives an income line with a slope greater

a sufficiently high tax may shift the equilibrium from the backward-sloping portion of the labor-offer curve to the positive-sloping portion and result in less labor being offered.

The Specified Workweek

An individual, when offering his services for a wage, typically enters into a contract calling for a specified number of hours to be worked per week or per day. Normally, a minimum number of hours must be worked and the work period is prescribed. More than the minimum may be called for, usually at the will of the employer, but this extra labor may be remunerated at premium rates. By law two types of maximum work periods exist; one sets a maximum work period beyond which premium rates (say time-and-one-half) must be paid for hours of work in excess of the maximum. The other sets an absolute maximum and does not permit work time for any one employer to extend beyond this limit. Examples of the absolute maximum are found in laws regulating the hours of work of women and children.

The minimum or maximum limits so imposed by the employer or by law may exceed or fall short of the equilibrium work period desired by the worker, given the wage rate. This can be illustrated in Figure 8.10. At wage rate $0Y/0X$, the worker prefers to work AX of his available time and he would receive a level of satisfaction indicated by indifference curve I_3. His income is therefore AG. If, however, work opportunities are limited to BX, he finds himself on indifference curve I_1, which is inferior in satisfaction to I_3. The individual prefers more income, but he cannot achieve the higher

---

than that of the progressive tax but less than that of the fixed tax. If the wage–offer curve is positively sloped, the point of tangency to an indifference curve of the income line net of the proportional tax will cause a smaller reduction in labor offered than with the progressive tax, but a greater reduction than with the fixed tax. The converse holds if the wage–offer curve is negatively sloped. The effect of a tax on labor time offered has been discussed by Kenneth Boulding, *Economic Analysis*, 4th Edition (New York: Harper & Row, 1966), pp. 644–646; by Richard Musgrave, *The Theory of Public Finance* (New York: McGraw-Hill, 1959), pp. 232–342, by Robin Barlow and G. R. Sparks, "A Note on Progression and Leisure," *American Economic Review*, Vol. 54 (June 1964), pp. 372–377; by J. G. Head, "Comment on Progression and Leisure," *American Economic Review*, Vol. 56 (March 1966), pp. 172–179. Among these authors only Musgrave considers the effect of a tax where a backward sloping labor supply curve exists. Musgrave is concerned not only with the effect of different taxes on work effort, given equal yields, but also with the effect of different taxes on yields, given the work effort.

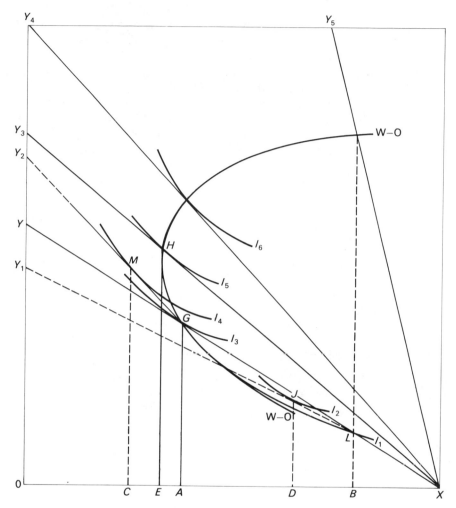

FIGURE 8.10. Overtime pay and moonlighting with given work periods.

level of satisfaction because of the restricted work period. For this reason he may be called an *income preferrer*. If, on the other hand, the work period is specified at *CX*, the individual finds himself on indifference curve I_1, earning *MC* amount of income. Even though his income exceeds his equilibrium income, the marginal rate of substitution of nonwork for income exceeds the wage rate—the individual gets more incremental satisfaction from marginal nonwork activities than he derives from the income earned by working *CA* longer. He is a *nonwork preferrer.*[15] If the specified work period is *AX*, the individual is a satisfied worker, being neither a nonwork nor a leisure preferrer.

Thus, if the required work period exceeds the equilibrium work period, the individual is a nonwork preferrer; if the required work period is less than the equilibrium period, the individual is an income preferrer. A backward-sloping labor supply curve is possible for either an income preferrer or a nonwork preferrer. In Figure 8.10, the offer curve is $W - 0$ which shows a maximum offer of work *EX* at wage $0Y_3/0X$. With a standard work period of *EX*, income lines with slopes different from $0Y_3/0X$ assure that this individual will be a nonwork preferrer. Income lines with slopes less than or more than that of XY_3 will result in a preference for work less than the standard. If, however, the standard work period were *AX*, between rates of pay represented by *XY* and XY_3, this same individual would be an income preferrer. He would prefer to work a longer-than-standard period, although the strength of his preference decreases at rates of pay above $0Y_3/0X$. It is apparent that at an existing rate of pay the desire to work a longer or shorter period of time than is required by the labor contract is not inconsistent with the concept of a backward-sloping supply curve (see Table 8.3).

Overtime Pay

Assume in Figure 8.10 that the standard work period is *AX* and the regular rate of pay is given by the slope of income line *XY*. The worker is satisfied. Now assume that the employer wishes to extend the work week to *CX*. There is no *regular* rate of pay which induces the worker voluntarily to offer more than *EA* additional hours of work, although the employer requires *CA* more work. However, by paying a premium wage equal to the slope of GY_2 where this slope exceeds the slope of *XY*, the individual willingly offers the necessary increment in work time. This suggests that premium pay for overtime may be a better method of eliciting extra work than by raising the regular rate of pay, and this may become more true the higher the regular rate of pay. It can also be shown that, given the premium rate indicated by GY_2, overtime of greater or lesser amount than *CA*, offered on a take-it-or-leave-it basis, converts the worker into, respectively, either a dissatisfied nonwork preferrer or a dissatisfied income preferrer. If the employer were able to convert *CX* into the standard work period, the worker would become

---

[15] These terms and this analysis is adapted from the article by L. N. Moses, "Income, Leisure, and Wage Pressure," *The Economic Journal* (June 1962), pp. 320–335. Moses used the terms *income preferrer* and *leisure preferrer*. For a mathematical analysis covering essentially the same ground, see Jan Mossin and Martin Bronfenbrenner, "The Shorter Workweek and the Labor Supply," *The Southern Economic Journal* (January 1967), pp. 322–331.

TABLE 8.3
AVERAGE WEEKLY HOURS AND HOURLY EARNINGS, GROSS AND EXCLUDING OVERTIME, IN MANUFACTURING INDUSTRIES, 1939–1970

	All Manufacturing Industries					Durable-Goods Manufacturing Industries				Nondurable-Goods Manufacturing Industries			
	Average Weekly Hours		Average Hourly Earnings			Average Weekly Hours		Average Hourly Earnings		Average Weekly Hours		Average Hourly Earnings	
Year or Month	Gross	Excluding Over-time	Gross	Excluding Over-time	Adjusted Hourly Earnings, (1967 = 100)	Gross	Excluding Over-time	Gross	Excluding Over-time	Gross	Excluding Over-time	Gross	Excluding Over-time
1939	37.7	—	$0.627	—	24.5	37.9	—	$0.691	—	37.4	—	$0.571	—
1940	38.1	—	0.655	—	—	39.2	—	0.716	—	37.0	—	0.590	—
1941	40.6	—	0.726	$0.691	25.0	42.0	—	0.799	$0.762	38.9	—	0.627	$0.613
1942	43.1	—	0.851	0.793	28.5	45.0	—	0.937	0.872	40.3	—	0.709	0.684
1943	45.0	—	0.957	0.881	31.0	46.5	—	1.048	0.966	42.5	—	0.787	0.748
1944	45.2	—	1.011	0.933	33.2	46.5	—	1.105	1.019	43.1	—	0.844	0.798
1945	43.5	—	1.016	0.949	34.6	44.0	—	1.099	1.031	42.3	—	0.886	0.841
1946	40.3	—	1.075	1.035	38.3	40.4	—	1.144	1.111	40.5	—	0.995	0.962
1947	40.4	—	1.217	1.18	44.0	40.5	—	1.278	1.24	40.2	—	1.145	1.11
1948	40.0	—	1.328	1.29	48.1	40.4	—	1.395	1.35	39.6	—	1.250	1.21
1949	39.1	—	1.378	1.34	50.3	39.4	—	1.453	1.42	38.9	—	1.295	1.26
1950	40.5	—	1.440	1.39	51.9	41.1	—	1.519	1.46	39.7	—	1.347	1.31
1951	40.6	—	1.56	1.51	56.0	41.5	—	1.65	1.59	39.5	—	1.44	1.40
1952	40.7	—	1.65	1.59	58.9	41.5	—	1.75	1.68	39.7	—	1.51	1.46
1953	40.5	—	1.74	1.68	62.1	41.2	—	1.86	1.79	39.6	—	1.58	1.53

TABLE 8.3—continued

Year or Month	All Manufacturing Industries					Durable-Goods Manufacturing Industries				Nondurable-Goods Manufacturing Industries			
	Average Weekly Hours		Average Hourly Earnings			Average Weekly Hours		Average Hourly Earnings		Average Weekly Hours		Average Hourly Earnings	
	Gross	Excluding Overtime	Gross	Excluding Overtime	Adjusted Hourly Earnings, (1967 = 100)	Gross	Excluding Overtime	Gross	Excluding Overtime	Gross	Excluding Overtime	Gross	Excluding Overtime
1954	39.6	—	1.78	1.73	64.1	40.1	—	1.90	1.84	39.0	—	1.62	1.58
1955	40.7	—	1.86	1.79	66.1	41.3	—	1.99	1.91	39.9	—	1.67	1.62
1956	40.4	37.6	1.95	1.89	69.6	41.0	38.0	2.08	2.01	39.6	37.2	1.77	1.72
1957	39.8	37.5	2.05	1.99	73.2	40.3	37.9	2.19	2.12	39.2	37.0	1.85	1.80
1958	39.2	37.2	2.11	2.05	76.2	39.5	37.6	2.26	2.21	38.8	36.6	1.91	1.86
1959	40.3	37.6	2.19	2.12	78.6	40.7	38.0	2.36	2.28	39.7	37.0	1.98	1.92
1960	39.7	37.3	2.26	2.20	81.2	40.1	37.7	2.43	2.36	39.2	36.7	2.05	1.99
1961	39.8	37.4	2.32	2.25	83.6	40.3	38.0	2.49	2.42	39.3	36.8	2.11	2.05
1962	40.4	37.6	2.39	2.31	85.7	40.9	38.1	2.56	2.48	39.6	36.9	2.17	2.09
1963	40.5	37.7	2.46	2.37	87.8	41.1	38.2	2.63	2.54	39.6	36.9	2.22	2.15
1964	40.7	37.6	2.53	2.44	90.0	41.4	38.1	2.71	2.60	39.7	36.8	2.29	2.21
1965	41.2	37.6	2.61	2.51	92.4	42.0	38.1	2.79	2.67	40.1	36.9	2.36	2.27
1966	41.3	37.4	2.72	2.59	95.5	42.1	37.8	2.90	2.76	40.2	36.8	2.45	2.35
1967	40.6	37.2	2.83	2.72	100.0	41.2	37.7	3.00	2.88	39.7	36.6	2.57	2.47
1968	40.7	37.1	3.01	2.88	106.1	41.4	37.6	3.19	3.05	39.8	36.5	2.74	2.63
1969	40.6	37.0	3.19	3.06	112.3	41.3	37.5	3.39	3.24	39.7	36.3	2.91	2.79
1970	39.8	36.8	3.36	3.24	119.6	40.3	37.4	3.56	3.44	39.1	36.1	3.08	2.97

Source: Economic Report of the President, 1971, p. 233.

a nonwork preferrer, but with the premium pay he is converted to a satisfied nonwork preferrer.[16] If the rate were $0Y_3/0X$ or greater and the standard work period were greater than EX_1, and if this individual were representative of a number of dissatisfied leisure preferrers, we could expect a movement to develop among these leisure preferrers for a shorter *workweek*. Because wages are higher in the United States, and because we might expect more leisure preferrers to exist where wages are high, this may explain why there has been more pressure in the United States for shorter workweeks than in other countries.

Moonlighting

A dissatisfied income preferrer is one whose standard work period is less than his equilibrium work period. It is this individual who is most willing to moonlight, that is, to accept secondary employment (see Table 8.4) or to work overtime. The individual would work overtime at the regular rate of pay. For example, if the standard work period in Figure 8.10 is BX, the individual would be willing to work AB extra hours per period of employment at the regular rate of pay. Premium or overtime rates for work in excess of BX would carry him to equilibrium on a higher indifference curve, and like the nonwork preferrer, premium rates would induce more work from the individual than would successively higher regular rates of pay. It can be seen in Figure 8.10 that an income line drawn from point H to point L would have a slope greater than XY_3, and therefore must be tangent to a higher indifference curve than I_5 at a work period to the left of EX. The dissatisfied income preferrer is likely to exert pressure for either higher rates of pay, a longer standard work period, or for more overtime with higher premium rates. Given the standard work period BX, it is likely in our illustration that the dissatisfied income preferrer would receive a wage increase sufficient to convert him into a satisfied worker—a wage equivalent to the slope of XY_5 would be necessary. General pressure for an extended standard work period has gone against the trend of the past two centuries, but in periods of recession when some firms practice a reduced workweek in order to distribute available work opportunities, such pressure might develop.

Dissatisfied income preferrers who cannot secure overtime employment are likely to moonlight. They will seek supplementary employment as long

---

[16] Moses defines a satisfied worker as one who is as well off, given the premium pay, as he would be at the regular rate of pay—that is, the premium pay carries him to the same indifference curve where he would be in equilibrium at the regular rate of pay, *op. cit.*, pp. 324–326. However, as I have used the term, a satisfied worker is one at equilibrium at the premium rate, and this equilibrium may represent either a higher or lower level of satisfaction than that at the regular rate of pay.

TABLE 8.4

PERSONS WITH TWO JOBS OR MORE, BY INDUSTRY AND CLASS OF WORKER OF PRIMARY AND SECONDARY JOB, SELECTED DATES, 1956–1979[a]

Item	May of—							Dec. of—			July of—	
	1970	1969	1966	1965	1964	1963	1962	1960	1959	1958	1957	1956
Primary Job												
Number (thousands)												
Total holding two jobs or more	4,048	4,008	3,636	3,756	3,726	3,921	3,342	3,012	2,966	3,099	3,570	3 653
Agriculture	276	273	335	416	405	386	364	332	321	629	858	866
Wage and salary workers	89	75	88	133	139	146	102	97	104	264	285	295
Self-employed workers	154	167	200	218	230	195	210	208	199	264	385	402
Unpaid family workers	33	31	47	65	36	45	52	27	18	101	188	169
Nonagricultural industries	3,772	3,735	3,301	3,340	3,321	3,535	2,978	2,680	2,645	2,470	2,712	2,787
Wage and salary workers	3,570	3,568	3,110	3,131	3,135	3,361	2,764	2,489	2,451	2,257	2,447	2,569
Self-employed workers	194	162	177	200	175	169	194	184	182	198	237	200
Unpaid family workers	8	5	14	9	11	5	20	7	12	15	28	18

Percent of total employed

Total holding two jobs or more	5.2	5.2	4.9	5.2	5.2	5.7	4.9	4.6	4.5	4.8	5.3	5.5
Agriculture	7.4	7.0	7.8	8.1	8.1	7.5	6.7	6.7	6.7	9.3	11.0	11.2
Wage and salary workers	7.4	5.8	6.6	8.4	8.8	8.8	6.2	6.7	7.7	13.2	12.1	13.4
Self-employed workers	8.0	8.5	8.9	8.6	9.3	7.5	7.5	7.6	7.2	8.1	10.7	10.9
Unpaid family workers	5.5	4.8	6.6	6.5	3.7	4.8	5.2	3.6	2.5	6.9	10.0	9.4
Nonagricultural industries	5.1	5.1	4.8	5.0	5.0	5.5	4.7	4.4	4.3	4.2	4.6	4.7
Wage and salary workers	5.2	5.3	5.0	5.2	5.3	5.9	5.0	4.6	4.6	4.4	4.7	4.9
Self-employed workers	3.7	3.1	2.8	3.0	2.7	2.7	3.0	2.8	2.8	3.1	3.7	3.3
Unpaid family workers	1.6	0.9	2.5	1.5	1.9	0.9	2.9	1.1	2.0	2.2	3.9	2.7

Secondary Job

Number (thousands)

Total holding two jobs or more	4,048	4,008	3,636	3,756	3,726	3,921	3,342	3,012	2,966	3,099	3,570	3,653
Agriculture	738	723	721	786	801	825	645	587	649	850	1,035	1,111
Wage and salary workers	122	121	139	167	185	188	176	135	130	362	506	485
Self-employed workers	616	602	582	619	616	637	469	452	519	488	529	626
Nonagricultural industries	3,310	3,285	2,915	2,970	2,925	3,096	2,697	2,425	2,317	2,249	2,535	2,542
Wage and salary workers	2,748	2,698	2,335	2,389	2,367	2,481	2,176	2,025	1,907	1,905	2,187	2,202
Self-employed workers	562	587	580	581	558	615	521	400	410	344	348	340

[a] Surveys on dual jobholders were not conducted in 1967 and 1968.
Note: Persons whose only extra job is as an unpaid family worker are not counted as dual jobholders.
Source: *Manpower Report of the President, 1971*, p. 250.

as the rate of pay in the second job exceeds the marginal rate of substitution of nonwork for income. In Figure 8.10 with standard work period BX and at a rate of pay given by the slope of XY, the individual is at point L on indifference curve I_1. Assume that supplemental work opportunities DB are offered, but at a rate of pay equal to the slope in income line LY_1. Line LY_1 has a smaller slope than line XY_1, indicating that the secondary job has a lower rate of pay than the regular job. Nevertheless, as long as the lower rate of pay yields an income line which has a greater slope than the indifference curve at point L, the income preferrer will always choose the opportunity for supplemental work because it carries him to a higher indifference curve than the one he is on at point L. Of course, the secondary job need not have associated with it a lower rate of pay than the primary job.

The Consumer Society

The data on persons working a longer workweek than 40 hours, the American standard workweek, support the above analysis, and seem to indicate that the American labor force is composed of substantial numbers of income preferrers. Most workers with workweeks in excess of the standard did not receive premium pay for the extra hours. In May 1965, one-third of American workers had a workweek in excess of 40 hours; and among these only 36.5% of nonfarm workers and 3% of farm workers earned premium pay. Moreover, the longer the workweek, the less likely were workers to receive overtime pay. Over 20% of workers having a workweek in excess of 48 hours had a second job, and the majority had a lower wage rate in the second job than in their primary job.[17] Generally, the longer-hour employees tend to be concentrated at the lower end of the earning scale, which is consistent with our analysis of the behavior of income preferrers.

Income preferrers and nonwork preferrers usually have distinctive characteristics. Income preferrers include "family builders." Family builders usually have a great need for income to house, educate, feed, and clothe children at the same time that opportunities for increased family income are restricted by the inability of wives to work because they must care for children. Consequently, the indifference map of family builders will reflect at moderate hours of employment a high marginal rate of substitution of nonwork time for income. In a related sense, the development of a taste for consumption goods, which requires a larger expenditure than has been customary, can convert a satisfied worker into an income preferrer.

[17] See the following articles in the *Monthly Labor Review*: James R. Wetzel, "Long Hours and Premium Pay" (September 1965); and "Overtime Hours and Premium Pay, May 1965," (September 1966), pp. 973–977; Peter Henle, "Leisure and the Long Work-week" (July 1966), pp. 721–727.

This phenomenon is typical in a newly industrializing, urbanizing economy which is also consumer oriented. Japan, Italy, and recently Russia have experienced such a consumer revolution. Income preferrers may also be found among those who associate high status, power, or security with income, and whose utility functions, because of their psychological propensities, generate high marginal utility for income that may even be subject to increasing returns.[18]

Leisure preferrers include those who have already established their homes and families, the elderly or infirm for whom much time must be spent in recuperative rest, or individuals whose consumption horizons are limited. It is probably true that the younger ages contain relatively more income preferrers and relatively fewer leisure preferrers while the opposite is true among the elderly. Of course, both types can be found at any age level. Since income and wage rates tend to change with age, as also do tastes, individuals may be alternatively one or the other at different times.

Salaried Professionals[19]

There exists a class of professional workers who are well educated, who work for salaries, and who enjoy their work. This group includes, among others, attorneys, staff and research physicians, scientists, and university professors. They are, at least academically, achievers and have learned, through the educational process that has led to their professional position, to delay gratification of current wants by substituting current effort for future superior rewards. Many of these persons are stimulated by their work, spend much of their waking hours thinking about or participating in their professional activities, identify themselves with their work, and indeed feel guilty, incomplete, or uncomfortable if they are separated too long from their professional activities. The nature of the activities associated with their profession provides motivation to these professionals to engage in the activities—sometimes these individuals are referred to as being self-motivated. In short, their work provides them with utility which may possess only small diminishing marginal returns over a substantial interval of time, and nonprofessional activities, often referred to as leisure, after a short interval of time may yield sharply diminishing marginal utility. In

[18] See Forest A. Bogan and Harvey R. Hamel, "Multiple Jobholders in May 1963," *Monthly Labor Review* (March 1964), and Vera C. Perrella "Moonlighters: Their Motivations and Characteristics," *Monthly Labor Review* (August 1970), pp. 57–64, for a description of the personal characteristics of moonlighters.
[19] This section has been adapted from my article "Income–Leisure Analysis and the Salaried Professional," *Industrial Relations* (February 1969), pp. 162–173. I use the term "leisure" in this section in place of the term "nonwork."

many of their activities, work and leisure may be indistinguishable. When an attorney entertains a client at a dinner, this may be work or leisure.[20]

Many salaried professionals are able to allocate the time devoted to their work-related and nonwork-related activities within a wide range of discretion. Their daily work schedule, although normally encompassing daylight hours, is sufficiently flexible to permit them to perform nonwork activities during the day, and to utilize early evening or nighttime hours or even weekend hours for work, instead of high priority weekday daytime hours. Thus, each activity can be performed at those times for which its total and marginal utilities are highest, or for which its time opportunity costs are lowest. A professor may play tennis in the afternoon and grade papers in the evening, a time ordering of the two activities which yields greater total utilities than if the ordering were reversed.

Although these professionals may control their use of time by exercising some free choice as to what portion of the day, week, month, or year will be allocated to different activities, ordinarily the time-intensive nature of many of their professional activities makes time a very restrictive constraint. (Stamina is a less meaningful constraint, partly because their control over their use of time permits them to pace themselves, and partly because their professional activities are not in general relatively effort-intensive.)[21] Finally, many professional workers earn an annual salary, and their current income is ordinarily invariant with respect to the length of time spent in their professional activities. Consequently, although income-earning opportunities may currently be limited, work opportunities are not.

As a utility maximizer, subject to an invariant income and to a meaningful time constraint, this class of workers might be expected to minimize the number of hours which they devote to their professional activities if these activities produce increasing marginal disutility, as it is normally assumed in conventional work–leisure analysis. On a conventional income–nonwork indifference map (Figure 8.11), the income line ($Y_1 Y_1$) would be horizontal to the time axis, and optimum satisfaction would be achieved where the income line touched the highest indifference curve (II_n) at zero hours of

[20] Harold L. Wilensky comments on the indistinguishability of work and leisure in the activities of executives in "The Uneven Distribution of Leisure: The Impact of Economic Growth on 'Free-Time,'" *Social Problems* (January 1961), p. 49. Robin Barlow, Harvey E. Brazer, and James N. Morgan in *Economic Behavior of the Affluent* (Washington: The Brookings Institution, 1966) make a similar point about the problem of measuring and classifying work. See p. 134.

[21] However, Barlow, Brazer, and Morgan, *Ibid.*, p. 137 report that in answer to the question of how their high-income respondents determined the number of hours they worked, fully one-half replied that "they were driven by the demands of their job or that they worked to the limit of their physical capacity."

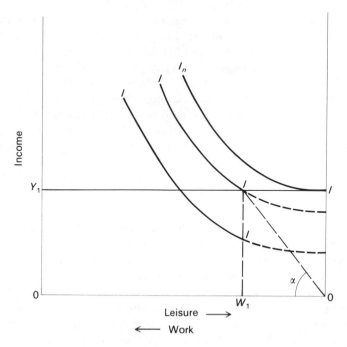

FIGURE 8.11. The income line of a salaried professional; $\alpha = OY_1/OW_1 =$ wage rate.

work. More realistically, one would expect a minimum number of hours $0W_1$ to be devoted to the job in order to prevent the employment contract from being annulled on the grounds of dereliction of duty. Indifference curves would not exist to the right of this minimum number of hours since a marginal decrease in hours of work would result in a total loss of income. Given the salary $(0Y)$ and the actual number of work hours $(0W)$, the wage rate is uniquely determined $(0Y/0W)$. The analytical problem, given conventional income–leisure analysis, is to determine the number of hours which are worked.

This analysis is contradicted, however, by studies which show that professional people, rather than working shorter hours, tend on the contrary to work longer hours than the standard workweek. Wilensky has found in a 1960 study of selected groups in Detroit that the higher the occupational strata, the greater the tendency of men to work long hours. "Only about a fifth of all lawyers and one-fourth of the professors work *fewer* than 45 hours per week while about one-half of the engineers and middle mass (a cross section of lower middle class and upper working class occupation) work that little."[22] James R. Wetzel found in a 1964 U.S. Department of Labor study that a disproportionate share of people who worked 60 hours or more a week come from the managerial occupations, from sales workers, and from *professional* and *technical* occupations.[23] Peter Henle has identified three types of individuals who tend to work long hours: (1) those people, such as professionals, who genuinely enjoy their work; (2) those persons who hold responsible positions, such as managers, who are either required or expected to work long hours; and (3) those persons who work long hours because of their need for additional income.[24]

Several explanations can be offered of the tendency of salaried professionals to work longer hours, a contradiction of the results predicted by income–leisure analysis. If it is assumed that work and leisure are perfect substitutes within a range of time, then the marginal rate of substitution of income for leisure is zero (the indifference curve is perfectly flat) within that range, since presumably work and leisure are indistinguishable and no extra income is necessary to bring forth the additional time spent in the "work–leisure" activity (see Figure 8.12). Consequently, the horizontal income line will be tangent to the relevant income–leisure curve up to the point where the latter begins its upward slope, i.e., where the two sets of activities cease to be perfect substitutes—where time requirements for nontransferable, nonwork activities approach an irreducible minimum. As income (salary) increases through periodic adjustments, the horizontal portion of the income–leisure indifference curves may terminate further to the left, further to the right, or remain unchanged, depending on whether the increase in income results in a stronger or weaker desire for nonprofessional leisure activities. Wilensky has suggested that longer hours of work are found among those with higher family incomes.[25] A study of the affluent has revealed that the median workweek of high-income workers was 48 hours and that one in four claimed to be working at least 60 hours a week.[26]

The propensity of salaried professionals to work long hours suggests another plausible explanation which is consistent with conventional income–leisure analysis (Figure 8.11). Income may still provide the motivation to

[22] *Op. cit.*, p. 42. High income, education, and entrepreneurship are other factors influencing long hours of work.

[23] "Long Hours and Premium Pay," United States Department of Labor, BLS Reprint No. 2472, 1966, p. 2.

[24] "Leisure and the Long Workweek," *The Monthly Labor Review* (July 1966), pp. 722–733.

[25] *Op. cit.*, p. 39.

[26] Barlow, Brazer, and Morgan, *op. cit.*, p. 134. "At an income level of $12,000 only one in six of those in the labor force worked 60 hours a week or more, whereas at an income level of $200,000, more than one in three did."

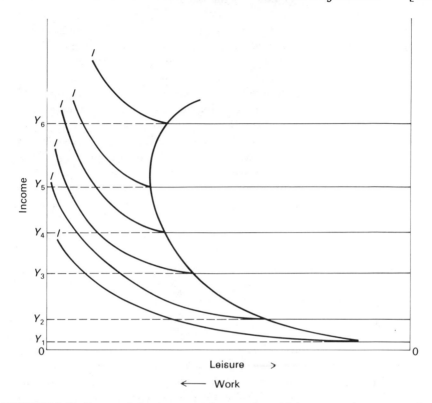

FIGURE 8.12. Income–leisure curves when work and leisure sometimes are perfect substitutes.

extend the hours of work, but the analysis here emphasizes the relationship between present work and future income instead of the relationship between present work and current income. Attorneys, professors, executives, and others regard the extra hours spent in professional activities as a form of investment in human capital, of which they already have a substantial amount. The work over and above the minimum amount[27] which is necessary to assure them the average minimum increment of income each year represents the human capital investment, and this yields a future incremental income, which is discounted by a time-preference rate of

[27] This includes an investment of time which may be regarded as maintenance cost; i.e., that amount of time which must be utilized to maintain proficiency within the field. For a complete discussion of the concept of investment in human capital, see Gary S. Becker, *Human Capital* (New York: Columbia University Press, 1964).

return and by a risk factor to yield a present value.[28] This present value of future income (V) represents an increment to current income (Y). The current wage rate (W), therefore, is not current income divided by current hours of work (H); rather, it is current income plus the present value of future incremental income divided by the hours of work $[W = (Y + V)/H]$. If current hours of work can be correlated with expected future income, then an income line can be constructed, using conventional income–leisure analysis, of which the tangent to the highest indifference curve yields the professional's optimum work hours with respect to income (see Figure 8.13). An explanation of why persons with higher incomes tend to work longer hours is that they have learned to associate present effort with future income and are continuing behavior which has been or is expected to be successful in achieving increased income.

One could expect the younger members of a profession to spend more time in work-related activities than do older members if for no other reason than the future income derived from the current human capital investment of older professionals is discounted over a fewer number of years so that the present value of incremental income is less. Age may also raise the effective discount rate and/or lower the marginal utility of money. Thus, within the higher-income groups, hours of work, although positively related to income, may be negatively related to age. This is consistent with the finding of Barlow, Brazer, and Morgan, who reported, "As age increased the median workweek gradually declined, from 52 hours for the high-income respondents aged under thirty-five to 40 hours for those age sixty-five and over who were still working."[29]

This analysis is not necessarily inconsistent with the previous analysis. Rather, it may be the expected future income which pulls the individual to the left on the horizontal portion of his indifference curves and persuades him to put "leisure hours" to work. Since future income depends on present

---

[28] The editor of a journal of economics in personal correspondence in 1968 has written that the estimated capitalized value of incremental salary income resulting from a published article is $7500. Ralph E. Balyeat of the University of Georgia, in a random sample of 307 colleges and universities in the United States, found that, as institutions increase in size and level of degree offered, the weight given to teaching activity decreases whereas the emphasis on research, publications, and public service increases. Furthermore, although little difference existed between private, state, and municipal institutions in their emphasis on teaching, the latter two tended to give greater weight to research and publication; "Factors Related to the Promotion of University Personnel," Mimeographed Report, 1966, p. 10. Lazarsfeld and Thielens have found that "regardless of their eminence (productivity), the proportion of full professors increases sharply with age," but that "age and productivity can compensate for each other" in that productive faculty members may become full professors at an age earlier than the average. See Paul F. Lazarsfeld and Wagner Thielens in *The Academic Mind* (Glencoe, Illinois: The Press Press, 1958), p. 405.

[29] *Op. cit.*, p. 134.

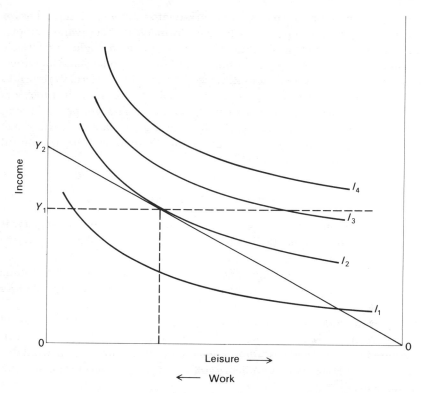

FIGURE 8.13. Future income and income–leisure analysis; $Y_1 \equiv$ current salary, $Y_2 \equiv$ sum of current and discounted future salary increments, $Y_2 - Y_1 \equiv$ present value of future salary increments.

effort, and since in most professions, continued investment in human capital is exceedingly time-intensive, long hours of effort are often necessary in order to yield any increment in future income. The fact that many professionals are permitted to establish their own work pace and work schedules permits them to select hours other than those for which the marginal utility of nonprofessional activities is extremely high. A rigid work pace or schedule might very well reduce the horizontal range of the indifference curves.

A third possible, but less plausible, explanation of the long hours of professionals is that the marginal utility of nonprofessional activities quickly becomes negative. Fear, guilt feelings, or feelings of incompleteness might produce disutility if a sizable proportion of one's time is used for nonprofessional activities. If guilt feelings or fear have earlier been induced in a person so as to alter his value structure concerning the desirability of kinds of activities, the result may be that he feels acutely uncomfortable if he is engaging in an unproductive or nonwork-related activity. I have known professors in graduate programs who seek to inculcate such values among their students. In such a situation, one can rise to a higher-preference function, given an income, by spending more hours in professional activities, and fewer in nonprofessional activities (see Figure 8.14). Attorneys return to the office in the evening to prepare themselves for a case; at night professors read books or journals or return to the laboratory. The prospect of losing the respect of one's peers because of failure in a court case or because one does not remain competent in one's academic discipline can be a powerful deterrent to the pursuit of leisure.[30]

Discussion Questions

1. "Purposive human activity, given the values of contemporary society, is essential for mental health." Is this statement true? Explain its implications to the theory of labor supply.
2. If every individual labor supply curve must have a negative slope at some high wage, how can a positively sloped aggregate labor supply curve be explained?
3. "A person works to get income to buy goods. But the consumption of goods requires time, and the more goods consumed, the more time is required. Therefore, the result is a decline in the amount of time available for work." How can our theory of labor supply accommodate this statement?
4. Has the development of part-time work caused increased female labor-force participation, or has increased female labor-force participation necessitated the provision of part-time work? Explain.

[30] The influence of the attitudes of a professor's campus or professional peers on his self-image is interestingly discussed by Paul F. Lazarsfeld and Wagner Thielens, *op. cit.*, pp. 148–152. The emphasis in the illustrations in the above paragraph is on the disutility associated with using one's time in nonprofessional activities. To be sure, one derives some utility from any voluntary participation in an activity A (which is a decreasing function of the time spent in that activity), but he incurs an opportunity cost in forgone utility from some other activity B, and this cost ordinarily can be expressed as an increasing function of the amount of time devoted to A. Part of this forgone utility has an economic character in that activity A consumes time which may be used in B to generate present or future income. However, there is a nonpecuniary side to the use of time in a nonoccupational activity. If a person identifies closely with his profession, if he values highly the respect and admiration of his peers, and if this esteem is acquired by accomplishments which require a high investment of time, then the failure to use time productively involves also an opportunity cost in these nonpecuniary rewards. Status in a profession obviously yields economic dividends, but the nonfinancial benefits can also be of significant importance. If the utility gained from using time in a nonwork activity is less than the utility forgone, then the net utility is negative; i.e., the activity yields disutility.

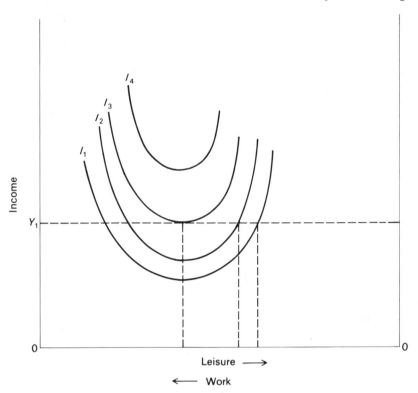

FIGURE 8.14. Income–leisure curves when leisure yields disutility; $Y_1 \equiv$ salary.

5. Since 1964, fiscal policy to encourage employment has led to income tax reductions. Yet our analysis in this chapter suggests that this can lead to a reduction in the amount of labor offered by a person. Is there a contradiction inherent in this national policy? Explain.

6. It has been found that long workweeks are found among persons who receive very low wages and among those who receive very high incomes. Does this mean that income–nonwork analysis is irrelevant in explaining work behavior? Explain.

7. Why might a society with an average age of 40 be less productive than one with an average age of 25? How would a society of average age of 15 compare with the other two?

8. Would the longer work hours of proprietors of retail establishments be explained by the same hypotheses that explain the long work hours of salaried professionals? Discuss.

9

Wages and Work in a Theory of Choice*

Introduction

Decision theory in economics has evolved from the hedonistic calculus. The economist assumes that an individual chooses to act or to engage in an activity because it yields *utility*, which is produced directly (intrinsically) by the activity or indirectly from some by-product of the activity, such as income. Activities yield utilities, then, as *outputs*. Activities also consume the time and energy of an individual, as well as goods and services, and these ingredients are identified as *inputs* into the set of activities. The magnitude of the inputs available to an individual constitute the constraint parameters that limit the number and kinds of activities in which he may engage. Rational behavior is defined as the selection by the individual of some optimum combination of activities so that the total utility derived from them is as great as the constraint parameters will permit.[1] Typically, economic

---

* Much of the material in this chapter has appeared in my article, "An Analysis of Work and Other Constraints on Choices of Activities," *Western Economic Journal*, Vol. 7, No. 3 (September 1970), pp. 213–225.
[1] A general statement of the optimizing principle is found in James M. Henderson and Richard E. Quandt, *Microeconomic Theory: A Mathematical Approach* (New York: McGraw-Hill Book Co., 1958), Chapter 2. It is summarized as follows: If the ratio of the marginal utility of an activity to its marginal cost exceeds the corresponding ratio of any other activity, expand the activity of the former and reduce that of the latter; if the ratio of the former is less than that of the latter, reduce the former and expand the latter. If the two ratios are equal, continue the level of each.

behavior has, however, been analyzed in terms of only one constraint, either income or time.

The Theory of Time

In the derivation of the individual labor supply curve, we have viewed the worker as making a choice between income and nonwork in the allocation of time. His preference function for income and nonwork, together with the wage rate and available work opportunities, determine his choice between the two. Income–leisure analysis has also been used to analyze such related hours of work phenomena as premium pay, moonlighting, the shorter workweek, and the backward sloping labor supply curve. As a general theory of choice, however, Becker has substituted an analysis which emphasizes that work and leisure both utilize combinations of time and goods, and which treats work as a special case of the use of time among a variety of activities.[2] This novel approach considers the household to be a producer of nonmarketed consumption goods and marketed factor outputs. Time as a resource constraint is transformed into "full income," a concept which is defined as the maximum money income achievable if *all* available time were devoted to earning income. Therefore, the opportunity cost of time devoted to each activity can be measured and this opportunity cost can be added to the costs of inputs of goods consumed in each activity to derive the total cost of the activity. The use of time and goods resources among a set of activities can be expressed in the equation

$$L(Z_1, Z_2, \ldots, Z_m) + p_i b_i Z_i = S \tag{9.1}$$

where L is the income forgone by engaging in an activity Z_i; p_i is the price of the goods input b_i for activity Z_i; and S represents full income. The consumer can use his time and other resources in consumption-type activities (nonincome yielding) or in production-type activities (directly or indirectly income yielding). A utility maximizer must choose among his activities subject to the full-income resource constraint S, which contains both goods and time because "time can be converted into goods through money income."[3] The optimum choice of activities requires that the ratio of the marginal utilities of any two activities must be equal to the ratios of the

---

[2] Gary S. Becker, "A Theory of the Allocation of Time," *The Economic Journal*, Vol. 75 (September 1965), pp. 493–517.
[3] *Ibid.*, p. 498. The concept of full income was suggested by Milton Friedman.

"full costs" of these two activities, which include the opportunity costs of the use of time and goods. [4]

If wages increase, the opportunity costs of consumption activities increase, and those consumption activities which use the most time have the greatest increase in opportunity costs. If goods can be substituted for the use of time, one would expect consumers to shift activities from time-intensive ones to goods-intensive ones, and for consumption activities to decrease. However, as we have seen in our previous analysis, whether productive (work) activities increase or not depends upon the relative strength of income and substitution effects. This is true also in Becker's analysis. Similarly, a lowering of the prices of goods used in consumption activities makes these activities less costly, the more so the more intensively the activity makes use of goods. This would tend to increase the time spent in the activity—the substitution effect—but if demand for the goods is elastic, more income is required to buy the goods, and more time may be spent in work in order to acquire the means to participate in that activity. The substitution effect would tend to be stronger the more time is required to utilize the complementary goods in the activity. An example might be skiing, or vacation travel to Europe when airlines reduce international fares.

Similarly, Becker concludes that increases in the productivity of productive time and consumption time yield an increase in full income, since the enhanced productivity has the effect of making more time available, and this increase produces income and substitution effect on the hours of work. If the productivity of productive time increases, less time is required for an activity, and the opportunity cost of the activity declines. The substitution effect would tend to cause the hours of work to fall; but the income effect could increase the demand for income to buy the complementary market goods used in the activity, and work time would tend to increase as a result of a negative income effect. It has generally been true that the productivity of both working and consuming time has increased, and the substitution effect for each might have negated one another so that hours of work from the substitution effect were not affected. The income effect could, however, work in various directions and produce various

---

[4] If the utility function is given by $U(Z_1 \cdots Z_m)$, differentiating with respect to each activity the LaGrange equation, $U - \pi(S)$, where π is the LaGrange multiplier, yields

$$\frac{\partial U}{\partial Z_i} = \pi(p_i b_i + L_i)$$

It follows that

$$\frac{\partial U}{\partial Z_i} \bigg/ \frac{U}{Z_j} = \frac{p_i b_i + L_i}{p_j b_j + L_j}, \qquad \text{where} \quad L_i \text{ is the cost of forgone earnings.}$$

results. If the income effect (and elasticity) for consumption is negative and that for work is positive the effect of each is to increase hours of work; if the respective income effects are positive and negative, hours of work would fall; and if both were negative or positive, the movement in hours of work would depend upon which effect was stronger[5] (see Table 9.1).

Since activities involve both time and goods costs, and since a rational consumer (or producer) tries to minimize costs, substitution occurs as their relative prices change. As wages (productivity of work time) increase, the opportunity cost of time used in nonwork activities increases, and as the price of inputs of goods into nonwork activities falls, the relative cost of time increases in these activities. To one who has observed the difference in the attitude toward time between persons in a developed economy and those in an underdeveloped one, Becker's observation which follows from the above sentences, is most illuminating[6]:

> "Since hours of work have declined secularly in most advanced countries, and so-called 'leisure' has presumably increased, a natural expectation has been that 'free' time would become more abundant (and be valued less). Yet, if anything, time is used more carefully today than a century ago. If there was a secular increase in the productivity of working time relative to consumption time there would be an increasing inducement to economize on the latter because of its relative expense. Not surprisingly, therefore, it is now kept track of and used more carefully than in the past."

Critique of the Theory of Time

As intriguing as this analysis is, it contains some conceptual gaps which require a reformulation of the theory of choice. The concept of full income may overvalue the resource constraint, for example. The diversion of time from work to leisure may not measure the money cost of the utility of leisure if some marginal time has no market value—that is, if either the workweek or work opportunity is limited. This is true if income is independent of worktime, although not of occupation, such as when a salary is paid. Also ignored is the possibility that work may have associated with it intrinsic positive utility, both total and marginal, within some range of time devoted thereto, while nonwork activities may yield intrinsic negative utilities within the respective range of time devoted to them. Therefore, the full-cost concept can fail to measure the money cost of the utility of activities.

---

[5] Becker's analysis of these effects is incomplete. *Op. cit.*, p. 506.
[6] *Ibid.*, p. 513. This provocative article is filled with many such gems of insight.

TABLE 9.1
AVERAGE WEEKLY HOURS OF WORK IN PRIVATE NONAGRICULTURAL INDUSTRIES, 1929–1970

Year or Month	Total Non-agricultural Private	Manufacturing			Mining	Contract Construction	Transportation and Public Utilities	Wholesale Trade	Retail Trade	Finance, Insurance, and Real Estate	Services
		Total	Durable Goods	Non-durable Goods							
1929	—	44.2	—	—	—	—	—	—	—	—	—
1930	—	42.1	—	—	—	—	—	—	—	—	—
1931	—	40.5	—	—	—	—	—	—	—	—	—
1932	—	38.3	32.5	41.9	—	—	—	—	—	—	—
1933	—	38.1	34.7	40.0	—	—	—	—	—	—	—
1934	—	34.6	33.8	35.1	—	—	—	—	—	—	—
1935	—	36.6	37.2	36.1	—	—	41.6	—	—	—	—
1936	—	39.2	40.9	37.7	—	—	42.9	—	—	—	—
1937	—	38.6	39.9	37.4	—	—	43.1	—	—	—	—
1938	—	35.6	34.9	36.1	—	—	42.3	—	—	—	—
1939	—	37.7	37.9	37.4	—	—	41.8	43.4	—	—	—
1940	—	38.1	39.2	37.0	—	—	41.3	43.2	—	—	—
1941	—	40.6	42.0	38.9	—	—	41.1	42.8	—	—	—
1942	—	43.1	45.0	40.3	—	—	41.4	41.8	—	—	—
1943	—	45.0	46.5	42.5	—	—	42.3	40.9	—	—	—
1944	—	45.2	46.5	43.1	—	—	43.0	41.0	—	—	—
1945	—	43.5	44.0	42.3	—	—	42.8	40.9	—	—	—
1946	—	40.3	40.4	40.5	—	—	41.6	41.3	—	—	—
1947	40.3	40.4	40.5	40.2	40.8	38.2	—	41.1	40.3	37.9	—
1948	40.0	40.0	40.4	39.6	39.4	38.1	—	41.0	40.2	37.9	—
1949	39.4	39.1	39.4	38.9	36.3	37.7	—	40.8	40.4	37.8	—

235

TABLE 9.1—continued

Year or Month	Total Non-agricultural Private	Manufacturing			Mining	Contract Construction	Transportation and Public Utilities	Wholesale Trade	Retail Trade	Finance, Insurance and Real Estate	Services
		Total	Durable Goods	Non-durable Goods							
1950	39.8	40.5	41.1	39.7	37.9	37.4	—	40.7	40.4	37.7	—
1951	39.9	40.6	41.5	39.5	38.4	38.1	—	40.8	40.4	37.7	—
1952	39.9	40.7	41.5	39.7	38.6	38.9	—	40.7	39.8	37.8	—
1953	39.6	40.5	41.2	39.6	38.8	37.9	—	40.6	39.1	37.7	—
1954	39.1	39.6	40.1	39.0	38.6	37.2	—	40.5	39.2	37.6	—
1955	39.6	40.7	41.3	39.9	40.7	37.1	—	40.7	39.0	37.6	—
1956	39.3	40.4	41.0	39.6	40.8	37.5	—	40.5	38.6	36.9	—
1957	38.8	39.8	40.3	39.2	40.1	37.0	—	40.3	38.1	36.7	—
1958	38.5	39.2	39.5	38.8	38.9	36.8	—	40.2	38.1	37.1	—
1959	39.0	40.3	40.7	39.7	40.5	37.0	—	40.6	38.2	37.3	—
1960	38.6	39.7	40.1	39.2	40.4	36.7	—	40.5	38.0	37.2	—
1961	38.6	39.8	40.3	39.3	40.5	36.9	—	40.5	37.6	36.9	—
1962	38.7	40.4	40.9	39.6	40.9	37.0	—	40.6	37.4	37.3	—
1963	38.8	40.5	41.1	39.6	41.6	37.3	—	40.6	37.3	37.5	—
1964	38.7	40.7	41.4	39.7	41.9	37.2	41.1	40.6	37.0	37.3	36.0
1965	38.8	41.2	42.0	40.1	42.3	37.4	41.3	40.8	36.6	37.2	35.9
1966	38.6	41.3	42.1	40.2	42.7	37.6	41.2	40.7	35.9	37.3	35.5
1967	38.0	40.6	41.2	39.7	42.6	37.7	40.5	40.3	35.3	37.0	35.1
1968	37.8	40.7	41.4	39.8	42.6	37.4	40.6	40.1	34.7	37.0	34.7
1969	37.7	40.6	41.3	39.7	43.0	37.9	40.7	40.2	34.2	37.1	34.7
1970	37.2	39.8	40.3	39.1	42.6	37.4	40.5	40.0	33.8	36.8	34.5

Source: *Economic Report of the President, 1971*, p. 230.

It is not inconceivable that for some persons, perhaps those in under-developed regions in particular, time may be a free good—that is, the sum of the time spent in all activities may yield maximum joint utilities at a total less than the total time available for those activities. Time, then, may have no economic cost, which may explain why some people are so willing to "waste" or ignore it. If not all time can be marketed, it is not possible to convert marginal time into equivalent goods via income. As a result, the concept of "full income" incorporating time and goods into a single resource constraint breaks down because substitution between the two is constrained.

The time-cost analysis also ignores the effort per unit of time expended in an activity, and it fails to recognize that this effort can be subject to increasing costs as time spent on an activity lengthens.[7] (An activity can be regarded as voluntarily completed when its marginal returns equal its marginal effort cost, and this completion criterion is satisfied at different time intervals for different activities.) Time as a constraint may validly be ignored if some other constraint, such as stamina, is more restrictive. The value of Becker's analysis is that he demonstrated that the failure to incorporate the time constraint, when it is appropriate, into economic analysis leads to misleading conclusions, but this can be said to be true of any appropriate constraint whose presence is analytically ignored. The nature and relevance to a theory of choice of other constraints is considered in the following pages.

Choice in Activities

Work has usually been treated as a choice activity in economic theory. Time is allocated optimally between work and leisure, given the wage rate, to determine the worker's income. This income, taken as a parameter, con-strains the person in his choice of goods. From the work–leisure analysis, the individual's labor supply function is derived, and from the theory of con-sumption his demand functions for goods are derived. Although the usual assumption is that time is fixed and independent of income, work time may increase if goods can easily be substituted for time-intensive activities. If goods can substitute for time in leisure activities, it can be shown on a conventional income–leisure indifference map that a higher wage may lead to a shift in the origin and an increase in disposable time. The income line shifts with the origin and is tangent to a higher indifference curve, at which point the amount of work may exceed that measured from the initial origin and determined by a lower, parallel income line. Hence, with higher wages the backward-sloping labor supply curve may not occur.

[7] For an earlier explanation of this phenomenon, see Alfred Marshall, *Principles of Economics*, 8th ed. (London: Macmillan and Co., Ltd., 1961), p. 438n.

In many respects, work is more of the nature of a nonchoice activity. Since an income in modern industrial society is essential to survival, most employees cannot exercise the choice of not working. Furthermore, choice is limited if work is offered on a "take it or leave it" basis—a block of work.[8] Marginal work decisions involve the whole block, and rationality requires that work be substituted for other activities up to the specified amount.[9] A worker, exercising his job options in a perfect labor market, would choose employment that would minimize his loss of utility if, under a given work constraint, he was forced to violate the time-optimizing condition. Yet, if a standard workweek exists with a small standard error, and if the productivity of a worker is given by his aptitude, skills, education, and experience, he may be faced with small variations in the amount of work required by employers. Hence, choice of employers even in a perfect labor market may not imply discretion over the amount of work.

Assume that activities are measured in terms of task units, and each unit in turn utilizes quantities of goods, time, or energy inputs. By representing any one activity along the horizontal axis and all other activities along the vertical axis, an indifference map showing orders of preferences between two sets of activities can be drawn. Budget lines for income, disposable stamina, and time define limits to the amounts of the two sets of activities that can be performed.[10]

The specification of a work period or number of work tasks affects the position of the budget lines for nonwork activities.[11] Work takes priority on

[8] Customarily, the prerogative to schedule the hours of work, the work shifts, and within broad limits, the quantity of work has been a management right, excludable from individual or collective bargaining.

[9] The marginal opportunity cost of nonwork will generally be infinitely large relative to the marginal opportunity cost of work.

[10] Individuals obviously are faced with different constraint patterns because they have different levels of resource endowments in terms of stamina and income. Although it may be argued that everyone is endowed with the same amount of time, differences in innate abilities and motivation influence the time cost per activity task and alter the available disposable time among individuals.

[11] If one of the activities is work, the position and slope of the indifference curves are affected by the task wage rate because the utility of work depends upon the utility of income. A higher task rate shifts the map to the right, indicating that the same quantity of work yields greater income and utility, and flattens the slope of each curve for any given quantity of work. Hence, for given time or stamina budget lines, the shifting indifference map plots out respectively a locus of points of tangencies. These loci, identifiable as time-pay and stamina-pay preference curves, relate the preferred amount of work for each type of input to each task rate of pay. These relationships are similar to that of the labor supply curve derived from an income–leisure indifference map, except that one of the wage-work preference curves is typically more restrictive than the other. The relationship between the work tasks identified in the time-pay preference curve and the amount of time spent in work in the labor supply curve depend upon the elasticity of the time cost per task, $e_t = (dt/dW)(W/t)$,

time and energy—the inputs of a laborer, given his human capital. From a fixed endowment of time and energy, after the performance of work a residue remains that can then be allocated among other activities. Given the task wage rate and required number of work tasks, the worker's income is determined. The slope of each budget line reflects the unit input cost of the activity relative to the set of other activities. Activities low in money or stamina costs may be high in time cost; similarly, input costs can vary with each activity. Hence, each budget line can have different slopes for each activity when paired with others. Also, any one constraint may be more restrictive than the others throughout the range of an activity. For a constraint that is more severe than others, the classical optimizing solution holds and the marginal rate of substitution of the activity for others equals the slope of the relevant budget line. The other constraints are not relevant for that activity, and in this sense they are "free goods."[12]

Budget lines will usually intersect, however, and form a boundary of feasible solutions, and by the Kuhn–Tucker theorem an indifference curve for any one activity must be tangent on the boundary to one or more of the constraints. Assume in Figure 9.1 for activity A and all other nonwork activities B that the income constraint (YY_0), the stamina line (SS_0), and the time constraint (TT_0) are such that time is for activity A a free good, and the income line intersects the stamina line from above at Z. Above point Z combinations of A and B will be limited by stamina, and below Z combinations will be constrained by income. Three possibilities are present. (1) Given sets of curves such as I_1 and I_3, stamina is the most restrictive constraint and the classical optimizing solution is relevant at a point above

---

where W is the number of work tasks performed and t is the time per task. Hours of work vary directly with W if $e_t \geq 0$ or $e_t < -1$, and inversely if $-1 < e_t < 0$. Higher wages may have different incentive effects upon the desire to work and the desire to work rapidly, depending on the level of income. Hence, dt/dW may assume different values at different income levels. The preferred amount of work may differ, however, from the required amount of work, and normally the latter is established independently of a worker's preferences.

[12] One may appropriately question the relevancy of the constraint pattern herein described, since substitution among inputs is ignored. Admittedly, goods (or services) may within limits serve as substitutes for time or energy inputs, thus relaxing the restrictions of the latter if the former endowment is more abundant. Similarly, within limits, time or stamina may serve as substitutes for one another. If perfect substitutability, without limit and with no restrictions, is assumed among inputs, this view of the constraint pattern is unrealistic because multiple constraints can be reduced to only one. If substitution possibilities are quite limited, on the other hand, the relevance of this approach is correspondingly enhanced. Moreover, if activities are identified by the types of goods used as inputs, the substitution of goods for time or stamina represents a different input mix and therefore a substitution of one activity for another.

Z. (2) Similarly, with curves such as I_5 and I_6, the classical optimizing solution holds at a point below Z where $\text{MRS}_{\text{BA}} = \angle\gamma$. (3) With sets of curves such as I_2 and I_4 and with boundary points of the feasible solution given by SZY_0, the MRS_{BA} exceeds $\angle\phi$ at and to the left of Z, and is less than γ at and to the right of Z. The classical solution in terms of income or

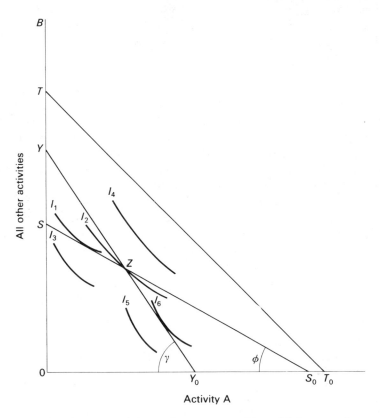

FIGURE 9.1. An activity preference map with multiple constraints.

stamina is not satisfied, yet the Kuhn–Tucker theorem proves that the activity would be used.[13] Both income and stamina constrain activities A and B, and time is still a free good.

[13] For a proof of this, see R. Dorfman, P. A. Samuelson, and R. M. Solow, *Linear Programming and Economic Analysis* (New York: McGraw-Hill Book Co., 1958), pp. 189–196.

Each budget constraint can vary as the work constraint is varied. The points of tangency of the indifference curves to the pattern of budget lines for income, disposable time, and disposable stamina, respectively, plot out income-preference, time-preference, and stamina-preference functions (lines), showing the amount of the activity that is preferred for each input with each specified work constraint. Given any specified amount of work, the constraint that is most restrictive on the activity can be identified from the preference curves. If for *n* activities one constraint is consistently more limiting, the remaining activities will be confined to types that use the scarce input sparingly and the other inputs relatively more intensively. For example, if a person spends a great amount of energy, but a small amount of time or money, in a strenuous sport, he may have to spend the remainder of the time in time-intensive activities which require lesser expenditures of energy, such as recuperative rest.

Situations occur in which the work constraint is zero—no work is permitted. Institutions may close to provide simultaneous vacations for their employees. On weekends and holidays, typically no work is performed. Disability or compulsory retirement may produce a zero work constraint. A change in work results in new constraints for nonwork activities, and income may become more restrictive than either time or stamina. Time-intensive or stamina-intensive activities may then be substituted for those that are goods-intensive. Weekends are spent in doing home chores, which may include such stamina-intensive ones as gardening, painting, or carpentry. Often, scheduled nonwork intervals are spent in time-intensive recreational activities such as "sleeping-in," watching TV, playing golf, or fishing. The retired or disabled may substitute time-intensive activities for stamina- and goods-intensive activities, since the time constraint is likely to be the least restrictive one.

Indeed, if the time constraint is relaxed suddenly because of a zero work constraint, the set of activities within a person's range of experiences, and hence range of choice, may be exhausted (that is, yield zero marginal utility) before time or stamina is exhausted, and the person may complain of monotony and be generally dissatisfied. If he seeks to engage in a low-utility-yielding activity with another—say, his wife—the second person may be conflicted. Demands upon the second person are being made that require a sacrifice of utility. This may explain why wives and mothers complain about having sick or retired husbands or vacationing children on hand. The constraint pattern has changed for the husband and children, but not for the wife. Both persons must learn to schedule their activities involving interpersonal interaction into a different pattern, and in particular the wife or mother must reappraise her utility functions with respect to time-intensive activities.[14]

Implications

Constraint Patterns and Economic Well-Being

The order of the constraints can reveal much about the individual. Since only three constraints (with the work constraint being a proxy for the income constraint in the allocation between work and nonwork) have been considered, there are six possible combinations, identified below, where Y represents income, S represents stamina, and T represents time.

		CATEGORIES			
A	*B*	*C*	*D*	*E*	*F*
S	S	T	T	Y	Y
Y	T	S	Y	S	T
T	Y	Y	S	T	S

For example, the activity patterns of workers in Western economies, whose income levels are relatively high compared to those in other parts of the world, might be traced. As a Western worker enters the labor force and during his period of family formation and development, category F may characterize the nature of constraints. Since vigor and health are features of youth, stamina may be the less restrictive constraint. The presence of a wife and the specialization which occurs in the home by role playing allows a wide variety of activities to be consumed with respect to time. Irregularity of employment also may increase the availability of time for nonwork activities. Income may be the most restrictive constraint, since lack of work experience and training yield low pay and inferior work opportunities at a time when activities are income-intensive.

As the worker moves into middle life and income needs are relaxed as children mature, and as experience and seniority lead to increased earnings,

---

[14] Each individual learns a sequence of activities that, if performed on schedule, permits him to maximize utility, given the pattern of constraint available to him. This sequence is of particular importance when the time constraint is more binding. When the ratio of the marginal utility to the marginal cost of one activity exceeds the corresponding ratio of another, the former is chosen. The marginal cost is an opportunity cost of inputs into forgone activities. The devoted husband (child) obtains high utility from socializing with the wife (mother) during conventional times because she allocates her undivided attention to them. A different utility output occurs if her attention is diluted by her attempts to perform activities simultaneously or out of sequence. Although the opportunity marginal cost for the husband (child) may be reduced—hence making the interaction with the wife (mother) a preferred one—it is, on the other hand, increased for the woman. At the time of the desired interaction, time is abundant for the one but scarce for the other.

depending upon the health of the worker, categories C or D become appropriate. Health problems may be consistent with C, but as would normally be true, good health in middle life is more appropriate to category D. College professors or research scientists would be faced, ordinarily, with the constraints in category D since their activities tend to be time-intensive and moderately remunerative.[15] Eventually, the worker reaches retirement and enters category E. Since work activity consumes the largest bloc of time, but also provides the major source of income, the retirement results in a reduction in the income flow and a release of a large bloc of time.[16] An interesting feature of this characterization is that workers in industrialized countries tend to be classified in categories D through F, in which income appears as the primary constraint in E and F and as secondary constraint in D. This is consistent with the patterns of low income in the United States; the aged and the young make up sizable proportions of this group.[17]

Labor in nonindustrial underdeveloped countries, however, may remain in category A throughout their work life, at best moving from A to E. Leibenstein and Yotopoulos[18] have written about the positive relationship among wages, stamina, and productivity, and Yotopoulos has even argued that landlords would find it in their long-run interests to raise wages above the existing market level, where they are suppressed because of the existence of substantial underemployment, in order to raise productivity and reduce unit labor costs. These authors recognize that low productivity (and wages and income) are a result of low stamina—i.e., that stamina is more restrictive than income or time. A peasant worker cannot increase his

[15] See my article, "Income–Leisure Analysis and the Salaried Professional," *Industrial Relations*, Vol. 8, No. 2 (February 1969), pp. 162–173.

[16] Robert J. Smith notes, "To an individual in his later years . . . used to being active, he may now find that an absence of scheduling poses problems for him. . . . In short, his days are now stretches of time which an earlier discipline will not fill up." "Cultural Differences in the Life Cycle and the Concept of Time," in Robert W. Kleemier, *Aging and Leisure* (New York: Oxford University Press, 1961), pp. 85–86. C. Northcote Parkinson has vividly described the relaxation of time as a meaningful constraint to "an elderly lady of leisure who can spend the entire day in writing and dispatching a postcard. . . . The total effort which would occupy a busy man for three minutes all-told may in this fashion leave another person prostrate after a day of doubt, anxiety, and toil." "Parkinson's Law," reprinted in *Managerial Economics and Operations Research*, Edwin Mansfield, ed. (New York: W. W. Norton & Co., 1966), p. 118.

[17] See James N. Morgan, Martin H. David, Wilber J. Cohen, and Harvey E. Brazer, *Income and Welfare in the United States* (New York: McGraw-Hill Book Co., Inc., 1962), Chapters 4, 16.

[18] Harvey Leibenstein, "The Theory of Underemployment in Backward Economies," *Journal of Political Economy*, Vol. 65 (April 1957), pp. 91–103. Pan A. Yotopoulos, "The Wage-Productivity Theory of Underemployment: A Refinement," *Review of Economic Studies*, Vol. 32 (January 1965), pp. 59–65.

income by performing more work tasks because he hasn't the reservoir of energy to do so. Thus, if his time rate of pay can be increased, he can obtain a larger income, consume more food, buy more health and stamina, and thereby increase the number of tasks which he can perform within the time interval, which would thereupon validate the increase in the rate of pay. The income may also improve his human capital and thus increase his productivity—both in the number and value of tasks. Whether the best method is to raise stamina through pay and income adjustments, as proposed by Yotopoulos, or through public health or welfare expenditures, or through fringe benefits such as the "hot lunch" program used in some countries, becomes a relevant question. The predominance of the last two methods and the violation of short-run profit maximizing principles of the former perhaps explain the relative absence of the former as a method of increasing productivity in underdeveloped countries. The indolence, laziness, sleepiness of the peasant or the "tobacco roader"—the stereotype of the American peasant—may be as much a health problem as it is one of value judgments. Stamina and income limit the activities that a peasant can do. The irregularity of employment varying from periods of extreme work activity in planting and harvesting seasons to almost complete idleness during other parts of the year produces intervals in which time is almost a free good. Even in periods of extreme work activity, the relative absence of highly synchronized, interpersonal activity, a characteristic of under-developed agriculture, permits wide variation in the time ordering (struc-turing) of activities.[19] These conditions undoubtedly produce an attitude toward the use of time and its interpersonal synchronization which places small importance or value upon it. Failure to perform a task at a given moment or to keep an appointment within a certain interval is not a serious breach of etiquette because the interruption in the schedule of another is minor—it creates a small loss of utility to the other person because the schedule is so flexible. Time is relatively free, not because one has more or less of it than anyone else, but because other constraints are more limiting on the number and kinds of activities in which persons customarily engage. Given this abundance of time relative to activities, much latitude is permitted in the scheduling and performance of the latter.[20]

[19] For example, during harvest season, all daylight hours might be spent in reaping. But the pace of work, the scheduling of breaks, even the area to be harvested can be varied within wide ranges.

[20] This interpretation of the value system of time is not inconsistent with that of Becker's, but perhaps it is more revealing because it calls attention to why time is relatively a "free good." Gary Becker, "A Theory of the Allocation of Time," *op. cit.*, pp. 513–514. That time may be a free good in underdeveloped countries is implicitly recognized by Staffan Linder, *The Harried Leisure Class* (New York: Columbia University Press, 1970), pp. 14, 16–19, 129.

Categories B and C are relevant to the affluent. Income does not limit the activities of persons in this category as much as do the other constraints. The activities of executives, merchants, and physicians, for example, might be affected by the order of constraints in B. As Barlow, Brazer, and Morgan have found,[21]

" . . . the high-income respondents who reported having opportunities to work more were then asked how they decided on the amount of work to do. . . . In fully one-half of the answers the respondents said that they were driven by the demands of their jobs or that they worked to the limit of their physical capacity."

Persons who have sufficient command over resources economize on the use of stamina and time, their two most relevant constraints, and often the economizing of time also involves economizing the use of energy. Dictaphones, intercom systems, messengers, secretaries, and other aids save steps and time for a busy executive. The periodic physical checkup protects the executive's health; the automobile may contain a telephone and is often driven by a chauffeur, freeing the executive to attend to other matters (use his time and attention) even while enroute from home to office. The executive jet permits him to move nationally and internationally at times most convenient to him, minimizing his loss of rest and most productive periods of the day.

Indeed, the "beautiful" people—the wealthy—have been called the *jet set* because they have adopted this rapid mode of transport which permits them to schedule more international activities of greater variety within a given interval of time. For those among the affluent who are not required to allocate their resources among work or leisure, and for whom time-intensive activities (which may also be goods-intensive) are numerous, time is the most restrictive of the constraints. Hence, to conserve the time of these "beautiful" people, fashion designers visit the "queens" rather than vice versa, personal secretaries handle their correspondence, governesses rear their children, and maids handle their grooming.

Labor Force Participation in Primary and Secondary Jobs

Morgan and Smith examined the hypothesis that families can exercise some choice over, and thereby augment, their level of real income by (1) expanding the incidence of the family's labor force participation (consistent

[21] Robin Barlow, Harvey E. Brazer, and James N. Morgan, *Economic Behavior of the Affluent* (Washington: Brookings Institution, 1966), p. 137.

with the added-worker hypothesis), (2) by extending the hours of employment of the breadwinner (moonlighting or overtime), or (3) by directly engaging in home production.[22] If this hypothesis is correct, it implies that income is the most restrictive of the constraints on the family's choice of activities. If a work constraint, however, exists and is absolutely binding on the set of work activities of the breadwinner, then real income must be increased via method (1) or (3). Even if opportunities for moonlighting or overtime exist, if the minimums permitted of these are in magnitudes in excess of time or energy limitations, then (1) or (3) will be chosen. Thus, method (2) will be chosen to increase family income only if the work constraint in all lines of work is not fixed and if income constrains the set of nonwork activities or, expressed differently, if time or stamina does not effectively constrain the supplemental work activity.[23] Method (1) is chosen by other members of the family only if the income constraint is effective in nonwork activities (that is, time and stamina are relatively free) *and* if for the breadwinner either time or stamina is the effective constraint in nonprimary work activities. Finally, method (3) is chosen over (1) or (2), (i) if the latter opportunities are limited, and (ii) if income in the performance of that activity is not the effective constraint. The family is willing to devote sufficient time and/or energy in the performance of an activity level such that little or no money expenditure is required.

Specialization in an activity takes place for a family member when the ratio of the marginal utility for an activity to any other continues to be greater over a substantial range of the effective constraint than the corre-

---

[22] "The Supply of Effort, the Measurement of Well-Being, and the Dynamics of Improvement," *American Economic Review*, Proceedings, LVIII, No. 2 (May 1968), pp. 31–39; Also see James N. Morgan and James D. Smith, "Measures of Economic Well-Offness and Their Correlates," *American Economic Review*, Proceedings, LIX, No. 2 (May 1969), pp. 45–62.

[23] This is consistent with the theoretical arguments of Moses. L. N. Moses, "Income, Leisure and Wage Pressure," *The Economic Journal* (June 1962). Moses identified as income preferrers those individuals whose prescribed work is less than that which they would freely choose. In this situation, the work constraint is less than that which is prescribed by the tangency of the most restrictive budget line to the work–nonwork indifference curve. Given the utility derived from the pay rate and reflected in the shape and position of the indifference curve relative to the budget lines, the person prefers to work more. The marginal utility of work (and income) relative to its constraint cost exceeds that of the marginal utility of nonwork relative to its constraint cost. If some other activity, which is an income substitute [either (2) or (3)] at the margin of its effective constraint, yields an increment of utility relative to input cost no less than that of any other nonwork activity, then the other income-like activity will be chosen up to that margin. Primary work would be preferred at the margin, but substitutes (moonlighting or home work) are chosen because of the nature of the constraint picture. Secondary work or work substitutes are inferior to primary work, however, and would not be chosen if primary work were not constrained.

sponding ratio for another member. In other words, the specialist develops a comparative advantage in that activity relative to other activities and relative to other members of the family.[24] At a margin of work, the marginal utility of a nonwork activity for the breadwinner relative to that of work may be so high owing to time or stamina constraints, that the breadwinner will consider permitting other members of the family to enter the labor force. The latter's corresponding ratio may be lower because of a comparatively more restrictive income restraint and less restrictive time–stamina constraints.

The exchange of labor for money in a work activity is a source of utility and affects the comparative advantage in the work of an individual. An increase in the exchange rate alters the money flow of the specialized work activity relative to that of other activities such that the former's marginal utility is increased. Alternatively, activities may be chosen which provide services that otherwise could be purchased if wages were higher, e.g., gardening, home maintenance, or auto repair. If opportunities for marginal work are zero so that the marginal utility of work approaches zero, then a comparative advantage in selected home-work activities can develop. However, where explicit secondary jobs are available and where time and stamina constraints are not yet effective, it is possible for a person to continue to have a comparative advantage in work even beyond the maximum workweek. It all depends upon the family's utility function for activities and the type of constraint patterns to which individual members of the family are subjected.

Economic Slack and the Use of Resources

If activities are subject to diminishing marginal utility, it is advisable to substitute one activity for another in order to increase total utility whenever the marginal utility relative to marginal input cost of one is less than the marginal utility of another relative to its marginal input cost. There is, nevertheless, a transfer cost in either time or stamina—perhaps in goods—in changing from one activity to another. Consequently, this transfer cost must be added to the marginal input cost of the second activity. If a relatively free input can be substituted for the scarce input used in the transfer cost, this latter cost can be reduced. This explains the use of jet travel or the hiring of personal servants such as chauffeurs, secretaries, or

[24] Over ranges of amount of any activities A and B, as long as $MU_{A_i}/MU_{B_i} > MU_{A_j}/MU_{B_j}$ for person i and any other family member j, then i has a comparative advantage in A and j has a comparative advantage in B. Family welfare can be maximized by permitting i to specialize in A and j to specialize in B.

valets. Apartment dwellings permit persons to live close to the place of employment or close to the center of the major time-intensive activities (such as recreational centers or centers of education). This reduces travel to and from these centers, a major transfer cost in terms of time.[25] The greater the variety of activities which are scheduled, the greater is the possibility of incurring transfer costs. Thus, most people, in organizing their activities, allow for a certain amount of slack in their use of resources. It is for this reason, for example, that the sum of an input into all activities may be less than the availability of the input in all but the most scarce of the inputs.

The more flexible a person is in performing his activities, or the more carefully he can schedule his activities, the less is the amount of the resource which goes to waste. While one waits to keep an appointment, letters may be written, phone calls may be placed, or books may be read. (Does this explain the presence of magazines in physicians' and dentists' offices?) Production schedules and standards minimize down-time of machinery, the expenditure of energies of supervision and labor, and use of materials. The control of slack optimizes the use of resources by reducing the transfer cost involved in moving from one activity to another.

Failure to allow for slack can also create problems. Students are well aware of professors who fail to organize their lectures carefully and, in order to avoid repeating preliminary material in another meeting, try to cram vital points into the minutes scheduled for transference between classes. Such attempts are often unsuccessful, and the professor must subsequently repeat himself in order to bring the students to the point of termination of the earlier lecture.

Industrial Relations

Work constraints ordinarily exist as parameters to individuals and typically place them in a state of disequilibrium with respect to activity choices. These work constraints may be formal, imposed by the employer, or informal and imposed by the worker's peer group. Thus, problems of soldiering on the job, featherbedding, absenteeism, or various work rules may be regarded as attempts by workers to adjust the formal parameter to a more preferred state. For example, for some persons it is possible that the work constraint is such so as to place them in the positively sloped region of their work–nonwork indifference map. In order to move to a more

---

[25] Why is this principle frequently violated by businessmen who commute long distances from suburbia to the city? Instead of residing close to his office, the family resides close to schools, shopping centers, and a pastoral environment. Time ordinarily is more restrictive to a businessman than to his family, and considerable transfer time from home to office is involved. Other noneconomic considerations, perhaps, explain these decisions, and they may be related to the risks to family welfare of central city habitation.

preferred indifference curve (level of satisfaction), an individual may attempt to reduce the average number of work tasks performed through soldiering or through absenteeism. If this problem is chronic among a work force, the employer may be compelled either to reduce the formal work constraint, or to impose sufficient sanctions upon violators of the constraint in order to correct the infractions. These sanctions in order to be effective must alter the indifference map of the person so as to shift the positively sloped portion above the work constraint. Compulsory overtime at premium pay may accomplish this or the imposition of a fine, demotion, discharge or threat thereof may produce a similar result. Given the amount of nonwork which is yielding positive marginal utility, the increased probability of a loss of wages or the loss of some other utility-producing opportunity (such as the promise of upgrading or promotion, or continued work) results in a loss of utility from an unauthorized reduction in work. This can occur only if the indifference curves are negatively sloped and convex from below. Sanctions can be imposed by either or both the employer and the work group and, whatever the source, can affect the shape and position of the indifference curves.

Similarly, given a task rate of pay and belief in the "lump-of-labor" theory, a performance of more than a given number of work tasks leads to a rightward shift in the indifference map, or, according to our representation, a leftward shift in the time and stamina budget lines. The effect is to reduce the order of satisfaction of the worker. Belief in this result conditions a worker to adhere to the work constraint norm established by his peer group. The lowering of utility occurs because workers believe that a work pace in excess of the group constraint cannot be preserved. The reduction either reduces employment opportunities by converting the work constraint to zero for some, or it produces a lower wage rate for others. Whether the belief in a lower wage rate is owing to the lower expected value of the wage, since the probability of earning a given wage is reduced through a lessening of employment opportunities, or owing to the competition of unemployed workers, the effect is the same in shifting the indifference map relative to the budget constraints. "Rate busters" are punished by the group in such a way as to negate the utility gained from the larger income which could be earned by exceeding the group norm. In this manner, group behavior can influence the work activity choices of individuals.

Belief in the lump-of-labor theory may, as industrial engineers have learned, negate the work-producing impact of an incentive wage. The level of work to which the incentive is directed may not, in the opinion of the work group, be sustainable. By the same line of reasoning, if the incentive rate successfully results in a level of work in excess of the formal norm, the rate itself may not be sustainable and may be reduced. If this occurs, the relation of the indifference curves to the budget constraints is worsened. Consequently, the informal norm is not likely to exceed the formal norm, and coupled with the lump-of-labor theory, it may actually be less.

An attempt to increase the level of work activities within a given work period and with no compensating increase in the rate of pay is called a "speedup." It frequently is one of the most vigorously resisted management innovations in labor relations. The reason for this is obvious, given the analysis here. The increase in work tasks requires greater time and/or energy inputs into work and reduces the availability of these resources, with no compensating increase in income, for use in nonwork activities. This causes the budget lines for time and stamina to shift to the left with respect to the set of nonwork activities, and correspondingly there is a reduction in total satisfaction experienced by the individual.

Where changes in work policy similarly and adversely affect either the utility functions or the constraint patterns of many employees, group action to correct or mitigate these changes can be expected. If the policy can be nullified by the collective adherence of individuals to the group's will, the sanctions imposed by the group probably will be informal. If, however, the work policy cannot be circumvented by informal but concerted group action, such as when the pace of an assembly line is increased, or when the utility functions of nonadherents to the group norm are more sensitive to countervailing sanctions of management, then the group action may be directed toward the employer, and a formal labor–management relationship may be established. Negotiations between management and work organizations then may turn toward matters which affect the utility functions of both, such as wages and those conditions of work related to the intrinsic utility of the job, or conditions of work which influence either the time or stamina costs of the job, or the work level to be imposed on the job.[26]

Productivity Increases

Productivity increases may occur in either or both work and nonwork activities. Furthermore, these productivity increases may appear as a reduction in inputs of time, energy, or goods per activity task, and the form of the appearance must be identified in order to distinguish the nature of the productivity increase.[27] An increase in the productivity or work

[26] For an analysis of bargaining developed in terms of utility theory, see Bevars D. Mabry, "The Pure Theory of Bargaining," *Industrial and Labor Relations Review*, Vol. 18, No. 4 (July 1965), pp. 479–502. For comment and reply, see R. E. Walton and R. B. McKersie, "The Theory of Bargaining," Vol. 19, No 3 (April 1966), pp. 414–435.

[27] For a comprehensive survey of techniques and practices in measuring productivity, see John T. Dunlop and V. P. Diatchenko, *Labor Productivity* (New York: McGraw-Hill Book Co., 1964).

ordinarily implies an increase in output per man-hour of employment,[28] which in turn suggests that the input of time per task has been reduced when stamina is the more restrictive constraint (see Table 9.2). A line of

TABLE 9.2
OUTPUT PER MAN-HOUR IN THE PRIVATE ECONOMY, 1961–1968 AND SELECTED PERIODS
(Annual rate of growth)

Year	Total Private Economy	Farm	Nonfarm
Year to year			
1960–1961	3.4	7.9	2.9
1961–1962	4.8	2.3	4.6
1962–1963	3.6	8.9	3.0
1963–1964	3.9	1.8	3.7
1964–1965	3.3	9.3	3.0
1965–1966	3.8	3.2	3.3
1966–1967	1.6	12.3	1.0
1967–1968[a]	3.3	([b])	([b])
Selected periods[c]			
1947–1961	3.2	6.1	2.5
1953–1961	2.6	5.2	2.2
1947–1968[a]	3.2	5.9	2.7
1961–1968[a]	3.5	6.1	3.3

[a] Estimated.

[b] Not available.

[c] Average annual rates computed from the least squares trend of the logarithms of the index numbers.

Source: *Manpower Report of the President, 1971,* p. 58.

work may use energy per task more intensely than it uses time so that the stamina constraint sets the limit to output. Even with a reduction in the expenditure of time per task, no increase in output may occur. Conversely, simply because output per man-hour has increased because of some production

---

[28] Increases in work productivity may be shown by the intersection of the budget line at a point on the work axis representing a greater number of tasks. The line is steeper because its slope, equal to the ratio of input cost per nonwork task to the input cost per work task, has been raised owing to the reduction in the latter input cost.

innovation does not imply that the time cost of the job has technically been reduced. If the work day has not changed, the innovation may have reduced the energy input of a worker in energy-intensive tasks, which then permits the worker to perform a larger number of tasks per work period, given his stamina. If slack time for recuperation has been programmed into a set of motions, it may simply reduce the need for recuperative rest and result in a reduction of scheduled slack time.

A productivity increase in work may reduce the time or energy input per task proportionately more than it increases the amount of work performed. If this occurs, not only may more work be preferred, but more of the resource will be available for use in nonwork. This implies a rightward shift of the budget line to the set of nonwork activities. With a larger number of work activities, income tends to be larger and this also increases the income available for nonwork activities.[29] A nonwork activity, which previously may have been excluded from the set of such activities because its inputs of time and goods were of such an intensive nature as to exceed the resources available to the individual, may, after the productivity increase, join the set of feasible activities. The growth of industries catering to recreational needs no doubt can be traced to the growing availability of time, income, and stamina which can be devoted to nonwork activities.

Productivity increases in nonwork activities also can affect the preferred amount of work. In the dichotomization of activities into work and nonwork, the latter is interpreted to include an index of a wide variety of activities. A productivity increase in any one nonwork activity will affect the index only to the extent that its relative weight in the index is affected. The development of an electric toothbrush, for example, is not likely to shift the stamina budget line perceptibly to the right in the work–nonwork space, although it is an energy-saving innovation (but perhaps not a time-saving one). On the other hand, the acquisition by a large family of an automatic clothes washer and dryer may perceptibly move to the right the intersection of both budget lines with the nonwork axis. The corresponding reduction in the slopes of these lines may result in tangency conditions with indifference curves at points corresponding to more or less work, depending upon the structure of the indifference map. If preferred work is increased sufficiently so that it now exceeds or at least equals required work, it may be that the nonwork innovation permits individuals to enter the labor force and

[29] As we have shown, the amount of time or energy spent at work need not increase, and it may even decrease. The hourly wage rate may, therefore, increase even though the task wage rate remains the same. Thus, productivity increases at work result in greater time rates of pay and increased hours of "leisure" with greater amounts of disposable energy to be consumed in nonwork activities.

participate therein. If it reduces preferred work below that required, the person may withdraw from the labor force.

Productivity increases which are time- and stamina-saving in nonwork activities are obvious, although they are commonly and nonspecifically identified as being *labor saving*. Less obvious, however, is a productivity increase in income. A productivity increase in income initially alters the slope and one, but not both, of the intersection points in nonwork activity space. Either a price reduction or a quality improvement of a good used in an activity will reduce the good's cost per activity task. Thus, price reductions relax income constraints, and conversely, price increases make income more restrictive on the choice of activities. If the price reduction occurs for a good which releases large amounts of time and energy from nonwork to work, and if work as a result increases, there is a secondary income effect. Not only is there a reduction in the slope of the income line in nonwork space but also the income line undergoes a rightward shift.

Taxation

Income–leisure analysis has been used to show the result on the supply of labor of an individual from the imposition of a tax[30] or a subsidy.[31] Similarly, activity analysis can be used to interpret the impact of a tax or subsidy. The results will be somewhat different from those of income–leisure analysis, for there it is assumed that work is measured in units of time and is a variable. In activity analysis, it is assumed that work is measured in task units, and that the amount of required work is a parameter. Although the worker may prefer more or less work, his preferences usually are not

[30] The effect of a tax on labor time offered has been discussed by Kenneth Boulding, *Economic Analysis*, 4th ed. (New York: Harper & Row, 1966), pp. 644–646; by Richard Musgrave, *The Theory of Public Finance* (New York: McGraw-Hill Book Co., 1959), pp. 232–242; by Robin Barlow and G. R. Sparks, "A Note of Progression and Leisure," *American Economic Review*, Vol. 54 (June 1964), pp. 372–377; by J. G. Head, "Comment of Progression and Leisure," *American Economic Review*, Vol. 56 (March 1966), pp. 172–179. The effect of an income tax normally is to decrease the hours of work if the pretax wage puts the worker on the portion of his labor supply curve which is positively sloped, and to increase the hours of work if the pretax wage places the worker on the negatively sloped portion of his supply function.

[31] See Richard Perlman, *Labor Theory* (New York: John Wiley & Sons, 1969), Ch. III, pp. 63–76. Also see C. T. Brehm and Thomas R. Saving, "The Demand for General Assistance Payments," *American Economic Review*, Vol. 54 (December 1964), pp. 1002–1018. A subsidy either may be a lump sum, in which case the normal result is to decrease the offering of labor, or it may be as a supplement to the wage rate. In the latter case, the effect on the supply of labor depends upon the point to which it moves the individual on his labor supply curve.

considered to be consistent with that which is required. The impact of taxation, either positive or negative, will thus be felt primarily in the set of nonwork activities. The imposition of a tax tied to wages moves the indifference map to the right relative to the constraints, which is analogous to a leftward movement, or reduction, in the budget lines. In addition, the budget line, particularly if the wage tax is progressive, will tend to have a smaller negative slope (flatter) relative to the indifference curves. The imposition of a fixed tax would tend to move the constraints to the left relative to the indifference map, but ordinarily it would not alter the slope of the curves. A subsidy, depending upon its method of bestowal, would have oppositely analogous effects. The general impact of a tax should be to decrease labor supply (measured in terms of work tasks). However, the shifted labor supply curve would diverge increasingly from the original as the wage rises, if the tax were not fixed. The amount of the divergence would depend upon the nature of the variable tax. Similarly, a subsidy would tend to increase the supply of labor, measured in terms of work tasks. Whether the change in the supply of labor measured in time is in the same direction as that measured in work tasks for either a tax or a subsidy depends upon the elasticity of the time cost per task.[32] This analysis, therefore, is not inconsistent with that of income–leisure analysis, but it does have the advantage of letting us examine more carefully its impact on nonwork activities.

If the required amount of work is not changed, however, the effect of a tax is to reduce the inputs of time and stamina available for nonwork activities. It may also change the order or restrictiveness of the constraints, and in particular, it may alter the order of the income budget line. One might show, for example, that the revenues from the tax are used to finance public projects which reduce the time or stamina costs of families engaging in common activities, such as busing children to school. For some families the benefit from this public function in terms of the use of these family resources may shift the budget lines to the right more than the tax shifts them to the left. The result may be an increase in the time and stamina resources of the family. The family's welfare still may be impaired by the tax if these augmented resources previously were free goods relative to income. By decreasing available income, which may have been originally the most limited resource, the family's welfare has been impaired. This

---

[32] Given: $W_0 \times t = T_w$ = hours of work. When $|e_t| = (dt/dW) \, W/t > 1$, T_w varies directly with W (the amount of work accomplished); T_w varies inversely with W as $|e_t| < 1$. Other things being equal, in terms of motivation it can be argued that a change in wages at different income levels has different incentive effects on the desire to work and the desire to work rapidly (W). Consequently, dt/dW may assume different values at different income levels.

example is even more true if the tax revenue is used for a purpose which is not contained in the activity set of the family.

Discussion Questions

1. Do most people consider the time cost of an activity? Should they? Might the time cost of attending, say, a union meeting explain the apathy of union members toward such meetings?
2. During what periods of the day, week, month, or year is time more likely to be a "free" good? Since the time of attorneys is valuable, why do you find many of them engaging in civic affairs? Why are physicians as active in these affairs as attorneys?
3. Why does the opening of a superhighway increase the geographical size of a labor market?
4. One might consider the stamina of one's eyes a constraint on how much TV he watches. Suppose color TV is easier on the eyes than black and white TV. Would the increased telecasting of football games correlate with an increase in sales of color TV sets? Since color TV sets are more expensive, how might the acquisition of such a set affect other activities?
5. Time-intensive activities have tended to become less so because goods are developed as input substitutes for time. What type of problems does this tendency pose for a bored retiree with a limited income?
6. It has been argued that all time and motion studies do is to remove an excess amount of slack in the performance of work activities. Comment. Must more slack be programmed for an undernourished labor force? What are the efficiency and productivity implications of your answer?
7. My secretary tells me that the purchase of a washer and dryer has actually increased her time expenditure in doing the family laundry. Prior to her purchase (and also her employment) she did these chores in a coin-operated washateria, using multiple washing and drying machines simultaneously? Why, then, did she buy her own laundry machines?
8. A family using a septic tank was compelled to pay a property assessment for the installation of a sewer line contiguous to their property. They claimed the assessment reduced their welfare. Appraise this claim.

10

Supply in the Labor Market

Aggregation

The aggregate labor supply curve for a labor market is influenced, but not solely determined, by the sum of the individual wage–offer curves. Each individual's labor supply curve turns backward at different wage rates, if indeed it turns backward at all. For example, one might expect the curve to turn backward at a lower wage for women with dependent children and with their husbands employed than for married men with dependent children and wives unemployed. On an *a priori* basis it is difficult to determine at what wage the aggregate quantity of labor supplied would become inversely related to higher wage rates. If the labor force is composed primarily of family builders—a probable situation if the average age of the labor force is under 30—an increase in the wage rate would probably increase the number of hours offered for work. The sum of additional hours offered by income preferrers would exceed the sum of hours withdrawn by leisure preferrers. In such a situation, a higher wage rate might also induce new entrants into the labor force—i.e., housewives who would prefer homework activities if lower rates were offered in the markets. Thus, higher wages could expand the quantity of labor supplied by increasing the number of hours of work offered by individuals and by increasing the numbers of individuals offering their services for hire.

Another possibility is that higher wage rates, while increasing the number of hours offered by each individual, reduce the number of individuals seeking employment. As Mincer and others have noted,[1] the family should be considered as the unit in which preferences for income and leisure

[1] Jacob Mincer, "Labor Force Participation of Married Women," in *Aspects of Economics* (Princeton: National Bureau of Economic Research, Princeton University Press, 1962).

are determined. The income of the husband is taken as a parameter by the wife in developing her preference for income and nonwork. A rise in the value of this parameter as a result of a wage increase received by the husband may increase the marginal utility derived from homework and decrease the marginal utility derived from income so that the indifference curves of the wife for income and nonwork shift upward and twist to the right. It takes a higher wage to induce the wife, therefore, to enter the labor force, and if the higher wage is not present in the occupations for which she is qualified, then she may withdraw from the labor force. Evidence strongly suggests that there is an inverse relationship between the income of the husband and the labor force participation of the wife, in terms of both permanent and transitional income.[2] T. Aldrich Finegan has hypothesized that the hours and earnings of wives similarly may affect the hours of work of husbands.[3]

The opposite situation may be true, however. Higher wages may reduce the hours of work of individuals but increase the number of individuals in the labor force. Secular data indicate that as wages have increased over time, the hours of work of males (and females) have contracted while the participation rate of females over time has expanded.[4] It was the apparent contradiction between this evidence and that in the preceding paragraph that led Mincer to undertake his study of the labor force participation of married women. He found the two to be consistent.[5] The former is true for selected points in time, but the latter is the trend. Over time, the female component of the labor force has increased, but females in higher-income families still tend to participate less in the labor force than those in lower-income categories.

It should be obvious that a simple aggregation of individual labor-offer functions cannot yield the total labor-supply function because these individual functions are not independent of one another. Since the number of individuals actively in the labor market depends upon the conditions which affect the labor-force participation rate, it is to a brief consideration of these conditions that we now turn.

The Labor-Force Participation Rate

A remarkable finding has been that the ratio of the labor force to population in the United States, England, New Zealand, Canada, and Germany has remained stable throughout the 20th century in spite of

[2] Clarence Long, *The Labor Force under Changing Income and Employment* (Princeton: Princeton University Press, 1958), pp. 7–8, 82–94. Mincer, *op. cit.*, finds a similar negative relationship. See also, W. G. Bowen and T. A. Finegan, *The Economics of Labor Force Participation* (Princeton: Princeton University Press, 1969).

[3] "Hours of Work in the United States: A Cross-Sectional Analysis," *Journal of Political Economy,*" LXX (October 1962), p. 457.

[4] Long, *op. cit.*, pp. 10–11, 117–140.

[5] *Op. cit.*

changes in the participation rate of the components of the labor force in terms of age, sex, and race.[6] There have been some short-run, transitional changes, caused primarily by war and great depressions, but from cyclical peak, the variation in the participation rate in the United States has been less than 2%. In the short run, from peak to trough, seasonably adjusted variation has been less than 3% since 1946, although seasonal variations do generate somewhat wider fluctuation. Although Long has found some evidence that depression (recession) does drive workers from the labor force (the discouraged-worker hypothesis) in greater numbers than have been attracted to the labor force (the added-worker hypothesis based on the desire to maintain family income), he finds that the peacetime labor force in full employment is not fundamentally different than in periods of less than full employment.[7]

Dernburg and Strand have found that in the early part of a recession, participation rates fall more rapidly as workers leave the labor force, but in later stages of the downturn, new entrants into the labor force compensate for withdrawals, and the participation rate subsequently declines more slowly.[8] Women and the very young and the very old males all seem to be subject to the discouraged-worker effect. When employment expands, discouraged workers are attracted back into the labor force while some of the previously added workers now withdraw, but the rate of reentry, net of withdrawals, varies with age and sex (see Table 10.1). Knowledge of these rates permits the calculation of elasticities of employment and labor-force participation by groups. The elasticity of group employment, e_1, is defined as the ratio of the percentage change in group employment to the percentage change in total employment; the elasticity of group labor-force participation with respect to total employment, e_2, is the ratio of percentage change in the group labor-force participation to the percentage change in total employment; the elasticity of group labor-force participation and group

[6] Long, *op. cit.*, pp. 20–26, 230–277.

[7] *Ibid.*, pp. 14–16, 20.

[8] Thomas Dernburg and Kenneth Strand, "Hidden Unemployment 1953–62; A Quantitative Analysis by Age and Sex." *The American Economic Review*, March 1966, p. 71. They calculated that over the period of 1952–1962, approximately one person left the labor force for every two who lost their jobs (p. 74). Jacob Mincer had criticized an earlier study of Dernberg and Strand, "Cyclical Variation in Labor Force Participation," *Review of Economics and Statistics*, Vol. XLVI (November 1964), pp. 378–391, by suggesting that their high correlation between the aggregate labor-force participation rate and (1) the employment-population ratio, and (2) the ratio of new unemployment-compensation exhaustions to the adult civilian population was owing to their model which was dangerously close to being tautological. However, in footnote 22, Mincer acknowledges that their later *AER* article, a manuscript which he had seen, was "less vulnerable to statistical doubt." See Jacob Mincer, "Labor Force Participation and Unemployment, A Review of Recent Evidence," in R. A. and M. S. Gordon, editors, *Prosperity and Unemployment* (New York: John Wiley and Sons, 1966), pp. 81–84, 109.

TABLE 10.1
EMPLOYMENT STATUS, BY COLOR, SEX, AND AGE, 1969–1970
(Numbers in thousands)

Employment Status, Sex, and Age	Total		White		Black and Other Races	
	1969	1970	1969	1970	1969	1970
Total, 16 years and over						
Civilian labor force	80,733	82,715	71,779	73,518	8,954	9,197
Employment	77,902	78,627	69,518	70,182	8,384	8,445
Unemployment	2,831	4,088	2,261	3,337	570	752
Unemployment rate	3.5	4.9	3.1	4.5	6.4	8.2
Men, 20 years and over						
Civilian labor force	46,351	47,189	41,772	42,463	4,579	4,726
Employment	45,388	45,553	40,978	41,093	4,410	4,461
Unemployment	963	1,636	794	1,371	168	265
Unemployment rate	2.1	3.5	1.9	3.2	3.7	5.6
Women, 20 years and over						
Civilian labor force	27,413	28,279	23,839	24,616	3,574	3,664
Employment	26,397	26,932	23,032	23 521	3,365	3,412
Unemployment	1,015	1,347	806	1,095	209	252
Unemployment rate	3.7	4.8	3.4	4.4	5.8	6.9
Both sexes, 16 to 19 years						
Civilian labor force	6,970	7,246	6,168	6,439	801	807
Employment	6,117	6,141	5,508	5,568	609	573
Unemployment	853	1,105	660	871	193	235
Unemployment rate	12.2	15.3	10.7	13.5	24.0	29.1

Note: Detail may not add to totals because of rounding.

Source: *Manpower Report of the President, 1971*, p. 16.

employment, e_3, is the ratio of the percentage change in group employment.[9] They have estimated for a change in total employment of 1000 that the labor force will increase by 454 and that unemployment will fall by 546.

[9] *Ibid.*, p. 81:

$$e_1 = \frac{dE_i}{dE} \frac{E}{E_i}, \qquad e_2 = \frac{dL_i}{dE} \frac{E}{L_i}, \qquad e_3 = \frac{dL_i}{dE_i} \frac{E_i}{L_i} = \frac{e_2}{e_1}.$$

These elasticities permit the calculation of the effect, on group employment and/or labor-force participation, of a 1% increase in total or group employment. See the comment by Alfred Tella that supports the Dernberg–Strand method of estimating the effect of the ratio of group to total employment on the labor-force participation rates. "Hidden Unemployment 1953–62; A Quantitative Analysis by Age and Sex: Comment," *American Economic Review*, Vol. LVI, No. 5 (December 1966), pp. 1235–1241.

The changes in employment are net of the offsetting effects of reentry of discouraged workers and withdrawal of the added workers. If the economy is operating at less than full employment, a movement to full employment would also enlarge the labor force. The relative changes in employment and the labor force would be reflected by the elasticity coefficient e_2. This implies that the actual labor force with less than full employment is smaller than the labor force would be at full employment. Therefore, a movement to full employment would require the creation of more jobs than would be indicated by the unemployment rate at less than full employment. The difference between the full employment labor force and actual employment is the manpower gap, and the difference between the manpower gap and actual unemployment is *hidden unemployment*. Hidden unemployment in 1962 for men was estimated to be 906 thousand and for women to be 1414 thousand, or a total of 2320 thousand. This would have raised the unemployment rate in 1962 from 5.6% of the labor force to 8.5%.[10]

Labor-force participation in the United States increased during World War II as about 20 million persons were drawn into either civilian or military employment. About 40% of these had been unemployed and the remaining 60% were net additions. The labor force as a percent of the population 14 years and older increased from 54.1% in 1940 to 62.3% in 1945 and fell to about 55.9% in 1947. During the war, for every 100 men taken into the military, about 70 persons were added to the labor force. About one-half of these additions were women whose husbands or husbands-to-be had gone to war, and the rest were made up of the young (students who now might be called "dropouts"), the old (the normally retired), and the heretofore unemployables. After the war, women retired from the labor force to begin their families, and many returning veterans delayed their reentry into the civilian labor force in order to extend their education. Thus, the school-directed veterans represented a withdrawal from the total labor force, although a large number of them took part-time jobs to supplement

[10] Dernburg and Strand, *ibid.*, pp. 88–90. Bowen and Finegan, *Economics of Labor Force Participation, op. cit.*, pp. 516–520 have found these estimates to be too high. Whereas Dernberg and Strand have used the employment-population ratio as a measure of labor market tightness, Bowen and Finegan have relied on the unemployment rate itself as a better measure. L. E. Galloway has found that hidden unemployment is found in all groups in his sample, although it is more heavily concentrated in certain subgroups. He reports that his study is consistent with the findings of others, including the Dernberg–Strand study and an earlier one by Tella. See, "A Note on the Incidence of Hidden Unemployment in the United States," *Western Economic Journal*, Vol. VII, No. 1 (March 1969), pp. 71–83. However, the results of a study by S. W. Black and R. R. Russell suggest that the Dernberg–Strand estimates of the potential labor force are too high for the period since 1958: "Participation Functions and the Potential Labor Force," *Industrial and Labor Relations Review*, Vol. 24, No. 1 (October 1970), p. 91.

their G.I. Bill of Rights' benefits. Changes in the normal participation rates of the young, the old, males, and females occurred during the war, but these returned very much to prewar rates with the ending of hostilities and the demobilization.[11] The war rates can, therefore, be regarded as exceptional.

There have been changes in the participation rates by sex; male participation rates have declined, female rates have increased. Although female participation rates are inversely related to their husbands' income, in general there has been a movement of women of all ages, regardless of marital status, into the labor force. In 1920 women comprised about 20% of the labor force, in 1970 they comprised over 40%. In 1968, 61% of employed women were married and over one-half of married women worked during the year.[12] Participation and education above high school are strongly, positively correlated. The demand for and the motivation of educated women to pursue careers is conducive to this positive relationship. Interestingly, Finegan has found a significant negative correlation between the percentage of females employed in an occupation and the hours of work of that occupation.[13] This is undoubtedly owing to the attraction for women of occupations which permit them to combine their employment careers with their role of homemaker. Long also notes that in combination with the shorter-hour movement, technological advances in homework and the increased willingness of husbands to assume some of the burden of household tasks together have freed women to take a more active role in the labor market.[14] In addition, smaller families have probably reduced the amount of homework required of wives and have shortened the period in which, as mothers, they concentrate upon close and constant supervision of children. As a result, women may tend to reenter the labor force more quickly.[15]

[11] During the war, many women gained employment experience which they otherwise would not have had, as evidenced by their increased participation rate. Although their rates fell following the ending of the war as they withdrew to raise children, it is possible that participation rates in the late 1950s and 1960s rose as a result of the return of many of these women after their children matured. The social mores regarding female employment certainly underwent a change, and this change together with earlier experiences might (1) induce a return to the labor force of wartime employees, or (2) relax family restrictions upon the entry of daughters into the labor force.

[12] Vera C. Perrella, "Work Experience of the Population in 1968," *Monthly Labor Review* (February 1970), pp. 58–59.

[13] "Hours of Work in the United States," *op. cit.*, pp. 463–465.

[14] *Op. cit.*, pp. 20–25. The decline in the workweek of males probably has facilitated their willingness to alter their traditional family roles.

[15] Malcolm S. Cohen had found that the single most important family demographic characteristic relating to labor-force participation of married females is the age distribution of children. "Married Women in the Labor Force: An Analysis of Participation Rates," *Monthly Labor Review* (October 1969), p. 33.

Participation rates have over the years undergone greater changes for the very young and the very old. For males under 25, participation rates have declined with each decade since 1890, and this is in part owing to compulsory school attendance and extension of educational opportunities in terms of incidence and duration of school attendance. It is also owing in part to the migration from rural to urban areas. The decline in participation rates is generally true in societies which are becoming proportionally more urban. In underdeveloped countries where the bulk of the population reside in rural areas, almost all members of the family are considered to be a part of the labor force. In Thailand, with over 80% of its population of 33 million in 1967 found in rural areas, and with 80% of its labor force employed in agriculture, forestry, and fishing, there is also about 80% of its population aged 15 years and over in the labor force. This participation rate is extremely high and is owing to the inclusion of almost all members of the rural family of age 15 and more in the labor force, since all perform work on the farm or in the family enterprise. As migration from rural to urban areas has accelerated in recent years in Italy, the labor force has actually declined as children and women withdrew when they entered the cities. Dernburg and Strand have found that the younger workers are more apt to suffer from the discouraged-worker effect as unemployment increases, and this would tend to lower participation rates.

Older workers have experienced relatively larger declines in participation rates. Undoubtedly, the extension of social security and industrial pension programs has facilitated retirement of those over 65. Long finds no evidence that the reduction is from a decreased ability to work. Instead, he believes that many older workers may have been pushed from employment by the increasing availability of better-educated women.[16] As job content has changed and hours of work have decreased, employers no doubt have preferred to substitute younger and better-suited women for older workers, and this may have led employers to change personnel policy to facilitate the employment of the former in preference to the latter. This is true also not only for males over 65 but also for males between 45 and 64 whose rates have also declined (see Table 10.2).

Although Long has found only a small decrease in participation rates of males between 25 and 44, there nevertheless has been a secular decline in this group's participation in the labor force. Dernburg and Strand found little change in participation rates in the 1953–1962 period, however, and

[16] *Op. cit.*, pp. 13, 30–33. Long also believes that better-educated women with previous employment experience may be preferred by employers over young, inexperienced, and inferiorly educated males. Thus, higher female participation rates may have *caused* lower male participation rates at young and old ages by either "pushing" the aged from jobs or "pulling" young males (preventing from entering) from the labor force.

TABLE 10.2
LABOR-FORCE PARTICIPATION RATES, BY COLOR, SEX, AND
AGE, 1960 TO 1980
(Annual averages in percent)

Color, Sex, and Age	1960	1965	1970	1975	1980
Total, 16 years and over	59.2	58.8	59.7	60.0	60.4
White, 16 years and over	58.8	58.5	59.4	59.7	60.1
Non-White, 16 years and over	63.0	62.1	62.4	62.4	62.4
Male, White, 16 years and over	82.6	80.4	80.5	80.3	80.4
Male, non-White, 16 years and over	80.1	77.4	78.3	78.5	79.0
Female, White, 16 years and over	36.0	37.7	39.6	40.4	41.1
Female, non-White, 16 years and over	47.2	48.1	48.0	47.9	47.5
Male, all races, by age	82.4	80.1	80.3	80.1	80.3
16–19	58.6	55.7	56.4	56.2	56.7
20–24	88.9	86.2	86.6	86.7	87.2
25–34	96.4	96.0	96.2	96.2	96.2
35–44	96.4	96.2	96.7	96.7	96.7
45–54	94.3	94.3	95.0	95.0	95.0
55–64	85.2	83.2	84.3	83.9	83.7
65 and over	32.2	26.9	25.1	23.4	21.8
Female, all races, by age	37.1	38.8	40.5	41.3	41.9
16–19	39.1	37.7	39.4	39.6	40.0
20–24	46.1	49.7	50.3	51.5	52.6
25–34	35.8	38.5	38.6	39.3	40.3
35–44	43.1	45.9	47.5	49.0	50.0
45–54	49.3	50.5	55.3	57.6	59.5
55–64	36.7	40.6	43.8	45.7	47.3
65 and over	10.5	9.5	9.8	9.8	9.9

Source: *Manpower Report of the President, 1969*, pp. 229, 231.

have concluded that participation of males age 25–64 in the labor force is almost automatic.[17] Black males and foreign-born white males had higher participation rates than native-born white males until 1930, but since then participation rates have declined for the former. In part this may be owing to a shift of Blacks to urban areas and in part to better educational opportunities which keep young males in school. The decline in immigration and the aging of the foreign-born population probably account for the decline in their participation rates.

[17] *Op. cit.*, p. 94.

Black females have had higher participation rates than white females, but as the former's rates have declined and the latter's rates have risen, differences by race have narrowed significantly. Thus, racial differences in participation rates have narrowed for both sexes, and Clarence Long believes that Blacks and Whites are moving towards common living and working patterns.

Characteristics of Labor Markets

Labor-force definitions conceal the existence of hidden unemployment. The increase in wages is normally a signal that the number of jobs at attractive wages have increased sufficiently to bring again into the labor market those who were previously discouraged. The degree of response in the offering of quantities of labor to a change in the wage rate depends upon the degree of competition in the labor market. From the supply side, the characteristics of a perfectly competitive labor market are as follows:

1. Homogeneity of labor
2. A sufficiently large number of buyers and sellers of labor so that no one buyer or seller can independently influence the wage rate
3. No barrier for entry into or exit from the market
4. Full information available to all of relevant market conditions in terms of alternative wages, employment opportunities, and conditions of employment

In addition, the time interval in which changes occur on either the demand or supply side of a labor market is sufficiently great so that the equilibrium level of wages and employment can be reestablished within that interval. An elaboration of these characteristics is in order.

Homogeneity of labor implies that each unit of labor, however measured, is equivalent to any other unit. At one extreme, if each unit of labor has the same skill, the same motivation, the same aptitudes, and expends the same amount of energy, then the units are homogeneous. It is sufficient, however, for each unit to have the same productivity, so that a unit of labor may be below average in some but above average in other determinants of productivity. Obviously, individuals do differ in basic aptitudes, in education, experience, training, and skill, in motivation, reliability, and ability to assume responsibility, and in physical strength and stamina. Moreover, deficiencies in these different characteristics rarely are balanced out by compensating proficiencies. If the market can be stratified or partitioned on the supply side in terms of the quality of labor, and each subset by quality is treated independently, then the homogeneity condition can at least conceptually be preserved. Employers are able to control in part the balance of desired characteristics through supervision, training, control of the work pace, inspection, and by the use of rewards and penalties. Minimum standards of employability are specified and workers meeting or exceeding these standards may be regarded as homogeneous. Deficiencies can be remedied somewhat by greater attention to one, several, or all of these instruments of control. Most of these measures to develop a homogeneous labor force per job category require an expenditure. If the supply of labor of a given quality is deficient at the going wage, a substandard quality of labor may be employed and raised to the quality required through an extension of the control measures. There is an accompanying increase in cost, however. Therefore, the necessity to develop homogeneity in a non-homogeneous labor force generates additional cost which is reflected in a function in which labor supply increases only as costs increase. However, conceptually this reflects an imperfection in the market.

The number of buyers of a given quality of labor may be large or small in a market, but what is of paramount importance is the size of the buyer relative to the size of the market. Implications of size are considered in detail in subsequent paragraphs. The numbers of sellers is usually large except in cases where unusual skills are required. However, it is possible that the extent of the market is enlarged with education and/or skill. If neither independent buyers nor sellers of labor are able to affect the wage, then the wage is determined or given for them, and any quantity of labor can be supplied to the buyer at the given wage. In terms of a graph, the supply curve is a horizontal straight line, parallel to the quantity axis.

Mobility Conditions

Conditions 3 and 4 of the list of characteristics are the mobility conditions. Obviously a worker cannot move to another job if he is not informed of the job, nor is he considered to be in the labor market unless he possesses the specifications required by the occupation. The knowledge condition not only refers to information about job vacancies, relative wage rates, and job content, but it also implies that the information required to perform the job is easily acquired. Entry and exit conditions imply that there are no institutional barriers to acquiring or changing an occupation, such as when exclusionary policies are adopted by unions. Workers are not only able to move into and out of jobs but they are willing to do so and actually will do so if wage differentials arise, such that benefits from changing jobs at least equal the costs. Consequently, psychological or emotional impediments to change do not exist.

Labor markets ordinarily do not contain the conditions necessary for perfect mobility (see Chart 10.1). Ignorance of job opportunities is

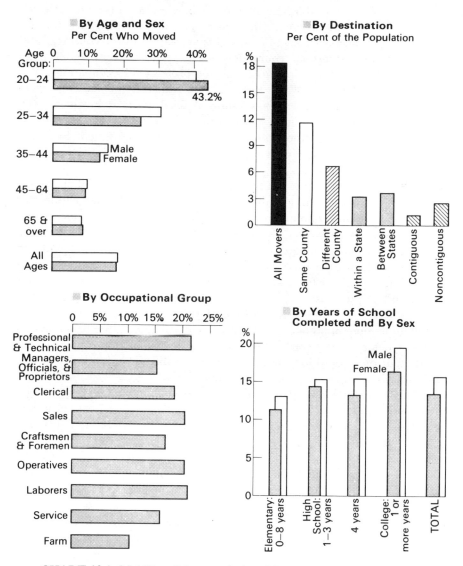

CHART 10.1. Mobility of the population, March, 1969 to March, 1970.
Source: The Conference Board, *Geographic Mobility in the Sixties*, Road Maps of Industry, No. 1666, May 15, 1971.

widespread, although public employment exchanges do exist to process job information.[18] Unions continue to impose barriers to entry into selected trades in spite of federal law to the contrary; employers still hire discriminately by sex, race, or religion, civil rights legislation to the contrary; and lack of capital and proper counseling prevent youths from undertaking training or further education necessary for professional occupations. The existence of differential wage rates is not sufficient in itself to yield occupational movement if loss of substantial fixed assets is involved, such as pension and seniority rights, resale value of the home, etc. As long as seniority systems and pension plans are in existence, movement from one company to another, even with no change in occupation, involves a cost. Benefits must exceed costs.

A job change may also involve a geographical change. A labor market necessarily has a geographical dimension and spatial mobility within this region has both an economic and a psychological cost. The residence site may or may not, however, be changed, depending upon the distance involved in the job change. The economic cost of commuting, with no change in residence, involves not only a monetary cost but a time cost as well.[19] The opening of an expressway through a city may link together labor markets previously separated by the time barrier of congested city traffic, and in like manner the opening of a superhighway may extend the spatial dimensions of labor markets over a wider region. Little or no savings in the monetary cost of commuting may result from the improved highway facility, but the savings in time may be considerable. The development of a rapid transit system may produce similar results.

A facility which reduces the time cost per mile of commuting enlarges the labor market because it permits a larger population to enter that market at reduced psychological costs. Psychological costs of job mobility are probably the basis of Adam Smith's comment that "a man is of all sorts of luggage the most difficult to be transported." Because of these psychological costs, a worker is particularly reluctant to change the geographic location of his residence. Such a change would require him, his wife, and children to leave their circle of friends and community attachments, and to leave the familiarity and security of an established home. Economically, there are costs in changing residences—cost of moving, risk of loss in the sale of their

---

[18] Joseph Shister has reported that over 75% of those seeking jobs for the first time obtain their jobs through personal friends, acquaintances, or relatives, through previous part-time work, or by random applications made at various job sites. *Economics of the Labor Market*, 2nd ed. (Philadelphia: J. B. Lippincott Co., 1956), p. 18.

[19] For an analysis of the time cost of transportation, see L. N. Moses and H. F. Williamson, Jr., "Value of Time, Choice of Mode, and the Subsidy Issue in Urban Transportation," *Journal of Political Economy* (June 1963), pp. 247–264.

house. Of course, a change in one's job also involves problems and risks of adjustments, so that improved commuting facilities which permit one to change jobs without changing residences do not reduce or remove all of these psychological costs.

It is apparent, therefore, that there are many types of barriers to movement. Some are physical, in a spatial sense; some are economic, involving out-of-pocket money costs that are in excess of the benefits of such a change; some are owing to lack of channels of or access to job information; many barriers are emotional in nature. All, however, limit the size of a labor market and impede adjustments to increases or decreases in the demand for labor. Normally, the greater the barriers the greater must be the size of wage increases in order to bring forth given increments in the quantity of labor offered.

Nevertheless, the population of the United States is relatively mobile. In a one-year period, about a fifth of the population moves from one house or apartment to another and about 6% move from one county to another, and in a ten-year period, over one-third of the population moves from one state into another.[20] Those who are most willing to move are the unemployed, the young, highly skilled workers, and professionals. In general among higher occupational levels, movement occurs to take a job; among lower occupations, movement occurs to seek a job.[21]

Perfect and Imperfect Labor-Supply Functions

The existence of the conditions for a perfect labor market, as has been already noted, generates for a firm a supply curve of labor which is perfectly elastic at the market-determined wage (Figure 10.1). The market-supply wage can be expected to increase as the quantity of labor offered increases because of the preference functions of individuals for income and leisure. The greater the barriers are to mobility, the greater will be the slope of the market-supply curve and the less will be its elasticity for any given quantity of labor. Given the market-demand curve, a steeper supply curve implies a higher equilibrium wage. The size of the firm relative to the market and the degree of heterogeneity of labor determines the degree of elasticity of the supply curve of labor to the firm. As we have noted previously, a given wage may call forth a sufficient *number* of workers to meet the employer's requirements, but if they are not of the *quality* he needs, he must incur training or control costs of increasing magnitude the more the profferred labor departs

[20] U.S. Department of Commerce, Bureau of the Census, *Statistical Abstract of the United States*, 1963 (Washington, D.C.: Government Printing Office, 1963), p. 38.
[21] Samuel Saben, "Geographic Mobility and Employment Status, March 1962–March 1963," *Monthly Labor Review*, LXXXVII, No. 8 (August 1964), pp. 873–881.

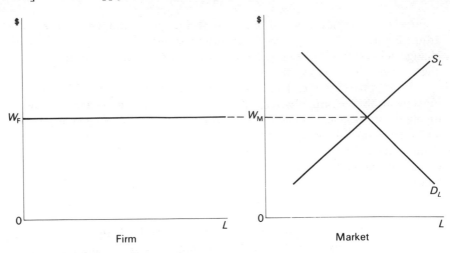

FIGURE 10.1. The firm's labor-supply curve in a perfectly competitive labor market.

from the standard. The likelihood of a market being unable to meet the employer's demand at a given wage is greater the larger the size of the employer relative to the market and the higher the quality of labor required by the employer. A small retail store in a large city may be able to obtain an unlimited labor supply, relative to its needs, at the prevailing wage, but an aerospace establishment employing physicists and engineers may quickly exhaust the available supply in that same city, regardless of the wage. An expansion of the retail store with the employment of more clerks can occur with no perceptible change in the wage rate (the firm is too small to affect the area's prevailing wage). An increase in the number of scientists to meet the needs of the expanding aerospace firm may be realized only if the wage is raised significantly in order to induce movement from other labor markets. The necessary increase will be influenced by the presence of psychic attractions of the firm's labor market (climate, schools, recreational facilities, housing, cultural facilities, etc.) and the proximity of the firm to other labor markets.

The magnitude of the wage increase necessary to bring forth additional job applicants will depend also upon the time interval scheduled for the expansion of the space firm. A crash program will require greater increases than an expansion program designed to increase slowly, say, over a ten-year interval. Training of scientists takes time. In the short run, the development of complementary technical personnel trained to do highly specialized tasks may be possible in order to conserve the activities of the more highly trained scientists, but these substitutes are labor costs which are apt to increase as the attempt to maintain homogeneity of effort is strengthened. The scientist and his bundle of technicians may be regarded as a homogeneous unit within which some substitution of technicians for scientists is possible, but which may quickly produce an extremely high marginal rate of substitution.

Thus, a firm's labor supply may be perfectly elastic, corresponding to a perfect labor market, or less than perfectly elastic, corresponding to an imperfect labor market. The former curve is perfectly flat, the latter is upward sloping. The two possibilities produce different average and marginal cost relationships.

In a perfect labor market, the firm's supply curve is perfectly elastic and average and marginal labor costs are both equal to the wage and therefore equal to each other.[22] This can be seen in Figure 10.2. Total labor cost for

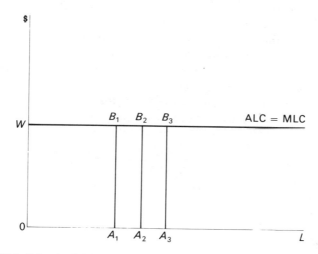

FIGURE 10.2. Marginal labor cost equals average labor cost in a perfectly competitive labor market.

$0A_1$ of labor is $0W \times 0A_1$, or area $0WB_1A_1$. Dividing $0WB_1A_1$ by $0A_1$ yields average labor cost, or the wage $0W$. Let labor be increased by one unit to $0A_2$—i.e., $\Delta L_1 = 0A_2 - 0A_1 = 1$. Total labor cost increases to $0WB_2A_2$ and the change in total labor cost, or marginal labor cost, is $A_1B_1B_2A_2$. This, however, is $1 \times 0W = 0W$, so MLC $= 0W$, the wage,

---

[22] Let W = wage which is a constant; L = the quantity of labor. Total labor cost (TLC) is given by $W \cdot L = $ TLC. TLC divided by L is average labor cost, or TLC$/L = $ ALC $= W$, taking $d(\text{TLC})/dL = Wd(L)/dL = W$. Thus, marginal labor cost MLC equals the wage, and MLC $= W = $ ALC.

and MLC = ALC. To hire additional labor in a perfect labor market, the firm incurs only the going wage in additional costs.

Marginal labor cost exceeds average labor cost when the labor market is less than perfect, for the supply curve is upward sloping. Since $L = f(w)$, therefore, MLC $= d(\text{TLC})/dL = w + Ldw/dL$. The slope of the supply curve is positive, so $dw/dL > 0$. Since L is positive, MLC $- W = Ldw/dL > 0$. Average labor cost and the wage for a given amount of labor are still the same. For this reason the supply curve of labor is sometimes referred to as the average labor cost *curve*.

$$W \cdot L = \text{TLC}; \qquad \frac{\text{TLC}}{L} = \text{ALC} = W.$$

An illustration of the relationship between marginal labor cost and average labor cost was provided to me by the vice president of a large company. We were speaking of a former student of mine who had been employed under the executive as an accountant. The executive expressed disappointment that the accountant had chosen to leave the company for employment with a competitor since the accountant had been such a valuable employee. The vice president was understanding of the move, since the accountant had been offered a $2000 increment in salary, yet he hated to lose such a promising employee. I asked the executive why he had

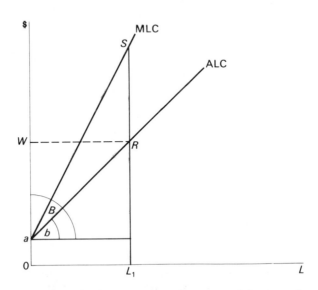

FIGURE 10.3. Marginal labor cost exceeds average labor cost in an imperfect labor market.

not met the offer of the competitor since the accountant was so valuable. The executive replied that the accountant was easily worth $2000 more per year; he was not, however, worth $32,000 more, which is what the total incremental cost would have been to the company. In order to keep the nth accountant, the wages of all of the $(n - 1)$ accountants would have had to be raised. This illustrates the principle that a rising labor-supply curve generates incremental (marginal) costs which exceed the wage (average labor costs) of the employees, including the marginal employee. If the labor-supply function is linear, it can be shown that the rate of increase of marginal labor costs is twice that of average labor costs,[23] and this is illustrated in Figure 10.3.

Wage Discrimination

Many firms practice wage discrimination within selected occupations. When wage discrimination is practiced, two conditions usually exist. (1) Each worker is paid a wage sufficient to keep him from actively seeking employment elsewhere—it is the minimum alternative cost wage. This wage is normally less than the employer would pay rather than to risk losing the employee. (2) The wage each person receives is known only to himself. The trick, of course, is to keep employees from sharing wage information with one another. This trick can be accomplished in at least one of two ways. One way is that the employee is led to believe that he is being paid what he is worth. To be paid a smaller sum than someone else, therefore, carries with it the implication that the lower-paid employee is inferior to the high-paid employee. Vanity might easily persuade an employee to keep his wage a secret. If he believes himself to be less valuable than his wage indicates, he is not likely to publicize this fact. If he feels he is paid more than others, out of consideration for the feelings of others, he may not wish to talk about his income if in so doing he believes he will make them feel inferior.

The second method is to develop a code of ethics in which it is considered most improper to divulge one's earnings. This code is especially strong among universities. A one-time colleague revealed that at the ivy league college where he teaches, such a code exists. By chance, he discovered that at his rank of full professor he was making less than recently employed assistant professors. The Department of Economics, in which he taught, then began to share salary information so that it was no longer possible to discriminate within the department. Nevertheless, other departments

---

[23] Let $W = \text{ALC} = a + bL$. Then $\text{TLC} = W \times L = aL + bL^2$; $\text{MLC} = d(\text{TLC})/dL = a + 2bL = a + BL$ where $a = $ constant, $b = $ slope of ALC, and $B = $ slope of MLC $= 2b$.

continued to follow the traditional code, and the practice of the Economics Department is regarded as alien. As a result, the Economics Department has improved its salary position relative to the university as a whole, according to the American Association of University Professors survey.

When wage discrimination is practiced on an individual basis, it is called first degree discrimination. In such a situation, the incremental cost of a marginal employee is that employee's wage. Thus, marginal labor cost equals average labor cost, and the curves corresponding to the two types of costs are coincidental. If a firm can successfully practice first degree wage discrimination, it can reduce its total labor costs. In Figure 10.3, if discrimination is not practiced, total labor cost is $0WRL_1$ or $0aSL_1$. When discrimination is practiced, total labor cost is $0aRL_1$, since the sum of marginal labor cost (now equal to ALC) is total labor cost. Savings in labor costs amount to WaR.

Discussion Questions

1. Because the income of the husband affects inversely the labor-force participation of the wife, is this sufficient reason to argue that the income of the wife will affect inversely the labor-force participation of the husband? Explain.
2. If the family is the appropriate unit for measuring labor-supply, why may not an aggregation of individual labor-supply functions not reveal the true total labor-supply function?
3. What are the difficulties of measuring the true size of the labor force during a recession? During a boom?
4. Why do labor-force participation rates among all groups in the population tend to increase during a major war?
5. What are the underlying bases for the trend of labor-force participation rates for Whites and Blacks to move toward common percentages? Does this imply that the labor market is becoming more competitive? Explain.
6. How can a small textile mill be a monopsonist in a highly competitive industry? Why might a large, oligopolistic manufacturer operate in a highly competitive labor market?
7. What are the forces at work in the United States making for increased labor-force mobility? For decreased labor mobility? Which set of forces is stronger? Why?
8. For many years during the 1960s, highly trained mathematicians, statisticians, and physicists enjoyed higher salaries than comparably educated professionals. Is this premium salary likely to continue through the 1970s? Explain. Will physicians continue to receive larger incomes

in the next decade than other comparably trained professionals? Defend your answer.

9. Why does first degree wage discrimination lead to reduced labor cost? Would this be true also for third degree wage discrimination? Explain.

10. Can wage discrimination be defended on economic grounds? If so, will this exempt the employer from the Equal Wage Law?

11

The Demand for Labor

The demand for a factor of production, as the Austrians first noted, is derived from the demand for the product it produces. The demand for labor as a factor of production is therefore a derived demand and is expressed in terms of variations in the quantity which the employer is willing to hire as the wage, the price of labor, is varied. The quantity of a given type of labor which will be employed by a firm is related to the output of the firm by the production function, and the output can be sold at prices determined by the demand for the product. In this chapter we shall first develop a diagrammatic analysis of the production function and show how a profit maximizer determines his demand for labor first when all factor inputs can be varied and then when only labor can be varied. In later chapters, we shall show how imperfections in product markets and/or factor markets can affect the demand for an employment of labor, and we shall examine the concepts of exploitation in relation to these imperfections. Of special importance is the impact of the union on the labor market. Technological change can also produce changes in factor demand, and the nature of inventions will be analyzed in order to explain these effects on demand.

Two-Variable Analysis of the Production Function

A production function which relates two types of inputs to output can be represented graphically by means of isoquants. Assume that labor L and capital C are the two types of inputs. A given combination of inputs yields a given quantity of output. Assume that combinations of inputs and the resulting outputs can be varied continuously, which implies that inputs and

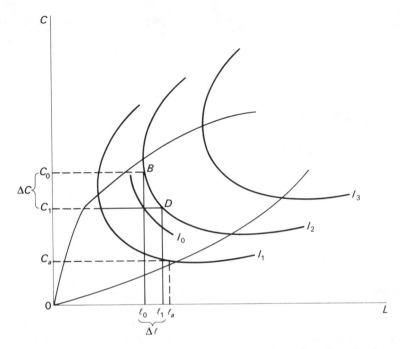

FIGURE 11.1. An isoquant map and the economic region of production.

outputs are infinitesimally divisible. Figure 11.1 represents a map of isoquants, where each isoquant I_i represents a given quantity of output. Each point, such as A, along an isoquant identifies the amounts of labor $0l_A$ and capital $0c_A$ required to produce the quantity of output represented by the isoquant. Since there is an infinite number of points along each isoquant, there is an infinite number of input combinations which yield the same output.[1]

---

[1] These isoquants can be visualized as the contour lines of a three-dimensional production surface. The perspective is one of looking directly down onto the surface, and each isoquant signifies the level or height of the surface. Ordinarily, the surface rises so that isoquants which lie above and to the right of other isoquants, i.e., in a northeastern direction, represent greater quantities of output. The map of isoquants is drawn so that discrete quantities of output are represented, and differences in quantities are shown by the distances between the isoquants. If the discrete isoquants whose quantity differences are constant get closer and closer together as we move in a northeastern direction along a vector drawn through the origin, this represents a perspective which implies that the slope of the surface is rising at an increasing rate. A scalar increase in the amounts of labor and capital, combined in the fixed proportions given by the slope of the vector, yields proportionately greater increases in output, and thus a surface with an increasing slope represents increasing returns to scale. An isoquant map thus described represents a production function yielding increasing returns to scale (homogeneous of degree greater than one).

Constant returns to scale can be represented by isoquants, differing by a constant amount, which lie at equidistant points along a vector drawn from the origin, and decreasing returns to scale can be shown by isoquants representing constant increases in output which have increasingly greater distances from one to the other as movement occurs up and to the right along the vector.[1a] Equal increments in output are represented for increasing returns to scale by points along a vector which lie closer and closer together.

The slope of an isoquant has been called by several names: the technical rate of substitution, the marginal rate of substitution, and the marginal rate of technical substitution. Any one is appropriate, but the marginal rate of technical substitution will be used in this book for consistency and we shall symbolize it by the letter S. The slope is negative, and is given by dc/dl. Holding labor constant at l_0, in Figure 11.1, a decrease in capital $(-\Delta c)$ from c_0 to c_1 reduces output $(I_0 - I_2 = -\Delta Q)$ and the decrease in output per unit decrease in capital is given by $\Delta Q_0/\Delta c_0$, which in discrete terms is the marginal product of capital $(\overline{MP}_C)$. Similarly, an increase in L from l_0 to l_1, holding capital constant at c_1, returns output to its original amount on I_2. The increase in output per unit increase in labor is given by $\Delta Q_0/\Delta l_0$, or the discrete marginal product of labor $(\overline{MP}_L)$. Now an approximation of the slope of I_2 between points B and D is given by the ratio $(\Delta c_0/\Delta l_0)$. Since $\Delta Q_0 = \overline{MP}_C \times \Delta c_0 = \overline{MP}_L \times \Delta l_0$, therefore, $\Delta c/\Delta l = MP_L/MP_C$. If we take the limit of the ratio as l_1 goes to l_0,

$$\lim_{l_1 \to l_0} \left(-\frac{\Delta c_0}{\Delta l_0} \right) = \frac{-dc}{dl} = \frac{-MP_L}{MP_C}; \tag{11.1}$$

the slope of I_2 at B is therefore $-dc/dl$ which equals the ratio at a point of the marginal product of labor to the marginal product of capital. Expressed as the marginal rate of technical substitution of labor for capital,

$$S_{LC} = \frac{-dc}{dl} = \frac{MP_L}{MP_C} \tag{11.2}$$

In other words, S_{LC} is the amount of capital which can be replaced by substituting one unit of labor for that capital without either increasing or reducing output. If we let B be any point on any isoquant, Equation (11.2) is generalized.

Isoquant curves may have a positive slope, but combinations of inputs at points where $dc/dl > 0$ are not within the economic range of production. In Figure 11.2, curve T_1 is a locus of points at which the S_{LC} of each isoquant

[1a] The slope of the production surface representing decreasing returns to scale consequently diminishes as input quantities are increased by some scalar multiple.

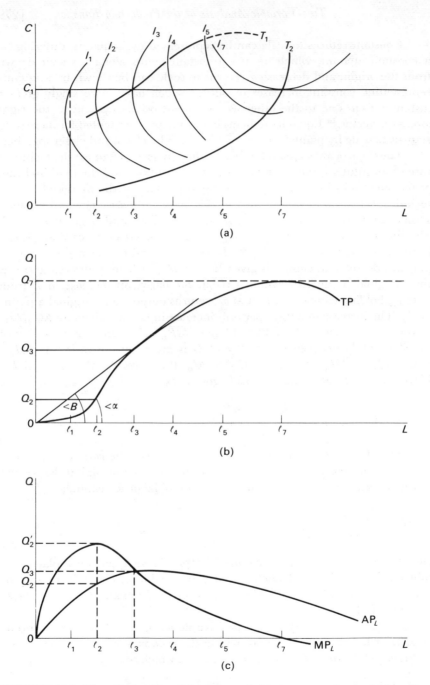

FIGURE 11.2. The relationship of the (b) total, (c) average and marginal product curve to an (a) isoquant map.

becomes infinitely large, i.e., $dc/dl = -\infty$. At points on an isoquant above and to the right of T_1, the S is greater than zero; the slope is positive. This means that if labor is increased, so also must capital or else total product will decline. If the marginal product of labor is positive and labor is increased without an increase in capital, total product must increase unless the marginal product of capital, given labor, is negative. If the marginal product of capital is negative, a decrease in capital, given labor, will increase total product, and we can see in Figure 11.2 that this occurs. An increase in labor can result in no change in product only if the positive marginal product of labor is offset by the negative marginal product associated with an increase in capital. Similarly T_2 is a locus of points at which the S_{LC} is zero— $dc/dl = 0$. If a combination of labor and capital is represented by a point on an isoquant to the right and below T_2, the S_{LC} is positive. A decrease in the amount of labor used must also be accompanied by a decrease in the quantity of capital used. By similar reasoning, we can show that the marginal product of labor must be negative, given capital, if the marginal product of capital is positive.

If in Figure 11.2(a) we fix capital at $0c_1$ and allow labor to increase, total product increases along the path indicated by TP in Figure 11.2(b). The slope of the total product curve is dQ/dl, or the marginal product of labor. The marginal product of labor is plotted in Figure 11.2(c). This slope is a maximum when the amount of labor is $0l_2$, indicated in Figure 11.2(b) by the angle α, and in Figure 11.2(c) we see that the marginal product of labor increases as labor is added up to $0l_2$. The average product of labor is defined as TP/$0l$, and this is indicated by the angle B in Figure 11.2(b). The angle is formed by drawing a vector through the origin to a point on the total product curve corresponding with a given quantity of labor— $\angle B = 0Q_3/0l_3$. It can be seen that at $0l_3$, the average product and the angle of the vector are at maximum, and this vector is also tangent to the total product curve at $0l_3$ and $0Q_3$. Thus, average product and marginal product are equal when $0l_3$ units of labor are used with c_1 units of capital. It can also be seen that any vector drawn from the origin to the total product curve at a point corresponding to an amount of labor less than $0l_3$ has a slope less than the slope of the total product curve at that point. This means that MP_L exceeds AP_L when labor used is less than $0l_3$. In Figure 11.2(c), we see that MP_L rises more rapidly than AP_L, reaches a maximum at $0l_2$, and AP_L reaches a maximum at $0l_3$, therefore, MP_L declines to equal AP_L at $0l_3$. The most northeasterly isoquant is reached at $0l_7$ in Figure 11.2(a); this is shown in Figure 11.2(b) with TP at a maximum, and in Figure 11.2(c) with MP_L equal to zero. Since TP is not zero at $0l_7$, then AP_L cannot be zero, and therefore in Figure 11.2(c) MP_L declines more rapidly than AP_L from $0l_3$ and beyond.

The Stages of Production

The three stages of production can be seen in Figure 11.2(c). Stage I, which is increasing average returns, occurs up to $0l_3$. In this stage marginal product exceeds average product. If in real terms labor is paid its marginal product, the total real wage payment $0Q_2'R'l_2$ will exceed the total product $0Q_2Rl_2$, and capital earns a negative return. This is consistent with our knowledge from Figure 11.2(a) that the marginal product of capital is negative. In stage II, from $0l_3$ to $0l_7$, both average and marginal product are diminishing but remain greater than zero. Except at the limits of this range, the marginal product both of capital and of labor is positive. In stage III, beyond $0l_7$, the marginal product of labor is negative. From Figure 11.2(b), it can be seen that a rational employer will not use a quantity of a factor whose marginal product is negative, because this means that total product is decreasing if that factor is variable. An economic input with scarcity value has a monetary opportunity cost, and the same output can be achieved with a smaller quantity of the variable input. Therefore, the smaller quantity of the input will be used, since, given the output, profits are maximized by minimizing costs. Stage III for labor is analogous to stage I for capital, for the marginal product of labor is negative in the former and the marginal product of capital is negative in the latter. If production is uneconomic in stage III because labor's MP is less than zero, so also must stage I be uneconomic. This leaves stage II as the only economic range of output. (This fact is used in Appendix B).

Since c_1 in Figure 11.2(a) was arbitrarily chosen, our analysis is general for the production map. It should now be obvious why combinations lying on or above isocline T_1 and lying on or below isocline T_2 are irrelevant for economic analysis, even though they may exist. In the remainder of this chapter, therefore, we shall deal only with maps whose isoquants are convex from below and whose S is negative.

Although we have derived the three stages of production in Figure 11.2, it is not necessary for stage I to exist. It depends on the production function. If diminishing marginal returns commence whenever any positive quantity of a variable input is used, stage I will not occur. Given capital, as equal increments of output are produced—shown by a horizontal line drawn from the given amount of the capital parallel to the labor axis—increasing quantities of labor are required to produce these increments. Isoquants representing equal increments of output cut the horizontal axis at increasing distances as we move from left to right. For example, in Figure 11.2(a), this is analogous to having the origin at $0l_3$ and $l_3l_4 < l_4l_5$ where $(I_4 - I_3) = (I_5 - I_4) = (I_7 - I_5)$.

From the preceding analysis, it can be seen that the short run, in which the quantities of some factors are fixed while the others are variable, can easily be represented. Variations in short-run production can be measured as the nonfixed inputs, here represented by labor, are varied, and from this variation, estimates of average and marginal product can be derived. This was essentially the method used by Marshall in his partial equilibrium analysis. Long-run production, in which all factors can be varied, is represented by the production map.

Isorevenue Curves

Isorevenue curves can easily be derived from the demand function which relates a range of quantities which can be sold by a firm at their respective prices. If the firm sells in a perfectly competitive market, each isoquant is changed into an isorevenue curve by multiplying the quantity of output which the isoquant represents by the market-determined constant price. Thus, an isorevenue map of a perfectly competitive firm contains individual curves of the same shape and relative position as the isoquants of the production map. If the firm sells in an imperfectly competitive market in which the demand for a product is normal, that is, price and quantity are inversely related, the shape of each isorevenue curve is unaltered but its relative position changes.[2] If price falls linearly with increasing quantity sold, the numerical value of price elasticity approaches 1. This means that total revenue approaches a maximum with increasing quantity of sales. Now if the range of output represented by the production map includes the quantity associated with unitary elasticity, there is a maximum value to which the isorevenue curves will tend. As movement occurs to the right, isorevenue curves corresponding to isoquants of equal increments lie closer and closer together in revenue terms until eventually an isorevenue curve of maximum value is achieved. The difference in revenue terms between isoquants is less and less along a vector drawn through the origin. This implies that there is a revenue limit to the range of combinations of inputs for producing output. Isorevenue curves R_i corresponding to isoquant curves I_i can be seen in Figure 11.3, parts (b) and (a), respectively. Given the linear demand function $P = 110 - 0.1Q$, the maximum revenue

---

[2] The slope of each isorevenue curve, given a combination of capital and labor, is equal to the marginal rate of technical substitution for that combination. The slope of an isorevenue curve is the ratio of the marginal revenue product of labor to the marginal revenue product of capital.

$$\frac{MRP_L}{MRP_C} = \frac{MR \times MP_L}{MR \times MP_C} = \frac{MP_L}{MP_C} = S_{LC}$$

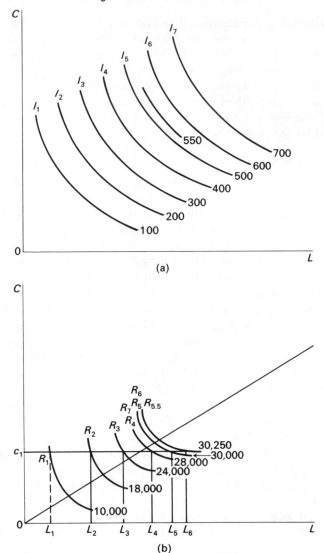

FIGURE 11.3 (a) and (b).

possible is $30,250 and the limit of combinations of inputs of labor and capital is found to lie along an isoquant between I_5 and I_6, representing an output of 550.[3]

[3] $TR = 110Q - 0.1Q^2$; $MR = 110 - 0.2Q$. Setting $MR = 0$, TR is a maximum at $Q = 550$. At $Q = 550$, TR is $30,250.

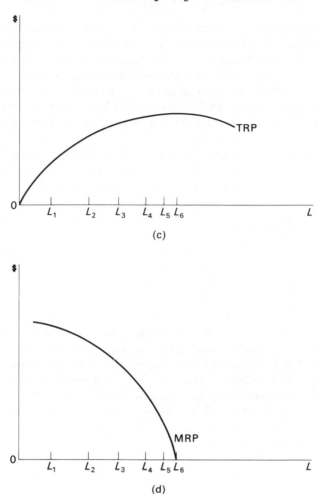

(c)

(d)

FIGURE 11.3. (b) The isorevenue map corresponding to (a) the isoquant curves, and (b) its relation to (c) total and (d) marginal revenue product curves.

Just as the marginal physical product can be derived from production maps (as in Figure 11.2), when capital is held constant and the quantity of labor is allowed to vary, so also can marginal revenue product curves be similarly derived. After diminishing returns have been reached, isorevenue curves under perfect competition will lie closer and closer together along a line perpendicular to the capital axis as labor is increased unit by unit, and the marginal revenue product consequently decreases. If imperfect competition in the product market prevails, declining elasticity of demand will assure that equidistant isorevenue curves represent declining differences in revenue as labor is increased unit by unit. Thus, the marginal revenue product of labor under imperfect competition declines not only because of diminishing marginal returns but also because total revenue increases at a decreasing rate. As the quantity of output is increased from using more and more of labor [see Figures 11.3(c) and 11.3(d)], it is then sold at declining prices. The MRP_L can be determined, given any quantity of capital, in this manner.

If factor prices are given, as they would be if a firm buys inputs in a perfectly competitive market, then the combinations of capital (C) and labor (L) which it is possible to use with a given outlay of money (TO) is determined by the following linear relation:

$$P_C \cdot C + P_L \cdot L = \text{TO} \tag{11.3}$$

For each outlay, the combinations form the points of an isocost curve whose slope is

$$-\frac{C}{L} = \frac{P_L}{P_C}, \tag{11.4}$$

given by the intersection of the isocost curve with, respectively, the capital axis and the labor axis.[4] A family of isocost curves, each of which is parallel to the others and which represents different expenditure outlays, can be constructed. Total outlay increases as movement occurs in a northeastern direction. The tangency of a given isocost curve with the highest possible isorevenue curve, or alternatively—which amounts to the same thing—the tangency of a given isorevenue curve with the lowest possible isocost curve, maximizes profits. At this point of tangency, the marginal rate of technical substitution, which is equal to the ratio of the marginal revenue product of labor to that of capital, is also equal to the ratio of the marginal cost of labor to that of capital.

$$S = \frac{MRP_L}{MRP_C} = \frac{P_L}{P_C} = \frac{MC_L}{MC_C}. \tag{11.5}$$

This is shown in Figure 11.4. The isocost line $c_n l_n$ is tangent to isorevenue curve R_3 at point A where c_0 of capital and l_0 of labor is utilized under

----

[4] At the isocost's intersection of the capital axis, $L = 0$ and $\text{TO} = P_C \cdot C$. Similarly, at the intersection of the labor axis, $C = O$ and $\text{TO} = P_L \cdot L$. So

$$C = \frac{\text{TO}}{P_C} \quad \text{and} \quad -\frac{C}{L} = \frac{\text{TO}/P_C}{\text{TO}/P_L} = \frac{P_L}{\text{TO}} \times \frac{\text{TO}}{P_C} = \frac{P_L}{P_C}.$$

Alternatively, $d\text{TO} = P_C dC + P_L dL = 0$. Hence, $-dC/dL = P_L/P_C$. Since the isocost curve is linear and negatively sloped, $dC/dL = -C/L$.

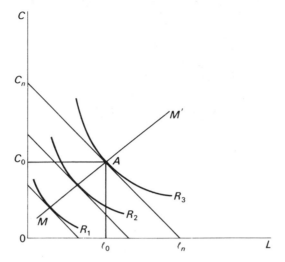

FIGURE 11.4. The minimum-cost isocline curve.

minimum cost and maximum profit conditions, given R_3. The locus of minimum cost–maximum profit points is given by the isocline MM', where each point along the isocline corresponds to a given revenue–cost combination. Point A may or may not represent the equilibrium combination of labor and capital. This depends upon whether point A yields a greater total profit than any other point along isocline MM'. If it does not, then some other point represents the equilibrium combination. If the monetary values of R_i and $c_i l_i$ are known, the equilibrium point can be easily determined.

Changes in the Wage Rate

A change in the price of labor alters the slope of the family of isocost lines, since the intersection of the labor axis is correspondingly affected. If the price of labor is increased, for each given expenditure less labor can be purchased. The opposite is true when the wage rate falls. Thus, the slope of the isocost curve which is C_i/L_i when C_i and L_i represent the intersection points of their respective axes, changes inversely with the ratio of factor prices;

$$\frac{C_i}{L_i} = -\frac{P_L}{P_C} \tag{11.6}$$

In Figure 11.5 as wages are decreased, the slope of the isocost curve, equal in amount to $C_0 P_C$, declines from C_0/L_0 successively to C_0/L_3, while concurrently the ratio of the wage rate to the interest rate declines. It can

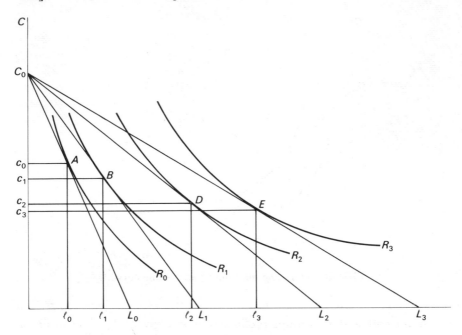

FIGURE 11.5. Deriving labor demand from an isorevenue map.

be seen that the quantity of labor which the firm is willing to employ increases from l_0 to l_3 as wages decline. If the firm were buying inputs and selling output competitively and if A were the equilibrium point when $W_0 = P_C \cdot C_0 / L_0$, then R_0 would equal $C_0 \cdot P_C$ and above normal profits would not be earned. A fall in wages from W_0 to W_1 would lead the firm to substitute labor for capital, and $l_0 l_1$ more labor and $c_0 c_1$ less capital would be used at the new equilibrium point B. Since competitive price is a constant, therefore, the new combination of labor and capital must have increased output, lowering average total cost and increasing profit. Thus, at B, above-normal profits would be earned. This, of course, is not a long-run equilibrium position since the excess profits attract new firms into the industry and industry price falls.

Each isorevenue curve in the map would correspondingly shift to the left as price declines, the magnitude of the shift depending upon the degree of elasticity of industry demand. The long-run equilibrium point will lie on an isorevenue curve which may lie to the left or right of R_0 in Figure 11.5, depending upon the magnitude of the price fall. In any event, since the new isorevenue curve will lie to the left of the original R_1, the expenditure will therefore decrease and the isocost curve will be parallel but to the left of

$C_0 L_1$. If the new isorevenue curve on which the equilibrium falls lies sufficiently to the left of R_0, it is possible that the long-run effects of a wage decrease might also decrease the amount of labor used by the firm. Although such a result is not probable, it does indicate the difficulties in deriving a long-run demand curve for a factor of production under conditions of pure competition. (See Appendix B).

A Monopolist's Demand for Labor

The difficulties in deriving a pure monopolist's long-run demand for labor are not so severe, because the isorevenue map is determined for all relevant price–quantity relationships. Since entry is impossible, a decline in the price of labor which increases monopoly profits cannot attract new firms into the industry. To the extent that the long-run marginal cost curve of the monopolist shifts to the right, output will increase and price will decline, given long-run demand for the product. On the isorevenue–isocost map a decline in the price of labor leads to a decline in the slope of each isocost curve in the family of isocost curves, and the maximum profit isocline (MM' in Figure 11.4) shifts to the right. This is so because points of tangency occur on each isorevenue curve to the right of the original tangency points. This assures that the monopolist long-run demand curve for labor is negatively sloped.

Determinants of the Elasticity of Labor Demand

If the slopes of the isorevenue curve were sufficiently steep (because of the nature of the production function), if industry product demand were sufficiently inelastic, if the supply of capital were sufficiently inelastic, and if labor costs were a significant part of total cost, then it would be possible for wages and the employment of labor to vary positively in the long run. The conditions determining the elasticity of the derived demand for a factor were first set forth by Marshall, restated by Pigou, and given a mathematical formulation by Hicks.[5] These four propositions are as follows:

I. The demand for labor is more elastic the more easily technology permits another factor to be substituted for labor.
II. The demand for labor is more elastic the greater the elasticity of demand for the product produced by labor.

[5] Alfred Marshall, *Principles of Economics*, 8th ed. (Macmillan Co., 1920), Book V, Chapter VI; A. C. Pigou, *Economics of Welfare*, 4th ed. (Macmillan Co., 1962), Book IV, Chapter V; John R. Hicks, *The Theory of Wages*, 2nd ed. (Macmillan Co., 1963), pp. 241–246. For a version of Hicks' mathematical proof of these properties under competition and constant returns to scale, see George J. Stigler, *The Theory of Price*, 3rd ed. (Macmillan Co., 1966), pp. 242–244, 346–347.

III. The demand for labor is more elastic the greater the elasticity of supply of cooperating factors.

IV. The demand for labor is more elastic the greater the ratio of labor cost to total cost.

The converse also holds for the degree of inelasticity of labor demand. In Appendix A these propositions are explained more fully by means of isoquant analysis.

Empirical Evidence of the Negatively Sloped Demand for Labor

Professors Reynolds and Gregory have attempted empirically to determine if the demand for labor has a negative slope.[6] Because the unemployment rates in Puerto Rico have been very high (over 10%), it was believed that minimum wages, established quasi-legislatively by industry boards, were in excess of the market-clearing wage. Changes in these board-determined wages, therefore, are not believed to be owing primarily to market-demand forces, but rather to political-welfare conditions. Hence, employment changes are likely to be a result of the wage changes, primarily. The authors assumed that linear homogeneous production functions existed in the industries under study, and by observing wage–employment levels for two sets of industries, one consisting of 37 industries in the period 1949–1954 and the other of 50 industries in the 1954–1958 period, they sought to measure the average elasticities of the wage–employment changes of each set of industries. If significantly negative, these elasticity coefficients, they concluded, would support their hypothesis of negatively sloped demand curves.

The authors assume that output varies proportionately with labor inputs; that is, $Q_2/Q_i = N_2/N_i = \alpha$, where Q_i represents output, measured in real value added and N_i represents the respective employment of labor, both when wage W_i applies. This assumption follows from the linear, homogeneous production function if capital is assumed to remain constant.[7] Because observed wage–employment combinations at different times need not lie on the same demand curve, the authors adjusted employment to

---

[6] Lloyd L. Reynolds and Peter Gregory, *Wages, Productivity, and Industrialization in Puerto Rico* (Homewood: R. D. Irwin, Inc., 1965), pp. 41–103. Also see Appendix B.

[7] A simple Cobb–Douglas production function can illustrate this:

$$Q_1 = aN_1^b C^d; \quad Q_2 = aN_2^b C^d, \qquad \text{where} \quad b + d = 1 \text{ and } C^d = \text{constant.}$$

Hence

$$Q_2/Q_1 = \frac{aN_2^b C^d}{aN_1^b C^d} = \frac{N_2^b}{N_1^b} = \left(\frac{N_2}{N_1}\right)^b.$$

determine the amount of labor that would have been employed, under given demand conditions, if the two observed wages had been in effect.

To illustrate (see Figure 11.6):

Observations		Demand A		
Employment	Wages	Employment	Wage	Comment
N_{1A}	W_1	N_{1A}	W_1	Observed
N_{2B}	W_2	$N_{2A} = (1/\alpha)N_{2B}$	W_2	Calculated[a]
		Demand B		
		$N_{1B} = \alpha N_{1A}$	W_1	Calculated[a]
		N_{2B}	W_2	Observed

[a] $Q_2/Q_1 = N_{2A}/N_{2B} = N_{1A}/N_{1B} = 1/\alpha$.

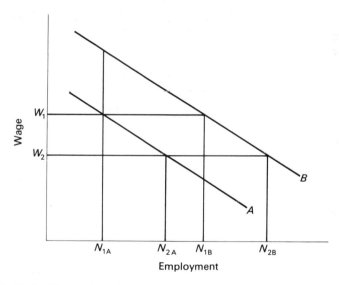

FIGURE 11.6. Observed and calculated wage–employment changes along two labor-demand curves.

From either Demand A or Demand B, observations for each industry were made and a corresponding linear regression equation whose slope parameter constituted an average elasticity coefficient was estimated. Because for both sets of industries the slope coefficient was significantly negative, the authors concluded that this supported the negatively sloped demand curve hypothesis.

This conclusion, however, may be in error. Their assumption of a linear homogeneous production function biased their observations in favor of their conclusion, for it is a mathematical property of such functions that the marginal productivity curve for an input has a negative slope.[8]

Since the authors have assumed that this condition holds in the function to which their empirical data were fitted, their conclusion is trivial. It has not been established that the demand for labor in Puerto Rico is negatively related to the wage rate.

Appendix A: An Analysis of the Determinants of Labor Demand Elasticity

The ease with which labor and another factor can be substituted one for the other is reflected in the rate of change of the slope of the isoquant S. The S is given by $-dC/dL = \text{MP}_L/\text{MP}_C = l_L/l_C$. As a point on the isoquant in Figure 11.7 moves from B to A, the slope becomes greater. This is $d(S_{AB})$, as B goes to A. The relative change in the slope is given by dS_{AB}/S_B. At B, the ratio of capital to labor is less than at A—i.e., $C_B/L_B < C_A/L_A$. As substitution of capital for labor occurs as we move from B to A, not only

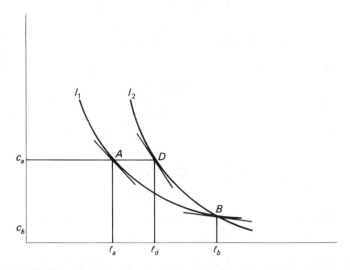

FIGURE 11.7. The elasticity of substitution is related to the slope of the isoquant curve.

[8] To show this, all we need to demonstrate is that $\partial^2 Q/\partial L^2 < 0$. Given $Q = aN^bC^{1-b}$, then $\partial^2 Q/\partial N^2 = [(b^2 - b)/N]Q$. Since $b < 1$, then $\partial^2 Q/\partial N^2 < 0$. In general for linear, homogeneous functions, $\partial^2 Q/\partial N^2 = -(C/N)\,\partial^2 Q/\partial N\,\partial C$, where $\partial^2 Q/\partial N\,\partial C > 0$, *normally*.

does this ratio increase but it increases at an increasing rate. The change in the input ratios is given by $d(C/L)_{AB}$ and the relative change is given by $[d(C/L)_{AB}]/(C/L)_B$ as B goes to A. To measure the relative change in the input ratios as a result of a relative change in S, the concept of the elasticity of substitution, E_s, has been developed.

$$E_s = \left(\frac{d(C/L)}{C/L}\right) \bigg| \left(\frac{dS}{S}\right) \tag{11.7}$$

The elasticity of substitution is also a measure of the ease by which labor can be substituted for capital and vice versa.[9] If the slope of the isoquant

---

[9] The elasticity of substitution is identical for the substitution of labor for capital and vice versa. To see this, consider the following:
Since

$$S = -\frac{dC}{dL} = \frac{f_L}{f_C} \quad \text{where } f_L = \frac{\partial Q}{\partial L} = \text{MP}_L \quad \text{and} \quad f_C = \frac{\partial Q}{\partial C} = \text{MP}_C,$$

therefore,

$$dC = -\frac{f_L}{f_C} \times dL = -SdL.$$

$$d(S) = \frac{\partial S}{\partial L} dL + \frac{\partial S}{\partial C} dC = \left(\frac{\partial S}{\partial L} - \frac{\partial S}{\partial C} S\right) dL \tag{i}$$

and

$$d\left(\frac{C}{L}\right) = \frac{L dC - C dL}{L^2} = -\frac{SL + C}{L^2} dL. \tag{ii}$$

Thus,

$$E_s = \frac{d(C/L) \cdot L/C}{dS/S} = \frac{S[-\{(SL+C)/L^2\} dL \cdot L/C]}{[(\partial S/\partial L) - (\partial S/\partial C)S] dL} = \frac{S}{LC}\left[\frac{-(C + LS)}{(\partial S/\partial L) - (\partial S/\partial C)S}\right] \tag{iii}$$

Since

$$\frac{\partial S}{\partial L} = \frac{f_{LL}f_C - f_{LC}f_L}{f_C^2}$$

$$\frac{\partial S}{\partial C} = \frac{f_{LC}f_C - f_{CC}f_L}{f_C^2} \tag{iv}$$

Therefore,

$$E_s = \frac{S}{LC}\left(\frac{-(C + LS)}{(f_{LL}f_C - f_{LC}f_L) - S(f_{LC}f_C - f_{CC}f_L)}\right) \cdot f_C^2$$

$$= -\frac{f_L f_C[C f_C + L f_L]}{L \cdot C[f_{LL}f_C^2 - 2f_{LC}f_L f_C + f_{CC}f_L^2]} \tag{v}$$

If we had used $d(L/C)$ and the differential dL, we would have obtained the same result.

increases more rapidly than from B to A, say, as from B to D, then $dS_{BD} >$ dS_{BA}, but this means that $d(C/L)_{BA} > d(C/L)_{BD}$ so that the relative change in inputs is smaller from points B to A than from point B to D. Therefore, the elasticity of substitution is less the steeper the isoquant between any two quantities of capital. The less the elasticity of substitution, the less labor will be substituted for capital. If I_1 is the appropriate isoquant, $l_A l_B$ amount of labor will be substituted for a reduction in capital of $c_A c_B$ amount, but if I_2 is relevant, then only $l_D l_B$ amount of labor is substituted.

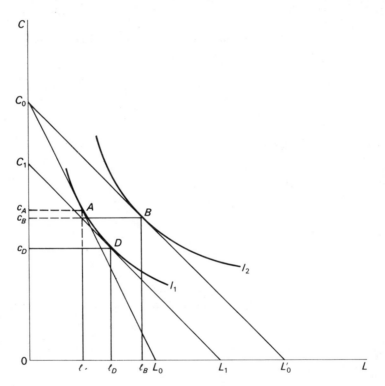

FIGURE 11.8. The relationship between the elasticity of substitution and changes in the wage rate.

To see the importance of the elasticity of substitution, consider in Figure 11.8 a decline in the wage rate of labor so that the slope of the isocost curve CL is less. The minimum cost point moves from A to B as output increases but with costs remaining constant. Labor in the amount of $l_A l_B$ is substituted for capital in the amount of $c_A c_B$. If the firm had not wished to increase output, however, with the lower price of labor it could produce the I_1 quantity at less cost, represented by isocost C_1L_1 which is parallel to C_0L_0'. Now C_1L_1 is tangent to I_1 at D, and the lower price of labor has led to a substitution of labor for capital. The substitution effect is measured by $l_A l_D$. If the average slope of I_1 had been less, and therefore the average elasticity of substitution had been greater, between A and D, more labor would have been substituted for capital, and the elasticity of the demand for labor would have been greater. The same relative wage change would have resulted in a greater relative use of labor.

Since isoquant curves cannot intersect, the greater (less) is the slope of any one of a family of such curves at a given quantity of either labor or capital, the more (less) steep must the slope of all of the other curves in the family be at the same labor or capital quantity.

The ability to produce the same output at lower cost has freed some of the monetary resources of the employer. With these excess resources, if he chooses to produce a larger output, he can employ either more of labor, more of capital, or more of both. Thus, a decline in the wage of labor results in a cost effect in the use of labor, which is measured by $l_D l_B$. The cost effect in the use of capital is given by $c_D c_B$. It can be seen in Figure 11.8 that if the employer chooses to increase output to I_2, the extra monetary resources will be allocated so that both more labor and capital will be used than if output had remained at I_1. The cost effect $l_D l_B$ would have been greater if the isoquants had a smaller slope at c_B amount of capital, or if the elasticity of substitution of labor for capital had increased at a greater rate as movement occurred to the right on each isoquant. Thus, the greater the increase in elasticity of substitution as labor is substituted for capital, the greater is both the substitution effect and the cost effect in the use of labor, and the greater is the relative use in the amount of labor when there is a given percentage change in the wage rate. This proves Proposition I.

The truth of Proposition II can be seen by referring again to an isorevenue map. A reduction in the wage rate reduces the slope of the family of isocost curves, and the new family of isocost curves will be tangent to isorevenue curves which lie to the right of the original points of tangency. The maximum profit isocline shifts to the right. The revenue difference between the new and the old point of tangency for an isocost curve of a given monetary amount will be greater, the greater the price elasticity of demand. As we have shown previously, except in the case of perfect elasticity of demand, the difference in revenue between isorevenue curves for given differences in quantity of product will be less and less as elasticity declines to unity. Thus, the new point of tangency will increase profits and revenue more or less as elasticity is more or less. Now the greater the increase in revenue and profits, the more willing will firms be to incur additional costs, and the greater will be the movement to the right along the new profit isocline. The greater the movement to the right along the new profit isocline, the greater the increase in the utilization of labor. Therefore, the greater the elasticity of product demand, the greater will be the increase in the utilization of labor from a given wage reduction.

In order to demonstrate the truth of Proposition III, we must modify our assumption of perfect competition in the factor market. If the firm is sufficiently large with respect to the capital market, different quantities of capital cannot be employed at a constant interest rate. To the extent that the firm is a monopsonist, increasing quantities of capital can be employed only at higher rates. The supply curve of capital, therefore, has a positive slope. The same may also be true for labor, but we are now interested in determining the effect of the supply elasticity of a factor cooperating with labor when wages are reduced. A less than perfect supply elasticity of capital is sufficient to make the isocost curve nonlinear.[10] To see this, let the supply curve of capital be given by the linear equation

$$i = a + bC \qquad (11.8)$$

An isocost curve of constant monetary amount K_i is expended on capital C or labor L, where the wage w of labor is treated as a constant.

$$K_i = iC + wL = aC + bC^2 + wL \qquad (11.9)$$

The total differential of the isocost curve is given by

$$dK_i = \frac{\partial K_i}{\partial C} dC + \frac{\partial K_i}{\partial L} dL = 0 \qquad (11.10)$$

or

$$\frac{dC}{dL} = \frac{-w}{a + 2bC} \qquad (11.11)$$

The slope of the isocost curve is given as the negative ratio of the marginal factor costs, and as C increases the slope becomes less negative and less steep. The opposite is true as C decreases. Thus, the isocost curve is concave from below.

If the wage rate is lowered, the slope of the isocost curve, at any given value of C—say, C_i—is less than at the higher wage rate, and this implies a rightward movement of K_i beginning with its original intersection of the

---

[10] Let K be some constant monetary sum which is expended on wages w for labor L, and on interest i on capital C, i.e., $K = wL + iC$. Both i and w are treated as constants. The total differential of K is: $dK = (\partial K/\partial L) dL + (\partial K/\partial C) dc$. Since $dK = 0$ along any isoquant, $dC/dL = -w/i =$ a constant. Thus the isocost curve represented by K is a straight line with a constant negative slope.

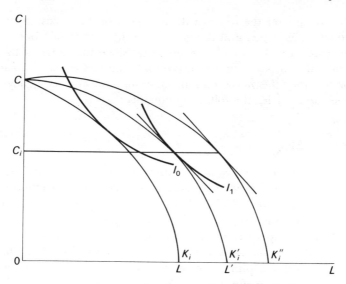

FIGURE 11.9. Concave isocost curves.

capital axis. This swing is illustrated in Figure 11.9. The elasticity of a linear supply curve is determined by the value of a in Equation (11.4),[11] where a is the supply price of capital if no capital is purchased by the firm. The greater the value of a with any given change in wages, the less will be the slope of the new isocost curve at any given value of C, and the greater will be its swing to the right. As the movement of the isocost curves to the right occurs, points of tangency to isorevenue curves occur which utilize greater quantities of labor. Therefore, the greater the elasticity of the supply

---

[11] This can be seen by the following: $a_0 > 0$, $a_1 = 0$, $a_2 < 0$,

$$e_s = + \frac{\Delta C}{\Delta i} \frac{i}{C}.$$

With supply curve C_0

$$e_s = \frac{i_0 R}{a_0 i_0} \cdot \frac{0 i_0}{i_0 R} = \frac{0 i_0}{a_0 i_0} > 1.$$

With C_1,

$$e_s = \frac{0 i_1}{a_1 i_1} = 1.$$

With C_2,

$$e_s = \frac{0 i_2}{a_2 i_2} < 1.$$

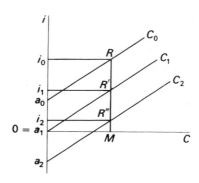

of capital, the greater the rightward movement of the isocost curve with a given reduction in wages, and the greater the utilization of labor.

The reason for this should be obvious. Since the slope of the isocost curve is now the (negative) ratio of the marginal factor costs instead of the factor price ratio, the maximum profit–minimum cost tangency (to the isorevenue curve) yields the following equality:

$$\frac{\mathrm{MRP}_L}{\mathrm{MRP}_C} = \frac{\mathrm{MC}_L}{\mathrm{MC}_C}. \tag{11.12}$$

Now the marginal cost of capital is greater, the greater the elasticity of supply—and, thus, the greater the value of a. A given reduction in wages lowers the marginal cost of labor, here treated as a parameter and equal to wages. The induced substitution of labor for capital lowers the expenditure on capital and reduces the marginal expenditure on capital by twice the price of capital. This increases the cost (output) effect by an amount equal to twice the price of capital (here given as $i = a + bC$). The augmented cost effect permits even more labor (and capital) to be purchased. Consequently, the greater is the elasticity of supply of capital, the greater will be the cost effect and the more labor it will be possible to employ.

If the supply curve of labor is also positively sloped, the slope of the isocost curve will depend not only upon the elasticity of supply of capital but upon the elasticity of supply of labor as well. The problem of estimating the effect on labor utilization is more difficult here, but it can be shown that the more elastic is the supply of capital relative to labor, the more will a given wage reduction result in an increase in the use of labor. Let the labor supply function be given by

$$W = \alpha + \beta L \tag{11.13}$$

so that

$$\frac{dC}{dL} = -\frac{\alpha + 2\beta L}{a + 2bc} \tag{11.11a}$$

It can be seen that a decline in wages, caused by an isoelastic increase in the supply of labor (a decline in β), will increase the utilization of labor, given b, if α is less and a is greater. This means that the slope of the new isocost curve will thereby be less, and the curve will swing more to the right.[12]

---

[12] There appears to be an ambiguity in the concept of elasticity of supply in the above analysis, where the firm is a monopsonistic buyer of both capital and labor. Can the student identify the "ambiguity" and explain its origin and nature?

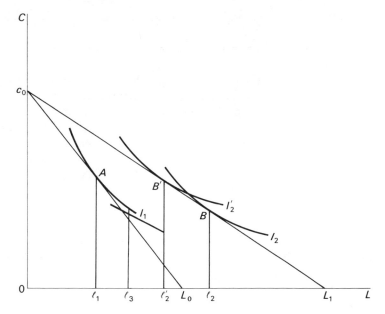

FIGURE 11.10. Changes in wage rates and the relation of labor to total costs.

Proposition IV—the demand for labor is more elastic the greater the ratio of labor cost to total cost—is illustrated in Figure 11.10. At a given wage and interest, and with an isoquant represented by I_1, the proportion of wages to total cost is given by $0l_1/0L_0$ when the isocost curve is C_0L_0.[13]

If wages are reduced so that the isocost curve of a given amount swings to the right, C_0L_1, the new minimum cost level of operations will use $0l_2'$ units of labor if I_2' is the relevant isoquant, or $0l_2$ units if I_2 is the appropriate isoquant. It is obvious that the share of labor cost to total cost is greater if I_2 is on the relevant isoquant map with I_1, since $0l_2'/0L_1 < 0l_2/0L_1$. Thus, the greater the new ratio of labor cost to total cost from a given wage reduction, the more elastic is the demand for labor. The substitution effect is given by l_1l_3 and the cost effect is l_3l_2' for I_2'; or l_3l_2 for I_2. The greater the cost effect, given the substitution effect, the greater will a given wage reduction increase the absolute and relative use of labor, and the greater will be the increase in the ratio of labor cost to total cost This holds for perfect competition if the isoquant map is replaced by an isorevenue map. Hicks, however, has shown that if the elasticity of substitution of inputs is

[13] $\mathrm{TLC/TC} = \dfrac{w \cdot 0l}{w \cdot 0L} = \dfrac{0l}{0L}$

greater than the elasticity of product demand, then this proposition will not be true [14]

Since the ratio of labor costs to total costs is greater at I_2 than at I_2', the elasticity of substitution from A to B on I_2 (Δ_2) is greater than that of A to B' on I_2' (Δ_2'). Since the cost effect is greater at I_2 for a wage decrease than at I_2', it can be shown that if the original wage rate had prevailed when the larger output was produced, then a reduction in output to I_1 would have reduced costs more from I_2 than from I_2'. Now as we have shown earlier, isorevenue curves, corresponding to isoquant curves of equal differences in output, get closer together in terms of revenue if product demand is less than perfectly elastic. It may be possible, if product demand has a sufficiently low elasticity and Δ is sufficiently large, to increase profits by reducing output when wages fall. If product demand is inelastic, revenue will rise, and the cost effect, from both lower wages and lower output, reduces costs. The greater is Δ the greater will be the cost effect, and the greater will be the reduction in output. If output is reduced sufficiently, even with the relatively greater substitution of labor for capital, less labor than was originally used may be employed.

Appendix B: The Labor Demand Curve When Labor is an Inferior Factor

We know that in the relevant range of production, stage II, the marginal product curve of a variable input is negatively sloped. Hence, the marginal revenue product curve, in either a perfectly or imperfectly competitive product market, must be negatively sloped. The price of the variable input varies inversely with the quantity demanded. Does this inverse relation hold, however, if multiple variable inputs are used?

Hicks and Samuelson have shown that the quantity demanded for an input varies inversely with its price, given either constant output or constant costs.[15] This is not true under all conditions if neither output nor costs are constrained. When more than one variable input is used, a change in the price of one of the inputs leads to a change in its use and may lead to a change in the quantity used of other variable inputs. As other variable inputs change, the input proportions may change which can cause the VMP curve of the specified input to shift. The actual demand curve for the input

---

[14] In perfect competition, the elasticity of product demand e_p is infinitely large, and therefore greater than the elasticity of substitution σ. If $\sigma > e_p$ then an increase in the relative labor cost will lower the elasticity of demand for labor. See J. R. Hicks, *op. cit.*, p. 245.

[15] John R. Hicks, *Value and Capital*, 2nd ed. (Oxford: Clarendon Press, 1953), pp. 319–323; P. A. Samuelson, *Foundations of Economic Analysis* (Cambridge: Harvard University Press, 1955), pp. 65, 73–74.

then will be the locus of points at which each possible price for the input is associated with its quantity on the relevant VMP curve.

Shifts in the VMP Curves

Factors in production always cooperate with one another in the sense that they utilize each other's properties in order to generate new utilities. However, a variety of combinations of factors is often possible in order to yield a particular product. If one factor may be used in place of a second factor in cooperation with a third factor, factors one and two are designated as substitutes. Factor one and factor two are each complementary to factor three. Another possibility is that factors one, two, or three may be neutral with respect to utilizing one another's properties. Hence, they are said to be independent.[16]. If the ratio of factors A and B changes, for example, through holding the quantities of A constant and allowing the quantity of B to vary, the factors are substitutes if the marginal product of A is increased (decreased) when the quantity of B is decreased (increased)—$f_{AB} < 0$; the factors are complements if the marginal product of A is decreased (increased) when the quantity of B is decreased (increased)—$f_{AB} > 0$; the factors are independent if the marginal product of A is unchanged when the quantity of B varies— $f_{AB} = 0$. The VMP curves of factors shift, therefore, in the manner in which their marginal products are affected as input ratios change.

Now, under certain circumstances, a change in the price of an input may lead to an increase in its use. The factor is designated as an inferior input and has a positively sloped demand curve. This is not the normal case, however, and it can be shown that a positively sloped demand curve requires that such a factor be a substitute to others. Assume that the product market is perfect, that two variable inputs (X_1, X_2) are used in combination with a fixed input $(\bar{X}_3)$, and that the production function $Q = f(X_1, X_2, \bar{X}_3)$ yields diminishing returns to scale. We have shown elsewhere that profits are maximized when factor inputs are used so that the value of their marginal products equal their factor price:

$$P \cdot f_i = w_i \tag{11.14}$$

where P = product price, f_i is the marginal product, and w_i is the competitive market price of the ith factor. The satisfaction of this condition also satisfies the cost minimization condition:

$$\frac{f_i}{f_j} = \frac{W_i}{W_j} \tag{11.15}$$

[16] If $Q = f(X_1, X_2, X_3)$, and $f_i > 0, f_{ii} < 0$, we define substitutable factors as $f_{ij} < 0$, complementary factors as $f_{ij} > 0$, and independent factors as $f_{ij} = 0$. See T. R. Saving, "Note on Factor Demand Elasticity," *Econometrica*, Vol. 31, No. 3 (July 1963), p. 556.

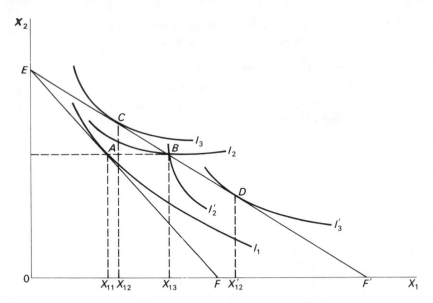

FIGURE 11.11. Effect of a wage rate change on different isoquant maps.

Therefore, as the ratio of input prices changes, the ratio of marginal products must change, and the ratio of inputs must change.

In Figures 11.11 and 11.12 are reproduced diagrams using isoquant and isocost analysis. Assume that point A in Figure 11.11 (X_{11}, X_{21}) is a profit maximizing, equilibrium point, with price ratio of F to E and costs reflected in isocost EF, and in Figure 11.12 let point A', (W_{11}, Q_{11}) represented on VMP_1. Points A and A' are consistent with respect to X_{11} and W_{11}. Now we permit W_{11} to decline to W_{12}, as shown in Figure 11.11 by a movement in the isocost line EF to EF'. The new minimum cost point may be at either point C or point D, depending upon the structure of the isoquant map.

If C holds when W_1 declines, VMP_1 shifts to the right, left, or remains stable as $f_{12} > 0, f_{12} < 0$, or $f_{12} = 0$. If $f_{12} > 0$, then VMP_2 lies to the right of VMP_1, and $Q_{12} > Q_{11}$ in Figure 11.12; this is consistent with $X_{12} > X_{11}$ in Figure 11.11. If $f_{12} = 0$, then no change in VMP_1 occurs, and $Q_{13} > Q_{11}$ is also consistent with Figure 11.11. However, if $f_{12} < 0$, then Q'_{12} may be greater or less than Q_{11}, depending upon how far VMP_1 shifts leftward. If VMP'_2 lies sufficiently to the left of VMP_1, $Q_{11} > Q'_{12}$ and a positively sloped demand curve, indicated by gg', may be formed if C were a profit maximizing point. Note that gg' depicts the relationship between the factor price and the quantity of the factor used when the factor is inferior.

If the factor is normal either dd' or VMP_1 depicts the demand curve for the factor; both are negatively sloped.

Next, assume that point D in Figure 11.11 is the new minimum cost point. Less of X_2 (see Figure 11.12) combines with a greater quantity of X_1. The VMP_1 moves to the left or to the right as $f_{12} > 0$ or $f_{12} < 0$. In order for factor demand to have a positive slope, Q_{12} must lie to the left of Q_{11}, which with less X_2 implies a decrease in output.[17] If $f_{12} > 0$, the demand curve will be positive.

A minimum cost condition in Figure 11.11 cannot be given by point B, since the tangency conditions for a minimum cost are not satisfied. However, as a point of reference B can be useful. Given B, the VMP curve in Figure 11.12 will not shift, since no change in X_2 occurs. If $f_{12} \geq 0$, VMP_1 is negatively sloped, as depicted. However, if $f_{12} < 0$, then VMP_1 will be positively sloped. The ratio X_2/X_1 falls as X_1 increases. Hence, units of X_1 have on the average less and less of X_2 with which to

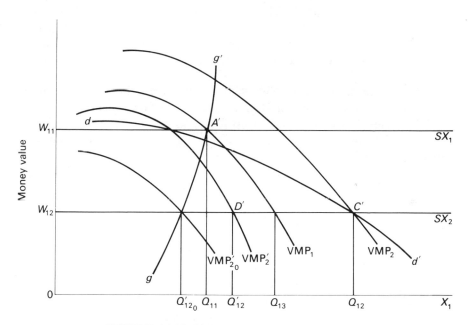

FIGURE 11.12. Shifts in the labor demand curve.

[17] Hicks defines a similar relationship as "regression." See *Value and Capital*, 2nd ed. (Oxford: Clarendon Press, 1953), pp. 93–96. "If the factor A and the product X are regressive, a substitution of A for B will lower the marginal product of B in terms of X, and therefore (at given prices of B and X) cause the supply of X to be contracted."

combine, which is analogous to holding X_1 constant and decreasing X_2. Since the marginal product of X_1, given X_1, increases along with decreases in X_2 when $f_{12} < 0$, it follows that the VMP curve of X_1 must slope upward, given X_2, when X_1 increases. Hence, again a substitution relationship between X_1 and X_2 could yield a positively sloped (short run) demand curve, here represented by the single VMP_1 curve.

Points C and D cannot be equilibrium points. Let us first assume that the inputs are not substitutes—i.e., $f_{12} \geq 0$. With reference to B, points C and A in Figure 11.11 reflect the uses of input X_1 in the following relationships, $X_{11} < X_{12} < X_{13}$, but in Figure 11.12, the relationships are $Q_{11} < Q_{13} < Q_{12}$. An obvious inconsistency exists since X_{12} should exceed X_{13} if C is an equilibrium point. Therefore, C must not be an equilibrium point. Equation (11.15) is satisfied at C, but Equation (11.14) is not. A movement of the isocost line parallel to EF' will occur along a scale line where the ratio X_2/X_1 is constant to some point, at which $X_{12} > X_{13}$, $MP_{x_1} = W_1/P$ and $MP_{x_2} = W_2/P$. As the inputs of X_1 and X_2 expand, individual and joint marginal products diminish due to our assumptions of a fixed X_3 and diminishing returns to scale, but the ratio of marginal products remains constant and equal to that at C. Short-run average fixed costs fall as output expands from A or C, and average and total variable costs rise from those at C.

If D is an equilibrium point when $f_{12} \geq 0$, the amount of factor 1 bears the relationship between D and B in Figure 11.11 such that $X_{12} > X_{13}$. In Figure 11.12, the relationship is $X'_{12} < X_{13}$. Hence, D cannot be an equilibrium point. Again, inputs will be changed in constant ratio, but this time they will decrease from the amounts used at D, until the amount of X_1 lies between Q_{11} and Q_{13} in Figure 11.12, and the new VMP curve lies to the left of VMP_1.[18] Equations (11.14) and (11.15) are then satisfied.

Our conclusion, therefore, is that if the marginal product of one input varies nonnegatively with the amount of another input ($f_{12} \geq 0$), neither C nor D in Figure 11.11 can be equilibrium points. Point C must move outward in a northeasterly direction, point D must move inward in a southwesterly direction, and in both cases, a negatively sloped demand curve, plotted along points where each price of the factor intersects the appropriate equilibrium VMP curve.

If $f_{12} < 0$ it is possible for C to be an equilibrium point if the VMP curve shifts to the left of VMP_1, as for example VMP''_{12}. If this occurs, Figures 11.11 and 11.12 are consistent with respect to amounts of X_1. However, if the curve shifts as far leftward as VMP'_{12}, C cannot be an

[18] Trout Rader has shown that where $f_{12} \geq 0$, output cannot fall if the price of a factor is reduced; i.e., $\partial Q/\partial W_i \geq 0$. "Normally, Factor Inputs are Never Gross Substitutes," *Journal of Political Economy* (January–February 1967), pp. 39–40. This implies that $X_{12} \geq X_{11}$.

equilibrium point, and amounts of both X_1 and X_2 must be reduced so that the ratio X_{22}/X_{12} is maintained and Equations (11.14) and (11.15) are satisfied. Similarly, D may be an equilibrium point as the VMP curve is shifted to the right, such as to VMP_2.

The significant conclusion to this discussion is that we have shown that the demand curve always has a negative slope in equilibrium if the inputs are in a normal, complementary, or independent relationship with one another ($f_{12} \geq 0$). Only if their relationship is one of substitutes ($f_{12} < 0$) can the demand curve have a negative slope (case C), but even when the substitute relationship exists, a negatively sloped demand curve is possible (case D).[19]

Discussion Questions

1. If isoquant curves intersect a vector through the origin so that equidistances between points of intersection along the vector are associated with quantities of output which differ by a constant amount, what type of production function is represented by the isoquant map and what returns to scale are implied?

2. Can an isoquant map be constructed for perfectly complementary inputs? For perfectly substitutable inputs?

3. Prove that the economic range of production implies stage II of the productive process.

4. (a) Why do not higher isorevenue curves necessarily imply lower prices in imperfect competition?

   (b) Why must maximum profit lie along an isocline curve which plots out points of tangency between isorevenue and isocost curves?

5. Give "common sense" explanations, if possible, of the four propositions determining the elasticity of demand for labor.

6. Is the elasticity of substitution an economic or a technological measure, or both? Explain.

7. It can be shown that if the elasticity of substitution of inputs is greater than the elasticity of product demand, then Proposition IV will not be true. Now, if in the long run, production occurs at an output where the production function yields constant returns to scale, show that in the long run, the fourth proposition must be valid. [Hint: Remember that marginal cost is positive and elasticity of demand = AR/(MR − AR).]

---

[19] These results, derived geometrically, are consistent with the more mathematically derived conclusions of D. V. T. Bear, "Inferior Inputs and the Theory of the Firm," *Journal of Political Economy* (June 1965), pp. 287–289.

8. How is an inferior factor of production analogous to the concept of an inferior consumption good? Suppose the supply of an inferior factor of production, with a positively sloped demand curve, is decreased. What will be the effect of the decrease in supply on wages and employment? How does this effect compare with that of a decrease in the supply of a normal factor?

12

Wage–Employment Determination
under
Imperfect Labor Market Conditions

Introduction

Markets may be either perfect or imperfect, and this applies to both product and factor markets. Perfect product markets have been described by the following properties[1]:

1. Active rivalry between buyers and sellers.
2. Maximizing behavior.
3. Homogeneous products per industry.
4. Perfect market knowledge.
5. Ease of entry into and exit from the market.
6. So many buyers and sellers of products that no one buyer or seller can influence the price.

Analogous conditions hold for the perfect factor market, which for our purposes is the labor market. Imperfect markets exist whenever any one of the above properties is violated.

---

[1] See Chapter 5, page 120, on The Marginal Productivity Theory.

Combinations of Product–Labor Markets

Four basic combinations of product–factor markets exist: (1) perfect product–perfect factor; (2) perfect product–imperfect factor; (3) imperfect product–perfect factor; (4) imperfect product–imperfect factor.[2] Although examples of perfect markets are rare, there are markets which approximate them. For example, a small retail store employing relatively unskilled labor may illustrate the first combination; a large hosiery mill in a small community approximates the second market structure; a spark plug factory in a large city can represent the third; and an automobile factory in a medium-sized city illustrates the fourth. The reader should seek to identify those features of these examples that place them within the appropriate market structure, as well as to consider those features which prevent them from being "ideal" examples of the respective structures.

Principles of wage–employment determination of the firm, based upon profit-maximizing objectives, can be derived from these market structures. Given the demand function for the product, the production function, and the supply function for the factor, the values for wages and employment can be derived.[3] Let us consider each market combination in turn.

[2] Of course, variations of these structures are possible and some will be considered later in the text, especially those involving oligopoly and oligopsony, and those involving bilateral monopoly. The market combinations were first examined by Joan Robinson, *Economics of Imperfect Competition* (London: Macmillan Co., 1933), Chapters 20–27.

[3] Let $Q_D = f(P) \equiv$ demand function; $Q = g(L, \bar{C}) \equiv$ production function; and $L = s(W) \equiv$ labor supply function; with $Q \equiv$ output of product; $P \equiv$ product price; $L \equiv$ labor; $\bar{C} \equiv$ capital, fixed in amount; and $W \equiv$ wages. Cost is given by $C = W \cdot L + r \cdot \bar{C}$, where $r \cdot \bar{C}$ represents fixed cost. To maximize profits π, differentiate partially with respect to labor the equation $\pi = p \cdot f(P) - C$; set it equal to zero:

$$\frac{\partial \pi}{\partial L} = \left[P \cdot f_l + f(p) \frac{dP}{dQ} \frac{\partial Q}{\partial L} \right] - \left[\frac{\partial W}{\partial L} \cdot L + W \right] = 0.$$

Now,

$$\left[P + f(p) \frac{dP}{dQ} \right] f_l = \left[\frac{\partial W}{\partial L_0} \cdot L + W \right] \tag{3.0}$$

or marginal revenue product = marginal labor cost. For combination (1), since $dP/dQ = 0$ and $\partial W/\partial L = 0$, Equation (3.0) becomes

$$P \cdot f_l = w \tag{3.1}$$

Combination (2) becomes

$$[P + f(p)(dP/dQ)]f_l = w \tag{3.2}$$

Combination (3) is

Perfect Product–Perfect Labor Market

In a perfect product market, the firm is too small to influence the price at which it sells its product. The product price is therefore a parameter, determined for the firm by industry supply and demand. Similarly, the firm is too small to affect the wage which it must pay for the labor it employs.

As a result, these price parameters are not within the control of the firm, and the firm must adapt to these market realities. In deciding whether to employ more or less labor—i.e., the employment decision—the firm must examine whether the revenue resulting from the sale of more or less additional output which a marginal laborer will produce will exceed, match, or be less than the cost of the extra laborer. The cost of the extra laborer is his wage; the extra revenue is simply the market price multiplied by the marginal worker's marginal physical product. The rule is this: If $P \times$ MPP $> W$, employ more labor! If $P \times$ MPP $< W$, employ less labor! If $P \times$ MPP $= W$, employment should be held stable. In each of these three situations, profits can be enhanced or losses can be reduced. Once action is taken on a marginal laborer, the rule is applied again and again until profits can be increased no further.

This is illustrated in Figure 12.1. Industry labor demand and supply in part (b) is determined at $\bar{W}$, which becomes the appropriate wage for the firm in part (a) for whatever amount of labor it decides to employ. If the firm employed $0N_1$ amount of labor, the VMP of labor is N_1R while the marginal labor cost (MLC), which also equals the average labor cost (ALC), is N_1S_1. The VMP exceeds MLC by RS and the firm is motivated to hire more labor. If $0N_2$ of labor were employed, MLC would exceed VMP by TC and the firm would reduce its employment. Only at $0N_0$ amount of labor does VMP $=$ MLC $= \bar{W}$ and are profits a maximum. A shift in either S_L or D_L, in Figure 12.1(b), would alter the market wage, and if the firm had been employing $0N_0$ labor, it would be faced with applying the profit-maximizing rule again. The firm can affect revenue and costs, not by changing wages and prices, but only by changing the amount of labor it utilizes. If by utilizing more labor it can increase revenues more than costs, the surplus accrues to profits; if by utilizing less labor it reduces costs more than revenues, the process adds to profits. The changing amounts of labor

---

$$P \cdot f_l = [\partial W / \partial L \cdot L + W] \tag{3.3}$$

Combination (4) is given by Equation (3.0). Since $dP/dQ < 0$ and $\partial W/\partial L > 0$, marginal revenue product [the left side of Equation (3.0)] is less than the value of the marginal product $[P \cdot f_l]$, and marginal labor cost [the right side of Equation (3.0)] exceeds the wage W. These equations can be solved for W and/or L.

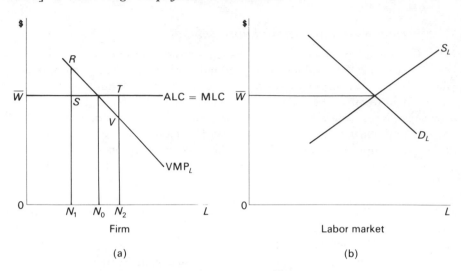

FIGURE 12.1. Perfect labor market–perfect product market. (a) Appropriate wage
for firm, based on (b) industry labor supply and demand.

influence sales through the effect on output and influence costs through the
change in the total wage bill.

Imperfect Product–Imperfect Labor Market

If perfect markets represent one extreme, then combination (4)
represents the other extreme. The firm is able to increase the sales of its
product only by decreasing its product price. This means that the revenue
accruing from the sale of the marginal product of the marginal worker will
be less than the price at which the marginal product is sold. Not only must
the price be lowered for the marginal product but the same decrease applies
to the total amount of that product offered for sale.[4] Hence, the marginal
revenue product (MR × MPP) is less than the value of the marginal
product (P × MPP). In a perfect product market, VMP and MRP
coincide. Since the firm employs labor from an imperfect market, the labor
supply curve is positively sloped and wages rise with expanded employment.
Not only do labor costs increase because higher wages must be paid to
marginally employed workers, but these costs increase because higher wages
must be paid to the total labor force employed in the firm.[5] Hence, the extra

[4] The exception, of course, is if the firm practices first-degree price discrimination.
[5] Except where first-degree wage discrimination occurs. Frequently, when a structure of
wages exists among a heterogeneous labor force, a rise in the base wage for the lowest skilled
labor is carried over into corresponding increases "across the board" for labor of higher
skills.

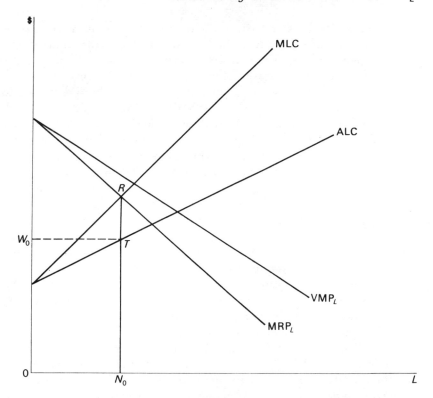

FIGURE 12.2. Imperfect labor market–imperfect product market.

or marginal cost of labor exceeds the wage rate. In a perfect factor market, the wage rate, ALC and MLC are all equal. (The student should determine for himself why this is so.) The firm supply-and-demand relationships for labor are illustrated in Figure 12.2.

The application of the profit-maximizing rule, given by the intersection of MRP and MLC, determines the optimum employment of labor. However, the wage is not measured at the point of intersection R. The wage associated with $0N_0$ amount of labor is read from the labor supply curve and is given by W_0. The wage is less than the marginal revenue product of the marginal worker.

Other Product–Labor Market Combinations

Combinations (2) and (3) are variations of combinations (1) and (4). In combination (2), the VMP curve coincides with the MRP curve, but MLC exceeds ALC (or S_L). In this market, as in (3), the revenue contribution of the marginal worker is greater than the wage, and both the wage and the employment decisions are within the discretion of the firm. In market (3), however, the wage is given to the firm by the larger labor market and only the employment decision is discretionary. The wage is equal to the revenue contribution of the marginal worker, although this revenue contribution is less than the value of his marginal product. The diagrammatic illustration of combinations (2) and (3) is left to the student.

As was noted in Chapter 5, Marshall used the concept of marginal net productivity. Marshall developed a procedure, used in the differential calculus of multivariable functions, by which only one variable is permitted to change while other variables are held constant. The effect of this change is noted and ascribed to the change in the variable. If the variable in question is the labor input, and the variables which are held constant are the other inputs to the production function, the prices together with the amounts of the latter make up the fixed costs of the firm. It is these fixed costs which are deducted from total revenue to derive the total net revenue function, and it is the derivative of the latter which is the marginal net revenue function. As described, this marginal function is the same as the marginal revenue function.[6] It may be, however, that all other inputs cannot be held constant; for example, as more labor is used, so must more raw materials and energy. If the market for these other variable inputs is perfect and their price is given to the firm, and if their inputs are used in fixed proportions with labor, their costs, along with other fixed costs, can be deducted from total revenue, but the derivative with respect to labor of this function will not be the same as the marginal revenue function.[7] Other more complicated possibilities of uses of variable inputs complementary with labor exist, of course. As far as we are concerned, the concept of marginal net revenue product is appropriate regardless of how it is calculated. It is this net revenue attributed to marginal labor in which we are interested. It

[6] That is,

$$P \cdot f(L) = R; \quad \frac{dR}{dL} = \left(P \frac{dQ}{dL} + f(L) \frac{dP}{dQ} \frac{dQ}{dL} \right) = \left(P + f(L) \frac{dP}{dQ} \right) \frac{dQ}{dL}$$

$$P \cdot f(L) - FC = R_N; \quad \frac{dR_n}{dL} = \frac{d(R)}{dL} - \frac{d(FC)}{dL} = \left(P + f(L) \frac{dP}{dQ} \right) \frac{dQ}{dL} - 0.$$

See the criticism of this concept explained in Chapter 5.

[7] Let labor be combined with energy (e) in the ratio α and with raw materials (m) in the ratio β. Hence,

$$R_n = P \cdot f(L, M, E) - FC - P_e \frac{L}{\alpha} - P_m \frac{L}{\beta};$$

$$\frac{dR_n}{dL} = [P + f(L, M, E)]f_l - \frac{P_e}{\alpha} - \frac{P_m}{\beta} < \frac{dR}{dL}.$$

can be less than the price at which the marginal product is sold because of imperfect market conditions; or it may be less than the marginal revenue of the marginal product because of internal diseconomies, such as higher administrative overhead or greater possibilities of slack or frictions in the utilization of resources; or for other reasons. Hereafter, when we refer to VMP or MRP, the net concept will apply.

Exploitation

Exploitation has been defined as the difference between the payment to a factor and the value of its marginal product, although for many years it was not clear whether this definition included the difference between VMP and *W*, or the difference between MRP and *W*. Edward Chamberlin demonstrated that it was MRP which was significant,[8] and hence in our combinations (3) and (4), that amount which is the difference between VMP and MRP with *N* employment is not to be construed as "exploitation." The concept of exploitation has been further defined as deliberate and nondeliberate.[9] Nondeliberate, or monopsonistic, exploitation occurs when the supply of labor is less than perfectly elastic; that is, as a buyer of labor, the employer, being sufficiently large relative to the market, possesses some monopsony power in that as he expands his purchase of labor, he can do so only at increasing labor costs. (If he were selling instead of buying, he would be called a monopolist.) The employer, by equating marginal labor cost with marginal revenue product, necessarily, but nonpurposively, pays as wages less than the workers' MRP because MLC exceeds the wage. In Figure 12.2, the measure of nondeliberate exploitation is given by *RT*. It should be noted that nondeliberate exploitation is apt to be slight if the slope of the labor supply curve is small, for in such a case MLC lies closer to the supply curve. Figure 12.3 illustrates this.

Deliberate exploitation has also been called "discrimination." It occurs when homogeneous laborers—workers of the same productivity—receive different wages, or when heterogeneous laborers—different productivity—receive the same wages. Examples of degrees of discrimination have been given in Chapter 9. If the discrimination is of first degree, where each laborer is paid only that wage which is necessary to secure his services, the marginal cost of labor coincides with the average cost of labor. In the case of homogeneous labor, all but the marginal worker are exploited, for all but

---

[8] Edward Chamberlin, *Theory of Monopolistic Competition* (Cambridge: Harvard University Press, 1933).
[9] Gordon Bloom, "A Reconsideration of the Theory of Exploitation," *Quarterly Journal of Economics*, Vol. 15 (May 1941), pp. 413–442.

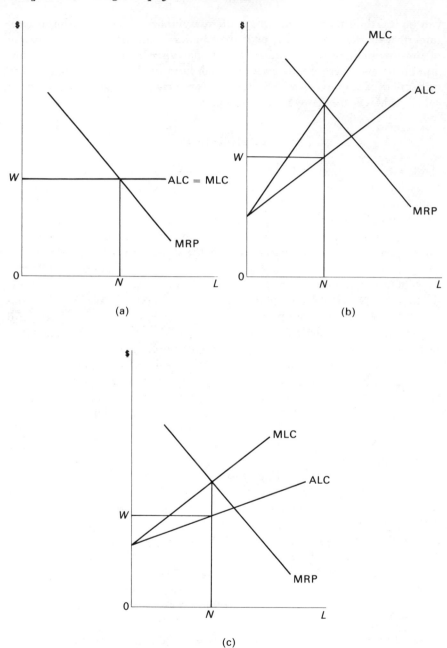

FIGURE 12.3. Degrees of exploitation: (a) none, (b) strong, (c) mild.

he are being paid a wage less than their MRP. Only one of these homo-geneous workers can be the marginal worker, however. If third-degree discrimination is practiced, then for the marginal "group" exploitation is reduced in the sense that the MLC curve lies in steps closer to the ALC curve with each step corresponding to a discriminated "group." If heter-ogeneous labor all receive the same wage, and if that wage is equal to the MRP of the least efficient group of workers, then workers of quality in excess of this least qualified group are exploited.

Allan Cartter has stated that the emotional impact of the term "exploi-tation" has impaired its analytical usefulness, and suggests instead the term "employer's monopsonistic wage advantage."[10] The term, originated by Marx to describe the exercise of economic power of the propertied capitalist over the nonpropertied laboring class, fell into disrepute during the cold war period in the decade after World War II. However, the term exploitation is essentially a technical one and in itself is devoid of ideological content.

The existence of exploitation has been questioned in the case of a variation of markets (3) or (4), i.e., where the firm is an oligopolist with a kinked product-demand curve. The discontinuity in the marginal-revenue curve is reflected in the labor-demand curve and is illustrated in Figure 12.4.

In the case of a perfect labor market, if the ALC curve intersects the MRP_L curve precisely at F or D, does exploitation occur for N labor? By our definition the answer is no. If the intersection is at some point between D and F, such as at E, one might argue that the oligopolist is as much the subject of exploitation as labor. In the case of an imperfect labor market, only if both the MLC and ALC curves lie within the DF gap can we deny, by definition, that exploitation exists. If the ALC curve lies below F, such as at G, and when MLC lies within DF, exploitation exists, but we cannot say whether it is by more than FG. The existence of the gap may introduce a range of indeterminacy in our estimate of the wage, although employment is specified. The employer is able to pay a wage up to ND, but the wage required to bring forth ON amount of labor to the oligopolist may be significantly below ND. Whether the employer pays more or less is a matter subject to his discretion. If we continue to assume that he is a profit maximizer, he will pay no more than the labor market requires, and the wage is not indeterminate.

The Rising MLC Curve and Employment Costs

Since the existence of exploitation is owing to a rising MLC curve, let us consider why such a curve occurs in imperfect labor markets. A firm

[10] Allan Cartter and Ray Marshall, *Labor Economics* (Homewood: R. D. Irwin, Inc., 1967), pp. 261–262.

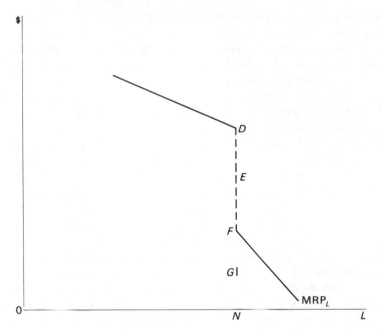

FIGURE 12.4. The MRP curve corresponding to the kinked demand curve.

sufficiently large relative to the market that wishes to employ more workers finds it can do so only if it raises wages. Higher wages are necessary to induce workers in adjoining labor markets to accept employment with the firm. If such a worker must increase his commuting time, some incremental wage is necessary to compensate him for the extra cost and time of commuting. If the worker cannot commute but must change his place of residence, a higher wage is necessary to induce him to bear the costs of moving. If the worker is currently employed in the same labor market, higher wages normally must be offered to induce him to undergo the psychic costs involved in changing jobs, not to mention reimbursement for loss of seniority and accumulated fixed fringe benefits which have accrued to him in his current position.

Viewed in Stigler's terms of the "economics of search," the firm is faced with a normal supply of job seekers, some employed in the labor market and some unemployed.[11] If the firm is unable to meet its manpower needs from this supply of job seekers, it must enlarge the supply of searchers for its

[11] George Stigler, "Economics of Search," *Journal of Political Economy* (Supplement, October 1962), pp. 202–204.

openings. One manner of doing this is to raise wages, which thereby raises the returns to search of job applicants at this firm. Similarly, the recruitment costs of the firm may rise as it pursues a more aggressive search of its own for qualified talent. These increased recruitment costs, while not reflected in actual wage rates, do increase the labor costs, and cause the average labor costs to rise.

In order to obtain additional employment, firms may be required through necessity to relax their hiring standards. If less-qualified labor is employed, it may be necessary to bring them up to the normal standard of proficiency through increased training and/or more careful supervision, both of which require greater outlays. The greater the deviation among new hires from average labor standards, the greater these incremental outlays. Either more intensive or a longer period of training may be required before normal productivity is attained. Perhaps a greater attrition rate results among the lower-qualified personnel for reasons of health, immaturity, or personality maladjustments. If output per man-hour declines when sub-normal labor is employed at the existing wage, average labor costs rise. Hence, even if the wage W is not increased to attract additional labor, average labor costs rise through incremental costs S of raising the marginal labor to standard efficiency or through reduced output per man-hour O:

$$\frac{W + S}{O} = \text{ALC}$$

The higher-than-normal unemployment rates of high school dropouts or of those with little or no work experience and the tendency of those over 45 who become unemployed to remain unemployed for extended periods of time is evidence of the reluctance of employers to incur higher labor costs. High school dropouts have demonstrated an unwillingness to accept the discipline which organized education imposes. It is normal for employers to reason that dropouts either have less innate capacity to absorb formal training or have less motivation to continue in a training program once undertaken. Employers may find that turnover rates are much higher among employees who have been high school dropouts, and hence training costs may be amortized over a much smaller period of employment. The latter is also true for the unemployed who are more advanced in age. Training cost per man-hour of future service is higher, the shorter the period of future employment. Inexperienced workers not only require more training, but the probability that these workers will change jobs is much greater. Job changing is much higher, the younger the labor force.[12] Hence, these

---

[12] G. Bancroft and S. Garfinkle, "Job Mobility in 1961," *Monthly Labor Review* (August 1963), p. 898. It declines rapidly beyond the age of 24.

categories of the unemployed find it very difficult to find jobs. Only when the supplies of the better educated, the young but not too young, and the experienced unemployed workers are exhausted will these categories receive favorable consideration for employment.

The Minimum Wage, the Union, and Exploitation

It has long been recognized that unions and/or minimum wage laws are capable of removing exploitation.[13] Assume in Figure 12.5 that the appropriate demand and supply curves of a firm for labor are given by MRP and L. Employment and the wage are determined, respectively, at $0N_0$ and $0W_0$, and exploitation exists in the amount RS. Assume further that a union is organized in the firm and obtains monopoly control over the services offered by the firm's employees (see Figure 12.6). The union then seeks to impose a wage increase upon the firm, enforced by the threat of a strike. If the strike is successful, the firm will be able to obtain no labor at wages

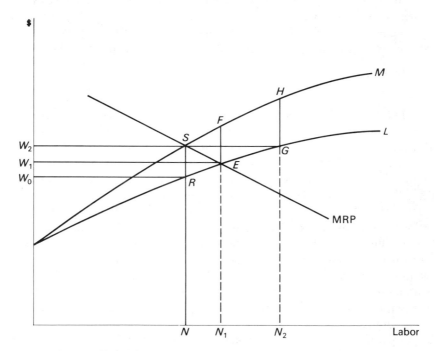

FIGURE 12.5. The minimum wage, exploitation, and employment.

[13] Joan Robinson, *Economics of Imperfect Competition*, p. 282.

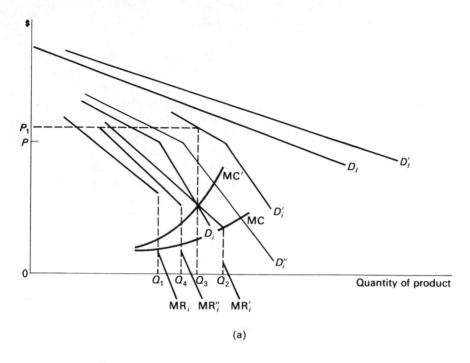

(a)

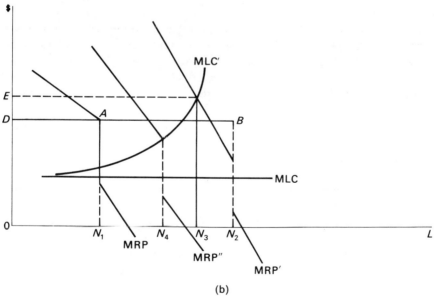

(b)

FIGURE 12.6. (a) Market shares and shifts in the kinked demand curve, and (b) equilibrium in the labor market.

below those set by the union. However, at the union wage, the employer can hire workers up to the amount constrained by the labor supply curve (L). Hence, for all practical purposes, what had previously been an upward sloping supply curve is now changed into a perfectly elastic one up to the point on the ALC curve established by the new wage. The MLC curve, M, now coincides with the modified ALC curve, and it is the intersection of this modified curve with the MRP curve which determines the level of employment. If the union sets the wage at $0W_1$, the new supply curve becomes W_1ES, the new MLC curve becomes W_1EFM, and the new level of employment is $0N_1$. The union has removed exploitation, although the wage increase is less than the previous level of exploitation, RS. However, employment can increase to $0N_1$. A union which has as its objective the desire to maximize membership might follow this wage employment policy. If instead the objective of the union is to maximize the wage of its members, subject to maintaining their positions, then the union might demand a wage increase to $0W_2$. The wage increase equals the previous level of exploitation, the new labor supply curve becomes W_2GL, the new MLC curve is W_2GHM, and the original level of employment $0N_0$ is maintained. A wage set above $0W_2$, however, would result in reduced employment.

Similarly, the minimum wage imposes a perfectly elastic labor supply curve, determined by fiat, upon the employer. Below the minimum wage, presumably sufficient penalties exist to prohibit an employer from offering a sublegal wage. At the minimum wage, the employer may utilize as much labor as the market will make available at that wage. As with the union, the imposition of the minimum wage, depending upon the size of the increase, may increase or have no effect upon the employment levels. Minimum wages in excess of the original amount of exploitation will reduce the amount of labor utilized by the firm.

The effect of unionization or the imposition of a minimum wage initially is to increase wages and possibly employment in the face of exploitation. Subsequent increases in either of these institutional forces, in the absence of changes in labor demand, will tend to decrease employment. Hence, the initial impact of these forces is to remove exploitation at no expense to employment opportunities. The evidence seems to support this result. Whenever union membership has increased rapidly in periods in which the expansion of aggregate demand has not obscured the union impact, wages in the unionized industries have increased relative to those in the nonunion sectors. This has been observed empirically in a number of studies. In one of the first studies of the impact of the union, Douglas found that in the early period of unionization, 1870–1914, wages rose appreciably, but in more mature stages of development, 1914–1926, the percentage increase in wages in unionized industries did not exceed that of wages in nonunionized industries.[14] A later study by Lewis found that unions had a greater impact on wages in the period 1935–1940, when union membership was increasing, than in the period 1953–1960, when membership was stationary.[15] Ross and Goldner also found that in general the greater the increase in unionization in industries between 1933–1946, the greater the increase in wages.[16] Evidence of the employment effects of minimum wage changes and unions is presented in the section on "employment effects."

The Share of the Market and Exploitation

This approach to exploitation leads us into an interesting interpretation of wage–price behavior. Let us assume that the demand for the product of an oligopolistic industry increases, as indicated in Figure 12.6(a), from D_I to D_I', and the demand for a representative oligopolistic firm increases from D_i to D_i'. If the firm were to maintain its market share, the demand curves for labor would shift proportionately to the right from MRP to MRP' with the discontinuity in the MRP' now beginning at less than $0D$ dollars.[17] If the labor market is perfect and ALC and MLC continue to intersect in the region of the discontinuity, the firm encounters no problem in maintaining its market share.[18] (The existence of considerable unemployment might create a condition under which employment expansion in the firm is possible with no increase in the going wage paid by the firm.)

If full employment or a situation close thereto exists, then MLC is likely to be upward sloping, as indicated by MLC'. When the MLC' curve is upward sloping, even though it intersects the gap in MRP, it may not do so in the gap in MRP'. If it intersects MRP' to the left of the gap, the firm will not be able to expand employment optimally from $0N_1$ to $0N_2$ so that, given the production function, it can maintain its share of the market. In fact, not only does exploitation now occur, but the firm is under pressure to raise the product price to $0P_1$ if it is not to violate the profit-maximizing output of $0Q_3$ and employment of $0N_3$. If it cannot raise the price because of industry (or government) pressure, MRP' shifts leftward to MRP'' where

[14] Paul Douglas, *Real Wages in the United States, 1890–1926* (Boston: Houghton Mifflin Co., 1930).

[15] H. G. Lewis, *Unionism and Relative Wages in the United States: An Empirical Inquiry* (Chicago: University of Chicago Press, 1963), p. 222.

[16] Arthur M. Ross and William Goldner, "Forces Affecting the Interindustry Wage Structure," *Quarterly Journal of Economics*, LXIV, No. 2 (May 1950), p. 268. See also Chapter 16 for a more detailed discussion of the unions' influence on wages.

[17] This is so not only because the discontinuity in MR_i' begins at a lower value than MR_i, but also because the marginal physical product of labor can be expected to decline with an increase in the usage of labor in the short run.

[18] In Figure 12.6(a), MC is taken to be consistent with MLC in Figure 12.6(b), and MC' is consistent with MLC'.

MLC″ intersects MRP″ at employment of $0N_4$, and the firm's market share is reduced.[19] If other firms, not necessarily domestic ones, have lower MLC curves, they will capture that portion of the market vacated by the first firm.[20] On the other hand, if all domestic firms have similar MLC curves and are protected by tariffs or quotas from international competition, all will initially offer a product supply of $0Q_4$ consistent with $0N_4$ amount of labor; all will be thereupon under pressure to permit the market to bid up the price; each will, as a result, tend to increase output to $0Q_3$ and labor to $0N_3$; and finally a consensus will be reached to fix product price at $0P'$ so that the new MRP′ intersects MLC′ at $0E$ (dollars).

It is meaningless in this situation to identify this seemingly administered price increase as induced by cost-push or demand-pull forces. Under full employment there is a simultaneous tendency for both prices and costs to rise in response to increased demand. The increased output demanded cannot be supplied unless labor is pulled away from other uses, and this necessarily incurs adjustment costs including overtime pay. Neither cost-push nor demand-pull forces are causes of the price adjustment effects. It is only those who wish to attach "blame" to a result which they deem to be undesirable that insist upon so labeling the phenomenon as one or the other. Instead, the culprit is the market structure together with the import restrictions. It is interesting, however, to note that a free trade policy is less likely to result in price increases in the oligopoly industry than is a restrictive trade policy, and the expansion of output is less likely to be restricted.

Employment Effects

The preceding studies identify wage effects but not employment effects. Studies of the impact of minimum wages, however, do identify employment effects. The initial 25-cent-an-hour minimum wage, established in 1938, reduced employment less than 0.05% immediately after it was applied, and these workers were largely concentrated in high-labor-intensity industries such as pecan shelling and tobacco stemming.[21] However, by 1940, effects were more adverse in the hosiery industry where, among low-paying firms, employment fell by almost 13%.[22] Other studies have supported the

[19] Consequently, D_i' shifts leftward to D_i'' and output becomes $0Q_4$.

[20] The phenomena described by this model have apparently occurred in the American steel market in the period 1968–1970. See A. F. Shorrocks, "Measuring the Imaginary; The Employment Effects of Imported Steel," *Industrial and Labor Relations Review*, Vol. 24, No. 2 (January 1971), pp. 203–215.

[21] J. F. Moloney, "Some Effects of the Fair Labor Standards Act upon Southern Industry," *Southern Economic Journal*, Vol. IX (July 1942), pp. 5–23.

[22] H. M. Douty, "Minimum Wage Regulation in the Seamless Hosiery Industry," *Southern Economic Journal*, Vol. XV (October 1948), pp. 176–189.

hypothesis that a rise in the minimum wage leads to a reduction in employment. David Kaun found that the number of noncorporate businesses and the number of production workers declined after the 1949 and 1956 increases, and Benewitz and Weintraub have confirmed the general negative relationship between increments in minimum wages and employment.[23] What these studies indicate is that apparently little exploitation existed among firms who were most affected by the minimum wage. This would be true, for example, if their labor supply were highly elastic at the preexisting wage, a condition not highly unique among firms using low-skilled workers in a labor surplus region such as the South. Many of the studies focused on this region of the country, primarily because the major impact of the early revisions of the Fair Labor Standards Act was felt by low-wage-paying industries concentrated in the South.

Adverse employment effects of wage changes can be mitigated, of course, by forces tending to increase labor demand. If labor demand increases, employment may even increase when and as wages rise. Either technological improvements, through raising the marginal physical product of labor, or expansion of product demand, through raising the marginal revenue of the marginal physical product, can shift the labor demand curve upward and to the right. Some of the employment effects of the minimum wage changes of 1938 and 1949 were obscured by the onset of war shortly after the increases went into effect. Similarly, the introduction of changes in 1945 and 1965 took place during an economic boom when a general expansion of employment accompanied rising economic activity. Nevertheless, for the careful observer, evidence of negative employment effects is present in official government documents, either in the form of continued decline in industries historically sensitive to minimum wages, or failure of sectors of newly covered industries to expand employment as rapidly as other uncovered sectors.[24]

Although the establishment of a union or the imposition of a minimum wage has the effect of altering the employer's labor supply curve, the market labor supply curve itself is not affected. Workers exist who would provide services below the institutionally established rate if they were permitted to do so; nevertheless, above this wage, expansion of the firm's labor force follows the path of the market supply curve. However, shifts in labor supply curves do occur. Ordinarily, these shifts occur because of migration patterns.

[23] David E. Kaun, "Minimum Wages, Factor Substitution, and the Marginal Producer," *Quarterly Journal of Economics* (August 1965), pp. 478–486; Maurice Benewitz and R. E. Weintraub, "Employment Effects of a Local Minimum Wage," *Industrial and Labor Relations Review*, Vol. XVII (January 1964), pp. 276–288.

[24] See, for example, studies by the U.S. Department of Labor, Wage and Hour and Public Contracts Divisions on Minimum Wages, 1965–1970.

Either workers move into the market attracted by higher wages, or leave the market for higher wages elsewhere. Occasionally such traumatic events as war, plague, inflation, or a major institutional policy, such as an increase in the limiting age of compulsory school attendance or the introduction of child labor legislation, can generate sudden shifts in the curves. Ordinarily, changes are gradual, however.

When barriers to entry into a labor market exist, such as when a trade union can control entry into the market or when capital requirements for buying the educational prerequisites to an occupation are relatively great, a wage increase, in the absence of compensating increases in product demand, results in unemployment. The unemployed workers are prevented from bidding down wages because they are prohibited from selling their services in the market. Hence, they must enter another market to seek employment, which shifts the supply curve of labor to the left in the original market and to the right, depressing wages, in the second market. A wage differential arises and persists between the two markets as a consequence.

The magnitude of the differentials will depend on the relative elasticities of demand for labor in the union and nonunion sectors, and on the relative quantities of labor employed by the two sectors. For example, if the degree of unionization is small, N_2N_1 in Figure 12.7(a) may represent a very small quantity of displaced labor, which may easily be absorbed by the very large sector in Figure 12.7(b) without substantial depression of the wage rate. Obviously, the relative elasticities influence the displacement and absorption capabilities of the two sectors.

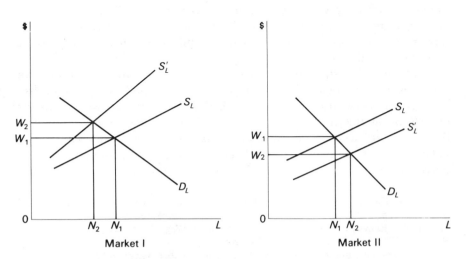

FIGURE 12.7. Wage differentials and shifts in labor supply (see text).

The employment effect of the wage increase may be obscured in the unionized or nonunionized sector if demand increases more or less simultaneously. (Also, if demand decreases, the effect may be erroneously dramatized.) Demand for labor may shift because of increases in aggregate demand generally occurring throughout the total economy (a macro influence), by growth forces peculiar to the unit, or by increases in the marginal productivity of labor. If demand increases sufficiently in the union sector, no unemployment effect need result from wage increase $W_1 W_2$. If demand is stable in the nonunion sector, the wage differential may not be as great; it may even narrow or disappear if, for example, as a part of a general increase in aggregate demand, labor demand also increases in the nonunion sector.

The ability of a union to preserve a superior wage position, of course, depends on its ability to maintain its control over the available supply of labor to the employer. This control is made easier if the sector in which the union functions as a broker of labor is itself expanding. Assuming that perfect immobility of labor is as rare as perfect mobility, over time the superior wage position should attract labor into the sector, shifting to the right the relevant ALC curve. The potentially competing source of labor to the unit, which the union must exclude, of course, is greater the less the labor demand curve increases. Consequently, if the sector does not grow with sufficient rapidity, we should expect the wage differential to narrow over time, or to fluctuate as demand fluctuates, as the competition of labor exerts its influence.

Long-Run Analysis of Wages and Employment

The marginal revenue product analysis is a short-run explanation of wage–employment phenomena. Long-run analysis, in which capital as well as labor can be varied, also predicts that increases in wages originating from supply-induced prices produce negative effects on employment in the absence of demand changes. Consider the isoquant map in Figure 12.8. Assume that the map of isoquant curves represents a linear, homogeneous production function.

Assume that point A is an equilibrium point on isocost curve FE. A rise in wages moves the isocost curve from FE to FE', and at the same total expense, FE, less output will be produced. Given the original cost, the new minimum cost point will be at B, and the new equilibrium point will lie on the vector $0B$. Some point below C, say D, will represent the tangency of an isocost curve $F'E''$, parallel to FE', to an isoquant curve below I_1. This is so because the increase in factor cost raises marginal cost, which intersects the product marginal revenue curve at a point corresponding to a lower

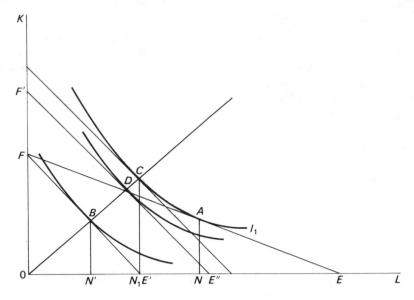

FIGURE 12.8. Substitution and output effects of wage changes.

output. If the same output had been produced, total cost would have been greater than $0F'$ and minimum cost would have been at C. If the firm were in long-run equilibrium in monopolistic competition, where TR = TC, the shift in the marginal cost curve, by intersecting the firm's MR curve at a point of greater elasticity of product demand, results in lower total revenue being earned. As a result, long-run total costs must be reduced below $0F$, and the new equilibrium point D may even lie below point B. Since, at points B, C, and D, less labor is utilized than at point A, under our assumed conditions, an increase in the price of labor will reduce its employment.

In Figure 12.8, point C represents the minimum cost position if the original output had been maintained at the new price ratio between capital and labor. It can be seen that less labor and more capital are used, and that capital has been substituted for labor. This is known as the *substitution effect* of a change in the price of labor, and it is measured by NN_1 in Figure 12.8. It is always negative. If costs had not changed, and output had been adjusted instead, $0N'$ quantity of labor would have been used. The *output effect* is measured by $N'N_1$, and this effect measures the change in the use of labor from one minimum cost point to another, given total costs, that is not offset by the substitution of factors when the price of labor is changed. The output effect is also negative when labor is a normal input, and the sum of the two effects is the total effect.

Another relationship can be identified, which shall be called the product market effect. If D is the new minimum cost condition which satisfies market equilibrium conditions,[25] we may also measure the wage-change effect on the employment of labor through its effect on equilibrium output. Normally, the relationship runs as follows:

$$\Delta W \rightarrow \Delta \text{MC} \rightarrow \Delta \text{MR} \rightarrow \Delta P \rightarrow \Delta Q\rho \rightarrow \Delta Q_L.$$

The arrow indicates a cause–effect relationship, and the relationship between ΔP and ΔQ_ρ is normally negative, whereas the other relationships are normally positive.[26] The sum of the substitution effect and the *product market effect* is given as the total market effect. In the illustration, this is $N_1 N_2$ and it normally is negative. If $N_1 N_2 > N_1 N'$, then D lies to the left of B; if $N_1 N_2 < N_1 N'$, as in the diagram, then D lies to the right of B.

Technological Change

Even if the price of labor does not change so that input price ratios remain constant, it is possible for capital to be substituted for labor if technological changes occur. This can be shown in Figure 12.9, where illustrations of three types of technical changes are presented.

Assume that one of points A, B, or D is an initial reference point. If point A on isoquant I is the initial reference point, a capital-using labor-saving technical change is illustrated by a shift in the isoquant curves from a family represented by I_1 to a family represented by I_2 where I_2 measures a greater quantity than I_1. (If the quantities had not changed, there would be no economic incentive for a firm to utilize the new technology.) If costs do not change, then B is the new minimum unit cost point at which more capital and less labor are utilized to produce a larger output. Such a technological improvement implies a flattening of the isoquant curves with respect to any given quantity of labor, such as q_1 or q_2. The marginal product of capital has increased, so that less capital is needed to substitute for a given amount of labor at each given quantity of labor (MP_L/MP_C falls as MP_C rises). By analogy, technical change which is capital saving but labor using can be illustrated by assuming point B to be the reference point and noting the effect of a shift in the family of isoquants from those represented by I_2 to those represented by I_1. Here I_1 measures greater output than I_2. At q_1, the MRTS on I_1 is greater than on I_2, which is to say that at q_1, I_1 has a steeper

[25] At B, we have $\text{MPP}_K/\text{MPP}_L = P_K/P_L$, but MRP_K and MRP_L are not necessarily equal to their respective marginal costs. At D, however, the respective MRP's do equal their marginal costs.

[26] For a proof that product price varies directly with input price, see C. E. Ferguson, *The Neoclassical Theory of Production and Distribution* (Cambridge: University Press, 1969), pp. 144–147.

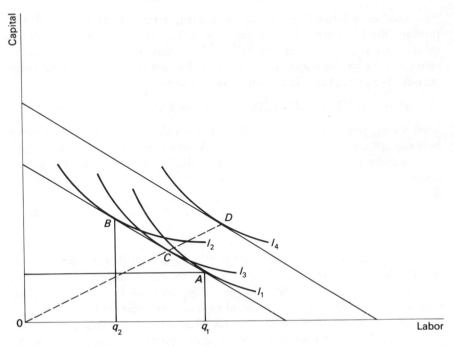

FIGURE 12.9. Employment effects of technological change.

slope than I_2. (The MP_L/MP_C for each q_L rises since MP_L has risen.) Minimum average costs have fallen as output, but not costs, has increased.

The third case of technological change (capital saving and labor saving) is neutral with respect to changes in the ratios at which capital and labor are combined, given constant input prices. Assume that D is an original equilibrium point. A neutral technological change shifts the isoquant of a given level of output down to I_3 at C, which lies along a straight-line vector from the origin. Since the marginal products of labor and capital change proportionately and since the input prices are constant, input proportions must be constant. The I_4 would, after the technological change, represent greater output at the same cost, and I_3 would represent the same output at lower cost; both result in lower unit cost. Normally, under such circumstances, output will expand to a point above D, and more labor and capital will be used. If a technical change occurs which is both labor saving and capital saving, but more one than the other, it falls appropriately into one of the first two categories.

It probably is true that the first and third categories are more typical than the second category. Only where labor is very cheap is there an incentive to develop a technology of the second type. For example, pedicabs (bicycle rickshaws) and three-wheeled taxis are used in the overpopulated Orient as substitutes for automobiles. Only to the extent that technical change is capital using and labor saving is there a tendency for less labor to be utilized. Even in this case, if the product demand is sufficiently elastic, a reduction in cost which makes possible a reduction in price may result in a disproportionate increase in the quantity that can be sold, so that an increase in labor utilization is possible.

As we have shown, an increase in the price of labor, in the absence of technological change, leads normally to a substitution of capital for labor and a reduction in the amount of labor employed. If product demand is expanding, the reduction may take the form of a fairly steady labor employment level, and price may rise to offset increased costs with no decrease in output. Even output may rise somewhat, although the increase will be less because of the increased wage bill. The increased wage bill, as has long been noted, can provide an incentive to entrepreneurs to develop labor-saving, capital-using techniques of production. If the cost of developing these techniques is less than the cost of the labor replaced plus the cost of the capital used in replacing them, it is economically profitable to fund research and development projects. Thus, an increase in wages may in the long run not only yield a substitution of capital for labor, but may induce labor-saving innovations. Through both influences, production can become less labor, and more capital intensive.

Exploitation and the Economics of Fringe Benefits

Lester has written that no theory exists "to give an adequate explanation of the great changes that have occurred in the wage–benefit mix in the American economy during the past two decades or to provide an objective basis for predictions regarding future developments in the wage–benefit mix and the distribution of compensation among different types of benefits."[27] This section shall show how the theory of exploitation—or rather the union's role in removing it—can explain the rise in supplemental wage payments.

In Table 12.1 and Chart 12.1 are presented recent data on the structure of employee compensation.[28] The 1968 data revealed that almost 20%, or

[27] Richard A. Lester, "Benefits as a Preferred Form of Compensation," *The Southern Economic Journal*, Vol. 33, No. 4 (April 1967), p. 495.
[28] Alvin Baumin, "Measuring Employee Compensation in U.S. Industry," *Monthly Labor Review*, Vol. 93, No. 10 (October 1970), pp. 17–24.

TABLE 12.1

LEVEL AND STRUCTURE OF EMPLOYER EXPENDITURES FOR
EMPLOYEE COMPENSATION, PRIVATE NONFARM ECONOMY,
1968

Compensation Practice	All Employees	
	Percent of Compensation	Dollars per Hour of Work
Total compensation	100.0	3.89
Pay for working time	82.8	3.22
Straight-time pay	80.4	3.13
Premium pay	2.4	0.09
Overtime, weekend, and holiday work	2.1	0.08
Shift differentials	0.3	0.01
Pay for leave time (except sick leave)	5.3	0.21
Vacations	3.1	0.12
Holidays	2.0	0.08
Civic and personal leave	0.1	0.01
Employer payments to vacation and holiday funds	0.1	([a])
Employer expenditures for retirement programs	6.0	0.24
Social security	3.3	0.13
Private pension plans	2.7	0.11
Employer expenditures for health and insurance programs[b]	3.7	0.15
Live, accident, and health insurance	2.2	0.09
Sick leave	0.6	0.03
Workmen's compensation	0.9	0.03
Employer expenditures for unemployment benefit programs	0.9	0.04
Unemployment insurance	0.8	0.03
Severance pay	0.1	([a])
Severance pay funds and supplemental unemployment benefit funds	([a])	([a])
Nonproduction bonuses	1.0	0.04
Savings and thrift plans	0.2	0.01

[a] Less than 0.05% or $0.005.

[b] Includes other health benefit programs, principally State temporary disability insurance
not presented separately.

67¢ per hour, of the total hourly compensation is paid to workers in the form
of (1) retirement programs, (2) leavetime pay, including vacation, holiday,
and sick pay, (3) health and insurance programs, (4) premium pay, including
overtime, late-shift differentials, and holiday pay, and (5) separation, and

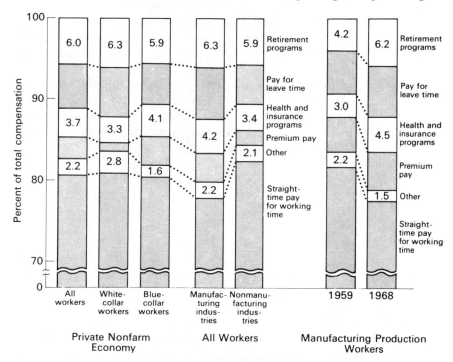

CHART 12.1. The structure of compensation for selected worker groups and industries, 1968, and manufacturing production workers, 1959–1968.

Source: Alvin Bauman, "Measuring Employee Compensation in U.S. Industry," *Monthly Labor Review*, October 1970, p. 18.

other types of pay. It does not include bonuses. The trend has been for these types of benefits to assume an increasing percentage of the total compensation of employees. "Between 1961 and 1969, about half the workers covered by major collective bargaining agreement settlements . . . received new or improved pension plan coverage; about half received a new or improved vacation program, and nearly two out of three got new or improved health and insurance programs."[29] That this trend is consistent with workers' preferences has been supported by studies cited by Lester.[30] A number of reasons have been put forth to explain this preference. Apparently, these reasons seem to suggest that the payments satisfy everyone's set of preferences: (1) workers receive preferential tax treatment and price savings through group purchases, together with convenience, in buying and paying for these

[29] *Ibid.*, p. 20.
[30] *Op. cit.*, pp. 485–495. Preferences for fringe benefits are analyzed more completely in my article "The Economics of Fringe Benefits," *Industrial Relations*, Vol. 12, No. 2 (Feb. 1973).

benefits through automatic deductions, where benefits are jointly contributive; (2) employers receive stability in their work force through reduction in turnover rates; and (3) unions receive membership stability and institutional survival.

Becker has suggested that employers who invest significant sums in the specific training of their employees find it to their advantage to pay part of the enhanced productivity of these employees in the form of deferred compensation—pension plans, separation pay, supplemental unemployment benefits—in order to discourage turnover and mobility of these workers.[31] Wages would be higher than in alternative employment using general skills, so that the economic incentive to change is reduced. The sum of supplemental forms of compensation and the wage rate is still less than worker productivity by at least the compounded cost of specific training. Unions whose membership is employed and whose employment is stable are likely to be more insulated from the possibility of losing their majority representative status. Moreover, to the extent that a bureaucracy develops within the union to administer the technicalities of the deferred forms of payment, the rationale for existence and the membership dependency are strengthened.

Robert Rice has examined the hypothesis that wage supplements are related positively to earnings, size of firms, and degree of unionization, and negatively to turnover rates.[32] The higher are earnings, the greater are the tax savings, given the progressive income tax structure, from deferred earnings. Put differently, if the worker had first been paid a higher wage equal to the premium on an annuity, he would have been unable, because of the tax, to have purchased an annuity of the same value and still retain the take-home pay that he has under the deferred-income plan. Simple regression coefficients were significant and of the correct sign for the relationship between the magnitude of supplemental benefits and earnings, turnover rates, unionization, and firm size. Multiple regression coefficients revealed that earnings were significantly related to size of benefits, but unionization was significantly related only for pensions. It was found that turnover rates were statistically insignificant, but this may be owing to the fact that either earnings are not a good proxy for specific training or that multicollinearity exists between turnover rates and some other independent variable. Lester has also found that the degree of unionization is positively related to the acceptance by employees of supplemental wage benefits. Weiss has found that larger firms pay higher wages and benefits, which is consistent with

---

[31] Gary S. Becker, *Human Capital* (New York: Columbia University Press, 1964).
[32] Robert G. Rice, "Skill Earnings, and the Growth of Wage Supplements," *American Economic Review: Proceedings*, Vol. 56, No. 2 (May 1966), pp. 583–592.

Rice's finding of positive correlation between earnings and wage supplements.[33]

The relationship between the magnitude of fringe benefits and large firms and unions suggests that supplemental benefits may be related to labor markets that are imperfect. As has already been noted in such markets, the marginal revenue product of labor may exceed the market wage necessary to bring forth the required amount of labor. The differential is retained by the employer as monopsony profits. The advent of a union can raise wages to equality with MRP without an adverse effect upon employment. However, this increase in wages may undermine the power of the union. If the labor in question is not in highly inelastic supply, and if the union is unable to control admission to membership as a condition of employment—that is, it is unable to erect barriers to employment—an increase in the wage rate may provide the employer with a large amount of labor from which he may selectively choose his employed labor force. One of the criteria for employment may be the applicant's negative attitude toward union membership.[34] In Figure 12.10, if the union succeeds in raising the wage from $0W_1$ to $0W_2$, the employer will be able to select $0N_1$ workers from a market supply of $0N_2$. The existence of N_1N_2 surplus labor available to the employer may represent a threat to the union. This threat can be reduced if the wage rate is increased only to $0W_3$, and if W_3W_2 is taken in the form of nonmarketable fringe benefits. The visible wage $0W_3$ attracts only $0N_3$ applicants to the firm, and the union finds it much easier to bar entry to N_1N_3 than to N_1N_2 workers. Membership carries with it the privilege of receiving higher real benefits and presumably this privilege strengthens the ties of employees to the union.

Employers may find that the arrangement tends to lower the ALC curve by lowering the variety of costs associated with turnover, of which training is only one part. Hence, even though the union is able to raise wages by W_1W_3 and add fringe benefits of W_3W_2, the employer may still be able to retain some monopsony profits because of the increased gap between MRP and the lower real supply curve of labor. One would expect turnover rates to decline as the longevity of those workers receiving fringe benefits increases. Vacation time and the capital value of pension and subrelated benefits increase with an employee's length of service. However, as an employee's length of service is extended, his future work life expectancy

---

[33] Leonard Weiss, "Concentration and Labor Earnings," *American Economic Review*, Vol. 56, No. 1 (March 1966), pp. 96–117.

[34] Although the employer may be committing an unfair labor practice in hiring upon the basis of antiunion sentiments, such a charge can easily be evaded by favoring applicants, say, with rural backgrounds where antiunion attitudes are more prevalent.

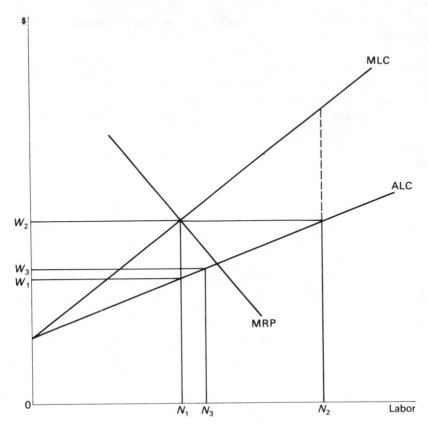

FIGURE 12.10. The effect of fringe benefits on the offer of labor to the firm.

is reduced. Hence, the wage differential in alternative employment that makes it economically feasible for an employee to change jobs becomes increasingly large, partly because it must be large enough to compensate a worker for the capital loss incurred from forgoing his accumulated fringe benefits and partly because the present value of the higher wage is less the shorter the period over which this wage is received. As long as the employer can maintain the wage differential below this critical level, economic motives of his labor force to change jobs will be largely absent. Of course, as the labor force ages, normal attrition from deaths, illness, and retirements will rise, but there may be a substantial lag before this occurs. During this interval, turnover costs may approach a minimum.

Lester quotes four studies made in 1952, 1959, and 1962 plus interviews in 1964 and 1965 with automobile workers in which employees reveal preference for benefits rather than wage increases.[35] The interval 1958–1965 represents a period of relative price stability in the American economy. To the extent that negotiated gains included modest wage increases *plus* these benefits, the workers could observe their real wage rise. Since the higher level of supplemental benefits represented greater security and reduced the need for higher personal savings, disposable personal income available for consumption purposes was correspondingly enhanced. To the extent that paid sick leave, disability, and medical insurance reduce the necessity of a contingency fund, spending can be greater for every level of income.

In periods of substantial price increases, such as the 1967–1970 period, worker preferences lean strongly toward wage increases. In fact, the higher cost of living tends to shift the labor supply curves leftward. Since wage bargains are negotiated primarily at three-year intervals, the expectation of inflation leads workers to seek to hedge against future declines in real earnings by building in higher wage rates. Unions are willing to support these demands because the leftward shift of the market labor supply curve means that the potential surplus labor at higher wage rates is removed. Workers' dissatisfaction at not receiving wage gains at a minimum pattern may represent a greater threat to union survival than the possibility of a surplus labor force, for employees can change bargaining representatives through decertification elections. Members may take for granted the protective role of unions, and if the union cannot protect them against inflation, the union may lose face with its membership just as much as if it were unable to process grievances effectively.

Thus, in periods of relative economic stability supplemental benefits have tended to register the greatest gains. This does not imply that the principle of a new type of benefit is necessarily established during so-called "normal" times. In fact, there is some evidence that these principles are established only when the union's power is at a maximum, which may well be when the labor market is the tightest. Hence, the general principle of pension plans was established during the first part of the Korean War and SUB ("Supplemental Unemployment Benefits") during the boom of 1955. Nevertheless, in terms of the magnitude of increases, 1957–1965 represents the period of greatest gain in these benefits. From 1950 through 1956, fringe benefits rose from 5% to 6.3% of total employee compensation, an increase of 26%. From 1957 to 1964, supplements increased from 6.3 to 8.8% of total compensation, an increase of almost 40%.[36]

[35] *Op. cit.*

[36] Based on *National Income and Product Accounts of the United States 1929–65, Statistical Tables,* U.S. Department of Commerce, Office of Business Economics (August 1966), Table 1.10. Not included are payments for time not worked. Various forms of premium pay, including overtime, shift pay, and holiday pay are included in wages and salaries and are not counted here as supplementary payments.

Employers find it to their advantage, aside from the effect on reducing turnover, to pay part of an employee's compensation in the form of fringe benefits. These benefits, not being a part of the basic wage, do not enter into overtime or premium pay calculations, nor need Social Security taxes be based upon them. Furthermore, in times of relative economic stability, firms may be able to grant supplementary benefits without disturbing existing wage patterns or establishing new ones in an industry; yet, they appear to satisfy the incessant cravings of unions and their members always for "more." In fact, by building into a supplementary benefit program multiple constraints, some more binding than others, firms may appear to be granting more than is actually involved. For example, SUB benefits were originally to be financed by a contribution of five cents per work hour to the SUB fund. However, such contributions were to cease when the fund amounted to a specified sum, determined by formula. Hence, over many of the early years of the program, firms were able to pay much less. Yet, union leaders and the automobile company were able to claim that a sizable settlement had been achieved. Similarly, pension contributions were tied in originally with Social Security payments. The employer limited his liability to a pension of, say, one hundred dollars per month. Hence, if Social Security payments advanced, the employers' contribution would be correspondingly reduced. Early in 1971 the U.S. Government began to frown upon the implementation of this practice and announced that the tax-exempt status of firms incurring expenses under such a pension program would be revoked if pension benefit contributions of employers were henceforth reduced. Until this time, however, employers could appear to be yielding more than they actually were. Union leaders complied in this deception, for it was to their advantage to have their members believe their leaders were winning more in collective bargaining than they actually were, particularly if market conditions prevented employers from granting liberal concessions.

Premium Pay as a Fringe Benefit

Why might employers be induced to pay overtime rates in excess of the legal requirement or to incur penalty payments for work time scheduled at times inconvenient to employees? Essentially, the labor market tends to compel these payments even in the absence of union pressure. In effect, labor is voluntarily withheld at certain times and persons will not exchange labor time for the customary rate of pay. Weekends, holidays, and evening hours carry especial attractions involving family activities and/or unique experiences. Hence, in order to be able to compel or require job attendance, the employer must raise the rate commensurate with the psychic satisfactions sacrificed by the labor force.

In 1971, Chrysler announced an agreement with the United Automobile

Workers to explore the possibility of scheduling a workweek consisting of four 10-hour work days in order to combat chronic absenteeism. Since much of Chrysler's work is under U.S. Government contracts, overtime pay may be required for hours over eight worked in any one day. If absenteeism occurs because of monotony or illness induced by fatigue, it is difficult to see how reducing the number of days will remedy the source of absenteeism. To be sure, the worker ostensibly sacrifices one-fourth rather than one-fifth of his pay, but if he is covered by sick leave, no sacrifice is involved. If the worker chooses to engage in other activities during his absenteeism, then the schedule change conceivably might remedy this problem. Michigan is not only a state filled with automobile assembly plants, but it is also a land of thousands of recreational lakes and ski slopes. Many of the affluent workers have second homes on lakes accessible through a superior highway system. Hence, it may well be that the absenteeism is simply a result of workers' choosing more leisure, given their high incomes. Whether a four-day week will satisfy their leisure preferences remains to be seen. Some absenteeism may be reduced through more desirable scheduling of leisure time, but absenteeism owing to other causes may increase. Hence, a prediction of no significant change in the absentee rate is reasonable. In fact, the labor supply curve is shifting to the left, and it may be that fringe benefits in the future must allow for even more paid nonwork time.

Discussion Questions

1. Does exploitation require an imperfect labor market? Was the labor market imperfect during the era observed by Karl Marx? Discuss the implications of your answers.
2. Suppose exploitation exists and a minimum wage law is enacted.

   (a) What will be the effect on wages and employment?
   (b) If no exploitation exists, what will be the effect on wages and employment?
   (c) What do your answers imply with respect to income distribution?
   (d) What do your answers imply with respect to continuing increments in the minimum wage?
3. Suppose a law was enacted taxing away all profits gained from wage exploitation. (Perhaps the revenues could be used for welfare payments.) For such a law, would a distinction between deliberate and non-deliberate exploitation be necessary? Discuss.
4. Either a free-trade policy or a policy to maintain the economy at less than full employment will tend to stabilize prices. Discuss.

5. Recruitment and training costs generate a rising curve of labor supply. Manpower policies to provide more efficient job information, therefore, may not eliminate exploitation or retard the rate of inflation. Discuss.

6. If unions could be prevented by law from seeking a further wage increase after their initial one, except when it can be shown that the demand for labor in the firms or industries organized by them has increased, then their wage–employment distortion effects would be minimized. Discuss.

7. Studebaker workers accepted a wage cut in order to preserve their jobs. Shortly thereafter the automobile company closed down. Does this prove that capital and labor are not always substitutes for each other?

8. Suppose a neutral technological innovation is introduced, but output is not changed. What does this imply with respect to the employment of labor and capital? If the change had been a labor saving one, does this imply that more capital would be used than formerly? Explain.

9. If real wages are to increase, must most technological innovations be labor saving? Discuss.

10. Fringe benefits have greater appeal to union officials and employers than to employees. Discuss.

13

Bilateral Monopoly and Bargaining Power

Introduction

One illustration of the imperfect labor market–imperfect product market is when a relatively strong union faces an oligopolistic employer. This situation has been identified as bilateral monopoly because both the seller of labor, the union, and its buyer, the oligopolist, possess monopoly-type powers. By law, the employer is required to recognize the union if it represents a majority of the company's employees, and although the company reserves the right to refuse to concede to union wage–employment demands, it does so only at considerable risk of a strike. Similarly, the company utilizes substantial amounts of labor in local labor markets, and its decision to hire more or less labor can have a market impact on the wages paid by other employers in the community. In the bilateral monopoly situation, economic analysis cannot predict the precise level of wages, even if the relevant supply and demand parameters are given. Under certain circumstances, it may be possible to explain the level of employment, however.

Let us examine the bilateral monopoly model to illustrate the problem of wage indeterminancy.[1] In Figure 13.1, the demand curve for labor, D_L, is the MRP curve. The market supply curve for labor, S_L, is the ALC curve, but if the union is a wage maximizer it will seek to equate the marginal cost of labor with the marginal curve to the demand for labor. Hence, the union in effect sells labor from the marginal labor cost curve M and this is, for all

[1] See William Fellner, "Prices and Wages under Bilateral Monopoly," *Quarterly Journal of Economics*, LXI, No. 4 (August 1947), pp. 503–532.

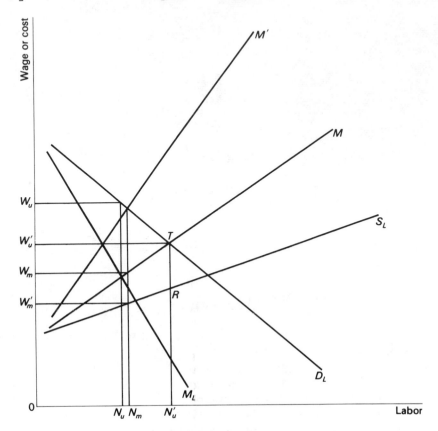

FIGURE 13.1. The bilateral monopoly labor market.

practical purposes, the labor supply curve. The union can maximize wages by seeking $0W_u$ wages, which if paid would lead the employer to utilize $0N_u$ quantity of labor. This represents a strong union–weak employer relationship.

The employer, on the other hand, regarding M as his appropriate supply curve, seeks to equate the curve marginal to it, M', with D_L, and if he is able to do so, would pay $0W_m$ wage and employ $0N_m$ labor. Hence, if the union and the employer are equally strong, the wage will tend to lie within W_uW_m and employment within N_uN_m. If the union is very weak relative to the employer, it is conceivable that the wage may even approach W'_m, the market supply wage.

If the union's primary objective is membership size, and if in order to attract members it is compelled to seek a wage higher than the market wage, this objective can be optimally satisfied at $0W'_u$ wage and $0N'_u$ employment. Normally, in a bilateral monopoly situation, the union seeks a given wage consistent with its expectation of a given or desired level of employment. However, it ordinarily has little control over the employment decision, which is regarded as a management prerogative.

If the wage–employment combination which the union seeks is consistent with the short-run demand–supply relationships, but causes a long-run disequilibrium situation, the union may attempt to protect its current employment position by imposing on the employer "make-work" rules. If such rules are not imposed, capital may be substituted for labor, and the new D_L curve may, at the existing wage, be consistent with less employment. Make-work rules, therefore, can be interpreted as a union policy designed to stabilize that demand curve for labor under which it seeks to influence the wage–employment relationship.

In the absence of a union, the strong employer can maximize profits by employing $0N'_u$ labor, consistent with the intersection of M with D_L. This is the same amount of labor that a membership-maximizing union would seek, although a range of indeterminancy, RT, in wages still would persist. It would be to the advantage of the employer and the union to agree to this desired employment position, but a condition thereto would undoubtedly require an acceptable division of the maximum income. Simulated bilateral monopoly experiments have been conducted by Fouraker and Siegel to determine if a cooperative relationship is a reasonable hypothesis.[2] They found that where the parties are able to learn through repeated negotiations and where they have sufficient information about the joint payoff, a cooperative pattern of behavior does tend to develop.

In established collective bargaining relationships which are approximations of the bilateral monopoly model, it can be concluded that settlements involving wages and employment will lie within ranges specified by the market parameters in which the parties operate. Although under firm profit-maximizing and union membership-maximizing behavioral assumptions[3] there is a tendency for a unique employment level to be established; this is not true for the wage rate. A unique wage is not established as an

---

[2] Sidney Siegel and Lawrence E. Fouraker, *Bargaining and Group Decision Making: Experiments in Bilateral Monopoly* (New York: McGraw-Hill Book Co., 1960). Donald L. Harnett has reported in a similar experiment that the parties to a bilateral monopoly price leadership model under complete information tend to reach a bargain at a price and quantity which equally divides the joint maximum payoff. See "Bargaining and Negotiation in a Mixed-Motive Game: Price Leadership Bilateral Monopoly," *Southern Economic Journal*, Vol. 33, No. 4 (April 1967), pp. 479–487.

[3] For a discussion of this and other assumptions of union maximizing behavior, see John T. Dunlop, *Wage Determination under Trade Unions* (New York: Macmillan Co., 1944), Chapters 3, 4.

equilibrium condition by these parameters, although they do permit the indeterminancy to be constrained within specified limits.

Qualifications to the Bilateral Monopoly Model

Wage–employment determination under bilateral monopoly conditions is further complicated by the fact that organized labor and management are not likely to share a common perception of present and future labor demand and supply function. These perceptions are clouded by self-interest where each party tends to see only that which it wishes to see. Management may be quite pessimistic with respect to the course of future demand, whereas labor may be equally optimistic. Management's view justifies a lower wage increase; the union's view favors a greater wage increase. Similar misconceptions can arise over the firm's labor cost functions.

Consequently, negotiations over wages ordinarily must pass through a phase in which the parties can communicate their perceptions to one another. In the process each tries to convince the other that his interpretation of the nature and magnitude of the real parameters is correct. A learning process occurs and some modifications in viewpoints occur. Ideally, the parties reach a consensus that approximates closely the real parameters, but this is not essential. In fact, each party's understanding of the magnitude of the parameters, although consistent, may be far from the true one.[4] Nevertheless, once a common understanding of the limits of bargaining is reached, a second stage is entered in which each, through the implied use of sanctions, seeks to obtain a settlement as favorable as possible to his own interests. This is the hard bargaining stage, and it usually is reached only as some deadline for the imposition of sanctions is approached. The process of bargaining, with its implications with respect to the use of power, is examined more closely later in the chapter.

Wage-Preference Analysis

A concept known as the "union wage-preference path" has been developed in order to identify a narrower range of indeterminancy of the

---

[4] If the first phase is unsuccessful, the parties will enter the second phase with vague and perhaps unrealistic ideas of what is obtainable. Bargaining power may not force a settlement before a strike occurs because of the imperfect framework on which each party bases its concept of power. It is still to the advantage of the union to have the employer believe that the labor-supply function is higher than the union believes it to be, and the employer still desires the union to underestimate the labor-demand function. Each party will attempt to secure these divergent beliefs through strategies and tactics. If the bargainers are sufficiently shrewd, however, these efforts are apt to result unintentionally in a clearer recognition of the realities of the situation.

wage–employment bargain.[5] It seeks to set the upper limit to the wage–employment bargain between unions and management under various possible levels of labor demand.

An indifference map of wage–employment combinations is assumed to exist. Along each indifference curve, the union derives the same utility from any combination of wages and employment. Greater utility is associated with combinations lying on higher curves. The sharp bend in the indifference curves means that a very high wage increase is necessary to compensate the union for the loss in utility associated with even a small reduction in employment, or that a very great increase in employment is necessary to compensate the union for even a small decrease in wages. The constraint which the union faces in realizing its wage–employment preferences is the demand curve for labor, here represented by the MRP curve. The MRP curve is also the employer's preference curve for wage–employment combinations in that, given any wage, the curve identifies the level of employment desired by the employer.[6] Given a set of labor demand curves, points of tangency between the union's indifference curves and the employer's preference curves plot out a locus which Cartter identifies as the union wage–employment preference curve. Because of the nature of the indifference curves, the positions of the sharp bends determine the position and shape of the wage–employment preference path (WPP). Implicitly, each MRP curve with respect to the indifference curve must have a smaller slope above the point of tangency and a greater slope below the point of tangency, which rules out a wide variety of labor demand situations to which WPP analysis can apply. Cartter believes that unions favor large wage increases rather than large employment expansion as demand expands, and they oppose wage reductions—even in the face of large contractions in employment—when demand decreases. These biases produce a kink in the WPP at the existing wage, P in Figure 13.2.

The WPP sets an upper limit to the wage–employment bargain, the supply curve of labor sets the lower limit. The range of bargaining in the bilateral monopoly model is narrowed if the WPP lies below the wages under each labor demand condition corresponding to W_u in Figure 13.1. Presumably, these W_u's plot out a locus determining the upper limit to bargaining, which we shall call WU. If WPP lies on or above WU, the range of bargaining is not narrowed.

[5] Allan M. Cartter, *Theory of Wages and Employment* (Homewood, Illinois: Richard D. Irwin, Inc., 1959), pp. 86–106. Also see Allan M. Cartter and F. Ray Marshall, *Labor Economics, Wages, Employment, and Trade Unionism* (Homewood, Illinois: R. D. Irwin, Inc., 1967), pp. 282–312.

[6] In Cartter, *ibid.*, pp. 95–98, it is demonstrated that the employer can maximize profits by moving to the right (and down) along the MRP curve, which is the labor demand curve.

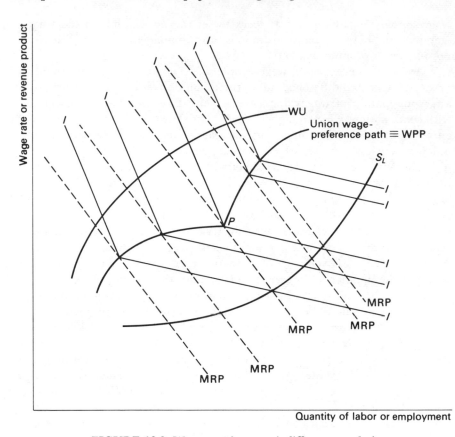

FIGURE 13.2. Wage–employment indifference analysis.

Lowell Galloway has developed an interesting application of wage-preference analysis by means of which he attempts to show that the union shop yields greater economic efficiency than the open shop.[7] Adopting Dunlop's assumption of a membership-maximizing objective, he assumes that the point of departure is at the point of the kink in the wage-preference path, where labor demand and supply are equal. In the absence of a union-shop clause, which provides the union with economic and institutional security, the union will seek to increase its membership by bargaining and obtaining higher wages. This is necessary because, under the open-shop arrangement made compulsory by right-to-work laws, membership is

[7] Lowell Galloway, "The Economics of the Right-to-Work Controversy," *Southern Economic Journal* (January 1966), pp. 310–316.

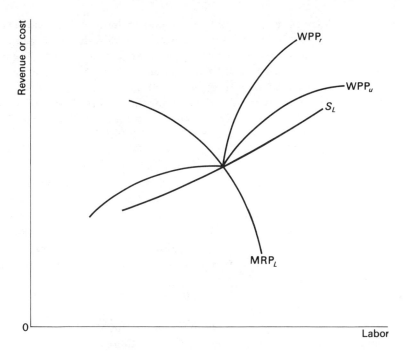

FIGURE 13.3. Wage-preference paths under open-shop and union-shop conditions.

completely voluntary and higher wages are necessary to attract members. On the other hand, under union-shop arrangements, the necessity to win and maintain employee affiliation is removed, and the union can substitute employment (membership) expansion for wage gains. As a consequence, under conditions of rising labor demand, the wage–employment indifference curves will be more steeply sloped in bargaining situations where right-to-work laws govern, than in situations where union-security provisions are permitted. This relative steepness of indifference curves plots out an open-shop wage-preference path (WPP$_r$) which lies above the wage-preference path under union-shop conditions (WPP$_u$). Economic efficiency is enhanced because wages and employment under the union shop lie closer to the market labor supply curve than under the open shop, and the misallocation of labor from the monopoly power of unions is reduced (see Figure 13.3).

Galloway has defended the central thesis of his argument against several challenges,[8] although he has acknowledged that one or more modifications

[8] Lewis Hill, "Comment," John M. Peterson and Darrel L. Spriggs, "Comment," *Southern Economic Journal* (January 1967), pp. 409–415. Also, Paul C. Roberts and Norman L. Brown, "Comment," *ibid.* (January 1969), pp. 265–266.

are in order.[9] Wage-preference analysis contains a basic fallacy, however, which negates the model used by Galloway to establish his argument. Furthermore, Galloway ignores a very important feature of the bilateral monopoly model as applied to collective bargaining, which may contradict his thesis. This oversight involves the concept of bargaining power.

The wage-preference path (WPP) plots out the preferred level of wages and employment of the union under varying conditions of labor demand— the MRP curves—and thereby tends to establish the upper limit of the wage–employment objectives sought by the union in bargaining.[10] The lower limit is established by the supply curve of labor. One of the conceptual difficulties of the WPP is that it can be identified only if the pattern of shifts in the demand for labor is known. Given the production function, the changes in the demand for labor depend upon shifts in the product demand function. As Joan Robinson has shown, in an imperfectly competitive world the patterns of possible shifts in product demand are infinite in number; therefore, the probability of parallel shifts in demand is infinitely small. If shifts in the production function are permitted, the identification problem is compounded. Although we may speculate about the shape of the wage–employment indifference curves, we cannot speculate meaningfully about the nature of the WPP unless we know the slopes of the MRP curves at each wage–employment point, for it is the tangency of these MRP curves to the indifference curves that determines the WPP.[11] It is conceivable that no tangencies exist under certain patterns of demand shift. Thus, if the WPP does not exist or cannot be identified, it is meaningless to argue that the "wage–preference path for the open shop will be more steeply sloped than that of the union shop above the respective equilibrium points."

[9] "Reply," *Southern Economic Journal* (January 1967), 416–418; and "Reply," *ibid.* (January 1969), p. 267.

[10] On this point, Roberts and Brown, *op. cit.*, are absolutely correct. The wage-preference path is not a path of equilibrium adjustments. Galloway in his reply ignores this fundamental point.

[11] In this sense, the question of the existence of the wage-preference path is analogous to that of a firm's supply curve in an imperfect world. As Peterson and Spriggs, *op. cit.*, have noted, "a particular pattern of indifference is predetermined in relation to the *current* wage–employment combination." The nesting arrangement of the indifference curves in effect determines the shape of the WPP since, according to Cartter's assumptions, the indifference curves are convex from below almost at right angles. This particular kind of convexity may make the tangency conditions even more difficult to satisfy. If no tangencies exist, the question may be asked—as Peterson and Spriggs imply—whether Cartter doesn't have the cart before the horse; i.e., whether the shape of the indifference map doesn't depend upon the existing wage *and* the nature of the shift in labor demand. The union and the employer may have different perceptions of the nature of the shift in the MRP curve, and a variation in perception may also occur between open-shop and union-shop labor organizations.

In a limited sense, it may be possible to conceive of the section of the WPP which lies between the demand curve for labor from which the present wage–employment combination is determined and the demand curve which is expected to prevail by the union during the period of a new labor agreement. Nothing is added, however, by attempting to develop the entire wage-preference path. The segment slopes may be significant in identifying the upper limits of the respective ranges of bargaining, but they are irrelevant for establishing Galloway's efficiency thesis, as Roberts and Brown have shown.

The existing wage, and movements therefrom, need not lie on the WPP, since wages in the bilateral monopoly model of collective bargaining need not lie on the MRP curve. The wage–employment point will lie on or near the MRP curve only if the bargaining power of the union is very strong relative to that of the employer. It will lie on or near the supply curve of labor only if the union is very weak relative to the employer. Thus, bargaining power determines the location of the wage–employment point, and even though this point is related to an existing MRP curve, it need not lie on the curve. Consequently, more relevant than the WPP to Galloway's thesis is the slope of the locus of points of actual wage–employment adjustments.

On the other hand, if a union is sufficiently strong to obtain the union shop but cannot, because of an open-shop (right-to-work) law, the locus of actual adjustments may lie close to the WPP segment. There is no reason to suppose that the slope of the WPP segment would be steeper if the right-to-work law did not exist, but we cannot infer that, therefore, the actual adjustment line is unaffected. On the other hand, if the open shop exists only because the union is not strong enough to win the union shop, the existing wage–employment point would lie below the MRP curve and be at a lower wage than in the former case, although it does not necessarily follow that employment may be greater. Changes in wages are likely to be less, and the slope of the actual adjustment line will probably be less than in the former case, regardless of the slope of the WPP. Ordinarily, the weaker bargaining power of the union in the market-determined open shop will generate a lower wage increase than in an open shop which exists only because it has been legally imposed. In either case, the slope of the WPP segment will depend upon how the union perceives the shift in the curve marginal to the new MRP curve, and the slope of the line of actual adjustments will depend on the union's bargaining power.

If the existence of a right-to-work law is taken as an indication of the relative political influence of union and employer groups, one might argue that these laws reflect an environment which confers more bargaining power on employers. If this is so, wages and wage changes may be lower than they otherwise would be if unions as a group had possessed political power sufficient to prevent the enactment or to secure the repeal of the laws. Again, the lower wages may or may not be associated with greater employment, so we cannot draw the conclusion—the converse of which was implied by Galloway's analysis—that right-to-work laws further economic efficiency. If, in fact, lower wages *and* greater employment do occur, then by Galloway's criterion, right-to-work laws do contribute to greater economic efficiency.

Bargaining Models[11a]

Bargaining refers to a procedure through which the parties to a transaction can argue, determine, and agree upon what each shall give and receive in the exchange that occurs between or among them. In this sense, bargaining is essentially the negotiations that take place over the terms of an agreement. A complete theory of bargaining should yield insight into several aspects of the procedure:

1. Who are the parties and why must they bargain?
2. What are the essential elements in bargaining, and why are they important?
3. How do the parties determine what terms to seek through bargaining and how are these terms evaluated?
4. How are these terms influenced by the bargaining process?
5. Under what conditions is an agreement reached?

This concept of the bargaining process is much broader than the concept of bargaining power in that the latter is primarily concerned with a solution to question (4).

Collective bargaining is essentially a two-party relationship in which ultimate choices and decisions are made by representatives of each of the two teams in bargaining. Of course, agencies and officials of the government, rival or cooperating unions, competing or cooperative employers, and, in some cases, suppliers and consumers do exert various forms of pressure in negotiation. Nevertheless, even under such complex bargaining arrangements as multiunion or multiemployer bargaining, the actual process of negotiations can be reduced in essence to a two-party or -team game, and the influence of outside parties can be incorporated into the valuations and judgements made by the actual participants (see Table 13.1).

[11a] Much of the material that follows has been adapted from my article, "The Pure Theory of Bargaining," *Industrial and Labor Relations Review* (July 1965).

TABLE 13.1
WAGE AND BENEFIT DECISIONS, 1965–1970

Measure	*Median Annual Percentage Rate of Increase in Decisions Reached in—*					
	1965	*1966*	*1967*	*1968*	*1969*	*1970*[a]
Major collective bargaining situations:[b]						
Wage and benefit change (packages):						
Over life of contract	3.3	4.0	5.2	6.0	7.4	8.9
First year	([c])	5.8	7.3	8.1	10.9	12.4
Negotiated wage-rate increases averaged over life of contract:						
All industries	[d]3.3	3.9	5.0	5.2	6.8	8.8
Manufacturing	([c])	3.8	5.1	4.9	5.8	6.6
Nonmanufacturing	([c])	3.9	5.0	5.9	8.5	12.3
Negotiated first-year wage-rate increases:						
All industries	3.9	4.8	5.7	7.2	8.0	10.2
Manufacturing	4.1	4.2	6.4	6.9	7.0	8.0
Nonmanufacturing	3.7	5.0	5.0	7.5	10.0	15.7
Wage increases in manufacturing:						
All establishments	3.7	4.2	5.3	6.0	6.2	7.0
Union establishments	3.6	4.1	5.5	6.5	6.9	7.7
Nonunion establishments	4.0	4.4	5.0	5.0	6.0	5.5

[a] Preliminary. Based on final data for first 9 months.

[b] Except for packages, data are for contracts affecting 1000 workers or more. Package-cost estimates are limited to settlements affecting 5000 workers or more (10,000 in 1965). The package cost of a few settlements affecting relatively few workers has not been determined.

[c] Not available.

[d] Based on settlements affecting 10,000 workers or more.

Note: Possible increases in wages resulting from cost-of-living escalator adjustments (except those guaranteed in the contracts) were omitted.

Source: Department of Labor. *Economic Report of the President, 1971*, p. 58.

The literature abounds with a variety of models, some more intricate than others, and it is perhaps impossible to identify one which is clearly superior to another. However, there are a number of popular models, made so in part by the esteem which their authors already merited in the field of labor economics, and brief summaries of four of these models will be presented. J. R. Hicks has developed a model which seeks to answer a simple but important question: To what extent can trade union pressure through the strike compel employers to pay higher wages (or grant more favorable terms to their employees in other respects) than they would if no such pressure had been exercised? He has called this the theory of industrial disputes, although he acknowledges that it is not intended as an analysis of the bargaining process. It is, however, an analysis of a very important element in that process.

Neil Chamberlain's model is representative of simple bargaining power models, and models of this type have usually considered only the method by which the terms of the agreement are influenced by the bargaining process. Jan Pen's approach is that of a general theory of bargaining and reflects the contributions of bargaining power models that apply to bargaining under conditions of uncertainty. Pen advances the work of such writers as Zeuthen and Shackle, although he goes beyond the contributions of this school. He is concerned not only with the manner in which wages are influenced by bargaining but also with how wages are subjectively evaluated by the bargainers and with the equilibrium conditions for settlement. Carl Stevens is not so much concerned with the process of subjective evaluation of wages as he is with the question of why the elements that characterize bargaining are important to the process. In all the models, there is much that is in common.

The Theory of Industrial Disputes

John R. Hicks perceives the threat of a strike and its costs to both parties as the essential feature of collective bargaining that brings about a negotiated wage settlement (see Table 13.2). The method by which the strike brings about agreement in the wage rate demanded by the union and that offered by the employer is illustrated in Figure 13.4. If the union anticipated that no strike would be necessary to obtain any wage increase, it presumably would seek the highest wage that is consistent with the employer's ability to pay—i.e., any higher wage might drive the employer out of business. In Figure 13.4 this is indicated as point *A*. Point *B* represents the existing wage, or a wage below which the employer could not attract or keep his labor force—a labor-market wage constraint. In the absence of an expected strike, this is the wage that the employer would offer. Any wage rate in excess of *B*, when multiplied by the man-hours to be worked in the future and discounted by an appropriate interest factor, represents the present value of future incremental labor costs to the employer as a result of the wage increase. However, strikes impose costs on the employer. Profits are forgone, fixed costs continue, customers are alienated, attrition in the firm's labor force occurs as the strike progresses, plant morale may suffer,

TABLE 13.2
WORK STOPPAGES RESULTING FROM LABOR–MANAGEMENT DISPUTES[a]

Month and Year	Number of Stoppages		Workers Involved in Stoppages		Man-Days Idle during Month or Year	
	Beginning in Month or Year	In effect during Month	Beginning in Month or Year (thousands)	In effect during Month (thousands)	Number (thousands)	Percent of Estimated Working Time
1945	4,750	—	3,470	—	38,000	0.31
1946	4,985	—	4,600	—	116,000	1.04
1947	3,693	—	2,170	—	34,600	0.30
1948	3,419	—	1,960	—	34,100	0.28
1949	3,606	—	3,030	—	50,500	0.44
1950	4,843	—	2,410	—	38,800	0.33
1951	4,737	—	2,220	—	22,900	0.18
1952	5,117	—	3,540	—	59,100	0.48
1953	5,091	—	2,400	—	28,300	0.22
1954	3,468	—	1,530	—	22,600	0.18
1955	4,320	—	2,650	—	28,200	0.22
1956	3,825	—	1,900	—	33,100	0.24
1957	3,673	—	1,390	—	16,500	0.12
1958	3,694	—	2,060	—	23,900	0.18
1959	3,708	—	1,880	—	69,000	0.50
1960	3,333	—	1,320	—	19,100	0.14
1961	3,367	—	1,450	—	16,300	0.11
1962	3,614	—	1,230	—	18,600	0.13
1963	3,362	—	941	—	16,100	0.11
1964	3,655	—	1,640	—	22,900	0.15
1965	3,963	—	1,550	—	23,300	0.15
1966	4,405	—	1,960	—	25,400	0.15
1967	4,595	—	2,870	—	42,100	0.25
1968	5,045	—	2,649	—	49,018	0.28
1969	5,700	—	2,481	—	42,869	0.24

[a] The data include all known strikes or lockouts involving 6 workers or more and lasting a full day or shift or longer. Figures on workers involved and man-days idle cover all workers made idle for as long as 1 shift in establishments directly involved in a stoppage. They do not measure the indirect or secondary effect on other establishments or industries whose employees are made idle as a result of material or service shortages.

Source: *Monthly Labor Review* (October 1970), p. 99.

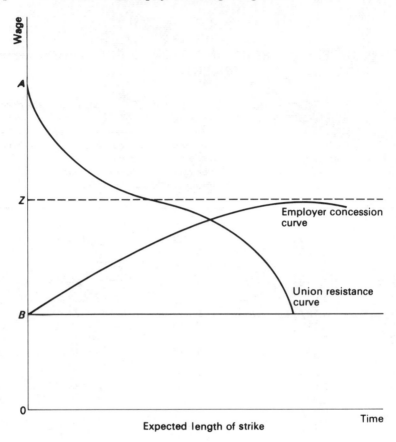

FIGURE 13.4. Hicks' model of wage bargaining.

etc. These costs also are a function of the duration of the strike. Presumably, the employer is indifferent between a given wage increase and a strike duration of some length if the present value of their costs are equal. The length of the strike which would equate strike costs with costs associated with a given wage in excess of B is measured along a path called the "employer's concession curve." Presumably, there is some wage such as Z whose present value of future costs will always exceed the costs of a strike of any duration. This wage Z may or may not exceed the maximum wage A, which the union would seek.

The union incurs costs of possible forgone wages if it seeks and wins a wage less than A. By the same token, the membership incurs the cost of lost income when they strike, and the longer the strike, the greater the loss of earnings. This loss of earnings reduces the net present value of the benefits derived from wage *A*. Presumably, the membership would find it to their economic advantage to accept a wage below *A* rather than to endure a strike longer than some specified duration: put another way, for each strike of a given duration there is a wage at which the union is indifferent between the strike and the wage. The path that traces the willingness of the union to strike for a period of time rather than accept a reduction in their wage demands is measured by the union resistance curve.[12] This curve indicates, in terms of the union's willingness to strike, its resistance to lowering its wage demands from *A* toward *B*.

The point *W* at which the union resistance curve intersects the employer's concession curve represents a wage which both would prefer, and hence would accept, rather than endure a strike longer than *t* duration. If both parties anticipated that the strike would last longer than *t* time, then *W* would be an acceptable wage to both during negotiations and a strike could be avoided if they could agree on *W*. If both felt that the strike would not last as long as *t*, then a strike would necessarily occur.

G. F. Shove observed in 1933 in reviewing *The Theory of Wages* that the interpretation of the "employer's concession curve" and the "trade union's resistance curve" is hazy and it seems impossible to extract from them the conclusions which are based upon them (while the employer's power of resistance and the union's belief about it are somehow left out of the picture).[13] The union resistance curve and the employer concession curve may be taken as truly representative of each party's position *at a point in time*. The difficulty, however, is that neither party actually knows the other's position; consequently, each must estimate these curves, and there is no necessary reason why their respective estimates should be the same. Moreover, if the positions of the parties change as bargaining unfolds, the respective curves which reflect their behavior should shift or change. Hicks, although he believes his diagram is sufficient for explaining how union pressure works, has lately acknowledged that a family of such curves is necessary to represent the developing levels of sophistication of the parties as bargaining unfolds.[14]

Bargaining Power

Chamberlain has defined *bargaining power* as follows: "The bargaining power of A is the cost to B of disagreeing on A's terms, relative to the cost

[12] In the words of Hicks, "Corresponding to each length of strike there will thus be a wage (or set of terms) which will be acceptable, if it cannot be improved except by prolonging the strike," *The Theory of Wages*, 2nd ed. (London: Macmillan Co., 1963), p. 354.
[13] "Review of the Theory of Wages," *The Economic Journal*, September 1933, reprinted in *The Theory of Wages*, 2nd ed., p. 263.
[14] *Ibid.*, p. 354.

to B of agreeing on A's terms.[15] The bargaining power of B is defined similarly. Thus, the relationship between the bargaining powers of the two parties can be shown in the following expression:

$$\frac{B.P.\ of\ A}{\text{cost to B of disagreeing on A's terms}}$$
$$\text{cost to B of agreeing on A's terms}$$

$$\frac{B.P.\ of\ B}{\gtreqless}\ \frac{\text{cost to A of disagreeing on B's terms}}{\text{cost to A of agreeing on B's terms}}$$

Each party can have substantial bargaining power. Each can make it much more costly to the other to disagree to their terms than to agree. Why then might they disagree? An analogous question is, "Why do countries go to war when each will lose by the conflict?" The answer seems to be that the party with superior power in a bargaining context can extract greater concessions from his opponent. If there is uncertainty as to who possesses superior power, so much more likely is a conflict. (In 1941 did Japan know it was weaker at that time than the United States?)

Chamberlain's concept of costs includes both economic and non-economic costs. He also recognizes that costs, and hence relative bargaining power, vary as terms are changed, although he does not express his power definition in terms of a functional relationship. Costs of disagreeing are identified as the losses owing to the overt nature of the disagreement. Costs of agreement include the sacrifices (monetary or otherwise) incurred by a party in accepting his opponent's offer, which ordinarily differs from his own demands. Costs, of course, are only one side of bargaining; benefits also accrue from the process, and ordinarily the two must be weighed in reaching agreement.

Although Chamberlain notes that bargaining power changes with the benefits or terms under consideration, he does not identify the motivational aspects of this process. When preferred terms are changed, the parties' willingness to accept or resist those changes is altered, and hence their goal orientation is transformed. The ability of the parties to influence one another's motives, to cause them to shift or change their proffered terms, is the essence of bargaining power. This is as much a communication problem as one of inherent ability to impose costs.

Because Chamberlain does not define relationships between terms and costs, he does not tell us under what conditions a settlement will be reached.

[15] Neil Chamberlain, *Collective Bargaining* (New York: McGraw-Hill Book Co., Inc., 1951), pp. 220–221.

In this sense, he does not provide us with a model of bargaining as complete as that of Hicks. He has distinguished the kinds of costs incurred in bargaining and how these costs influence relative power, and he has noted that power is essential in winning a favorable settlement. In this sense, his approach is similar to that of Hicks.

The Chamberlain costs can be interpreted also in terms of the traditional economic model of labor demand and supply. The relevant costs and revenue functions are the average cost of labor (ALC) and the average net revenue product (ANRP). If A, the union, seeks and obtains a benefit, say, in wages, the labor costs to the employer, B, are increased. However, not to grant the benefit imposes the costs of conflict on B, and this results in lowering the ANRP curve of the employer, since a strike interrupts the sales of a firm. Thus, the employer is faced with the possibility of reduced profits from granting the benefit, owing to a leftward shift in the ALC curve, and reduced profits from not granting the benefit, owing to a leftward shift in the ANRP curve. In Figure 13.5(a), the higher labor costs impose on the employer a reduction in profits equal to $W_1P_1E_1F_1$ minus $W_2P_2E_2F_2$. The loss of net revenue resulting from a strike or other conflict is shown in Figure 13.5(b) by the difference between $W_3P_3E_3F_3$ and $W_3P_3E_4F_4$. (The MRP curve need not be affected, unless other inputs are allowed to vary.) The employer is motivated to concede the benefits if the loss of revenue is greater than the loss resulting from higher costs; that is, if the net yield of the employer at that benefit level is negative.

The union is faced with the possibility of gain by a leftward shift of the ALC curve (in Figure 13.5(c), from ALC_1 to ALC_2), since this cost to the employer is revenue to the union. However, along with this gain comes the probability of conflict occurring, which will result in a rightward shift of the ALC curve (in Figure 13.5(c), from ALC_2 to ALC_3) as the costs of conflict are deducted from the gross revenue of the union. Presumably, the union will pursue benefits as long as the estimated change in the ALC curve (ALC_3) lies far enough to the left of the original curve (ALC_1) so that $W_3P_3N_20$ is greater than $W_1P_1N_10$. (Note that the employer will hire from the ALC_2 curve, for this curve represents his out-of-pocket money costs.) Thus, the union is motivated to seek benefits as long as the resulting net revenue (which is equal to $W_2P_2N_20$ minus the costs of the conflict, $W_2P_2P_3W_3$) is greater than the revenue originally received; that is, as long as the net yield of the union at that benefit level is greater than zero.

Presumably, the greater the benefit sought, the greater is the shift to the left of the ALC curve. However, the possibility of obtaining this large benefit would most likely affect the willingness of both the employer and the union to bear conflict. Thus, the ANRP curve would also tend to shift more to the left, and the costs to be deducted from the union's revenue curve (the

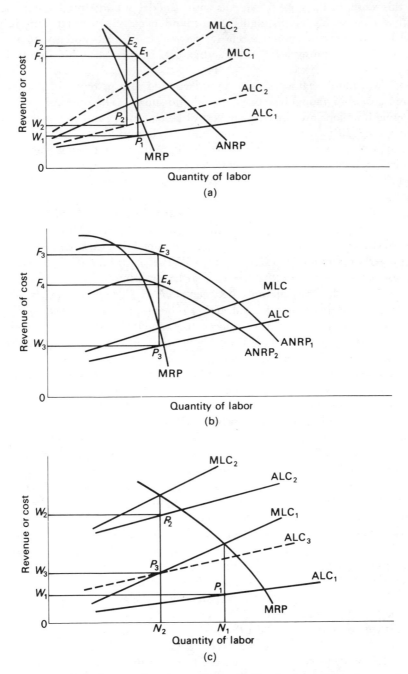

FIGURE 13.5. Costs and revenue effects of collective bargaining (see text).

employer's ALC curve) would be greater. Thus, the union and the employer seek, via bargaining, to shift one another's net-yield functions by shifting the revenue and cost functions. The union seeks to influence management's net-yield function through a shift in the ANRP and ALC curves so that at each benefit level either or both of the ANRP and ALC curves are lower than management had assumed them to be. The union also seeks to reduce its own costs of conflict necessary to achieve a level of benefits so that it may net more of the benefits from a leftward shift of the ALC curve. Management attempts to increase the costs of conflict to the union in order to reduce the union's estimate of its net-yield function. Management also tries to insulate itself from the effects of conflict in order to prevent a decrease in its ANRP curve.

Utility Functions and Bargaining Power

Jan Pen has developed a model which, unlike Chamberlain's, recognizes that the terms of the bargain can be transformed into utility functions.[16] He calls these functions "ophelimity functions" after a term first used as a substitute for the word utility by Vilfred Pareto, an Italian economist of the late 19th and early 20th centuries. Similarly, estimates of the cost of bargaining can also be expressed in such subjective terms. In addition, Pen attaches probability estimates (risk valuation factor) to these functions in estimating the likelihood of various costs being experienced. His bargaining power model can be expressed as follows[17]:

Bargaining power of labor:

$$\phi_L \left(\frac{L_{wl} - L_w}{L_{wl} - L_c} \right) - F_l(E_w - E_c) \gtreqless 0 \qquad (13.1)$$

Bargaining power of employer:

$$\phi_E \left(\frac{E_{we} - E_w}{E_{we} - E_c} \right) - F_e(L_w - L_c) \gtreqless 0 \qquad (13.2)$$

Since $(L_{wl} - L_w)$ represents the cost of agreement to labor—i.e., what labor loses if it accepts the offer under consideration—and since $(L_{wl} - L_c)$ represents the cost of disagreement to labor—the difference between what labor desires and what it gains from conflict—and, finally, since $(E_w - E_c)$

---

[16] Jan Pen, *The Wage Rate under Collective Bargaining* (Cambridge, Massachusetts: Harvard University Press, 1959).
[17] $\phi_{L \text{ or } E}$ = labor's (or employer's) risk-valuation factor; L_{wl} or E_{we} = functional value of utility of labor's or employer's utility of settlement for desired wages; L_w or E_w = utility of wage under consideration; L_c or E_c = wage after a strike; F_l or F_e = risk of resistance factor.

represents the employer's will to resist—the employer's current offer minus what he is forced to pay—Pen's model can be reformulated in these terms:

$$\text{Prob. } L \text{ or } E \left(\frac{\text{cost of agreement}}{\text{cost of disagreement}} \right)$$

$$- \text{ Prob. } L \text{ or } E \text{ (opponent's will to resist)} \gtreqless 0 \qquad (13.3)$$

Pen states that a settlement will be reached when both the buyer's and seller's estimated costs of agreement relative to the costs of disagreement are equal to the opponent's estimated will to resist. Pen recognizes that each party's estimate of the equations will differ and that the purpose of bargaining is to bring about a common estimate of the equations.

Pen's model represents a substantial advance over other bargaining power models, although in its final form it is reducible to substantially the same set of relations identified by Chamberlain. Pen does recognize a functional relationship between wages and the satisfaction derived from each wage level, but he does not integrate noneconomic benefits with his functional relationships. Conceptually, if economic and noneconomic benefits yield utilities, and if cost or revenue functions are transformable into utility functions (and vice versa), a merger of the two types of benefits is theoretically permissible. Pen also recognizes the existence of uncertainties, and his use of probability factors is an improvement over other models.

Pen notes that one of the most important functions of bargaining is the transmission of the information between the parties so that they can reach compatible estimates of the magnitude of the relevant variables in order for agreement to be reached. Behaviorally, the parties observe that the other's will to resist has stiffened. This suggests that Pen could have formulated his equation in these terms:

$$\text{expected (cost of disagreement} - \text{cost of agreement)}$$

$$- \text{ expected (opponent's will to resist)} \gtreqless 0. \qquad (13.4)$$

The first term reduces for labor, as an example, as follows:

$$\phi[(L_{wl} - L_c) - (L_{wl} - L_w)] = \phi[L_w - L_c] \qquad (13.5)$$

or labor's expected will to resist. Hence, as reformulated, the equilibrium condition for parties I and II is simply

$$\text{expected will to resist}_I \geq \text{expected will to resist}_{II} \qquad (13.6)$$

The wage in question in this case favors party I, who possesses the greater power. For party II to be favored, the inequality sign would be reversed. If the will to resist is interpreted in terms of a party's willingness to incur strike action, then this formulation is very similar to Hicks'. Pen requires that Equations (13.1) and (13.2) must both equal zero for an equilibrium to exist, but this appears to be too stringent a condition.

A model of bargaining power must show how the equilibrium conditions are reached when a disequilibrium condition prevails. Pen's model does not show this. It simply tells us whether the parties are motivated to seek or to resist a change in benefits. Since the essence of bargaining power is the ability of a party to alter the utility functions, an ability to change power relationships depends upon the capacity to alter the opponent's estimate of these utility functions.

Bargaining as a Conflict Situation

Stevens developed an approach that views bargaining as a conflict situation[18] in which the parties are called upon to make choices between two undesirable alternatives. This approach is described in an "avoidance–avoidance" model[19] in which the union's goal and the management's goal represent extreme ultimate positions. The distance separating the two extreme positions is measured in terms of a range of wage rates. If management settles on the union's terms, management loses; if it settles on its own terms, a conflict is precipitated in which management also loses. Management's motivation to avoid a settlement on the union's terms increases as the union's terms are approached in bargaining (*AA* in Figure 13.6), and an increasing risk of conflict also motivates management to avoid a settlement on management's terms (*BB* in Figure 13.6). The point of intersection of the two avoidance curves determines a compromise position and a point of possible settlement (*E*). The union has a similar set of avoidance curves. In bargaining, a party attempts to raise the avoidance curve *AA* or to lower the avoidance curve *BB* in order to bring about a settlement favorable to itself. A settlement can be reached only if both parties arrive at the same value for *E*, and furthermore, both parties must be aware that such an *E* exists.

The model used by Stevens is based, with only minor changes, on the avoidance–avoidance model developed by Dollard and Miller[20] to explain some features of behavior in which anxiety is induced by a situation in which there are no alternatives available to a subject except two undesirable goals. In the Dollard and Miller model, the level of anxiety is inversely associated with the distance, either spatial or temporal, from a goal. As the goal is approached, the level of anxiety increases according to the slope of the avoidance gradient, and the subject is increasingly motivated to avoid

[18] *Strategy and Collective Bargaining Negotiations* (New York: McGraw-Hill Book Co., 1963).
[19] Stevens, *op. cit.* (see note 1), p. 15.
[20] John Dollard and Neal E. Miller, *Personality and Psychotherapy* (New York: McGraw-Hill Book Co., 1950), pp. 359–364.

FIGURE 13.6. An avoidance–avoidance model of bargaining.

achieving the goal. If a subject is forced to choose between two undesirable goals such as remaining hungry or obtaining food from a source fraught with danger, the subject will find himself unable to escape from a frustrating situation, and his behavior will be vacillatory, indecisive, and erratic. Presumably, the level of anxiety increases because, through experience, the subject has learned to associate a negative benefit with the achievement of the goal. Achievement of the goal has not been rewarding; it has been punishing. Correction of neurotic behavior induced by such a situation, Dollard and Miller believed, requires achievement of a goal that produces a reward, but the learned behavior of a neurotic prohibits him from approaching too close to the goal for fear of punishment. As the subject "avoids" one goal by retreating from it, he approaches an undesirable opposing goal that also compels him to retreat. The neurotic, therefore, is a victim of competing drives that keep him in a state of tension. He is caught in the middle. The function of the psychoanalyst is, then, to lower through therapy the approach gradient to goal one to such an extent that retreat from goal two forces him to achieve goal one. A drive to achieve goal one can be induced also by raising the approach gradient of goal two so that the two gradients intersect only after goal one has been achieved.

There are some difficulties in adapting the avoidance–avoidance model to an analysis of collective-bargaining behavior. First of all, even though collective bargaining is a tension-producing situation, it is not analogous to vacillating, neurotic behavior, nor are the alternative goals always limited to two competing goals. In fact, there are numerous alternative goals, and, in the process of bargaining, these goal opportunities are explored. Neurotic collective-bargaining behavior would perhaps exist where both parties either refused to negotiate or continued to bargain without end because they were afraid of the results. In this respect, the symbiotic relationship could continue, but both parties would continue to suffer from unresolved problems inherent in the ill-suited terms of the relationship.

The avoidance–avoidance model is inappropriate for a second reason. Achievement of an agreement is a typical consequence of collective bargaining. As a result the parties have been rewarded in the sense that the anxieties generated in negotiations have been relieved. This experience should condition the parties to seek to approach a settlement goal. In this respect, the avoidance gradient should be a decreasing, not an increasing, function of the distance from the goal. (Perhaps a modification of the Dollard and Miller "approach–avoidance" model[21] might be more suitable for analyzing collective-bargaining relationships if this type of psychological approach is to be used, although other limitations of this approach, which will be identified later, suggest that some other analytical structure can be more fruitful.)

A third difficulty lies in the fact that the concept of the wage rate is not a good substitute for the concept of "distance" from a goal. Under Stevens' concept of distance, equilibrium is achieved at some intermediate wage rate between two opposing goals. This is not a solution in the Dollard and Miller sense, for neither of the opposing goals is achieved, vacillatory behavior continues, and anxiety (conflict) is not relieved. The parties remain in conflict in the intrapersonal sense. Under the Dollard and Miller model, either goal must be achieved before intrapersonal conflict is reduced. During collective bargaining, goals are continually undergoing modification in the intrapersonal sense. Consequently, opposing goals (represented by the end vertical lines in Figure 13.6) move horizontally closer together as successful bargaining progresses, and there are shifts not only in the positions of the gradients but also in the end points. The goal parameters of Stevens'

[21] *Ibid.*, pp. 355–359, 366–367.

model are, in fact, variables in collective bargaining. The failure to recognize this forces Stevens to assume that an intermediate point between two goals is an equilibrium position. This is an equilibrium position that describes indecisive, neurotic behavior, and thus, it may be a psychological equilibrium, but it is not an economic equilibrium in the sense that the terms of the bargain are thereby established at that point.

Apart from the inappropriateness of the avoidance–avoidance model for analyzing collective-bargaining behavior, it has other limitations as a general theory of bargaining. The model does not suggest how the goals sought by the parties or the position and slope of the avoidance gradients are established. Stevens denies that utility theory (or variations thereof) is appropriate for analyzing conflict behavior. "Utility theory is essentially a nonconflict theory of choice behavior."[22] Rather, Stevens takes both the goals and the strength of the tendency to avoid as data. He does not tell us what causes the avoidance tendency or what determines its strength. Furthermore, he fails to identify the forces that drive a party to seek a goal when there are costs or dissatisfactions associated with its achievement. He simply does not recognize the positive aspects of achieving a goal. If an understanding of the essence of these forces is to be achieved, an analysis in terms of a subjective evaluation of the degree of response to a stimulus (pain-and-pleasure or utility analysis) must be made.

The failure of the model to explain how goals are established and why they are modified during bargaining reduces the goals to mere bargaining limits, which may not represent the true aspirations of either of the parties. Although Stevens recognizes the existence of an avoidance–avoidance model for each of the parties, he does not suggest how the two models are interrelated, that is, how a change in an avoidance curve in one model might affect an avoidance curve in another model.

Stevens suggests that equilibrium is achieved at a point where estimates of the avoidance gradients of each party intersect at a wage rate identical for each party, when both parties are aware of that intersection point. It is true that both parties must be aware that conditions compatible with a settlement have been reached. However, it is necessary for only one of the parties to be willing to accept a level of benefits within the range in which the other party is willing to concede, rather than submit to the pressures that the conceder feels he will be forced to experience by the seeker. Stevens' model fails to recognize that a range of benefits can exist within which a settlement is possible, and it fails to identify that range. Consequently, the

---

[22] Stevens, *op. cit.* (see note 1), p. 14. Nevertheless, on p. 56 of his book, satisfactions are related to outcomes.

equilibrium in Stevens' model is possible only at a point, and this is an unduly restrictive equilibrium condition.

Summary

Since gains rarely accrue to labor without some accompanying monetary or psychological loss to management, and vice versa, the collective-bargaining relationship can be characterized as a situation in which the interests of the parties are opposed. One party obtains benefits only if the other party concedes something of value. Typically, in our culture, valuable items are not relinquished willingly or freely when no object of equal value is offered in return. A party must be forced or coerced into his concession if he is not rewarded for so doing.

The ability of one party to win a concession from a second is influenced by one's ability to reward or punish the second and by the second's estimate of this ability. The motivation to seek a concession depends upon the amount of pleasure (reward) the party associates with the benefit, together with his *estimate* of the amount of pain he must endure in order to coerce the concession from his opponent. This *estimate* in turn depends on the party's *estimate* of the value of the concession to the opponent, which determines the opponent's willingness to resist the concession. The party's ability to punish the opponent depends upon the party's capacity to endure pain and the receptivity of the opponent to the forms of punishment. This receptivity is influenced by the opponent's ability to insulate himself from the actions of the party. The amount of information available to both parties and the effectiveness of the process through which information is transmitted are important in formulating estimates of the magnitude of rewards and punishments. Goals and alternatives are important, for they influence the estimates of the amount of pleasure.

The ability to influence the opponent's estimate of the rewards or punishments to which he can be subjected by a party is an element in the party's power over the opponent. This ability is highly relative, both to the specific level of benefits being sought and to the available forms of rewards and punishments, which in turn are related to environmental conditions. A party's willingness to reward or punish an opponent depends on the magnitude of the goal desired and on the estimated sacrifice required to obtain the goal. Indeed, bargaining involves a process by which rewards and punishments are communicated and ascertained in relation to goals, and the assessments of pleasure versus pain obtained from a course of action relative to the pleasure or pain imposable upon an opponent are subject to change during the course of negotiations.

Appendix: The Net Gain Theory of Bargaining

A model of bargaining between X and Y based upon the foregoing ideas must consider the following elements:

1. An estimate by X of the utility (pleasure) he receives in securing a benefit of a particular magnitude. As the level of benefits B varies, so does the amount of utility. Hence, $U_{xx} = f(B)$.
2. An estimate by X of the sacrifice of utility (pain) which he must be willing to undergo in order to compel Y to give up a given level of benefits. This utility sacrifice, D, is a monotonically increasing function of the level of benefits. Hence, $D_{xx} = g(B)$.
3. An estimate by X of the utility experienced by Y of keeping (not conceding) the benefit desired by X. (This can also be expressed as the retained utility available to Y because he did not give up the benefit.) The relationship can be expressed as: $U_{yx} = h(B)$.
4. An estimate by X of the utility sacrificed by Y in enduring the punishments inflicted by X to obtain a given benefit level $D_{yx} = k(B)$.

Party Y is assumed to make a similar set of estimates. Each party seeks to influence the other's estimates. Since the estimates are based on future behavior and are uncertain, they must be appropriately reduced by a probability factor.

The net gain (N) to X from seeking a level of benefits B_0 is given by

$$N_{xx} = f(B_0) - g(B_0) = U_{xx}(B_0) - D_{xx}(B_0). \qquad (13.7)$$

Differentiating the net gain function of N_x, with respect to the benefit index, gives us the rate of change of net utility as benefits increase, and net utility is a maximum when the differential function N'_{xx} is equal to zero. We shall call N' the marginal net gain function.

Similarly, the net gain to Y as seen by X is given as

$$N_{yx} = h(B_0) - k(B_0) = U_{yx}(B_0) - D_{yx}(B_0) \qquad (13.8)$$

and its rate of change is N'_{yx}. In this manner, N_{yy} and N_{xy} can be obtained, along with N'_{yy} and N'_{xy}, where N_{yy} represents the net gain of Y as seen by himself and N_{xy} represents the net gain of X as seen by Y. The derivatives of N_{ij} might be as plotted in Figure 13.7.

In Figure 13.8(a), party X perceives his optimum benefit level as being B_1, but he estimates Y's optimum benefit level at B_2. At the same time, in Figure 13.8(b), party Y estimates X's optimum benefit level to be

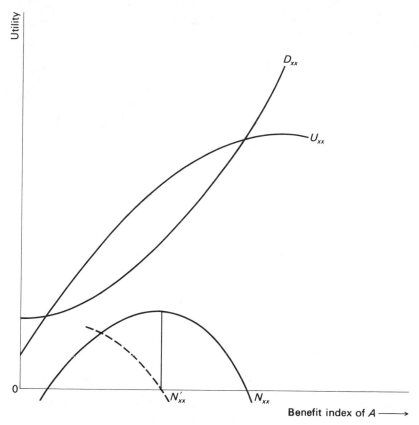

FIGURE 13.7. Deriving the net-gain function from bargaining.

B_4, whereas Y believes his optimum benefit level to be B_3. Hence, both parties are correct in recognizing that Y will seek a benefit level less than that of X. However, there is no reason why B_1 must equal B_4 or why B_2 must equal B_3. Now, if B_1 is less than B_3, where Y is the employer and X the union, the employer is willing to concede a greater benefit than the union will initially demand, and an agreement should be reached in short order. The parties need only communicate this fact. On the other hand, as is typically the case, B_1 may be greater than B_3, and settlement cannot occur as long as this condition obtains.

Consider again Figure 13.8(a). The union seeks to move the employer's N_y' curve so that it has zero utility at or to the right of the zero utility point on its own N_x' curve. To do this, the union must change the employer's perception of the rewards and costs associated with the benefits under

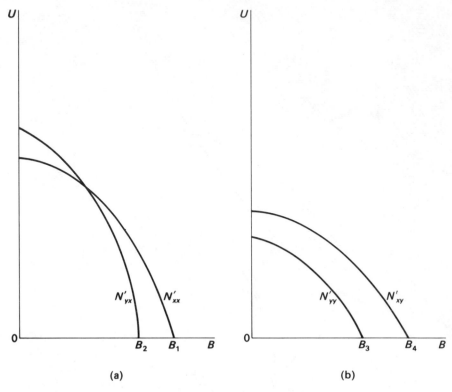

FIGURE 13.8. Perceptions of net gain functions. (a) Benefits of both parties as perceived by X. (b) Benefits of both parties as perceived by Y.

negotiation. Similarly, in Figure 13.8(b), the employer wishes to shift the union's marginal net gain function so that its zero utility point lies to the left of the zero utility point on the employer's marginal net gain function. Analogously, the employer must change the union's perception of the rewards and cost associated with each level of benefits. Whichever party is more successful in altering the other's marginal net gain function is able to obtain more favorable settlement terms.

The functioning of bargaining, then, is to provide an arrangement wherein the parties can communicate with one another and by this process alter one another's N' function so that an agreement becomes possible. The essence of bargaining power is the ability of one party to alter the other's perception of his N' function more than his own is changed. Specifically, the union wishes not only to maintain the zero utility point on its own N'_{xx} function as far to the right as possible, while at the same time it maneuvers the employer to shift the latter's zero utility point on his N'_{yy} function as far to the right as possible. Management's objective is similar but it seeks to move the point to the left. Shifts in the marginal net gain functions are accompanied by shifts in the parent net gain functions, but these are changed by altering the U and D functions. Ordinarily, an attempt by the union to increase the D_y function leads to either an increase in its D_x function (a longer strike hurts both) or a reduction in its U_x function (a counteroffer of another type of benefit, such as agreeing to a loosening of existing work rules). Similarly, an attempt by the employer to increase the U_x function can lower his own U_y function. As a result, bargaining maneuvers produce interrelated changes in net gain and marginal net gain functions of both parties.

In the preceding formulation, agreement is reached when for a benefit level B_0,

$$\max N_{xx} \geq \max N_{yy} \qquad (13.9)$$

This condition simply requires that for a settlement to be reached, the optimum settlement for the union must be equal to the optimum concession of the employer.

It should be noted that in bargaining the union can influence the employer's perception of his utility functions (U_{yy}, D_{yy}) and those of the union (U_{xy}, D_{xy}), and the employer can influence the union's perception of the set of utility functions (N_{xx}, D_{xy}, U_{yx}, D_{yx}). The initial perception of one's own and one's opponent's functions is important in determining the tactics and strategies to employ in bargaining; although the cross perceptions need not equal the self-perceptions at equilibrium—i.e., if $N_{xx} \neq N_{yx}$ and $N_{yy} \neq N_{xy}$, an equilibrium is still possible—it is not only necessary that Equation (13.9) hold, but also the following relationships must hold: $N_{xx} \leq N_{yx}$ and $N_{yy} \geq N_{xy}$. Otherwise, the parties will not perceive that a settlement is possible. Hence, restated, the equilibrium condition is

$$\max N_{yx} \geq N_{xx} \leq \max N_{yy} \geq N_{xy}. \qquad (13.10)$$

The terms will tend to favor the party with the greater bargaining power, which is defined here as the ability of one party to change the zero utility point of its opponent's marginal net gain curve more than his own zero utility point is changed. This can be expressed as follows: Since $N'_{ii} = 0$ when $U'_{ii} = D'_{ii}$, a change in $N'_{ii} \rightarrow \Delta(U'_{ii} - D'_{ii})$. Hence, the bargaining power of the union is greater if $\Delta(U'_{xx} - D'_{xx}) > \Delta(U'_{yy} - D'_{yy})$. Similarly, the bargaining power of the employer is greater if $\Delta(U'_{yy} - D'_{yy}) > \Delta(U'_{xx} - D'_{xx})$.

This model suggests the importance of the use of appropriate strategies and tactics in bargaining and also the importance of maintaining lines of communications. Presumably, the exercise of bargaining power shifts the B values of employers and unions into the desired relationship. A successful strategy that misleads the opponent into underestimating the true value of his own net gain function and into overestimating the value of his adversary's net gain function, of course, is desired. Nevertheless, there is a danger that (1) the party himself will be so influenced that he will overestimate his bargaining strength and underestimate that of his opponent and (2) the party will not correctly convey the true parameters of his net gain function to his opponent, so the opponent will fail to evaluate properly the party's strength and his own. A strategy based on bluff or misinformation may jam the communication channels between the two parties and prevent a settlement that otherwise would have occurred without conflict. If management cannot develop an approximation of the true positions of the net gain functions, it will not be able to estimate the ultimate (realistic) objective of the union, and this ignorance may very well cause management to fail to make the necessary concessions that would lead to a settlement. A similar result may obtain with the union, so that a stalemate results and the possibility of a peaceful settlement is forgone. Overt conflict will then be necessary to communicate a more realistic appraisal of the net gain functions.

The Concession Process

The above analysis suggests how parties seek to manipulate one another into offering or revealing concessions. These concessions are generated through the exercise of bargaining power, and in the process of shifting net gain functions, the union concedes B leftward as the management concedes B rightward.

J. C. Cross has another view of the concession process. Cross has stated that the very essence of the bargaining process is contained in the dynamic process of disagreement–concession–agreement. In a recent book he has illustrated one means by which this process is implemented.[23] Time, he argues, is the most important variable in the rate of concession, because time has a cost. "If it did not matter when people agreed, it would not matter whether they agreed at all." He applies discount rates to the costs involved in bargaining and assumes that parties adjust their estimates of their opponents' concession rates through a learning process, so that if the actual concession rate exceeds the expected concession rate, the expected concession rate is revised upward, and vice versa. The greater the discrepancy between the actual and the expected concession rate, the faster will the expectations change. The making of concessions through shifts in the concession rate, consequently, is influenced by (1) the ability to hold out or

[23] *The Economics of Bargaining* (New York: Basic Books, 1969), Chapters III and IV.

to "outwait" one's opponent, and in turn this ability is influenced by the costs determined by the discount rates, and (2) the sensitivities of the parties to learning. "Agreement," Cross states, "is defined by the situation in which the sum of the player's demands," determined by their concession functions, "is equal to the available supply of benefits." Viewed in terms of the net gain model, strategies involving "waiting" or involving attempts to alter the estimates of discount rates as well as costs would affect the magnitude and timing of shifts in the relevant net gain functions.

Cross assumes that the parties are bargaining over the division of a single product M_i and that each party, I or II, has a single-variate utility function related to quantities q_1 and q_2 of this good. Further, he assumes that the marginal utility functions are positive and subject to diminishing returns:

$$U_1 = f(q_1) \quad \text{and} \quad U_2 = g(q_2)$$

Each party initiates a demand for a share of the good q_i, and estimates the time it will take the opponent to concede so that the equilibrium condition is satisfied, i.e., $q_1 + q_2 - M = 0$. If the opponent's rate of concession per unit of time is given by r_2, then the expected time to reach agreement is

$$\frac{q_1 + q_2 - M}{r_2} = w. \qquad (13.11)$$

The present value of I's demand is given by

$$q_1 = f(q_1)e^{-aw} \qquad (13.12)$$

where a is I's rate of discount. The cost of bargaining is the present value of a stream of costs C_i per time i, or

$$Z = C_1 \int_0^w e^{-ax}\, dx = \frac{C_1}{a}(1 - e^{-aw}) \qquad (13.13)$$

The net utility value to I of insisting on a given division of the good q_1 is thus defined as

$$U_1 = f(q_1)e^{-aw} - Z = f(q_1)e^{-aw} + (C_1/a)e^{-aw} - (C_1/a). \quad (13.14)$$

Utility is maximized by differentiation of Equation (13.14) with respect to q_1, setting it equal to zero and solving for the optimum q_1, where $dw/dq_1 = 1/r_2$,

$$\frac{dU_1}{dq_1} = \left(f(q_1) + \frac{C_1}{a}\right)\frac{a}{r_2} - f'(q_1) = 0, \qquad (13.15)$$

or, marginal cost of U_1 is set equal to the marginal return of U_1. As noted above, I changes his conception of r_2 as $-dq_2/dt$ (the rate of concession of II) exceeds or is less than r_2; if II's actual concession rate exceeds the expected concession rate, I revises r_2 upward—i.e., $dr_2/dt > 0$; if II's actual rate is less than expected, r_2 is revised downward—i.e., $dr_2/dt < 0$. The greater I's error, the more rapidly he revises r_2.

To find I's concession rate $(-dq_1/dt)$, Equation (13.14) is differentiated with respect to time and solved for dq_1/dt. It is found that I's actual concession rate varies as does the change in the estimate of II's concession rate. If I revises II's concession rate upward, I will increase his demands and $dq_1/dt > 0$. If I revises II's concession rate downward, I will decrease his demands and $dq_1/dt < 0$.

The analysis is symmetrical for player II in estimating player I's rate of concession r_1 and in adjusting his demands, q_2.

Cross illustrates the bargaining process, in terms of the above analysis, as follows. Assume that both parties start with demands that exceed the total product, $q_1 + q_2 > M$, and each expects a positive rate of concession from the other. Further, assume that II does not concede. Then I will therefore lower his r_2 and also lower his demand q_1. In reducing his demand, II will make a judgement as to whether I's actual rate of concession is above or below his estimate, and II will adjust his estimate of r_1 accordingly, and also his demand q_2. If both concession rates are below expectations, both concede their demands and the parties move to a settlement. If one person learns more quickly than the other, he may actually increase his demand, which further motivates his opponent to concede more rapidly. Convergence to a settlement is still possible if the party increasing his demand does so at a slower rate than the party conceding so that $(q_1 q_2)$ falls, even though one q_i is rising while the other is falling.

The major flaw in this analysis is that it is unrealistic to expect each party to believe that it will be his opponent who will concede, and that his own initial demand will not change.[24] This assumption is in reality a mathematical requirement in order to simplify the solution of the maximization process. This assumption may be valid among first-time, inexperienced bargainers, but it certainly is not valid for any experienced negotiator. It also may be valid for a bargainer who uses Boulwareism tactics, but invalid for one who, because of uncertainties in the settlement point of the opponent, inflates his initial demands and engages in blue sky bargaining. In such situations, the party is fully aware that his initial position will change.

Hicks Revisited

It is possible to derive the Hicks model from the net gain model, assuming a set of net gain functions at a point in time. Figure 13.9 depicts

[24] Edward Saraydar makes this point in his astute review of the Cross book in *Industrial and Labor Relations Review*, Vol. 23, No. 4 (July 1970), pp. 592–593.

the process by which the union resistance curve is derived. In both figure parts (a) and (b), point A is the union wage goal (where we are considering wages as the sole subject of negotiations). If the union is offered its goal at A, it need not strike. Nevertheless, its goal A is in part determined by its willingness to incur costs (bear pain) or to strike. The greater the distance that A is, say, from C [Figure 13.9(a)], the greater is the additional cost the

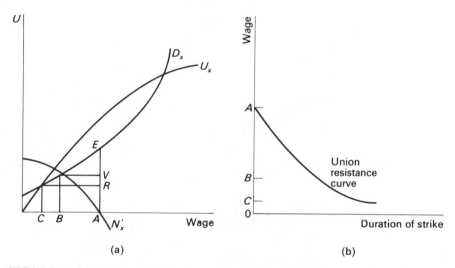

FIGURE 13.9. Deriving Hicks' union resistance curve from the net gain model. See text.

union would endure in order to obtain A. Thus, if C is the employer's offer, so that the union does not have to strike to get C, the union would be willing to experience RE more cost to secure A. If B were the offer, the union, although willing to give up AD amount of pain to obtain A, finds that the extra pain it would have to sacrifice in order to get A (since presumably it believes that it would take RV cost to move the employer to an offer of B from C) would only be equal to VE. As B approaches A, then V approaches E, so that VE approaches zero. If we view the extra cost RV in terms of the union's willingness to strike (or extend the duration of the strike), we obtain the union's resistance curve [Figure 13.9(b)]. The RV, therefore, is transformed into the union's resistance curve as B moves from D to A.

However, in this derivation, the target wage is not determined because the pleasure (U) function is ignored. We need not only the cost function but also the pleasure function which measures the utility derived from the

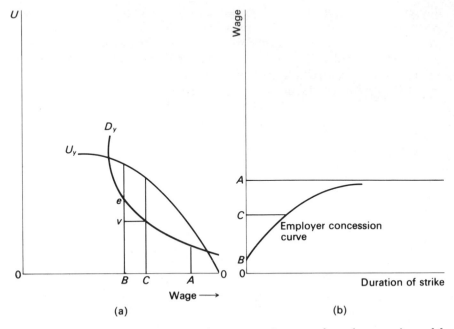

FIGURE 13.10. Deriving Hicks' employer concession curve from the net gain model. See text.

benefit level in order to obtain the target wage. As A is approached, dU approaches dD, and it is the equality of these two differentials that determines the optimum wage goal.

Figure 13.10 presents the process by which the employer's concession curve can be derived from the net gain model. In both (a) and (b) of Figure 13.10, assume that point B represents the employer's goal and is the point where the benefit from a low wage (resulting, say, in higher profits) is just offset by the pain of a low wage (the strike cost necessary to get the wage accepted by the union). In Figure 13.10(a), if the union asks for C when the employer seeks B, then the employer would be willing to incur ve additional pain (to bear that much longer a strike). As C approaches A, the ve increases and the corresponding strike duration lengthens in Figure 13.10(b). Obviously, the higher the wage demand with which the employer is confronted, the greater the pain he is willing to endure, because the higher wage takes him further and further from B.

It is just as valid to say that the employer seeks to approach B as to say that he seeks to avoid the higher wages represented by C or A. Viewed from the approach context, the diagram in Figure 13.11 can be constructed,

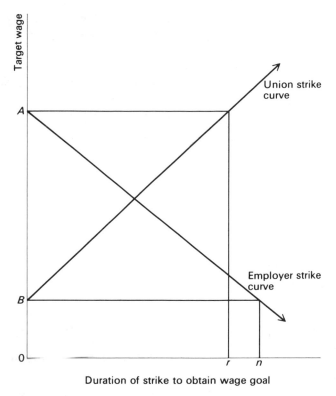

FIGURE 13.11. An alternative formulation of the theory of industrial disputes.

which is the converse of the Hicks diagram. If management's target wage were *A* and if this were the union's demand, management would not take any strike. If the target wage were *B* and the union demanded *A*, however, then management would strike for *U* weeks rather than grant it. Similarly, if management offered *B*, and this were the union's goal, the union would not have to strike to obtain *B*; but if management offered *B* when the union sought *A*, the union would strike for *r* weeks to obtain *A*.

None of the curves in Figures 13.9, 13.10, or 13.11 corresponds to the marginal net gain curves. They would correspond only if the marginal utility associated with varying levels of benefits were constant (that is, in Figure 13.9(a), $dU = dE$ = some constant). We know that this contradicts our experience. Higher benefit levels do yield greater pleasure than lower benefit levels, but the rate of change of this pleasure need not be constant. The marginal net gain from different benefit levels must be considered as a function of both marginal pain and marginal pleasure, which themselves are functionally related to benefit levels. If the bargaining process is viewed only as an exercise to avoid pain, or marginal pain, and if this yields an unclear concept of a goal, there really is no way to measure the magnitude of pain one is willing to bear to obtain the goal. Only insofar as the concept exists of a goal which is sought because it satisfies, yields utility, can we determine the pain one is willing to endure to achieve the goal. In this sense, the net gain model has features not unlike the Dollard and Miller "dual approach–avoidance model."[25]

Discussion Questions

1. In the bilateral monopoly model, explain the nature of wage–employment decisions (who benefits the more) for the following situations.

    (a) Weak employer–strong union.
    (b) Strong employer–weak union.
    (c) Strong employer–strong union.
    (d) Weak employer–weak union.

2. Why might a union seek a membership-maximizing objective rather than a wage-maximizing objective? Are the two objectives inconsistent? Why is a wage-maximizing objective not necessarily an income-maximizing objective?

3. It has been observed that an implicit assumption of wage-preference analysis is that unions derive relatively greater marginal utility from wages than from employment in recessions and vice versa during prosperity. Evaluate this assertion with respect to the analysis and to the real world. Is such an assumption consistent with a membership-maximizing objective?

4. Hicks' theory of industrial disputes, although widely criticized, has had amazing survival power—perhaps more so than the other models cited in this chapter. How can this be explained?

5. According to Chamberlain's model of bargaining power, is the power of the union independent of the power of the employer?

6. How important in bargaining power is the ability to bluff? One of the tactics sometimes used in bargaining is to develop an irrevocable threat —a sort of doomsday bomb, which may lead to the destruction of both parties. Why would such a tactic be used?

7. Would bargaining be necessary, or even fruitful, in a world of perfect knowledge? Explain.

[25] Dollard and Miller, *Personality and Psychotherapy, op. cit.*

8. Why are wage goals altered during bargaining? Are there circumstances under which wage goals must remain relatively fixed? If so, would a bargainer be accused of negotiating in "bad faith"?

9. (a) One of the criticisms of the net gain theory of bargaining is that it is not "behavioral." Evaluate this criticism.

   (b) Can the net gain theory develop hypotheses which can be tested empirically, or is it merely "impressionistic"? Explain.

10. (a) How important is time in collective bargaining? In answering this question, consider such bargaining situations as those involving the railroad industry, the West Coast shipping industry, and public service negotiations.

    (b) Since events necessarily must occur in a time dimension, is it "time" or the events which condition the concession rate? Explain.

14

Wage Differentials

Nature of Differentials

The existence of a wage structure implies the existence of differences in wages, or wage differentials. To the extent that different occupations require different skills and degrees of training, an occupational wage structure may be said to exist. To the extent that a single firm utilizes the services of labor dispersed throughout a variety of occupations, then the firm's occupational structure is also its wage structure. Since firms producing similar products are identified as an industry, the composite wage structure of the member firms comprise the industry occupational and wage structure. Workers, firms, and industries of necessity must possess a geographical location, and therefore the wage structure of a region reflects the occupational structure of the firms and industries located therein. To the degree that particular firms and industries or occupations are unionized, a union wage structure will exist which may differ from that of nonunionized firms or industries. To the extent that occupations are filled by members of particular races or sex, wage differentials by race or sex may exist. Thus, numerous bases exist for classifying wage differentials.

Although there are market forces at work which tend over time to reduce wage differences, we cannot expect them to be eliminated. Adam Smith observed 200 years ago that where workers were free to choose occupations and free to move among them, they would allocate themselves in such a way so as to equalize the net advantages among them. This implies that the tendency toward equality is among all the attributes of a job, and not just toward equality in wages. On the contrary, Smith noted that wages,

377

in fact, would tend to differ owing to different conditions of employment which make jobs more or less attractive.[1]

Rottenberg has expounded upon these basic premises of Smith and has shown how they are relevant to understanding the workings of the labor market.[2] Workers make choices among available jobs on the basis of "expected" net advantages; sometimes they make errors in judgment, but their choices are nevertheless rational. "If the goal is A, choice which leads to achievement of A is rational; choice which leads to the achievement of B, when the chooser believes it leads to A, is also rational." The evidence suggests, claims Rottenberg, that only where nonpecuniary advantages are equal will wages alone influence the choice of workers, and consistent with Smith, the trend appears to show that this occurs. If between any two jobs the nonpecuniary advantages of one exceed those of another, a higher wage will tend to exist in the latter sufficient to compensate workers for the relative disadvantages. If sufficient time is permitted to allow the labor market to work itself out, where the assumptions of Smith are valid, his predictions seem to be substantiated.

Smith had assumed that the labor market is perfectly competitive, and Rottenberg has argued that in the long run the market approaches the competitive state. Other classical economists, John Stuart Mill and J. E. Cairnes, have developed the concept of noncompeting groups in order to explain how imperfections in the labor market can prevent wage differentials from narrowing.[3]

The barriers to movement among occupational levels in the final analysis were perceived to be of an educational and capital character. In the absence of state subsidization of education and in the presence of class barriers to entry into the better schools, these barriers could effectively stratify British employment opportunities and thereby limit occupational choice. To the extent that they still exist, choice is limited among occupations.

The principle by which wage differentials under competition are eliminated works the same regardless of their classification, either assuming that nonpecuniary advantages are equal or that differentials narrow to that

[1] Adam Smith, *The Wealth of Nations* (New York: The Modern Library, 1957), p. 100. Also, see Chapter 3 of this text for an earlier discussion.
[2] Simon Rottenberg, "On Choice in Labor Markets," *Industrial and Labor Relations Review*, Vol. 9 (January 1956), pp. 183–199. Some economists believe that Rottenberg's argument is tautological; i.e., "if wages differ among occupations, workers must have accepted employment in those jobs because of nonpecuniary attributes of the jobs, because to do otherwise would be irrational." However, this is not what Rottenberg is implying or intending to imply. Rather, he is trying to demonstrate that the push and pull of market forces, reflected in wage differentials, *tends* to allocate workers to jobs in a rational manner.
[3] J. E. Cairnes, *Some Leading Principles of Political Economy Newly Expounded* (London 1874), pp. 66–67. See also Chapter 4 in this text for an earlier discussion.

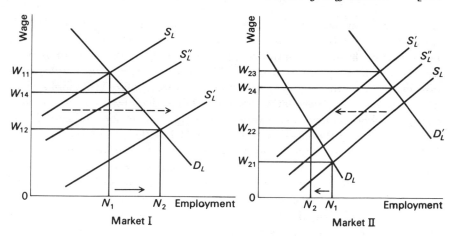

FIGURE 14.1. How wage differentials are eliminated in perfect labor markets.
(See text.)

amount necessary to compensate for them. Assume that in one market—
occupational, industrial, regional, racial, or otherwise—short-run demand
and supply conditions yield a wage higher than wages in other similar
markets, $W_{11} > W_{21}$. The higher wage attracts labor from other markets
into the preferred one, increasing its labor supply and reducing labor supply
in those experiencing emigration (see Figure 14.1). Employment expands in
market I and contracts in market II, so that $W_{12} = W_{22}$. If demand in
any one market increases so that a disequilibrium results between the two
markets, W_{23} in II and W_{12} in I, adjustments in labor supply once again
bring wages into equality at $W_{14} = W_{24}$. This implies that a number of
long-run trends will be evident in terms of the two labor markets.

1. Wage differentials will narrow.
2. Labor will move from low-wage sectors to high-wage sectors.
3. Employment will expand relatively more in high-wage sectors than
   in low-wage sectors, given demand in the two sectors.
4. Although wages may rise and fall in the short run, they will tend to
   some uniform level between the two sectors. In the long run,
   however, changes in the demand for labor can either increase or
   decrease the utilization of labor. Hence, low long-run correlation
   between wages and employment are implied.

Observations over periods of time, however, may not support these
implications because of a variety of complications. First, either demand in

sector I may increase more rapidly than the supply of labor through immigration, or labor demand in sector II may decrease more rapidly than labor supply through emigration. In either event, wage differentials need not narrow, although movement of labor between sectors and employment changes occur in the predicted direction. However, wages and employment need not have low correlation. Second, labor demand and supply may increase in both sectors so that wages and employment both increase. If the natural growth of the labor force in sector II is sufficiently large to permit both emigration to sector I and an increase in labor supply, labor supply and employment can both increase with expansion in demand. Wage differentials need not narrow; labor and employment move in the predicted direction in sector I. Although in sector II employment appears to contradict the simple prediction, the movements are quite consistent with the competitive hypothesis. Finally, significant positive correlation between wages and employment is possible.

Demand may increase more rapidly than supply in sector I simply because capital substitution for labor occurs. Whereas the disequilibrium between the two sectors originally generated a wage differential, the capital–labor substitution could generate dissimilarities between the two markets which inhibit the transfer of labor. For example, if the capital substitution upgraded the occupational mix, the lag in the acquisition of upgraded talents could retard the expansion of supply relative to demand in sector I, decrease the reduction in supply relative to demand in sector II, and cause the differential to persist over a longer period of time. Other illustrations of changes are possible that are quite consistent with the predictions of competitive theory, but which on the surface appear not to be. Hence, in empirical observations, results which appear to contradict the competitive hypothesis must be interpreted with caution.[4] To refute the competitive hypothesis, it must clearly be shown that all allowances have been considered and that the results still are inconsistent.

It is logical to suppose that, in fact, most labor markets do exhibit imperfect features, and that the persistence of wage differentials is caused by imperfect knowledge of labor market conditions, by barriers to movement or to entry or exit in the form of restricted opportunities or high capital

---

[4] For example, see Charles T. Stewart, Jr., "Wage Structure in an Expanding Labor Market: The Electronics Industry in San Jose," *Industrial and Labor Relations Review*, Vol. 21, No. 1 (October 1967), pp. 73–91. Stewart states that the failure of earnings to increase more rapidly in an industry growing by leaps and bounds than in similar industries elsewhere or in industries not growing so fast contradicts common sense and the competitive hypothesis, but that is what his findings show. However, the competitive hypothesis is not contradicted if labor supply is increasing more rapidly in that industry in that region than elsewhere. There is some evidence to indicate that this is what actually happened, and Stewart's failure to demonstrate otherwise weakens his conclusion.

requirements, or by monopoly-type restrictions. Furthermore, the homogeneity postulate of competitive theory is at variance with the normal distribution of native skills in a population. The observation of labor market behavior over an extended interval of time may suggest that these barriers "ought to be reduced with the passage of time," but institutional features and cultural traits of a market may be such that in fact little or no reduction in imperfections does occur. The concept of the long run in theory is not paralleled by the passage of a given number of years. To be sure, a decade or two may be a better approximation of the long run than a year or two, but the imperfections in a labor market may be so deep-rooted that the former interval still does not approach the conceptual interval in which any adjustment is supposed to be possible. Reder has noted that in the short run the competitive hypothesis does not appear to be very reliable, and that it can hardly be said to be firmly established as an explanation of wage phenomena even for long periods; but it has at least survived reasonably well the tests to which it has been put.[5]

Occupational Wage Differentials

To the extent that occupations require different degrees of education and training, they will utilize different degrees of skill.[6] Presumably, earnings in occupations requiring higher levels of skill and training will be sufficiently greater than earnings in occupations using lower levels of skill to induce workers to acquire the necessary investment in human capital. Any rate of return on human capital greater than that necessary to induce such training presumably will attract new entrants into these preferred occupations, and rates of return will fall as a consequence, and skill differentials will narrow. Rates of return may rise if the cost of acquiring advanced education or training is lowered; the extension of free or low-cost public education at all levels and the provision of manpower training opportunities both tend to lower this cost. It is possible for ratios of occupational earnings by skill to fall while at the same time differences between earnings actually widen. Ordinarily, it is sufficient for mobility to be induced in response to excessive earnings differentials, although a rise in the earnings ratio will also generate such movement.

[5] Melvin W. Reder, "Wage Differentials: Theory and Measurement," *Aspects of Labor Economics* (Princeton: Princeton University Press, National Bureau of Economic Research, 1962), pp. 288–289.

[6] Jacob Mincer has noted a significant positive relationship between the amount of on-the-job training and the educational and prejob training requirements, "On-the-Job Training: Costs, Returns and Implications," *Journal of Political Economics* (October 1962 Supplement), p. 59. We shall use "occupational levels" as synonymous terms.

The data in this country indicate that over time, skill differentials have narrowed. Studies by the U.S. Department of Labor have shown that the ratio of an index to skilled labor to one of unskilled labor has declined from 1904 to 1953 (see also Table 14.1).

> "White-collar workers had smaller relative increases than did production workers. The highly skilled craft worker earns more per hour on the average than the semiskilled or unskilled man, but the difference is not as great as in earlier years. Average earnings of highly skilled manufacturing workers in 1904 were more than 100% above the earnings of the least skilled, 65% larger in the period 1937–1940, and by 1952–1953 they were only 37% higher. Just as the earnings of the unskilled have increased proportionately more than those of skilled workers, so the latter have tended to overtake the earnings of salaried professional workers such as teachers, engineers, and scientific personnel."[7]

A more recent U.S. Department of Labor study has shown that the skilled–unskilled wage index remained at 137 in 1962, possibly indicating that the skill differential had stabilized.[8] There is evidence, however, that the skilled–unskilled ratio varies with the business cycle, rising in periods of unemployment and falling in periods of full employment, although the general long-run trend has been downward. Consequently, examination of the ratio over a period as short as a decade can be misleading, particularly if one point of comparison represents a full-employment period and another represents a period of substantial unemployment. The former will tend to lie below the negative trend line and the latter above it, and may suggest a stability that does not exist. On other grounds, Rice has argued that the skilled–nonskilled wage differential may have narrowed less than indicated by such indices if fringe benefits or wage supplements are counted as a part of earnings. He has found that earnings correlate positively with such benefits, which is consistent with the arguments of Oi and Mincer that these benefits are used by employers to convert into a fixed factor labor that has

---

[7] Bureau of Labor Statistics, U.S. Department of Labor, *Economic Forces in the U.S.A.*, in *Facts and Figures* (Washington, D.C.: Government Printing Office, 1960), p. 76. These findings were based on studies by Harry Ober, "Occupational Wage Differentials, 1907–1947," *Monthly Labor Review*, Vol. 71 (August 1948), pp. 127–134; and Toivo Kanninen, "Occupational Wage Relationships in Manufacturing," *Monthly Labor Review*, Vol. 76 (November 1953), pp. 1171–1178.

[8] Richard Perlman has adjusted Kanninen's data to make it more consistent with the data used by Ober, and finds that in 1953, skilled wages were 45% higher rather than 37%. "Forces Widening Occupational Wage Differentials," *Review of Economics and Statistics*, Vol. 40 (May 1958), pp. 107–109.

TABLE 14.1
MEDIAN EARNINGS OF YEAR-ROUND, FULL-TIME MALE CIVILIANS,
BY OCCUPATION, 1939, 1958, AND 1968

	Earnings in Dollars			Percent Increase		
Occupation Group	1939	1958	1968	1939– 1958	1958– 1968	1939– 1968
Professional, technical, kindred employer	2100	6730	10,542	220	57	402
Farmers and farm managers	430	1878	3,353	337	79	680
Managers, official, proprietors	2254	5909	9,794	162	66	335
Clinical, kindred workers	1564	4856	7,326	210	51	368
Salesworkers	1451	5371	8,292	270	54	471
Craftsmen, foremen, kindred	1562	5346	7,958	242	49	409
Operatives and kindred	1268	4502	6,773	255	50	434
Service workers	1019	3961	5,898	289	49	479
Farm laborers and foremen	365	1479	2,870	305	94	686
Laborers, except farm	961	3732	5,606	288	50	483

Source: U.S. Department of Commerce, Bureau of the Census, Current Population Reports: *Income of Persons in the United States, 1958*, Series P-60, no. 33, p. 51; *Statistical Abstract of the United States, 1970.*

received, at the employer's expense, substantial forms of specific training.[9] Hence, the sum of wages and fringe benefits of skilled workers may have increased at a greater percentage than the sum received by unskilled workers, not because the wage component increased at a greater rate, but because the fringe benefits increased proportionately more for the skilled workers. Among homogeneous occupations where presumably skill differences are minimal, it has been found that wage dispersions have narrowed during the 20th century.[10] In the light of Rice's findings, this narrowing of

[9] Robert G. Rice, "Skill, Earnings, and the Growth of Wage Supplements," *American Economic Review*, Vol. 56 (May 1966), pp. 503–593.
[10] Paul G. Keat, "Long-Run Changes in the Occupational Wage Structure, 1900–1956," *Journal of Political Economy*, Vol. 68 (December 1960), pp. 584–600. Part of this decline may be explained by the study of Raimon and Stoikov. Although they were testing the spillover effect of blue-collar earnings (they found little), in the process they indicated that white-collar employment was becoming an increasing proportion of the employed labor force (48.5% by 1975). They also noted that the market for white-collar labor exhibits more characteristics of the competitive labor market in terms of knowledge of employment opportunities, ability to move, and transferability of skills. Hence, to the extent that this component of employment is increasing, the competitiveness of the labor market is increasing, and occupational wage dispersion should therefore be expected to narrow. See Robert L. Raimon and Vladimir Stoikov, "The Effect of Blue-Collar Unionism on White-Collar Earnings," *Industrial and Labor Relations Review*, Vol. 22, No. 3 (April 1969), pp. 358–374.

wage dispersion among ostensibly homogeneous occupations might also be illusionary if fringe benefits are considered. Yet, it is known that between semiskilled blue-collar workers and white-collar workers, the former have increasingly acquired the type of fringe benefits long associated with the employment package of the latter—wage supplements that guarantee stability in income, paid vacations, sick leave, paid holidays, coffee breaks, better work environments, etc. This suggests that, considering fringe benefits, compensation dispersion may have narrowed more than that reported.

The Job-Vacancy Hypothesis

One explanation consistent with existing data about occupational wage differentials is the job-vacancy hypothesis.[11] This model seeks to explain variations in skill differentials by noting that as the labor market tightens, employers have the choice of lowering quality standards and/or of raising wages to fill their vacancies. Which method they will use will depend upon (1) the risk of property loss if standards are lowered; (2) the degree of collusion among the employers in fixing wage rates; (3) the willingness and ability to upgrade workers from lower grades in order to fill expanded skill requirements (although promoted workers receive higher wages, the firm's wage structure need not be changed. The process is reversible); (4) the relative advantages of upgrading workers through supplemental training or through recruitment at higher employment standards; the choice is one of minimizing costs.[12]

Firms utilize a hierarchy of skills. If the firm pays above the market rate, say the union rate, and there exists a labor reserve in the economy, then the firm will enjoy a "labor slack." This slack represents a supply of applicants in excess of requirements among which the firm can choose selectively. However, as demand expands and the labor reserve is reduced, the slack tends to disappear. The firm is increasingly faced with the necessity of raising wages to attract workers of the necessary skills from other sources,

[11] Melvin W. Reder, "The Theory of Occupational Wage Differentials," *American Economic Review*, Vol. 44, No. 5 (December 1955), pp. 833–852. This theory has been modified slightly in his "Wage Differentials: Theory and Measurement," in *Aspects of Labor Economics, op. cit.*, pp. 269–276.

[12] Recognition of this phenomenon had earlier been noted by Lloyd Reynolds, who suggested that the most common type of mobility occurred among occupations *within* the firm. See his *The Structure of Labor Markets* (New York: Harper and Bros., 1951), p. 139. A description of the process of intrafirm occupational mobility in the Waltham Watch Company is given by H. M. Gitelman, "Occupational Mobility Within the Firm," *Industrial and Labor Relations Review*, Vol. 20, No. 1 (October 1966), pp. 50–65. Gitelman finds that mobility had been greatest in the second half of the 19th century during periods of prosperity. See p. 59. Interestingly, he makes no reference to Reder's model.

or of substituting workers of lesser skills, perhaps with additional training, for those outside the firm with greater skills. Another alternative is to alter the production process so that lower-skilled workers can perform simpler tasks.[13] As either of these alternatives is used, the excess supply of workers with lower skills is absorbed, and labor shortages begin to appear at these lower skill levels. The upgrading of the firm's labor force has not necessitated changes in the wage structure, but at the lower levels as shortages develop, market wages tend to rise. As rates on unskilled jobs are driven up relatively to skilled jobs, the differential between the two narrows. During the two world wars, the labor reserve was exhausted, and skilled margins contracted. In the intervals between and after these wars, the reoccurrence of the labor reserve did not lead to a widening of the differentials, because the concept of the socially acceptable minimum wage had undergone a change so that employers were obligated to pay higher minimum wages. Hence, the job-vacancy hypothesis implies that during periods of labor shortages, the skill margin will decline, and that during periods of labor slack, a rise in the social minimum wage will restrain its widening.[14] This apparently occurred during the great depression.

A corollary of this hypothesis is that the easier it is to substitute lower levels of skill for higher levels of skill, the lower the skill differential will be. The general level of educational attainments in a country or region will affect this ability to substitute, as also will the minimum qualifications for employment. Similarly, the higher the capital–labor ratio, the less will be the tendency for unemployment at any social minimum wage (because of

[13] Howard G. Foster describes how this process works in the construction industry during seasonal and cyclical peaks. See "Labor-Force Adjustment to Seasonal Fluctuations in Construction," *Industrial and Labor Relations Review*, Vol. 23, No. 4 (July 1970), pp. 528–540. This same process of upgrading or promoting workers from within, with additional attention being given to training, is described by Peter B. Doeringer and Michael J. Piore in *Internal Labor Markets and Manpower Analysis* (Lexington: D. C. Heath and Co., 1971). They, too, completely ignore Reder's theory, although there are many parallels between their analysis and his.

[14] Robert Evans, "Note on Wage Differentials, Excess Demand for Labor, and Inflation," *Review of Economics and Statistics*, Vol. 45 (February 1963), pp. 95–98. Evans has attempted to test the Reder hypothesis that skill differentials narrow during periods of labor shortages. He found that differentials tended to narrow in the Civil War and the two world wars more during periods of rising prices rather than during periods in which the "labor reserve" is reduced. However, during the two world wars, the labor market was already close to full employment, and the greater responsiveness of the wage differentials to price changes than to reductions in unemployment does not seem to damage Reder's hypothesis. To do so, Evans would have had to show that there was no narrowing of wage differentials as unemployment moved from, say, 7% to 2 or 3%. He might have been able to offer support for the inflation hypothesis as being more explanatory than Reder's if he had shown that the wage differential narrowed during periods of inflation when unemployment was increasing, such as in 1957–1958 or 1969–1970.

higher worker productivity), and therefore the less will be the differential. It has been observed that since semiskilled jobs in the South are less frequent than, say, in the Far West, less substitution among skills is possible, and the differential is wider in the South and narrower in the Far West. Because the United States generally has lower employment standards than Australia or Western European countries, the skill differential is narrower in these countries than in the United States. To the extent that the government can raise educational levels or provide increased manpower training opportunities, it indirectly could contribute to a narrowing of the differential. Similarly, a commitment of the government to maintain a low labor reserve (high employment) could lead to a narrowing of differentials.

Perhaps this theory explains why unskilled workers are more subject to cyclical unemployment than skilled workers. The reverse process of downgrading skills falls more heavily upon the lowest-skilled workers. It also can explain variations in income distribution shares. Lower wages and greater unemployment reduce annual earnings of the unskilled relative to the skilled. Moreover, an increase in the aggregate supply of unskilled labor relative to aggregate demand would tend to depress the income share of this component of the labor force.

The Labor-Shortage Hypothesis

Another model concerning the origin of wage changes supplemental to the job-vacancy hypothesis is that short-run scarcities of skilled labor in the post-World War II period influenced the size of wage increases in the United States economy.[15] Consider a labor market with excess labor supply —unemployment. Wages for skilled labor will be bid upward (1) to the extent that increases in the demand for labor occur in sectors which utilize advanced skills, (2) to the extent that these skills are in inelastic supply, and (3) to the extent that mobility between firms and/or industries occurs. Unskilled labor, however, will more likely bear the burden of unemployment, so that its labor supply will be highly elastic. Consequently, changes in labor demand will tend to raise wages of the skilled but not the unskilled. If the latter rise, it is because institutional forces exist that tend to maintain the wage structure. So far, this line of reasoning is consistent with the job-vacancy model.

Next, consider those skills of a general nature which are easily transferable. When above-normal unemployment exists, only the skilled are apt to have much mobility because only for them are the uncertainties of securing another job minimal after a quit. Where these uncertainties are

[15] Sara Behman, "Wage-Determination in U.S. Manufacturing," *Quarterly Journal of Economics*, Vol. 82, No. 1 (February 1968), pp. 117–142.

large, less mobility among the skilled occurs. Hence, the young are more mobile than the middle-aged or aged. On the basis of this analysis, the following hypothesis should be true:

1. Voluntary quitting is greater in industries using relatively more skilled labor, and this quitting is more pronounced in periods of labor shortages.
2. In firms where skills are a larger proportion of total employment, increases in wage rates are positively related to new hire rates. Suppose it is found that industries with a greater proportion of skilled employment have higher annual quit rates and that quit rates rise and fall with the business cycle. However, this evidence would be consistent with the job-vacancy hypothesis that upgrading occurs as labor reserves disappear among skilled workers. Firms that upgrade may promote from within, or they may accept applications for higher-skilled positions from employees at the next lowest skill level who transfer from other firms. To the extent that employees are hired from outside the firm and this expanded market for upgraded skills attracts labor from other firms, then quit rates will rise. When demand falls and upgrading opportunities are fewer, existing employment compares more favorably with the uncertainties of better employment elsewhere, and quit rates fall.

To test the second hypothesis, first suppose wage changes are related to new hires by sector and suppose we find significant positive relationships between new hires, skills, and wages, where data on wages are average hourly earnings. To the extent that a firm expands its skilled labor force as a proportion of its total labor force by upgrading, it will have more workers at higher pay. The change in weighting of hourly wages will increase the average hourly rate, even if there is no change in the wage structure. Although the labor-shortage hypothesis suggests that the wage structure of skilled workers will rise (suggesting a widening of the skill differential), this is suggested also by the job-vacancy hypothesis.[16] Second, suppose we find a significant negative relation between increases in semiskill proportions and wages. The job-vacancy hypothesis implies that greater substitutability of lower skills for higher skills will occur the greater is the semiskill component in the labor force. If shortages of skilled labor develop and firms elect to simplify the tasks assigned to the skill, making them more of a semiskilled nature, new hires will be at the semiskilled level. If labor reserves of semi-skilled workers exist and wages do not increase as new hires at this level

[16] To support the hypothesis, it must be shown that wage rates *per skill level rise* as skilled employment increases proportionately.

increase, the weighted average of the hourly wage rate will decline. Thus, such a negative relation would follow from the job-vacancy analysis.

It must be concluded, therefore, that such tests of the labor-shortage hypothesis are equally supportive of the job-vacancy hypothesis.[17] The two models do not appear to be mutually exclusive, or even inconsistent.

The "job-vacancy hypothesis" explains mobility as being induced, not by changes of the wage structure, but by vacancies within the existing wage structure which pay wages higher than are currently received elsewhere. Hence, upgrading opportunities are sufficient to generate mobility. The labor-shortage analysis has some of these features, but it asserts that quit rates should be higher, as should new hire rates, in industries using high proportions of skilled labor. These changes are induced by changes in the wage structure, which in turn explain or influence many of the changes in United States wages. In an opposite vein, it has been argued that it is not the highly paid who are most likely to quit, because their opportunities for improvement are more limited. Instead, quit rates should vary negatively with unemployment rates (opportunities for better jobs exist) and positively with relative wage changes. In support of the job-vacancy model, it was found that almost 80% of the variations in quit rates were explained by (1) unemployment and (2) wage changes, but unemployment explained more of the quit rates than did wages.[18] It was also found that quit rates vary negatively with higher-paying jobs, casting doubt upon the labor-shortage model.

Industrial Wage Structure and Wage Differentials

Occupational wage differentials should not correspond to industry wage differentials, since industries utilize occupations of different skill levels to different degrees. To the extent that there has been a narrowing of the occupational wage differentials, one might expect that industrial differentials also would narrow. It is possible, of course, that high-paying industries might increase their proportion of highly skilled occupations and that low-paying industries might decrease their proportion of highly skilled jobs, so that, even in the face of narrowing occupational differentials, industrial differentials might widen. This would be owing to the weighting factor of a different distribution of high-skill, high-wage occupations among industries. However, to the extent that a tendency to a more even distribution of levels of skill occurs, a narrowing of occupational differentials would imply a narrowing of industrial differentials. It has been found in the period 1899–

---

[17] This is precisely the conclusion that must be drawn from Behman's tests, *op. cit.*
[18] Alan K. Severn, "Upward Labor Mobility: Opportunity or Incentive," *Quarterly Journal of Economics*, Vol. 82 (February 1968), pp. 143–151.

1950 that relative wage dispersion among 84 industries has been stable, as has been the relative ranking of industries.[19] A narrowing of the wage dispersion might have been expected if the skill proportions had remained stable, and if no barriers to mobility among industries had existed. That no narrowing occurred suggests either that changes in skilled proportions are correlated with the wage ranking of industries or that changes in employment which might have led to a narrowing of wage dispersion may have been inhibited by the development of barriers to entry into high-wage industries.

It is sufficient to establish that the labor market is efficient if it can be shown that labor tends to move from lower-paying to higher-paying industries. In the real world in selecting a period for observation, we cannot reproduce comparative static equilibrium positions as we can via diagrams. Hence, we can never be sure that our experiment reproduces the conditions underlying our hypothesis. To overcome this difficulty, criteria have been developed that attempt to establish that the labor market has allocated resources efficiently, and in the process it is recognized that a wage structure will exist among sectors of the economy, consistent with competition, because there exist real economic costs of changing jobs.[20] However, it is argued that the existence of the following conditions is sufficient to show efficient allocation in the face of these costs; efficiency is not impaired by noneconomic barriers to movement.

1. Sectors paying higher wages also have greater absolute wage increases than lower-paying sectors. If the sector wage structure remains constant, this condition is implied. High positive correlation between sectoral wages and sectoral wage changes tends to maintain the wage structure.
2. Unemployment will be distributed proportionately over sectors by level of sectoral employment. High sectoral correlation between employment and unemployment suggests this.[21] Implicit here is the

[19] D. E. Cullen, "The Interindustry Wage Structure, 1899–1950," *American Economic Review*, Vol. 66, No. 3 (June 1956), pp. 353–369.

[20] L. E. Galloway, "Labor Mobility, Resource Allocation, and Structural Unemployment," *American Economic Review*, Vol. 53, No. 4 (September 1963), pp. 698–701. For an adaption of the following argument, see my "Comment on Structural Unemployment, Labor Market Efficiency and the Intrafactor Allocation Mechanism in the United States and Canada," *Southern Economic Journal*, Vol. 39, No. 2 (October 1972), pp. 307–309.

[21] Galloway is in error here. An efficient (competitive) labor market need not allocate cyclical national unemployment evenly. Assume, as is usually the case, that changes in sector demand are uneven. If wages and prices remain unchanged, output and employment will differ among sectors, depending upon the respective changes in product demand and the elasticities of demand. Hence, unemployment will initially differ among sectors. If disproportionate unemployment occurs and is to be remedied, unemployed workers from

assumption that aggregate demand changes proportionately by sector.

3. Through time, there is no appreciable change in the distribution of sector wage rates.[22]
4. Through time, there is no appreciable change in the rank order of the sector wage rates.[23]

Conditions 1, 3, and 4 relate to the constancy of the wage structure. Condition 2 measures the distribution or allocation of unemployment, given a constant wage structure. It should be noted that the failure to show that all of these conditions do hold does not imply, however, that the labor market is not an efficient allocator. If these conditions cannot be established, it may mean that adjustments in the direction of efficient labor allocation have not been completed in the period of observation, that the conditions themselves are unreal or contradictory (as footnotes 21 and 22 suggest), that there is error in the statistical tests, or that the conditions assumed by the

sectors suffering greater than proportionate unemployment must move to sectors suffering less than proportionate unemployment.

To the extent that workers suffering disproportionate unemployment undercut and replace workers in industries suffering relatively less unemployment, unemployment is redistributed. But if it is the high-wage industries that suffer relatively the greater unemployment, it is the low-wage industries which must reabsorb them. Lowering wages in the low-wage industries may either widen the differential or increase reported unemployment in them as inferior workers are displaced. (In this situation, the redistribution of unemployment is illusory, for employment falls less in the low-wage industries.) On the other hand, if it is the low-wage industries that suffer relatively the most unemployment, the mechanism to reallocate labor will not work, no matter how efficient the labor market. Inferior workers will not replace superior workers, even at lower wages, or else they would have done so before a recession. In conclusion, this condition does not appear to be a necessary one.

[22] In the previous footnote, we have shown how a labor market, efficiently allocating labor, can disturb either the dispersion of wage rates by industry or the rank ordering of industry wage rates. Hence, finding that conditions 3 and 4 are violated may lend support to the efficiency hypothesis, contrary to Galloway's argument. However, it should be noted that Cullen's results indicate that industry wage dispersions had not increased in the period 1890–1950. H. Gregg Lewis has estimated that unions have, in the late 1950s, caused the relative inequality of average wages among industries to be about 6–10% higher than it otherwise would have been. *Unionism and Relative Wages in the United States: An Empirical Inquiry* (Chicago: University of Chicago Press, 1963), p. 292. As a significant source of imperfection in the labor force, this distortion in the interindustry wage structure does not appear to be large.

[23] F. W. Bell uses this measure of dispersion in his article, "The Relation of the Region, Industrial Mix, and Production Functions to Metropolitan Wage Levels," *Review of Economics and Statistics* (August 1967), see pp. 370–371.

model and for which they are sufficient to demonstrate efficiency are not pertinent to the observations.[24]

The conclusion must be, therefore, that the criteria do not provide us with a conclusive answer as to whether or not the labor market efficiently allocates labor, although the evidence does indicate that the forces of competition work in the expected direction in terms of occupational wage movements and regional employment movements and suggests that they may also apply in terms of industrial wage and employment adjustments.

Labor Mobility and the Industrial Wage Structure

The efficiency by which the industrial wage structure allocates labor among industries has been questioned on a different basis.[25] Suppose that, unless changes in demand or productivity are dramatic and substantial, the industrial wage structure is influenced more by custom and/or institutional features such as unions, wage patterns, or internal wage structures to the firm than by competitive forces. If this is true, then (1) employment adjustments to substantial changes in demand, which produce changes in wage differentials, are implied in the competitive hypothesis, but (2) changes in employment in response to differentials existing within a given wage structure are not so implied. In both situations the equilibrium state of the labor market is relevant. The second case—which follows from the job-vacancy hypothesis—is consistent with the competitive hypothesis and in fact is implied by it if disequilibrium exists within the existing wage structure. In the first case, changes in employment need not move strongly in the direction of wage changes resulting from demand changes if the system were already in disequilibrium. In Figure 14.2, if the disequilibrium situation, W_1 and N_1, exists between two sectors, ordinarily we would expect employment to expand in sector II and contract in sector I. However, if supply is more elastic in I than in II an increase in demand raises wages slightly in I and expands employment greatly, whereas an expansion of demand in II raises wages more and expands employment less. Shifts of labor supply leftward in I and rightward in II may proceed slowly in the

---

[24] As a result, conclusions based upon tests of these criteria must be taken with caution. For example, M. A. Zaidi, "Structural Unemployment, Labor Market Efficiency and the Intra-factor Allocation Mechanism in the United States and Canada," *The Southern Economic Journal*, Vol. 35, No. 3 (January 1969), pp. 205–213. Zaidi considers efficiency in terms of interindustrial and interregional allocation of labor.

[25] Lloyd Ulman, "Labor Mobility and the Industrial Wage Structure in the Postwar United States," *Quarterly Journal of Economics*, Vol. 79, (February 1965) pp. 73–97. He, too, questions Galloway's assumption of the necessity of a constant wage structure to demonstrate labor market allocative efficiency. See pp. 78 and 81.

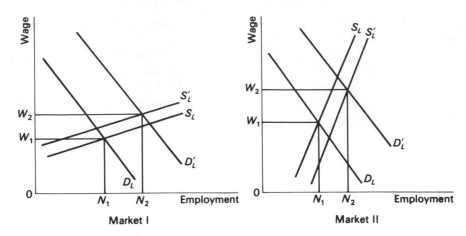

FIGURE 14.2. Labor markets in disequilibrium. See text.

face of wage differentials if quality differences impair the substitutability of the two. Expansion of demand in both sectors, especially if uneven, may obscure the magnitude of employment changes, yet the labor market can be allocating workers in the predicted direction. Unless disequilibrium situations are recognized, questionable conclusions may result from a casual inspection of data.

Because wage changes have shown little relationship to employment changes in 57 industries and because little relationship existed between the original level of earnings and employment changes, an erroneous conclusion has been drawn that neither the job-vacancy hypothesis nor the competitive hypothesis is supported by industry data. Data also have shown that quit rates vary inversely with wage rates, which also has led to the erroneous conclusion that high-paying industries do not have to pay higher wages to maintain their labor force, and hence are not compelled by the market to raise wages. As we have seen in the preceding paragraph, the magnitude of employment changes need not parallel the magnitude of wage changes if demand increases unequally and if labor supply has different elasticities among industries. If, as the evidence indicates, higher-paying firms utilize superior grades of labor, increases in the demand for the scarce supply of this grade may necessitate greater wage increases if the firm's labor force is to remain intact. Little increase in employment may result. If unemployment exists or the labor force is increasing, employment would expand cross sectionally and zero wage level–employment correlation would not be unusual. "Yet the additional workers employed in high-wage industries could have been recruited from among those previously employed in low-paying industries, which in turn would be required to recruit from among the ranks of the unemployed and new entrants into the labor force."[26] If unemployment exists and demand is expanding, the results of Ulman's evidence are consistent with both the job-vacancy and the efficient allocation of labor hypotheses. Hence, the findings rejecting these hypotheses do not necessarily follow.

Interindustry Wage Variations

Nevertheless, imperfections do exist in labor markets, and the failure of the studies cited here to refute the competitive hypothesis does not imply that competitive forces are always dominant. It suggests, however, that other approaches should be used. One such theory that utilizes assumptions of imperfections in labor markets is the theory of interindustry wage variations.[27] Others have noted the influence of productivity[28] and the degree of unionization as forces explaining wage determination in United States industry. Although productivity changes explain a substantial amount of wage variation, employment and wages changes do not correlate highly. Also, variation in wages among industries within groups by degree of unionization is greater than among the groups.[29] Hence, a more systematic model than the competitive one is necessary to explain wage variation in United States industry (see Table 14.2).

The interindustry wage-variation hypothesis acknowledges that there are both internal and external forces on a firm, influencing its wages. Productivity is an internal force; degree of unionization and the nature of and changes in product demand are external forces. Under competition in the product market, increases in productivity and corresponding reductions in cost must be passed on to the customers of the firm through lower prices. If oligopoly power is possessed by the firm, it may be able to capture the lower costs as profits by exercising control over prices and output. In the absence of unions, the greater profits act as a permissive force which can enable firms to raise wages; the union, however, acts as a positive force to

[26] For similar reasons, Severn also does not accept Ulman's conclusions regarding the job-vacancy thesis. He believes that Ulman implicitly assumes full employment, which is not a part of the job-vacancy hypothesis. Alan K. Severn, "Upward Labor Mobility: Opportunity or Incentive," *op. cit.*, p. 145.

[27] J. W. Garbarino, "A Theory of Interindustry Wage Structure Variation," *Quarterly Journal of Economics*, Vol. 64 (May 1950), pp. 282–305.

[28] John T. Dunlop, "Productivity and the Wage Structure," in *Income, Employment, and Public Policy* (New York: W. W. Norton, 1948), pp. 341–342.

[29] A. M. Ross, *Trade Union Wage Policy* (Berkeley and Los Angeles: University of California Press, 1948), pp. 113–133; Paul H. Douglas, *Real Wages in the United States, 1890–1926* (Boston: Houghton Mifflin Co., 1930).

TABLE 14.2

INCREASES IN AVERAGE GROSS HOURLY EARNINGS OF PRIVATE NONAGRICULTURAL PRODUCTION OR NONSUPERVISORY WORKERS, 1960–1970

	Percentage Change per Year					
Industry	1960– 1965	1965– 1966	1966– 1967	1967– 1968	1968– 1969	1969– 1970[a]
Total private	3.2	4.5	4.7	6.3	6.7	5.9
Mining	2.3	4.5	4.6	5.0	7.5	6.7
Contract construction	3.7	5.1	5.7	7.3	8.4	9.2
Manufacturing	2.9	4.2	4.0	6.4	6.0	5.3
Durable goods	2.8	3.9	3.4	6.3	6.3	5.0
Nondurable goods	2.9	3.8	4.9	6.6	6.2	5.8
Wholesale and retail trade	3.5	4.9	5.2	7.1	6.7	5.9
Wholesale trade	3.1	4.6	5.5	5.9	5.9	6.5
Retail trade	3.7	4.9	5.2	7.5	6.5	6.1
Finance, insurance, and real estate	3.4	3.3	4.5	6.6	6.2	5.1
Services	5.7[b]	5.9	5.5	6.1	8.2	8.0
Transportation and public utilities	5.2[b]	2.6	4.2	5.6	6.1	6.1

[a] Preliminary.

[b] Data not available for years 1960 through 1963; percentage change from 1964 to 1965.

Note: Data relate to production workers in mining and manufacturing, to construction workers in contract construction, and, generally, to nonsupervisory workers in all other industries.

Source: Department of Labor. *Economic Report of the President, 1971*, p. 57.

compel increases in wages. In either event, if productivity gains occur in firms located in oligopoly industries, these firms are more apt to grant wage increases and pay higher wages. Thus, it is hypothesized that wage variations among industries can be explained primarily through changes in productivity and by its index of concentration. This index is determined by the size of the industry market controlled by the firm. Firms having similar indices of concentration will rank in industry wage structures corresponding to their productivity ranking. Examining 1923–1940 data, Garbarino finds that the correlation between wage changes and changes in output per man-hour is 0.60; the relationship between the degree of concentration and wage changes is 0.67; and taking the two together, about 0.86 of the deviations in wages are explained.

He found a low relationship between wages and degree of unionization, but a strong relation between degree of unionization and degree of concentration.[30] Garbarino examined the extreme wage variations and found that in low-paying industries, both the degree of unionization and the index of concentration are low. However, in seven industries that pay extremely high wages, four had more than 60% of their employees in unions, four had substantial increases in employment, and one ranked fairly high in the index of concentration.[31] Thus, Garbarino concluded that his model successfully explains much of the interindustry wage variation in the observed interval.

Industrial Concentration and Wages

Firms which enjoy oligopoly power may be able to pay higher wages, and unions in such firms may be able to extract greater wage concessions. However, the greater financial resources of the oligopoly may also give it greater bargaining power vis-à-vis the union by permitting it to hold out against a strike over a longer duration. Hence, any explanation which relates wages to the degree of industry concentration and degree of unionization must include a variable representing the monopsony power of the corporation in the labor market.[32] One view holds that the greater the

[30] In a multiple regression equation in which wages are dependent upon productivity, the index of concentration, and the degree of unionization, the coefficient of the degree of unionization may not be significantly different from zero because of the high intercorrelation between unionization and concentration.

[31] "Interindustry Wage Structure Variation," *op. cit.*, pp. 304–305.

[32] For such an explanation see Leonard W. Weiss, "Concentration and Labor Earnings," *American Economic Review*, Vol. 56, No. 1 (March 1966), pp. 96–117. An explanatory equation would be of the form $W_1 = b_0 + b_1 C_i + b_2 V_i - b_3 M_i$ where i is the industry index, W is the industry wage rate, C is the concentration index, V represents the proportion of workers in the industry under collective bargaining agreements, and M is the interaction variable which measures the relative strength of the oligopoly vs. the union. Earlier, H. Gregg Lewis had used this same approach in a study of the effect of concentration on wage changes in manufacturing and had found the coefficient to be negative. See his *Unionism and Relative Wages in the United States* (Chicago: University of Chicago Press, 1963), pp. 159–161 and 177–178. Weiss indicates that he developed his model independently of Lewis and concurrently with him. Whereas Lewis analyzed relative rates of change in earnings over time, Weiss considered relative magnitudes of annual earnings cross sectionally for 1959. A test of the influence of concentration on wage changes over an interval of time has been performed by Bruce T. Allen, "Market Concentration and Wage Increases; U.S. Manufacturing, 1947–1964," *Industrial and Labor Relations Review*, Vol. 21, No. 3 (April 1968), pp. 353–366. Allen finds that throughout most of this period, employees in concentrated industries received larger wage increases than did workers in competitive industries. He does not consider, however, the influence of unions on these increases.

organizational strength of a union, the greater will be its ability to raise wages in any industry, competitive or oligopolistic.[33] However, in competitive industries, unless the union can organize a critical area, such as a strategic local labor market—e.g., in trucking—or the industry in a limited region in which organization is to the marked advantage of the industry— e.g., coal mining—it is not likely to develop much organizational strength which would permit it to raise wages. Strong oligopolies do contribute to the development of the organizational strength of unions and hence unions can exact high wages from these industries, but the stronger the oligopoly the less is the union's relative strength in securing wage gains, even in highly organized industries.[34] Bargaining power in this bilateral monopoly situation then determines the wage outcome.

Of interest is the finding that wages paid in concentrated industries are not higher than necessary to attract the quality of labor used therein, an argument which had been used to support the case that the labor market did not allocate labor resources efficiently. Instead, on the basis of a variety of personal characteristics, higher wages were found to be payments for superior workers and that "their earnings contain little or no monopoly rent."[35] Hence, concentrated industries pay higher wages partly because they are unionized and partly because they employ "superior" workers.

An intraindustry test of the hypothesis concerning the effect of market– union concentration on wages has been made for the newspaper industry.[36] A newspaper's share of total citywide newspaper circulation has been taken as a measure of market concentration. Wages were found to be negatively related to the degree of concentration, and this relation was not offset by the impact of unionization or of city size. This led to the conclusion that monopoly can depress wage rates. The results appear to refute earlier findings. Two points of clarification, however, may remove the inconsistency. First, even though the degree of unionization may be substantial, the

---

[33] H. M. Levinson, "Unionism, Concentration, and Wage Changes: Toward a Unified Theory," *Industrial and Labor Relations Review*, Vol. 20, No. 2 (January 1967), pp. 198–205.

[34] Weiss has found that great oligopoly power can and does hold union power in check. For semiskilled males, "unionization seems to raise annual earnings by about 16 percent when concentration is low, but to have no effect when concentration is high. Concentration seems to raise earnings by about 33 percent when unions are weak, but by only 13 percent when they are strong." *Op. cit.*, pp. 104–105.

[35] *Ibid.*, p. 115. For another detailed study of the influence of personal characteristics on wages, see Sherwin Rosen, "On the Interindustry Wage and Hours Structure," *Journal of Political Economy* (March-April 1969), pp. 249–273. Rosen finds a positive relationship between unionization and wages.

[36] John H. Landon, "The Effect of Product-Market Concentration on Wage Levels: An Intra-Industry Approach," *Industrial and Labor Relations Review*, Vol. 23, No. 2 (January 1970), pp. 237–247.

organizational strength of the unions may be weak because of (1) a large number of unions present in the newspaper industry, (2) weak commitment of the labor force to unionization (i.e., the newspaper industry may have a disproportionate number of white-collar workers or female employees), and (3) the financial resources of the union may be small. Weak organizational strength impairs ability to obtain wage increases. Second, the concentration index may be nonrepresentative. The availability of newspapers from nearby cities may not be revealed in the index used in the study. Moreover, newspaper circulation ignores the competition of other media—radio, TV, magazines. Hence, the share of the newspaper in the local media market may be relatively small, even though the share in the newspaper circulation of the local market is large. As a result, earlier findings of a positive relationship between wages and degree of concentration, as well as wages and degree of organization, may not be contradicted by this study.

Summary

Wage differentials arise from a number of sources, as economists have long recognized. These differentials arise from human capital differences, from inherent differences in ability, from employment tastes that differ, and from varying job requirements. Competitive labor-market theory implies that differentials which exceed those necessary to equate net advantages among jobs will in time disappear. It also implies that employment changes will be responsive to excess wage differentials.

Skill differentials in occupations have appeared to narrow in the 20th century, although recently there is some evidence that they may have stabilized. If fringe benefits are included in compensation comparisons, it is possible that the highly skilled, who may enjoy more of such benefits, have maintained their relative advantage over the nonskilled. Reder has developed a theory which explains compression of the wage structure during periods of tightening labor markets as a process of upgrading within the job hierarchy. Labor scarcities are felt more at the bottom of the hierarchy than at intermediate levels or at the top, and wages of the less skilled labor force are correspondingly bid up more than those of the more skilled.

Tests by Evans and Behman on the surface appear to refute Reder's hypothesis. Evans found that wage differentials in periods of extreme labor shortage did not narrow. Behman found that quit rates correlated positively with industries utilizing greater proportions of the skilled, and she concluded that wage rates are positively related to quit rates as the proportion of skilled to total employment increases. If the skilled quit more readily to take higher-paying jobs, the skill differential need not narrow. Upon closer examination, it is found that neither author has tested hypotheses that are inconsistent with Reder's theory; hence, Reder's theory has not been refuted. Severn has conducted independent tests, and contrary to Behman, finds that quit rates vary inversely with levels of skill. In general, Severn's tests support Reder's job-vacancy hypothesis.

A number of studies have sought to determine if the industrial wage structure has narrowed, as competitive labor-market theory would imply. However, the theory of competition assumes a static economy where disturbances that have produced disequilibrium are allowed to work themselves out, *ceteribus paribus*, as the market returns to equilibrium. Unfortunately for the testing of hypotheses, the real world does not grant the *ceteribus paribus* assumption, and tests that fail to support the competitive hypothesis may be invalid because other disturbances occur to perpetuate the disequilibrium. Studies by Cullen and Ulman seem to refute the competitive hypothesis; in the first case because the industrial wage structure was found not to have narrowed, in the second case because changes in employment do not correlate significantly with changes in wages. Both studies are suspect because they assume movement from one equilibrium position to another. Other studies by Zaidi and Galloway have found that the labor market does appear to have allocated labor efficiently, although the evidence that is has done so among industries is less clear.

However, imperfections do exist in the labor market, and such imperfections can affect wages. Garbarino, Weiss, Lewis, and Levinson have studied the influence of industrial concentration and unionization on wages. Their findings that concentration does appear to raise wages, and that oligopoly power tends to hold union power in check are generally consistent. The failure of Landon to find this to be true in local labor markets where newspapers hold monopoly power may be owing to a too restrictive definition of the market in which newspapers compete.

On the basis of the analysis and evidence presented in this chapter, we must agree with Reder and Rottenberg that over time the competitive labor-market model does provide reasonably good predictions concerning the movement of wages and employment.

Discussion Questions

1. How valid are the observations of Smith, Mills, and Cairnes on the nature of wage differentials to this phenomenon today?
2. Suppose an industry is growing rapidly, as evidenced by employment growth, yet wages in that industry are no higher than in other industries with slower rates of growth. Is the competitive hypothesis refuted? Explain.

3. Based upon what you have learned in this chapter concerning the skilled–unskilled wage differential, what would you predict about this differential during the last half of the 1960s? The first half of the 1970s? Substantiate your answer.

4. The "internal labor market" is one in which the jobs within a firm are allocated to employees on some rational basis—i.e., efficiency, seniority, nepotism, or friendship. Does Reder's theory of occupational wage differentials include the concept of an internal labor market? Does your answer explain the neglect of Reder's model in the literature of the "internal labor market"?

5. Severn suggests that quit rates among the highly skilled should be lower than among the semiskilled because their opportunities for improvement are fewer. Would this hypothesis also apply to the highly educated? If we find that mobility correlates positively with the level of education, would this finding refute Severn's hypothesis? Explain.

6. Does the finding of stability in the industrial wage structure offer any suggestion as to what employment decisions a young person should make who is entering the labor market for the first time? If occupational wage differentials are narrowing, does it matter what occupational choices are made? Explain.

7. Is it to workers' short-run advantage to have an efficient labor market? Their long-run advantage? Discuss.

8. How can the theory of human capital contribute to an understanding of wage differentials? If labor that receives higher wages is defined as being of better quality, is the human-capital hypothesis verified? Must labor be more productive in order to be of higher quality? Explain.

15

Regional Wage Differentials

Introduction

It has previously been noted that an industry located in different parts of the country may utilize different occupational mixes. In one region an industry may use proportionally more skilled employees, in a second region it may use proportionally more semiskilled employees, and in a third it may rely on a mix heavily weighted with unskilled occupations. There is even more diversity in the skill mix among industries. Furthermore, some industries are confined to a small geographic area; some tend to exist in large cities; others are found fairly widely distributed across the nation; and still others tend to locate only in smaller cities and towns. The configuration of this occupation–industry–location mix is reflected in the wage patterns peculiar to the regions of the country, for this mix affects the demand for labor in any particular region. Interacting with these forces influencing labor demand are the labor supply characteristics of the region.

Regional Labor Demand

The regional demand for labor is affected by a number of forces. The resource endowment of a region obviously attracts industry and undoubtedly influences the composition of industry within a region. However, labor resource endowment is a supply influence, so we are here referring to nonlabor resource endowment. Of especial importance is the supply of capital resources available to the region, which influences the capital–labor ratio, in turn the productivity of labor, and ultimately the wage-paying capability of firms.[1] Capital can either be generated internally through

[1] Lowell E. Galloway, "The North–South Differential," *Review of Economics and Statistics*, Vol. 65 (August 1963), p. 270.

regional savings or it can flow into or out of the region. Obviously, the mobility of capital is important in determining the expansion or movement of industry into or out of a region. The expansion and development of industry provides jobs and determines the magnitude of the demand for labor. The type of industry developing or existing within a region determines the demand for labor by occupation, and this affects the wage pattern of a region. Regions which contain industries utilizing high levels of occupations will possess a wage pattern dominated by high-wage jobs. If the industries located or locating in a region are growth industries, the demand for labor will be expanding, and the wage-paying capabilities of these firms will tend to be high. Consequently, not only is the mix of industry by wage-paying characteristics important in determining the wage level of a region, but whether those industries are growing or declining will influence the future demand for labor in that area. Finally, the elasticity of substitution of capital for labor is an important influence in determining the development of employment opportunities. Normally, if both capital and labor are mobile, the elasticity of substitution will tend to be higher in a period of time than if either or both are relatively immobile. To the extent that high-wage industries are growth industries, the tendency of capital to substitute for high-wage labor may be offset by expanding output. Yet, the increase in employment in any expanding industry will tend to be greater the less the elasticity of substitution.

Regional Labor Supply

Forces affecting labor supply may operate either on the elasticity of supply or on the quantity supplied at any wage rate. Ordinarily, costs of living tend to be higher in cities than in rural areas. Hence, the subsistence component of wages will be higher in cities and a higher wage is normally required to bring forth a given offer of labor. Consequently, the urban–rural mix of a region will be an important determinant of the supply of labor. Moreover, population growth rates historically have been higher in rural areas, generating greater increases in the labor force.[2] New entrants in the labor force are apt to be in greater supply in a rurally dominated area than in an urban one, and because of lower educational attainments and a tendency toward inferior schools, these new entrants are apt to possess less training. Hence, the unskilled component of the labor force is apt to be greater in rural areas, and a labor surplus, given relative declines in the demand for this type of labor, is more likely to exist. However, mobility of the young

[2] H. M. Douty, "Wage-Differentials: Forces and Counterforces," *Monthly Labor Review*, Vol. 91 (March 1968), pp. 74–81.

tends to be greater, and hence the elasticity of supply may be greater in nonurban regions.[3] The concentration of minority groups—Blacks, Mexican-Americans, Indians—may also affect the nonskilled component of the labor force of a region, since these ethnic groups tend to have lower levels of educational attainment, and unemployment, mortality, and debility rates by age tend to be higher.[4] Taken together, the interaction of labor demand and supply determinants influences the wage pattern and average level of wages within a region, and, hence, accounts for the regional wage structure in the United States.

Urban Wages

It has been suggested that urban wages are higher than those found in rural areas. Moreover, wages tend to be higher the larger the metropolitan area.[5] As we have noted, schools tend to be better and educational attainments are higher, implying that a better quality of labor is to be found in the city. Moreover, the cost of living tends to be higher, which puts a higher floor under wages than in rural areas. Although the elasticity of supply of the unskilled labor force tends to be higher in rural areas, it probably is true that the elasticity of the skilled labor force is greater in the city than in rural areas. In part this is owing to the greater geographical mobility of the better trained and educated, and also the city permits greater spatial mobility within it across occupational and industrial lines.[6] Put another way, where occupational and industrial wage differentials exist within a city, the labor market is more likely to generate movement from low wage to high wage sectors because spatial barriers to movement are minimal.[7] This implies a diffusion of wages in an upward direction, consistent with the job-vacancy and wage-differential hypotheses of labor market allocation. To the extent that metropolitan areas also represent consumer and industrial markets, they offer locational advantages to industries. Because of the high cost of

[3] Robert L. Raimon, "Interstate Migration and Wage Theory," *Review of Economics and Statistics*, Vol. 44 (November 1962), p. 429.
[4] *Ibid.* Recent data indicate that the educational gap between non-Whites and Whites is narrowing. See William Deutermann, "Educational Attainment of Workers," *Monthly Labor Review*, Vol. 93, No. 10 (October 1970), p. 11.
[5] Douty, *op. cit.* See also, Victor R. Fuchs, *Differentials in Hourly Earnings by Region and City*, Occasional Paper No. 101 (New York: National Bureau of Economic Research, 1967).
[6] F. W. Bell, "The Relation of the Region, Industrial Mix, and Production Function to Metropolitan Wage Levels," *The Review of Economics and Statistics*, Vol. 49 (August 1967), p. 368.
[7] For a description of mobility barriers that do exist in the city when the urban transit system decays, see William Tabb, *The Political Economy of the Black Ghetto* (New York: W. W. Norton, 1970), pp. 68–69, 118–119.

living, high-wage, high-productivity firms are more likely to survive in the city, and this is truer the larger the city. The greater supply of skilled labor in the city also encourages firms with high-skill occupational mixes to prefer the city over a rural or less urbanized area.[8] Similarly, the presence of financial institutions, transportational facilities, vocational schools, etc., provides the firm with complementary resources. Thus, there is an interaction between supply forces and demand forces which on balance gives cities a comparative advantage in attracting industry.

By city size, Table 15.1 indicates the differences in hourly wages paid

TABLE 15.1
AVERAGE HOURLY WAGES BY CITY SIZE,
OF INDUSTRIAL WORKERS, 1959

Size (*in 1000*)	Wage Rate (\$)
Rural	2.00
Under 10	2.12
10–100	2.23
100–250	2.39
250–500	2.43
500–1000	2.56
1 thousand and over	2.84

Source: Bureau of the Census, 1960.

in urban–rural locations in 1959. However, in recent years there has been a tendency for new industry to avoid central urban locations, and instead to move to the suburbs. About 65% of all new industrial construction between 1954 and 1965 occurred outside the central cities, although most of this construction occurred within standard metropolitan areas.[9]

Size of Differentials

There are two related questions associated with the phenomenon of regional wage differentials: (1) What is their magnitude? (2) How do we explain

[8] Consistent with the job-vacancy thesis, firms that newly locate in an area may need only a small nucleus of top-level skills. The transfer of the next lowest level of skill from other firms in the area to the higher-skill vacancies in new firms permits the worker to upgrade his skill and his wage at the same time. The presence of multiple types of news media and grapevine networks permits wide dissemination of knowledge of these job vacancies, resulting in an elastic labor supply curve.

[9] *Manpower Report of the President, 1967* (Washington: U.S. Government Printing Office, 1967), p. 87.

them? The answer to the first question leads logically to the second. We have already suggested some of the causes of the differentials, but methodological problems exist as to how to measure the impact of each cause. First, let us consider the size of these differentials and in the next section consider the cause of the differentials.

Table 15.2 shows average hourly earnings of production workers in manufacturing by selected states in selected areas. It is generally true for states not listed that wages tend to be related to those in states to which they

TABLE 15.2
AVERAGE HOURLY EARNINGS OF PRODUCTION WORKERS IN MANUFACTURING BY STATE AND REGION, APRIL 1970

Area, by Land	Average Hourly Earnings
I. West	(3.833)[a]
California	3.75
Oregon	3.73
Washington	4.02
II. North Central	(3.830)[a]
Illinois	3.61
Michigan	4.12
Ohio	3.76
III. Mountain	(3.45)[a]
Colorado	3.51
Idaho	3.15
Montana	3.68
IV. Northeastern	(3.16)[a]
Massachusetts	3.19
New Jersey	3.39
Vermont	2.90
V. Great Plains	(3.08)[a]
Kansas	3.13
Nebraska	3.13
South Dakota	2.98
VI. Southwest	(2.97)[a]
New Mexico	2.70
Oklahoma	3.06
Texas	3.15
VII. South	(2.49)[a]
Georgia	2.63
Mississippi	2.40
North Carolina	2.45

[a] Unweighted average.

Source: U.S. Department of Labor, *Employment and Earnings*, Vol. 17, No. 1 (July 1970), pp. 83–86.

TABLE 15.3
REGIONAL INCOME PER WORKER AS PERCENTAGE OF UNITED STATES AVERAGE, 1880–1950

| | *Year* | | | | |
Area	1880	1900	1920	1930	1950
United States	100	100	100	100	100
New England	121 (IV)	118 (IV)	108 (V)	113 (IV)	99 (V)
Middle Atlantic	132 (III)	125 (III)	121 (II)	122 (I)	112 (II)
East North Central	110 (V)	112 (V)	110 (III)	117 (II)	112 (II)
West North Central	99 (VI)	108 (VI)	95 (VI)	92 (VI)	97 (VI)
South Atlantic	46 (IX)	48 (IX)	67 (VIII)	63 (IX)	75 (VIII)
East South Central	55 (VIII)	52 (VIII)	60 (IX)	58 (VIII)	68 (IX)
West South Central	64 (VII)	68 (VII)	80 (VII)	71 (VII)	87 (VII)
Mountain	150 (II)	144 (I)	110 (III)	94 (V)	102 (IV)
Pacific	172 (I)	142 (II)	122 (I)	114 (III)	114 (I)

Source: R. A. Easterlin, "Long-Term Regional Income Changes, Some Suggested Factors," *Papers and Proceedings of the Regional Science Association*, Vol. IV, 1958, p. 317.

are contiguous. For example, Kentucky's wage rate is closer to Ohio's than to Georgia's; Arizona's wage rate is intermediate between California's and New Mexico's, as is Pennsylvania's with respect to Ohio's and New Jersey's. In Table 15.3 is presented another view of the trend of regional earnings in the interval between 1880 and 1950. The regional classification is somewhat different from Table 15.1 and earnings are expressed as income per worker as a percent of the United States average. Rank is in parentheses beside the index, and it is interesting to observe that the rankings of the top four regions has undergone numerous changes in the seventy-year interval; only the Pacific and the Middle Atlantic regions have retained their position in the top three. The bottom three regions (all in the South) have remained at the bottom, with the South Atlantic and the East South Central vying for the lowest rank.

Because the southern states have historically been at the bottom of the national wage structure and because the northern states (New England, Middle Atlantic, and East North Central) have consistently ranked above the national average, the wage differentials between the two broad regions have been the subject of numerous studies. Because of their relatively proximate geographical relationship and because the wage differentials have persisted over time, economists have tended to use these broad regions as a base from which to study the geographical allocations mechanism of the

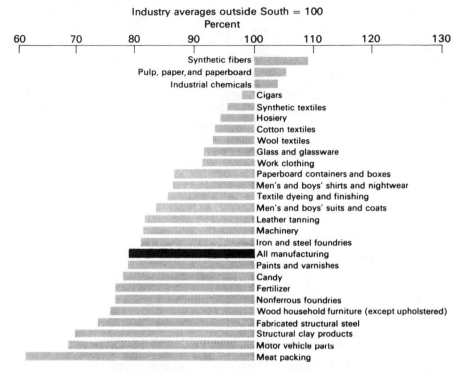

CHART 15.1. Straight-time average hourly earnings, South as percent of remainder of United States, all manufacturing and selected manufacturing industries.

Source: Bureau of Labor Statistics, U.S. Department of Labor, Industry Wage Surveys, Various Dates, 1962–1966. From H. M. Douty, "Wage-Differentials: Forces and Counter-forces," *Monthly Labor Review* (March 1968), pp. 74–81.

labor market. Chart 15.1 depicts the manufacturing industry structure of the South and a comparison of the straight-time average hourly earnings in the South and in regions outside the South. Only a few industries in the South pay above the national industry average. The data in Chart 15.1 compare with data developed elsewhere which indicate that average hourly earnings in the South are only about 80% of the national average.[10] Data in Tables 15.2 and 15.3 suggest that this differential may be narrowing over the long run.[11] For example, the unweighted average of hourly earnings in the Southwest and South is about 84% of the unweighted national average.

[10] Fuchs, *op. cit.*, p. 32.
[11] Douty holds this view, *op. cit.*, p. 80, although he believes the differentials will persist for a long time.

Others have noted that the wage differential has been stable since World War II[12]; whether this is only a lull in the long-run tendency or a permanent condition remains to be seen.

Average hourly earnings are measured by summing for each region the total industry annual wage bill and dividing that wage bill by the man-hours worked during that year. Differentials are then measured by subtracting one region's average from another or that region's average from the national average. Although the measures are composite ones and give us an indication of the relative size of a region's wage structure, they reveal little about the cause of the differences. They also tell us little about the size of the differential if each region enjoyed full employment of its labor force. To the extent that the relative-earnings coefficient measures relative-productivity rankings of regions or serves as a welfare index for the regions, it may be misleading. As an average-productivity index or as a welfare index analogous to per capita income, but applied to the labor force, the region's total wage bill perhaps should be divided by the region's total labor force, adjusted for hidden unemployment. Hence, regions with above average unemployment would have a lower average, and the differentials may widen or narrow as the dispersion of unemployment rates widens or narrows among regions.

The Source and Nature of Regional Differentials

Regions possess characteristics. These characteristics are variously identified, but for our purposes, the employment structure of a region is distinguishable by (a) employment by industry, (b) occupational employment, (c) occupational wage pattern, (d) urban–rural employment patterns, (e) personal characteristics of the labor force—composition by age, sex, race, educational attainments, and (f) degree of unionization. These employment characteristics have all been used to identify the source of wage differentials among regions, because only the employed receive wages (see Appendix). Scholars who study the origin of regional differentials have approached the problem in essentially this manner: in respect to one or more of these characteristics, what would the wage structure, and hence, the relative wage position, have been for region A if it were homogeneous in terms of this characteristic with the rest of the nation or with some other region B? In order to answer this question, a modified average wage has been developed which standardizes the region in terms of the characteristic.

Hanna first used the standardization procedure to demonstrate that a simple comparison of state wage levels is misleading because employment patterns differ by regions. Each state's wage structure was adjusted by using

[12] Richard Perlman, *Labor Theory* (New York: John Wiley, 1969), pp. 132–139.

the national employment pattern as the standardization norm, and wage comparisons by state were thereby derived.[13] Wonnacott has raised a basic objection to the use by Hanna of national employment patterns as a standardizing norm on the grounds that such a norm may be irrelevant to the actual employment pattern of many states.[14] To overcome this difficulty, he constructs a 49 × 49 matrix, representing the 48 contiguous states and Washington D.C., in which the element in each row is the wage pattern of the row state multiplied by the employment pattern of the column state. Correspondingly, the element in each column is the employment pattern of the column state multiplied by the wage pattern of each row state. Hence, every element simultaneously provides us with the answers to the following questions for any two states represented by the element:

1. If state M (N) had the employment pattern of state N (M), what would be its average wage and what would be the differential?
2. Given the employment patterns as they exist in M and N, what would be the differential if the wage pattern in M (N) were the same as the wage pattern in N (M)?

Such a procedure permits states to be ranked by order of distribution of employment in high-wage industries and by order of distribution of high-wage patterns in industries. The midwestern and western states ranked highest in wages; the southern states ranked lowest.[15] In terms of distribution of employment in high-wage industries, the ranking is less pronounced, although midwestern states tended to rank in the upper half and southern states exhibited a strong tendency to rank in the lower half.[16] This technique accounts for much of the source of wage differences between states.

A somewhat similar approach has been used to derive data for two labor market phenomena: (1) the effect on employment of a capital–labor substitution, and (2) the process by which wage levels are diffused over a metropolitan employment structure.[17] The regions used for comparison are

[13] F. A. Hanna, *State Income Differentials, 1919–1954* (Durham, N.C.: Duke University Press, 1959). Also, see his earlier article, "Contribution of Manufacturing Wages to Regional Differences in Per Capita Income," *Review of Economics and Statistics*, Vol. 33 (February 1951), pp. 18–28, in which the employment patterns of the North were applied to southern wage patterns.

[14] R. J. Wonnacott, "Wage Levels and Employment Structure in United States Regions: A Free Trade Precedent," *Journal of Political Economy*, Vol. 72 (August 1964), pp. 414–419.

[15] *Ibid.*, p. 416.

[16] *Ibid.*, p. 417.

[17] F. W. Bell, "The Relation of the Region, Industrial Mix, and Production Function to Metropolitan Wage Levels," *Review of Economics and Statistics*, Vol. 49 (August 1967), pp. 368–374.

65 standard metropolitan statistical areas (SMSA), and in each SMSA an area effect and a mix effect are then calculated. The area effect is defined as the difference between the actual area wage bill, $\sum W_{km} e_{km}$, and the wage bill which would have resulted if the average national industry wage W had been paid to employment e in each industry k in the area m. It is reduced to a ratio in order to obtain a pure number.

Area effect:
$$\frac{\sum_k W_{km} \cdot e_{km} - \sum_k \bar{W}_k \cdot e_{km}}{\sum_k \bar{W}_k \cdot e_{km}}.$$

Industries include only those in manufacturing. To the extent that area industry wages exceed national industry wages, the area will have a higher wage pattern.

The mix effect is defined as the difference between the wage bill in the area if the national industry wage pattern had been applied to the employment pattern and the wage bill which would have been received if the average wage of all industries in the nation, $W_{\bar{n}}$, had been paid to the employment pattern in the area.

Mix effect:
$$\frac{\sum_k \bar{W}_k \cdot e_{km} - \sum_k W_{\bar{n}} \cdot e_{km}}{\sum_k W_{\bar{n}} \cdot e_{km}}.$$

To the extent that the national industry wage is greater than the national average wage of all industries, the SMSA will have higher wages. The SMSA's were ranked in terms of area-effect ratios and mix-effect ratios and the SMSA's were classified into one of the four combinations of favorable–unfavorable ratios (favorable area–unfavorable mix, unfavorable area–favorable mix, etc.). (See Appendix.)

The area-effect data have been used to derive production function parameters for a number of industries. Given the parameters, it is possible to determine the employment effect on a SMSA if the wage structure of another SMSA were imposed upon it. If the wage structure of a high-wage city were imposed on the industry employment pattern of a low-wage city, the low-wage city would experience a substitution of capital for labor, and given the output of each industry in the low-wage city, employment in each industry would decline corresponding to the appropriate elasticity of substitution.[18]

To the extent that each SMSA possesses a set of key industries whose wage patterns are determined by the wage contour to which they belong, and to the extent that these industries dominate the wage decisions of other firms in the area through the competition for labor in the local market, then their wage patterns will be diffused throughout the area.[19] Hence, the mix

[18] *Ibid.*, p. 392.
[19] *Ibid.*, p. 373.

effect will be transmitted to the area effect, because if industry wages in the area for key industries tend to be greater than the over-all average national wage, then the industries in the area will tend to pay their employees more than the national industry average. This in turn will lead to a rise in the capital–labor ratio as capital substitution occurs, and employment expansion in the area owing to industry growth will be mitigated by the use of more capital for less labor. With a given area effect, variations in the mix effect will influence the output–labor ratio, determined from the production function, and the level of employment required to produce any given level of output. Similarly, results of holding the mix effect constant and varying the area effect can be shown.

Wages have also been standardized to determine differences in the North–South employment mix.[20] If the East–South Central and South Atlantic states had had the same employment patterns as did the Middle Atlantic states, the ratio of their average wages to those of the Middle Atlantic states would have been, respectively, 85 and 86%, instead of 78 and 79%.[21] In other words, employment in the Middle Atlantic states is more heavily concentrated in high-wage industries than is employment in the South. It is also argued that these wage differentials exist because of lower capital–labor ratios in the South, which have been derived from its historical scarcity of nonland capital and which have persisted because of barriers to mobility of resources into and from the South. Although it is true that capital–labor ratios are lower in the South than in the North, it is not obvious that these ratios are a cause of low wages rather than a consequence. This question will be discussed later, however.

A somewhat different approach has been used in measuring the source of wage differentials between the South and non-South.[22] Whereas the studies of regional wage differences identified above may be said to have sought explanation for regional wage differences in forces influencing labor demand—employment patterns, wage patterns, capital–labor ratios, and capital–labor substitution—the study seeks to explain wage differentials in terms of labor supply forces. It involves standardizing the labor force of the South and non-South regions in terms of four "quality" characteristics— age, sex, race, and education. The nonstandardized average southern wage is 80% of the non-South wage; after "quality" standardization, southern wages rise to 93% of the non-South level. Thus, if there were no differences between the quality of the labor force in the South and that in the non-South,

[20] L. E. Galloway, "The North–South Differential," *Review of Economics and Statistics,* Vol. 45 (August 1963), pp. 264–272.

[21] *Ibid.,* p. 265.

[22] See the pamphlet by Victor Fuchs, *Differentials in Hourly Earnings by Region and City Size, 1959,* Occasional Paper No. 101 (New York: National Bureau of Economic Research, 1967).

average hourly earnings in the former would more closely approach those of the latter. In fact, if the educational level is permitted to vary, with other qualities being standardized, the southern wage index varies directly with the level of schooling, although a differential still exists at each educational level. The differential is greater for low levels of education than for high levels.[23]

City size can affect the regional wage differential. If industries were located in cities in the South of the same size as those in the non-South, the wage level of the South would be 92% of that of the non-South. Therefore, estimates show that in 1959, one-third of the regional wage differential was owing to labor force "quality" differences, one-third was owing to differences in the location of industry by city size, and one-third was left unexplained.[24] Although it is possible that the degree of unionization may explain somewhat this residual difference, the high correlation between unionism and city size probably means that the effect of unionization is largely explained by city size. It would be surprising, indeed, if all the forces influencing labor supply had been identified, or if the forces which were identified explained all differences in wages.[25] It would amount to saying that prices (wages) are determined unilaterally by either demand or supply forces.

Prior to 1971, one important variable that had not been standardized was differences in the cost of living between northern and southern cities. This omission has now been remedied.[26] Using 1963 data for five northern and five southern cities, raw unweighted average hourly wages were 8.5% higher for northern cities, but cost-of-living adjustments revealed that the average *real* wage was 1% higher in the South than in the North. After standardizing for regional and industrial effects, *money* wages in the South were found to be 12.4% lower than the average for the total ten cities. However, hourly *real* wages in the South were only about $0.08 lower, and this was statistically insignificant. Annual real earnings differed only by $42.59, again an insignificant difference. Moreover, even after allowances were made for differences in the sex and color composition of the labor force and the capital–labor ratios, differentials remained of the same order of magnitude and were insignificant. Hence, it is argued that no real wage differential now appears to exist between the North and the South if the cities studied are representative of the two regions.

[23] *Ibid.*, pp. 22–26.
[24] *Ibid.*, p. 32.
[25] An attempt to identify the variables contained in the interindustry labor demand and supply functions has been made by Sherwin Rosen, "On the Interindustry Wage and Hours Structure," *Journal of Political Economy* (March–April 1969), pp. 249–273.
[26] P. R. R. Coelho and M. A. Ghali, "The End of the North–South Wage Differential," *American Economic Review*, Vol. LXI, No. 5 (December 1971).

Regional Differentials and Labor-Market Efficiency

The existence of wage differentials under competitive conditions between regions should induce the movement of labor to high-wage regions, the movement of capital to low-wage regions, the substitution of capital for labor in high-wage regions and vice versa in low-wage regions. The net effect of this activity should bring wages into some sort of parity between the two regions. Of course, wages could still differ by some amount sufficient to compensate labor or capital for incurring the costs of movement, although in the long run these costs per hour of work should become very small; this is especially true for labor of relatively young age. Wages could also differ sufficiently to cover inherent advantages of regions that make life more pleasant or reduce the cost of living, although quite frequently wages in areas with desirable climates are higher than wages in climatically less desirable regions (California vs. Wisconsin). Similarly, wages might differ if the quality of labor differs among regions, although these differences presumably would become minimal over the long run. Failure of wages to converge would indicate significant barriers to adjustment—imperfection in the labor market.

Studies have been made to see if regional reallocation of capital and labor are consistent with the labor-market efficiency thesis. The evidence supports the conclusion that "the labor market in either the United States or Canada is a reasonably efficient intrafactor allocation of labor between regional sectors of that market."[27] This conclusion is based upon evidence (1) that the interregional wage structure has remained stable, (2) that unemployment correlates with the level of employment by region, and (3) that the wage dispersion and rank order of regions has remained stable. Because interregional wage levels change slowly, the findings with respect to the stability and dispersion of interregional wages are to be expected over the relatively short period of the data studied. To the extent that employment and high capital–labor ratio industries are found in population centers, and to the extent that industries with high capital–labor ratios (durable goods industries) are recession prone, we would expect unemployment to vary with regional employment. Hence, these findings in the interval studied, it seems, simply do not imply efficient labor-market allocation. The findings are consistent with the industry employment mix of the regions and the

[27] M. A. Zaidi, "Structural Unemployment, Labor Market Efficiency and the Intrafactor Allocation Mechanism in the United States and Canada," *Southern Economic Journal*, Vol. 35, No. 3 (January 1969), p. 212. Also see L. E. Galloway, "Labor Mobility, Resource Allocation and Structured Unemployment," *American Economic Review* (September 1963). For a critique of these conditions, see Chapter 14.

economic forces at work during the interval, and they carry no necessary implication regarding the reallocation of labor among regions. Hence, the milder conclusion seems to be less controversial, "At least, the labor markets are no more inefficient in allocating labor regionally in 1964 than they were in 1953,"[28] although it is not clear that the evidence merits even this conclusion.

There are two other aspects of the allocation process of the labor market among regions.[29] One aspect relates to the process of the upgrading of labor within a given wage structure by which workers in lower-paying jobs move to higher-paying ones. The other aspect explains the allocation process in terms of wage structure differentials in which labor moves from low-paying sectors to higher-paying sectors. Presumably, other things remaining equal, differentials in wage structures will narrow as a result. However, if other things do not remain equal, a narrowing of differentials is not implied. Observers of the first aspect of labor-market allocation have propounded a job-vacancy thesis as the prime determinant of labor mobility; i.e., workers move more (1) in response to job openings than (2) in response to wage differentials. Some proponents of the job-vacancy thesis have concluded that the labor market is not an efficient allocator in response to wage differentials. This is an erroneous conclusion. Wage differences exist within a wage structure. If vacancies exist in jobs paying higher wages, or job vacancies at the same wage are present in firms providing greater advancement opportunities, job movement drift is from jobs with low net advantages to jobs with high net advantages, and this is all that is implied in the competitive labor-market analysis (of which the existence of wage differentials is a component of the sum of advantages). Hence, on *a priori* grounds there appears to be no essential difference in the two versions of how the labor market operates as an allocator; rather, perceptions are merely focused upon two mechanisms utilizing the same principle by which the choice of jobs is made.

Raimon's findings confirm the compatibility of the two views of the labor market. He finds that there was high correlation (0.86) between the net in-migration to states and their average earnings and income in the interval 1950–1957 level; moreover, he finds high correlation between net in-migration and changes in the volume of employment (0.89). Taken together, he concludes that the job-vacancy and the wage-difference hypotheses tell the same story.[30] Interestingly, he finds that the young (ages 20–29) tend to dominate among the interstate movers, and evidence

---

[28] *Ibid.*, p. 212.
[29] R. L. Raimon, "Interstate Migration and Wage Theory," *Review of Economics and Statistics*, Vol. 44 (November 1962), pp. 428–438.
[30] *Ibid.*, pp. 430–433. In fact, he finds that the correlation coefficient between changes in employment and the earning level, by state, is 0.72.

that their labor force attachment is strong is revealed by the fact that net population changes from in-migration by state relate strongly to employment volume changes. This is to be expected because among the young not only can the fixed costs of moving be amortized over a longer period, but also the expected gains from job search will be received over a longer period, which increases the capitalized value of a job change.[31]

It is not certain that the labor market will in the future generate changes in employment in the predicted direction. Between 1947 and 1959 wage increases of industries reducing production employment have exceeded wage increases of industries increasing production employment. Labor-market theory would indicate that firms paying higher wages would attract more labor than those paying lower wages, other things being equal[32]; evidence does not refute this even though it does cast doubt on the allocation hypothesis. It is predicted that high-wage firms will substitute capital for labor, that the motivation to do this will be stronger, the higher the wage level, and that the level of employment may fall with a sufficiently high elasticity of substitution and a sufficiently low expansion in product demand. To the extent that the capital–labor ratio rises as a result, labor productivity will rise, and greater wage changes are thereby possible. If the type of labor utilized in those industries has a relatively inelastic long-run supply curve, wages are more likely to rise. If this trend persists, the movement from low-wage to high-wage industries may be adversely affected.[33] Yet, if industry wage differentials narrow and if the skill mix becomes more concentrated in high-wage industries, the semiskilled can move (and probably will move as employment is reduced) from high-wage industries to lower-wage industries and still get more pay. This is possible if semiskilled wages in the lower-paying industries are higher than those in the higher-paying industries, where the relative wage position in the industry is determined more by the skill mix than by differences in wages by occupations. Semiskilled workers can still upgrade their position by moving from industries having lower concentrations of high-skill workers.

---

[31] See George Stigler, "Information in the Labor Market," *Journal of Political Economy*, Vol. 70, No. 5, Part 2 (October 1962 Supplement), pp. 94–105, for an analysis of the process of human capital investment through job search. Also in the same issue see Larry A. Sjaastad, "The Costs and Returns of Human Migration," pp. 80–93. Sjaastad argues that net migration is not the only mechanism for removing earnings differentials. Gross migration considers both in-migration and out-migration. To the extent that a state has both high-wage and low-wage industries, both types of migration are compatible with labor-market theory. He also considers both monetary and nonmonetary costs of moving. For the young, in particular, both are apt to be less.

[32] *Op. cit.*, p. 436.

[33] This is Raimon's opinion. *Ibid.*, pp. 436–437.

The North–South Differential

Even though the southern states have increased their volume of employee employment relative to the rest of the country, their volume of total employment relative to the non-South has not increased. Rather, the movement in the South from farm employment, largely self-employment, to nonfarm employment had produced this phenomenon.[34] This again is evidence of the labor-market reallocation process operating through the job-vacancy mechanism. The net effect is to raise the earnings level of the South, to reduce the labor surplus hidden in agriculture, and ultimately to set the stage for narrowing the differential. However, the differential may be preserved if low-wage industries concentrate in the South. Unskilled labor will find it can earn as much in the South as elsewhere, and this will tend to stabilize the out-migration from the South.[35] Similarly, the mobility of industries with low capital–labor rates into the South will be stabilized as the unskilled differential narrows between regions. Hence, to the extent that the South contains essentially a mixture of low-wage industries, the regional differential will persist. However, it may be argued that this process sets the stage for the eventual migration of capital-intensive industries into the South. Presumably, even low-wage manufacturing industries utilize some proportion of skilled labor, small though it may be. As low-wage manufacturing industries expand employment, the supply of skilled labor also expands proportionately. Now if the skilled–semiskilled–unskilled wage structure internal to firms or industries is relatively compressed in the South—i.e., the skilled–unskilled differential within the southern firm is lower than in firms in other regions—the possibility of upgrading the wage level of the skilled employees by changing jobs is substantial. This condition may well attract into the South firms which utilize a higher skill mix in anticipation that they will be able to secure the necessary skilled labor force by raiding other firms. Hence, the job-vacancy mechanism, coupled with the wage-differential mechanism, may eventually lead to further narrowing of the South–non-South wage differential.

Although there has been substantial out-migration of labor from the South, the relatively high rate of natural population growth has been sufficient to permit this and at the same time provide a growing southern labor force. Although southern manufacturing employment has expanded more rapidly than in other regions, the unskilled labor reserve has not yet

---

[34] *Ibid.*, p. 435.
[35] Richard Perlman, *Labor Theory* (New York: John Wiley, 1969), p. 134. This position appears to place Perlman in the school which narrowly adheres to the job-vacancy view of the labor-market allocative process.

been exhausted. Interestingly, the industries concentrated in non-South regions have grown more rapidly in terms of employment expansion than industries concentrated in the South, even though southern employment has expanded more rapidly than in other regions. This apparently contradictory phenomenon has a simple explanation. The non-South regions have had expanding industries which require expanding employment. As a result, wages rise. The rise in wages is less, the more that in-migration occurs from the South, and although substantial in-migration has occurred, it has not been sufficient to stem the rise in wages. As a result, low wage–low productivity–low capital firms located in the non-South find it difficult to survive in these regions. Because capital is more mobile than labor, these firms have tended instead to move to the South. The industries of which they are a part, while not growing rapidly on the national scene, are declining in employment in the non-South and increasing in employment in the South. As firms move South, displaced employees in the non-South are reabsorbed by expanding industries. Because of the growth of these low-wage industries in the South, the wage differential with other regions has tended to be preserved. Although in time more capital-intensive industries, utilizing labor of higher skills, may be expected to be attracted southward by the wage differential, this process has not yet gathered much momentum. It has been retarded also by the willingness of skilled labor in the South to migrate to other regions, and this tendency has tended to reduce the regional differential among the most highly skilled employees. As a result of these and other developments, there appears to be a consensus among students of the North–South wage differential that it will continue to exist for quite some time into the future.[36]

Summary

Regional wage differences are reflected in the labor demand and supply conditions peculiar to each region. Labor demand is influenced by the physical and capital resource endowment of the region, together with the type of industries located therein. Labor supply is affected by labor force characteristics, including age distribution, educational level, racial composition, and the urban–rural configuration of the population. Urban wages tend to be higher than rural wages, and regions such as the South and Great Plains states, with larger rural populations, tend to have lower average wages.

[36] Indeed, it should continue to exist if the cost-of-living differential does in fact offset the monetary differential, for no real wage differential would exist. Policies to remedy the monetary differential would represent a misallocation of resources. See Coelho and Ghali, *op. cit.*

Because each region has a mix of unique characteristics, to determine the influence of any one characteristic requires comparing wage data among regions on the basis of that characteristic alone. Various standardization techniques have been employed to achieve this basis for comparison. Hanna has compared regions, using the national employment pattern as a standardization norm. Bell has compared wage–employment patterns in 65 metropolitan areas to determine the area effect—where a modified area wage bill, computed by applying national industry wages to area industry employment, is subtracted from the actual area wage bill. A mix effect is determined also by subtracting from the modified area wage bill of the area effect the product of the average industrial wage and the area employment. This permits Bell to estimate the employment effect on an area if the wage pattern of another area is imposed upon it. Wonnacott has developed a 49-state matrix by which he can estimate wage patterns and differentials from applying the employment pattern in one state to that of any other, or the wage pattern of one state to that of any other.

Galloway and Fuchs have studied the causes of the North–South differential. Galloway applies the employment patterns of the North to the South in order to measure the hypothetical differential owing solely to the lower wage structure of the South. Fuchs, on the other hand, standardizes labor force characteristics in order to determine the influence which age, sex, race, and education have upon regional wages. Fuchs considers also urban–rural differences in the two regions as a source of wage differentials.

Zaidi, Galloway, and Raimon have examined regional wage and employment movements to determine if the reallocation of labor among regions has been consistent with the predictions of labor-market theory. All three authors agree that the evidence does not refute, and hence—by implication—supports competitive theory. However, the prognosis of a narrowing North–South differential in the next decade is not favorable. Mobility of capital into the South and labor from it do not appear to be of sufficiently large magnitudes for such an adjustment in wage differentials to occur that quickly.

Appendix

Consider two regions in which one, m, has a greater average wage, W_m, than the average wage, W_n, of the other region, n. The ratio of employment in a high-wage industry i in region m to total employment is given by e_{im}/E_m. As this ratio is high or low, employment in m is concentrated in high- or low-wage industries. The ratio of skilled to unskilled workers, S_{im}, reflects the skill mix of the industry, and the wage per skill level in industry i is given by W_{sim}. Now, given that $W_m > W_n$, what are the possible sources of this differential? They can be classified as follows:

I. Average wages by industry are greater in m than in n, but the employment patterns by industry are the same in each region: $W_{\text{im}} > W_{\text{in}}$, and $e_{\text{im}}/E_m = e_{\text{in}}/E_n$. This may be owing to the following reasons.

(a) The skill mix by industry is greater in region m than in n, but wage rates by skill are equal: $S_{\text{im}} > S_{\text{in}}$; $W_{\text{sim}} = W_{\text{sin}}$.

(b) Wages by skill are greater in m than in n, but the skill mix is the same by industry in each region; $W_{\text{sim}} > W_{\text{sin}}$; $S_{\text{im}} = S_{\text{in}}$.

(c) Some combination of (a) or (b), but if $W_{\text{sin}} > W_{\text{sim}}$, then $W_{\text{sin}}/W_{\text{sim}} < S_{\text{im}}/S_{\text{in}}$. Similarly, if $S_{\text{in}} > S_{\text{im}}$, then $S_{\text{in}}/S_{\text{im}} < W_{\text{sim}}/W_{\text{sin}}$.

II. Average wages by industry in region m equal those in n, but employment in i in region m is a greater proportion of total employment in m than in n. $W_{\text{im}} = W_{\text{in}}$; $e_{\text{im}}/E_m > e_{\text{in}}/E_n$. This is owing to either of the following:

(a) The skill mix by industry and the wage by skill in m are equal to those in n; $S_{\text{im}} = S_{\text{in}}$; $W_{\text{sim}} = W_{\text{sin}}$.

(b) The skill mix by industry in m is greater or less than the skill mix in n, as the wage by skill is less or greater in m than in n. $S_{\text{in}} \gtreqless S_{\text{im}}$ as $W_{\text{sim}} \lesseqgtr W_{\text{sin}}$.

III. Wages by industry and employment in high-wage industries both are higher in m than in n. $W_{\text{im}} > W_{\text{in}}$ and $e_{\text{im}}/E_m > e_{\text{in}}/E_n$. Consistent combinations are the following.

(a) The skill mix by industry in m is higher than in n if wages by skill are the same: $S_{\text{im}} > S_{\text{in}}$; $W_{\text{sim}} = W_{\text{sin}}$.

(b) The skill mix by industry in m equals that in n, but wages by skill in m exceed those in n: $S_{\text{im}} = S_{\text{in}}$; $W_{\text{sim}} > W_{\text{sin}}$.

(c) As the skill mix by industry in m is less than that in n, so must the wages by skill be greater in m than in n. The converse is also true. If $S_{\text{im}} < S_{\text{in}}$, then $S_{\text{in}}/S_{\text{im}} < W_{\text{sim}}/W_{\text{sin}}$; if $W_{\text{sim}} > W_{\text{sin}}$, then $W_{\text{sin}}/W_{\text{sim}} < S_{\text{im}}/S_{\text{in}}$.

These possibilities explain how characteristics (a), (b), and (c) noted earlier in combination can explain the source of wage differentials.[37] It may be argued that characteristics (d), (e), and (f) influence regional wage patterns through their impact on (a), (b), and (c). Hence, an approach using (d), (e), or (f) is also possible as a source of explanation of regional wage patterns in which (a), (b), and (c) are by-passed.

Standardized wages can be constructed in a variety of forms in order to standardize the average wage bill in terms of some norm of comparison.

[37] See p. 408.

For example, answers to the following questions require wage computations of different forms. Assume W_{km} refers to wages in m area in k industries, and e_{km} refers to employment in m area in k industries; similarly assume W_{kn} and e_{kn}, where n may be another region or even the national employment pattern (see p. 409).

1. What is the actual differential in average hourly earnings? Average hourly earnings are, respectively for m and n areas,

$$\bar{W}_m = \frac{\Sigma_k W_{km} \cdot e_{km}}{\Sigma_k e_{km}} \quad \text{and} \quad \bar{W}_n = \frac{\Sigma_k W_{kn} \cdot e_{kn}}{\Sigma_k e_{kn}}.$$

The differential is $\bar{W}_m - \bar{W}_n$, where $\bar{W}_m > \bar{W}_n$. The index is expressed as $\bar{W}_n / \bar{W}_m = E_{mn}$.

2. If region m had the employment pattern of n, what would be its average wage and what would be the differential?

$$\bar{W}_{mn} = \frac{\Sigma_k W_{km} e_{kn}}{\Sigma_k e_{kn}}.$$

An index of the differential is given by $\bar{W}_n / \bar{W}_{mn} = E_{\overline{mn}}$ and the degree by which differences in employment patterns explain the differential is given by $E_{\overline{mn}} - E_{mn}$.

3. A similar computation to that in question 2 follows if the employment pattern in m existed in n.

$$\bar{W}_{nm} = \frac{\Sigma_k W_{kn} \cdot e_{km}}{\Sigma_k e_{km}};$$

the index is $\bar{W}_{nm} / \bar{W}_m = E_{\overline{nm}}$, and the effect on the differential is $E_{\overline{nm}} - E_{mn}$.

4. Given the employment patterns as they exist in m and n, what would be the differential if the wage pattern in m were the same as the wage pattern in n?

$$\bar{R}_{mn} = \frac{\Sigma_k W_{kn} \cdot e_{km}}{\Sigma_k e_{km}};$$

the index is $\bar{W}_n / R_{mn} = F_{mn}$; the effect on the differential is given by $F_{mn} - E_{mn}$.

5. Similarly, what would be the differential if the wage pattern in n were the same as in m, given the employment patterns?

$$\bar{R}_{nm} = \frac{\Sigma_k W_{km} \cdot e_{kn}}{\Sigma_k e_{kn}};$$

$F_{nm} = \bar{R}_{nm} / W_m$ is the new index; and the differential effect is $F_{nm} - E_{mn}$.

Questions 2 and 3 are concerned with employment pattern effects, and questions 4 and 5 consider wage pattern effects. It should be noted that not all the possibilities of combinations of (a), (b), and (c) from page 408 which explain differentials are considered. In particular, although recognition of different weights of industry employment in any two regions is noted, different distributions of skill by industry in terms of the skill mix are not contained in these standardization procedures. Yet, these last four standardization procedures (2–5) are essentially the form in which variations in characteristics (a), (b), and (c) have been analyzed.

An examination of these standardization results can indicate whether the wage differential, given $W_m > W_n$, is owing to (i) a more favorable employment pattern in m than in n, (ii) a more favorable wage pattern in m than in n, or (iii) a combination of both (i) and (ii). For example, in question 2, if $E_{\overline{mn}}/E_{mn} < 1$, the differential has been widened and this implies that employment in n is more favorable than in m; hence, the wage pattern in m must be more favorable. If $E_{\overline{mn}}/E_{mn} > 1$, the wage differential has been lowered and the employment pattern is more favorable in m. In question 3, if $E_{\overline{nm}}/E_{mn} > 1$, this implies that the employment pattern is more favorable in m. If $E_{\overline{nm}}/E_{mn} < 1$, the employment pattern is more favorable in n and the wage is more favorable in m. In questions 2 and 3 if the index ratios equal 1, the employment patterns are the same, and the wage pattern is more favorable in m. Similar results can be derived for questions 4 and 5.

Discussion Questions

1. "The increase in employment in any expanding industry will tend to be greater the less the elasticity of substitution of capital for labor." Explain.
2. "In essence, the basic determinant of regional wage differentials is the skill mix of the industries located in the regions." Evaluate this statement.
3. (a) Why have southern wages historically ranked at the bottom among regions?
   (b) Do urban areas have a comparative advantage in attracting "quality" labor? Explain.
4. "Standardization procedures in measuring regional wage differentials result in a distortion of wage patterns. Hence, they conceal as much as they reveal the source of the true regional wage differentials." Discuss.
5. "Regions that are capital-poor, have substantial numbers of non-Whites, are proportionately more rural, utilize less skilled labor, and tend to pay lower wages." What manpower policies, if any, are implied by this statement?

6. Suppose it is found that the degree of unionization in the industries of a region is correlated positively with the relative wage ranking of regions. What other characteristics of the regions would you expect to find that correlate with the degree of unionism? Is unionism, then, a cause or effect of a region's wage rank? Discuss.

7. What is the evidence to support the thesis that "workers move more in response to job openings than to wage differentials"? If true, can the market be an efficient allocator of labor? What are the implications of your answer to the persistence of regional wage differentials?

8. Evaluate the impact of the following on the North–South wage differential.

   (a) Contemporary manpower policies.
   (b) The Civil Rights Act.
   (c) School busing.
   (d) The Equal Pay Act.

16

Union–Nonunion Wage Differentials

One of the major institutional changes in the labor market in the 20th century is the growth and spread of labor (trade) unions. To the extent that unions seek control of employers' labor force, or at least that portion of the labor force contained in the bargaining unit represented by the union, and to the degree to which unions use this control, we may say that they represent a source of monopoly in the supply of labor.[1] This monopoly power is used to influence the wage rate and other terms and conditions of employment, including the magnitude of employment. Hence, the existence of unionized sectors and nonunionized sectors, and of gradations in between, may give rise to differences in wages. In earlier chapters, we have considered the theoretical effects of the introduction of a union in the determination of wages. In this chapter, we shall consider some evidence as to the impact of the union on wages.

Wage Differentials between Unions and Nonunions

Unions may or may not obtain higher wages for their members than are paid to nonunion employees. Although economists have been searching for

---

[1] For a discussion of the extent to which unions possess monopoly power and their ability to affect the market for labor, see E. S. Mason, "Labor Monopoly and All That," *Annual Proceedings, Industrial Relations Research Association*, 1955, pp. 188–208.

the answer to this question for over 40 years, and although the weight of the evidence tends to support an affirmative reply, their studies have by no means revealed a consensus. Data on wages and hours for the period from 1890 to 1926 were examined by Paul Douglas, who found that earnings initially increased rapidly in industries that were becoming unionized.[2] Yet, in more latent stages of organization, wages in these same industries did not rise any more rapidly than in industries with low degrees of unionization. In fact, over the whole period wages in nonunionized industries in percentage terms rose more than did wages in unionized industries—237 to 206%, respectively.[3] On the other hand, because the union wage base was initially much higher than the nonunion base, Butler was able to demonstrate from the Douglas data that wages between 1914 and 1926 actually increased nominally almost twice as much in unionized as in the nonunionized industries.[4] Caution against drawing firm conclusions from these studies, of course, is in order, since data for the period were scarce and the degree of union influence was limited to relatively few sectors in the economy.

The ability of a union to secure wage changes and the magnitude of wage differentials over time between union and nonunion sectors should bear some relationship to the degree of control of the union over entrance into its particular labor market. For example, industrial unions using nonskilled labor may be less able to influence wages in periods of slack demand than craft unions, which can control supply through apprenticeship programs. For this reason the impact of unemployment may be greater among skilled occupations than among nonskilled occupations during periods of weak demand.

In periods of strong demand, where unemployment rates are near the frictional minimum, the competition of employers for scarce labor may bid up wages for the unskilled or semiskilled as well as for the skilled. Again, industrial unions, although assuming credit for these increases, may have had little or no influence on the wage rise. Milton Friedman[5] and Albert Rees[6] have expressed strong doubt that industrial unions have been able to cause wages to increase appreciably more than they otherwise would have risen in the absence of such unions. If product demand is elastic, or if the union exercises weak control over its supply of labor, or its labor costs are a

[2] *Real Wages in the United States, 1890–1926* (Boston: Houghton Mifflin Co., 1930).

[3] *Ibid.*, p. 564.

[4] *Labor Economics and Institutions* (New York: The Macmillan Co., 1961), p. 370.

[5] "Some Comments on the Significance of Labor Unions for Economic Policy," in *The Impact of the Union*, David M. Wright, ed. (New York: Harcourt, Brace, and World, Inc., 1951), pp. 204–234.

[6] "Wage Determination in the Basic Steel Industry," *American Economic Review*, Vol. XL, No. 3 (June 1951), pp. 389–404.

high proportion of total costs, union power will correspondingly be less. A high elasticity of product demand at the competitive price restricts the ability of an employer to pass on wage increases in the form of higher prices. This will tend to increase his resistance to wage increases. The natural consequence of reduced employment and loss of jobs also serves to constrain the union. If the union control over the labor supply is weak, the employer can find it easier to substitute low-wage nonunion labor for the higher-priced organized labor. Finally, the higher the percentage of total costs are labor costs, the greater will be the reduction in employment opportunities. In coal, clothing, steel, and automobiles, wages rose more rapidly in the post-World War I period when unions were weak than in the post-World War II period when unions were strong. The conditions, in one form or another, which characterize the impotency of unions on wages are present in these industries. Friedman attributes the rise in wages in these industries, although in the latter period ostensibly initiated by unions, primarily to market forces operating through expanded demand.

Rees has also examined the process of wage change in the steel and coal industry during inflationary periods and reaches conclusions consistent with those of Friedman. Both recognize that industrial unions may cause short-run rigidities in wages, preventing their decline during recessionary periods, but that in the long run the same impotency of these unions on wages as revealed during the upswing would also limit their ability to prevent ultimately the decline in wages. Although Rees examined industries in the manufacturing sectors, he felt that the absence of a close relationship between the degree of unionization and wage changes would be found in other economic sectors as well, and that the relationship would be even smaller once the degree of concentration in the industry was considered. [7]

It has also been found that although the degree of unionization and wages was positively correlated in concentrated industries, the higher wages could also be explained as a payment for superior quality of labor. [8] These findings, therefore, are not inconsistent with the position taken by Rees, although they apply to only the oligopolistic sector of the economy. Yet, unions appear to be more stable and relatively stronger in this sector.

Supplemental studies to the Douglas work have been made which tend to support his findings. Levinson performed a more inclusive study for the

---

[7] Albert Rees, "Union Wage Gains and Enterprise Monopoly," *Essays on Industrial Relations Research* (Ann Arbor, Detroit: University of Michigan, Wayne State Institute of Industrial Relations, 1961), p. 133.

[8] Leonard Weiss, "Concentration and Labor Earnings," *American Economic Review*, Vol. 56, No. 1 (March 1966), pp. 96–117. See also A. W. Throop, "The Union–Nonunion Wage Differential and Cost–Push Inflation," *American Economic Review*, Vol. LVIII, No. 1 (March 1968), pp. 79–99.

interval 1913–1933, covering between 7 million and 11 million workers.[9] The data show that over the interval percentage increases in union wages were greater for all wage classes than in nonunion wages.

For the period 1933–1947, Levinson examined wage changes in selected industries with different degrees of unionization.[10] Percentage wage increases tended to follow the degree of unionization for the two highest wage classes in the intervals 1933–1942, 1933–1946, 1933–1947, but in the lowest wage class, the degree of unionization appears to have had little influence during these intervals. In a later study for the period 1947–1958, Levinson found almost zero correlation between wage changes and degree of unionization in the interval 1947–1953, but significant positive correlation from 1953 to 1958.[11] A similar study by Ross and Goldner for the period 1933–1946 also showed that the greater the degree of unionization, the greater the absolute wage increase over the stated intervals.[12] H. Gregg Lewis has concluded from his studies, with the exception of the war years and the immediate postwar period, that since the late 1930s the average wage of unionized employees has been from 10% to 15% higher, relative to the average wage of nonunionized employees, than they would have been in the absence of unionism.[13]

Others have used different methodology in studying the union–nonunion differential. In one study, by comparison of the wage rates of union and nonunion workers in plants of similar sizes, in the same industry, occupation, and region, and by adjustment for sequential changes in wage rates of firms within the same time interval, it was found that wage differentials between union and nonunion plants were statistically insignificant.[14] This finding suggested that unions, therefore, had little or no effect on wage differentials.

[9] H. M. Levinson, *Unionism, Wage Trends and Income Distribution, 1914–1947*, Michigan Business Studies, Vol. X, No. 4 (Ann Arbor: Bureau of Business Research, School of Business Administration, June 1951), p. 47.

[10] *Ibid.*, pp. 60–61.

[11] Cited in H. Gregg Lewis, *Unionism and Relative Wages in the United States: An Empirical Inquiry* (Chicago: University of Chicago Press, 1963), p. 176. Lewis notes that results of a study by William Bowen over the same intervals showed positive correlation, as does Lewis' own calculations. The original reference is H. M. Levinson, *Postwar Movements of Prices and Wages in Manufacturing Industries*, Study Paper No. 21, Joint Economic Committee, Eighty-Sixth Congress, 2nd Session (Washington: U.S. Government Printing Office, 1960).

[12] Arthur M. Ross and William Goldner, "Forces Affecting the Interindustry Wage Structure," *Quarterly Journal of Economics*, Vol. 64, No. 2 (May 1950), p. 268.

[13] *Op. cit.*, pp. 5, 190. For a perceptive review of Lewis' book, see M. W. Reder, "Unions and Wages: The Problem of Measurement," *Journal of Political Economy*, Vol. 73 (April 1965), pp. 188–196.

[14] John E. Maher, "Union, Nonunion Wage Differentials," *American Economic Review*, Vol. XLVI, No. 3 (June 1956), pp. 336–352.

The methodology of this study contained some weaknesses, however; such omissions as the exclusion of the influence of union employees who might be a plant minority, but who might have a substantial influence on the wage structure, biases the results of the study. An adjustment in the data revealed significant differences in relative union–nonunion wages in three of the seven industries.[15] Kaun found in a study of the impact of the 1956 minimum wage increase that there was a significant difference in union–nonunion wages in these industries even after establishment size, city size, operation methods, product type, and ownership were standardized.[16]

Although the evidence is mixed and undoubtedly confusing to the beginning student, the weight of the evidence does seem to support the hypothesis that higher wages are associated with unionized sectors than with nonunion sectors. Moreover, the degree of unionization of an economic unit and the amount of the wage changes do show a strong positive relation.

Intrasector Wage Differentials

It has earlier been observed that skilled–unskilled differentials have narrowed,[17] and this tendency should be reflected in the wage structure of the firm and industry. Of interest is the extent that the union contributes to the compression. It may be argued that a union is internally a political unit, and, to the extent that it is, wage differentials within the economic unit with which it is affiliated should narrow. In part this may be achieved by regulating the output per worker, which tends to make the labor force of a unit a more homogeneous group.

Rees has noted that in the past industrial unions have tended to compress the skill differential, primarily because the wages of the least skilled workers were raised more than those of the most skilled.[18] One method by which this compression occurs is by forcing the multiplant company with varying regional locations to pay equal wages for identical jobs in every plant. In the South, the effect of this action has been to raise the wages of the unskilled relative to the skilled. The narrowing of wage differentials occurs also between production and nonproduction workers. The wage gains from collective bargaining among production workers in the manufacturing and extractive industries do not always transfer to the

---

[15] Lewis, *op. cit.*, pp. 80–96.

[16] David E. Kaun, "Union–Nonunion Wage Differentials Revisited," *Journal of Political Economy*, Vol. 72, No. 4 (August 1964), pp. 403–413.

[17] See Chapter 14.

[18] Albert Rees, "The Effects of Unions on Resource Allocation," *Journal of Law and Economics* (October 1963), pp. 69–78.

salaries of nonproduction workers.[19] To the extent that the wages of the latter initially exceeded the wages of the former, a narrowing of the differences occurred. In part this was owing to less unionization among white collar workers, and in part to the greater competitiveness of the labor market for clerical employees.

One of the causes of the narrowing of the skill differential is the upward trend of the society's concept of what is an acceptable social minimum wage, and this concept is influenced in part by union wage policy and its ability to implement it.[20] Certainly, the minimum-wage laws are partially a result of union pressure. The demands of unions for private pension plans have done much to reduce the resistance of employer groups to improvements in Social Security benefits, and the improvement of social insurance and its extension to disabilities, medical care, and unemployment compensation has received strong labor support. These programs tend to raise the reservation price in the offering of labor services and hence raise the social minimum wage. Similarly, the rise in fringe benefits, many of which are income-tax exempt, has been encouraged by the enactments of a sympathetic Congress. In fact, the economics of the firm has been substantially influenced by the laws passed by legislative bodies in general whose members are sensitive to labor votes and have responded to union political pressure.

Union Benefits and Labor Turnover

A source of wage differentials favorable to union members may be attributed to an indirect effect of labor organizations. Suppose that a lower rate of labor turnover is associated with union membership. It is possible that this lower turnover rate may yield a higher-weighted average wage than the average wage in firms with higher turnover rates. If longevity increases with reduced turnover, as it must over time, and if wage increments are associated with longevity, as they frequently are, then an average older labor force will tend to earn higher wages. There is also evidence that as the wage rates rise the quit rate falls. It may be that employees who earn high wage rates are faced with fewer opportunities to improve their economic position through job changes.[21] Consequently, a finding of a negative relation between the degree

[19] R. L. Raimon and Vladimer Stoikov, "The Effect of Blue-Collar Unionism on White-Collar Earnings," *Industrial and Labor Relations Review*, Vol. 22, No. 3 (April 1969), pp. 358–374.
[20] Melvin W. Reder, "The Theory of Occupational Wage Differentials," *American Economic Review*, Vol. 65, No. 5 (December 1955), p. 439.
[21] A. K. Severn, "Upward Labor Mobility: Opportunity or Incentive?", *Quarterly Journal of Economics* (February 1968), pp. 148–151.

of unionism and quit rates would not be surprising. Moreover, the older the labor force, the greater tends to be its reluctance to make changes.

A frequent contention is that union membership is a determinant of turnover rates. A U.S. Department of Labor study has attributed this to three factors, pensions, seniority, and grievance procedures. "Pensions are more common in high-wage firms, and much more common in unionized firms which are likely to have strict seniority rules and effective grievance procedures which minimize the necessity of changing jobs to obtain satisfactory work situations."[22] Nonvested pension programs provide an employee with an equity in his job; to leave his job would involve a substantial capital loss which increases with the length of his tenure. Even with vested programs, there is often some loss incurred from a job change. Although unions have been proponents of vested pension programs, which would tend to permit workers to have more job mobility, the resistance of employers to this form has limited the ability of unions to secure wide adoption of the principle of vesting. This is understandable, for one of the tradeoffs of a pension fund is the lower costs incurred by an employer from reduced labor turnover. Vesting to some extent negates this tradeoff. Seniority rights also bestow benefits upon workers which have a capital value. Security from layoffs, priorities to job and shift assignments, to promotion, to vacation schedules all have utilitarian and/or monetary value and are associated with seniority. Even the grievance procedure can reduce labor turnover. Penalty separations are less likely to be invoked under a grievance procedure. The system of industrial jurisprudence has reduced the capriciousness with which capital punishment in the plant—the discharge— has been invoked. The grievance procedure, by providing a method to remedy real or imagined injustices, also has reduced the compulsion among disgruntled employees to quit in order to secure release from a situation that may induce anxiety.

The largest element in the accession rate is new hires; in the separation rate, the largest elements are quits and layoffs. During recovery and prosperity, quit rates rise and layoff rates fall; the reverse is true during recessions. Accession rates tend to rise during recovery and fall during recession. These rates for recent years are presented in Table 16.1. It is

---

[22] Hugh Falk, "Effects of Private Pension Plans on Labor Mobility," *Monthly Labor Review* (March 1963), p. 287. As workers become older, all indices of turnover, both accessions and separations, fall rapidly. This is particularly true of quits. Moreover, this decline in quit rates is much more obvious among industries with pension plans than among those with no programs. Vladimer Stoikov and Robert L. Raimon have found that the degree of unionization, the level of annual wages, and recent wage increases all correlate negatively with the quit rate. "Determinants of Differences in the Quit Rate Among Industries," *American Economic Review*, Vol. LVIII, No. 5 (December 1968), pp. 1284–1298.

TABLE 16.1
LABOR TURNOVER RATES IN MANUFACTURING, 1959–1970
[per 100 employees]

Year	Total Accessions	New Hires	Total Separations	Quits	Layoffs
1959	4.2	2.6	4.1	1.5	2.0
1960	3.8	2.2	4.3	1.3	2.4
1961	4.1	2.2	4.0	1.2	2.2
1962	4.1	2.5	4.1	1.4	2.0
1963	3.9	2.4	3.9	1.4	1.8
1964	4.0	2.6	3.9	1.5	1.7
1965	4.3	3.1	4.1	1.9	1.4
1966	5.0	3.8	4.6	2.6	1.2
1967	4.4	3.3	4.6	2.3	1.4
1968	4.6	3.5	4.6	2.5	1.2
1969	4.7	3.7	4.9	2.7	1.2
1970	4.0	2.5	4.6	2.0	1.9

Source: U.S. Department of Labor. *Monthly Labor Review* (October 1971), p. 78.

possible that unions may have little influence on total separation rates. Although their policies may reduce quit rates, by the same token they may increase layoff rates as firms adapt to rigid wage policies by reducing the labor force more. It is also possible that, by pushing for compensation policies during layoffs, unions motivate firms to stabilize employment more. Instead of increasing the new hire rate during expansion, the firm may instead schedule overtime for existing employees, or subcontract work for outside firms to provide.

The Union Impact on Employment

From our earlier analysis, to the extent that unions are able to increase wages, under given conditions of the demand for labor, it was shown that the firm will reduce the amount of labor which it will employ. This reduction in employment may be avoided, however, if exploitation exists and the wage increase does not exceed the magnitude of exploitation. Consequently, unions may be more successful in avoiding the unemployment effect in early periods of collective bargaining during which exploitation is more likely to exist. The unemployment effect may also be avoided in the short run if the demand for labor increases, owing either to an increase in product demand or improvements in labor productivity. The unemployment effect may not be visible if the displaced labor moves to the nonunion sector. Hence, there are a number of situations in which unemployment in the short run may not be observed as a consequence of union wage pressure. Yet, in the long run our analysis has suggested that wage increases can induce a substitution of capital for labor, which can result in a net reduction in employment if the degree of substitution exceeds the degree of expansion of product demand.

If unions succeed in raising wages, employment may expand less in industries in which they have a high membership incidence than in those in which their membership incidence is low. In the absence of other changes, this could imply a widening of the interindustry wage structure. The occurrence of this effect, along with the greater dispersion in the inter-industry wage structure, could alter the ranking of industries by earnings. Some confirmation of this reasoning may be inferred from the finding that the interindustry wage dispersion has, in the post-World War II period, increased.[23] (We have noted in an earlier chapter some conceptual problems in these findings which cast doubt upon their validity.)[24] The study by Cullen,[25] which revealed stability from 1889 to 1950 in the relative spread of wages by industries and the ranking of industries by wages, has been cited as support for the contention that unions have not raised wages. Cullen's findings, however, do not necessarily support this conclusion. Suppose, initially, that high-wage industries were subject to some union influence, whereas low-wage industries were not. Now, if these patterns of unionization persisted throughout the period, one would expect little or no change in the wage ranking of these industries. Moreover, to refute Cullen, others have found that wage dispersion has not remained stable, but in the post-World War II period that it had significantly increased. If unions had no influence, instead of remaining stable or increasing, wage dispersion theoretically should have decreased. The implication is that wage distortion may, indeed, have resulted from the shifts of labor from unionized to nonunionized industries. It has been estimated that in 1957 about 1.7 million workers could have been transferred out of the union sector as a result of bargaining.[26]

---

[23] J. E. Maher, *Labor and the Economy* (Englewood Cliffs, N.J.: Allyn and Bacon, Inc., 1965), p. 319. Lewis, *op. cit.*, p. 282; has computed the increase in the wage dispersion within industries to be about 4% in the 1950s. Among industries the increase in the order of dispersion has been about 6–10% (p. 292).

[24] See Chapter 14, p. 398. Essentially, it has been shown that the conditions tested may not be logically consistent, and it appears that an inferior measure of dispersion has been used.

[25] D. E. Cullen, "The Interindustry Wage Structure, 1899–1950," *American Economic Review*, Vol. XLVI, No. 3 (June 1956), pp. 353–369.

[26] Rees, *op. cit.*, p. 71. He bases this upon an employment effect of 15% arising from a 15% wage effect caused by the presence of unions.

Exploitation implies, along with continued levels of employment, that employers may offer less resistance to wage increases. Hence, a number of studies suggest that unions may have been able to remove exploitation during their early periods of organization. Douglas found evidence that relative earnings of unionized labor rose appreciably in their earlier period of development, but in the more mature stages, wages in unionized industries did not increase percentagewise more rapidly than did wages in non-unionized industries.[27] Lewis found that unions had a greater impact on wages in the period 1935–1940, when membership was increasing, than in the period 1953–1963, when membership was stationary.[28] Ross and Goldner found that during the period of rapid expansion of industrial unions, 1933–1946, wages tended to increase more rapidly the greater the degree of unionization of industries during this period.[29]

U.S. Department of Labor studies of the impact of minimum wages seem to indicate that unemployment effects were greater the less expansionary was aggregate demand in the economy, and vice versa. Although increases in the minimum wage are not a direct result of collective bargaining, their employment effects are theoretically similar to those resulting from negotiated wage increases.[30] In general, when labor demand has remained relatively stable, increases in minimum wages have resulted in reduced employment in those industries most affected by the law.

The long-run effect on employment of an increase in wages may be the substitution of capital for labor. As Simler has noted:

> "Employers can escape the threat of union-inspired increases in money wage rates by instituting reductions in the labor coefficient (either via routine substitutions of capital for labor within the framework of given production functions or by setting up new production functions which embody labor-saving innovations)."[31]

The percentage of reduced employment from the substitution of capital for labor which a given percentage increase in wages will generate, given the cost of capital, is determined by the elasticity of substitution. Estimates of the elasticity of substitution for 19 selected industries have been computed from data in the 1958 *Census of Manufacturers*; thirteen of them have an

[27] Douglas, *op. cit.*, p. 564.

[28] Lewis, *op. cit.*, p. 222.

[29] *Op. cit.*, p. 268.

[30] See pp. 322–325 for an earlier analysis of the theoretical and empirical effects of minimum wage laws.

[31] N. J. Simler, "Unionism and Labor's Share in Manufacturing Industries," *Review of Economic and Statistics*, Vol. XLIII, No. 3 (August 1961), p. 378.

elasticity coefficient not significantly different from 1.[32] This coefficient of 1 implies that for a given percentage increase in the ratio of the price of labor to capital, the ratio of the amount of labor to the amount of capital will be reduced by the same percent, given the level of output. Translating this, if the wage structure of Detroit were imposed on Memphis for industries existing in both cities, and assuming no change in output, labor employment would be reduced 34.3% through the operation of the elasticity of substitution function.[33]

Capital substitution and other labor-saving techniques can produce substantial long-run effects on employment. Others have found that in manufacturing for a 10% increase in the ratio of the price of labor to capital, somewhat less than a 10% reduction occurs in the labor–capital ratio; in the primary industries somewhat more than a 10% reduction occurs.[34]

Union Influence on Wages throughout the Business Cycle

The influence of unions on the relative wage structure can be expected to vary as business conditions expand or contract. In the short run, when labor is apt to be least mobile, lack of growth in demand in the unionized sector will tend to weaken the ability of the union to increase wages, since its control over the potential competitive labor supply weakens. However, the union may be able to prevent wages from falling as rapidly in periods of sagging demand and, therefore, preserve or even widen the differential as unemployed labor inundates the nonunion sector. In periods of expanding demand, and particularly in periods of rapid inflation, there is reason to believe that union and nonunion wage differentials will be at a minimum, during periods of mild inflation or periods of economic instability, wage differentials should reappear; and during periods of economic decline, wage differentials may even widen, particularly in industries where unions have tight control of the labor supply. These implications follow also from the wage-rigidity hypothesis and have been succinctly summarized as follows:

" . . . Under given conditions of excess demand, employers will raise wages less when they are dealing with a union than otherwise

[32] F. W. Bell, "The Relation of the Region, Industrial Mix and Production Function to Metropolitan Wage Levels," *Op. cit.*, p. 371.
[33] *Ibid.*, p. 372.
[34] K. J. Arrow, H. G. Chenery, B. S. Minhas, and R. M. Solow, "Capital–Labor Substitution and Economic Efficiency," *Review of Economics and Statistics*, Vol. LXIII, No. 3 (August 1961), pp. 225–250.

because the difficulty (cost) of obtaining a subsequent decrease would be less if there were no union. Conversely, in the presence of excess supply, unions prevent wage reductions that would occur in their absence."[35]

If this hypothesis is true, in periods of excess demand, wages rise more in nonunionized sectors than in unionized sectors; in periods of substantial excess supply, wages in unionized sectors are less apt to decrease than in nonunionized sectors.

Levinson's study of the influence of the degree of unionization on wage increases seem to offer some support to both of these hypotheses.[36] In the period of rapid inflation between 1914 and 1920, nonunion wages increased proportionately more in the high- and low-wage classes than did union wages, while wages in the middle class increased by almost the same percentage. In the inflationary period 1945–1947, wages in the highest wage class increased more the more heavily unionized the sector; in the middle class, the degree of unionization appears to have had no influence whatsoever, and in the lowest-wage class, the wage increase was inversely related to the degree of unionization. Thus, between the highest- and lowest-wage classes, a narrowing of the differential occurred with the greatest narrowing coming from the least unionized sectors. In another study, Levinson also has found weaker correlation between the degree of unionization and wage increases in the greater inflationary period (1947–1953) than in a less inflationary period (1953–1958).[37] Between 1966 and 1968, an inflationary period, average hourly compensation increased at an annual rate of from 6.1 to 7.4% for all industries. However, for all industries in which collective bargaining occurred, negotiated increases amounted annually to only 3.6–5.5%.[38] In a period of relative price stability (1923–1929), union wages in all classes increased more than nonunion wages. In periods of recession, union wages either increased (1920–1923) or decreased less (1929–1933) than nonunion wages decreased. Hence, Levinson's studies generally support the wage-rigidity hypothesis and the wage-differential-movement hypothesis. Other data are also compatible with the two hypotheses,[39] and H. Gregg

---

[35] M. W. Reder, "Unions and Wages: The Problem of Measurement," *op. cit.*, p. 191.

[36] "Unionism, Wage Trends, and Income Distribution, 1914–1947," *op. cit.*, p. 47.

[37] *Postwar Movements of Prices and Wages in Manufacturing Industries*, quoted in Lewis, *op. cit.*, p. 176.

[38] *Economic Report of the President, 1969*, p. 46, 47.

[39] *Op. cit.*, p. 268.

Lewis has also found that the effect of unions on relative wage rates runs contracyclically, falling in prosperity and rising in depression.[40]

Unions and the Real Wage Differential

That real wages and productivity increase proportionately has long been apparent. For example, between 1919 and 1960, labor productivity increased at an annual rate slightly less than hourly real wages—2.4 to 2.6%, respectively.[41] However, the data in Table 16.2 indicate that real wage increases in the 1960s have lagged behind productivity increases. Between 1960 and 1970, average annual percentage increases in output per man-hour and real wages were, respectively, 2.56 and 1.81. The data for the period 1919–1970, then, support the statement by the Council of Economic Advisers, "Despite year-to-year variations, and certain limited periods of apparently nonproportional growth, both productivity and earnings have risen strongly and consistently, and their movement has been essentially parallel."[42]

The effect of unions on real wages is by no means obvious. There is ample evidence that if money wages rise more rapidly than productivity, then prices tend to increase, which erodes the purchasing power of the wage increase. If unions can continuously increase money wages more rapidly than inflation occurs, then real wages received by their membership may increase. Yet, it is not certain that unions are even responsible for money wage increases. Some economists have noted the influence of pattern bargaining or wage rounds as a step-by-step process of advancing wages,[43] but as we have noted above, others have argued that these wage increases would have occurred in any event. All unions have done is to take credit for the wage increases. As a matter of fact, if labor agreements have fixed wages for a specified period during which inflation occurs, unions may even be responsible for lowering the real wages of their membership. This is precisely what appears to have occurred in the latter part of the 1960s in a number of large industries. Labor agreements had been entered into in 1967 and

---

[40] *Op. cit.*, pp. 73–75. Lewis finds that the effect of unions on average wages relative to nonunion employees' average wage correlates positively with unemployment and negatively to the rate of price changes.

[41] John W. Kendrick and Ryuzo Sato, "Factor Prices, Productivity, and Economic Growth," *American Economic Review*, Vol. LIII, No. 5 (December 1963), p. 979.

[42] *Economic Report of the President, January, 1964* (Washington, D.C.: Government Printing Office, 1964), p. 89.

[43] John E. Maher, *Labor and the Economy* (Englewood Cliffs, N.J.: Allyn and Bacon, Inc., 1965), p. 319. He has computed the basic pattern established in nineteen industries from 1946 through 1960 (see p. 363). See Otto Eckstein, "Money Wage Determination Revisited," *Review of Economic Studies* (April 1968), pp. 133–143.

TABLE 16.2
INDEX OF OUTPUT PER MAN-HOUR AND AVERAGE, HOURLY EARNINGS IN CONSTANT DOLLARS, PRIVATE NONFARM INDUSTRIES, 1947–1970
[1957–1959 Base period]

	Index of Output per Man-Hour		*Average Gross Hourly Earnings*	
Year	*Number*	*Percent Increase[a]*	*In 1957–1959 Prices*	*Percent Increase[b]*
1947	74.1	—	1.45	—
1948	76.5	3.2	1.46	0.6
1949	79.5	3.9	1.54	5.5
1950	84.4	6.2	1.59	3.2
1951	86.3	2.3	1.60	0.6
1952	87.0	0.8	1.64	2.5
1953	89.6	3.0	1.73	5.5
1954	91.6	2.2	1.76	1.7
1955	95.7	4.5	1.83	4.0
1956	95.2	− 0.5	1.90	3.8
1957	97.2	2.1	1.93	1.6
1958	99.7	2.6	1.94	0.5
1959	103.1	3.4	1.99	2.6
1960	104.4	1.3	2.03	2.0
1961	107.4	2.9	2.05	1.0
1962	112.3	4.6	2.11	2.9
1963	115.7	3.0	2.14	1.4
1964	120.0	3.7	2.18	1.9
1965	123.6	3.0	2.23	2.3
1966	127.7	3.3	2.26	1.3
1967	129.0	1.0	2.30	1.8
1968	133.4	3.4	2.36	2.6
1969	134.2	0.6	2.39	1.2
1970	134.4	0.1	2.41	0.7

[a,b] Average annual percent change 1947–1970 was 2.63 and 2.23, respectively.

Sources: *Economic Report of the President, 1969*, pp. 264, 266;
Monthly Labor Review (October, 1971), p. 100.

1968 with only limited cost-of-living clauses contained in them. The substantial inflation of 1969 and 1970 exceeded these limited allowances, and real wages of many union members actually declined.

Nevertheless, there is some evidence that unions have increased the real wages of their membership relative to the real wages of nonmembers. Lewis has found this differential to be in the neighborhood of 6%.[44] Perhaps one

[44] H. G. Lewis, *Unionism and Relative Wages in the United States, op. cit.*, p. 9.

reason for this relatively small differential is that many nonunionized firms and industries match the wage increases of the unionized ones so as not to provide a motive to their employees to seek union representation.[45] Hence, although there appears to be some support for the contention that unions redistribute the increases in real wages in favor of their membership, this evidence is by no means conclusive. Perhaps union members consist of employees who possess more human capital and whose productivity increases more rapidly. Hence, they would receive higher real wages and real wage increases even if no union represented them.

Unions can also influence the trend to real wages through their influence on technological change. Labor-saving innovations by definition result in increases in output per man-hour, the most commonly used index of productivity. Unions may either speed up or delay technological change. If the ratio of the cost of labor to that of capital increases more rapidly than the ratio of the productivity of labor to capital, firms will be motivated to substitute capital for labor. In fact, labor-saving innovations may be sought for other reasons. The risks of strikes and other manifestations of labor disputes which threaten continuous plant operations may lead employers to automate production processes as much as possible. Then, by maintaining a large supervisory force that is capable of operating the plant on an emergency basis for an extended period, the firm can minimize the shutdown impact of organized labor. This, of course, is an unplanned and undesired consequence of union wage pressure and bargaining tactics, yet it can happen where technological conditions are favorable. Unions have also been known to resist technological change, although in the long run their efforts have usually failed. Yet, during this interim period, improvements in output per man-hour are less than they would have been without the obstructionist tactics of unions.

That real compensation has increased between 1947 and 1968 can be seen in Table 16.3. This percentage increase is somewhat greater than that cited for the period 1960–1970 (Chart 16.1) because the data in this table include fringe benefits and other supplemental payments. Again, real wages and productivity are shown here to increase at about the same rate.

Unions and the Distribution of Income

Interest in the distribution of income arises for a number of reasons. To some, a substantial inequality in the distribution of income represents a social injustice. It is unethical, immoral, an outrage against humanity for the mass of society to live near the subsistence level while a few privileged ones

[45] Harold M. Levinson, *Unionism, Wage-Trends, and Income Distribution, 1914–1947, op. cit.*, pp. 71–73.

TABLE 16.3
CHANGES IN COMPENSATION, PRODUCTIVITY, UNIT LABOR COST, AND OUTPUT PRICE IN THE PRIVATE ECONOMY SINCE 1947

	Percentage Change per Year		
Sector and Item	*1947–1966*	*1966–1967*	*1967–1968[a]*
Total private economy:			
Average hourly compensation:[b]			
Current prices	5.2	6.1	7.4
Constant prices[c]	3.1	3.2	3.3
Output per man-hour	3.5	1.6	3.3
Unit labor cost	1.7	4.4	3.9
Implicit GNP price deflator	2.0	3.1	3.6
Private nonfarm:			
Average hourly compensation[b]			
Current prices	4.9	6.0	7.2
Constant prices[c]	2.8	3.1	3.2
Output per man-hour	2.9	1.1	3.4
Unit labor cost	1.9	4.8	3.7
Implicit GNP price deflator	2.2	3.5	3.6
Manufacturing:			
Average hourly compensation:[b]			
Current prices	5.1	5.3	7.0
Constant prices[c]	3.0	2.4	3.0
Output per man-hour	3.2	0.6	2.8
Unit labor cost	1.8	4.7	4.2
Implicit GNP price deflator	2.0	2.6	([d])

[a] Preliminary.

[b] Wages and salaries of all employees and supplements to wages and salaries such as employer contributions for social insurance and for private pension, health, unemployment, and welfare funds, compensation for injuries, pay of the military reserve, etc. Also includes an estimate of wages, salaries, and supplemental payment part of the income of the self-employed.

[c] Adjusted for changes in the consumer price index.

[d] Not available.

Note: Data for each sector relate to all persons.

Sources: Department of Commerce, Department of Labor, and Council of Economic Advisers.

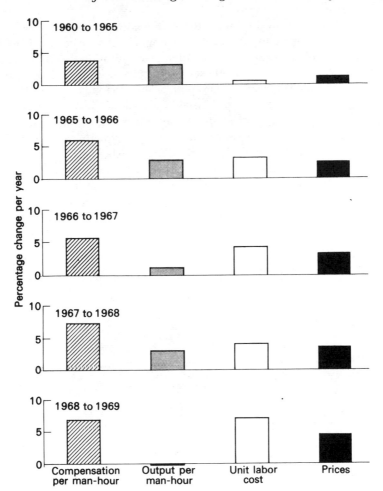

CHART 16.1. Changes in compensation, productivity, labor costs, and prices; private nonfarm sector.

Note: Data relate to all employees.

Sources: Department of Labor and Department of Commerce.

receive a large proportion of the nation's income. To those concerned with political power, income inequality can represent a cause of political instability, and this knowledge can be used as an instrument to enlist the support of the poor to change the political structure of society which supports such inequality, or to enlist the support of the rich to preserve the structure that has smiled so favorably upon them. Economists are interested in the nature of income inequality because of its implications for economic growth. If those who receive wages have a smaller share of the national income and a lower propensity to save than those who receive nonwage income, then it can be shown that the growth potential of an economy is more favorable than if wages were a greater percentage of national income.[46] A greater supply of savings is thereby available for investment purposes, and the capital accumulation so necessary for economic growth can proceed at a faster rate. The model can also be modified to show that if labor has a greater propensity to save than capital owners, then a favorable income distribution for economic growth requires an increase in labor's share.

The degree of income inequality in an economy can be measured by a Gini Coefficient. To understand this measure, consider Figure 16.1. Measured

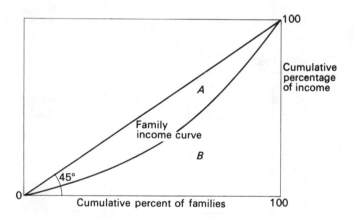

FIGURE 16.1. A Lorenz curve of income distribution.

on the horizontal axis from left to right is the cumulative percentage of families receiving income. Measured vertically is the cumulative percentage of income received by the appropriate percentage of families. Perfect equality in income distribution would be represented by a 45° straight line from the origin, along which at equal distances given cumulative percentages of families receive the same cumulative percentages of income. If the cumulative percentages of income are plotted for successive, cumulative family incomes, a family income curve will be generated which deviates to

[46] Such a model has been developed by Nicholas Kaldor, "Alternative Theories of Distribution," *Review of Economic Studies*, Vol. 23 (1955–1956), pp. 83–100.

the right from the 45° line. The more to the right is the family income curve, the greater is the inequality in income distribution. The total area under the 45° line represents a perfect income distribution and this is equal to the areas of A + B. The deviation from perfect income distribution is given by area A. Hence, the Gini index is defined as

$$G = \frac{A}{A + B},$$

and the greater is this coefficient, then the more unequal is the distribution of income. In the United States, family income distribution had, until about 1948, been becoming more equal and the Gini index had been declining as area A decreased. After 1948, however, family income distribution has apparently stabilized. This is shown in Table 16.4. Why this has occurred

TABLE 16.4
DISTRIBUTION OF FAMILY INCOME IN SELECTED YEARS, IN QUINTILES, 1935–1970

	1935		1947		1957		1966	
		Cum.		Cum.		Cum.		Cum.
Quintile	%	%	%	%	%	%	%	%
Lowest Quintile	4.1	4.1	5.1	5.1	5.0	5.0	5.4	5.4
Second Quintile	9.2	13.3	11.8	16.9	12.6	17.6	12.3	17.7
Third Quintile	14.1	27.4	16.7	33.6	18.1	35.7	17.7	35.4
Fourth Quintile	20.9	48.3	23.2	56.8	23.7	59.4	23.7	59.1
Highest Quintile	51.7	100.0	43.3	100.0	40.5	100.0	41.0	100.0
Top 5%	26.5	—	17.5	—	15.8	—	15.3	—
Mean Income	—	—	($3566)		($5483)		($8423)	

Source: *Bureau of the Census, Current Population Reports.*

is an unsettled question. Some argue that trade unions reached the peak of their strength in 1947, and since greater income equality had paralleled the rising influence of unions, unions somehow must have been responsible for the trend. With the rise of more restrictive labor relations legislation in 1947 the economic and political power of unions ceased to grow and measures to redistribute income were thereupon stabilized. This is a rather tenuous cause-and-effect hypothesis, however. A more likely explanation is that tax policy, which is more instrumental in redistributing income, itself had stabilized, and that this tax policy was a reflection of political sentiments which also had reached a middle-of-the-road stance as economic and international conditions returned to a more normal level.

Unions and the Misallocation of Resources

To the extent that unions introduce imperfections into the labor market, impose barriers to the entry of labor into selected occupations, restrict output through make-work rules, and increase labor costs in excess of the increase in output per man-hour, social costs are involved. Albert Rees has attempted to estimate the dollar cost to society in 1957, the welfare loss, of the policies of unions.[47] He estimated the loss of real output from the transfer of labor from high-productivity to low-productivity industries to be 600 million dollars. Adding this to the costs of misallocation of resources within industries, he arrives at an estimate that is less than 0.3% of GNP. He notes the difficulty in estimating losses from make-work rules, but estimates in the railroad industry have placed such losses from feather bedding at less than 0.1% of GNP. This would suggest that union monopoly costs the country in loss of output not more than one-half of 1% of GNP. Offsetting this welfare loss, of course, must be the gain in satisfaction which accrues to the members of unions in obtaining some control over their own work lives, and this apparently has been possible only through the introduction of a monopoly element—unions—into the labor market.[48]

If the Cobb–Douglas production function is relevant to the American economy, will the share of labor income then be a constant, no matter what wage policy may be pursued? A number of economists have observed that in Western economies, labor does appear to receive a relatively constant proportion of national income, although its share varies from one country to another. Weintraub in the United States is perhaps one of the strongest proponents of the belief that labor's share is a "magic" constant.[49] However, at least a superficial examination of the evidence does not support this contention. In Table 16.5, it can be seen that there has been a mild drift upward since the 1920–1928 period in the proportion of national income received in the form of employee compensation. The one exception, during the period

[47] "The Effects of Unions on Resource Allocation," *Journal of Law and Economics* (October 1963), pp. 69–78.

[48] For a discussion of the conflict between optimum resource allocation for the benefit of consumer satisfaction vs. the producer (worker) satisfaction, see Neil W. Chamberlain, *Collective Bargaining* (New York: McGraw-Hill Co., 1951), pp. 368–369.

[49] Sidney Weintraub, *A General Theory of the Price Level, Output, Income Distribution and Economic Growth* (Philadelphia: Chilton Co., 1959), p. 41. See also the perceptive review of this book by Abba P. Lerner, "On Generalizing the General Theory," *American Economic Review*, Vol. L, No. 1 (March 1960), pp. 121–143.

TABLE 16.5
EMPLOYEE COMPENSATION AS PERCENTAGE OF NATIONAL INCOME, 1919–1970

Year or Period	Percent	Year or Period	Percent
1919	55.8	1948	63.1
1920	61.5	1949	64.7
1921	66.5	1950	63.7
1922	60.0	1951	64.6
1923	60.2	1952	66.7
1924	60.0	1953	68.3
1925	68.5	1954	68.8
1926	60.1	1955	67.8
1927	61.0	1956	69.1
1928	60.1	1957	69.6
1929	58.9	1958	70.0
1930	61.6	1959	69.5
1931	66.0	1960	70.8
1932	73.6	1961	70.9
1933	73.0	1962	71.2
1934	70.0	1963	71.1
1935	65.4	1964	71.0
1936	66.1	1965	69.8
1937	65.1	1966	70.2
1938	66.6	1967	71.5
1939	66.1	1968	72.1
1940	63.9	1969	73.3
1941	61.9	1970	74.9
1942	61.9	—	—
1943	64.3	1920–28	60.5
1944	64.4	1929–38	66.6
1945	64.0	1939–48	64.6
1946	64.1	1949–58	67.4
1947	64.0	1959–64	70.7
—	—	1965–70	72.2

Source: Computed from U.S. Department of Commerce, *Survey of Current Business*, April, 1971.

1939–1948 can in part be explained by the rigid wage controls imposed during World War II.

This drift upward may be owing to a variety of reasons. Increased urbanization, the advent of the welfare state, and militant union wage policies have been put forward as possible explanations. It is more likely that unions have encouraged this drift, not so much from their wage policies, but from their political support of the welfare state. The growth of the service sector, utilizing more educated labor may also be partly responsible for the upward trend in employee compensation. Indeed, the substantial investment in human capital may have altered the ratio between it and physical capital so that labor now receives a larger relative share. The larger share represents not only payment for physical labor but also a return to the educational and training investment of a worker. If this has occurred, and if the Cobb–Douglas function can approximate the aggregate production function, this implies that either a shift in the parameters is occurring, or that a meaningful variable has been omitted from the equation.

Appendix

What has happened to labor's share in national income? Has it remained stable since 1947, as has family income; has it declined; or has it increased? Let us first dichotomize the economy into two types of inputs; labor inputs, represented by L, and nonlabor or property inputs, represented by K. If we let W represent the average wage of labor and r represent the average payment for the use of property, we can represent factor shares in one of two ways.

$$wL + rK = Y \qquad \text{or} \tag{16.1}$$

$$\frac{wL}{Y} + \frac{rK}{Y} = 1 \tag{16.1a}$$

$$\frac{wL}{rK} = \lambda \tag{16.2}$$

National income is represented by Y and is distributed between labor income (wL) and property income (rK). The ratio of labor's share to property's share is given by λ. As λ increases or decreases, labor's relative share increases or decreases. Whether or not λ increases or decreases depends upon the magnitude of the coefficient measuring the elasticity of substitution between labor and capital in the aggregate economy.

The concept of the elasticity of substitution is a simple one, yet it is one which seems to give students a great deal of trouble. Let us define it as the percentage change in the property–labor ratio divided by the percentage change in the wage–property payment ratio. Or

$$\frac{d(K/L)}{(K/L)} \div \frac{d(W/r)}{(W/r)} = e_{LK} \tag{16.3}$$

$$e_{LK} = d\left(\frac{K}{L}\right)\frac{L}{K} \div d\left(\frac{W}{r}\right)\left(\frac{r}{W}\right) = \frac{d(K/L)}{d(W/r)}\frac{WL}{rK} \tag{16.3a}$$

Now, we know from marginal productivity theory, cost minimization occurs when the following condition is satisfied.

$$\frac{MP_L}{MP_K} = \frac{W}{r} = \frac{K}{L} \tag{16.4}$$

Therefore, an increase in wages, holding property payments constant will lead to a substitution of property for labor. From Equation (16.2) we see that λ will increase if the ratio (W/r) increases in greater proportion than the ratio (L/K) decreases. But if the ratio (L/K) decreases, then the ratio (K/L) must increase, and this is implied by the substitution of K for L. Hence, we can say that λ will increase if the ratio (W/r) increases proportionately more than the ratio (K/L) increases. This is precisely what Equations (16.3) and (16.3a) state. From (16.3a), if $d(K/L)$ is greater than $d(W/r)$, labor's share will rise relative to capital's share. This implies an elasticity of substitution greater than 1. Similarly, with an elasticity of substitution equal to 1, an increase in wages relative to property payments will not alter labor's share; if e_{LK} is less than 1, a relative rise in wages will reduce labor's share.

Next, let us define national income as being the monetary valuation (P) of real national output (Q).

$$WL + nK = Y \equiv P \cdot Q \tag{16.1b}$$

$$\frac{W}{P} L + \frac{r}{P} K = Q \tag{16.1c}$$

Equation (16.1c) tells us that the real wage paid to labor and the property payment received by owners of property exhaust national product. [Factor shares in Equation (16.2) are not affected by this modification.] The real wage of labor is equivalent to the marginal product of labor, and the real property payment is equivalent to the marginal product of property. Therefore, we can rewrite Equation (16.1) as

$$\frac{\partial Q}{\partial L} L + \frac{\partial Q}{\partial K} K = Q \tag{16.1d}$$

This is a property of a linear, homogeneous function. Let us consider one of the earliest forms of an aggregate production function—the Cobb–Douglas type—

$$Q = AL^{\alpha}K^{\beta} \tag{16.5}$$

with A, α, and B defined as parametric constants, and $\alpha + B = 1$. The marginal product of labor is

$$\frac{\partial Q}{\partial L} = \alpha AL^{\alpha-1}K^{B},$$

and the relative share of labor is

$$\frac{(\partial Q/\partial L)^L}{Q} = \frac{\alpha A 1^{\alpha-1} K^B \cdot L}{AL^\alpha K^B} = \alpha$$

The marginal product of property is

$$\frac{\partial Q}{\partial K} = BAL^\alpha K^{B-1},$$

and the relative share of property is

$$\frac{\partial Q}{\partial K}\frac{K}{Q} = \frac{BAL^\alpha K^{B-1} \cdot K}{AL^\alpha K^B} = B$$

Therefore, with a Cobb–Douglas production function, the relative shares of labor and property are constant. It can be shown that the elasticity of substitution for such a function is 1. Since from (16.4),

$$\frac{MPL}{MPK} = \frac{W}{r}; \qquad \text{therefore,} \qquad \frac{W}{r} = \frac{AL^{\alpha-1}K^B}{BAL^\alpha K^{B-1}} = \frac{\alpha K}{BL}, \quad \text{and}$$

$$\frac{K}{L} = \frac{B}{\alpha}\frac{W}{r}$$

Substituting this result into (16.3a), we get

$$\frac{B/\alpha\, d(w/r)}{d(w/r)}\left(\frac{\alpha}{B}\frac{K}{L}\right)\left(\frac{L}{K}\right) = 1.$$

Discussion Questions

1. Intuitively, does it appear that unions ought to be able to raise wages more for their members than nonunion members can raise their wages on their own? Interpret your answer so that it can be consistent with the empirical findings.

2. Why might a greater degree of competition in the labor market for white-collar workers be associated with a narrowing of the differential between white-collar and blue-collar workers? Are there other causes for this narrowing?

3. On the one hand it is argued that the minimum wage tends to narrow wage differentials, but on the other hand it is argued that the minimum wage increases income dispersion. Are these two viewpoints inconsistent? Discuss. What has been the impact of the union on the minimum wage?

4. Is it in a union's self-interest to support vesting of pension benefits? In view of this union support, why are not most pension plans of the vested category?

5. "Unions tend to convert labor costs from variable into fixed costs." Explain. If true, what effect would this tendency have upon the short-run price policy of affected firms?

6. How can unions ignore the possibilities for the substitution of capital for labor in the face of wage increases? Are employers, in granting wage increases, affected more by short-run or long-run considerations? Are the time perspectives of unions and employers consistent? Discuss.

7. Explain the ratchet effect of union wage policy. Does the upward drift of wages guarantee an upward drift in prices? Explain.

8. If the evidence is so overwhelming that the long-run real wage increases parallel to increases in labor productivity, why then do unions seek wage increases in excess of productivity increases?

9. How can the increasing share of employee compensation in national income in recent decades be explained? In Mexico, employees' share in national income is closer to 50%. Why the difference?

10. Suppose the empirical evidence convincingly shows that unions retard technological advance, distort the efficient allocation of labor, generate cost–push inflation, accentuate balance-of-payment deficits, and deter the increase in real wages. What impact is this likely to have on national labor relations policy? Would your answer be the same if the empirical evidence is mixed?

17

Group Wage Differentials:
The Economics of Discrimination

In the United States, the capital value of a white worker is greater than that of a non-White. This is so because the typical White has higher average earnings than the non-White, the life expectancy at birth is greater and work-life expectancy at 16 is longer. Similarly, the earnings of the typical male worker exceed those of the typical female worker. Why these earning differentials exist is the subject of this chapter. In part they exist because of wage differences within occupations, in part because the average durations of the work year differ, and in part because the rate and duration of unemployment vary by color or sex. In the first section of the chapter, the magnitude of the differentials shall be considered; in the second section, the theory of discrimination will be summarized; in the next section, empirical evidence of the source and nature of discrimination will be examined, and in the fourth section, selected remedial proposals will be considered.

Dimensions of Differentials

To be a non-White with the same years of schooling as a White usually means that the former will receive less earnings than the latter. This condition has changed somewhat in the past few years, however, as the ratio of non-White to White earnings has risen. From 1965–1968, this ratio of earnings for persons with an elementary school education has risen from

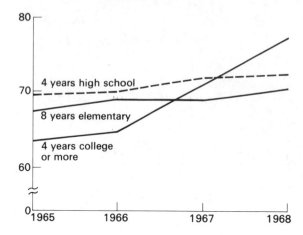

CHART 17.1. Average annual earnings of Blacks and other minorities as percent of earnings of Whites; men working full time all year, 1965–1968.

Source: U.S. Department of Labor, *U.S. Manpower in the 1970s: Opportunity and Challenge*, p. 7.

TABLE 17.1
OCCUPATIONAL DISTRIBUTION OF NON-WHITES, 1960–1970
[Percentages]

	Year			
Occupation	*1970*	*1969*	*1965*	*1960*
White-collar workers	27.9	26.2	19.5	16.1
Professional and technical	9.1	8.3	6.9	4.8
Managers, officials, proprietors	3.5	3.0	2.7	2.6
Clerical workers	13.2	12.9	8.2	7.3
Sales workers	2.1	2.0	1.8	1.5
Blue-collar workers	42.2	42.8	41.0	40.1
Craftsmen and foremen	8.2	8.5	6.8	6.0
Operatives	23.7	23.9	21.5	20.4
Nonfarm laborers	10.3	10.5	12.6	13.7
Service workers	26.0	26.7	31.6	31.7
Private household	7.7	8.5	12.6	14.2
Other	18.3	18.2	19.1	17.5
Farm workers	3.9	4.2	7.8	12.1
Farmers and farm managers	1.0	1.0	1.8	3.2
Laborers and foremen	2.9	3.2	6.0	9.0

Source: U.S. Department of Labor.

about 68% to slightly more than 70%; the ratio for those with a high school diploma is somewhat higher, rising from slightly below 70% to about 72%; and for college graduates, the greatest improvement has been registered, from 61% to 77%. These relative gains of non-Whites are illustrated in Chart 17.1.

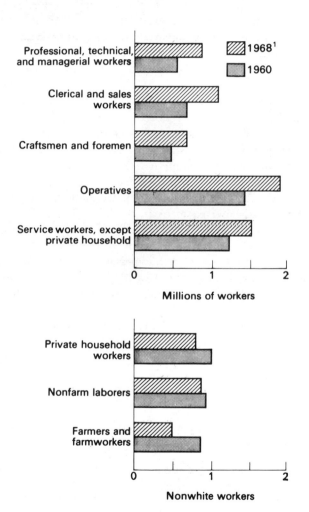

CHART 17.2. Non-White employment shifted to better jobs between 1960 and 1968.
[1] Data for 1968 preliminary.
Source: U.S. Department of Labor. *Manpower Report of the President, 1969*, p. 40.

In part, non-Whites have lower earnings because they are concentrated in low-wage occupations. In Table 17.1 and Chart 17.2 are presented the data on non-White workers by occupation for selected years from 1960 to 1970. Blacks in 1967 comprised 10.8% of the labor force.[1] Because in the higher occupations the percentage of non-Whites is less than this, they are obviously under-represented, and in lower occupations they are over-represented. The degree of improvement in selected higher occupations required to bring the proportion up to the national proportion is compared with the actual improvement in Chart 17.2.

In part the upward drift in occupational upgrading is a result of higher educational attainments of non-Whites. In March 1970, it was estimated that the median years of school completed for Whites 18 years and over was 12.4 years and for non-Whites of the same age category, 11.7 years, a difference of less than one year. In October 1952, the respective attainments were 11.4 and 7.6 years, a difference of almost 4 years.[2] Non-Whites are closing the gap, although in higher age categories and for certain minorities the educational gap is still substantial.[3] The gap is being closed by the expanding educational achievements of the young non-Whites. The occupational significance of this can be seen in the distribution of jobs by educational level, as shown in Chart 17.3. In 1980 almost 1 million Black college graduates are expected to be in the labor force, a fourfold increase since 1960; from 1952 to 1970, Black college graduates increased 260% compared to an increase of 74% for White graduates.[4]

Nevertheless, Blacks continue to experience more unemployment than Whites, a factor also reducing annual earnings. In Chart 17.4 are presented unemployment rates for selected years between 1961 and 1968. Although unemployment rates have fallen in the interval, non-White men, women, and teenagers experienced substantially heavier unemployment rates than for corresponding groups of white persons. The group most heavily hit among the races, of course, is the teenagers who have less schooling and work

---

[1] Claire C. Hodge, "The Negro Job Situation; Has It Improved," *Monthly Labor Review*, Vol. 92, No. 1 (January 1969), pp. 21, 25.

[2] William Deuterman, "Educational Attainments of Workers, March 1969 and March 1970," *Monthly Labor Review*, Vol. 93, No. 10 (October 1970), p. 10.

[3] For example, American Indians have median educational attainment of only 8.4 years of schooling. See Alan L. Sorkin, "American Indians Industrialize to Combat Poverty," *Monthly Labor Review*, Vol. 92, No. 3 (March 1969), p. 21. Only about 40 or 50% of the young people complete high school. Wages of Indians in factory employment for plants located on the reservation averaged in 1966 between $1.60 to $2.00 per hour, compared to a national average of $2.83.

[4] Deuterman, "Educational Attainments of Workers," *op. cit.*, p. 11.

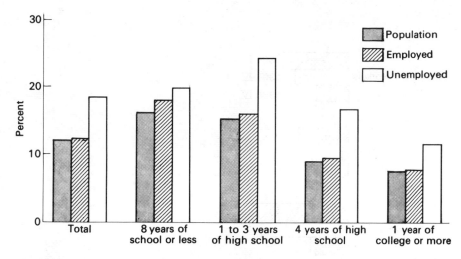

CHART 17.3. Blacks as a percent of population, employed, and unemployed, March 1970 (persons 18 years old and over).

Source: William Deuterman, "Educational Attainments of Workers, March 1969 and March 1970," *Monthly Labor Review*, Vol. 93, No. 11 (October 1970), p. 13.

experience. Ordinarily, as years of schooling increase, rates of unemployment decline. This is seen in Chart 17.3. Although rates of Black unemployment reached the lowest level in 10 years in March 1970, the rates for Blacks were still greater at each educational level than they were for Whites, and with the increase in unemployment later in 1970, it again fell more heavily upon Blacks and other minority groups.[5] Employment among high school

[5] At the end of the 3rd quarter of 1970 the national unemployment rate was 5.2%. By age, sex, and race it was:

	White	Non-White
Men, 20 years and over	3.6	6.1
Women, 20 years and over	4.7	7.1
Both sexes, 16–19 years	14.0	30.0
	4.9	8.5

To the extent that unemployment is heavier among those missed by census takers, "the hidden population," and since the latter are more than proportionately represented among Blacks, these data may understate the degree of unemployment among Blacks. See Denis F. Johnston and James R. Wetzel, "Effect of Census Undercount on Labor Force Estimates," *Monthly Labor Review*, Vol. 92, No. 3 (March 1969), pp. 3–13.

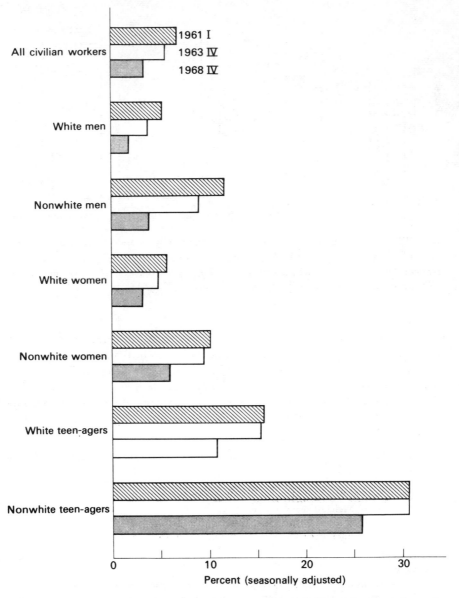

CHART 17.4. Unemployment rates, giving percent of civilian labor force in each
group who are unemployed.

Source: Department of Labor.

graduates has been unevenly distributed by race in the lower occupational categories. About three-fourths of non-White graduates held semiskilled or unskilled jobs, whereas only about one-half of White employed graduates had jobs at these levels.[6]

Dropouts from school are more numerous among Blacks than among Whites (see Chart 17.3), and this undoubtedly influences the differential employment potential among races. If dropouts leave school before age 16, legal restrictions may bar them from jobs; even between ages 16 and 18, child labor certificates may be required or hazardous jobs may be closed to them, both of which impair their opportunities. The unemployment rate for dropouts is double that of high school graduates of the same age, although the difference between unemployment rates for Black dropouts and graduates (in October 1969, 19.1 and 15.8% respectively) is substantially less than the corresponding difference between White dropouts and graduates.[7] Because of the rapid growth of young people in the 1960s (for both Whites and Blacks the increase was 43%), and because of the relative decline in non-skilled jobs, job opportunities were relatively scarce for these untrained, inexperienced entrants into the labor force. Hence, their unemployment rates were high. The ratio of youth to adult unemployment rates was 3.3 in 1960, 4.3 in 1964, and 5.5 in 1969. The estimated increase in the 16–19 age category of the labor force in the 1970s is 11% over-all, but it will be 9% for Whites; it will continue at 43% for non-Whites. Hence, the racial unemployment rate *differential* will probably continue until 1980 and the rate itself will probably remain high for non-Whites. To the extent that unemployment in any skill category reduces wages, or at least prevents them from rising as rapidly and to the extent that unemployment rates vary with the duration of unemployment, annual earnings will be reduced for those groups having greater unemployment rates. Therefore, the racial wage and earnings differential also will persist throughout the seventies.

There also exists a wage-earning differential by sex. Women in May 1969 received median weekly earnings of $87, and the median rises to over $100 only for those women with college educations.[8] Average weekly earnings for private nonagricultural workers, male and female, for the same

---

[6] Howard Hayghe, "Employment of High School Graduates and Drop-outs," *Monthly Labor Review*, Vol. 93, No. 8 (August 1970), p. 41. Among drop-outs, however, there appeared to be no difference in the level of jobs held by Blacks and Whites.

[7] *Ibid.*, p. 37. In 1960, Black dropouts had an unemployment rate of 30% compared to 16% among White dropouts. In 1968, the rate for Black dropouts was 23%, for Whites only 12%.

[8] Robert L. Stein, "The Economic Status of Families Headed by Women," *Monthly Labor Review*, Vol. 93, No. 12 (December 1970), p. 8.

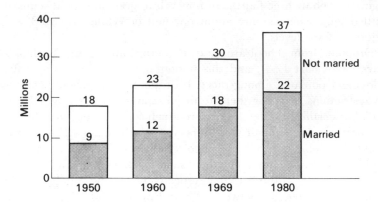

CHART 17.5. Women in the labor force.

month were $113.[9] The increase in the labor force participation of women since 1950 is presented in Chart 17.5, and changes in the labor force participation rate is shown in Chart 17.6. Part of the earnings differential is explainable by the concentration of women in lower-skilled jobs, by the greater proportion in part-time employment, and by the high turnover rate of women in employment. A Labor Department report indicated in 1968 that an average of 28 million women worked during the year, but over 37 million held jobs at some time during the year—an indication of a high quit rate. Moreover, among women who were heads of families, over 70% worked in 1967, but only 38% worked all year at full-time jobs.[10] These turnover rates undoubtedly influence many employers' willingness to hire and train female employees, except perhaps at a lower wage rate. In academic employment, women in the natural sciences were promoted at a rate comparable to their male counterparts, but not so in the social sciences. In all faculties, female academic salaries were lower than males' at each rank.[11]

Married women with husbands who work add to family income (see Chart 17.7) and in so doing may lift the family out of the poverty category. Women who are heads of families who work, however, are much more likely to receive incomes which are within the poverty category ($3700 for a

[9] U.S. Department of Labor, Bureau of Labor Statistics, *Employment and Earnings*, Vol. 16, No. 1 (July 1969), p. 77.
[10] Stein, "The Economic Status of Families Headed by Women," *op. cit.*, p. 7.
[11] A. E. Bayer and H. S. Astin, "Sex Differences in Academic Rank and Salary among Science Doctorates in Teaching," *Journal of Human Resources*, Vol. 3, No. 2 (Spring 1968).

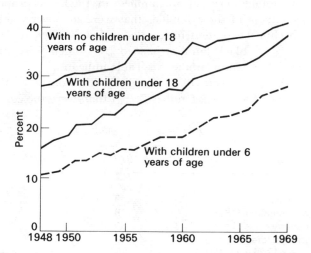

CHART 17.6. Labor force participation rate of married women, husband present.
Source: U.S. Department of Labor. *U.S. Manpower in the 1970s: Opportunity and Challenge*, p. 8.

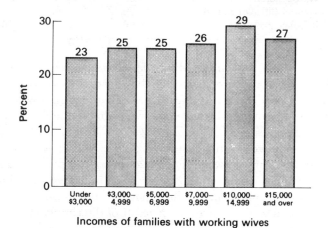

Incomes of families with working wives

CHART 17.7. Median percent of family income contributed by wives' earnings, 1968.
Source: U.S. Department of Labor, *U.S. Manpower in the 1970s: Opportunity and Challenge*, p. 9.

family of four in 1969), since incomes of families headed by males are more than twice those of families headed by women. In 1970, families with women as head totaled 11% of all families; in 1960, the proportion was 10%. The percentage of these families that were in poverty was 36% in 1970, but with children present in female-headed families, the percentage increased to 47%.[12] Black families headed by women were much more likely to be poor than white families, as Table indicates.[13]

Not only, in 1970, were Black families with women at the head a greater percentage of all Black families (27%) than were the corresponding

| Characteristic | Percent of Families in Each Category | |
	March 1970	March 1960
White		
All Families	9	9
with children	9	8
In Poverty	30	20
with children	40	25
In Central Cities of SMSA	12	10
in poverty	39	24
Black		
All Families	27	22
with children	31	25
In Poverty	53	32
with children	59	35
In Central Cities of SMSA	29	23
in poverty	66	28

White families (9%), but among Black families headed by females, more were poor (53%) than were White families headed by females who were poor (30%). Poverty in both groups is heavier in central cities, but Black families headed by females who were poor were almost double the percentage of such White families.

Although we have identified earnings differentials by race and sex, part of which may be owing to wage differences or to occupational and unemployment differences, and even though we have indicated that these differences result in placing some within poverty categories, we have not determined that these differences are a result of discrimination. It is to this matter that we now turn.

[12] Stein, *op. cit.*, pp. 3, 4.
[13] *Ibid.*, p. 4.

The Theory of Group Differentials

Labor Supply

Let us assume that there exist two groups, A and B, where A is the favored group and B incurs discrimination. Because of current or past discrimination, A is also the wealthier group. This wealth may be in the form of physical capital from which an income is received or in some other more intangible form. It is not necessary for any particular person in group A to own the capital as long as he is a member of a family who shares the income receipts or equivalent opportunities with him. A parent's willingness and ability to sustain a child influences the latter's reservation wage for entering the labor force, for example. Other forms of intangible capital, of course, include such things as access to credit markets at low or lower interest charges, better knowledge of job opportunities and fewer psychological barriers to mobility, or more job contacts through friends and acquaintances. Not to be excluded are the educational advantages possessed by A, both qualitative and quantitative, although these also influence the productivity and demand for labor.

To show how capital differences affect the labor supply functions of representative members of A and B, let us engage in income–leisure analysis. Assume that A and B each possess the same income–leisure preference function I_i illustrated in Figure 17.1. Party A possesses capital equivalent to an income stream of $0_L C$, and party B possesses none. If the two parties are faced with a wage rate equal to $0_w Y/0_w 0_L = W_1$, the appropriate income line for B is $0_L Y$ and the amount of labor time offered by B is $0_L Q_B$. For A the appropriate income line is CY', and he offers $0_L Q_A$ amount of work. For each wage, the income line for B rotates through the origin at 0_L and for A it rotates through point C. For upward portions of the labor supply curve, B will offer more labor at each wage than A. Generalizing from this, it can be argued that the market labor supply curve for group B lies below and to the right of the market supply curve of group A. For any given amount of labor, group B will accept a lower wage than group A.

The wage at which labor force participation is initiated is lower for members of group B, $0B$ in Figure 17.1(b), than for group A, $0A$ in Figure 17.1(b). To shift BS_B to the left to coincide with AS_A, an income subsidy to group B equal to $0_L C$ in Figure 17.1(a) is necessary. A negative income tax or child welfare payments may characterize the subsidy. After the subsidy,

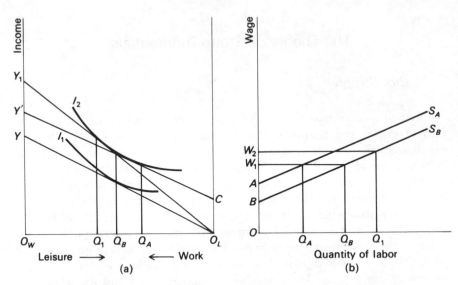

FIGURE 17.1. How wealth differentials alter labor supply curves. See text.

at any given wage, B will offer the same amount of labor as A.[14] To shift S_A sufficiently to the right to coincide with BS_B requires the imposition of a fixed tax per period equivalent to 0_LC. After the tax, since B and A now proceed from the origin 0_L, a wage equal to $0_wY_1/0_w0_L$ is necessary to bring A back to his original indifference curve and B up to that level. Note, however, that at the higher wage, both B and A offer the same amount of labor, 0_LQ_1, which exceeds the earlier offer of either.

Labor Demand

With B willing to offer the same quantity of labor at a lower wage, if both A and B have the same marginal revenue product schedule, the employer will prefer to employ more of B. If, however, they are faced with the same demand schedule for labor, it may be argued that they are, in the mind of the employer, perfect substitutes (see Figure 17.2). In this event, if the wage of B is at or below the reservation wage of A, $0A$, the market will

---

[14] The point that a person may reduce his hours of work if assistance payments are increased has been made by C. T. Brehm and T. R. Saving, "The Demand for General Assistance Payments," *American Economic Review*, Vol. 54, No. 6 (December 1964), p. 1005.

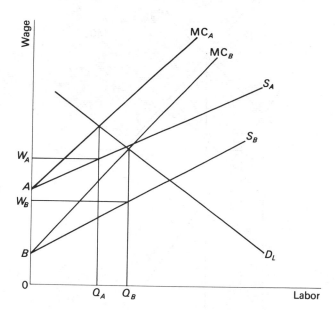

FIGURE 17.2. Labor markets of groups with equal productivity but different wealth endowments.

not employ A.[15] If the wage of B is only slightly higher than the reservation wage of A, some of A may sell their services in the market, but the employment distribution will be heavily weighted in terms of B. In certain occupations for example, Blacks or females tend to dominate; domestic service, particularly in the pre-World War II South, was almost completely composed of Blacks; sales clerks in small shops or variety stores were almost completely female, often made up of high school girls or female dropouts.

If members of groups A and B are not perfect substitutes, their marginal productivity schedules will differ (see Figure 17.3). In order for a wage differential to exist to Bs disadvantage, B must have a lower MRP for any given employment level. This lower MRP curve may follow from lower

---

[15] On an isoquant map, the isoquant curves would be straight lines with slopes equal to 1. The isocost line would have a slope less than 1; hence, no point exists at which the employer is indifferent to employment of members from the two groups. The minimum cost solution would therefore lie on the axis representing B as input.

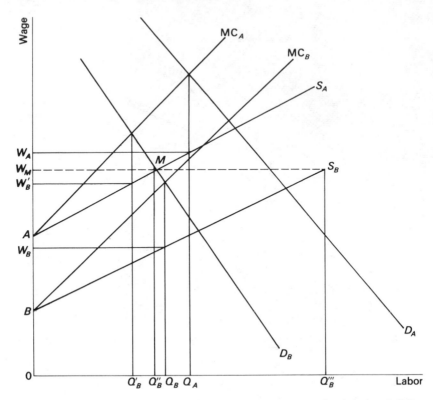

FIGURE 17.3. Labor markets of groups with different productivity and different wealth endowments.

quality or quantity of education and/or training, poorer health or stamina, or a lesser degree of labor force commitment.[16] The lower MRP of B may also be illusory, existing only as a result of the prejudices of the employer. However, to the extent that these prejudices form a belief structure upon which decisions and behavior are based, they are perceived as real. It is possible that integration of groups A and B generates differences in productivity schedules of each where none might exist if segregation were practiced.[17] Males and females may flirt or otherwise distract one another,

[16] Such as that which a young female may have who plans to work continuously only until she begins her child-bearing and -rearing life cycle. One may also identify this commitment in terms of motivation or desire to achieve specified goal levels in the employment endeavor.
[17] Finis Welch gives an innovative analysis of this phenomenon. See "Labor Market Discrimination: An Interpretation of Income Differences in the Rural South," *Journal of Political Economy*, Vol. 75, No. 3 (June 1967), pp. 229–231.

resulting in wasted time and effort, or even greater accident rates. Blacks and Whites may not cooperate as well, reducing their complementary nature as inputs.

If the differences in the productivity schedule are sufficiently large as illustrated in Figure 17.3, there will not only be a wage differential $(0W_A - 0W_B)$ between the two groups, but less of B will be employed compared to A $(0Q_B < 0Q_A)$. If the labor supply schedule of B can be made to coincide with that of A (through policy implementations), the wage differentials will be reduced $[(0W_A - 0W_B) > (0W_A - 0W'_B)]$, but the employment differential will widen $[(0Q_A - 0Q_B) < (0B_A - 0Q'_B)]$. Hence, the willingness of the discriminated group to accept lower wages can enhance the employment opportunities of its members.

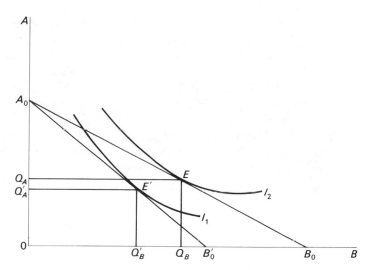

FIGURE 17.4. The effect of a relative increase in the wage of B on employment of A and B.

In Figure 17.4, consider an isoquant map using labor from group A and B, with E as an equilibrium point.[18] A rise in the wage of B moves the isocost line leftward from $0B_0$ to $0B'_0$, and under the same cost constraint reduces the amount used of A and B, but the use of B as illustrated tends

---

[18] At E, the (i) necessary and (ii) sufficient conditions are both satisfied.

   (i) $W_A/MP_A = W_B/MP_B$, and $W_B = W_A(MP_B/MP_A)$, where $MP_B < MP_A$. Hence, $W_B < W_A$.

   (ii) $MC_B = MRP_B$; $MC_A = MRP_A$.

to decrease more than A. Point E' may not be an equilibrium point, but because marginal costs have increased, a reduction in output is implied. The reduction in the use of B is owing not only to the substitution effect of A for B, but also is a result of the output effect. Moreover, since it is assumed that A and B are complementary, the latter figure is more general than the former because the substitution of A for B increases the ratio of A to B, decreases the ratio of B to A, and with the movement of the new ratios tends to move the MRP curves more closely together.[19] The same type of effect on the relative use of A and B is produced when a minimum wage is enacted above the existing wage of B but below that of A. Employment of B is reduced relative to that of A, and output is reduced which can lead to a reduction in the use of A when the output effect dominates the substitution effect. Moreover, the imposition of a minimum wage increases the unemployment level of B, partially because less of B is employed and partially because more of B offers their services at the higher minimum wage W_m. In Figure 17.3 with S_B as the supply curve of B, assume W_m is enacted. The $W_m MS_B$ now becomes the supply curve of B in which its marginal cost is coincidental with average cost between W_m and $W_m M$. Under the assumed demand conditions for B, employment of B falls from $0Q_B$ to $0Q_B''$, and unemployment becomes $0Q_B''' - 0Q_B''$.[20] Consequently, it is consistent with this analysis that unemployment rates for Blacks, particularly Black youths whose labor supply schedules may tend to lie below White youths' labor supply schedules, will be higher. Similarly, unemployment rates for females may be affected more as a result of minimum wage enactments than for males, although the discouragement effect on females may induce them to withdraw from the labor force, and this may hide the impact on their unemployment rates.

The Effect of Equal Wage Laws

An antidiscrimination law may be said to do two things: (1) it requires the employer to demonstrate no preference in hiring one applicant over another if the applicants, members of different groups, are equal in qualifications; (2) wages paid to members of each group must be equal for essentially the same set of tasks. As we have seen, if either the supply or demand schedules, or both, differ between groups, wage and employment differentials will exist. Compliance with the law in such circumstances

---

[19] The MRP schedule for A tends to shift leftward relatively more as proportionally less of B is used with A. See Chapter 11 in which is described the demand curve for an input when multiple variable inputs are used.

[20] The astute student will recognize that employment of B may lie to the left or right of $0Q_B''$ as D_B is affected by the smaller employment of A. Reference to Figure 17.4, our isoquant map, suggests, however, that $0Q_B'' < 0Q_B$.

cannot be expected among rational, economic men unless violations carry some penalty. Unless the penalty is sufficiently severe, the employer may decide that the cost of the penalty risk is less than the cost from eliminating the differential, and may conclude that continued discrimination is more profitable. Hence, the magnitude of the expected value of the penalty is of importance in appraising the success of an antidiscrimination law in achieving its objective.

To simplify our analysis, let us initially assume that productivity differences are believed to exist between two groups, and that labor supply conditions are such that the wage for group A is higher than the wage for group B, and the supply of labor for each group is perfectly elastic at its respective wage. Profit maximization and cost minimization are achieved when

$$\begin{cases} w_A = \text{MRP}_A \\ w_B = \text{MRP}_B \end{cases} \quad \text{and} \quad w_B = w_A \frac{\text{MRP}_B}{\text{MRP}_A}.$$

If the law requires that $w_A = w_B$, and $\text{MRP}_B < \text{MRP}_A$, it will violate the rational profit-maximizing behavior of an employer to abide by the law. If a penalty P is imposed such that its infliction reduces the MRP_A to equality with the MRP_B; i.e., $\text{MRP}_A - P = \text{MRP}_B$, violations may still occur if enforcement is lax or uncertain. The expected value of P, the probability of its imposition times the value of P, is given by $E(P)$, and it is less than P in proportion to the probability of the violation not being detected. Hence, the magnitude of the penalty must vary inversely with the degree of enforcement if discrimination is to be eliminated. It is the difference between the expected value of the penalty and the MRP_A that must be made less than or equal to the MRP_B so $(\text{MRP}_A - E(P)) \leq \text{MRP}_B$. Hence $E(P) \geq \text{MRP}_A - \text{MRP}_B$.[21]

---

[21] In the case where the supply curves of labor originally are not perfectly elastic for the two groups, it can be shown that the expected value of the penalty depends upon the elasticity of labor supply of the favored group, e_{sa}, and its wage, w_a. Profit maximization occurs where $\text{MC}_A = \text{MRP}_A$, $\text{MC}_B = \text{MRP}_B$. MC_A is defined as the derivative of the wage bill, $W_A = w_a L_a$ with respect to the quantity of A, L_a.

$$\text{MC}_A = \frac{dW_a}{dL_a} = w_a + L_a \frac{dw_a}{dL_a} = \text{MRP}_a.$$

Similarly,

$$\text{MC}_B = \frac{dW_b}{dL_b} = w_b + L_b \frac{dw_b}{dL_b} = \text{MRP}_b.$$

Therefore,

Penalties usually contain two types of costs: punitive and remedial. The punitive cost α is the fine for a willful violation; the remedial cost is the reimbursement to the aggrieved for the loss incurred by him. Hence, the employer who discriminates against N employees for t duration in the amount $w_A - w_B$ may be subject to the following penalty.

$$P = \alpha + N \cdot t \cdot (w_A - w_B).$$

Strong enforcement of the law requires that α be high when t is small. An employer also may be able to reduce the expected value of the penalty if he can keep N small, but there is a positive relationship between the value of N and the probability of enforcement. For example, the more hiring an employer does, the more chances he has to discriminate in employment, and the greater the probability that a disgruntled and rejected applicant will file a complaint. If an employer, however, can reduce N sufficiently, perhaps by reducing the turnover of A by increasing $(w_A - w_B)$ less than N, he may be able to exercise some control over the magnitude of the penalty. If such a practice occurs, it is possible that a civil rights act may result in greater rather than less employment discrimination. In fact, employers are less apt to oppose a civil rights act, the milder are its penalties and the weaker is the scheduled enforcement.[22]

$$w_a = \mathrm{MRP}_a - L_a \frac{dw_a}{dL_a}; \; w_b = \mathrm{MRP}_b - L_b \frac{dw_b}{dL_b};$$

and the wage differential,

$$w_a - w_b = \mathrm{MRP}_a - \mathrm{MRP}_b - L_a \frac{dw_a}{dL_b} + L_b \frac{dw_b}{dL_b}.$$

Elasticity of labor supply is given by $e_s = (dL/dw)(w/L)$. Thus,

$$w_a - w_b = \mathrm{MRP}_a - \mathrm{MRP}_b - \left(\frac{w_a}{e_{sa}} - \frac{w_b}{e_{sb}} \right).$$

If, through law, w_a is set equal to w_b, then as we have earlier shown, $e_{sb} = \infty$, and $\mathrm{MRP}_a - \mathrm{MRP}_b = w_a/e_{sa} = E(P)$. Therefore, to eliminate wage differentials with productivity differences and with positive-sloping labor supply curves, the expected value of the penalty varies directly with the wage of A and inversely with the elasticity of labor supply of A.

If the labor supply curve of each group is identical and a straight line, then the penalty is equal to $(w_a - w_b)/e_s$, where $e_{sa} = e_{sb}$. If the common labor supply curve is not a straight line, the expected value is $w_a/e_{sa} - w_b/e_{sb}$. A labor supply curve which is concave from below requires a smaller expected value than one which is convex from below.

[22] An unplanned consequence of a weak civil rights act may be that various disgruntled, vigilante-type minority groups embark upon a self-enforcement crusade in which their own set of penalties are imposed upon violators. The success of the civil rights movement may, as a result, depend upon which group can most successfully deprive the other of their respective civil rights.

To the extent that w_B is raised to equality with w_A, even in the original absence of perfect elasticity of labor supply, the existence of separate supply schedules, one lower than the other, may generate greater unemployment rates among the discriminated class. The smaller output also tends to reduce the employment of the favored class. In this respect, in the absence of complementary policy, the twin objectives of equal pay and equal employment opportunities are self-defeating. As we have seen, a sufficiently large penalty coupled with a sufficiently large degree of enforcement may bring wages into equality and coerce the employer into a state of indifference in employment between the two groups.[23] However, the higher wage induces, as we have seen, new entrants of B into the labor force who may be unable to obtain jobs.

If civil rights legislation is to achieve its twin objectives, companion welfare policies are required, and these companion policies are more important the less the emphasis given to penalties and enforcement. One policy may simply be to subsidize the employment of group B sufficiently to bring the sum of the MRP_B and the subsidy up to equality with the MRP_A. The subsidy may be tied to manpower training programs developed and controlled by employers, such as those instituted under the Job Opportunities in the Business Sector (JOBS), in which employers are reimbursed an average of $3000 per trainee for the extra cost of counseling and training disadvantaged workers in order to raise their productivity. Provisions of higher welfare payments to capital-poor families in group B may reduce labor force participation rates, and shift its labor supply schedule to a point coincidental with that of group A. This alone is not sufficient to induce employers to hire them indiscriminately, but given other policies designed to affect the net marginal productivity schedules, the unemployment problem may be reduced. Various supplemental manpower training programs designed to remedy the labor force quality inadequacies of the unemployed in B also may tend to increase the MRP_B.

Employers who are compelled to hire indiscriminately at equal wages may upgrade or promote discriminately. Hence, if the productivity of group B employees is judged on the basis of real or imaginary performance to be inferior to that of group A employees, and if evaluations of potential productivity determine the type of jobs into which new employees are channeled, it may be that employees of group B tend to be placed into "dead-end jobs," whereas employees in group A are placed in jobs where chances of upward movement are better. David Taylor found, for example, that non-Whites were more apt to be found in janitorial jobs than in

---

[23] That is, when $w_B = w_A$, and $MRP_A - MRP_B = E(P)$, then $w_A = MRP_A$, $w_B = MRP_B + E(P)$, and $w_B/w_A = MRP_B + E(P)/MRP_A = 1$.

material-handling jobs, both of which paid comparably and which required low skills.[24] In fact, the proportion of Blacks in material handling varied inversely with the wage position of the firm. Material handlers can be promoted or upgraded, whereas janitors are more likely to represent dead-end jobs. Similarly, in the basic steel industry, Richard Rowan found that Blacks have not tended to move up the occupational hierarchy and that they remain concentrated in blue-collar jobs in which they have experienced few changes in their occupational level.[25]

The Discrimination Parameter

Becker has developed the theory of discrimination in a somewhat different fashion, although the approach is not completely dissimilar.[26] He identifies three components of market discrimination: employer, employee, and consumer. Each component is said to have a taste for discrimination measured by a discrimination coefficient ($DC = d$). The over-all measure of the rate of market discrimination is given by $R = (w_A - w_B)/w_B$. No market discrimination exists, obviously, if $R = 0$ and if A and B are equally productive. (Becker does not make it clear that A and B must be otherwise homogeneous in productivity if R is to be a valid measure of discrimination.) The employer has a taste for discrimination if he is willing to employ homogeneous units of A and B only if he pays B a lower wage than A; i.e., $w_A > w_B$. His taste for discrimination is measured by the differential d added to the wage of B which makes the ratio of the net wage of B to the actual wage of A equal to the ratio of the marginal products of the two groups. His minimum cost position under competition in the labor market is given by $MP_A/MP_B = w_A/w_B(1 + d)$. Implicit in this formulation is awareness that the employer believes, correctly or not, that the marginal product of A exceeds that of B.[27]

Consumers also have preferences toward purchasing the products produced by either groups A or B, or a mixture of both. This preference, or bias, is reflected in their willingness to purchase commodities produced by either group. Presumably, the consumers differentiate between the same product in the same manner as they would between products made in two different countries—i.e., toys made in Hong Kong or Germany. Their willingness to buy identical quantities from each group is expressed in price differentials. Hence, produce demand curves are believed to be not identical

---

[24] "Discrimination and Occupational Wage Differentials in Markets for Unskilled Labor," *Industrial and Labor Relations Review*, Vol. 21, No. 3 (April 1968), pp. 375–390.
[25] "Negro Employment in Basic Steel," *Industrial and Labor Relations Review*, Vol. 23, No. 1 (October 1969), pp. 29–39.
[26] Gary Becker, *The Economics of Discrimination* (Chicago: University of Chicago Press, 1957).
[27] Apparently, discrimination occurs only if this belief is erroneous.

between the two groups. Therefore, even if no differences exist in the physical productivity of the two groups, differences can exist in marginal revenue products because of consumer discrimination. One might expect, for example, positive correlation between the bias of an employer toward the productivity of a member of group B and the bias in his estimate of the extent of consumer discrimination. Consequently, even though consumer discrimination no doubt does exist, it can be subsumed under the employer's discrimination coefficient, which is made a function of the former. (Becker does not clearly indicate this.)

Somewhat related is the argument that the capital–labor ratio may influence the degree of discrimination between Blacks and Whites.[28] Industries which are capital intensive and of large scale tend to have a high degree of impersonalization between employer and employee and between customer and producer. On the other hand, retail and service industries, which tend to be small and labor intensive, tend to have personal intergroup relations. In the former, impersonalization leads to more objectivity and less discrimination, whereas in the latter visual awareness of color can trigger attitudinal responses which are based upon stereotyped opinions regarding racial capabilities. This suggests the hypothesis that wage discrimination is less in capital intensive, large-scale industries.

Another source of discrimination is the employee's willingness to work in integrated groups. Let W be the money wage of A earned when working only with other members of group A and W_{ab} be the money wage of A earned when working with members of both groups A and B. If working in an integrated group generated a rate of dissatisfaction to an A employee equal to r, then his net wage is $W_{ab}(1 - r) < W_{ab}$. The cost to A of choosing not to work with members of group B (i.e., of choosing a segregated work group) is given by $C = (W_{ab} - W_{aa})/W_{ab}$. As C is greater than, equal to, or less than r, the A employee will choose to work, be indifferent to working, or prefer not to work with members of group B. In effect, this formulation implies that the segregated labor supply curve of group A lies to the left of its integrated labor supply curve. The premium paid by an employer to A employees in an integrated work environment also becomes a source of wage differentials between A and B, and the premium may be deducted from the wage of B employees.[29] The result is that the employer views the integrated labor supply curve of B. The existence of preferences for discrimination can, therefore, yield differences in labor supply curves. However, to the extent that A embodies more capital than B, the complementary nature of A and

[28] Raymond Franklin, "A Framework for the Analysis of Interurban Negro–White Economic Differentials," *Industrial and Labor Relations Review*, Vol. 21, No. 3 (April 1968), pp. 370–371.
[29] As Becker observes, *op. cit.*, pp. 16–20, if $W_{ba}(1 - d) > W_{bb}$, it is to the advantage of B to "trade" with A, even with discrimination.

B is reflected in a higher integrated marginal revenue product curve than a segregated marginal revenue product curve for B. Similarly, integration may alter the marginal revenue product curve for A, particularly if elements of B substitute for elements of A. In any event, the magnitude of the employer's taste for discrimination is dependent also upon his estimate of his employees' tastes for discrimination, as well as upon his estimates of their relative marginal productivities and the consumer's preference for discrimination. Taken together, the employer's estimates of the relative positions of marginal revenue product curves and labor supply curves determine the magnitude of wage differentials between members of the two groups. Becker's analysis, therefore, can be modified to essentially the same form as our earlier presentation.

To the extent that wage differentials are removed, through effective enforcement, the discriminated group receives a benefit. However, costs are incurred in the enforcement procedure, and from the standpoint of society, it pays to enforce equal wage laws only as long as the benefits exceed the costs. Thurow and Rappaport have applied cost–benefit analysis to the investigation by the U.S. Government of alleged violations of the minimum wage, overtime, and equal pay laws.[30] These investigative aspects of enforcement have declined as a deterrent as time has passed, yet it remains a significant risk factor in the employer's discounting of benefits through violation of the law. Insofar as society is concerned, the haphazard selection of cases to investigate reduces the benefit to society through enforcement procedures. It has been found that a more careful selection of cases can raise employee benefits by as much as tenfold. This would justify, in a social context, a greater expansion of enforcement expenditures, and can increase the risk factor to employers of being apprehended.

Finis Welch has expanded on Becker's analysis of employer discrimination.[31] He divides the labor of an individual into two components, physical labor N and educated labor E, which are assumed to be complements of one another.[32] Furthermore, units of physical labor are considered to be perfect substitutes among groups, units of education are complementary among groups, and members of two groups are generally assumed to be complementary as inputs. Integration increases output by less than the sum of the positive marginal products of the components of the two groups because of

[30] Lester Thurow and C. Rappaport, "Law Enforcement and Cost–Benefit Analysis," *Public Finance/Financee Publiques*, Vol. 24, No. 1, 1969.

[31] "Labor Market Discrimination: An Interpretation of Income Differences in the Rural South," *op. cit.*, pp. 228–232.

[32] He argues that they cannot be substitutes, but his proof is questionable. See pp. 228–229, 240. The E of the group is defined as $\sum_i r_i n_i$, where r_i is the number of units of education and n_i the number of laborers in a group.

friction from interpersonal interaction. The losses from this friction have been identified as type 1 losses, resulting from the interaction of physical labor components, and type 2 losses resulting from interaction of educational components. These losses comprise the discrimination coefficients for physical labor and for education, and they are imposed upon the minority group. A one-to-one relationship between members of two integrated groups is assumed. The minority group bears the integration loss because output increases would not be reduced by group friction if laborers from only the majority group were employed.

From the employee's point of view, integration is desirable because it increases his wage. This follows from educational differences between the two groups. The incentive to integrate would be removed if educational differences were eliminated.[33] Discrimination in wages would still occur under integration if frictional losses continued to be incurred, but since wages under segregation would then be higher than wages under integration, employees from the two groups would not seek integrated employment. This formulation has the advantage of identifying the composition and source of the discrimination coefficient imposed by the employer.

The Source of Group Wage Differentials

His formulation of the nature of group wage differentials has permitted Welch to test empirically some of the implications of his theoretical analysis by examining the White–non-White income differentials for rural farm males in the South in 1959. He considers the discrimination resulting (1) from physical labor and (2) from education. The latter is further broken down into derived discrimination from inferior quality of schooling. A Black with eight years of schooling, the standard educational unit, earns on the average about $860 a year less than a White with the same education and of the same age. The composition of the differential is divided as follows: (1) $250 in discrimination against the physical labor of the Black; (2) $230 owing to the inferior quality of the Black's education; and (3) the remaining $380 is assumed to be market discrimination against education. Other findings were as follows:

1. A non-White with no schooling earns only 81% as much as a comparable White, implying a discrimination coefficient of 19% against physical labor.
2. Comparisons of the quality of schooling received by Whites and

---

[33] *Ibid.*, p. 232. Welch acknowledges, however, the restrictive character of his assumptions which lead to this conclusion.

non-Whites—based on expenditures per pupil, teacher salaries, and size of secondary schools—revealed that non-Whites acquire only 73% as much education as Whites for equivalent years of attendance. Moreover, since non-Whites attend school fewer days per year, they receive only 91% as much schooling per year of enrollment. This reduces the relative quantity of schooling for non-Whites to 66% as much as for Whites.

3. Ignoring quality differences in education, unit increases in school attendance (prorated on a unit of eight years) increase income for a non-White at a rate of only 28% of the corresponding increase in income for a White.

4. On the average, equivalent education returns only 32% as much to a non-White as to a White. Hence, the discrimination coefficient is owing to the inferior quality of schooling received by the non-White; 63% is the impact of market discrimination against the non-White's education.

The findings suggest that the improvement of the quality of schooling is perhaps more feasible in removing the income differentials than trying to eliminate market discrimination. The latter is influenced more by sociological phenomena and is more difficult to eliminate.[34] Of course, the analysis is in terms of wage rate differentials, but the empirical study is based on earnings differentials. Since the market discrimination estimate is a residual, it may include differences in earnings owing to different periods of employment during the year. Although the opportunity to work a greater proportion of the year may be related to race, and thus may include a form of discrimination, it is not *de facto* a component of the discrimination coefficient. Hence, it is possible that the market discrimination coefficient would be much smaller if adjustments were made in, say, cyclical variations in job opportunities.

The relationship between unemployment and economic discrimination has also been studied.[35] The unemployment rate for Black males has consistently exceeded that of White males for decades. In part, this may be owing to Blacks' being concentrated in occupations and/or industries which have, on the average, larger unemployment rates. Even within broad

---

[34] *Ibid.*, p. 239. R. L. Lassiter has also noted that Whites have more incentive to invest in education than non-Whites since their rate of return from education is higher. Moreover, he finds that the quality of education for non-Whites is lower, "The Association of Income and Education for Males by Region, Race, and Age," *Southern Economic Journal*, Vol. 32, No. 1 (July 1965), pp. 15–22.

[35] Harry J. Gilman, "Economic Discrimination and Unemployment," *American Economic Review*, Vol. 55, No. 5 (December 1965), pp. 1077–1096.

occupational categories, Blacks may be concentrated in the lower strata of those categories in which unemployment rates, although lower than in lower occupational categories, are higher than in higher intraoccupational strata. Standardizing the data in terms of occupational distribution results in a reduction of the White–non-White unemployment rate differential by 100% in 1940, 42% in 1950, and 38.5% in the period 1953–1961. Hence, this cause of unemployment differences has been diminishing. Similarly, standardizing for differences in education, industry, and age within occupations eliminated up to 50% of the White–non-White unemployment rate differential. In the South, 68% of the differential was eliminated, and in the non-South 43% was eliminated. Nonracial characteristics, those associated with labor force quality, explained much of the unemployment variations.

Two hypotheses are used to account for the unexplained residuals in unemployment variation. One hypothesis explains the residual differences in male unemployment rates as owing to incomplete statistical control over the skill factor with respect to educational and on-the-job training differences. This hypothesis has been rejected because no significant support existed for these corollaries to the hypothesis: (1) unemployment rates and qualitative differences are most pronounced in the highest skills; (2) larger rate differences are found among older than among younger males because the skill difference between races widens with age owing to less on-the-job training for non-Whites; (3) a higher unemployment rate differential exists in the South because educational differences are greater in this region; (4) as educational differences decline over time, so do unemployment rate differentials.[36] The second hypothesis explains the residuals as owing to the existence of increasing wage rigidity over time among non-Whites in the presence of discrimination. If wages were flexible for non-Whites, greater variations in wages than in employment would occur. To the extent that legal and institutional restrictions reduce this flexibility more for non-Whites than for Whites, variations in unemployment for non-Whites will increase. In the South where enforcement of these causes of rigidity is less stringent, there should be less variation in unemployment. Evidence tends to support this, and Gilman concludes that unemployment rate differential residuals are explained more by employment discrimination in the face of growing wage rigidity than by failure to identify more carefully variations in skill. Thus, unemployment rate differentials appear to be owing both to group quality differentials and to discrimination.

Other studies have tended to confirm that wage differentials are in part explained by differences in characteristics associated with labor force quality. For example, the higher wages paid by concentrated industries can

[36] *Ibid.*, pp. 1086–1090.

largely be explained by the higher "quality" of the employees.[37] Poverty, at least among Whites, is associated with old age and with factors which tend to reduce labor force participation rates.[38] However, in support of the discrimination hypothesis, among unskilled workers in Chicago, non-Whites employed at the same wage as Whites tended to have higher qualifications. The apparent wage equality was made less so because of the higher commuter costs of Blacks, who tend to travel further to work than Whites.[39]

Remedies for Group Wage Differentials

It is illegal for firms subject to Federal law to discriminate on the basis of sex, race, color, religion, or age. The Equal Pay Act of 1963 forbids unequal pay for equal work, regardless of sex; the Civil Rights Act of 1964 forbids discrimination; Executive Order 11246 prohibits discrimination after October 1967 by federal contractors, and The Age Discrimination in Employment Act of 1967 protects workers in the age category 40–65. The costs of enforcing these acts are high, and employers have used a number of excuses in order to evade them. Employers have argued that women on a group basis require larger fringe benefits and this has necessitated wage differentials by sex; the inability of women to do heavy lifting has also been claimed as justification for lower wages; similarly, differences in training costs have been cited.[40] The courts, however, have examined these rationalizations carefully. In the *Wheaton Glass* case, it was ruled that "Jobs must be only substantially equal, not identical, to permit job comparisons under the Act; there must be a rational explanation for the amount of the wage differential, and it is the employer's burden to provide it; and the employer's past history, if any, of unequal pay practices is an important factor in determining whether there is a violation of the Act."[41] Although penalties under the Act can be high if differentials are substantial, long-standing, and applied to a large part of the employer's labor force, enforcement does not appear to have been vigorous or widespread, and thus, whatever compliance with the Act may occur, it is primarily a voluntary decision.

James Tobin has argued that the economic status of Blacks can best be

---

[37] Leonard W. Weiss, "Concentration and Labor Earnings," *op. cit.*, p. 115.

[38] Joseph D. Mooney, "Urban Poverty and Labor-Force Participation Rates," *American Economic Review*, Vol. 57, No. 1 (March 1967) pp. 104–119.

[39] David P. Taylor, "Discrimination and Occupational Wage Differentials in Markets for Unskilled Labor," *op. cit.*, pp. 384–390.

[40] Robert D. Moran, "Reducing Discrimination: Role of the Equal Pay Act," *Monthly Labor Review*, Vol. 93, No. 6 (June 1970), pp. 32–33.

[41] *Ibid.*, p. 33.

improved by policies designed to assure a tight labor market.[42] In such a market, Black unemployment rates are reduced; employers undertake training programs to upgrade the skills of marginal Black workers; full-time employment would increase annual earnings; the employment of male family heads would lend stability to the Black family and self-respect to the male; it would assist the migration of Blacks from the rural South. Although other policies can improve the economic position of Blacks, these remedies are of a second order of importance to that of maintaining a high level of economic activity. The former is a complement to the latter, and the basic problems will remain if full employment is not maintained.

More radical approaches have been proposed.[43] Suppose the ghetto is viewed as a colony of the larger society, which is subject to imperialistic exploitation by other economic institutions in the society. Moreover, if the Black business community is characterized by low capital–labor ratios, high competition, and submarginal firms, then attempts to develop Black business ventures, "Black Capitalism," may not have much chance for success. In addition, consider the efforts of large corporations to improve the Blacks' employment position as merely "sops" to integration pressures—"tokenism" —and note that funds for corporate programs of ghetto development are among the first to be cut back when civil rights agitation subsides. Regard as inadequate attempts to break up the ghetto through subsidization of housing in integrated neighborhoods, or manpower policies to assist in locating, training, placing, and counseling submarginal Blacks in better occupations. Unless programs are adopted that are as massive as the problems they face, believe that they will not succeed. If these attitudes are strongly held, they can form a basis for believing that a major restructuring of society, led by Blacks themselves with White support, is in order.[44]

---

[42] James Tobin, "On Improving the Economic Status of the Negro," *Daedalus* (Fall 1965), pp. 878–898, reprinted in *Readings in Labor Economics and Labor Relations*, ed. by Richard Rowan and Herbert Northrup (Homewood: Richard D. Irwin, Inc., 1960), pp. 496–509. Almost a restatement of Tobin's position was taken by Johnson's Council of Economic Advisers in *The Economic Report of the President*, 1969, "Combating Poverty in a Prosperous Economy," Chapter 5 (Washington: U.S. Government Printing Office, 1969), pp. 151–179.

[43] William K. Tabb, *The Political Economy of the Black Ghetto* (New York: W. W. Norton and Company, Inc., 1970).

[44] There are undoubtedly some Marxist overtones to this approach. It calls for Whites to support those Blacks who are on the cutting edge of the struggle, the militant groups that refuse to go slow and accept token reforms. Second, these Whites should build a White movement for radical social change. The continued apathy and resistance of the White working class may impose a barrier to Black improvement, and because of the symbiotic relationship of all members of society, to their own improvement as well. "Racism hurts Whites in ways which must be made clear." *Ibid.*, p. 145.

Another view holds that if Blacks are to obtain economic advancement, working class differentials must be removed.[45] Because the preponderance of the ghetto's labor force is used in customer-contact employment with low capital–labor ratios, wages are low in these establishments. This is because of low productivity and partly because of discrimination. Because the ghetto isolates the Black from better employment opportunities, wage differentials persist, and Blacks come to regard themselves as inferior because they receive lower wages. Franklin calls this "a feedback effect." Blacks, because of this attitude, tend to underestimate their potential, motivation is adversely affected, and those who have made it to "middle class" status tend to reject their lower class brothers in order to protect themselves from this stereotyped opinion. Hence, they tend to reenforce it. However, the feedback effect also influences the status of middle class Blacks, and therefore it is to their advantage to neutralize this effect. This, however, requires, at a minimum, upgrading the lowest-class Black to the status of the lowest-class White. How this is to be done remains the essence of the problem, for which no new insights into ways to solve the problem have yet been proposed.

Summary

In this chapter, data are first presented to show that Blacks have lower education, are concentrated in lower-paying jobs, and have greater unemployment at all ages and occupational levels than Whites. Women receive lower weekly earnings, have lower labor force participation rates, and as heads of households are more likely to be poor than males. These two groups represent the largest number of persons who have experienced discrimination in the United States.

Economic analysis shows that groups with lower income from property tend to offer less labor in the labor market. This implies a higher labor supply curve. In occupations in which each group has the same productivity, therefore, those who are willing to work for lower wages are more likely to be employed. However, if productivity of the capital-rich group is regarded as being greater, both wages and employment of this group can exceed that of the capital-poor group. Also, it is shown that an increase in the minimum wage can decrease employment more in the disadvantaged than in the advantaged group. To remedy the inequities between the two groups, either the advantaged group can be taxed in order to increase its labor supply curve, or the disadvantaged group can be subsidized to decrease its labor supply curve, or some combination of the two policies can be utilized to

---

[45] Raymond S. Franklin, "A Framework for the Analysis of Interurban Negro–White Economic Differentials," *Industrial and Labor Relations Review* (April 1968), pp. 367–374.

bring the supply curves of the two groups together. In addition, measures can be taken concurrently to increase the productivity of the disadvantaged group in order to eliminate demand sources of wage differentials.

A theory of discrimination is developed in which it is shown that the number of penalties and the degree of enforcement influence the willingness of employers to comply with a civil rights act requiring equal pay and employment among groups. The greatest success in achieving economic equality among groups requires companion policies of strict enforcement and enlightened welfare policies designed to upgrade the productivity and employability of deprived groups. Gary Becker's earlier model of discrimination is shown to reach conclusions similar to those of the model developed here.

A number of studies have been examined which seek to measure the extent of discrimination. Welch found that discrimination did occur in employment, but that wage differentials also reflected differences in education quality between Blacks and Whites in the rural South. This quality differential may be owing to an indirect form of discrimination, however. Gilman found that employment discrimination is present because Blacks are concentrated in the lower-paying jobs in each occupational category. (Also, see Table 17.1.) He also found that where wage discrimination is more possible, owing to exclusions or nonenforcement of minimum wage laws, employment variability among groups is reduced. Weiss, Mooney, Taylor, Rowan, and others have found similar evidence of discrimination.

Finally, the proposals of a number of scholars to remedy the sources of discrimination have been presented. Tobin, although in favor of manpower programs to assist the disadvantaged, believes that a maintenance of sufficient aggregate demand to provide jobs is the critical element in upgrading their economic position. Rabb believes that Black and White radical groups must take a militant stand in order to compel society to provide a greater degree of social justice than the tokenism that it has provided up to 1970. Franklin notes that wage differentials breed an inferiority complex among the disadvantaged which saps their motivations and aspirations, and which must be eliminated if the vicious circle of poverty is to be escaped.

Discussion Questions

1. How can the occupational upgrading of non-White workers in the past decade be explained?
2. Suppose non-Whites and females achieve complete economic equality with Whites and males, respectively. Will poverty be eliminated? Discuss.

3. Administrators of civil rights statutes stress the desirability of persuasion and voluntary compliance over court enforcement of violations. What are the advantages and disadvantages of this preferred technique from the standpoint of government administrators? Of employers? Of minority groups?
4. Examine the labor supply implications of the negative income tax. How will this policy affect the wage–employment opportunities of minority groups?
5. "A lessening of racial tensions can improve productivity and lessen discrimination." Discuss.
6. To what extent do consumers contribute to wage discrimination?
7. (a) An employer who pays a comparably educated and trained woman less than her male counterparts is not necessarily discriminating. Discuss.
   (b) Should an employer be required to select his employees indiscriminantly with respect to age, if age is not a criterion for the job?
8. "Only through *Black Power* can Blacks secure economic justice." Discuss.

Part IV

THE MACRO THEORY OF

THE LABOR MARKET

18

The Macro Theory of Wages and Employment

The revolution in economic thought known as Keynesian economics can be said to be an outgrowth of the development of the theory of imperfect competition. Just as Joan Robinson and Edward Chamberlin analyzed the impact of market imperfections on price and output variables at the micro level, Keynes analyzed the impact of market imperfections on price and employment variables at the macro level. Imperfect knowledge of future events was shown to affect attitudes toward the store-of-value function of money and estimates of the expected yield from investment; trade unions introduced imperfections in the labor market which made for downward rigidities in wages and greater variations in unemployment; immobilities in the short run impaired the substitution of factors of production, created bottlenecks in production, and transformed increases in aggregate demand into price rather than output increases. Because of the immediate practical importance of the *General Theory of Money, Interest, and Employment* and because of the new perspectives which it provided in developing contra-cyclical policies, his work has received more attention. Phrased differently, the macro applications of the theory of imperfect competition perhaps filled more of a gap than did the micro applications, and hence the revisions were more dramatic and evident. Thus, Keynes is as much a member of the School of Imperfect Competition as are Sraffa, Robinson, Chamberlin, and Triffin.[1]

---

[1] Piero Sraffa, "The Laws of Returns under Competitive Conditions," *Economic Journal*, Vol. 36 (1926), pp. 535–550; Joan Robinson, *The Economics of Imperfect Competition* (London: Macmillan and Co., Ltd., 1933); E. H. Chamberlin, *The Theory of Monopolistic Competition* (Cambridge, Mass.: Harvard University Press, 1933); Robert Triffin, *Monopolistic Competition and General Equilibrium Theory* (Cambridge, Mass.: Harvard University Press, 1949).

To throw modern macro theory into sharper relief, we shall first present the neoclassical macro theory of wages, money, and employment. Following this, we shall analyze the theoretical contributions of modern macro economics and evaluate the implications of this revision on the functioning of the total economy.

The Neoclassical Theory of Wages, Money, and Employment

The neoclassical system is of more than historical interest. Modern macroeconomic theory has two major schools. One traces its lineage directly from the neoclassical model, with only minor modifications to account for some of the most potent criticisms of Keynes. This is the *monetarist* school, among whom are such noted economists as Milton Friedman and Don Patinkin.[2] The second school has evolved directly from the Keynesian model and it may be said to represent the mainstream of current macroeconomic thought. Paul Samuelson has said, "We are all Keynesians now."

A formal statement of the neoclassical relationships may be helpful to the student. In addition to the functional specifications, a graphical exposition is given to assist the student in visualizing the relationships.

An aggregate production function is assumed for the economy in which real national output y is related to inputs of labor N and capital K. Capital in the short run is assumed to be fixed, $\overline{K}$, although over time the capital stock is enlarged through net investment. Hence,

$$y = f(N, \overline{K}). \tag{18.1}$$

This function is subject to diminishing marginal returns and is illustrated in Figure 18.1(a). Given the production function and $\overline{K}$, maximum output is reached at y_0. Profit maximizing is assumed among the competitive economy's entrepreneurs, so that labor is employed up to the point where the marginal product of labor equals the real wage (w/p). The marginal product function constitutes the aggregate demand for labor, D_n:

$$D_n = \frac{dy}{dN} = \frac{w}{p} \tag{18.2}$$

where w is the money wage and p is the price index. The function is graphed in Figure 18.1(b) and because of diminishing returns has a negative slope. The aggregate supply of labor is assumed also to be a function of the real

[2] Milton Friedman, ed. *Studies in the Quantity Theory of Money* (Chicago: University of Chicago Press, 1956); Don Patinkin, *Money, Interest, and Prices: An Integration of Monetary and Value Theory*, 2nd ed. (New York: Harper and Row, 1965).

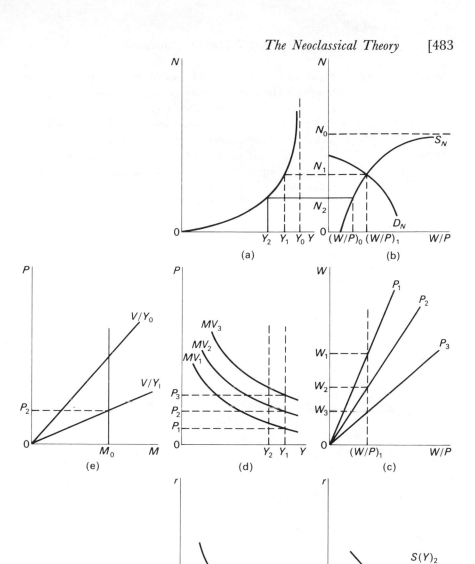

FIGURE 18.1. The neoclassical model of income, wages, prices, and employment; (a) the labor–output function, (b) the labor market, (c) the wage–price relation, (d) the price–income relation, (e) the money–price relation, (f) the interest–income relation, (g) the investment–savings market.

wage. This wage compensates labor for the loss of utility from forgone leisure, and as we have seen in the income–leisure analysis in earlier chapters, higher wages are necessary to elicit more labor effort from an individual. Presumably, there exists some wage at which an individual will proffer no more labor. Individual labor-supply curves are aggregated and are normally positively sloped. Below a biological or institutionally established minimum wage $(w/p)_0$, no labor will be offered, and beyond some amount of labor (N_0) no wage will induce more labor force participation.

$$S_N = N_S \left(\frac{w}{p}\right) \tag{18.3}$$

Full employment is defined as the wage and employment level at which, at a determined wage, the demand for labor is equal to the supply of labor.

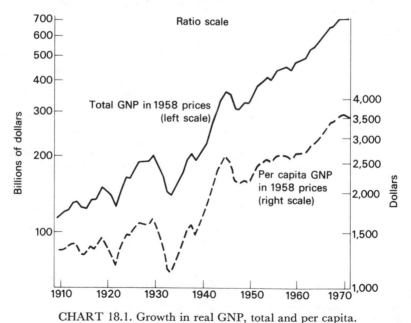

CHART 18.1. Growth in real GNP, total and per capita.

Source: Department of Commerce. *Economic Report of the President, 1971*, p. 109.

TABLE 18.1
ECONOMIC AND MANPOWER DEVELOPMENTS, 1968–1970

				Change			
				1968–1969		*1969–1970*	
	1968	*1969*	*1970*	*Number*	*Percent*	*Number*	*Percent*
(Billions)							
GNP in current dollars[a]	$865.0	$931.4	$976.8	$66.4	7.7	$45.4	4.9
GNP in 1958 dollars[a]	707.2	727.1	724.3	19.9	2.8	−2.8	−0.4
(Thousands)							
Total civilian employment	75,920	77,902	78,627	1,982	2.6	725	0.9
Nonfarm payroll employment[a]	67,915	70,274	70,669	2,359	3.5	395	0.6
Unemployment	2,817	2,831	4,088	14	0.5	1,257	44.4
(Percent)							
Unemployment rate	3.6	3.5	4.9	—	—	—	—
Weekly earnings (private nonfarm production workers) in current dollars[a]	$107.73	$114.61	$119.78	$6.88	6.4	$5.17	4.5
Consumer Price Index (1967 = 100)	104.2	109.8	116.3	—	5.4	—	5.9
Weekly earnings in 1967 dollars[a]	$103.39	$104.38	$102.99	$0.99	1.0	− $1.39	−1.3

[a] 1970 data are preliminary.

Source: *Manpower Report of the President*, 1971, p. 7.

All workers who wish employment at that wage can find it. In Figure 18.1(b) this is at $0N_1$ employment and $(w/p)_1$ real wage.

The level of full employment also determines the level of real aggregate output [Figure 18.1(a)]. (See also Table 18.1 and Chart 18.1.) Real aggregate output, when multiplied by the price index P, equals aggregate money output Y,

$$P \cdot y = Y \qquad (18.4)$$

The value of P is influenced by monetary characteristics. From the equation of exchange, we know the following relation:

$$M \cdot V = P \cdot y = Y \qquad (18.5)$$

Now, if M, the quantity of money, is fixed by the monetary authorities, and if v, the rate at which money is spent, is given by stable institutional arrangements, the price level P follows from the level of aggregate output established by full employment. It follows from (18.5)

$$P = (v/y)M \qquad (18.5a)$$

Equation (18.5a) states that the price level varies directly with the velocity of money v and its quantity M, and inversely with the level of aggregate output. A different relationship between P and M is defined, given v, for each y, and this is illustrated by the straight lines v/y_i, in Figure 18.1(e), where $y_0 < y_1 < y_2$. The full-employment output and the given quantity of money establishes a point on a specific v/y_i curve and the price level can then be read from the vertical axis. For a given M, the relationship between P and y is a rectangular hyperbola, and higher hyperbolas represent greater quantities of M. The relationship between P and y for various levels of M is given by the hyperbolas MV_i in Figure 18.1(d).

$$P \cdot y = vM \qquad (18.5b),$$

where $MV_1 < MV_2 < MV_3$.

The real wage $(w/p)_1$ determined in Figure 18.1(b) and the price level determined in Figure 18.1(c), permit the money wage to be derived. For any given money wage w_i, the real wage increases as P declines. Similarly, for any given real wage, the money wage increases as the price increases. Finally, with a given price level, the real wage increases with the money wage. These relationships are illustrated in Figure 18.1(c) by rays from the origin, the slope of each representing a specific price $(P_0 > P_1 > P_2 \cdots)$. Hence, given the real wage from Figure 18.1(b) and the price level from Figure 18.1(d), the money wage w, is determined. The diagrams in Figures 18.1(a–e) are sufficient to determine the equilibrium output, its monetary value, equilibrium full employment, wages, and the price level.

The interest rate and the level of savings and investment are incidentally determined. The interest rate is assumed to be related inversely to the real money supply

$$r = r(P/M) \qquad (18.6)$$

or alternatively,

$$r = r(v/y) \qquad (18.6a).$$

Given the money supply M, the lower the price level, the lower will be the rate of interest. This follows from the desire to hold a fixed proportion of income in the form of cash.

$$1/v = M/P \cdot y \qquad (18.5c)$$

Given v, a decline in P releases idle balances, which flow into loanable-funds institutions, depressing the interest rate. The lower interest rate discourages savings, increases consumption, and encourages investment, since both savings and investment are assumed to be dependent upon the rate of interest. The increase in consumption and investment, in real terms, generates increases in y. Hence, r is inversely related to y. This relationship is shown in Figure 18.1(f). Given y, P and M, then r is uniquely determined.

Savings are related not only to the rate of interest, but also to the level of income. The higher the level of income at any given interest rate, the greater is the level of savings.

$$S = S(r, y) \tag{18.7}$$

At any income level, savings vary positively with the rate of interest. Investment is assumed to vary inversely with the rate of interest since the marginal productivity of capital, expressed as a ratio to its cost, is set equal to the cost of money expressed as the interest rate by profit-maximizing entrepreneurs. Given diminishing returns, more investment occurs only in response to lower interest rates:

$$I = i(r) \tag{18.8}$$

The relationships between the interest rate and savings and investment are shown in Figure 18.1(g).

These seven diagrams depict the relationships identified in the neo-classical macroeconomic system, and the seven dependent variables—N, y_0, P, W, r, S, and I—are determined simultaneously. In the system, the production function, the labor supply function, the savings function, the investment function, the quantity of money and the rate at which it is spent, and the interest–income function are given to us. Changes in M produce changes in Y, P, and W, but do not disturb the magnitude of the real variables. An improvement in technology or an increase in the capital stock can shift the production function to the right. Normally, unless the technological improvement is very labor saving (after Hicks),[3] the demand for labor will also increase, the real wage will rise, and real output will expand. In the absence of an increase in the money supply, prices will fall,

---

[3] A very labor-saving innovation permits the same output with greatly reduced quantities of labor. If increments of labor beyond the new amount result in substantial diminishing marginal returns, it is possible that the marginal product of labor under the new production function at the original quantity of labor will be less than under the old production function. The new marginal product curve therefore twists in its shift, part lies above the old curve when small amounts of labor are used and part lies below the old curve when larger amounts of labor are used.

but wages will normally decrease by a smaller proportion. The interest rate will fall and savings and investment will increase. Similar results can be explained for increases in the supply of labor and changes in the investment or savings functions.

Criticisms of Neoclassical Macro Theory

Keynes was a critic of received macro theory. In particular he was critical of the quantity theory of money as an explanation of the process by which price level changes, employment, and levels of real output were determined. Aggregate demand was expressed as the quantity of money M multiplied by its income velocity V, or MV. Keynes argued that this measure, while useful as a summary statement, obscures the underlying behavioral relations, and, moreover, when expressed as a part of the equation of exchange and the quantity theory of money, it is valid only as a special case.[4] In addition, he criticized received theory as dichotomizing real and monetary sectors without providing logically consistent links between the two. The former develops the theory of relative value and the latter the theory of money prices. In Figure 18.1, parts (a–c) are related to the real sector, and parts (d–g) are related to the monetary sector. Although the real and monetary sectors are related by parts (d) and (c), it is difficult to see the relationship between parts (e–g) and the remaining parts in a behavioristic sense. The Keynesian system attempts to remedy this independent dualism.

Keynes also felt that the flow of causation was incorrect in the neoclassical system. What appeared as a cause in the neoclassical system was in reality a result. Given the aggregate production function, real aggregate output was determined along with the real wage by the level of full employment, defined as the equilibrium level of employment between the demand and supply of labor. With a specified quantity of money, the amount of which is determined by the central bank, the wage and price levels are simultaneously determined, as is the rate of interest, which distributes output among investment and consumer goods. These relationships can be traced in Figure 18.1. The amount of money was viewed as a passive agent whose functions were merely to serve as a medium of exchange and as a unit of account, and the former function was accomplished by adjusting various price levels to consistency with the second function. To the contrary, Keynes noted that money was an active agent in determining the level of aggregate demand and, hence, output. Money also functions as a store of

[4] John Maynard Keynes, *The General Theory of Employment, Interest and Money* (New York: Harcourt, Brace & Co., 1936), pp. 292–299. In essence, the quantity theory of money assumes that the elasticity of output with respect to the money supply is zero, and the elasticity of price with respect to the money supply is 1.

value, and permits its holders to make judgments in a time perspective as to *when* to use it—to spend or demand goods and services with it now or in the future. The demand for money as a wealth item depends upon the holders' expectations of its future value (whether prices will rise or fall), and since it bestows utility upon its holders, interest must be paid to them to relinquish it. How much interest is paid depends (1) on the strength of the desire to hold money (the liquidity preference schedule), and (2) on its availability (the quantity of money). (In this sense, the rate of interest is viewed as a price, determined by the demand for and supply of money.) The interest rate then operates to determine the amount of savings (consumption) and investment forthcoming; i.e., aggregate demand. The level of aggregate demand then determines the level of aggregate output, via the aggregate production function. The level of aggregate output determines the level of employment. Depending upon how close this last level is to full employment, changes in wages and prices may occur. However, if full employment has not been reached, wages and prices need not increase, say, from an increase in the quantity of money. Certainly, prices need not increase in the same proportion as the money supply. The flow of causation has originated from the quantity of money, through the interest rate to aggregate demand, on to aggregate supply, and last to the level of employment—completely the reverse of the neoclassical argument.

Keynes also modified the neoclassical concept of full employment. In the neoclassical system, this is determined by the intersection of the demand for labor and the supply of labor. Keynes implicitly rejects the neoclassical concepts of the flow of causation in the demand for labor and of the effective supply of labor. Since it is the level of aggregate money demand which determines via the production function the level of aggregate output, the demand for labor can be viewed as derived from the demand for output. Output and employment are determined simultaneously from aggregate demand, and from the aggregate production function is derived the marginal product of labor—or the demand for labor in real terms. However, the level of aggregate demand may not generate full employment, in which case the marginal product of labor will be higher, given diminishing returns, than it would be under full employment. In the neoclassical system, it is the level of full employment which determines the level of output and, simultaneously, the real wage.

If aggregate demand is sufficiently deficient, it is possible that entrepreneurs will believe that no extra output beyond that determined by effective demand can be sold, in which case the marginal revenue product of labor (as distinct from the marginal physical product of labor) may suddenly go to zero for marginal increments of labor beyond that specified by the output generated by effective demand. Hence, the money demand curve for labor may have a range of complete inelasticity at the aggregate-demand-determined employment level[5] (see Figure 18.2).

The labor supply function is viewed as being perfectly elastic over a wide range of employment. The wage[6] at which much of the aggregate labor supply curve is linear is determined by such institutions as trade unions, the legal minimum wage, or employers' concept of the just wage (which ordinarily is close to the area or industry prevailing wage). This view of the labor market suggests (1) that money wages are rigid in a downward direction because of these institutional forces which are slow to change, and (2) that employment can and will expand without an increase in the money wage level (index) over a substantial range. However, there exists some level of employment which can be obtained only if wages are increased. At this point, the labor supply curve indicates a positive relationship between employment and wages, and the elasticity of employment with respect to wage changes approaches zero rapidly as employment increases. Full employment, therefore, under Keynes' perception, exists within some narrow employment range where the employment elasticity varies between infinity and zero.

Do these latter implications mean that potential workers can be attracted into the labor force at existing wage rates in contradiction to the conclusions of income–leisure analysis? If aggregate demand expands and real marginal product declines with expanded employment, implying rising prices with a constant money wage, will employment still expand? If so, does this not imply, even more perversely, that the supply curve of labor is negatively sloped in real terms? Satisfactory answers to these questions have continued to perplex and elude economists.[7] The answers are (1) the income–leisure analysis is not invalidated, and (2) the concept of the money illusion, in which additional workers accept employment at declining real wages, is not a perverse one. These answers are perfectly obvious if one recalls that Keynes is viewing the world as an imperfectly competitive one, whereas the neoclassical economists perceived it as being perfectly competitive, in which knowledge, foresight, and factor mobility are unconstrained.

---

[5] Another interpretation has been expressed by E. J. Mishan, "The Demand for Labor in a Classical and Keynesian Framework," *Journal of Political Economy*, Vol. 72 (December 1964), pp. 610–616. Mishan recognizes that money demand for labor can shift with changes in the stock of money. His supply curve for labor, however, differs from the analysis below, and he does not consider the possibility of a range of perfect inelasticity in the MRP curve.
[6] Technically, this wage should be viewed as an index of a structure of wage rates, just as the price level in aggregate terms is treated as an index.
[7] For example, the discussion by Richard Perlman, *Labor Theory* (New York: John Wiley, 1969), pp. 143–165, although plausible and involved, misses the point.

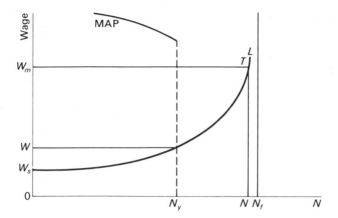

FIGURE 18.2. Money wages and the aggregate labor supply curve.

The supply curve of labor to which Keynes refers is that which is perceived by employers. It is an aggregate one, not the personal, individual one derived from income–leisure indifference curves. The individual supply curves thereby derived show the amount of labor a person would supply at a series of wages, *if* he could sell his labor in the market. Keynes' point is that the unemployed worker cannot sell his labor in the market because (1) there may not exist job vacancies at the market wage because of insufficient aggregate demand, and (2) institutionally imposed rigidities (imperfections) in the wage prohibit competitive downward bidding of wages, and make superfluous the willingness of unemployed workers to offer their services at lower wages. Now, if workers exist who are willing to offer services at lower wages, it cannot be said that their willingness contradicts income–leisure analysis. Consider Figure 18.2 where $0W_m$ represents the institutionally determined minimum wage. Note that W_m is not a single wage, but an index of wages determined in many micro labor markets. It represents a wage structure. Similarly, $0W_s$ is the subsistence wage index, and it lies substantially below $0W_m$. It is possible for some micro labor markets to pay wages close to $0W_s$, but the position of $0W_m$ indicates that these markets are a small portion of the aggregate labor market. Employers view the labor supply curve as $W_m TL$, in which employment can expand to $0N$ at wage $0W_m$. Labor force participation is governed, however, by the supply curve $W_s TL$. The supply curve to which Keynes refers is $W_m TL$; that to which the neoclassical economists referred is $W_s TL$. In Keynes, terminology, $0N_f$ refers to maximum full employment, but it is approximated by a point between $0N$ and $0N_f$. Employment is determined by aggregate demand and is indicated by $0N_y$; unemployment is given by N_yN, and these members of the labor force would be happy to accept employment in their respective micro markets at wages consistent with the index $0W_m$; in fact, substantial numbers would accept employment at wages which vary downward from $0W_m$ to $0W$ if such employment were available. But it isn't. Many of the unemployed will become discouraged and will appear to withdraw from the labor market. Hence, unemployment may appear to be less than N_yN.

Now, allow aggregate demand to expand and move $0N_y$ toward $0N$. As micro markets expand on a cross-sectional basis, unemployed workers are reabsorbed. Many if not most will move into lower-paying jobs, some of which are openings developed because of expanded production and sales, and other openings result from upgrading within and among firms, consistent with the job vacancy hypothesis. Those who are upgraded receive higher wages, although the wage index need not change. Most of those who are reemployed receive money wages in excess of that required to induce their labor force participation. If, under output expansion, diminishing returns operate and prices creep upward, there is no decline in the real wage of the newly employed, because any real wage in excess of zero represents a higher real wage than their unemployed wage (assuming no unemployment compensation). As long as the real wage received by them exceeds that necessary to bring forth their participation, they will accept employment. Similarly, for the employed who are upgraded, even though the money wages in their new positions may purchase less than before expansion, they may still be better off. For the most skilled, whose upgrading opportunities are limited, there may be a decline in the real wage, but their labor force participation is not apt to be impaired by this decline. Those of intermediate levels of skill who were unemployed because the wages of inferior jobs were insufficient to induce their labor force participation, are drawn back into the labor force as job vacancies develop at money wages, modified in real terms by price increases, consistent with the over-all index.

Consequently, what appears to be a money illusion from an aggregate perspective turns out to be something else when viewed cross-sectionally at micro levels. Employment can expand consistent with a constant aggregate wage level in the face of creeping prices as long as the institutionally determined wage exceeds that necessary to keep the unemployed in the labor force.[8] That employment can expand with rising aggregate demand at constant wages is consistent with the findings of a number of economists;

---

[8] It is possible that this wage may even rise if employment weights in higher-paying labor markets increase more than proportionately, yet in each labor market for each job, the money wage need not have changed.

discouraged persons do reenter the labor market to accept employment at existing wages when job vacancies occur.[9]

If wages are viewed as the principal source of variable costs and if they tend to be rigid as employment expansion occurs, marginal costs will fall or rise as the marginal product increases or declines.[10] In imperfectly competitive product markets in a deep recession, it is possible, but irrational in the profit-maximizing sense, for marginal costs to first fall as expansion gets underway. In such markets, prices also are apt to be rigid, so real wages are apt not to decline. As we have shown above, for numerous sectors of the labor market, real wages should actually increase through reemployment or upgrading. However, as diminishing returns set in, the rise in marginal costs should expand, feeding the recovery. As full employment is approached and bottlenecks occur in selected micro factor markets, the competition for scarce labor would begin to bid wages up.[11] The level of profits not only motivates firms to expand but it provides the funds with which to pay higher wages. Trade unions, sensitive to the profit levels of firms, exercise their increased bargaining power to extract wage concessions from employers. It is possible for the action of unions to influence the level of employment at which wages tend to rise. Depending upon the rapidity of the expansion and the timing of the expiration of major collective bargaining agreements, a case could be made for an advance or a retardation of the advance in wages as a result of union influence. Because there are major agreements expiring at frequent intervals, wage increases may be initiated somewhat earlier in the presence of strong unions than where either weak unions or no unions exist.[12] Hence, rising profits can be expected to precede rising

[9] See Jacob Mincer, "Labor Force Participation of Married Women," in *Aspects of Labor Economics*, National Bureau of Economic Research (Princeton: Princeton University Press, 1962); Clarence Long, *The Labor Force under Changing Income and Employment* (Princeton: Princeton University Press, 1958); James N. Morgan, "The Supply of Effort, the Measurement of Well-Being, and the Dynamics of Improvement," *American Economic Review*, Vol. 58 (May 1968); J. D. Mooney "Urban Poverty and Labor Force Participation Rates," *American Economic Review*, Vol. 57, No. 1 (March 1967); A. K. Severn, "Upward Labor Mobility: Opportunity or Incentive," *Quarterly Journal of Economics*, Vol. 82 (February 1968); Kenneth Strand and Thomas Dernburg, "Cyclical Variations in Civilian Labor Force Participation," *Review of Economics and Statistics*, Vol. 46 (November 1964); also see their article "Hidden Unemployment 1953–62," *American Economic Review*, Vol. 56 (March 1966).

[10] Marginal cost is defined as marginal variable cost/marginal product, or W/mp.

[11] This process is consistent with Melvin Reder's "Theory of Occupational Wage Differentials," *American Economic Review*, Vol. 65 (December 1955), pp. 833–852.

[12] See the articles by Otto Eckstein and Thomas A. Wilson "The Determination of Money Wages in American Industry," *Quarterly Journal of Economics*, Vol. 76 (August 1962), pp. 379–414; "Money Wage Determination Revisited," *Review of Economic Studies* (April 1968), pp. 133–143.

wages, with the lag being influenced by the degree of imperfections in the labor market, including union strength.

Under traditional macro theory, flexible wages and prices will bring about an equilibrium state at full employment. By way of illustration, let us suppose that the Vietnam War subsides and brings about, through a reduction in military expenditures, a temporary decline in aggregate demand. In Figure 18.1(a), this would be represented by a movement downward on the aggregate production function to y_2, and in Figure 18.1(g) by a leftward shift of the saving function to $S(y)_2$. Employment would decline, as would output, and the lowering of money wages from the competition of the unemployed would, given prices, result in a decrease in the money and real wage [see Figure 18.1(b)]. However, with no change in the money supply or velocity, and with a new, lower level of income y_2 [Figure 18.1 (e and d)], it would appear that either prices must rise or income must again increase. Yet with lower money costs and a perfectly competitive market, prices cannot rise. In fact, given the lower wages and income, a lower MV is possible. The excess money (idle balances) instead will enter the money market, security values will rise, and the interest rate, pushed upward by the leftward shift of $S(y)$, will fall. As interest rates decline, investment increases [Figure 18.1(g)]. Output, as a consequence, must expand and employment rises again to the full employment output Y_1, as the savings function shifts back to $S(y_1)$. Hence, flexible wages and prices, under competition, assure full employment.

Keynes disagreed. Expectations of future wages and prices play a role in economic behavior which the neoclassicists did not acknowledge. Because money functions also as a store of value, declining wages (and prices) lead holders of money to believe that its value (purchasing power) will increase. This is the same as saying holders of money expect wages and prices to continue to fall. It is to their advantage to hold onto money, not spend it, and velocity V therefore declines. Aggregate demand represented by MV in Figure 18.1(d) also would decline correspondingly, say, from MV_2 to MV_1. Consequently, it is possible for output to stabilize at y_2; employment to stabilize at N_2, and equilibrium unemployment of N_2N_1 to exist. Full employment is not guaranteed by flexible wages and prices.

The response to this criticism was that Keynes had ignored the "real balance effect" on the money supply of a fall in wages and prices. Because the purchasing power of money would have increased, people would hold more money than they need or are accustomed to holding. According to the cash balance hypothesis, people hold money in some fixed relationship to their needs, and this ratio is determined largely by prices and their income.[13]

[13] The necessity to explain why people have such a propensity to maintain this relationship led Milton Friedman in 1957 to develop the permanent-income hypothesis as a determinant

Not wishing to maintain such a large "real balance"—i.e., money–goods ratio—they will purchase either interest-earning securities or goods. Persons who desire more future income will buy securities, the purchase of which may in turn lower the interest rate, because the increased demand for securities raises their price and, given a fixed monetary yield, lowers their rate of return. The lower rate of interest encourages investment spending, which maintains velocity and therefore aggregate demand and employment. Even if interest rates do not fall, other persons will decrease savings directly and thereupon purchase more consumption goods. In Figure 18.1(g), a decrease in savings as a result of price reductions will tend to shift the savings function to the left; however, in Figure 18.1(d), the decline in price tends to increase income along a given MV, and this increase in income tends to shift the savings function back to the right. Even if the two shifts offset each other so that there is no change in the interest rate, the intersection of the savings and investment functions, which yields the original levels of savings and investment, will be at a higher income because consumption has risen. Either directly or indirectly, income increases as a result of price declines, which have generated a shift in the savings function. This effect of an increase in real balances has been called the *Pigou-effect*, after its proponent. Again, flexible wages and prices, via increases in real monetary balances, assure full employment.

Keynes had overlooked the possibility that consumption might be directly stimulated via the real balance effect, but he did consider the effect of a decline in prices in stimulating spending via the interest rate effect. If real balances increase and real consumption expenditures remain constant, the resulting increases in real and monetary savings need not find their way into financial intermediary institutions. Instead, the released cash balances may be hoarded. Why? Financial investors are aware that there exists a minimum level to which the rate of interest can decline. This is determined among other things by the costs of making and administering a loan. Suppose the market interest rate is in the vicinity of this minimum. This implies that bonds have high monetary value. If the interest rate were to

---

of consumer spending. According to the Friedman hypothesis, consumers expect to receive a normal amount of income over their lifespan, based on income earned in their experience of the past several years. Hence, they believe current income to be permanent. Increases in income, real or otherwise, that may occur are viewed as temporary deviations from the normal income stream, and consumption expenditures, as a consequence, are not based upon the "temporary" income. Rather, these expenditures will continue to be based on the normal stream. Only after the new income stream has been received for a few years will the recipients come to regard it as permanent and only then will they adjust their consumption expenditures upward. In the meantime, savings will have increased. See Friedman, *A Theory of the Consumption Function* (Princeton: Princeton University Press, 1957).

rise, the value of bonds would decline. Since the market rate of interest is regarded as being as low as it possibly can be, there is little probability that the value of bonds will rise through a further decline in interest rates, but there is a much greater probability that interest rates will rise and produce a proportional loss in the value of bonds. The probability that a large capital loss may occur can cause holders of wealth to prefer to keep it in liquid form—money—rather than in financial obligations. Hence, interest rates may not decline, investment expenditures are not induced to expand and may even not be maintained, velocity will not be maintained, and aggregate demand will not expand. The important conclusion, therefore, is that if the demand for money as a store of value is perfectly interest elastic, a liquidity trap will exist, and flexible wages will not automatically assure full employment.

Cannot the decay of existing capital equipment in the long run stimulate sufficient investment at the low rate of interest where the liquidity trap exists to bring about an expansion in demand and a restoration of full employment? This is true, Keynes acknowledged, but "in the long run we are all dead." In the meantime, unemployment exists. If the desire is one of lowering the rate of interest in order to stimulate investment, how much simpler it would be to increase the nominal quantity of money sufficiently to bring about the result rather than by advocating a lowering of wages and prices. The latter can only destroy confidence, whereas the former policy will maintain it. All the good results from a lower interest rate will accrue, but none of the harmful effects of a flexible wage and price policy will be experienced.

Implicit in this "long-run" argument is an answer to the "real-balance" effect on consumption expenditures. In the short run, falling wages and prices may deter current expenditures if the expectation is that the spiral will continue downward. But once the downward spiral has ended, and wages and prices have stabilized at lower levels, then the real-balance effect can operate. But if wages and prices again turn upward as expansion gets under way, the real-balance effect tends to be reversed. Only if, in the long run, the lower levels are maintained, will the real-balance effect be realized. To those interested in long-run consequences, the real-balance effect is important. In the short run, it may not be.

The Modern Macroeconomic Theory of Wages, Money, and Employment

Let us examine the modern macroeconomic system more formally. The supply of money is determined largely by the Central Bank, although the commercial banking system does have some capacity to expand the money supply. Since commercial bank income is earned from charging interest on loans, it is to these banks' advantage to increase loans as the interest rate rises; i.e., to expand bank deposit money. This can be accomplished through narrowing of extralegal reserve margins, through more effective use of excess reserves of other banks in the system, or by encouraging shifts of idle balances from demand deposits to time deposits which carry lower reserve requirements. Ordinarily, however, the elasticity of the money supply is quite low. We might represent the money supply M_s by a function

$$M_s = M(M_0, r) \tag{18.9}$$

where M_0 is the supply determined by the Central Bank and r is the interest rate. In Figure 18.3(b), the M_s is shown to have a steep positive slope.

The supply of money is held, necessarily, by persons, but for a variety of reasons. The medium-of-exchange function of money motivates persons to hold money to finance transactions or to provide for contingencies in intervals within which money income is received (that is, at intervals at which the stock of money is replenished for the individual). Money is also held as a wealth item, as a store of value, and the motive to hold money varies with the strength of a person's belief that money will rise or fall in value (prices will fall or rise, respectively). Money in this sense is hoarded for purposes of speculation if its value is expected to rise; it is dishoarded if its value is expected to fall. The greater the belief that its value will rise, the greater the rate of interest must be to induce persons to relinquish their hold on money; i.e., to exchange it for some debt asset issued by a financial institution. For example, if the price of bonds is very high (low-interest yield), speculative holders of money may expect bond prices to fall. To induce them to exchange money for bonds, the interest rate must rise. The store-of-value function of money, the most liquid of assets, imparts utility to its holder precisely because he has preference for liquidity.

The money supply, therefore, is held either for transaction purposes or for speculative purposes. As aggregate income increases, more transactions occur, and given the income velocity of money, more money is required to fulfill the medium-of-exchange function. These relations can be expressed as follows:

$$M_t = M(Y) \tag{18.10}$$

The transaction demand for money M_T depends upon the level of money income Y. This is illustrated in Figure 18.3(a).

$$M_l = M(r) \tag{18.11}$$

The liquidity preference for money depends upon expected movements in the interest rate, which are a proxy for movements in the value of money.

$$M_s = M_t + M_l. \tag{18.12}$$

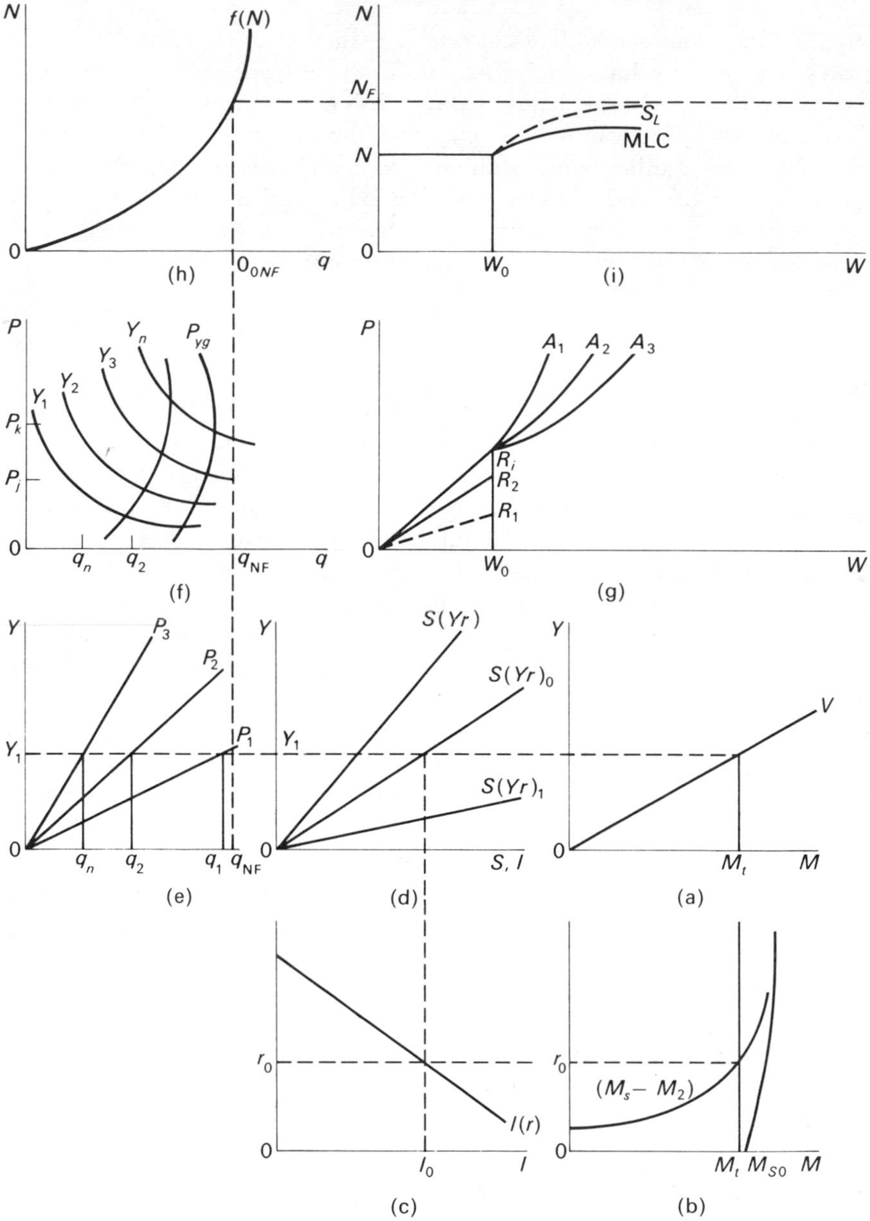

FIGURE 18.3. The modern macro model of income, wages, prices, and employment; (a) the income–money relation, (b) the money–interest relation, (c) the investment market, (d) the savings–investment–income relation, (e) the money–real income relation, (f) the price–output relation, (g) the price–wage–productivity relation, (h) the labor–output relation, (i) the labor market.

Equation (18.12) is an identity which recognizes that the supply of money must be held, but it is held for different reasons. The transaction demand for money schedule can be represented, therefore, as a function of the liquidity preference schedule,

$$M_t = M_s - M_l \tag{18.10a}$$

The liquidity trap at which M_l has an interest elasticity of infinity is at r_e in Figure 18.3(b). Given the relationship between Y and M_t in Figure 18.3(a), and given the money supply function in Figure 18.3(b), for each level of income there is an interest rate which distributes the money supply between its two uses. This interest rate influences the level of investment, as illustrated in Figure 18.1(c).

As in the neoclassical system, investment is shown to be a function of the rate of interest. However, the modern macro investment demand function is different from that of the neoclassicists. The payoff from investment decisions occurs in the future, and uncertainty reduces the expected value of the payoff. This affects the expected yields from investment. Hence, investment demand schedules can shift not only from changes in technology which affect the marginal productivity of capital, as observed by the neoclassicists, but also from shifts in investors' expectations regarding the future payoffs. These expectations are based upon beliefs about the strength or weaknesses of future markets. To distinguish the investment demand schedule from that of the neoclassicists, it is called the marginal efficiency of capital. In Figure 18.3(c), this function is represented:

$$I = I(r). \tag{18.13}$$

The level of savings depends only partially upon the rate of interest. However, savings have been found to be more dependent upon the level of income than upon the rate of interest; in fact, savings are inelastic with respect to the interest rate

$$S = S(Y, r) \tag{18.14}$$

The relationship among savings, the level of income, and the interest rate is shown in Figure 18.3(d). Savings increase with income, given any rate of interest; alternatively, at any income level, more savings occur as the interest rate rises ($r < r_0 < r_1$); or, given the level of savings, as income rises, it requires less interest to maintain that level. Figure 18.3(a–d) illustrates how these relationships simultaneously determine the equilibrium level of money income Y and the rate of interest. There is some interest rate which allocates the supply of money between transaction and speculative uses and which at the same time yields a level of investment that is consistent with a level of savings at some income level. At this income level, the transaction need for money is consistent with that amount allocated by the interest rate.

This income level represents aggregate money demand. The amount of real output which this level of aggregate demand will induce depends upon the price level. Since

$$Y = p \cdot q \tag{18.15}$$

then the greater the price level, the less is the output for any given Y. In Figure 18.3(e), the Y is related to q by a map of constant price rays, with $P_1 < P_2 < P_3 \ldots$. Given q, the Y is greater as the price ray is higher. Hence, for any given Y, a rectangular hyperbola defines the relationship between p and q. In Figure 18.3(f) a map of such hyperbolas represents varying levels of Y, and higher hyperbolas represent greater income. For any level of aggregate demand [Figure 18.3(d)], the hyperbola is specified in Figure 18.3(f), and a range of output–price relationships is determined. For ranges of output q_i, levels of employment N_i are determined in Figure 18.3(h). For each level of employment, the wage and marginal labor cost is determined from the marginal cost of labor curve MCL in Figure 18.3(j). (Labor quantity is determined from the MCL curve, where $W \leq$ MCL.) Prices are related to marginal labor cost by the following equation:[14]

$$P_i = W \frac{(1 + e_{WN})}{MP_i}$$

Because the money wage is constant up to $0N$ amount of employment, e_{WN} is zero and MCL $= W$ for amounts of labor up to this point. This relationship is illustrated in Figure 18.3(g) by $W_0 R_i A_1$. Angle $R_i 0 W_0$ varies inversely with the marginal product for each N_i along curve $0f(N)$ in Figure 18.3(h); the angle increases with declining marginal product as N_i increases. Hence, as N_i increases, $W_0 R_i$ rises, where $W_0 R_i = P_i$. For any given level of aggregate demand, a price and output level consistent with the supply function of labor can be found. For example, on a given aggregate demand hyperbola, select some price–output quantity. This output quantity is associated in Figure 18.3(h) with a given employment level N_i and MP_i; N_i is related to wages and MCL in Figure 18.3(i). The wage–price relation is given at $W_0 R_i$ in Figure 18.3(g) if employment is perfectly wage elastic at $0W_0$, and along segment RA_1 if employment is less than perfectly wage elastic. If the price at $W_0 R_i$ is not consistent with P_i in Figure 18.3(f), then the quantity must change. If, for example, $W_0 R_k > P_k$ in Figure 18.3(f),

---

[14] This is derived as follows: $P \cdot MP = MCL$; or $P = MCL/MP$. But MCL $= d\mathrm{TLC}/dN = (w + dw/dN) \cdot N$, where TLC is total labor cost. The elasticity of wages with respect to employment is $e_{wn} = dW/dN \cdot N/W$. Hence MCL $= w(1 + e_{wn})$.

then output q_j and employment N_j must expand, MP_j will decline from MP_k, and W_0R_j in Figure 18.3(g) will increase from W_0R_k toward the new, lower P_j in Figure 18.3(f).

The real wage is approximated by $MC/P = MP$. Where $MC > W$, the real wage is less than the marginal product. In Figure 18.3(g) it is also shown that shifts in the productivity of labor ($A_1 < A_2 < A_3 \cdots$) can raise the wage rate with no increase in the price level. These shifts, of course, are reflected in rightward shifts of the aggregate output curve in Figure 18.3(h).

The Phillips Relation

The Phillips relationships are between wage–unemployment or price–unemployment. The influence of sector unemployment rates—structural unemployment—on this relationship can be expressed as a measure of the relationship between changes in the money supply parameter and changes in such dependent variables as aggregate demand Y, aggregate output q, money wages W, and prices P. These measures are given as elasticity coefficients. Modern macro theory explains the influence of coefficients in micro sectors on the aggregate coefficients.[15] The aggregate production function as a summation of micro production functions implies that

$$q = \xi q_i = \xi f_i(N_i) = f(N) \tag{18.16}$$

$$q_i = f_i(N_i) \tag{18.16a}$$

Moreover, the level of aggregate demand generates, through the response of firms, aggregate output, and the magnitude of the aggregate output response depends upon how close the economy is to full employment. This closeness is, in turn, reflected in how close the micro sectors i are to full employment of the factors which they utilize. If the elasticity of factor supply approaches zero and micro markets expand cross sectionally with increases in aggregate demand, then the elasticity of output in the respective micro sectors will approach zero.

The elasticity of output in certain micro markets can approach zero before the elasticity in other micro sectors. Bottlenecks occur unevenly across the economy and constrain increases in output. In those sectors where bottlenecks do occur, wages will tend to increase through competitive bidding for scarce resources, marginal costs will rise, and prices will tend to increase. Hence, as aggregate demand increases, depending upon the extensiveness of factor scarcity in micro sectors, part of the increase will be

[15] See Chapters 20 and 21 of the *General Theory*. Also see E. S. Phelps, ed. *Microeconomic Foundations of Employment and Inflation Theory* (New York: W. W. Norton & Co., 1970).

reflected in price increases and part in output increases. Mobility of labor between sectors can mitigate the wage and price increases, so the magnitude of increases depends also upon the degree of imperfection in the labor market.[16]

When full employment is reached, increases in aggregate demand will be dissipated completely into increases in prices, and the quantity theory of money is validated, but only in this special case. If there is substantial unemployment, and if this is reflected cross sectionally in micro labor markets, increase in aggregate demand, experienced cross sectionally, can increase output in each sector with little or no increase in sector prices. In this case, almost all of the aggregate demand is reflected in output increases. Both full employment and substantial unemployment represent extreme or limiting situations, and the majority of situations lie somewhere in-between. It is this in-between situation that is reflected in the tradeoff between the wage–price increase and a reduction in unemployment. This is the "Phillips curve" relationship.

Definitions and mathematical relationships between elasticities are given in the appendix to the chapter.

The Inflationary Process

The effect on the price level from an increase in the money supply, e, depends (1) upon what happens to aggregate demand as a result of a change in the money supply e_y, and (2) what happens to the price level as a result of an increase in the aggregate demand e_p. If the liquidity preference function is perfectly interest elastic, moderate increases in the money supply will have no effect on aggregate demand. The interest rate is unaffected, and money savings and investment therefore do not change. This is the case of the liquidity trap in which increases in the money supply simply flow into hoards, and e_y is zero. At the other extreme, where the liquidity preference function is completely interest inelastic, increases in the money supply will flow into transaction balances as the desire to hold money for speculative purposes is zero, and aggregate demand will increase proportionately with changes in the money supply. The availability of funds for spending and the desire to spend (not to hoard) generates the aggregate demand increase, and e_y can be as much as 1. The former is the extreme Keynesian effect; the latter is the extreme neoclassical effect.

---

[16] For example, the supply of certain skilled trades or highly trained personnel may be exhausted as demand expands. In time, of course, the market can produce these skilled personnel, but in the short run, these factors receive economic rent as part of their wages. As this analysis suggests, the existence of the possibility of structural unemployment and its impact on prices is contained in the theoretical framework of macroeconomic theory.

The effect on the price level as a result of a change in the aggregate demand depends on e_q, the elasticity of supply, and e_w (more generally, e_m), the elasticity of wages. As aggregate demand increases, output normally expands and requires more employment. Hence e_q measures the effect on output and employment as a result of an increase in aggregate demand. At full employment e_q is zero. This means that increases in output and employment in response to an increase in aggregate demand will generate accelerating increases in wages. The effect of the increase of aggregate demand, through output and employment, on wages will be reflected in sharply rising marginal costs and will be transmitted into price increases, the magnitude of which is measured by the elasticity of prices.

For example, as e_w goes to 1 as full employment is approached, then prices will tend to increase proportionately with aggregate demand. Any increase in aggregate demand is primarily in the form of price increases rather than output since e_q goes to zero. If e_w goes to infinity before e_q goes to zero, price will increase more rapidly than aggregate demand and output will decline. This result recognizes that rising wages in response to increases in aggregate demand, assuming a given production function, can generate strong inflationary pressures. The possibility exists of sharply rising wage increases, the closer that full employment, à la Keynes, is approached.

Another view, equally acceptable, is that rising prices, as full employment is approached, generate attempts to increase output, causing competitive upward bidding of wages in order to attract the labor input necessary to increase the desired expansion in output, and these increases in wages generate, perhaps with a lag, rising costs, which with the expanded demand encourage still further price increases. The loop in Figure 18.3(f–j) can proceed in either direction, but depends upon initial increments in aggregate demand from Figure 18.3(e).

Appendix

As we have shown, changes in the money supply affect aggregate demand, aggregate demand affects aggregate supply or prices in greater or lesser degree, depending upon the level of employment. If full employment, either in micro or macro terms, exists, wages and prices (not necessarily or usually in that order) will increase. Hence, the elasticities should be related in this sequence also. First, let us define the appropriate elasticities.

1. The effect on price of a change in the quantity of money is given by

$$e = \frac{M}{p}\frac{dP}{dM} \qquad\qquad (18.17a)$$

2. The effect on aggregate demand from a change in the quantity of money is given by

$$e_y = \frac{M}{Y}\frac{dY}{dM} \tag{18.17b}$$

3. The effect on output from a change in aggregate demand is given by

$$e_q = \frac{Y}{q}\frac{dq}{dY} \tag{18.17c}$$

This can be derived from the graph in Figure 18.3(e).

4. The effect on price from a change in aggregate demand is

$$e_p = \frac{Y}{P}\frac{dP}{dY} \tag{18.17d}$$

This can be derived from the graph in Figure 18.3(f).

If we multiply e_p by e_y, we get e. Hence, the effect on price of a change in the quantity of money is transmitted in chain-link fashion through the effect of the money quantity change on demand, and the effect of the demand change on price. However, the effect of the demand change on price is transmitted through the effect of the demand change on wages and output.

5. The effect of the change in demand on money wages is:

$$e_w = \frac{Y}{w}\frac{dw}{dY} \tag{18.17e}$$

The elasticity of output, the effect of a change of aggregate demand on output, approaches zero as full employment is approached. It is easy to show that e_q goes to zero as e_N, the elasticity of employment with respect to an increase in demand, goes to zero.[17]

$$e_N = \frac{dN}{dY}\frac{Y}{N} \tag{18.17f}$$

---

[17] $e_q = Y/q \cdot dq/dY$. This approaches zero as dq/dY goes to zero. But $dq/dY = dq/dN \cdot dN/dY$, which goes to zero as dN/dY goes to zero. At full employment, by definition, $dN/dY = 0$ because $dN = 0$. Q.E.D. The definition of full employment used by Keynes has also been adopted by Robert Solow in "A Policy for Full Employment," *Industrial Relations* (October 1962), pp. 1–14. He notes, "It is probably sufficient to define full employment as that degree of unemployment at which further increments of increased demand result primarily in money wage increases rather than in increased employment," p. 3.

Define the elasticity of employment with respect to output as

$$e_{Nq} = \frac{dN}{N} \frac{q}{dq} \qquad (18.17g)$$

This is represented by the graph in Figure 18.3(h).

Therefore, $e_N = e_q \cdot e_{Nq}$ \qquad (18.17f.1)

Also, define the elasticity of wages with respect to employment as

$$e_{WN} = \frac{dw}{w} \frac{N}{dN} \qquad (18.17h)$$

This can be derived from the graph in Figure 18.3(j). Hence, alternatively,

$$e_w = e_q \cdot e_{Nq} \cdot e_{wn} \qquad (18.17e.1)$$

Now Equation (18.17e.1) implies that e_w approaches infinity as full employment is approached if e_{Nq} goes to zero more slowly than e_{WN} goes to infinity.[18] Since e_w is zero up to the employment level $0N$ in Figure 18.3(j) and goes from zero to infinity between $0N$ and $0N_F$, it is obvious from the mean value theorem that at some intermediate employment level within NN_F, e_w must equal 1.

The relationship among e_p and e_q and e_w is given by[19]

$$e_p = 1 - e_q(1 - e_w) \qquad (18.18)$$

The elasticity of price is related by this formula to the elasticity of output and the elasticity of wages, all with respect to changes in aggregate demand. As a side relation, it can be shown that the elasticities of price and output sum to 1.[20]

$$e_p + e_q = 1 \qquad (18.19)$$

---

[18] Under the type of labor supply function hypothesized by Keynes, this ordinarily will be true. This is particularly true if full employment is reached at a level where $dq/dN > 0$; i.e., where additional output could be obtained if additional labor were available. Since $e_w = e_q \cdot e_{Nq} \cdot e_{wN}$, and since $dq/dN > 0$, and therefore $dN/dq > 0$ as full employment is approached in Figure 18.3(h), it follows that e_{Nq} must go to zero more slowly than e_{wN}. This is so because dN/dw goes to zero as full employment is approached while dq/dN goes to some value greater than zero as full employment is approached. At full employment they are both zero, but only dN/dw approaches zero in the neighborhood of full employment. *Q.E.D.*

[19] For the derivation of this result, see Keynes, *General Theory, ibid.*, p. 285. A more general formula is given by $e_p = 1 - e_q(1 - e_m)$, where e_m is the elasticity of marginal labor cost with respect to aggregate demand. If MCL $= W$, then both e_m and e_w equal zero, but e_m approaches infinity more rapidly than e_w when MCL $> W$.

[20] Given that $Y = p \cdot q$. Hence $dY = p \cdot dq + q\,dP$. Dividing through by Y, we get $dY/Y = dq/q + dp/p$. Multiplying both sides by Y/dY gives us $1 = Y/q \cdot dq/dY + Y/P \cdot dP/dY$, or $1 = e_q + e_p$. *Q.E.D.*

This means that as e_q varies from 1 to zero, with expanded output and employment, e_p varies from zero to 1. If e_q goes to zero before e_w goes to 1, Equation (18.18) is consistent with Equation (18.19). As long as e_w is zero, up to $0N$ in Figure 18.3(j), Equations (18.18) and (18.19) are the same. If e_w becomes 1 before e_q becomes zero—i.e., wages increase proportionately with aggregate demand before full employment is reached —then prices will increase in equal proportion to aggregate demand and wages. If e_w rises above 1 before e_q goes to zero, then both prices and wages will rise proportionately more than aggregate demand. From Equation (18.19), the elasticity of output will become negative. Increases in aggregate demand are dissipated in increases in prices at the expense of real output. Real output declines, even though aggregate money demand increases. This result can be seen in Figure 18.3(f) along the equilibrium curve for price, aggregate demand, and real output—P_{yq}; above Y_n, real output declines and price increases as aggregate demand increases. This is viewed as a perverse condition, however, but it is a possibility. It sets the stage for runaway inflation which can have as deleterious effect on output as can deficient demand.

Discussion Questions

1. "If workers had perfect knowledge, there would be no money wage illusion, and hence there would be no range in which the supply curve of labor is perfectly elastic." Discuss the validity of this statement. Is imperfect knowledge the only feature of the labor market contributing to an elastic supply of labor?

2. "If the neoclassical economists had recognized and incorporated the imperfections in the market economy into their analysis, Keynesian analysis would be superfluous." Discuss.

3. According to the neoclassical economists, there can be no involuntary unemployment. On what assumptions is this conclusion based and why? Keynes argued that only a fool would prefer flexible wages and prices when variations in the supply of money could produce the same policy objectives. Explain.

4. Defend both of the following propositions:

    (a) Union wage policy acts as a stabilizing force in the economy.
    (b) Union wage policy acts as a destabilizing force in the economy.

5. Explain the probable effect on income, wages, prices, and employment in Figure 18.3 of the following, assuming no other changes.

    (a) A decrease in the slope of $0V$ in Figure 18.3(a).

(b) An increase in M_1 in Figure 18.3(b).
(c) A shift to the right of $I(r)$ in Figure 18.3(c).
(d) A movement from A_1 to A_2 in Figure 18.3(g).
(e) A rise in N_F in Figure 18.3(j).

6. Discuss the assertion that the Phillips relation showing the tradeoff between the rate of change of wages or prices and the rate of change of unemployment is implied in the Keynesian analysis.

7. It has been suggested that a reduction in the level of structural unemployment (imperfections in the labor market) would lessen the tradeoff between inflation and unemployment. Interpret this suggestion, using Figure 18.3.

8. (i) Prove

    (a) $E_p \cdot E_y = E$.
    (b) $E_q \to 0$ as $E_N \to 0$.
    (c) $E_p = 1 - E_q(1 - E_w)$.
    (d) $E_p + E_q = 1$.

(ii) Define these elasticities.

19

The Macro Analysis of Unemployment

Introduction

In the preceding chapter it was shown that pre-Keynesian economics viewed full employment as being determined by the intersection of the labor demand and labor supply curves, and this level of employment determined real national output, which via the quantity of money, was translated into an aggregate price level and money national income. The money level of wages was determined by the price level multiplied by the real wage, or marginal product. Keynes reversed the order of causation, noting that aggregate demand determined simultaneously the price level, the level of output, and the demand for labor. Equilibrium among the variables may or may not be at full employment. Ordinarily, aggregate demand will not be sufficient to generate full employment, so that unemployment may persist, but because of institutional rigidities—slow to change—money wages will remain relatively constant. An expansion of aggregate demand can increase output and employment, at first with no increase in money wages as the unemployed willingly accept jobs at the going rate. Prices may or may not increase, depending upon the degrees of imperfection in product and labor markets. If oligopoly in product markets is substantial and expansion in these markets absorbs initially much of the increase in demand, then shifts of the kinked demand curve, with the kink remaining at the existing price, implies shifts in the labor demand curves in which the rising marginal labor cost curve may continue to remain in the marginal revenue product gap. Prices and real wages then remain constant, oligopoly profits may increase, although

509

the share of these profits in national income may decline. Whether the share of profits as a whole declines depends upon the relative importance of oligopoly in the economy and what happens to profits in other product markets.

As aggregate demand continues to expand and full employment is approached, wages and prices then begin to rise. Increasingly, increments in demand result in smaller increments in real output and employment, and larger increments in wages and prices. The rate of change of aggregate demand and the rate of change of underlying real parameters in the economy, such as the stock of capital and labor, the level of technology, the money supply, and the psychological preference functions of consumers and investors, all influence, as we shall see, the rate of change of wages, prices, and the unemployment rate. The society is unevenly affected by rates of change of wages, profits, prices, and unemployment, and different groups in the economy have different perspectives about these rates of change. The ideal situation would be one in which wages and profits both increase, prices remain constant or decline, and the unemployment level falls to the absolute minimum, all in a context of economic growth. Experience has indicated, unfortunately, that these conditions rarely, if ever, occur simultaneously, and that society is often forced to choose between, say, inflation or unemployment, as goals. It is to a consideration of these socioeconomic objectives that we now turn.

Labor Market Implications and Changes in the Labor Force

In the previous chapter, Figure 18.3 provided us with an illustration of the process by which the level of aggregate demand was related to the level of output, employment, wage, and price. Parts (a–c) of Figure 19.1 below correspond to parts (e, f, h), respectively, in Figure 18.3. In Figure 19.1, let us examine the relationships among equilibrium aggregate demand, output, employment, unemployment, wages, and prices. Consider Y_0 in (a), which is assumed to be consistant with an equilibrium interest rate, level of savings and investment, and money supply. Equilibrium levels of output, employment, wages, and prices are, respectively, q_0, N_0, W_0, and P_0 and relevant functions are $Y_p f_0$ in (a), $P_{\bar{y}q}$ in (b), $f(N)_0$ in (c), $W_0 L_0$ in (d), and $W_0 R_0 f_0'$ in (e). Unemployment is measured as $N_0 N_{F0}$. This level of aggregate demand represents, therefore, an equilibrium at less than full employment. In the neoclassical system, the unemployed would bid down wages, product competition would force prices down, interest rates would fall, and real aggregate demand and employment would increase as Y_{pf} and $P_{\bar{y}q}$ each

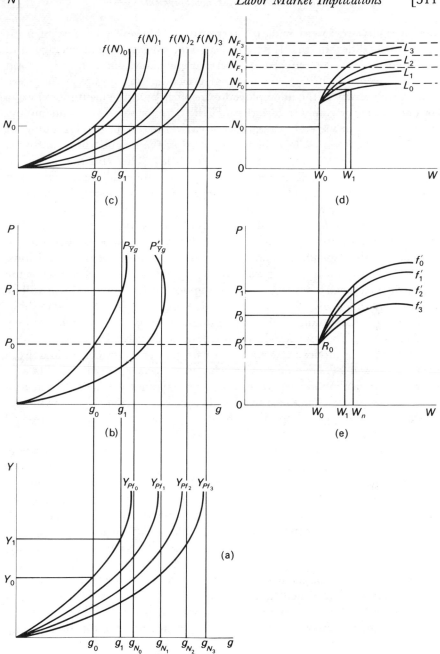

FIGURE 19.1. The modern macro model; (a) the money–real income relation, (b) the price–output relation, (c) the labor–output relation, (d) the labor market, (e) the price–wage–productivity relation.

shifted rightward in (a) and (b), respectively. However, because of institutional rigidities in the Keynesian system, wages do not change and unemployment is not reduced. Kuh has argued that the unemployed and the employed are, in fact, members of noncompeting groups because the value productivity of the unemployed is insufficient at the institutional wage for employers profitably to hire them.[1] The cure for this level of unemployment requires an increase in aggregate demand to $0Y_1$ in (a). Output q_1 at $0Y_1$ is consistent with a level of employment in the neighborhood of $0NF_0$, but wages rise to $0W_1$ and prices increase to $0P_1$. The reduction in unemployment has resulted in prices which increase proportionately more than wages or employment, and real wages decline as a consequence. The increase in aggregate demand could have resulted from monetary policy which increased the money supply, or from fiscal policy that increased private spending—consumption or investment—via tax reductions, or through increased public spending. The increase in aggregate demand could have resulted also from favorable shifts in the marginal efficiency of capital or the liquidity preference function. The resulting decline in unemployment will be viewed favorably by the previously unemployed, by those who have succeeded in upgrading their employment position via the job vacancy mechanism, by labor unions who attract new membership from the expanded employment and appear to be able to win greater wage concessions from employers, and by some employers who have received higher profits as a result of the decline in real wages and who have not yet been caught in a price–cost squeeze. On the other hand, almost everyone will deplore the rapid increase in prices, especially those who receive pensions, salaries, and other forms of fixed income.

Let us now introduce some dynamic elements into our analysis and note the consequences. Because of population growth, we can expect the labor supply function to increase over time such that more labor N will be offered at any given wage. This is reflected in the movement upward of W_0L_i, and the level of full employment increases correspondingly. This means that, given Y_1 and q_1, with succeedingly greater increases in labor supply in a given interval of time a smaller wage increase will occur within that time interval. However, given q_1, succeeding larger increases in labor supply mean succeedingly larger levels of unemployment as the full employment level increases. Consequently, price increases will be less with a growing labor force for any level of aggregate demand, but unemployment levels will be higher. Alternatively, with a given production function $f(N)_0$,

---

[1] Edwin Kuh, "A Productivity Theory of Wage Levels—An Alternative to the Phillips Curve," *Review of Economic Studies* (October 1967), p. 339. Their inferior productivity is related to inadequacies of human capital which cannot be repaired in the short run.

increases in aggregate demand over a given interval of time will be accompanied by smaller wage and price increases the more the supply of labor increases, but unemployment levels may nevertheless increase with aggregate demand. This may well characterize the phenomena of the period of the late 1950s and early 1960s when wage and price increases were mild, the labor force expanded rapidly as the postwar babies matured, and unemployment rates remained at high levels as aggregate demand increased. However, another dynamic force must be included in order to interpret this period more accurately. This is the expansion of the production function as a result of technological improvements and capital growth.

If within the interval in which aggregate demand and the labor supply are increasing so also is the real aggregate production function, then more favorable effects on prices and unemployment are possible. In Figure 19.1(c), let the production function shift rightward from $f(N)_0$ to $f(N)_i$. For any level of aggregate demand, say Y_1, less labor is required; and for any given level of labor supply, prices will be lower. As long as the amount of labor required by the shifting production function is less than the amount supplied at the institutionally fixed wage, then wages will be correspondingly lower. Stated differently, as aggregate demand increases, for any given supply function of labor, wages (as qualified) and prices will increase by less the greater the shift in the aggregate supply function. It is possible, with sufficient increases in productivity, for increases in aggregate demand to be transformed completely into output increases; employment will expand as necessary with increases in wages along a given labor supply function, say $W_0 L_0$, but the productivity of labor rises sufficiently so that no price increase is necessary. This is illustrated in Figure 19.1(e) as f_0' shifts downward towards f_3', and wages may increase to $0W_i$ with no increase in price, P_0'. If the labor force is also increasing along with increases in aggregate supply, wage increases will be less, and it is possible that either prices will decline or profits will increase, depending upon the extent of product market competition. If prices decline, even more of the increase in aggregate demand can be transformed into aggregate output, with a corresponding reduction in unemployment.

In order for the ideal situation to occur in the economy of constant prices, rising wages and profits, minimum unemployment, and economic growth, there must be a balance in the growth sectors of the economy. Aggregate money demand must grow sufficiently to utilize the growing labor force. Since the growth in aggregate supply ordinarily results in a requirement of less labor as an input for any given level of real output, the increase in aggregate demand must be sufficient to compensate for this employment-depressing condition. Hence, aggregate demand must be growing at a rate at least equal to the sum of the growth rates of aggregate output supply and aggregate labor supply. Expansion toward full employment across dynamically shifting labor supply curves raises money wages, but shifts in marginal productivity functions may be sufficient to offset the increases in marginal labor costs so that no price increases are necessary.[2] If aggregate demand expands less rapidly in a given time interval than this necessary rate, then unemployment results. If aggregate demand expands more rapidly, then price increases result. Ordinarily, the expansion of labor supply can be controlled only slightly; it is a result of fixed institutional and past historical forces. Some control can be exercised over the shift in the aggregate supply function, but it is obvious that successful price–unemployment experience depends primarily upon policies influencing aggregate demand.

Changes in educational policy which encourage young people to extend their years of schooling, or in pension programs which lower the age of retirement, or in female labor force participation rates may affect the shift in the labor supply function. The former two should retard its increase, the latter should advance it. Other institutional changes can affect the slope of the curve as it approaches full employment, and hence the elasticity of wages with respect to employment. Manpower policies to reduce imperfections in the labor market would tend to increase dN/dw and reduce dw/dN. Such programs as a system of national job exchanges to disseminate knowledge of vacancies more fully and to facilitate interregional placements, or retraining programs for displaced workers with obsolete skills, or subsidized moving and relocation allowances to facilitate movement from labor surplus to labor shortage areas, all would increase the elasticity of labor supply in micro markets. As a result, bottlenecks in micro markets would be reduced and wages need not rise as much in order to obtain on either the micro or macro level the required labor. On the other hand, the existence of trade unions can lower dN/dw or increase dw/dN through the establishment of barriers to entry to occupations with excess demand. Escalator clauses in labor agreements which adjust wages quarterly to changes in the consumer price index will tend to shift the institutional wage to the right for any given amount of labor demanded. Similarly, trade unions' political pressure to raise the legal minimum wage will tend to increase the institutional wage.

To the extent that wages increase by more or by less with a given increase in real output, prices will tend to rise by more or less. Hence, the more inelastic—the smaller the coefficient of e_{wn}—is the supply of labor, the greater will be the price increase, and the more will a given increase in aggregate demand be reflected in price rather than output gains. Trade unions may also affect the magnitude of price increases by their policies

---

[2] Given $P = \text{MLC}/f_i'$. If $\Delta\text{MLC} = \Delta f_i'$, then P remains constant. Recall that f_i' is MP, or the real wage.

toward productivity improvements. Barriers to the introduction of technological change or make-work rules may impede the rightward shift of the production function in Figure 19.1(c), the downward shift of the marginal production function in Figure 19.1(e), and hence the magnitude of the price change with any given wage change. Although productivity improvements may yield a favorable impact on prices for the over-all economy, they can be, at the micro level, extremely deleterious to the welfare of the union and its members. Technological unemployment in one sense is even more damaging than cyclical unemployment. Subsequent increases in demand need not restore the lost job opportunities of those workers experiencing technological unemployment. However, expanding demand can enlarge employment opportunities if the latter has been the source of unemployment. In an industry which experiences a more rapid rate of labor-saving innovations than expansion of product demand, employment will decline. As an institution concerned with survival, the prospect of declining membership is indeed unpalatable to a union. Hence, resistance to technological change makes sense to the isolated union, although it may not be in the interests of society in general.

Can this model allow us to identify the cause of inflation as being demand–pull or wage–push? If the rate of increase in aggregate demand exceeds the rate of growth in productivity and the labor force, is not this unambiguously demand–pull? Our answer might be yes if we could be sure that excessive demand occurred in the absence of any barriers to productivity increases or labor mobility. Alternatively, given the rate of shift of our supply functions, does not wage–push inflation occur when trade union policy leads to an increase in the elasticity of wages with respect to employment or a shift in the institutional wage level? Again, to answer this, we need to know what is happening to aggregate demand. Our answer might be yes if we could determine that these changes were independent of pressures of excess demand on microsectors of the economy which themselves could generate these changes.

Unemployment

The magnitude of unemployment depends upon its definition. This definition varies among countries. It also varies among economists, a difference which has led to unnecessary arguments over semantics rather than substance. To examine how changes in definitions can affect magnitudes, let us consider the U.S. Census definition and how it has changed in recent years.

Prior to 1940, the Census defined the labor force, which consists of the employed and unemployed, as being composed of persons in the non-institutional population of age ten years or over. From 1940 to 1967, the age criterion was changed to 14 years or over, and since 1967, it has applied only to persons 16 years or more. The shift from the farm and family farm employment to the city, and the upgrading in educational levels has brought about this change in definition. Some of those in the labor force are in the armed forces; the remainder are in the civilian labor force. Those who are not in the labor force are in institutions—schools, prisons, hospitals—are too old to work, are disabled, are housewives, or are not looking for work because they believe no work exists. This last group includes seasonal workers who are employed only during certain periods of the year. It also includes discouraged, but prospective employees who estimate the cost of search to exceed the benefits derived from continuing the search for a position.[3] Ordinarily, the number of discouraged persons excluded from the labor force definition because they are not actively in the labor market varies directly with the unemployment rate. Bowen and Finegan, for example, have found that a 1% increase in unemployment leads to more than a 1% decrease in the participation of married women, to a 1.5% decrease in men 65 years or older, and for male teenagers, a 1.9% decrease.[4] (See Chart 19.1 and Table 19.1).

To be counted as employed, one must be at work at least for one hour in the survey week if he receives a wage; if he is engaged in a family enterprise, he must work at least 15 hours during the week. If persons were not at work, but had a job, but for a variety of acceptable reasons they were not on the job at the time of the survey, they are counted as employed. Prior to 1967, workers who were on strike, were looking elsewhere for jobs (even though they had not quit their current job), or were off work because of weather conditions, were considered to be unemployed. Now the unemployed are those who were currently available for work, were looking for work, *and* did not work. Previously to 1967, the availability criterion was not applied to the current search but only to the time at which employment was desired. College seniors interviewing on-campus recruiters for postgraduation employment are no longer considered as being unemployed. The unemployed also includes those persons who have not looked for work because they are on temporary layoffs or, because they have a job scheduled to begin within 30 days. Otherwise, if they have not actively sought a position within the past four weeks, they are not counted as being in the labor force. Prior to

[3] This may be owing to low probability of finding a job combined with low earning prospects. See Lowell E. Galloway, "A Note on the Incidence of Hidden Unemployment in the United States," *Western Economic Journal*, Vol. 1, No. 1 (March 1969), pp. 71–83. Estimates of the number of discouraged workers were 700,000 in 1967 and 1968, declining to 600,000 in 1969. The number of these workers is about 20 to 25% of those who are officially listed as unemployed. See Paul O. Flamm and Paul M. Schwab, "Employment and Unemployment Developments in 1969," *Monthly Labor Review* (February 1970), p. 53.

[4] William G. Bowen and T. Aldrich Finegan, *The Economics of Labor Force Participation* (Princeton: Princeton University Press, 1969), pp. 180, 341, 431–436.

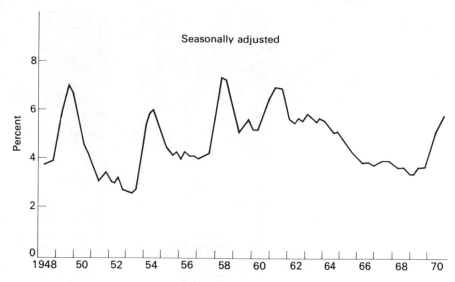

CHART 19.1. Unemployment rate of civilian labor force (data relate to persons 16 years of age and over).

Source: Department of Labor, *Economic Report of the President*, 1971, p. 38.

1967, failure of the unemployed to look for work because they believed no work to exist did not automatically exclude them from the labor force.

This view of the labor force is based upon the belief that voluntary participation in the market is an appropriate criterion. Those who wish employment sufficiently to "look for it" and are capable of performance at the time of their search are "in" the market; those whose preference for employment is not sufficiently strong to motivate an active search are not counted as in the market. Certain excuses for failure to undertake an active search are acceptable as reasonable—temporary layoff, job in the near future; other excuses are not. Refusal to accept a proffered job is not sufficient to repudiate evidence of availability, capability, and active search. The proffered position must be compatible with the applicant's work experience and/or training, regardless of whether that experience and training is currently relevant. Whether this person is any less in the labor market than the discouraged worker may be an academic question, but it is not a definitional one. The definition states that the worker with obsolete skills to sell is more in the labor market if he is actively trying to sell them.

A more extreme view of the labor force is that which is possible in a regimented society. Manpower utilization rates in the United States during World War II were significantly higher than in normal peacetimes. Rates

TABLE 19.1
PERCENT DISTRIBUTION OF THE TOTAL LABOR FORCE, BY COLOR, SEX, AND AGE, 1960 to 1980

(Numbers in thousands)

Sex and age	1960			1965			1970			1975			1980		
	Total	White	Non-White	Total	White	Non-White	Total	White	Non-White	Total	White	Non-White	Total	White	Non-White
Both Sexes															
16 years and over															
Number	72,104	64,210	7,894	77,177	68,627	8,551	84,617	75,055	9,560	92,183	81,436	10,746	99,942	87,872	12,072
Percent	100.0	100.0	100.0	100.0	100.0	100.0	100.0	100.0	100.0	100.0	100.0	100.0	100.0	100.0	100.0
16 to 24 years	17.6	17.5	18.8	20.3	20.1	21.5	22.4	22.1	24.6	22.8	22.4	26.1	22.6	22.1	26.2
25 to 44 years	44.2	43.8	47.7	41.7	41.3	45.4	39.5	39.1	42.7	40.5	40.2	43.0	43.4	43.1	45.6
45 to 64 years	33.5	33.9	30.1	33.9	34.4	29.9	34.3	34.9	29.9	33.0	33.7	28.3	30.6	31.2	25.9
65 years and over	4.7	4.8	3.4	4.0	4.1	3.1	3.8	3.9	2.8	3.6	3.7	2.5	3.4	3.6	2.3

Male

16 years and over

Number	48,933	44,119	4,814	50,946	45,862	5,084	54,958	49,263	5,695	59,355	52,946	6,409	64,063	56,822	7,241
Percent	100.0	100.0	100.0	100.0	100.0	100.0	100.0	100.0	100.0	100.0	100.0	100.0	100.0	100.0	100.0
16 to 24 years	16.6	16.3	19.3	19.2	18.8	22.4	21.4	20.9	25.0	21.9	21.4	26.3	21.7	21.1	26.1
25 to 44 years	45.8	45.6	47.2	43.5	43.4	44.8	41.8	41.7	43.2	43.2	43.1	44.3	46.3	46.2	47.5
45 to 64 years	32.7	33.1	29.7	33.2	33.6	29.5	33.0	33.4	28.8	31.3	31.9	26.8	28.7	29.3	24.1
65 years and over	5.0	5.1	3.8	4.2	4.3	3.4	3.8	3.9	3.0	3.5	3.6	2.7	3.3	3.4	2.3

Female

16 years and over

Number	23,171	20,091	3,080	26,232	22,765	3,467	29,657	25,792	3,865	32,827	28,490	4,337	35,881	31,050	4,831
Percent	100.0	100.0	100.0	100.0	100.0	100.0	100.0	100.0	100.0	100.0	100.0	100.0	100.0	100.0	100.0
16 to 24 years	19.9	20.2	17.9	22.5	22.8	20.2	24.2	24.2	24.0	24.6	24.4	25.9	24.2	23.8	26.3
25 to 44 years	40.9	39.8	48.6	38.4	37.1	46.3	35.2	34.2	41.9	35.7	34.8	41.0	38.3	37.6	42.8
45 to 64 years	35.0	35.7	30.8	35.5	36.2	30.7	36.9	37.7	31.5	36.1	36.9	30.7	33.8	34.7	28.6
65 years and over	4.1	4.3	2.7	3.7	3.9	2.8	3.7	3.9	2.5	3.7	3.9	2.4	3.7	4.0	2.3

Source: *Manpower Report of the President, 1969*, p. 233.

in the Soviet Union tend to be higher than in the United States, and indeed the Soviet perspective on labor force participation tends to regard work as a universal duty of Soviet adults rather than as an elective activity.[5] Consequently, all those who are capable of work are considered to be part of the "normal" labor force. The difference between those who are employed for 35 hours a week or more and this group is much larger than the difference between the U.S. Census definition of the labor force and those who are employed. Estimates by the Soviets of the unemployed in the United States includes the estimate by the Census, plus those seasonal workers who currently are not in the labor force, the "hidden" unemployed, those with a job but not working, those partially employed for less than 35 hours a week, and students who have had some work experience during the year. These estimates indicate that unemployment in the United States is from three to five times higher than that reported.[6] No doubt, this estimate reflects to some extent Soviet propaganda about the relative inefficiency of the United States economy in maintaining full employment, but there are grains of truth in the estimates.

The unemployment rate is taken as a ratio of the unemployment count to the civilian labor force. If there are errors in the estimate of the unemployed, then this rate will be too high or too low as the errors are positive or negative. To the extent that hidden unemployment exists, the errors will be negative; those discouraged workers who have withdrawn from the labor force are identified as the "secondary" labor force, or the "labor reserve." The theoretical concept of the unemployed ordinarily includes this labor reserve, even though it is omitted from the statistical measure. Similarly, the theoretical concept of full employment differs from the Census definition of the labor force.

The neoclassical view of full employment, as we have noted, is that level of employment at which all persons who wish to work for a given real wage can find jobs at that real wage. Persons who would be willing to enter the labor market and work at higher real wages are not considered to be unemployed. As we have seen, such workers may be counted among the unemployed by the Census definition. If they are willing to accept real wages at or below the equilibrium wage but cannot find employment under these conditions, then they are involuntarily unemployed. However, this condition was viewed at worst as a temporary one. Under the neoclassical view, full employment is determined by labor market supply and demand

---

[5] Michael J. Lavelle, "Soviet Views on American Unemployment, 1953–63," *Kyklos*, Vol. 21, No. 2, 1968, pp. 313–325. Lavelle notes that the Soviet Union is primarily concerned with maximizing output, and hence tends to operate with a "forced draft" concept of the labor force.

[6] *Ibid.*, pp. 316–317.

forces. It recognizes that employment expansion is possible, given supply, under changes in demand that increase the real wage; or under changes in supply, given demand, that decrease the real wage.

The modern macro concept of full employment is one based almost entirely on labor supply conditions. Essentially, full employment is defined as a level in which further increases in labor demand result primarily in increases in wages rather than employment.[7] Keynes believed that expansion of employment up to the full-employment level at the existing institutional money wage level was a possibility, after which wages would increase with extreme rapidity. This view of the labor supply function perceives a right angle at full employment. If the marginal labor cost function is taken as the relevant labor supply function, this perception is perhaps more closely approximated. (See Figure 18.2 in the preceding chapter.) From either perspective, the range of employment over which the elasticity of the supply function (e_{wN}) goes from zero to infinity is relatively small. This is illustrated in Figure 19.2, which is an adaptation of Figure 19.1(d). There appears, therefore, to be some tradeoff between the level of unemployment and the magnitude of wage increases.

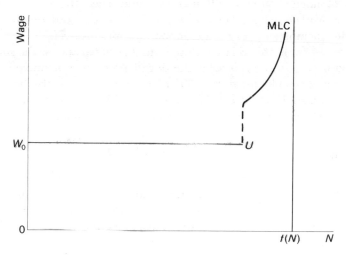

FIGURE 19.2. The aggregate MLC curve.

[7] In addition to Keynes, this definition, for example, has been used by Robert M. Solow in "A Policy for Full Employment," *Industrial Relations*, October 1962, p. 3. Richard Lipsey has used a definition very similar to this in "The Relationship between Unemployment and the Rate of Change of Money Wage Rates in the United Kingdom, 1862–1957: A Further Analysis," *Economica* (February 1960), pp. 14–15.

A variation in the concept of full employment recognizes that the demand for labor in terms of the sum of the employed plus the number of job vacancies may be, in fact, equal to the sum of the employed and the unemployed. Hence, if job vacancies equal in number the unemployed, full employment is said to exist.[8] The implication is, of course, that jobs exist for all those who are seeking them and that it is only a matter of time until anyone who is unemployed in such a labor market will be able to obtain employment. This concept also recognizes that the labor market is continuously in a state of flux as workers die, retire, fall ill, change jobs, and enter or reenter the job market. Consequently, vacancies are continuously developing. Particularly, as workers leave one job for another, there is a normal period of time which elapses as the search process takes place. Similarly, as workers enter the labor force, either for the first time or after a period of interruption, they will be classified as unemployed until their search is fruitful. Viewed in this manner, unemployment has the character of being a pool or reservoir, the level of which is governed by the inflow into the pool of those who begin their search for work and the outflow of those who successfully find vacancies. The fewer the vacancies and the larger the number of applicants, the longer is the search process. The average duration of unemployment will increase, and since the rate of outflow declines as workers who otherwise would have found jobs remain unemployed, the unemployment rate thereupon increases. Conversely, the smaller the number of applicants relative to the number of vacancies, the shorter is the period of search, the shorter is the duration of unemployment, and the lower is the unemployment rate. The minimum to which the average duration of unemployment can be reduced, and hence the minimum level of unemployment, is identified as frictional unemployment.

The Labor Pool and Job Vacancies

It may or may not be true that this minimum level of unemployment is established when the number unemployed is equal to the number of vacancies. This may be a necessary condition for frictional unemployment to exist, but imperfections in the labor market can prevent it from being a sufficient condition.

Reder has expanded on his theory of occupational wage differentials to develop a theory of unemployment.[9] The ability of an unemployed worker to find employment depends upon the hiring standards established by an

[8] See Solow, *ibid.*, p. 2. This definition is not satisfactory to all economists. For a contrary view, see Richard Perlman, *Labor Theory* (New York: John Wiley, 1969), pp. 167–196.
[9] Melvin Reder, "Wage Structure and Structural Unemployment," *Review of Economic Studies*, Vol. 31 (October 1964), pp. 309–322.

employer. As demand expands and employment increases, vacancies develop. Employers may delay in filling these vacancies in an attempt to attract higher-quality labor. If the supply of labor at a given quality in a particular labor market sector is scarce, the employer has two options: (1) either to raise wages, or (2) to lower hiring standards. Rapid increases in marginal labor costs as wages rise can persuade an employer to lower hiring standards instead. This can be accomplished by upgrading his existing labor force or through accepting job applications from prospective employees whose training and/or experience are consistent with a related job lower in the hierarchy. As a result, the vacancy "waiting" period attributed to the employer declines, and positions are filled. This waiting period can sometimes be negative, as when an employer hedges by retaining skilled members of his labor force when demand for his product declines because he anticipates difficulty in attracting workers of equal quality should demand increase again in the relatively near future.[10] The willingness of employers to accept reduced quality may be impaired by union apprenticeship standards, but the dilution effect appears to be general in varying degree throughout the western world. Moreover, this view of the labor market in its more limited sense suggests that employment opportunities open up for new entrants at the bottom of the occupational hierarchy. Those with the lowest levels of skill must wait in the "vestibule" for employment opportunities. They enter at the lowest rung of the occupational ladder and must wait their turn for further advancement opportunities through the vacancy mechanism. When demand declines, the unskilled are the first to be laid off, as they are bumped downward by the more skilled. When demand expands, they are also the last to be hired. Hence, according to this theory the unskilled incur more unemployment and also of longer duration.

This approach is also consistent with the queue theory of unemployment. Job applicants are viewed as being ranked by prospective employers in order of quality. As employment opportunities expand, the queues become shorter and applicants are accepted by employers more quickly. The unemployment duration becomes shorter and unemployment declines. Queues become longer and progression proceeds more slowly when demand declines; unemployment thereupon increases.

Reder also notes two offsetting effects on unemployment from changing demand: (1) a frictional effect, and (2) a ladder effect. Because the unskilled

---

[10] *Ibid.*, p. 310. Such hedging by employers no doubt explains the lack of a close relationship in the short run between employment and output found by George Wilson, "The Relationship Between Output and Employment," *Review of Economics and Statistics*, Vol. 42 (February 1960), pp. 37–43. The relationship is more clearly established in intervals as long as a year. Wilson's data were quarterly.

TABLE 19.2
SELECTED UNEMPLOYMENT RATES, 1961–1970
[Percent] [a]

Group of Workers	1961–1965 Average	1966	1967	1968	1969	1970
All workers	5.5	3.8	3.8	3.6	3.5	4.9
Sex and age:						
Both sexes 16–19 years	15.9	12.8	12.8	12.7	12.2	15.3
Men 20 years and over	4.4	2.5	2.3	2.2	2.1	3.5
Women 20 years and over	5.4	3.8	4.2	3.8	3.7	4.8
Race:						
White	4.9	3.4	3.4	3.2	3.1	4.5
Black and other races	10.4	7.3	7.4	6.7	6.4	8.2
Selected groups:						
White-collar workers	2.8	2.0	2.2	2.0	2.1	2.8
Blue-collar workers	7.1	4.2	4.4	4.1	3.9	6.2
Craftsmen and foremen	4.8	2.8	2.5	2.4	2.2	3.8
Operatives	7.3	4.3	5.0	4.5	4.4	7.1
Nonfarm laborers	11.8	7.4	7.6	7.2	6.7	9.5
Private wage and salary workers in nonagricultural industries	5.9	3.8	3.9	3.6	3.5	5.2
Construction	12.8	8.1	7.4	6.9	6.0	9.7
Manufacturing	5.6	3.2	3.7	3.3	3.3	5.6

[a] **Number of unemployed in each group as percent of civilian labor force in that group.**
Source: Department of Labor. *Economic Report of the President,
1971*, p. 40.

bear more of the brunt of unemployment and since it is more difficult for members of this group to find jobs, frictional unemployment tends to be greater among them. Any change in demand that was felt cross sectionally across skill levels in changing absolute employment requirements would have less proportional effect on the unemployment rate of the unskilled. This is owing to the larger base value of unemployment among the unskilled. For example, consider the following distribution of employment and unemployment by skill level.

Level of Skill	Level of Employment	Level of Unemployment		New Unemployment	
		No.	%	No.	%
Skilled	1.98 mil	0.02 mil	1	0.04	1.98
Semiskilled	9.60 mil	0.40 mil	4	0.42	4.12
Unskilled	7.2 mil	0.8 mil	10	0.82	10.22

The same absolute increase across skill levels raised unemployment by 98% for the skilled group, 30% for the semiskilled, and only 22% for the unskilled. The ladder effect, on the other hand—because those with lower skills are bumped off jobs by those with higher skills—tends to increase unemployment rates inversely with the level of skill. Frictional effects may tend to dominate when demand changes are relatively small, but ladder effects may tend to dominate when demand changes are large. If the two effects offset one another, there should be no change in the skill distribution of unemployment. If unemployment is increasing or decreasing slowly, the unskilled proportion may decline or increase respectively, through the frictional effect. A rapid increase or decrease in unemployment should alter substantially the proportion of unskilled among the unemployed.

This theory of unemployment therefore explains the changing composition of unemployment and indicates why unskilled rates are higher than skilled rates. It indicates also why frictional unemployment—not to be confused with the frictional effect—rises with declining aggregate demand. If the process of finding jobs takes time, and the amount of time is related to the number of vacancies compared with the number of job seekers, then the duration and level of unemployment rise with declining vacancies. Just as molecular friction rises as gases are compressed, so also does frictional unemployment rise as applicants are compressed by fewer job vacancies. To reduce frictional unemployment to some minimum level requires as a cure an increase in the number of vacancies, and this in turn requires an increase in aggregate demand. This view regards deficient demand as the principal cause of unemployment.

Structural Unemployment

Another group of economists has put forth the thesis that structural imbalances have developed within the economy between the composition of the demand for labor and its supply. Changes in consumer preferences have altered the structure of demand; as a result, the mix of growing and declining industries has changed. Declining industries generating primary employment and centered in geographical locations have produced regional unemployment. Skills have become obsolete as vacancies in expanding industries require different educational and on-the-job experiences from those of declining industries. The shift of low-skilled uneducated minority groups to an urban environment, and the flight of industry to the suburbs have resulted in accessibility barriers. The relative decline in the number of unskilled jobs in general has compounded the employment problems of these minority groups. Hence, regional, industrial, and occupational shifts in the demand for labor have made it more difficult to match job vacancies with the skills of the unemployed, have lengthened the search process, have introduced new barriers to movement, and in general have increased the level of unemployment and its duration. In fact, proponents of the structuralist hypothesis cite as evidence the increase in the proportion of the unemployed who have experienced "long-term" unemployment of over 26 weeks. (See Chart 19.2.)

It is difficult to see how this concept of unemployment differs from "frictional" unemployment. In fact, it has been argued that structural unemployment represents that increase in unemployment which is owing to changing forces in the economy impairing the efficiency of the operation of a competitive labor market—an increase in the degree of imperfection in the labor market. It is not due to deficient aggregate demand. To the extent that structural unemployment develops in an economy, then for any given level of aggregate demand, frictional unemployment will vary with the degree of structural imbalance. As structural imbalance grows, the level of frictional unemployment grows. Changes in structural unemployment can be measured, therefore, by observing the level of unemployment at a given level of aggregate demand and subtracting from it that level of unemployment which would have existed when aggregate demand was at that level during some earlier period. (Implicit, of course, is the assumption that the labor force is unchanged.) If this earlier level of unemployment is interpreted as "normal" frictional unemployment, then total unemployment at the later date is the sum of frictional and structural forces. The distinction, however, does not appear to be valid, since in a dynamic economy, the ease or difficulty of adjusting to changing labor market requirements is in part a function of how rapidly these changes are occurring. It is questionable if normal frictional unemployment exists, and if this is true the distinction becomes meaningless.

One economist has sought to identify structural unemployment as "the number of unemployed minus the unemployed who can fill vacancies," whereas frictional unemployment consists of those who are able to fill

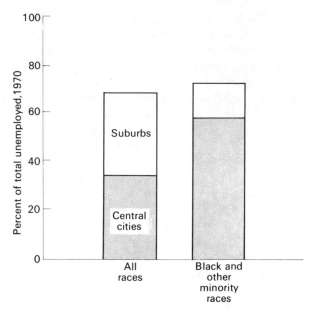

CHART 19.2. Metropolitan areas contain more than two-thirds of the nation's unemployed and nearly three-fourths of the Black unemployed.

Source: Department of Labor, *Manpower Report of the President*, 1971, p. 87.

vacancies.[11] If all those who are unemployed can find vacancies for which they are qualified, then all of unemployment is frictional. If all the unemployed have no qualifications which meet the standards set by the vacancies, then all unemployment is structural. If the qualified unemployed exceed the number of vacancies, then unemployment is presumably owing to deficient demand.

If Reder's theory of unemployment is valid, then the above set of definitions is not relevant. First, according to Reder the standards established for vacancies are variable, falling in periods of excess labor demand and rising during periods of excess labor supply. Therefore, during periods of deficient aggregate demand, we would expect a larger proportion of the unemployed to fail to meet the job standards of vacancies. Second, during periods of deficient demand, the unskilled would bear disproportionately the burden of unemployment. In periods of stable or rising demand, as general upgrading occurs, we would expect a large number of vacancies to be filled by the employed who advance up the hierarchy of jobs. Consequently, only

[11] Perlman, *op. cit.*, p. 168.

those vacancies at the bottom of the ladder would be relevant for the less skilled unemployed. A sizable proportion of the unemployed would be unable to meet the qualifications of the vacancies, but this would not mean that structural unemployment had increased. As Reder has noted, "When the demand for labor at higher rungs falls below the level at which the current rate of ladder ascent can be maintained, unemployed workers begin to pile up in the vestibule leading to the ladder."[12] Furthermore, he notes that evidence of structural imbalance could only be observed by "comparing two or more periods of varying unemployment percentages," never from one period alone.

A trial-and-error test has been suggested for discovering the amount of frictional and structural unemployment in the economy.[13] However, this test implicitly assumes (1) a relationship between wage and price changes, (2) a relationship between wage changes and the unemployment rate, and (3) a social preference function for competing combinations of price increases and unemployment rates. Assume from Figures 19.1 and 19.2 that we are able to derive a price–unemployment equilibrium curve which associates changes in the price level with varying levels of unemployment. This curve represents the trade-off possibilities between inflation and unemployment with which an economy is confronted. This curve is represented by the P_1U_1 curves in Figure 19.3. Assume also that the members in the economy have preference functions for combinations of the two, represented by the set of indifference curves p_1u_1 in Figure 19.3, where more preferred combinations lie on curves approaching the southwest origin. Assume that there is no inflation and the unemployment level is at $0X_2$. Increases in aggregate demand under the existing economic structure can lead to a desired inflation–unemployment trade-off position at point a, with X_3a amount of inflation and $0X_3$ amount of unemployment. Deficient demand unemployment is therefore measured by X_3X_2. Two types of policies may restructure the economy and reduce unemployment by shifting the price–unemployment trade-off curve to the left. (1) An industry relocation policy could assist industries in sectors of excess labor demand to move to sectors with deficient labor demands through a program of subsidies, tax concessions, or reserve investment funds.[14] Such a policy would tend to bring jobs to workers and

---

[12] Melvin Reder, "Wage Structure and Structural Unemployment," *op. cit.*, p. 319.

[13] R. G. Lipsey, "Structural and Deficient-Demand Unemployment Reconsidered," in A. M. Ross, ed., *Employment Policy and the Labor Market* (Berkeley: University of California Press, 1965), pp. 210–218, 243–355, reprinted in B. J. McCormick and E. Owen Smith, eds., *The Labor Market* (Baltimore: Penguin Books, 1968), pp. 245–265.

[14] See Paul Burrows, "Manpower Policy and the Structure of Unemployment in Britain," *Scottish Journal of Political Economy*, Vol. 15, No. 1 (February 1968), pp. 77–83 for a discussion of policy to accomplish a reorientation of sector demand.

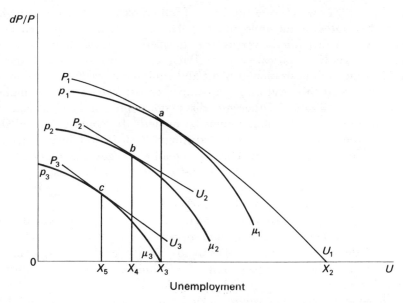

FIGURE 19.3. Types of unemployment and social inflation–unemployment preference functions.

reduce imbalances among geographic labor markets. (2) Manpower policies could retrain workers in skills in scarce supply, subsidize employers for on-the-job training, reduce the vacancy-waiting period described by Reder, and subsidize workers in relocating to areas of excess labor demand. To the extent that these policies yield social and economic benefits at least equal to their costs, they could continue to be pursued at no net cost to society. Assume that this point is reached at b, and unemployment is now at $0X_4$. The X_4X_3 measures the amount of structural unemployment that can be removed by policies other than those associated with changes in aggregate demand. Frictional unemployment is measured as a residual by $0X_4$.[15]

These policies to improve the structural balance of the economy not only reduce unemployment, but they also reduce the rate of inflation. The first prescription, however, calls for the removal of as much unemployment as the public's tolerance for inflation will permit by expansion of aggregate demand. Thereafter, the society could experiment with ways to reduce further the remaining unemployment. Initially, the trial-and-error technique calls for the society to act as though deficient demand is the cause of unemployment. It is possible that structural unemployment may have a secular

[15] Lipsey, "Structural and Deficient Demand Unemployment," *op. cit.*, pp. 246–250.

trend upward, in which case the level of full employment occurs at higher and higher rates of unemployment.[16] However, tests of the structural unemployment hypothesis versus the deficient demand hypothesis are difficult to verify empirically. Ordinarily, tests must be undertaken at levels in which full utilization of plant and equipment occur and the unemployment rate at this level must be compared with rates at earlier periods of full capital utilization. Otherwise, distinctions between deficient demand and structural unemployment cannot be made.[17] It should be added that there is nothing in this analysis to distinguish structural unemployment from frictional unemployment. Policies to reallocate aggregate demand on a sector basis to areas of surplus labor and to retrain and reallocate surplus labor to areas of surplus demand amount to a prescription of how to reduce frictions in the operation of a labor market.

Although Lipsey suggested that structural unemployment would trend upward, the evidence does not seem to support this hypothesis. Kalachek has examined the corollary that changes in structural unemployment would be reflected in higher unemployment rates among vulnerable industries employing blue-collar workers. He found for the period 1958–1960 lower unemployment rates than would have been predicted by the 1947–1957 experience of these industries.[18] A geographical and industrial corollary of the structural hypothesis is that more changes occur in unemployment in certain sectors than in others so that the correlation of unemployment among sectors is reduced. Galloway found that for the period 1958–1960 correlation coefficients for sectors in the United States were larger than for the 1948–1956 period,[19] and Zaidi using Galloway's technique, arrived at similar results for the United States and Canada in comparing the period 1958–1962 with that of 1954–1957.[20] Both Zaidi and Galloway have concluded that the structural hypothesis was not supported. R. A. Gordon examined the incidence of unemployment among groups who ordinarily would be expected to bear the burden of structural unemployment most heavily—non-Whites, teen-agers, and other unskilled workers—and found that their unemployment rates relative to their labor force participation had not increased in the early 1960s over the rates of the 1950s. Rather, they had declined. He

---

[16] Using the definition of full employment as a level in which further increases in demand result in higher prices rather than greater output or employment.

[17] *Ibid.*, p. 261.

[18] E. D. Kalachek, *The Determinants of Higher Unemployment Rates, 1958–60* (Cambridge: Unpublished Doctoral Dissertation, M.I.T., 1963), pp. 49–71.

[19] Lowell C. Galloway, "Labor Mobility, Resource Allocation, and Structural Unemployment," *American Economic Review*, Vol. 53, No. 4 (September 1963), pp. 711–712.

[20] M. A. Zaidi, "Structural Unemployment, Labor Market Efficiency and the Intrafactor Allocation Mechanism in the United States and Canada," *Southern Economic Journal*, Vol. 35, No. 3 (January 1969), pp. 211–212.

concluded, therefore, that structural unemployment was not evident among these groups.[21] Lipsey, however, would urge caution in accepting the findings of such studies, since they all examined unemployment during periods of depressed economic activity in which there is now general agreement that deficient-demand unemployment cannot be distinguished between structural unemployment.[22]

Another corollary of the structural unemployment hypothesis is that long-term unemployment should increase as displaced workers with obsolete skills and those whose levels of skill traditionally are low, find it increasingly difficult to secure employment. Simler has examined the existence of long-term unemployment—defined as that over 15 weeks, U_L—and of very long-term unemployment—that over 26 weeks, U_{LL}—for the period 1947–1963.[23] He has found that both types of long-term unemployment were higher for the 1958–1963 period than for the earlier period, but he also found that current unemployment rates U_t and unemployment rates that lagged one year U_{t-1} were also higher, as was the percentage of the long-term unemployed over age 45, L_{45}. The equations are of the following type.[24]

$$U_L = a + bU_t + cU_{t-1} + L_{45} \qquad (19.1)$$

$$U_{LL} = \alpha + \beta U_t + \gamma U_{t-1} + L_{45} \qquad (19.2)$$

Equation (19.1) predicted very well the actual long-term unemployment rates for the period 1958–1963, but Equation (19.2) underpredicted the actual very long-term unemployment rates. This has led Simler to explain this phenomenon in terms of the length of time in which the unemployment rate lies above some critical level. If unemployment rates fluctuate within certain limits, the unemployed may reasonably expect to find employment

[21] R. A. Gordon, "Has Structural Unemployment Worsened?" *Industrial Relations*, Vol. 3 (May 1964), pp. 53–77.

[22] Lipsey, "Structural and Deficient-Demand Unemployment," *op. cit.*, p. 262.

[23] N. J. Simler, "Long-Term Unemployment, the Structural Hypothesis, and Public Policy," *American Economic Review*, Vol. 54, No. 6 (December 1964), pp. 985–1001.

[24] *Ibid.*, pp. 990–991, 993. Regression equations based on 1947–1957 data revealed the following:

$$U_L = -2.575 + 0.322\,U_t + 0.0684\,U_{t-1} + 0.0470\,L_{45} \qquad (19.1a)$$
$$ (0.743) \quad (0.0288) \qquad (0.0287) \qquad (0.0195)$$

$$R^2 = 0.933, \quad \bar{S} = 0.0896$$

and,

$$U_{LL} = -1.454 + 0.129\,U_t + 0.0614\,U_{t-1} + 0.0268\,L_{45} \qquad (19.2b)$$
$$\phantom{U_{LL} =\ } (0.402) + (0.0155) + (0.0155) \qquad (0.0105)$$

$$R^2 = 0.903, \quad \bar{S} = 0.0484$$

within, say, 14 weeks. If the unemployment level rises above some critical level and varies thereafter above that level, not all of the unemployed in a cyclical downswing will be able to find employment during the succeeding upswing. The unsuccessful applicants enter the ranks of the long-term unemployed. With each cycle, more enter into these ranks. He also hypothesizes that the skills of the unemployed decline relatively to those who are employed as the duration of unemployment lengthens, or at least employers believe this decline to take place. Hence, in later cycles, an upward trend develops in the rate of long-term unemployment or skills decay and as the long-term unemployed find it increasingly difficult to find jobs.[25]

This upward trend in the long-term unemployed is not owing to structural changes in the economy, but rather it is itself an outgrowth of chronic deficient demand. An increase in demand sufficient to remove the short-term unemployment will not, however, reduce the rate of the long-term unemployed. The over-all unemployment rate at full employment may even appear to have risen. Manpower policies to impart new skills to the long-term unemployed are a necessary supplement to policies designed to increase aggregate demand if unemployment is to be reduced to the original frictional levels. Simler notes that whereas manpower policies by themselves cannot reduce either short-term or long-term unemployment caused by deficient demand, neither can removal of deficient demand remove all of the unemployment which it earlier had induced.[26]

It should be noted that the effects of persistent excess demand since 1965 have cast some doubts upon this last conclusion. A Department of Labor Study found in 1969 that one person in eight was unemployed for longer than 15 weeks, and that only long-term unemployment had been declining since 1965. In 1969, such unemployment was the lowest it had been since the Korean War.[27] Although we cannot be sure that structural unemployment has in fact increased, it now seems apparent that the persistent unemployment rate above 5% between 1958 and 1964 was due primarily to deficient demand. It would seem that the structuralists have yet to prove their point.

---

[25] *Ibid.*, pp. 996–998. Burrows has also found this to be true in England in the 1956–1966 period, *op. cit.*, pp. 82–83.

[26] *Ibid.*, p. 1000. Paul A. Samuelson has referred to the structurally unemployed as a core made of ice which "can be melted over a period of time by adequate effective demand, or it can become solidified from inadequate over-all demand." See *Economics*, 8th ed. (New York: McGraw-Hill, 1970), p. 802.

[27] Fraim and Schwab, "Employment and Unemployment Developments in 1969," *op. cit.*, p. 51.

Discussion Questions

1. (a) The existence of substantial amounts of oligopoly can lead to an expansion of employment with no increase in prices, even in the face of diminishing aggregate marginal product. Discuss.

   (b) Suppose the aggregate production function is linear over a substantial range of the expansion in aggregate demand. What will be the effect on real wages and prices?

2. Because of a large number of new entrants into the labor force in the 1960s, inflation as a result of the Vietnam War was less than it would have been if the war had occurred in the 1970s, when labor force growth so far has been less rapid. Discuss.

3. In order for wages and profits to rise, for unemployment to be at a minimum level and prices to remain stable, the growth in aggregate demand must balance the real growth forces in the economy. How might manpower policy affect the real growth forces and aggregate demand? Which type of policy is apt to be more effective in the 1970s and why—that affecting aggregate supply or that affecting aggregate demand?

4. (a) Suppose that in the 1970s, a restrictive labor policy curtails the bargaining power of organized labor. How might this affect inflation and unemployment during this decade?

   (b) If along with a restrictive labor policy, a vigorous antitrust policy is pursued, would this tend to improve employment opportunities? Explain.

   (c) Why are manpower policies helpful in remedying technological unemployment? Would such policies weaken the strength of unions? Are manpower policies a sufficient remedy? Explain.

5. Distinquish between structural and frictional, and voluntary and involuntary unemployment. Are these distinctions helpful to policy makers?

6. It has been suggested that in the Soviet Union much labor is misallocated (for example, over one-third are still employed in agriculture) and hence their productivity is suboptimal. Discuss the relative merits of a more efficient allocation of labor, utilizing some unemployment, versus the utilization of labor in less productive pursuits with no unemployment.

7. (a) Contrast and compare the "job vacancy" and "queue" theories of unemployment with the concept of structural unemployment.

   (b) Is Lipsey's test to measure structural unemployment empirically feasible? Outline a procedure to implement this test.

8. (a) Is structural unemployment worsening? Cite evidence to support your answer.
   (b) How can union policy contribute to structural unemployment? To deficient-demand unemployment?
9. Is structural unemployment a long-run or short-run phenomenon? Is the time dimension important insofar as economic policy is concerned? Discuss.

20

The Relationship between Inflation
and Unemployment

Inflation may be defined as a weighted average increase in the level of prices. From microtheory, students have learned that prices may rise from an increase in demand, given supply; from a decrease in supply, given demand; or from some combination of an increase (decrease) in demand in excess of (less than) an increase (decrease) in supply. In traditional macrotheory, the assumption of full employment of resources implied fixed supply. Consequently, price changes were caused by either excess or deficient demand; price rose if the former condition existed, but fell if the latter held. The Keynesian modifications, recognizing the existence of conditions of less than full employment, explained how expansions in aggregate demand can be translated into either an expansion in output or an increase in the price level. The existence of unemployed resources permits output expansion in response to increases in demand; as full employment is approached (unemployment diminishes), further increases in demand are translated into price level increases. The rise in prices as unemployment decreases, therefore, is explained in theory by the elasticity of price with respect to aggregate demand; this elasticity in turn is a function of the elasticities of output and wages.[1]

---

[1] These elasticity relationships were explained in Chapter 18, pp. 503–506. Also see J. M. Keynes, *The General Theory of Employment, Interest and Money* (New York: Harcourt, Brace, 1936), Chapters 20, 21.

The fall in prices, however, may not be as sensitive to decreases in demand or rising unemployment in modern macrotheory as it was in traditional theory. The existence of market imperfections permits rigidities in wages and prices as unemployment increases. Consequently, within limits as demand increases and decreases, the coefficients of price and wage elasticity may have values close to zero.

The movement of wage rates in the United States over the course of the period 1860–1959 was examined to see if wages indeed had been rigid during cyclical downswings, as hypothesized by Keynes.[2] Wages had paralleled the general rise in productivity over the 99-year period, giving a strong upward bias to their movement. Variations of wages about this trend line, in fact, should be the appropriate base with which to measure the impact of cyclical variations on wages. Substantial evidence was found that wages do, in fact, tend to lie below this trend line in cyclical downswings, which indicates that wage variations at least are sensitive to movements in the level of economic activity. Interestingly, the findings do not refute the assumption of rigid money wages in periods of unemployment in the short run; the findings do tend to support the hypotheses concerning the relationship between elasticities of price, output, and wages.

Post-Keynesian modifications of macrotheory have acknowledged the other two sources of change in the aggregate price level.[3] Just as changes in supply can affect prices in microtheory, so can changes in the general price level emanate from changes in aggregate supply. Unlike inflation induced by demand–pull forces, changes in supply that result in higher resource or product costs can *push* up prices; hence, price increases from this source have been designated *cost–push* inflation. This explanation is the logical opposite of the Keynesian recognition of downward rigidities in wages and prices owing to monopoly influences, when aggregate demand decreases. If monopoly powers can prevent a fall in wages and prices, perhaps they can also initiate their increase.

Modern macro theory has also explained the origin of inflation as a combination of demand–pull and cost–push forces. Although the economy is treated aggregatively, modern theory recognizes that it has component sectors that are themselves aggregates of microparts. In some sectors, excess demand can exist; in other sectors, whereas demand may not be declining, cost-push forces may be dominant; in other parts of the economy deficient demand and an absence of rigidities may yield falling resource and product

[2] Clarence Long, "The Illusion of Wage Rigidity: Long and Short Cycles in Wages and Labor," *Review of Economics and Statistics*, Vol. 4 (May 1960), pp. 140–161.

[3] For an excellent review of the literature on inflation, see M. Bronfenbrenner and F. D. Holzman, "Survey of Inflation Theory," *American Economic Review*, Vol. 53, No. 4 (September 1963), pp. 543–561.

prices; yet the same condition of deficient demand in still other sectors can encounter forces that resist a lowering of prices. The weighted combination of all these sector demand and supply forces determines whether aggregate demand and prices are rising or falling.

In this chapter the various theories of the origin of inflation will be presented, and the results of empirical studies will be examined in the light of these theories.

Demand–Pull Inflation

If an increase in the rate of growth of demand occurs when the economy is operating close to full employment, shortages of specialized resources, including skilled labor, may develop which constrains the ability of producers to increase supply. Either through a process of competitive bidding among purchasers or by unilateral action by suppliers in attempts to ration the limited supply, prices begin to rise. The increase in prices at first results in an increase in profit margins as costs lag behind and motivates producers to expand supplies.[4] Although producers may attempt to overcome shortages of critical personnel through the substitution of less- for more-skilled laborers, eventually the supply of even the less-skilled unemployed workers will be absorbed. Continued demand for their services will lead employers to raise their wages in an attempt to attract additional workers, either into the labor force or from other areas of employment. Higher labor costs result either from using a greater mix of less productive workers or from higher wages, and a second round increase in prices is initiated in order to maintain profit margins. As long as the banking system permits sufficient credit expansion to finance the attempts to expand aggregate supply, the increase in aggregate demand will be sufficient to accommodate the higher prices. In a sense, inflation has begun to feed upon itself. Eventually, however, the banking system exhausts its ability (or willingness) to expand credit; high interest rates discourage further borrowing; and consumers react negatively to higher prices.

The upward spiral of prices and costs comes to an end as limits to the expansion of aggregate demand operate to lower the rate of increase of buying below the rate of increase of aggregate output. Inventories, unplanned, accumulate, and output is curtailed. Layoffs reduce the size of the work force and idle plant capacity develops. Special sales in the form of price reductions occur as firms seek greater liquidity through reduced inventories. Surplus labor, unemployed but seeking jobs, bids wages down as

---

[4] Long has found that wages have tended to lag behind price increases. "The Illusion of Wage Rigidity," *op. cit.*, p. 150.

they accept employment at lower rates of pay. With lower costs and the competition generated by excess productive capacity, firms are motivated to lower prices. Increases in aggregate demand in the expansion phase of the cycle have "pulled up" wages and prices; deficient demand in the contraction phase has "pulled down" wages and prices. In both phases, prices and unemployment have moved counter to one another. Hence the movement has come to be regarded as an index of the relationship between aggregate demand and aggregate supply.

Proponents of "demand–pull" inflation have recognized that full employment in the economy does not mean a zero rate of unemployment. Rather, because of the lack of perfect mobility of labor or of perfect knowledge of job opportunities, workers in the process of changing jobs will not immediately move from one job to another. These frictions in the operation of the labor market will produce a backlog of workers seeking jobs, even where jobs are plentiful. Full employment may be considered as the minimum level of this frictional unemployment in a labor market in which the number of job vacancies is not less than the number of job seekers. As the unemployment rate approaches this frictional minimum, inflationary pressures accumulate. As the unemployment rate increases beyond the frictional rate, deflationary pressures grow. If demand is such that the unemployment rate hovers in the vicinity of this frictional rate, therefore, the price level will remain relatively stationary. What, then, is the rate of unemployment at which the price level remains constant; where neither inflationary nor deflationary pressure is experienced?

One study suggests that in the United States stable prices occur at an unemployment rate of between 5 and 6%.[5] The experience between 1954–1971 of prices and unemployment is presented in Chart 20.1. Although the price level as measured by the GNP implicit price deflator index revealed an increase of between 1 and 2% whenever the unemployment rate measured between 5 and 7%, as it did in the interval 1958–1964, there is reason to believe that this represents reasonable price stability. According to the Council of Economic Advisers, "Considering the availability of new products

[5] "Analytical Aspects of Anti-Inflation Policy," *American Economic Review*, L, No. 2 (May 1960), pp. 192–193.

Level of Unemployment as Percentage of Labor Force	Price Increase (%) per Annum
6–7	−1
5–6	0
4	2–3
3	4–5

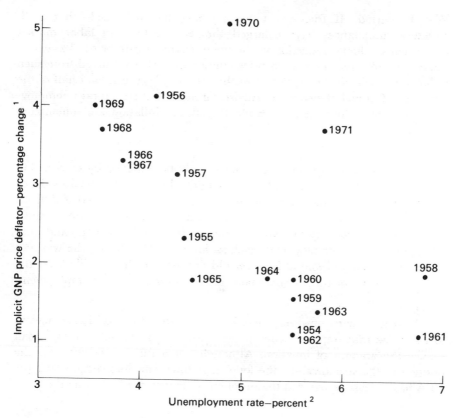

CHART 20.1. Price performance and unemployment.

[1] Change during year, calculated from end of year deflators (derived by averaging fourth quarter of a given year and first quarter of subsequent year).
[2] Average for the year.

Sources: Department of Commerce, Department of Labor, and Council of Economic Advisers.

and quality changes not fully reflected in the index, there has been little if any real erosion of the purchasing power of the consumer's dollar."[6]

One of the nuances of the controversy concerning the existence of structural unemployment, discussed in the preceding chapter, has been whether the frictional unemployment rate has increased in the post-World

---

[6] *Economic Report of the President, January 1964*, p. 35. The average annual change in the consumer price index was 1.2%; the wholesale price index over the whole period increased by only 0.1%.

War II period. If frictional unemployment has increased—that is, if structural imbalances have enlarged the imperfections in labor market adjustments—then a reduction in the unemployment rate below 5% would imply a more rapid increase in prices than had earlier occurred from such reductions. Prior to the expansion of the economy in the second half of the 1960s, the Council of Economic Advisers denied that structural unemployment may have increased the tradeoff between inflation and unemployment[7]:

> Economic expansion could eventually be impeded by shortages in strategic categories of skills and training, but the statistical evidence reveals no such shortages enroute to 4% unemployment. It is difficult to believe that an economy that was able to absorb the dramatic shifts needed to convert to war production in World War II and that operated at unemployment levels as low as 1.2%, during the war and more recently (1953) at 2.9%, could not move rather readily, over the space of two or three years, to our interim target of 4% unemployment.

In recent years, however, the CEA has modified its position somewhat to recognize that improvements in the operation of the labor market can reduce the amount of inflation. Although not a full agreement with the position of the structuralists, the following statement does suggest that the CEA has at least recognized the problem of structural employment[8]:

> The efficiency of labor markets is reflected in the matching of job opportunities and available manpower. The fit is never perfect; while in some areas and for some skills "help wanted" signs prevail, there are simultaneously many unemployed persons whose skills or locations do not fit the needs of employers. Continued job vacancies tend to pull wages up and thereby attract labor. In areas of excess supply, however, wages are rarely subject to strong downward pressures. Thus, unmanned jobs and jobless men do not offset each other in influencing average wages. The better the labor markets operate, the higher the level of employment and the lower the volume of job vacancies that can accompany any degree of upward pressure on average wages.
> There are a number of ways that a better and more flexible fit of available manpower and job opportunities can be achieved. Workers

[7] *Economic Report of the President, January 1964,* p. 182.

[8] *Economic Report of the President, January 1969,* p. 98. See Chapter 3 for a more complete discussion of manpower policies designed to remedy labor market imbalances.

can move more easily between occupations and geographical locations if they are given improved information about job opportunities and if they are not confronted with barriers to entry into certain occupations. They can be aided by training programs which are more closely oriented toward skills that are in short supply. And the productivity of employed labor can be improved by the removal of restrictive work practices.

Measures of these kinds can both alter the level of employment consistent with reasonable price stability and add significantly to the real output at a given level of employment.

Phillips Curves for the United Kingdom

The pioneering study of the relationship between wages and unemployment was made by A. W. Phillips.[9] He hypothesized that wages should be affected nonlinearly by the level of unemployment, rising more when unemployment rates are low and employers are bidding wages up, and falling less when unemployment levels are high and workers are resisting wage cuts. Moreover, the wage change should also be related to the rate of change of unemployment since this rate of change influences the expectations of employers regarding the future scarcity of labor. If unemployment levels are rapidly declining, employers might be more willing to raise wages in order to secure or retain labor if they believe its scarcity will increase at a time when the demand for their products is increasing. The movement and level of unemployment are taken as proxies for the existence of excess demand—demand–pull—in the economy. Finally, the cost of living of workers, particularly for food, as evidenced by the change in import prices can affect the movement of wages with any given level of unemployment. The movement of import prices can be interpreted as a cost–push force which begins to operate only after such prices change by at least 5%. To test these hypotheses, the movement of wages and unemployment was examined during the course of business cycles from 1861 through 1957.

For each set of cyclical upswings and downswings, wage–unemployment observations plot out a loop. The rate of change of wages during the upswing appears to be higher for any given level of unemployment than the rate of change during the downswing for that level of unemployment. Hence, along a curvilinear regression line, with declining rates of unemployment, observations tend to lie above the line, and with increasing rates of unemployment, they tend to lie below the line. The loop is illustrated in Figure 20.1 and the number associated with each observation can be taken to refer to an

---

[9] "The Relation Between Unemployment and the Rate of Change of Money Wage Rates in the United Kingdom, 1861–1957," *Economica* (November 1958), pp. 283–299.

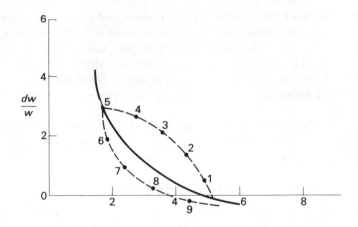

Percent unemployment

FIGURE 20.1. The loop of a Phillips Curve.

annual observation in a nine-year cycle. Observations 3 and 8 each represent
the same rate of unemployment, but the relative changes in wages, dw/w,
for point 3 is higher during the upswing than in the downswing at point 8.
In general, wage changes were found to be higher the lower was the unemployment rate, consistent with the first hypothesis, and the rate of change
of unemployment and its sign, reflected in the loop behavior of the observations, affected the magnitude of the wage change, consistent with the second
hypothesis. Significant deviations from these patterns in the early 1920s, the
mid-1930s, and late 1940s can be explained by changes in food or import
prices.

There appeared to be a tendency for the loops to widen in the later
years of the period under observations. In part this was attributed to the
spread of trade union activity, which through collective bargaining could
generate a lag in wage adjustments after changes in unemployment had
occurred. An observation of wage changes in a particular time period,
therefore, would be in the graph associated with the unemployment rate of
that period rather than the more appropriate rate of some earlier period.
For example, in Figure 20.1 if the wage associated with observation 3 were
plotted against the employment at observation 2, the deviation from the
regression line would be greater. By lagging wage changes seven months
after unemployment rates in the 1948–1957 interval, much smaller deviations from the regression line were found.[10]

[10] *Ibid.*, p. 297.

The regression lines have come to be called Phillips curves. They purport to show the average rate of unemployment which is associated with an average rate of wage change. For example, Phillips found that in England an unemployment rate of 5.5% would be associated with a zero change in wage rates—stable wages; and that with an annual productivity rate of increase of 2%, assuming that the rate of price change equals the rate of wage change minus the productivity increase rate, a rate of unemployment of about 3.5% would be associated with a stable price level.[11] Hence, Phillips curves may relate either wages and unemployment or prices and unemployment.

Phillips Curves for the United States

A similar study for the periods 1890–1932 and 1947–1957 has been made for the United States.[12] The United States data did not fit as closely to the regression line as those found in England. This in part was attributed to the greater size of the United States which permitted greater wage–employment dispersion, in part to the use of average hourly earnings rather than wage rates as the dependent variable, in part to the more consistent unemployment statistics available for England. When wholesale prices—a proxy for food prices—were introduced as an explanatory variable in the 1890–1932 period, the explained variance increased significantly. However, consistent with Phillips' hypothesis, minor changes in the price index affected wage changes very little. In the post-World War II period the consumer price index appeared to be the only significant variable in explaining the movement of wages, whereas earlier both the employment rate and its rate of change were significant as explanatory variables.[13] In a follow-up study for the years 1948–1958, the use of quarterly data converts the unemployment rate and its rate of change into significant explanatory variables.[14] Thus a Phillips curve appears to be relevant also for the United States,[15] although the relationship between changes in the wage rate and in the unemployment rate do not appear to be as strong as in England. (See Chart 20.2.)

[11] *Ibid.*, p. 299.

[12] R. R. France, "Wages, Unemployment, and Prices in the United States, 1890–1932, 1947–1957," *Industrial and Labor Relations Review*, Vol. 15 (January 1962), pp. 171–190.

[13] France felt that wage rates rather than average hourly earnings might be more sensitive to unemployment movements. He found, for example, when allowance was made for fringe benefit changes, the relationship between average hourly labor costs and unemployment deteriorated. Also, he felt that annual data revealed a much less sensitive relationship than quarterly or monthly data. *Ibid.*, pp. 184–186.

[14] K. M. McCaffree, "A Further Consideration of Wages, Unemployment, and Prices in the United States, 1948–1958," *Industrial and Labor Relations Review* (October 1963), pp. 60–74.

[15] See also the study by Paul A. Samuelson and Robert M. Solow, "Analytical Aspects of Anti-Inflation Policy," *op. cit.*

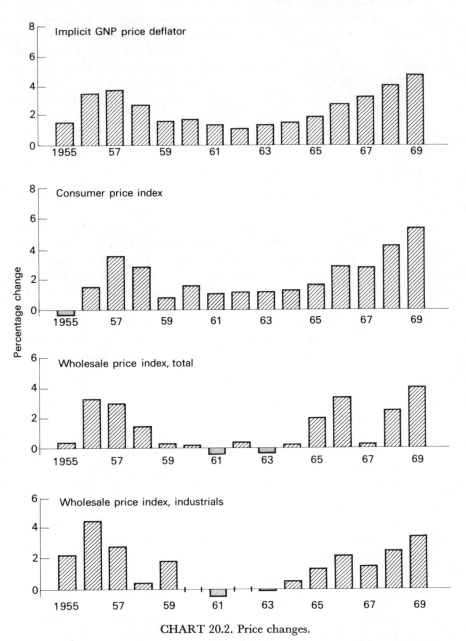

CHART 20.2. Price changes.

Sources: Department of Commerce and Department of Labor. *Economic Report of the President,*
1970, p. 55.

Cost–Push Inflation

If demand is not increasing, but prices are rising, is this not *prima facie* evidence that some forces in the economy are pushing up prices? This phenomenon appeared in the periods 1956–1958 and 1970–1971 and was attributed to the combined monopoly power of big unions and big businesses. It is claimed that these organizations have the economic strength to impose wage and price increases in the absence of market conditions conducive to such increases. Even though reduced sales and greater unemployment may result, the increases occur nevertheless. The phenomenon has been labeled by a number of terms: cost–push,[16] mark-up,[17] or administered price[18] inflation.

A simplified version of the process attributes the initial action to strong unions, who by virtue of some institutional or random occurrence, find their bargaining power sufficient to win a wage increase in excess of productivity gains. The rise in unit labor costs imposes a profit squeeze upon the firm or industry which, seeking to earn a given target rate of return, responds by raising prices. The increase in price is an administrative decision in the same sense as the union's demand for a wage increase. It is a result of a conscious decision. The price leader in an oligopoly industry initiates the price increase, knowing full well that rival firms will follow because they are subject to the same cost pressures from the wage increase. Prices are marked up in unison in order to earn a desired rate of return.

Alternatively, a country that imports a large portion of its food supply, such as England or Japan, may find that imported food prices rise because of world market conditions. This raises the cost of living of working men, who spend a large portion of their income on food. In order to protect the purchasing power of their wages, they seek a "markup" in them. The increase in wages may be demanded by their unions during periodic contract negotiations, or such increases may be contained in escalator clauses allowing cost-of-living adjustments already present in labor agreements.

A relevant question is whether unions possess sufficient strength to compel an increase in wages in the face of deficient aggregate demand. If the unemployment rate is high or is increasing, can the union successfully win a wage increase if the membership is reluctant to strike because they

[16] Franklyn D. Holzman, "Inflation: Cost–Push and Demand–Pull," *American Economic Review*, L, No. 1 (March 1960), pp. 20–42.

[17] Gardner Ackley, *Macroeconomic Theory* (New York: The Macmillan Co., 1961), pp. 452–459.

[18] Jules Backman, Gardiner C. Means, and William J. Donald, *Administered Prices, Administered Wages and Inflation* (New York: National Industrial Conference Board, Inc., 1957).

fear replacement and loss of jobs? How great is the possibility that the employer may elect to "take" a strike and seek to operate by using as strike breakers workers recruited from the unemployed? Moreover, how willing is an employer, even an oligopolist, to grant a wage increase if he believes that the market will not accept an increase in price? After all, a union's relative bargaining power is dependent upon its membership's willingness to undergo a strike and an employer's unwillingness to take a strike. How, then, have unions affected the relationship between prices and unemployment?

Unions and the Phillips Curve

It has been argued that structural changes in the economy can alter the Phillips curve. One such structural change that has been mentioned is the degree to which the labor market is organized into trade unions.[19]

One group of adherents, on the one hand, believes that unions may worsen the inflation–unemployment tradeoff. A natural consequence of monopoly in declining demand is to reduce output rather than price, and to the extent that a union is a monopoly element of labor supply, it may accept greater unemployment rather than wage reductions. Moreover, in expanding demand the union may be more sensitive to increased prices and profits, and reduce the lag between price and wage changes. Hence, for every unemployment level, a reduction in the lag raises the rate of wage change and the Phillips curve correspondingly shifts upward.[20] Arguments also have been put forth that automatic wage adjustment clauses—the escalator clauses—will increase the slope of the Phillips curve, since it is general price increases or productivity changes and not those specifically related to the micro market that govern the wage adjustment. Similarly, barriers to labor mobility erected by unions will increase frictional unemployment and shift the curve. On the other hand, another group of adherents holds that the existence of long-term labor agreements will tend to increase the lag between wage increases and reductions in unemployment, and the Phillips curve will shift leftward as a result. This will tend to improve the inflation–unemployment tradeoff. A third school simply asserts that unions will have no influence. All three schools can cite empirical studies which support their position.

[19] Phillips himself cited the growth of unions and their activities as an explanation of deviations and shifts in his curves. *Op. cit.*, pp. 292, 293, 298. Also, see K. M. McCaffree for a discussion of possible effects of unions on wages, "U.S. Wages, Unemployment, and Prices," *op. cit.*, pp. 69–70.

[20] R. G. Lipsey, "The Relationship between Unemployment and the Rate of Changes of Money Wage Rates in the United Kingdom, 1862–1957: A Further Analysis," *Economica* (February 1960), p. 17.

Data from earlier studies support the conclusion that, whereas in the 19th century unemployment and its rate of change explained much of the variation in wage changes, these variables lose their significance in the 20th century as an explanation of wage changes.[21] Part of the reason for this is that unemployment rates have varied much less in this century, particularly since 1912, and that wage changes have continued to vary widely in the face of relatively stable unemployment rates. Thus, other factors must be exerting influence on the wage rate changes. The effects of trade unions were examined, along with other variables such as changes in profits and in price levels. Changes in trade union membership explained a significant portion of the variance in wage changes. These changes in union membership, it is argued, are a better index of union militancy and strength in raising wages than the level of union membership, and it is the militancy of trade unions that produces changes in wages. The British experience revealed that the membership changes coincided with wage changes better than when lags were introduced. Do workers join unions because unions raise wages, do wage increases cause workers to join unions, or do workers join unions before wage increases occur? No definitive answer is given, but the finding that changes in union membership correlate significantly with nonlagged changes in prices suggests that they are simultaneous occurrences. Perhaps it is the fall of real wages as prices increase that attracts workers into unions, who promise them action to gain compensating increases in wages. It was also found (1) that changes in trade union membership correlated positively when changes in profit levels lagged six months, and (2) that little relationship existed between the unemployment rate or its rate of change and the rate of change of union membership; hence, the latter cannot be taken as a proxy for the former.

Although there is no doubt that membership changes in England are related to wage rate changes, we do not know if trade union activity caused wages to change. Because unemployment rates have been relatively stable and low over the period in which a relationship between wages and trade unions is found to exist, it may be that unions merely take credit for changes in wages which primarily occurred as a result of profit changes and price changes—that is, from market interactions of supply and demand. However, an important conclusion is that a policy to maintain a stable level of unemployment as an antiinflation objective is not likely to succeed if other

[21] A. G. Hines, "Trade Unions and Wage Inflation in the United Kingdom, 1893–1961," *Review of Economic Studies*, Vol. 31 (1964), pp. 221–251. A later study reaches the same conclusion, "Unemployment and the Rate of Change of Money Wages in the United Kingdom, 1862–1963: A Reappraisal," *Review of Economics and Statistics* (February 1968), pp. 60–67.

relevant variables are ignored. Some control over trade union activity may be required.

Studies of union influence on wages in the United States have given mixed support to the influence of unions. A comparison of the period before the Great Depression with the post-World War II period revealed that, for given levels of unemployment, wage increases in the United States were greater in the latter period than in the former.[22] This is attributed to the growth of unions and the spread of collective bargaining in the later period. Mild evidence exists to show (1) that in the union sector wages are less sensitive to unemployment levels than they are in the nonunion sector, and (2) that the Phillips curve of the unionized sector tends to shift upward and of the nonunionized sector tends to shift downward.[23] These data appear consistent with the hypothesis that unions introduce rigidities into the wage adjustment process and accentuate wage lags, which in turn lower the slope of the Phillips curve. In both the upswing and downswing of a cycle, wage changes occur more slowly in the unionized than in the nonunionized sector. One consequence of these lags is that unions may exert pressure for wage increases after the peak of a cycle has passed; the illusion is thus created that unions push up wages and prices even when demand does not justify it. In reality, the union may only be responding belatedly to earlier demand–pull pressures. Wage dispersion about unemployment rates, then, is somewhat greater in the unionized sector. Noneconomic forces operating through union pressure can increase the erratic wage behavior pattern found in organized markets and contribute to wage dispersion. On the other hand, the degree of union organization in metropolitan labor markets apparently has had little influence on wage changes.[24]

Another study on the effect of unions on the Phillips curve has found that the relative sensitivity of wages in the unionized sector varies with the level of unemployment and with changes in consumer prices. Using union concentration data in 19 two-digit manufacturing industries, they are classified into (I) "strongly organized" and (II) "weakly unionized" industries.[25] The two groups are further subdivided into A and B sectors;

[22] R. R. France, "Wage, Unemployment, and Prices in the United States, 1890–1932, 1947–1957," *op. cit.*, pp. 187–190. To compare two "normal" subintervals in the two broad periods, he chose 1923–1929 and 1953–1959 and found that wage increases were almost twice as large in the latter.

[23] K. M. McCaffree, "U.S. Wages, Unemployment and Prices," *op. cit.*, pp. 71–73.

[24] W. P. Albrecht, "The Relationship between Wage Change and Unemployment in Metropolitan and Industrial Labor Markets," *Yale Economic Essays* (Fall, 1966).

[25] Gail Pierson, "The Effect of Union Strength on the U.S. Phillips Curve," *American Economic Review*, Vol. 58, No. 3 (June 1968), pp. 456–467. The union concentration data are based upon the percentage of workers in each industry covered by collective bargaining agreements as calculated by H. M. Dounty for 1958.

the A sector consists of the five most organized industries in I; the B sector consists of the five least organized industries in II. The average percentage organized in A is 87; in B it is 45. It was found that the consumer price index influenced wages in groups I and A more than in groups II and B. In fact, little significance can be attached to the influence of consumer prices on wages in groups II and B, but in groups I and A, a 1% change in consumer prices will produce 0.33 and 0.45% changes in wages.[26] Hence, the evidence here that union strength can shift the Phillips curve is somewhat stronger than that offered by other studies. The Phillips curve of strong union sectors converges toward that of weaker union sectors as unemployment is reduced from 5 to 4% if consumer prices are held constant.[27] On the other hand, permitting consumer prices to vary causes wages in the strong union sector to increase more than in the weak sector with a given reduction in unemployment. Whether or not the strong-sector curve is more or less steeply sloped than the weak-sector curve, therefore, depends upon the relative strength of the reaction to the consumer price changes. Thus, unions may not reduce the slope of the Phillips curve.[28]

These results must be interpreted with some caution. For example, we need to know the specific unemployment rates in groups I and A compared with groups II and B when the economy has an over-all unemployment rate of 4%. If the former groups are more sensitive to changes in aggregate demand, we might have an unemployment distribution as tabulated:

	Unemployment Rate in			
National Unemployment Rate	*I*	*A*	*II*	*B*
4	3.8	3.5	4.2	4.5
5	5.5	6.0	4.5	4.8

Therefore, to measure the effect of the union on the over-all Phillips curve, we cannot assume that unemployment is evenly distributed and calculate the wage changes for each sector at any aggregate level of unemployment. For example, at an aggregate level of unemployment of 5%, wages may not

[26] *Ibid.*, p. 461.

[27] *Ibid.*, pp. 463, 464. This is true even when "spillover" effects are taken into account.

[28] John Vanderkamp has studied organized and unorganized sectors of the labor market in Canada and his findings are similar to those of Pierson. Wage changes in organized sectors are more sensitive to price changes than in unorganized sectors, and the unemployment parameter is smaller in the organized sector. See "Wage and Price Determination: An Empirical Model for Canada," *Economica* (May 1966), pp. 201–203. Vandercamp cautions against reaching the conclusion, however, that unions impair the competitiveness of the Canadian labor market.

be rising any more rapidly in the strong sector than in the weak sector, not because unions have less influence but because this influence is negated by higher unemployment rates. Similarly, at a 4% aggregate level of unemployment, wages in the strong sector may be increasing much more rapidly than in the weak sector, not because the strong sector is more sensitive at a given level of unemployment, but because its rate of unemployment is less than in the weak sector. Pierson does not examine the question of the distribution of unemployment rates by sector, although it would appear to be a relevant line of inquiry in order to appraise the magnitude of the influence of unionism on the Phillips curve.

Although the evidence of the impact of unions on the Phillips curve is somewhat mixed, unions do appear to have some influence. That the British and United States experiences are somewhat different is probably a result of the differences in the institutional forms which collective bargaining assumes in the two countries. Studies in the United States have examined the relationship of the amount of unionization to changes in wages and unemployment, whereas Hines' study of the British economy found that the amount of unionization was less significant than the change in union membership. Although there is some evidence that the periodicity with which labor agreements are negotiated does introduce lags in the wage adjustment process which would tend to lower the slope of Phillips curves, it is probably true that the increased sensitivity of wages to price changes brought about by union-sponsored escalator clauses at least offsets the lag effect. This sensitivity, taken with the evidence of an upward shift in the Phillips curve, indicates that unions have tended to increase wage adjustments at given levels of unemployment. (See Table 20.1)

Mixed Inflation

The economy can be viewed in terms of its component sectors and/or intertemporally. The total economy is the sum of its parts, and what happens in these parts can have macro implications. Similarly, the economy is changing over time. Aggregate demand may be growing or declining, but experience, buttressed by statutory commitments to maintain economic stability, has taught micro decision makers that wide variations in aggregate demand in either direction will not long be tolerated. These two perspectives of the economy provide the basis for explaining the process of inflation as a combination of both demand–pull and cost–push forces. In one instance, one set of forces may be stronger than the other set, whereas at another time the two may be acting concurrently with almost equal strength.

The rise in prices in the immediate post-World War II period of 1945–1948, during the Korean War in the early 1950s, and during the Vietnam

TABLE 20.1
FIRST-YEAR CHANGES IN WAGE RATES IN COLLECTIVE BARGAINING
AGREEMENTS COVERING 1000 WORKERS OR MORE NEGOTIATED
IN THE FIRST 9 MONTHS OF 1970

| | *Percent of Workers Affected* | | | |
| | | | Nonmanufacturing | |
Type and Amount of Wage-Rate Action[a]	*All Industries*	*Manufacturing*	*Total*	*Construction*
Total increases	100	100	100	100
Under 5%	1	1	1	(b)
5 and under 7%	6	11	2	(b)
7 and under 9%	25	46	12	5
9 and under 11%	20	31	12	11
11 and under 13%	10	3	15	14
13 and under 15%	5	2	6	16
15% and over	33	5	52	53
Number of workers (thousands)	2,601	1,009	1,592	504
Mean adjustment (%)	13.2	8.5	16.0	17.5
Median adjustment (%)	10.2	8.0	15.7	15.7

[a] Percent of estimated average hourly earnings, excluding overtime.
[b] Less than 0.5%
Note: Data are preliminary. Detail will not necessarily add to totals because of rounding.
Source: Department of Labor. *Economic Report of the President, 1971*, p. 59.

War in the middle and late 1960s is generally acknowledged to be a result primarily of demand–pull forces, although cost–push forces may have accelerated the rise in prices. However, the inflationary tendencies of the periods 1956–1957 and 1969–1971, during which the level of aggregate demand had stabilized and then turned downward, were attributed to a combination of cost–push and demand–pull forces. One version attributes the inflationary process in these latter periods as being a result of (1) an uneven distribution of demand forces among sectors of the economy and (2) the ratchet effect of wages and prices in concentrated industries.[29] In

[29] C. L. Schultz, *Recent Inflation in the United States*, Study Paper No. 1, Joint Economic Committee, U.S. Congress (Washington: U.S. Government Printing Office, 1959). Empirical support for the Schultz hypothesis has been offered by W. G. Bowen and S. H. Masters, "Shifts in the Composition of Demand and the Inflation Problem," *American Economic Review*, Vol. 54, No. 6 (December 1964), pp. 975–984.

some sectors of the economy, demand may be increasing, whereas in other sectors it may be stable or declining. Yet the over-all weight of these different manifestations may be reflected in stable or declining aggregate demand. Resource immobilities may generate shortages in the expanding sectors and force up wages and prices therein. Demand–pull may be said to be operating in these sectors. In sectors experiencing a decrease in demand, opposition to wage cuts by unions and to price cuts by oligopolies may result in a greater reduction in output and employment rather than in lower prices and wages. This tendency of wages and prices to rise under conditions of growing demand and to stabilize under conditions of deficient demand has been called a "ratchet" or stair-step effect. Since prices and wages, but not necessarily employment, are rising in some sectors, and since in other sectors wages and prices are not falling as unemployment increases, the tendency in the over-all economy is for prices and wages to rise while unemployment is rising. (See Chart 20.3.)

This tendency may be reinforced by a third set of sectors in which aggregate demand has stabilized. Costs can rise in this third set from at least two causes. First, firms in anticipation of rises in demand may have increased capacity, utilizing more capital intensive—human or physical—resources. Failure of demand to expand as forecasted results in operation of facilities at less than full capacity and at higher unit costs. Second, wage increases negotiated in an earlier period to take effect at a later date or in other industries with current expansions in demand, which then are transferred by sympathetic effects into the industry in question, can result in larger labor costs. These higher costs are then reflected in higher prices as firms attempt to offset them. In all three sectors, the net effect is one of rising wages and prices and increasing unemployment owing partly to demand–pull forces and partly to cost–push forces.

Unions seek wage increases in industries unable to raise prices without a reduction in output and employment. Sometimes, firms agree to wage increases when the demands for their products will not permit offsetting price increases. Reasons for these actions have been suggested in the "dilemma model."[30] Suppose unions ask for wage increases that can lead to higher prices and/or unemployment. If restrictive monetary and fiscal policies to combat inflation succeed in retarding aggregate demand so that unemployment rates increase to recessionary levels, the issue of unemploy-

---

[30] Variations of this model have been developed by W. A. Morton, "Trade Unionism, Full Employment and Inflation," *American Economic Review*, XL, No. 1 (March 1950), p. 26; Gottfried Haberler, "Wage Policy, Employment and Economic Stability," in *The Impact of the Union*, David McCord Wright, ed. (New York: Harcourt, Brace and World, Inc., 1951), p. 39; and W. C. Bowen, *The Wage-Price Issue* (Princeton, N.J.: Princeton University Press, 1960).

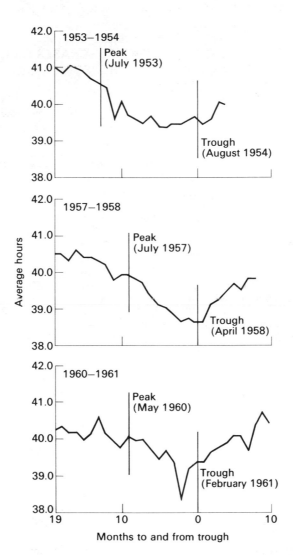

CHART 20.3. Average weekly hours of factory production workers in three recession periods, seasonally adjusted (peaks and troughs refer to business cycle peaks and troughs as determined by the National Bureau of Economic Research).

Source: Hazel M. Willacy, "Changes in Factory Workweek as an Economic Indicator," *Monthly Labor Review*, Vol. 93, No. 10 (October 1970), p. 26.

ment is made a political one. The government is admonished for its inhuman policies that deprive men of work and dignity. In election years the incumbent administration, seeking reelection, is under heavy pressure to relieve the unemployment,[31] and it can be expected to respond by loosening

TABLE 20.2
JOBS GENERATED BY GOVERNMENT PURCHASES OF GOODS AND SERVICES, 1970 AND PROJECTED 1980
[Thousands of jobs]

Sector and Industry	Total Jobs[a]		Jobs Generated by Federal Purchases		Jobs Generated by State and Local Purchases	
	1970[b]	Projected 1980	1970[b]	Projected 1980	1970[b]	Projected 1980
Total	86,839	101,867	8,922	8,924	13,338	18,371
Public sector	16,160	19,899	5,249	4,955	9,717	13,587
Federal Government	6,060	5,791	5,213	4,906	91	85
General government	5,168	4,851	5,168	4,851	—	—
Civilian	2,008	2,178	2,008	2,178	—	—
Military	3,160	2,673	3,160	2,673	—	—
Government enterprises	892	940	45	55	91	85
State and local government	10,100	14,108	36	49	9,626	13,502
General government	9,591	13,464	—	—	9,591	13,464
Government enterprises	509	644	36	49	35	38
Private sector	70,679	81,968	3,673	3,969	3,621	4,784
Agriculture	3,756	3,156	41	55	85	115
Mining	659	584	44	42	62	72
Construction	4,086	5,427	202	364	1,027	1,390
Manufacturing	19,953	22,133	2,011	1,918	1,200	1,544
Transportation and warehousing	2,872	3,086	251	182	208	234
Wholesale and retail trade	17,474	20,282	221	281	264	435
Other	21,879	27,300	903	1,127	775	994

[a] The number of jobs differs from the number of persons employed.
[b] Preliminary.
Source: Estimates by Department of Labor, Bureau of Labor Statistics.
Manpower Report of the President, 1971, p. 162.

[31] Political analysis predicted that the outcome of the 1972 presidential election would depend more upon domestic economic issues than upon any other single variable. See "A Drive to Beat Inflation—and Democrats," *Time* (October 18, 1971), p. 11.

credit, lowering taxes, or increasing federal spending—all devices to expand aggregate demand. When and if demand increases sufficiently to reabsorb the unemployed labor force, the prior wage and price increases will be validated. Expecting this sequence of events to happen, unions and businessmen are not constrained from raising prices and wages by the prospect of reduced output and greater unemployment, because they know at worst that these conditions will only be temporary. The implication of this analysis is that if the parties believed that the government would not take action to reduce unemployment, unions would be less willing to press excessive wage demands and employers would be less willing to accede to them. It is charged that the willingness of the government to supply enough demand to offset the cost–push forces is precisely why these latter forces tend to develop. (See Table 20.2.)

The government must choose between either sustaining excessive wage and price behavior or permitting unemployment, or must seek another action by which it might deter unwarranted inflationary pressures. Between 1962 and 1965, wage–price guideposts were established, and invoked by Presidents Kennedy and Johnson, by which unions were admonished not to seek wage increases greater than the average annual increase in productivity in order to abate cost pressures upon prices. In August 1971, President Nixon imposed a three-month wage–price freeze, followed in November 1971 by wage–price controls of a more stringent nature than those contained in the guideposts.[32] If organized labor and business fear such controls and believe that they are more likely to be invoked than are policies to raise aggregate demand enough to eliminate unemployment, then it is possible that these parties may mitigate their search for higher wages and prices.

Empirical Studies

Lipscy has reexamined the data for England used by Phillips and has developed an alternative explanation of the phenomenon of the loops which is consistent with the explanation of mixed or demand–shift inflation.[33] First, he considers the relationship between wage changes and unemployment changes. These changes occur in micro markets and the sum of the effects in all micro markets is revealed as the Phillips curve. Micro markets

---

[32] These controls and the events leading up to them are described in more detail in the following chapter.

[33] R. G. Lipsey, "The Relationship between Unemployment and the Rate of Change of Money Wage Rates in the United Kingdom, 1862–1957: A Further Analysis," *Economica* (February 1960), pp. 1–31. Lipsey also finds that there is no evidence that loops have narrowed. Moreover, he finds that the cost of living offers little by way of explanation of wage changes, but that the changes in the price level explain 17% more of the variance in wages.

can experience varying gradations in the demand for labor, from excess demand to excess supply. Presumably, in the micro markets, wages respond to excess demand or supply for labor, whose proxy is the unemployment rate. It is argued that the relationship between wage changes and decreasing unemployment will tend to be nonlinear, because as labor becomes scarce in micro markets, employers will bid up wages. Proportional reductions in the unemployment rate are accompanied by greater than proportional increments in the rate of wages. Whereas wages can become extremely large, it is unlikely that unemployment will be reduced to zero, and impossible for it to become negative. Hence, percentage changes in wages must exceed percentage changes in unemployment rates as the latter decrease. On the other hand, as surplus labor develops in micro markets, wages can fall proportionately with unemployment rate increases. Therefore, at unemployment rates below that at which wage changes are zero, the relationship between unemployment rate changes and wage changes will tend to be linear.[34]

This nonlinear relationship at positive changes in the wage rate and the linear relationship at negative changes in the wage rate are crucial to Lipsey's hypothesis about the nature of the micro Phillips curve. Now, assume that an increase in aggregate demand is transmitted to some micro markets, whereas in other micro markets demand may be stable or even declining. Wages in the expanding markets will increase along micro Phillips curves at an increasing rate as unemployment in these markets is reduced.

Wages in stable markets may at worst be declining linearly. The weighted effect of all wage changes will be that the nonlinear increases dominate the linear declines, and at the macro level, wage rates will increase. As increases in demand spread into all markets, nonlinear weights are increased and wage increases appear at the macro level to be accelerating as overall unemployment is reduced. Next, assume that aggregate demand is declining and this decline is distributed more evenly over micro markets than when it was increasing. The linear relationship will have a greater weight, and wage changes will appear to be less at each unemployment rate in the cyclical downswing than in the preceding upswing. There are no loops at the micro level; the level of excess labor demand determines on each micro Phillips curve the appropriate wage rate. The loops at the macro level are a statistical illusion produced by the aggregative weighting process. In particular, the Phillips explanation that employers' expectations of labor shortages induce them to raise or lower wages in an attempt to hoard or dishoard labor is an unnecessary assumption.

[34] A proof of this is offered by Lipsey, *Ibid.*, No. 1, p. 15.

This view of the aggregate Phillips curve carries with it a number of interesting implications. Unless the distribution of unemployment among micro markets is specified, no predictions are possible concerning the rate of change of wages in response to changes in unemployment rates. In particular, this suggests that changing distributions of unemployment, perhaps brought about by structural changes in the economy, can generate shifts in the Phillips curve.[35] In policy terms, if the distribution of unemployment among micro markets can be made more equal, or if the labor market can be made more competitive, the wage–price–unemployment tradeoff can be made less unfavorable. That structural changes may have occurred in the English economy in the post-World War II period was suggested by his finding that "there is evidence of a more rapid increase in wages in response to demand and prices in the period since the second world war than in the period prior to the first world war."[36]

Structuralists might argue either that changes in the pattern of demand among micro markets may have altered the weights of wage changes in them or that the Phillips curve of each micro market may itself have shifted. Assume for example that the national level of unemployment remains constant, but that changes in demand result in declining industries in specific regions, and unemployment rates in those regions increase greatly. In other regions, expanding demand for products of their industries results in labor shortages. Wages in the labor surplus region may not change, but wages in the labor shortage regions will tend to rise, perhaps rapidly, but certainly more rapidly than if no labor scarcity had been experienced. More even distribution of unemployment would alleviate both labor surpluses in some markets and labor scarcities in others. Thus, on the macro level, wage changes will appear greater with the demand shift than if demand had remained more evenly distributed with a given unemployment level. This is a structural change on the product demand side, and it is essentially the explanation offered by Shultze of the rise in prices which occurred in 1956 and 1957 in the United States. A perfectly competitive labor market would, of course, reallocate quickly labor from surplus areas to shortage areas, and micro markets would tend to operate at the same point on their respective Phillips curves—i.e., wage changes and unemployment changes would tend to be more uniform among micro markets. Consequently, perfectly competitive labor markets would imply a stable Phillips curve in the face of demand shifts. Alternatively, a macro curve with loops implies an imperfectly competitive labor market; certainly, it suggests that changes in micro demand for labor occur too rapidly for adjustments among micro labor markets to be made.

[35] *Ibid.*, p. 19.
[36] *Ibid.*, p. 30.

The alternative structuralist view is that institutional or technological changes in the economy alter the slope and position of the micro Phillips curve. For example, the development of strong unions in particular sectors may increase the slopes of the Phillips curves, because unions may exercise their bargaining power in pushing up wages more rapidly than labor supply conditions require. Technological change may alter the skill requirements and impair mobility from labor surplus areas with unskilled labor or with obsolete skills to labor shortage areas where higher skills are required. As a result, these skill imbalances can increase the slopes of micro Phillips curves in shortage areas.

The suggestion that conditions in micro markets determine the nature and position of the macro Phillips curve has led to an examination of the wage–unemployment relationship in disaggregated markets.[37] Such markets consisted of 73 SMSA areas, as well as industrial and occupational submarkets located within and across the SMSA areas. In order for a stable macro Phillips curve to exist, the micro relationships must be essentially identical. If they are not, the predictive value of a macro Phillips curve is impaired since one does not know which one of a large number of macro Phillips curves is relevant. Local and national unemployment rates, rates of change of prices, and rates of change of employment were found to be significantly related to changes in average hourly earnings. Moreover, the relationships were found to vary widely among SMSA areas, leading to the conclusion that no stable macro Phillips curve exists.[38] Some relationships were more sensitive to local unemployment rates; others were found to be more sensitive to national rates. Those labor markets which geographically were more isolated had wages that varied more with local unemployment rates than with national unemployment rates. Also, the dominance in an area of key economic groups, particularly industries which were more sensitive to national trends, made wage changes in that area more likely to be associated with national unemployment rates. The existence of oligopolistic industries is a case in point, although interestingly, unions did not appear to affect the sensitivity of an area to either local or national trends, except where the unions were found in concentrated industries. Interestingly, some cities which had high unemployment rates, 10% or more, for up to 10 years still experienced increases in average hourly earnings not too different

[37] "The Relationship between Wage Changes and Unemployment in Metropolitan and Industrial Labor Markets," *Yale Economic Essays* (Fall 1966), pp. 279–341.

[38] He qualifies this conclusion by noting that his observations, based on annual data for 1950–1962, occurred with only small changes in the unemployment rate and the price level. Hence, the observations were clustered within a relatively narrow range of the Phillips curve. *Ibid.*, p. 339.

from the national pattern.[39] Relatively few cities had annual increases in these earnings of less than 1.5%. This phenomenon suggests implications with respect to structural unemployment. This pattern of wage increases in the face of high unemployment retards the expansion of employment in the area, and it also provides incentive for unemployed workers to remain in the area by preventing wage differentials to develop or widen between the surplus labor area and other sectors in the economy.

This study tends to support Lipsey's theory. Both studies recognize that micro markets are important in identifying macro wage–employment relations. Moreover, they both agree that the distribution of unemployment among sectors must be known before any relationship can be identified. Albrecht's specification of a linear relationship in his regression equations does not correspond with Lipsey's hypothesis concerning the nature of micro market Phillips curves. However, this type of equation has been used with good results elsewhere for United States data.[40]

Discussion Questions

1. How can it be argued that wages vary with the business cycle if wages tend to be rigid in periods of unemployment?
2. Has deficient demand in the contraction phase of the cycle during the post-World War II period "pulled down" wages and prices? How would the demand–pull proponents interpret this phenomenon?
3. Does the acknowledgment of the existence of structural unemployment undermine the demand–pull theory of inflation? Discuss.
4. Does the Phillips curve validate the demand–pull theory of inflation? Is it consistent with the cost–push theory of inflation? Of what policy use is the Phillips curve, if any?
5. If economic concentration is a contributing cause to inflation, and if inflation is regarded as a social ill, why then are such concentrations of economic power not regulated more?
6. In an earlier chapter it was observed that union bargaining power influenced the ability of the organization to secure wage increases for its members. During what phase of the cycle is union bargaining power apt to be the strongest? Is this consistent with a cost–push theory of inflation? Discuss.

[39] *Ibid.*, p. 338.
[40] See the article above by R. R. France, *op. cit.* France and Albrecht both used annual data. Perhaps if Albrecht had used quarterly data some of his nonsignificant variables would have been found to be relevant.

7. (a) "Inflation begets inflation." Is there any evidence to support this assertion?

   (b) "Suppose we find in one time segment of an inflationary spiral that demand–pull forces are stronger, but that at another time cost–push forces are stronger. Can we regard the whole period of inflation as being caused by "mixed" forces?

   (c) If economic decision makers act on the basis of what they believe to be true, at the present or in the future, can all inflation be appropriately described as "demand–pull" induced? Discuss.

8. According to Lipsey, would a Phillips curve exist if demand were apportioned uniformly to all sectors of the economy? If unemployment were apportioned uniformly among sectors? How does Albrecht's data relate to these questions?

21

Do Phillips Curves Really Exist?

The Monetarists' View of Inflation and the Phillips Curve

Milton Friedman, one of the most articulate spokesmen for the monetarist school, has written, "Inflation is always and everywhere a monetary phenomenon, resulting from and accompanied by a rise in the quantity of money relative to output."[1] Essentially, Friedman believes that if the quantity of money is permitted by the monetary authorities to grow more rapidly than the level of output, undesired cash balances will initially accrue. The magnitude of cash balances—liquidity—desired by the inhabitants of a country varies according to institutions, wealth, and customs: in the United States it may be equivalent roughly to four weeks of income; in India, to ten weeks of income. An unwarranted increase in the quantity of money will increase cash balances above normal because someone must hold the money supply. In attempting to draw down cash balances to the desired level, spending will increase, there will be higher aggregate demand, and prices will rise if the supply of output cannot be increased accordingly. The increase in prices will reduce real wages if monetary wages lag behind, leading to an expansion in employment, or a reduction in unemployment. Eventually, the reduction in unemployment and real wages leads employers to bid up money wages and labor to seek higher wages until the level of money cash balances again bears the desired relationship to money income.

We may thus view the desire for cash balances as either a desire for real liquidity, in the sense that a person wishes to hold sufficient monetary wealth which can be transferred quickly into real goods and services, or a desire for real income. The amount of these goods and services one is

[1] *Dollars and Deficits: Living with America's Economic Problems* (Englewood Cliffs, N.J.: Prentice-Hall, Inc., 1968), p. 98.

accustomed to consuming is obviously related to one's real income, and particularly to the flow of permanent real income which a person expects to receive in the future. These expectations are slow to change; hence, when an increase in real income occurs, which is viewed as temporary when cash balances increase before prices do, the extra balances can be drawn down by savings (financial investments), which in turn lowers the money interest rates. Loans expand and increased spending in turn bids up resource and product prices and restores cash balances to the desired real level.

This view of inflation places Friedman and the monetarists solidly in the demand–pull school. In fact, Friedman denies that cost–push, either in the form of wage push or profit push, can *cause* inflation.[2]

"Unless the cost–push produces a monetary expansion that would otherwise not have occurred, its effect will be limited to at most a temporary general price rise, accompanied by unemployment, and followed by a tendency toward declining prices elsewhere." Producers may believe that cost–push forces are operating, because the higher prices which they must pay for resource inputs, including labor, impose additional costs upon them which they in turn try to pass on in higher prices. Yet, it was the original increase in the nominal money supply which initiated the price increases, and only a further increase in the money supply, providing extra spending capability, can sustain the continuation of inflation.

If the money supply continues to expand more rapidly than output over a period of time and prices continue to rise, cash holders will come to expect continuing inflation. Eventually, attempts to bring inflation under control by stabilizing the money supply will lead to a stabilizing of price changes, but only belatedly. The inflationary psychology, i.e., the belief that inflation will continue, generates pressure among those who enter into long-term contracts for the sale of resources or products—such as organized labor—to continue to push for price and wage increases in order to offset the anticipated ill effects of continued inflation. A stabilized money supply will not sustain the increased monetary expenditures on the same level of output that has been inflated by price increases, and so contraction in production and employment materializes. If the inflationary psychology is sufficiently strong, prices may continue to rise, but at a decreasing rate, over an extended period even while unemployment is increasing. Eventually, however, if the money supply remains stabilized, inflation will dissipate. The danger, Friedman fears, is that government will step in too soon and attempt to remedy the unemployment by relaxing its controls upon the money supply. If this occurs, inflation may not abate.[3]

---

[2] *Ibid.*, p. 101.
[3] This sounds very much like the inflationary periods of 1956–1957 and 1969–1971.

Although this line of reasoning suggests that Friedman may belong to the "mixed inflation" school, this is not true. He acknowledges the existence of the ratchet effect owing to union pressures to resist wage reductions, and the ability of oligopolies to resist price reductions. Moreover, he recognizes the possibility that government may validate cost–push forces through ill-conceived monetary policy, and therefore he acknowledges the likelihood of a "dilemma model." Yet, Friedman believes that wages and prices are not absolutely rigid, and that if those representatives of government who make and implement economic policy would demonstrate sufficient patience, reductions in the money-output ratio would eventually bring about wage and price reductions. Furthermore, the "dilemma model" is not a necessary process of inflation. Again, all that is required is continued restraint in bringing the money supply into the proper relationship with real aggregate output.[4] Therefore, Friedman is not a proponent of the "mixed inflation" school; rather, he would declare that members of this school, if they acknowledged the true impact of monetary policy, would properly be categorized as members of the demand–pull school.

The Natural Rate of Unemployment

How do Friedman's views of inflation fit into the concepts of structural unemployment and Phillips curve analysis? Stated briefly, Friedman recognizes that structural unemployment and short-run Phillips curves exist, but in the long run, Phillips curves do not exist.[5] More specifically, in any economy in any era there exists a natural rate of unemployment which is determined by the set of economic institutions, statutes, labor market information, etc. The natural rate changes as these determinants change. This rate of unemployment is "natural" because, given the structural characteristics of markets, it is an equilibrium rate in the Walrasian sense.[6] Real wages are stable and rise secularly in line with increases in real

[4] It is not full employment that brings about inflation, declares Friedman. It is full employment *policy. Ibid.*, p. 39.

[5] For a succinct statement, see Milton Friedman, "The Role of Monetary Policy," *American Economic Review*, Vol. 55, No. 1 (March 1968), pp. 7–11.

[6] This rate of unemployment has variously been termed as "normal," "full employment," or "warranted." See Edmund C. Phelps, ed., *Microeconomic Foundations of Employment and Inflation Theory* (New York: W. W. Norton & Co., 1970), p. 13. This rate is not quite the same as the frictional unemployment rate, for it need not represent the rate at which job vacancies equal the number unemployed. The rate will be above zero if population and the labor force are growing and if technological change continues. In the former case, new entrants into the labor market need time to search for jobs, as do displaced workers in the latter case. See G. C. Archibald, "The Structure of Excess Demand for Labor," *Microeconomic Foundations of Employment and Inflation Theory, op. cit.*, pp. 212–223.

productivity. Moreover, the structure of real wages realized is consistent with the structure of anticipated real wages.

Now, suppose this "natural rate" of unemployment is 5%, but for some reason the Council of Economic Advisers perceives it to be 4%. Moreover, suppose the economy has reached a level in the vicinity of the natural rate, with reasonable price stability. A national goal of full employment is interpreted to mean that policies must be implemented to reduce the rate to 4%. Policies designed to improve the structural efficiency of the economy in matching men with jobs would be appropriate. Improving labor market information, improving the competitiveness of product and labor markets, extension of educational and training programs are all cases in point of desirable policies. However, policies designed only to increase aggregate demand through fiscal manipulations or additions to the money supply will, in the long run, tend to be self-defeating.

The Expectational Hypothesis

With stable wages and prices, no anticipated increases exist in either, other than perhaps the anticipated increase in real wages that are consistent with underlying real trends in the economy. An increase in the money supply, by raising spending through the cash balance effect, will lead to an increase in prices and money wages. The labor force, with lagged beliefs about the stability of the price level, interprets these money wage increases, termed nominal market increases by Friedman, as representing an increase in future real wages. This is so because, even though the members of the labor force may believe the wage increases are permanent, they regard the price increases as temporary. In reality, however, real wages have declined and employers are motivated to expand employment. Others, in the mistaken belief that real wages have risen, accept the offered employment. For a time, unemployment declines as prices rise. This is all consistent with the Phillips analysis.

In time the labor force becomes aware of the true effect on real wages of the higher prices and nominal wages, and unemployment begins to drift back to the natural level, as workers who originally were unwilling to offer their labor at lower real wages begin to withdraw into the secondary labor force. If the monetary authorities do not intervene, the natural rate will be reestablished at a higher wage and price level. However, if the perception of full employment has not changed, additional money will be pumped into the economy and the process will repeat itself. Soon, members of the labor force will begin to anticipate a given rate of inflation and they will seek to maintain their anticipated level of real wages by building into their wage contracts escalator provisions to offset price increases. Hence, after a lag, nominal wage increases will tend to parallel price increases. Wage increases

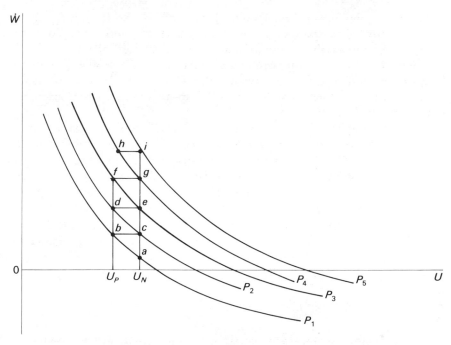

FIGURE 21.1. The natural rate of unemployment and short-run shifts in Phillips curves; $\dot{W}$ ≡ rate of change of money wages, U_P ≡ perceived full employment rate, U_N ≡ natural unemployment rate, P_t ≡ Phillips curve at time t.

have adapted to expected price increases, and as this dynamic equilibrium relationship is approached, unemployment again will drift back towards the natural rate. This return to the natural rate of unemployment has been in the face of a greater expansion of the money supply. Friedman, therefore, concludes that to maintain a rate of unemployment below the natural rate, increases in the money supply will have to accelerate, and this implies an acceleration in the rate of inflation and wages.[7] This can be represented in Figure 21.1. At point a, wages are rising at the secular real rate. To move the unemployment rate to U_P, the rate of change of wages must be consistent with that at point b in time interval 1. Adaptation to that rate of wage and price inflation returns the unemployment rate to U_N at point c, as P_1 shifts upward to P_2. Wages must rise at a higher rate in period 2 in order to return the unemployment rate to U_P, as represented by point d; again,

---

[7] The converse is also true. To maintain an unemployment rate in excess of the natural rate, deflation must accelerate.

adaptation to the higher rate of wage change shifts P_2 to P_3 and U_N again is approached. The tradeoff between wage changes and unemployment occurs only temporarily because of unanticipated rates of inflation.

The net effect of this process is a long-run vertical line at U_N, with no long-run tradeoff between unemployment and the rate of change of wages (or prices). Hence, there is no long-run Phillips relation under the expectational hypothesis.

How long will it take for participants in the economy to adapt to new rates of inflation? For rates of inflation peculiar to the United States, Friedman believes it will take up to 20 years for the effects to work themselves out. Initial recognition of danger in the rate of inflation will take between two and five years, and initial reactions will take about the same length of time (labor agreements run for about 2.7 years and wage rounds following key bargains may run as long as three to five years). Thus, the time dimension of this ultimate adaptation of unemployment to inflation is similar to that of the "Pigou" or "real balance" effect. In fact, it is merely a manifestation of the real balance effect.

Microeconomic Foundations of the Expectational Hypothesis

The "expectational hypothesis" has been given a microeconomic interpretation. The Phillips tradeoff between wage inflation and unemployment is interpreted as a short-run phenomenon. In the long run, as expectations adapt to higher rates of wage changes, unemployment and wage-rate changes are shown to be independent, consistent with the Friedman model. However, the Phillips curve phenomenon is attributed to a variety of microeconomic manifestations. Fundamental to this interpretation is the concept of the labor market. Prospective or existing employees are viewed as participating in the labor market in search of jobs. Each participant is faced with imperfect knowledge of the true distribution of wage rates among jobs, but the participant possesses some concept of the dimensions of the distribution. This concept is formed by sampling the job market or by various sources of incomplete or imprecise information. Hence, he has a set of expectations concerning the real benefits bestowed by jobs in the labor market. From his indifference map for income and leisure, he has formed a reservation "real" wage that determines acceptable employment for him. In his search process, he is motivated to accept employment when he believes he has found a job meeting his reservation wage. If he has mistaken the real benefits conferred by the job because he has incorrectly inferred the purchasing power of money wages; i.e., he has incorrectly anticipated the rate of change of money prices, he will seek adjustments in the future.

On the other side of the labor market, individual employers are searching—recruiting—workers. Wages are used as an instrument of recruitment policy. The higher the wages relative to other employers, the more successful will be the recruitment policy. Each employer also possesses a concept of the distribution of wages among jobs offered in the labor market, and the employer seeks to establish that wage which will enable him to staff his firm, consistent with the costs and productivity constraints under which the firm must operate. An expansion in aggregate demand, by expanding the output requirements of firms, leads to an expansion of job vacancies. From the natural or "equilibrium" level of unemployment, this allows employment to expand. In the process, each firm raises offered wages in an attempt to recruit new workers or retain old ones by slowing down the rate of quits. Imperfect knowledge of the wage structure and/or actions based on a lagged wage structure leads employers to expect an increase in employment from offering higher wages. Initially, as unemployment is reduced below the "natural" rate, some expansion of employment will occur. However, as workers learn of the true changes in the real wage, unemployment tends to return to the natural state, and the employer learns that the labor market is simultaneously adjusting the wage structure upward. Therefore, to maintain the same recruitment rate, employers, acting individually, will have to accelerate their rate of wage increases.

From this micro view of the labor market comes several explanations of short-run Phillips curves. Quit rates are viewed as being inversely related to the rate of unemployment, and unemployment duration is positively related.[8] The lower the unemployment rate, the higher the quit rate and the shorter the duration of unemployment. Now, people quit jobs to accept other employment at higher rates of pay; similarly, if the average duration of unemployment is reduced, this means that searchers are finding jobs at rates of pay equal to or above their reservation wage. In both cases, the weighted average of wage rates tends to increase as unemployment is reduced. This is consistent with the Phillips curve. This condition is temporary, however, because accompanying higher prices frustrate expectations of higher real wages, and labor market adjustments return unemployment to the natural rate at the higher wage rate structure.

Job vacancies also play a role in creating the Phillips curve illusion. The greater the number of job vacancies, the easier it is for the unemployed to secure the types of jobs they are seeking. Similarly, the more job vacancies there are, the greater is the tendency of workers to move to higher rates of pay. Job vacancy growth, consequently, can produce a Phillips curve

---

[8] C. C. Holt, "Job Search, Phillips' Wage Relation, and Union Influence: Theory and Evidence." See also, "How Can the Phillips Curve be Moved to Reduce Both Inflation and Unemployment," in E. S. Phelps, *Microeconomic Foundations of Employment and Inflation Theory*, *op. cit.*, pp. 53–123, 224–256.

relation. This is true even when wage rates are trending upward, for if the increase in wage rates exceeds the expected change in wages, unemployment will be drawn down as workers accept employment under the mistaken belief that their reservation real wage has been met. It is the magnitude of job vacancies that influences jointly the rate of wage inflation and the rate of unemployment.[9]

Just as a landlord in renting his apartments must build into his rent structure the probability that his apartments will be empty part of the time if he is to receive adequate compensation for their rental, so must a laborer obtain a wage that compensates him for the probability of unemployment in that job. Moreover, in accepting a job the worker foregoes the opportunity to seek and obtain another job, possibly at higher wages. These elements enter into the reservation wage standards adopted by workers. If this reservation wage is not immediately obtainable in his job search, the labor force participant must "wait" while he continues his search.[10] Some, such as housewives or children, may even retire from active labor force participation until their reservation wage is met. If new jobs open up from an expansion in aggregate demand, the period of "waiting" is reduced for obtaining the reservation rate. Again, if expectations of real wages are frustrated by unexpected price changes, withdrawals will occur and the natural rate of unemployment will be restored. Obviously the reservation standard, the period of wait, and the availability of jobs are all related to the duration of unemployment.

Frictional Unemployment and the Phillips Curve

Combining the job search hypothesis of Stigler, the theory of occupational wage and employment structure of Reder, and the Phillips curve, a number of economists have approached macroeconomic theory from a somewhat different perspective.[11] Charles Holt, a member of this school, has developed a model which relates frictions in the labor market, that interfere with job

[9] See E. S. Phelps, "The New Microeconomics in Employment and Inflation Theory," and "Money Wage Dynamics and Labor Market Equilibrium," *ibid.*, pp. 1–26, 124–166. Phelps claims that the vacancy rate determines "unemployment and thus excess demand and the rate of inflation," *ibid.*, p. 13. This may be questionable, however. To this author, it seems that job vacancies can more properly be regarded as a manifestation of the level of aggregate demand.

[10] D. F. Gordon and Allan Hines, "On the Theory of Price Dynamics," in Phelps, *ibid.*, pp. 369–393.

[11] The works of representatives of this new approach are found in Edmund S. Phelps, ed., *Microeconomic Foundations of Employment and Inflation Theory* (New York: W. W. Norton, 1969).

search, to the shape and position of the Phillips curve.[12] The labor market is perceived as consisting of unemployed workers searching for jobs, whose willingness to accept wages of a given magnitude is inversely related to the duration of their search (unemployment), T_U. Similarly, employers are searching for workers to fill vacancies, and the magnitude of their wage offers is positively related to the duration of their search, T_V. It can be shown that as unemployment expands, the duration of unemployment expands and both workers' willingness to accept and employers' willingness to offer lower wages increase. The opposite is true as the level and duration of unemployment decline.

Consider the following definitions[13]:

$$F = \frac{P \cdot V \cdot U}{T_S} \qquad (21.1)$$

$$T_U = \frac{U}{F} = \frac{T_S}{P \cdot V} \qquad (21.2)$$

$$T_V = \frac{V}{F} = \frac{T_S}{P \cdot U} \qquad (21.3)$$

where $P \equiv$ probability of a job hire from a job interview; $V \equiv$ number of vacancies; $U \equiv$ level of unemployment; $T_S \equiv$ search time per interview; $F \equiv$ flow of new hires per time period. If, for example, search time is two weeks, the number of vacancies is one hundred and the probability of a successful interview is 0.02, the average duration of unemployment will be

$$T_U = \frac{2 \text{ weeks}}{0.02(100)} = 1 \text{ week.}$$

It can be seen that the shorter the search time per interview, the greater the probability of finding a job; and the greater the number of vacancies, then the shorter will be the average duration of unemployment. The worker's education, skill, and experience will influence P, the efficiency of labor market information channels will affect T_S, and the state of sector demand will determine V. Similar relations determine T_U. It can be shown that the degree of segmentation and imbalance among segments of a labor market affects T_U and T_V.

Next, consider the neoclassical implication of perfect foresight on the state of the Phillips curve. Given the level of full employment, some frictional unemployment will exist. Now assume that aggregate demand increases,

[12] "Improving the Labor Market Trade-Off Between Inflation and Unemployment," *American Economic Review*, Vol. 59, No. 2 (May 1969), pp. 135–146.
[13] *Ibid.*, p. 138.

causing unemployment to decline, wages to increase, and prices to increase, all consistent with a Phillips curve. However, real wages will remain unchanged if wages and prices increase proportionately, and when this is recognized by the labor force, employment and unemployment will return to the original level. However, wages and prices will remain at the higher level, and combined with the initial unemployment level, the Phillips curve will then shift upward. The neoclassical condition implies shifts in the Phillips curve with inflation. However, if a money illusion exists with respect to the wage rate, if vacancies at higher-paying jobs develop unevenly with respect to micromarkets, or if worker expectations lag behind changes in aggregate demand and money wages, then a nonshifting Phillips curve is possible.

Whether or not the Phillips curve shifts, is an empirical question. Improvements in labor market information which lowers T_S, or in labor force skills that raise P, or in aggregate demand that lowers U and raises V, all combined can improve the inflation–unemployment tradeoff. These policies, in effect, will generate a shift in the Phillips curve.

An Empirical Test of the Expectational Hypothesis

An empirical test of the expectational hypothesis raises the question of whether the time dimension for negating the tradeoff between inflation and unemployment is irrelevant for policy purposes, as Friedman implies. If the tradeoff occurs only temporarily, but temporary means an interval of twenty years, it may be that the authorities cannot ignore a rate of unemployment which the society deems undesirable, even if it may be "natural."

Solow has examined the expectational hypothesis and has formulated a model which permits empirical testing of its validity.[14] His expectations equation is

$$P^*_{t+1} = (1 - \theta)P^*_t + \theta P_t$$

where P^*_t is the expected rate of inflation in period t; the P_t is the actual rate of inflation in that period; and θ is the rate of learning when the expected rate of inflation P^*_t differs from the actual rate. If $\theta = 0$, zero learning, then there is no rate of learning, and the actual rate of inflation is independent of the expected rate. A zero value of θ also means that the expected rate of inflation is constant. If θ has a value of 1, then the expected rate of inflation in the next period equals the actual rate of inflation in the preceding period. Solow claims that Friedman's model implies that $\theta = 1$ and this he calls the

[14] R. M. Solow, *Price Expectations and the Behavior of the Price Level* (Manchester: University of Manchester Press, 1969).
[15] *Ibid.*, p. 8.

"strict expectations hypothesis."[15] With $\theta < 1$, we have the adaptive expectations model, in which adjustments to past inflation are not complete.[16]

His regression model relates the actual rate of price changes to wages, labor input per unit of output, a plant capacity utilization index, two dummy variables representing the Korean War period, and the Wage Guideline period, and finally a variable representing the expected rate of inflation. Various θ's are assumed, and the coefficient for the expected rate of inflation variable varied between 0.37 and 0.55. Little improvement occurred in the explanation of the variance of the actual rate of inflation for values of θ greater than 0.4. Solow concluded, therefore, that "these estimates offer no support whatever to the expectations hypothesis in its strict form."[17] Rather, the evidence suggested that there did exist a tradeoff between the rate of inflation and real determinants of output (for example, the proportionate level of capacity utilization). However, he found that in the long run, the tradeoff was less than in the short run. For example, given $\theta = 0.4$, "if money wage rates begin to rise 1% a year faster, prices will rise only 0.25% a year faster at once, but as expectations adjust, the rate of inflation eventually rises to become a little more than 0.4% a year faster. . . ."[18] This is understandable, he argues, because the United States' pattern of inflation has been irregular, and this is not conducive to perfect adaptation of expected future rates of inflation from erratic past rates. Studies of the British and American economies lead Solow to conclude that in both countries, expectations in both the short and long runs do adapt to recent past inflation, although the tradeoff is more pronounced in the short run than in the long run. It would be well to remember that Solow argues that a Phillips-curve tradeoff occurs if aggregate demand causes prices to change at a rate less than the change in wage rates. This condition implies an increase in output and a reduction, perhaps, of unemployment of labor and/or plant capacity.

In fairness to Friedman, it should be noted that Solow's strict expectations model requires an adjustment in a much shorter period than Friedman specified. Solow uses a period equal to one year, so that if $\theta = 1$, complete adjustment, expectations of price changes in the current year are equal to the rate of price changes one year earlier. Friedman has never intimated that adaptations could occur so quickly. Indeed, *initial* adaptations occur only in a period of from two to five years. The finding of Solow of $\theta = 0.4$ is more consistent with Friedman's estimate of the rate of adaptation, since this θ implies that 40% of the adaptation occurs in the first year. Presumably, at

[16] For another formulation of the expectations model, see Robert E. Lucas and Leonard A. Rapping, "Real Wages, Employment, and Inflation," in Phelps, *op. cit.*, pp. 257–305.
[17] *Ibid.*, p. 14.
[18] *Ibid.*, p. 15.

a minimum, complete adaptation to an initial change in the rate of inflation would take 2.5 years, well within the period specified by Friedman. Also, the latter might argue that Solow's finding that long-run (20-year) tradeoffs are smaller than short-run ones is precisely what his analysis implies. Only in an extreme case, with no intervening shocks, would there be no long-run tradeoff.

Relevant to the "expectation hypothesis" is the question of the timing of wage–price adjustments. If wage adjustments to price changes, or vice versa, occur within a year, a basis for rapid learning of the relationship between wages and prices exists, and Solow's test would be more relevant. However, if price–wage lags, or vice versa, occur over a longer duration, then the Friedman interpretation of the expectational hypothesis is more relevant. Cargill has found, using annual data for England and the United States dating back to the 18th century, that, "When there is a time difference (of several years) between prices and wages, it tends to result in a wage lag; however, there are many instances where no meaningful time differences exist, implying that prices and wages are coincident."[19] Since annual data are used, this means that any lag that occurred in the short run did so within the year.[20] In the long run it could be argued that Friedman's hypothesis implies a price–wage lag, yet Cargill's data reveal a wage–price lag. Thus, it would appear that Solow's results take on increased relevance in the light of Cargill's study.

Discussion Questions

1. Paul McCracken, in leaving his post in late 1971 as Chairman of the President's Council of Economic Advisers, confessed that he was less of a supporter of the Friedman School than when he first took the job. Assuming that the monetarist's view of inflation is valid, how can McCracken's statement be reconciled with their view of inflation?
2. Is there really such a thing as the "natural rate of unemployment"? Is this question as important as, "Does the Phillips curve really exist?" Must we choose between the two questions in our quest for an understanding of how to control inflation?

[19] Thomas F. Cargill, "An Empirical Investigation of the Wage-Lag Hypothesis," *American Economic Review*, Vol. 59, No. 5 (December 1969), p. 810.
[20] Interestingly, for the 1947–1965 period, price changes in United States manufacturing have been found to be significantly related to wage changes lagged one and two quarters. See Calvin B. Siebert and Mahmood A. Zaidi, "The Short-Run Wage–Price Mechanism in U.S. Manufacturing," *Western Economic Journal*, Vol. IX, No. 3 (September 1971), pp. 278–287.

3. Are employment commitments short-term or long-term commitments? If expectations of employment benefits are not realized by labor force participants, what labor market adjustments are appropriate? What policy implications follow from the "expectations hypothesis"?
4. If Phillips curves do not exist in the long run, but do exist in the short run, of what value is this knowledge?

22

Productivity, Profits, and Wages in an Incomes Policy

Wage Stabilization Programs

In earlier chapters we have examined the relationship between wage rate or price changes and the unemployment rate, the so-called "Phillips curve," together with the underlying theory behind this relationship. We have also considered the effect of labor organizations on these relationships, and the importance of expectations in influencing the inflation–unemployment trade-off. In this chapter we shall examine an alternative policy which has often been used to reduce the rate of inflation when the economy is operating close to full employment. This other policy in England has variously been called "an incomes policy" or a "wage–price freeze"; in this country it has been associated with wage–price stabilization programs, and during the Kennedy–Johnson administration, it was called the "wage–price guide-posts."

Wage stabilization programs were used during both World War II and the Korean War to prevent inflation when the economy was subjected to rapid increases in aggregate demand and faced serious manpower and other resource shortages. During World War II, not only were wages frozen to a level 15% greater than that which existed in the Spring of 1941, but rents and prices were also tightly controlled, and the Federal Reserve System pursued such an easy money policy that the interest rate approached the lowest level in the history of the country. During the Korean War, a Wage Stabilization Board passed on and approved wage increases in a mild attempt to restrain wage and price increases. Wage–price stabilization boards in the construction industry in early 1971 were proposed on a voluntary self-regulatory

575

basis by the Nixon administration, and a wage–price freeze was imposed in August 1971. In November, the freeze was lifted and in its place wages and prices were subject to regulation.

Peacetime attempts to restrain wage and price increases in this and other advanced industrial countries have generally resulted from balance-of-payments difficulties. When the domestic price level rises relative to that in other countries, imports tend to increase as domestic consumers shift their purchases from home to foreign produced goods; similarly, exports tend to fall as foreigners alter their buying patterns. In order to relieve the imbalance in trade and the resulting payment problems which threaten a country's international liquidity position, attempts are made to bring the domestic price level in line with foreign prices. In general, if prices are rising on the international scene, this readjustment can be accompanied not by deflation, but through price stabilization programs. By limiting general wage increases to increases in productivity, labor costs can remain stable, and since these on an aggregate basis determine about 75% of costs, pressure to increase prices can be reduced. Stable prices on the domestic scene represent an improvement in the international competitive position of American industry if price levels in other countries continue to increase.

The Wage–Price Guidelines

The existence of large, powerful unions and corporations was recognized as a force in the economy which could substantially affect the movement of wages and prices. The exercise of monopoly power, and its transmission via pattern setting to other sectors, permitted wide discretion in wage–price setting. If wages and prices were to be established fairly by the exercise of discretion, guidelines were necessary. The essential guideline was, of course, the rate of increase in productivity. The Council of Economic Advisers stated the wage–price guidelines as follows[1]:

> The general guide for noninflationary wage behavior is that the rate of increase in wage rates (including fringe benefits) in each industry be equal to the trend rate of over-all productivity increase. General acceptance of this guide would maintain stability of labor cost per unit of output for the economy as a whole—although not, of course, for individual industries.

[1] *Economic Report of the President, January 1962* (Washington: U.S. Government Printing Office, 1962). It is interesting that in the *Economic Report of the President, 1964*, the CEA stated that the guidelines were to be used as a standard for wage and price decisions, and the exceptions included in the modifications were expected to apply only to relatively few cases.

The general guide for noninflationary price behavior calls for price reduction if the industry's rate of productivity increase exceeds the over-all rate—for this would mean declining unit labor costs; it calls for an appropriate increase in price if the opposite relationship prevails; and it calls for stable prices if the two rates of productivity increases are equal.

Important modifications in these two guideline principles are the following:

1. Wage rate increases would exceed the general guide rate in an industry which would otherwise be unable to attract sufficient labor; or in which wage rates are exceptionally low compared with the range of wages earned elsewhere by similar labor, because the bargaining position of workers has been weak in particular local labor markets.

2. Wage rate increases would fall short of the general guide rate in an industry which could not provide jobs for its entire labor force even in times of generally full employment; or in which wage rates are exceptionally high compared with the range of wages earned elsewhere by similar labor, because the bargaining position of workers (elsewhere) has been especially strong.

3. Prices would rise more rapidly, or fall more slowly, than indicated by the general guide rate in an industry in which the level of profits was insufficient to attract the capital required to finance a needed expansion in capacity; or in which costs other than labor costs had risen (*sic*).

4. Prices would rise more slowly, or fall more rapidly, than indicated by the general guide in an industry in which the relation of productive capacity to full employment demand shows the desirability of an outflow of capital from the industry; or in which costs other than labor costs have fallen; or in which excessive market power has resulted in rates of profits substantially higher than those earned elsewhere on investments of comparable risk.

The wage–price guidelines were essentially voluntary, relying not on fiat for their enforcement, but upon the pressure of public opinion. Accompanying the guidelines was a certain amount of "jawboning"; the Council of Economic Advisers watched closely significant collective bargaining agreements and industry pricing behavior and identified those that were considered to be inflationary. (Chart 22.1 shows the changes in the 1960s.)

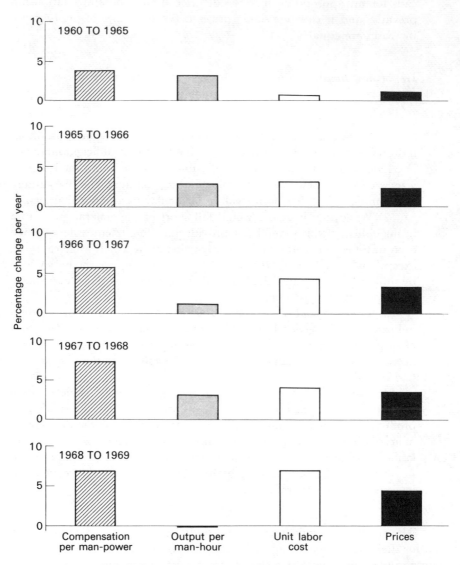

CHART 22.1. Changes in compensation, productivity, labor costs, and prices for private nonfarm sector. Data relate to all employees.

Sources: Department of Labor and Department of Commerce, *Economic Report of the President, 1970*, p. 52.

That behavior which was considered to be out of step with the guidelines—excessive—was condemned as unpatriotic or not in the national interest and wide publicity was given to this judgment. If voluntary adjustments were not forthcoming, vague threats of legislation or of redirecting massive federal purchases to those firms who did cooperate were used. At times, government stockpiles were released on the market to drive prices downward, and removal of tariffs or lowering of import quotas was advocated as retaliatory measures against uncooperating unions and firms.

The guidelines policy sought to impose the burden of proof on the union–firm that "excessive wage–price increases" were necessary. The modifications to the general guideline principles indicated acceptable reasons for departing from the general principles. Criticisms poured in from all sources: academicians, union and business leaders, politicians. The complaints varied: (1) The guidelines interfered with natural market forces; (2) admonitions without effective sanctions won't work, leading therefore to the imposition of sanctions and ultimate wage–price controls; (3) income shares of labor and capital will be frozen by the guidelines, implying that these shares are now distributed equitably; (4) the guidelines, together with the modifications, are so loose that parties can behave as they wish and justify their actions through rationalizations provided by the modifications. It is interesting that critics of the guidelines in the early 1960s reversed their position in the 1969–1971 inflationary–recession period and called for a new incomes policy, an appeal which President Nixon at first firmly resisted. Table 22.1 shows the changes from Fall 1967 to Fall 1970.

CRITICISMS   Two of the most articulate critics of wage–price controls have been Arthur Burns and Milton Friedman. In addition to fixing the proportion of wages and profits in national income, and hence implying that the existing distribution was equitable, Burns feared that such controls would lead to the demise of the free-market competitive system.[2] By freezing prices,

---

[2] See Arthur F. Burns, "Wages and Prices by Formula," *Harvard Business Review* (March–April 1965), pp. 57–64. Dr. Burns has expressed a varying attitude toward government policy to promote wage–price restraint. In this article, he examines some of the weaknesses of the guideline approach and expresses the belief that these controls are ineffective, misdirected, and inappropriate to a free market economy. Earlier in a 1958 address to the American Assembly, he had called upon the government to take steps to control inflation. "What we need more than anything else at this juncture is a national declaration of purpose with regard to the level of prices that could have a moral force such as the Employment Act . . . ," reprinted in "The Threat of Inflationary Psychology," in Arthur M. Okun, ed., *The Battle Against Unemployment* (New York: W. W. Norton, 1965), p. 69. After becoming chairman of the Board of Governors of the Federal Reserve System in 1970, Burns went on record in favor of wage–price guidelines, although in testimony before the Senate subcommittee on financial institutions on March 31, 1971, he felt that wage and price control authority delegated to the President should be limited to six months.

TABLE 22.1

CHANGES IN COSTS AND PRICES IN THE TOTAL PRIVATE NONFARM ECONOMY AND IN NONFINANCIAL CORPORATIONS, 1967 III TO 1970 III

Item	Percentage Change (Seasonally Adjusted Annual Rates)				
	1967 III to 1968 III	*1968 III to 1969 III*	*1969 III to 1970 III*	*1969 III to 1970 I*	*1970 I to 1970 III*
Total private nonfarm economy:					
Labor compensation per man-hour	7.2	6.8	7.0	7.2	6.8
Output per man-hour	2.5	0.0	1.4	−1.3	4.2
Unit labor costs	4.5	6.8	5.5	8.6	2.5
Real compensation per man-hour	2.7	1.2	1.2	1.1	1.3
Prices (deflator)	3.5	4.5	4.7	4.5	4.9
Nonfinancial corporations:					
Total price per unit of output[a]	2.5	3.7	4.2	4.1	4.2
Labor compensation	2.4	5.6	5.7	8.5	3.0
Corporate profits and inventory valuation adjustment	3.6	−5.8	−12.4	−25.5	2.9
Other costs	2.2	5.5	9.2	10.7	7.7
Capital consumption allowances	0.0	3.7	8.9	11.0	6.9
Indirect business taxes plus transfer payments less subsidies	2.0	4.9	9.3	9.5	9.0
Net interest	13.0	15.4	10.0	13.8	6.3

[a] Current dollar cost per unit of 1958 dollar gross product originating in nonfinancial corporations.

Sources: Department of Labor and Department of Commerce.
Economic Report of the President, 1971, p. 45.

a successful guidelines policy would cause resources to be misallocated, and if prices were not permitted to adjust freely to market forces, rationing and black market would be inevitable.[3] Too much reliance on a guidelines

---

[3] Compulsion would be a natural consequence if voluntary compliance was withheld. Voluntary compliance by unions and corporations with monopoly powers cannot be expected because it requires a surrender of their control over market forces, one of the chief reasons for their existence. This same view has been stated by Ben W. Lewis, "Economics by Admonition," *American Economic Review*, Vol. 49 (May 1959), pp. 384–398.

policy might encourage the government to rely less heavily on monetary and fiscal restraint to control inflation,[4] and it could cause the government to pursue less vigorously anticost–push policies toward minimum wages, antitrust, and free trade. These shortcomings would become evident if the guidelines were successful. However, Burns did not believe they would or could be successful. They were implemented when unemployment was sufficient to reenforce them; he accurately predicted that they would not succeed when markets became tighter, which they did in 1965. After mid-1966 the guidelines for all purposes were abandoned. Other drawbacks to successful implementation of the guidelines were (1) inadequate and belated statistical data on specific productivity movements, (2) lack of appropriate wage–price indexes, and (3) rationalizations of unions and firms which permitted them to conclude that they qualified as exceptions. These drawbacks reduced the guidelines to mere "exhortations" or admonitions. He believed that instead of wage–price controls, the government should pursue a policy to make the economy more competitive. This would involve a more vigorous antitrust policy, greater controls upon labor unions, a reduction in tariffs and import controls, labor market policies designed to retrain and encourage mobility of labor, and refinement in monetary and fiscal controls.

Somewhat similar to Burns' views on the wage–price guideposts are those of Friedman. Economic control of prices, wages, rents, interests, and foreign currencies as a means of combating inflation merely "suppresses" it.[5] He regards open inflation as bad, but suppressed inflation is even worse. Basically, it distorts the price system, which he regards as the most efficient allocating system yet invented. By not allowing prices to perform their rationing function, all sorts of administrative gimmicks are employed to patch up the economy, and multitudinous illogical arrangements, employing outlandish subterfuges, develop. Jobs are redefined or upgraded in order to grant hidden wage increases, coupons are used to ration purchases, instead of money, encouraging counterfeiting and black markets. These in turn require further restrictive controls. Not only does suppressed inflation violate the logic of economics, but it does not attack the source of inflation. Friedman likens economic controls of prices to trying to control the action of a thermometer. The latter merely registers heat; it does not produce it. Similarly, prices register forces in the economy. Just as one can't stop the action of a thermometer without breaking it unless one does something about

---

[4] Burns believed that the implementation of monetary and fiscal policy should be cued, not to the unemployment rate as it currently is, but to the vacancy–unemployment ratio, because this ratio is a much more sensitive measure of the state of the economy than the unemployment rate.

[5] Milton Friedman, *Dollars and Deficits: Living with America's Economic Problems* (Englewood Cliffs: Prentice-Hall, Inc., 1968), pp. 97–121.

the source of heat, neither can the government hold down the rise in prices without destroying the economic system. Attempts to evade the controls, reasonable and in accord with economic philosophy (and therefore moral), lead to disrespect for law and order. Moreover, such controls violate human freedom and dignity and are inconsistent with a democratic society.

A RETORT   In reply to the critics of stabilization policy, it has been recognized that policies to make the economy more competitive would reduce the adverse relationship between inflation and unemployment, but such policies can only be implemented in the long run.[6] In the short run, the realities of the Phillips curve in most industrialized countries have required some type of wage restraint policy as a stop-gap action. A wage–price restraint policy is primarily a method of marshaling public opinion against those sectors of the economy which, because of their size and economic power, can exercise discretion in wage or price setting. These are imperfect markets, and stabilization policy is intended to produce the same kind of results that would occur in perfectly competitive markets. Hence, the charge that wage–price restraint would impair the competitive free market simply doesn't conform with the facts. Also, stabilization policy will have little effect on income distribution, which historically has been slow to change in any event, and allowance for a small degree of error in the implementation of the policy can permit prices to vary annually, say, by 1%, which is all the flexibility that the economy requires to allocate its resources efficiently. In addition, there are difficulties in applying statistical measures of a productivity index. Caution is in order against allowing unions and firms to use estimates of productivity gain as a bargaining matter—it is something to be discovered, not argued about.

Moreover, inflationary pressures can build up in local markets if local monopolies, such as in the construction industry, are permitted to exploit their power. Stabilization policy may be ineffective here. Instead, changes in government wage policy, such as those contained in the public contracts laws, can be more appropriate. It is indeed interesting that President Nixon employed this specific device early in 1971 in order to compel cooperation from the construction sector as an initial step in a wage–price stabilization program. Under discretionary authority delegated by Congress, the President could invoke wage–price controls for up to six months if he decided to use them. Initially, Nixon suspended the Bacon–Davis act with respect to the construction industry in order to elicit cooperation from management and industry.

[6] Robert Solow, "The Case Against the Case Against the Guideposts," in George P. Schultz and Robert Z. Aliber, eds., Guidelines, Informal Controls, and the Market Place (Chicago: University of Chicago Press, 1969), pp. 41–54.

The 1971 Wage–Price Controls

The rapid increase in prices in 1968 and 1969 led the monetary authorities to impose tight restraints on the growth of the money supply in 1969, so much so that interest rates reached the highest levels of the century. The restrictive policies succeeded in curtailing spending, and by late spring of 1970 it was clear that the economy was entering a recessionary period. Throughout 1970 and 1971 unemployment rates continued an upward trend. Although there was mild abatement in the rise of the consumer price index, the increase in the price level in 1970 was about 5.5% and almost 4.0% in 1971. These were politically unacceptable rates of inflation. Moreover, labor contracts negotiated in 1971 did not reflect the state of the economy. Agreements in such major industries as steel, automobiles, communications, railroads, and the postal system called for an annual increase in labor costs of over 10% during the following two or three years. A 7.6% increase throughout the economy in the hourly rate of pay, projected on an annual basis, during the second quarter of 1971 was offset by only a 2.8% annual increase in the rate of productivity—causing a 4.6% rise in unit labor costs. There seemed to be no end in sight to the cost–push inflationary forces, as firms raised prices to offset these higher costs. In the meantime, the balance of trade became unfavorable for the first time since the beginning of World War II.

Repeated requests from businessmen, members of Congress and the chairman of the Federal Reserve System eventually led President Nixon to announce in mid-August 1971 a wage–price freeze to last for three months. This action was contrary to statements only two months earlier that such controls would not be imposed. Under the presidential order, wage or price increases that had not taken effect before the date of the order, August 15 (even though they may earlier have been agreed upon or announced), were prohibited during the three-month freeze. Termed "Phase I," a Cost of Living Council was appointed to administer the freeze. The freeze relied heavily upon public support, principally in the form of voluntary adherence to the controls or of complaints of violations which were investigated by agents of the Bureau of Internal Revenue. By October, the freeze began to show some results. In that month, the Consumer Price Index rose by 0.1%, the smallest monthly increase since February 1967.

In mid-October, President Nixon announced his follow-up program, Phase II, to take effect on November 13. Retroactive wage and price increases were not permitted to take effect after the freeze expired. Two operating boards were established to formulate and administer standards and guidelines for wage and price increases: the Pay Board, consisting of fifteen members, five each to represent the public, business, and labor, and the Price Commission, composed of seven public members. These two boards were coordinated through the Cost of Living Council, chaired by the Secretary of the Treasury. The Pay Board established the guideline that wage and fringe increases must be held to a total average annual increase of 5.5%, regardless of prior negotiated contract commitments. The five labor representatives on the Pay Board, headed by the President of the AFL–CIO, voted *en mass* against this action, whereas the remaining ten members voted for it. On a case-by-case basis, the Pay Board could consider exceptions to this constraint. The standards were at first to apply to all forms of employee compensation, including those paid to executives.

The Price Commission declared that prices would be permitted to rise only sufficiently to cover increases in costs. Productivity increases which lowered costs were included in the calculations. Per unit profit increases were disallowed through price increases. The goal was to bring the level of price increases down to an annual rate of 2 or 3%. To facilitate these actions, firms and unions were divided into three groups. The top group, firms with annual sales of over $100 million and labor organizations with more than 5000 members, were required to submit requests for pay or price increases to the Pay Board or Price Commission, respectively, 30 days before the increases would take effect. The appropriate board would then rule on the legitimacy of the increase. The second group was composed of firms with sales of $50–100 million and labor organizations with membership between 1000 and 5000. This group could implement increases without formal approval, although the same prior notice must be given and excessive increases could be nullified. The third group consisted of the remaining firms and unions. It was felt that these were the "followers" and not the initiators of inflationary action.

Phase II has pleased neither organized labor nor business, but the former has been more vocal in its opposition. However, the program apparently did succeed in modifying the inflationary psychology which gripped the economy. Whether or not business and labor regard these forms of government economic controls as being sufficiently odious to constrain their future behavior remains to be seen. However, the programs do represent an alternative to the "dilemma" model of mixed inflation described in Chapter 20.

Macro Implications of Union Wage Policy

Labor organizations are a fact of life in modern industrial society. As a monopoly element in labor supply, the impact of these organizations is to decrease the degree of adaptability of labor resources to changing market conditions. Labor unions, therefore, represent a major source of imperfections in the labor market. Let us briefly examine how union wage policy can affect prices, employment, and economic growth.

1. If trade unions resist wage reductions during recessions, this rigidity may stabilize economic spirals downward. In a contraction phase, stabilizing the price level may prevent wholesale destruction of confidence. If the store-of-value function of money is sufficiently enhanced, the economy's insatiable desire to hold money may seriously retard production, which in an industrial society implies a breakdown in the functioning of the highly interdependent exchange-oriented economy. Money loses its medium-of-exchange importance. By preventing this, rigid wages may aid in the avoidance of deep depressions such as that experienced in the 1930s.

2. During recovery, unions may succeed in reducing the lag of wage increases behind price increases. Whereas the accentuation of this lag in the downswing of the cycle may have a stabilizing effect, the reduction of this lag in the upswing by negotiated cost-of-living adjustments, through annual-improvement factors, and through periodic negotiated wage increases in anticipation of expected price increases may generate more rapid inflation.

3. Aggregate demand depends to a great extent on the effect of union wage policy on the components of spending. If the demand for labor is income inelastic, a rigid wage policy can maintain aggregate demand in periods of economic decline and can restrain the expansion of demand in boom periods so that capital creation may occur at a rate sufficient to increase supply in a reasonable relationship to expanding demand. As a result, significant price increase may not occur.

(a) During recession, rigid wages may maintain consumer expenditures. A floor under consumer purchases is also likely to sustain investment expenditures. To maintain consumer spending, a redistribution of income from segments of the population with low propensities to consume to segments with high such propensities is required. This implies an increase in labor's share of national income.

(b) An improvement in the international balance-of-trade position may be prevented if rigid wages in a recession prevent price declines. Export industries may contract more or expand less than imports, with a consequent reduction in net foreign trade F. This implies an improvement in terms of trade (the ratio of imports to exports) and helps prevent the decline in the real wage. Although failure of real wages to decline may inhibit expansion of employment, if F is small, the total effect on spending may be minimal. On the other hand, the effect of unions, through the price level, on the balance of payments may lead a concerned nation to impose restraints on the ability of unions to raise wages. These policies may permit a higher level of unemployment to persist or may impose direct controls on wages and prices.

(c) A redistribution of income from persons with high propensities to consume to those with low such propensities facilitates capital growth and allows investment to expand more rapidly than consumption. A wage policy that directs increased labor costs more into fringe-benefit funds than into wage increases may, even with a shift in the distribution of income in favor of the labor sector, permit the rate of savings to increase more rapidly than the rate of consumption. Labor costs per man-hour worked that increase proportionately to increases in output per man-hour worked are favorable to noninflationary economic growth.

4. The wage policy of unions may speed up inflation if the following sequence occurs.

(a) Money wages are increased more rapidly than productivity and are in a form in which they can be immediately spent.

(b) Actual or expected wage increases in excess of productivity increases lead firms to raise prices to cover higher unit labor costs.

(c) The resulting price increases stimulate spending by producing expectations of future price and wage increases.

(d) Increased spending is directed into the consumer durable-goods industry, which then infringes upon the capital-goods industry for available resources.

(e) An expected decline in profits, resulting from an expected redistribution of income, discourages potential investment spending and economic growth. On the other hand, by using political pressure on the government to maintain aggregate demand through monetary and fiscal policies, unions may contribute to an economic environment favorable to investment.

5. To the extent that unions force money wages to rise more rapidly than productivity, workers with low productivity may be unable to obtain employment. Labor agreements impose contractual limitations upon employers not to pay wages below the union scale, even though the productivity of these now submarginal laborers merits only lower wages. As a result, hidden unemployment may develop.

6. Employers are more sensitive to union wage pressure under conditions of full employment. Even without unions, severe shortages of labor in periods of rising demand are favorable to wage increases as firms raid one another for needed employees. With unions, employers are even more sensitive to the potentiality of strikes through which they may lose nonloyal customers and irreplaceable employees.

Empirical Evidence

In recent years a number of studies have been made concerning the effectiveness of the wage–price guideposts. Essentially, these studies have examined whether or not the guideposts have affected the Phillips curve relationship. If the guideposts have been successful in achieving their objective, price inflation should be less at given levels of unemployment. Related to these studies are companion studies which seek to determine if wage rate changes are more sensitive to profit or productivity changes than to the level of unemployment or its rate of change. If, for example, prices and/or productivity advance at a greater rate than do wages, the share of income going to profits may increase. If trade unions are particularly sensitive to the rate of profit, they may respond by asking for wage increases not only sufficient to restore labor's share to its prior proportion, but also sufficient to hedge against future offsetting reductions. This competition of both labor and management for larger respective shares of industries' income, it is argued, can initiate a wage–price spiral. Hence, relevant to a study of the effectiveness of the wage–price guideposts are these studies which seek to determine if monopoly elements in the economy influence the pattern of wage–price adjustments. An examination first of the latter set of questions and second of the impact of the wage–price guideposts seems to be the most logical order of presentation.

Wages, Profits, and Productivity

Since 1860 real wages and productivity have moved closely together, but "money wages have not tended to lead productivity, employment, or wholesale prices during cyclical expansion: if anything, they have lagged." [7] If wages lag behind price and productivity increases in cyclical upturns, then profits will tend to increase. When profits and aggregate demand are expanded, it has been argued, then the bargaining power of unions is at its strongest. Under membership pressure, and because of comparisons made among union leaders on the basis of their accomplishment, general widespread wage gains will result from union pressure. Depending upon market conditions, wage advances may either catch up or pass previous price increases, and these wage gains may currently or eventually result in even larger price increases. Thus, a wage–price spiral can be initiated as a result of profit gains initially induced by a wage lag. [8]

Data for the United States in the period 1935–1959 indicate that wages have responded to lagged profits, although the relationship is less close in the interval since 1948. [9] However, in this study, unemployment was not

[7] "The Illusion of Wage Rigidity of Long and Short Cycles in Wages and Labor," *Review of Economics and Statistics*, Vol. 4 (May 1960), p. 150.

[8] N. Kaldor, one of the first proponents of this view, believed that unions in their wage demands would respond to profit rates of the preceding year and to production increases more than they would to the pressures of unemployment, as suggested by the Phillips analysis. See his "Economic Growth and Problems of Inflation," *Economica* (November 1959), pp. 293–295.

[9] Rattan J. Bhatia, "Profits and the Rate of Change in Money Earnings in the United States, 1935–1959," *Economica*, Vol. 29 (1962), pp. 255–262. Yale Brozen has argued that a two-year lag between profits and wage increases exists in the United States. See "Down the Collective Bargaining Road to Recession," *Economics and Business Bulletin*, Vol. 23, No. 2 (Winter 1971), p. 17.

used as an explanatory variable. It is possible that the explanatory power of profits on wages in the latter period is owing to the fact that unemployment variation was much smaller than in the earlier period. Consequently, the impact of unemployment variation on wages may have been constrained, so that other forces such as profits are relatively more important in explaining the variation in wages. A study for the United Kingdom for selected periods in the interval 1870–1958 revealed that changes in unemployment explained wage variations better than did the profit rate, although in the period after World War II, profits did have some impact on wages.[10] Unions were stronger in this later period.

Profits may be a proxy for a more fundamental determinant of wages, namely, the marginal value product of labor. If this is true, perhaps productivity is more closely related to wages than is the level of profits. United States data for 1950–1960 gave a better explanation of wage variation when *productivity* and unemployment variables were used than when *profits* and unemployment variables[11] were used. Similarly, in Canada the ratio of profits to GNP was rejected as an explanatory variable for wages, but in industries where unions were strong, the productivity variable had significant explanatory power, although it did not among industries in which unions were weak.[12]

Essentially, then, the wage–profit–productivity relationship has more support in the United States and Canada than elsewhere. This may be owing to the particular form of collective bargaining practiced in these countries and to the more independent relationship between labor unions and political parties than exists elsewhere. It should be noted, however, that the evidence cited in the United States and Canada is based on post-World War II data, and that in England, profits did have some impact on wage rates during this period. It should be emphasized that a finding that wages and profits are related does not imply that wages and unemployment are not. It may well be that, given a level of unemployment, it is the rate of increase of productivity, or the rate of change in profits, that motivates

[10] R. G. Lipsey and M. D. Steur, "The Relation Between Profits and Wage Rates," *Economica* (May 1961), pp. 137–155.

[11] Edwin Kuh, "A Productivity Theory of Wage Levels—An Alternative to the Phillips Curve," *Review of Economic Studies* (October 1967), pp. 333–360. R. R. France found that wages and productivity were likely to vary in opposite directions, "Wages, Unemployment, and Prices in the United States, 1890–1932, 1947–1957," *Industrial and Labor Relations Review* (October 1963), pp. 183–184. In part this is owing to rigid wages in the upswing, in which productivity is apt to be increasing, and to rising wages at the peak, at which time productivity is likely to be decreasing. Perhaps the use of a lagged productivity variable would have yielded a better measure of the relationship.

[12] John Vanderkamp, "Wage and Price Level Determination in Canada," *Economica* (May 1966), pp. 205–206.

unions to seek wage increases. The magnitude of the increase sought and the union's ability to obtain it may well be a function of the level of unemployment.

The Spillover or Wage-Round Hypothesis

Because corporations and unions are closely related in "key groups" by product markets or factor links, wage increases in any one component can be spread throughout the key group. If one key group, because of unique demand conditions, establishes a particularly desirable wage package, then through coercive or invidious comparisons made by union leaders of other key groups, the settlement tends to be generalized over other highly related, concentrated "key groups." The process of transference of these wage gains does not stop, however, among centers of economic concentration. They are spread through nonconcentrated sectors that fear the threat of unionization, that are compelled by Federal contract laws to pay the "prevailing wage," or that attempt to maintain their relative position in labor markets. This has been identified as "sympathetic pressure" or "spillover effects." Moreover, the interval of time in which these wage gains are generalized throughout the economy may take many months, or several years, and although initiated during a cyclical upswing may continue into a recession. These interrelated wage bargains and the interval in which they are spread have been defined as "wage rounds."[13]

To test this hypothesis, wage behavior in manufacturing industries from 1948 to 1966 was examined on both a time series and cross-sectional basis. Seven "wage rounds" were identified in this interval. On a cross-sectional basis, for the first five rounds no significant evidence was found that the degree of unionism had influenced wages, although this in part was attributed to the spillover effects of union wage pressure into the nonunion sectors. A significant relationship between wages as the dependent variable and profits and unemployment levels as independent variables existed in these five rounds, which supports the hypothesis concerning the "key group," wage-round process of wage determination.[14] However, for the sixth and seventh wage round, the earlier regression equations did not predict well. Instead

[13] Otto Eckstein and Thomas A. Wilson, "The Determination of Money Wages in American Industry," *Quarterly Journal of Economics*, Vol. 70 (August 1962), pp. 379–387. Also see Otto Eckstein, "Money Wage Determination Revisited," *Review of Economic Studies* (April 1968), pp. 133–143.

[14] They note, however, that the distribution of profits and unemployment in the economy affects the change in wages. Also, to prevent inflationary wage pressures, they state that the higher the level of profits, the higher then must be the rate of unemployment. *Ibid.*, p. 406.

[15] Gail Pierson, "The Effect of Union Strength on the U.S. 'Phillips Curve,'" *American Economic Review*, Vol. 58, No. 3 (June 1968), pp. 458–461.

of wage gains spilling over from manufacturing into other sectors, apparently the opposite had occurred. Indeed, evidence existed of a breakup of old key groups and the establishment of new ones. Construction became a key group and a pattern setter. As a theory of wage determination, the "key-group, wage-round hypothesis" apparently did not pass the test. This is not to say that profits and unemployment do not significantly affect wages, but that support is lacking for the hypothesis that wage gains are spread throughout the economy through institutional channels of key groups in response to these variables.

Additional support for the profit–wage relationship and its dispersion via "spillover" effects has been found by Pierson.[15] In the subsector where unions were strongest, the rate of change of profits was found to affect wages significantly, and after allowing for spillover effects into sectors where unions were weakest, both lagged profits and changes in profits were found to have a significant relation to wages. Although Pierson believes that this supports the key-group hypothesis, it should be noted that the spillover effect does not depend upon the "key-group concept." Hence, a wage spillover between organized and unorganized sectors can occur even if key groups do not exist.

In summary, profits and value productivity are variables that reflect in part the strength of the demand for labor. Theoretically, these variables together with the unemployment rate, which indicates somewhat the labor supply condition, should have an impact on wage changes. Those studies that find that they do not, therefore, require close examination. Insofar as the United States is concerned, there is consistent evidence that wages have been influenced by these variables since World War II. One would expect one set of variables to have more explanatory power than another, depending upon whether excess labor demand (deficient labor supply) or excess labor supply existed (deficient labor demand). Both labor productivity and profits can be expected to have higher wage sensitivity (1) in tight labor markets and (2) where strong unions exist. The degree of sensitivity should be greater where the two conditions are combined. It should be noted that the two conditions can exist in specific industries when excess labor supply exists. The construction industry in 1971 is a case in point. Empiricists might well divert their attention to a consideration of these implications.

The Impact of Stabilization Policy

INITIAL STUDIES   A number of studies have been made which have specifically addressed themselves to whether or not the guideposts have had any impact on wages and prices. Using quarterly data, it was found that the Korean War Wage Stabilization Program had suppressed the wage adjustments which would have been expected to occur at the low levels of unemployment existing in 1951–1953.[16] Inclusion of the Korean War quarterly data in regression equations increased the unexplained variance, whereas exclusion of these quarterly data increased the explained variance. The effect of the Wage Stabilization Board may have been not only to suppress wage increases, but to delay the timing of their implementation. Hence, lags of wage changes behind unemployment rate changes could increase dispersion. Another scholar included, as an independent variable in regression equations, a dummy variable to account for the effect of the wage–price guideposts beginning in 1962. At assumed unemployment rates of of 4 and 5%, inclusion of the guideposts made a difference.[17] Wage increases without allowance for the guideposts were higher than when allowance was made for them, indicating that the dummy variable suppressed wage increases. Moreover, the dummy variable had more effect on wage increases in strongly unionized industries than in weakly unionized industries, suggesting that the more monopolistic the union, the greater the effect of the dummy variable.

A more systematic examination has been made of the guidepost effects. The purpose was to determine whether wage (and price) changes were smaller than they would have been without the 3.2% voluntary wage-change guidelines established early in the Johnson administration. Some economists had argued that the guideposts were not effective since wage settlements had been greater than 3.2%. Perhaps concern about deviations around this figure is not as relevant as whether the wage changes were smaller than they would have been in the absence of the guideposts. Initially, two general regression equations were computed in which quarterly wage changes in manufacturing, W, were related to changes in the consumer price index, $\dot{C}$, to the reciprocal of the unemployment rate, U^{-1}, to the average after-tax profit rate expressed as a percentage of equity, R, and to the quarterly change in the profit rate, ΔR.[18]

---

[16] McCaffree, *op. cit.*, pp. 67–68.

[17] Gail Pierson, "The Effect of Union Strength on the U.S. 'Phillips curve,' " *op. cit.*, pp. 456–467.

[18] G. L. Perry, "Wages and the Guideposts," *American Economic Review*, Vol. 57 (September 1967), pp. 897–904. The two equations are as follows:

I. (1947–1960)

$$W_t = -4.313 + 0.367\,\dot{C}_{t-1} + 14.711\,U_t^{-1} + 0.424\,R_{t-1} + 0.792\,\Delta R_t \qquad R^2 = 0.88$$
$$(0.054) \qquad (2.188) \qquad (0.068) \qquad (0.176)$$

II. (1953–1960)

$$\dot{W}_t = -4.712 + 0.680\,\dot{C}_{t-1} + 18.421\,U_t^{-1} + 0.360\,R_{t-1} + 1.244\,\Delta R_t \qquad R^2 = 0.80$$
$$\phantom{\dot{W}_t = -4.712 +}(0.132) \qquad (3.050) \qquad (0.120) \qquad (0.300).$$

Next, estimates of wage changes, as percentages, were computed from each equation for quarters beginning in 1962 through the first quarter of 1966. These estimated wage changes were then compared with actual wage changes; and for both equations, beginning the third quarter of 1962, *estimates* were consistently higher than the *actual* changes. (Moreover, Equation II gave consistently higher estimates, and hence deviated more from the actual, than did Equation I.) This suggests that the guideposts were effective, because actual wages in the 1962–1966 period were less than predicted wages in both equations.

However, to guard against the possibility of spurious correlation, additional tests were conducted. First, two periods were selected of comparable economic activity, with and without guideposts, i.e., 1954–1957 and 1963–1966, and then the ratio of wage changes in visible industrial groups were compared with those in invisible industrial groups.[19]

$$R_i^W = \left(\frac{W_t}{W_{t-1}} \right) 1950\text{s} \Big/ \left(\frac{W_t}{W_{t-1}} \right) 1960\text{s}$$

With few exceptions, the R_i^W was higher for visible industries than for invisible industries, suggesting that the former were more sensitive to the guideposts. A similar ratio was calculated for employment changes, R_i^E; with few exceptions, the R_i^E for the invisible industries exceeded the R_i^E for visible industries. This also was consistent with the guideposts. Employment in the 1950s would change relatively less than in the 1960s if wage increases were relatively greater in the 1950s than in the 1960s. The evidence appears to support the effectiveness of the guideposts, and the burden of proof had now been shifted to those who declared them to be ineffective.

THE LABOR RESERVE HYPOTHESIS   Simler and Tella have reexamined the evidence on the effect of the guideposts and have suggested an alternative explanation for the wage–price stability of the first half of the 1960s.[20] Specifically, they rejected the technique of introducing a dummy variable into the regression equations, ostensibly to account for the effect of the guidepost. "Merely saying the dummy variable represents the guidepost would not, of course, make it so. The dummy could represent anything one

---

[19] *Ibid.*, pp. 899–902. Perry adopted a somewhat different approach than did Pierson in identifying those industries which are most sensitive to the guideposts. Whereas Pierson classified industries on the basis of unionization, Perry let a panel of experts make the selection.

[20] N. J. Simler and Alfred Tella, "Labor Reserves and the Phillips Curve," *Review of Economics and Statistics* (February 1968), pp. 32–49.

wished, or nothing, and the regression would be the same."[21] Instead, they used a broader concept of the labor force to include secondary workers as well as primary workers, which tends to reduce variations in its size over the cycle because it includes those members who are added during the recovery and who drop out during the recession.[22] Unemployed secondary workers are normally excluded from unemployment statistics, but nevertheless constitute a labor reserve which, by increasing the available supply during expansionary periods, inhibits the rise in wages. Only when the expansion has exhausted, or nearly so, the supply of both primary and secondary workers will acceleration in wage increases be evident.

Estimates of the primary and secondary labor force under full employment were made to derive the potential labor force.[23] The difference between the potential and the actual labor force in any period of time measures the labor reserve, which, when added to the official unemployment estimate, measures adjusted unemployment. The adjusted unemployment rate is the ratio of adjusted unemployment to the potential labor force. Inclusion of the difference between this variable and the unemployment rate (both expressed as reciprocals) in the Perry equations produced a significant change in the estimated value of the rate of change of wages, W, between 1961 and 1964. Lower values of W were found for this period, a time during which considerable labor reserves were present in the economy. This was true whether W represented changes in the straight-time average hourly earnings of manufacturing production workers or "changes in wages and salaries per man-hour in the private nonfarm sector of the economy." Hence, Simler and Tella concluded that the labor reserve model is a better predictor of wage changes than the Perry Model; the Simler–Tella model makes no allowance for the guideposts.

Simler and Tella next examined the question of whether there has been a structural change in the economy. Using the equation based on 1948–1957

---

[21] *Ibid.*, p. 33.

[22] Earlier studies on this phenomenon were made by Tella, and Thomas Dernberg and Kenneth Strand have reported their findings on the incidence of "hidden unemployment." A definitive study on labor force participation is that by William G. Bowen and T. Aldrich Finegan, *The Economics of Labor Force Participation* (Princeton: Princeton University Press, 1969). Bowen and Finegan found that labor force participation rates are higher in markets where unemployment rates are lower. Tella, Dernberg, and Strand had sought to estimate the extent of hidden unemployment at various unemployment rates. Bowen and Finegan found that their estimates of variation in the labor force with respect to unemployment rates, although of the proper sign, were too large, and that their estimates of hidden unemployment were too high. This later finding would undoubtedly have some effect on the Simler–Tella study.

[23] Simler and Tella, *op. cit.*, pp. 36–38.

data, changes in wages were predicted for the 1953–1964 period and these predictions W_1 were compared with those W_2 made from an equation based on 1953–1964 data. If $W_2 > W_1$, this suggests that a structural change has occurred. Using Perry's equation, such a change was found to have occurred; the labor reserve model revealed no such change, however, since $W_1 > W_2$.[24] Phillips curves were derived also from the two models, holding variables other than unemployment rates and wage rate changes constant. Structural changes between the 1948–1957 period and the 1953–1964 period would be revealed by shifts in the Phillips curves. The Perry model revealed an upward shift in the Phillips curve, indicating that the inflation–unemployment tradeoff had worsened as a result of the structural shift. The labor-reserve model also indicated that the Phillips curve had shifted, but only slightly and in the opposite direction, when average hourly manufacturing wage changes were used as the dependent variable. When nonfarm wages per man-hour were used, however, the curve had twisted as its slope was reduced; at unemployment rates above about 3.5%, the 1953–1964 curve lay above the 1948–1957 curve; below the 3.5% rate, the 1953–1964 curve lay below the 1948–1957 curve. Simler and Tella used these results to conclude that structural changes in the neighborhood of full employment had not worsened the unemployment–inflation tradeoff.

The implication of the Simler–Tella study is that hidden unemployment in the early 1960s, and not the wage–price guideposts, suppressed wage changes. Also, even though there is some evidence that structural changes may worsen the inflation–unemployment rate tradeoff at high levels of unemployment, the opposite is true at levels of full employment. The evidence presented by Pierson and Perry that some industries are more sensitive to wage–price guidelines than others was not examined. Indeed, it is difficult to see how the labor-reserve model could explain this phenomenon, because it may well be that the sensitive industries are less affected by the potential competition of the labor reserve. Although the labor-reserve model may cast some doubt on the efficacy of the wage–price guidelines, it may well be that the guidelines tend more to hold down wage–price increases in sensitive industries, and the labor reserve fulfills this function in the nonsensitive industries. This is, of course, an empirical question yet to be resolved. If it is true, however, then both Simler–Tella and Perry–Pierson are correct in stating, respectively, that (1) the labor reserve in periods of less-than-full employment retards wage increases, and

[24] *Ibid.*, pp. 43–44. However, a more recent study suggests that structural change is a secular feature of the labor force, and that Simler–Tella did not eliminate all secular instability in labor force behavior by including a labor reserve variable in their equations. Arthur D. Butler and George D. Demopoulous, "Labor-force Behavior in a Full Employment Economy," *Industrial and Labor Relations Review*, Vol. 24, No. 3 (April 1971), pp. 375–388.

(2) the wage–price guideposts have suppressed wage increases during their existence.[25]

The Guidelines, "Wage Rounds," and the Labor Reserve

Otto Eckstein has argued that the guidelines could not have had sufficient impact to explain the errors in the calculated wage changes for the sixth and seventh wage rounds. He added data on the "labor reserve" to his own regression equation, and finds better results.[26] In fact, he finds that the labor reserve correlates highly with wage-round results. When the labor reserve is low, the wage-round variables (profits, key industries, spillovers, unemployment) explain wage changes; when the reserve is high, the wage-round variables lose much of their explanatory power. Thus, by incorporating the labor reserve into his model, Eckstein is able to salvage it.[27] Not only unions have responded to the guidelines by moderating demands for wage increases, but the existence of hidden unemployment has apparently also weakened the magnitude of wage increases negotiated in rounds during the guidepost period.

Summary

There is a continuing precedent in this country to establish a wage–price stabilization policy whenever rising prices pose a sufficient threat to the economic welfare of the country. Such policies have been adopted in wartime when inflationary pressures are obvious, but they have also been adopted when less-than-full employment exists. In the latter case, the policies seem to be a response to chronic balance-of-payment deficits, which became critical in the first half of the 1960s and early in the 1970s. Although inflation in the late 1960s and early 1970s was caused more by the Vietnam

---

[25] Behman has offered still another hypothesis to explain the damped wage changes in the 1962–1965 period. She notes that wages are determined by two sets of forces: (1) labor-market forces, in which the price of labor relative to other factors is important via substitution effects, and (2) market-power forces, including concentration in industries and in unions. She found that relative factor prices after 1962 were sufficiently unfavorable to labor, in terms of the least-cost input combination, to suppress wage increases. This substitution potential may explain why the labor reserve was able to suppress wages in industries in which its employment normally would not be expected. Sara Behman, "Wage Changes, Institutions, and Relative Factor Prices in Manufacturing," *Review of Economics and Statistics*, Vol. 51, No. 3 (August 1969).

[26] "Money Wage Determination Revisited," *Review of Economic Studies, op. cit.*, p. 140. He notes that Jacob Mincer has found errors in Tella's estimate of the labor reserve, which reduces its influence.

[27] *Ibid.*, p. 141. Eckstein has since reported that the 1967–1970 wage round (the eighth) tended to fall once again into his model.

War than perhaps has been recognized, it was the balance-of-payments deficit which precipitated the monetary crisis that led to the Nixon controls. Reaction to these controls has been similar to that to the guideposts, and critics have attacked these policies as a departure from the laissez-faire principles implicit in a democratic competitive economy. Defenders of the policies have observed that the presumption of a competitive economy is fallacious and that the controls simply seek to bring about a result which would be achieved if the economy were perfectly competitive.

The institutional structure of the United States economy is viewed in part as being either the cause of, or the vehicle through which is spread, inflation. Although there exists historical evidence of a lag in wages behind productivity changes, attention has been focused on the lag in wages behind profits—a corollary of the wage–productivity lag hypothesis. Increments in profits are presumed to motivate union leaders to seek wage gains which, if in excess of productivity gains, can generate inflation. Evidence seems to support the existence of both a wage–profit lag and a wage–productivity lag in the United States, although elsewhere the evidence is mixed.

The process of diffusing such excess wage gains is through key groups related through union comparisons, product markets, and prevailing wages. Wage gains by one component of a key group is spread throughout the group and throughout other groups via a spillover effect. This process seemed to hold true in the 1948–1960 period, but did not explain the two wage rounds in the first half of the 1960s. Later it was discovered that by including a variable for hidden unemployment, a reasonably close prediction of wage changes resulted from the wage-round equations. Hence, unemployment is a factor influencing the magnitude of wage adjustments, and these wage adjustments occur at periodic intervals which can be distinguished as rounds.

Generally, equations which related wages to productivity, profits, and registered unemployment gave estimates of wage changes in excess of actual ones, in the period when guidelines were in effect. Including a dummy variable for the period, labeled the Guidelines, yielded estimated wage changes close to the actual, and this led some observers to conclude that the guideposts had constrained wage increments. Others found that adjustments in the level of unemployment, to account for hidden unemployment, produced the same effect on predicted wage changes. These latter observers concluded that it was hidden unemployment, not the guideposts, that had limited the power of unions to obtain wage increments. Even though the hidden unemployed were not directly involved in these labor markets where unions were strong, their threat as a potential indirect substitute for union labor—particularly through linked markets—was transmitted to organized labor and constrained their wage demands.

It would be surprising if the guideposts or the Nixon stabilization policies did not have some effect in moderating wage demands. If nothing more, they changed the climate in which bargaining power is exercised. It may be that stabilization policy is a clearer and more direct signal that the Government will not validate inflationary wage increases, but will instead tolerate, or continue to tolerate, a condition of underemployment in the economy. Consequently, it may take both a stabilization policy and unemployment in the economy to hold down wage and price increases, since the two taken together create and enforce an antiinflation psychology. Hence, studies that show that one or the other is responsible for retarding wage increases need not be contradictory, yet neither one alone may tell the whole story.

Appendix: A Macro Model for Wage–Price Policy, the Balance of Trade, and Unemployment

I. A wage–price stabilization program, such as that instituted by President Nixon in late 1971 or the earlier Guidelines in the Kennedy–Johnson administrations, seeks to maintain, as an ideal objective, a constant price level through the process of limiting wage increases to productivity increases. In this appendix it will be shown that under certain assumptions, if wage–price policies can be effectuated, then less unemployment and an improvement in the balance of payments, as well as greater price stability, result.

II. The following relationships are implicit in a wage–price stabilization policy. Relative changes in aggregate wages, W, are to be set equal to relative changes in aggregate output per man-hour, A.

$$\Delta W/W = \Delta A/A \qquad (22.1)$$

This implies that unit labor costs, U, will remain constant, so that wages increase in constant proportion to average output.

$$W/A = U \qquad (22.2)$$

It is also implicit in the wage–price policy that unit labor costs are more or less a constant proportion of prices, P.

$$U/P = a \qquad (22.3)$$

or, from (22.2),

$$W/P = aA \qquad (22.3a)$$

Now, one of the purposes of the wage–price policy is to stabilize domestic (export) prices, P, and in so doing improve the balance of payments.

Implicit in this analysis is the assumption that foreign (import) prices, P_m, will continue to rise over time, and the international competitive position of domestic products will gradually improve. Using indifference analysis for export and import goods, it can be shown that the ratio of exports, X, to imports, M, is inversely related to their respective prices. If we assume, where α is a constant,

$$X/M = \alpha P_m/P \qquad (22.4)$$

so that

$$PX/M = \alpha P_m \qquad (22.4a)$$

it follows that the relationship between domestic prices and the trade ratio, X/M, is a rectangular hyperbola for each given level of foreign prices.

Now, when certain conditions hold, the level of national income, Y, is related positively to the trade ratio.

$$Y = f(X/M) \qquad (22.5)$$

Let the money supply vary directly with the trade ratio.[28]

$$M_s = g(X/M) \qquad (22.5a)$$

As the trade ratio increases, foreign exchange and/or gold flows into the country, expanding the money supply.[29] A cooperative (or passive) central bank facilitates this relationship. The interest rate, i, is assumed to be inversely related to the money supply,

$$i = i(M_s) \qquad (22.5b)$$

and the level of investment, I, is inversely related to the interest rate.

$$I = I(i) \qquad (22.5c)$$

Equating I with the level of savings, S, which is in turn related to the level of income,

$$I(i) = S = S(Y) \qquad (22.5d)$$

our circle of relationships is complete.[30] (See Figure 22.1.)

The income identity, where Q is real national output, is

$$Y = PQ = \sum_i P_i Q_i \qquad (22.6)$$

---

[28] This follows automatically under a freely fluctuating exchange rate or the gold standard.
[29] The money supply may be highly inelastic, but greater than zero, with respect to changes in the trade ratio.
[30] $(X/M) \to M_s \to i \to I \to S \to Y$. Hence, we have Equation (22.5). Government spending and taxation can be included as parameters.

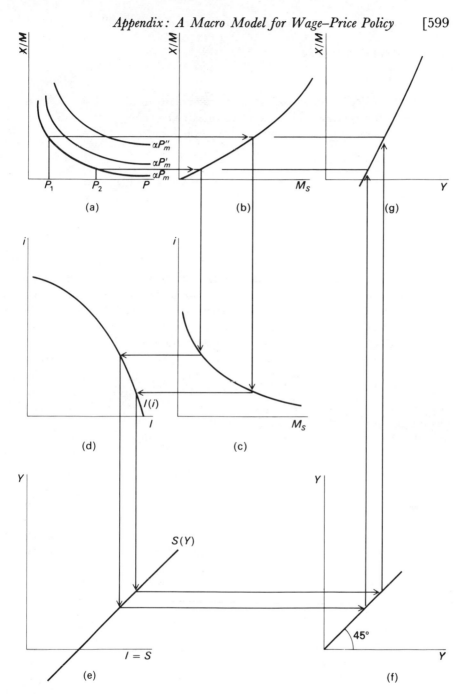

FIGURE 22.1. The terms of trade–income relationship, via the price level, the money supply, investment, and savings. (See text.)

and can also be written as

$$Q/Y = 1/P \tag{22.6a}$$

If, as productivity increases owing to improvements in technology, T, or to increases in the capital stock, K, output remains constant, then, with rising output per man-hour less employed labor, E, is required

$$Q = Q(E, K, T) \tag{22.7}$$

Given the labor force, L, divided between the employed, E, and the unemployed, V, unemployment must increase as E declines.

$$L = E + V \tag{22.8}$$

Our system is now complete.

These relationships can be illustrated in Figure 22.2. In Figure 22.2(a), the relationship between wages and prices, derived in Equation (22.3a), is illustrated. The slopes of the vectors are equal to the ratio of unit labor costs to price (a constant) times the output per man-hour (average labor product). The greater the slope of the vector, the greater the average product. From Equation (22.4a) the product of the export–import ratio times the domestic price level is a rectangular hyperbola equal to a constant times the foreign price level, P_m, illustrated in Figure 22.2(b). Given the domestic and foreign price levels, the trade ratio is determined. In Figure 22.2(c) the relationship between the trade ratio and income is shown.[31] Given the trade ratio, income is determined, and from Figure 22.2(d) this income level, together with the given domestic price level, expressed inversely as vectors, determines real output. The higher the price level, the less is the slope of the vector. Given the labor force and the level of productivity, output is inversely related to unemployment. Increments in productivity through improvements in technology or additions to capital stock can shift q_i upward, so that with any given level of output, more unemployment occurs. This is shown in Figure 22.2(e). Hence, given the level of output, productivity, and the labor force, the level of unemployment is determined. Of interest in this analysis is the effect (i) of wage changes in excess of productivity, (ii) of a variable import price–domestic price ratio when productivity increases, and (iii) of wages that rise consistent with productivity increases, so that domestic prices are fixed when import prices rise.

(i) To show the first effect, let wages rise but domestic prices stay fixed at $0P_2$ in Figure 22.2(a); let no change occur in productivity in Figure 22.2(e). Import prices rise in Figure 22.2(b). In Figure 22.2(f), it can be

---

[31] See Equations (22.5a)–(22.5d) and Figure 22.1.

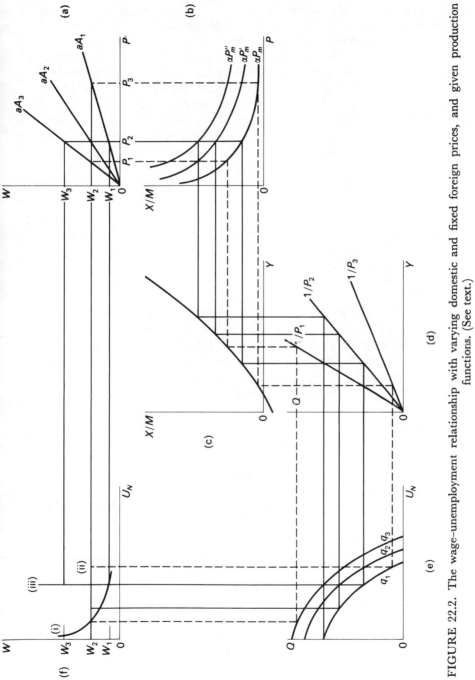

FIGURE 22.2. The wage–unemployment relationship with varying domestic and fixed foreign prices, and given production functions. (See text.)

seen that as wages rise with import prices, unemployment decreases along line (i), and in Figure 22.2(e), consistent with the rise in employment, real income, Q, rises (and since prices are fixed, money income also rises).

(ii) To show the second effect, let wages be fixed at $0W_2$; import prices remain constant at P_m as productivity increases, leading to a decline in domestic prices from $0P_3$ to $0P_1$. As domestic prices fall, the trade ratio and money income grow [Figure 22.2(c)] and real income [in Figure 22.2(e)] grows. In Figure 22.2(f) it can be seen that unemployment declines. Hence, when productivity grows faster than wages, and the ratio of import to domestic prices rises, real national income grows and unemployment contracts [as shown by the horizontal line labeled (ii) in Figure 22.2(f)].

(iii) The third effect can be shown by letting wages grow in accordance with productivity so that domestic prices remain constant, as in Figure 22.2(a). As import prices rise, the trade ratio and money income expand; and because prices are constant, real income expands. However, no change need occur in the unemployment rate, as can be seen by the vertical line labeled (iii) in Figure 22.2(f).

III. There are a number of implications from this analysis:

A. If wages rise more rapidly than productivity, then unemployment can fall and real national income can rise if domestic prices rise sufficiently less rapidly than foreign prices. Consequently, a policy of permitting wages to increase, but not domestic prices, may result in less unemployment. However, if import prices fall relative to export prices, unemployment will rise and national income will fall. As unemployment goes to zero, it is very unlikely that prices can remain rigid.

B. If wages are fixed and prices are flexible downward when productivity increases, then real national income grows and unemployment declines if import prices do not fall.

C. Conversely, it can be shown that if wages and domestic prices are both fixed when import prices rise, even with no increase in productivity, real and money income will rise and unemployment will decline. This situation is more realistic than implication B because domestic prices are not likely to be flexible downward.

D. If wage increases are constrained to productivity increases, domestic prices are fixed and import prices rise, then national income (real and monetary) will increase, but unemployment need not decline. If the labor force is growing, it may even increase.

E. If wages increase less than productivity and domestic prices are fixed when import prices are increasing, not only will real and money national income rise, but unemployment will decrease.

The importance of this analysis with respect to stabilization policy which seeks (1) to control inflation, (2) to reduce unemployment, and (3) to improve the balance of payments is that the guidepost formula will accomplish (1) and (3) but not (2), as seen in implication D. However, if policy consistent with implication E is imposed, all three objectives may be capable of being achieved.[32]

Discussion Questions

1. How do wage–price controls interfere with natural market forces? If natural market forces produce undesirable results, should policy attempt to alter these results? What is the argument in favor of allowing natural market forces to operate and what are the implicit assumptions behind this argument?
2. (a) Why are sanctions needed to make an incomes policy work?
   (b) Should an economist be concerned with whether a given income distribution is "equitable"? Should a politician? Should organized labor?
3. Evaluate the effectiveness of the Pay and Price Boards established by President Nixon. What evidence is needed to demonstrate that wage–price controls have been successful? Unsuccessful?
4. Can the theory of "wage rounds" explain the negotiated wage settlements of the early 1970s? Explain. How can the inflationary psychology explain the willingness of employers to grant substantial wage concessions in a period in which production, sales, and profits are declining?
5. Are profits a good proxy for productivity? Why would wage increases tend to follow profit increases? How can unions affect the lag between profit changes and wage changes?
6. Conservative economists have tended to change their minds about the desirability of pursuing a *laissez-faire* economic policy once they have assumed a policy-making position in Washington. Why? Suppose Professor Friedman were to be appointed as the new Chairman of the President's Council of Economic Advisers. What wage–price policy might

[32] These policies, to be effective, require that the monetary authorities do not nullify the effect of the trade ratio on the money supply. This appears to have been the case in the August 1971–March 1972 period of the Nixon wage–price controls during which, with an adverse balance of trade, the money supply was allowed to increase. With a sufficiently loose monetary policy, the trade ratio may be negatively related to income, so that with moderate increases in wages, prices can continue to rise, but output and unemployment are little affected. An appropriate modification of the diagram in Figure 22.2, showing a negative relationship between X/M and Y, can reveal just this result.

he recommend to the President in view of the current state of the economy?

7. Discuss the impact of the labor reserve on the Phillips curve. Does this suggest that a new definition of the labor force is desirable? If you were President of the United States, what definition of unemployment would you seek and what control over labor market information would be in your interest?

8. (a) Since net foreign trade comprises only about 4% of GNP in the United States, why should the government be concerned with the balance of payments.

   (b) How is national wage policy related to the balance-of-payment policy? Identify the linkages.

   (c) Why is it so difficult to achieve full employment, price stability, a satisfactory balance of payments, and economic growth all at the same time? Which objectives are most important, and why?

23

Macroeconomic Models of
Manpower Planning

Introduction

The provision of an infrastructure suitable for the viable development of the economy is a minimum objective in the over-all formulation of macro-economic plans. This infrastructure includes the educational system, which is primarily responsible for developing the human resource base of the economy. To facilitate the development of the educational infrastructure through the process of planning, a number of models have been developed,[1]

---

[1] A growth model has been developed by Jan Tinbergen and Hector Correa, "Quantitative Adaptation of Education to Accelerated Growth," *Kyklos*, Vol. 15 (1962). This model has been expanded and developed by Jan Tinbergen and H. C. Bos, "A Planning Model for the Educational Requirements of Economic Development," O.E.C.D. Study Group in the Economics of Education, *The Residual Factor and Economic Growth*, O.E.C.D., Paris, 1964. Reprinted in Mark Blaug, ed., *Economics of Education*, Vol. 2 (Baltimore: Penguin Books, 1968), pp. 125–151. A linear programming model has been used by Samuel Bowles to solve an objective function for maximizing national income from educational activities. "The Efficient Allocation of Resources in Education," *Quarterly Journal of Economics*, Vol. 81, No. 3 (1967), also reprinted in M. Blaug, *Economics of Education*, Vol. 2, *op. cit.*, pp. 168–201. See also Irma Adelman, "A Linear Programming Model of Educational Planning—A Case Study of Argentina," in I. Adelman and E. Thorbecke, eds., *The Theory and Design of Economic Development* (Baltimore: The Johns Hopkins Press, 1966), and Dennis Maki, "A Programming Approach to Manpower Planning," *Industrial and Labor Relations Review*, Vol. 23, No. 3 (April 1970), pp. 397–405. Peter Armitage and C. Smith have developed a model for measuring flows of students through the educational system and into the labor market, "The Development of Computable Models of the British Educational System and Their Possible Uses," *Mathematical Models in Educational Planning*, O.E.C.D., Paris, 1967. Also in Blaug, *op. cit.*, pp. 202–237. Input-output models can be adapted also for manpower planning. Given an input–output transaction matrix and time series on sectoral output and employment, sectoral employment multipliers and consistent employment projections can be obtained.

the solution of which leads to balanced economic growth and/or to optimum allocation of resource inputs and educational outputs. Conceptually, these models can provide valuable insights into the nature of the data needed to estimate the parameters used in the structural equations, and they can permit the planners, through sensitivity analysis, to ascertain the effects of different policies.

Data limitations can impair the usefulness of the models, however. Manpower forecasting, even in advanced countries with well-developed statistical series and institutions to collect and process data, incurs many handicaps. The problems are compounded in less-developed countries where data are sparse and often unreliable, and where the means of collecting them are either nonexistent or seriously deficient. Moreover, since decisions concerning the direction and magnitude of the "economic plan" are just as likely, if not more so, to be made on political grounds rather than economic ones, models may be misdirected in the answers provided by their solutions. The solutions may provide answers to those questions of greatest interest to the economists who construct the models, but the answers may have little utility to those who construct and/or implement the economic plans. Instead of asking the question, "What rate of economic growth will optimize the use of available manpower resources?" a more appropriate question might be, "Will full employment be achieved given the planned rate of economic growth?" Instead of the question, "What educational priorities should be established, given the manpower needs of the economy consistent with varying rates of growth?" the appropriate question might be, "Will the given educational priorities satisfy the manpower needs of the economy at its planned rate of growth?" Rather than solving a model to find the optimum flow of teachers into the educational system, given the optimum educational priorities, perhaps the model should reveal whether the planned flow of teachers into the educational system, given the educational priorities, is sufficient to achieve the educational plan. Thus, models may have varying degrees of usefulness.

Three approaches to manpower planning will be described in this chapter. The first model to be discussed has been developed by Jan Tinbergen in collaboration with Hector Correa and H. C. Bos. It is a balanced-growth model. The second approach, still in an embryonic form, describes the procedure by which manpower estimates can be derived from a Leontief input–output matrix for sectors of the economy. The third approach is a model combining elements of the first two by means of which, given projections of the Gross National Product, manpower demands can be forecast by educational levels and matched with forecasts of educational supply. Manpower imbalances can then be identified for the total economy by sectors and by educational level. The model is adaptable for policy recommendations. It has been applied as a case study to the economy of Thailand.

The Tinbergen–Correa–Bos Model

This model, hereafter identified as the TCB model, is a rather straightforward educational planning one which is capable of modification to meet a variety of policy considerations. It depicts an educational structure which supplies trained manpower into the labor force at different levels. The rate of growth of output is limited by the rate of growth of each sector of the labor force through the output–labor relationship, specified by a simple, aggregate production function for each type of labor. However, if output grows more slowly than a sector of the labor force, unemployment in that sector may occur. Balanced growth occurs, given the output–labor relationships, when the labor force sectors are supplied with just enough trained labor to match the requirements for economic growth.

The structure of the model is illustrated in Chart 23.1. Students, S, enter the secondary educational system and during a six-year period identified as the time-interval unit, progress through the system. Some of the secondary graduates enter the labor force, S_L, while the remainder continue on to higher education, S_H. Similarly, the S_H from the preceding time interval constitute the students who enter into higher education and progress during a six-year interval through the higher educational system, H. Graduates from the higher educational system may enter into teaching either at the secondary level, T_{HS}, or at the higher educational level, T_{HH}, or they may enter the higher-educated labor force L_H. The number of teachers entering into either secondary schools or higher education is determined by the size of enrollments and the respective student–teacher ratio, α_S and α_H. The labor force, divided into the two sectors by educational level, is augmented by graduates from each level, but is reduced by the rate of withdrawals, W_S or W_H, from each sector. The labor force may be augmented also by foreign manpower imported into each sector, L_{SF} or L_{SH}. Finally, given the output–labor ratios of each labor force sector, the rate of absorption into employment of each type of educated labor is determined by the rate of growth of real national income, Y.

The given parameters are the rate of growth of output, the withdrawal rates, output–labor ratios, and teacher–student ratios. For each rate of growth, the model provides solutions for the required labor force by educational levels, for rates of entry into the labor force sectors, for enrollments in secondary and higher education, and for the number of new teachers to service these enrollments. If the rate of growth exceeds the capabilities of the educational system within a specified period of time, the model can be adapted to determine the magnitude of foreign-trained sources of labor that will permit the income growth rate to be achieved. Parameters can be estimated by econometric procedures.

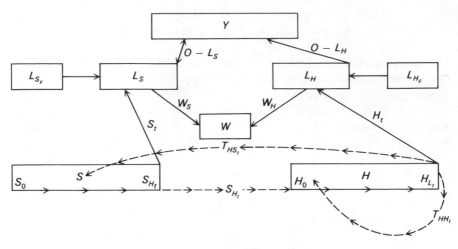

CHART 23.1. A diagrammatic scheme of the TCB model.

Glossary

$S_t \equiv$ secondary students in time t

$H_t \equiv$ students in higher education at time t

$S_{H_t} \equiv$ students continuing in higher education in time t

$S_L \equiv$ secondary students entering the labor force

$T_{HS_t} \equiv$ graduates from higher education beginning teaching in secondary schools

$H_{L_t} \equiv$ students from higher education entering labor force in time t

$T_{HH_t} \equiv$ higher education graduates beginning teaching in higher education

$L_S \equiv$ secondary trained labor force

$L_H \equiv$ higher education trained labor force

$Y \equiv$ real national income; $\dot{Y} = dY/Ydt$

$W_S \equiv$ withdrawals from L_S in time t

$W_H \equiv$ withdrawals from L_H in time t

$0 - L_S \equiv Y/L_S$

$0 - L_H \equiv Y/L_H$

Other modifications of the TCB model are possible. Although output–labor ratios are expressed linearly, nonlinear formulations are derived which are capable of relating employment both to output and to per capita income. Growing output–labor ratios imply that for a given increase in real national income, less labor is required to produce it. Although the TCB model is a two-sector one with time units of six years, educational levels and corresponding sectors of the labor force can be disaggregated and time units can be specified for a shorter interval. Withdrawal rates from the labor force are given, but they can be modified to reflect past rates of entry and current age distributions. Similarly, allowances can be made for student drop-out rates in the progression through the educational system. Variations are possible in the student–teacher ratios, permitting flexibility in the educational system to accommodate increased enrollments. Thus, a variety of alterations are possible in the model to permit a growth rate in the labor force sufficient to accommodate increases in the demand for labor via growth in real national income.

Suppose an increase in the economic rate of growth is required within some specified time interval. More trained labor will be required. In an interim period, foreign aid may supplement or supply the trained labor in the quantities required. Alternatively, policies could be undertaken to lessen the withdrawal rate from each segment of the educated labor force. With a given inflow into the labor force and a smaller attrition rate from it, the labor force increases at a greater rate. For example, the age of retirement may be delayed, or child care centers may permit women to maintain their participation rate when motherhood occurs. Another possibility is to increase the number flowing through the educational system. If teacher–student ratios are maintained, this implies an increase in the number of teachers required in the educational system. In an interim period, the number of graduates entering the teaching profession may be diverted from those entering the higher-educated labor force. This condition would result from the one-period lag of higher-education enrollments behind increased secondary enrollments. (This lag can be avoided by diverting more graduates from secondary education into higher education, thereby diminishing temporarily the flow of secondary graduates into L_S.) Consequently, a temporary shortage could occur in the supply of the higher-educated labor force. However, by decreasing the teacher–student ratio—i.e., by increasing class size or by putting teachers on overtime—these temporary shortages could either be avoided or mitigated. Hence, the model can accommodate a number of policy changes, which would be reflected in the values assigned to the parameters.

The model is reasonably complete and it is internally consistent. It does possess a number of deficiencies, however. The production functions from which output–labor ratios are estimated are relatively simple ones which do not permit substitution of capital for labor or one type of labor for another. Moreover, technological progress is not reflected in growing output–labor ratios. Failure to account for the possibility of skill substitutions or for growth in labor productivity means that the rate of growth of real national income is not strictly constrained by the rate of growth of the labor force sectors. The authors of the TCB model do acknowledge that graduating students may decide not to enter the labor force, but their labor force participation is not related to causative, independent variables. Instead, this decision to enter or not to enter the labor force is subsumed under given parameters. Somewhat related to this criticism is the absence of any explanation of why some secondary graduates choose to enter the labor force or why others choose to continue their education. Modification of the model at this point to incorporate rates of return to investment in education would remedy this omission. Finally, no recognition is given of attrition rates of teachers. Although technically teachers are a part of the higher-educated labor force, L_H, in the TCB model they are treated as a separate component. Consequently, it appears that the withdrawal rate W_H from L_H does not include the withdrawal of teachers from this profession. Indeed, this withdrawal rate is one of the major problems of underdeveloped countries in maintaining an adequate supply of teachers.

Employment Projections from an Input–Output Matrix

Employment projections can be obtained from an input–output transaction matrix and from time series on sectoral output and employment. From the time series data, simple regression equations provide estimates of the employment–output relationships. These equations are normally of the form $E_i = a_i + b_i X_i$ where E_i is the total employment (in man-year) in industry i and X_i is the gross output (deflated) in millions of dollars. If no time series data exist for an industry in the area defined by the input–output study, national employment in that industry can be correlated with the portion of national income earned in that industry. The resulting relationship can then be adjusted to represent the relationship between employment and output for the defined area. The slope (b_i) of the above regression equation represents the direct employment effect resulting from a change in final demand for that industry.

To illustrate the process by which employment projections and manpower demand can be estimated, let us take a simple example of an economy. Assume that the economy consists of three sectors: agriculture (I), manufacturing (II), and services (III). To produce its output each sector uses as inputs in its production function an amount of labor, part of its own output,

TABLE 23.1
INPUT–OUTPUT MATRIX

Buyers of Inputs [Millions of dollars]

Producers of Output		*I*	*II*	*III*	Consumption *C*	Total Production
Agriculture	I	497	620	367	1000	2484
Manufacturing	II	994	207	367	500	2068
Services	III	248	621	367	600	1836
Labor value		745	620	735	—	6388

and part of the output of the other two sectors. That portion of the output of a sector that is not used in the form of inputs is consumed, say, by households. (We may also regard households as providing the labor input.) Consequently, each sector is a producer of output and a user of inputs. We can set up a table (Table 23.1) of this relationship, using hypothetical quantities expressed in millions of dollars. Each row represents the output of that sector which goes as inputs to sectors or to final demand. Each column represents the amount of the outputs of the row sectors used as inputs by the column sector. If we consider only the intersectoral input–output relationship—the technical production relation—we are then concerned only with the first three rows and the first three columns. If we divide the element in each row by the output corresponding to the sector, we get the following table:

	x_1	x_2	x_3	
x_1	0.2	0.3	0.2	
x_2	0.4	0.1	0.2	(23.i)
x_3	0.1	0.3	0.2	

This table is called the technical coefficient matrix A and each a_{ij} cell shows the dollar amount of the product from row i which is used as an input to produce one dollar's worth of output of column j. We can express our input–output relationship also in the following form:

$$0.2x_1 + 0.3x_2 + 0.2x_3 + 1000 = x_1 \qquad (23.1)$$

$$0.4x_1 + 0.1x_2 + 0.2x_3 + 500 = x_2 \qquad (23.2)$$

$$0.1x_1 + 0.3x_2 + 0.2x_3 + 600 = x_3 \qquad (23.3)$$

where x_1, x_2, and x_3 represent the total value of output, respectively, of agriculture, manufacturing, and services. Alternatively, the relationships can be expressed as follows:

$$0.8x_1 - 0.3x_2 - 0.2x_3 = 1000 \qquad (23.1a)$$

$$-0.4x_1 + 0.9x_2 - 0.2x_3 = 500 \qquad (23.2a)$$

$$-0.1x_1 - 0.3x_2 + 0.8x_3 = 600 \qquad (23.3a)$$

and these three equations can be expressed in matrix form as $(\mathbf{I} - \mathbf{A})\mathbf{X} = \mathbf{C}$ where $(\mathbf{I} - \mathbf{A})$ is the adjusted technical coefficient matrix,[2] $\mathbf{X}$ is the sector

[2] Formed by subtracting the A matrix from the identity matrix I.

output matrix (here a vector), and C is the final sector demand matrix (vector). A solution for the value of the output matrix is given by

$$\mathbf{X} = (\mathbf{I} - \mathbf{A})^{-1}\mathbf{C}$$

An analogous algebraic operation would be a solution of this equation for x:

$$ax = c$$

$$x = \frac{1}{a} \cdot c = a^{-1}c$$

Just as a^{-1} is the inverse of a, so $(\mathbf{I} - \mathbf{A})^{-1}$ is the matrix inverse of $(\mathbf{I} - \mathbf{A})$. The matrix $(\mathbf{I} - \mathbf{A})^{-1}$ is the technical requirements matrix and is given by the following:

$$\begin{bmatrix} 1.719 & 0.781 & 0.625 \\ 0.885 & 1.615 & 0.625 \\ 0.547 & 0.703 & 1.563 \end{bmatrix} \tag{23.ii}$$

If this matrix is multiplied by $\mathbf{C}$, the consumption, or final-demand vector, the values for x_i are determined. These are shown in the last column of Table 23.1. Multiplying the x_i values by the appropriate a_{ij} cells gives us the input–output cell values for sectors I, II, and III in Table 23.1.

Next, let us assume that for every dollar of output of sectors I, II, and III, the following values of labor are used as inputs, respectively: $L_1 = 0.3$; $L_2 = 0.3$; $L_3 = 0.4$; and each L_i is the fixed labor–output ratio for each sector i.

We can multiply the cells of row i of the technical coefficient matrix by the appropriate L_i to transform it into a labor coefficient matrix, which tells us the monetary value of labor required as inputs to produce one dollar of output for each sector; then we can take the inverse of this labor coefficient matrix to obtain a labor requirements matrix,[3] and multiply the labor requirements matrix by the final demand vector C. This product determines the total value of labor required by each sector to produce its output. Alternatively, we can obtain the labor requirements matrix by multiplying each cell of row i in the technical requirements matrix—$(\mathbf{I} - \mathbf{A})^{-1}$—by the

[3] Each cell of the labor requirements matrix shows the direct and indirect labor required from the row sector needed to increase the portion of column sector output going to final demand by one dollar. The sum of the columns of the inverse matrix shows the total direct and indirect labor requirements necessary to deliver one dollar's worth of output to final demand.

TABLE 23.2
MANWEEKS OF LABOR, BY SECTOR AND SKILL LEVEL
[Millions]

	Sector			
Skill	I	II	III	Total
H	0.8765	1.24	1.6334	3.7499
S	2.6295	3.10	1.6334	7.3629
U	5.2590	1.86	4.9002	12.0192
Sector Total	8.7650	6.20	8.1670	23.1320

appropriate L_i;[4] this product can then be multiplied by C. The values of labor obtained are identified in the last row of Table 23.1.

Manpower requirements can be obtained, given the distribution of labor inputs by skill level into each sector, and given the average wage for each skill level in the economy. Assume three skill levels of labor in the economy: highly skilled H, semiskilled S, and unskilled U. The average weekly wages for each level are:

$$W_H = \$150.00 \qquad W_S = \$100.00 \qquad W_U = \$66.67$$

The labor force distribution by level of skill in each sector is

$$\begin{array}{cccc} & I & II & III \\ H & 0.1 & 0.2 & 0.2 \\ S & 0.3 & 0.5 & 0.2 \\ U & 0.6 & 0.3 & 0.6 \end{array} \qquad \text{(23.iii)}$$

It follows that the average weekly wage in sectors I, II, and III, respectively, are \$85, \$100, and \$90. Dividing the respective average weekly wages into row 4 of Table 23.1, we find the following labor force requirement in manweeks as shown in Table 23.2.

Next, assume a planning commission for the economy desires to increase final demand in manufacturing from \$500 million to \$600 million, a 20% increase. Translated into labor requirements, the extra \$100 million will require initially and at a minimum at least \$30 million of labor. This is the direct requirement of additional labor. But to produce a final-demand

[4] The labor requirements matrix is:

$$\begin{bmatrix} 0.5156 & 0.2344 & 0.1875 \\ 0.2656 & 0.4844 & 0.1875 \\ 0.2188 & 0.2813 & 0.6250 \end{bmatrix}$$

increment in manufacturing of $100 million requires also more inputs, not only from the agricultural and service sectors, but also from the manufacturing sector itself. Hence, total outputs and inputs in all three sectors must increase. Repeating the process, we derive the new labor requirements in the three sectors:

[Millions]

Labor Requirements

Sector	New Final Demand	Old Final Demand	Increment	L	H	S	U
I	$769	$745	$24	0.282	0.0282	0.0846	0.1692
II	669	620	49	0.490	0.0980	0.2450	0.1470
III	762	735	27	0.300	0.0600	0.0600	0.1800
Total	2200	2100	100	1.072	0.1862	0.3896	0.4962

The value of the direct labor force increment Δl_d is $30 million; the value of the total increment, both direct and indirect Δl_t is $100 million, yielding an employment multiplier $\Delta l_t/\Delta l_d$ of 3.33. In real terms, the direct requirement increment of man-weeks of labor is 300,000; the total increment is 1,072,000 man-weeks, giving a real employment multiplier of 3.57, a slightly higher value. Similar employment multipliers can be computed for skill levels.

If the employment data collected in the input–output study are disaggregated, then additional information can be easily obtained on employment impacts resulting from output changes. For instance, if the employment data are disaggregated on the basis of sex or age, then employment changes can be shown also on this basis. Any disaggregation then can be obtained in the initial stage and can be maintained throughout the impact and multiplier analysis.

The most serious fault of this second procedure for estimating the impact of demand on employment is the underlying assumption that labor inputs vary proportionately with changes in output. This assumption is a simplification of the true functional relationship that exists between employment and output, particularly in the long run. However, if it is further assumed that each firm is operating at a profit-maximizing output, no excess capacity can exist. This assumption, combined with the assumption that production techniques are fixed in the short run, leads to the conclusion that the linear assumption may be theoretically reasonable for the short-run period.

A Model of Manpower Imbalances: A Case Study for Thailand

The method by which manpower forecasts can be derived when data limitations exist necessarily must be direct and simple. Output is defined as Gross Domestic Product (GDP) measured in constant prices, and exponential growth trend equations by economic sector can be derived, from which estimates of real output for future years can be made. Also, growth rates for the output–labor ratios for each economic sector are based on time series data for real GNP and sector employment. These growth rates are used to estimate the output–labor ratios for future years. Given the equations and projected growth rates, the amount of employed labor required in each sector to produce that level of output can be computed. Summing the sectors yields the aggregate demand for labor that can be expected in the terminal years.[5]

The difference between the projected demand for labor by sectors in either terminal year and a base year is the incremental amount of labor needed. Next, the expected incremental demand for labor is converted into educational requirements by deriving an estimate of the distribution by educational level of the employed labor force for each sector. Summing by educational levels across the sectors yields the incremental demand for educational attainments of the projected employed labor force.

The supply of labor by educational levels is then estimated. Essentially, this is accomplished by estimating growth rates in enrollments in the first grade and applying average drop-out rates between each grade level in subsequent grades and years. Dropouts are presumed to enter the non-institutional population from which, after an appropriate lag for maturation to age 15, a given proportion—determined by labor force participation rates—enters the labor force. Aggregation of dropouts at each level permits estimation of increments to the labor force. The estimated aggregate supply is then compared with the estimated aggregate demand to determine the expected levels of unemployment. Similarly, expected needs for labor by

---

[5] Up to this point, there are strong similarities in estimating manpower demand between this model and that used in the O.E.C.D.'s Mediterranean Regional Project. For a discussion of the O.E.C.D.'s methodology, see R. G. Hollester, *Planning Education for Manpower Needs: A Technical Evaluation of the First Stage of the Mediterranean Regional Project*, Paris, O.E.C.D., 1966, reprinted in M. Blaug, *Economics of Education*, Vol. 1, *op. cit.*, pp. 338–350. Chinnawoot Soonthornsima has also used this basic technique for forecasting sectoral employment and unemployment in Thailand. United Nations Economic Commission for Asia and the Far East, "Sectoral Output and Employment Projections for Thailand: 1970–1980," *Sectoral Output and Employment Projections for the Second Development Decade*, Bangkok, 1970, pp. 291–335. For a less technical presentation of this method, see B. D. Mabry and T. Kompur, "Manpower Imbalance in Thailand," *Western Economic Journal*, Vol. X, No. 4, (Dec. 1972).

educational level are compared with expected available supplies in order to estimate the extent of structural educational imbalance in the economy. This imbalance provides a basis for recommending changes in national policy.

Forecasting Thailand's Manpower Imbalances

Labor Force and Population

Thailand, with approximately 35.9 million people in December 1971, has experienced rapid and sustained economic growth since 1946. It is essentially an agricultural economy in which about 79% of the labor force is employed. The labor force, consisting of persons 15 years of age or over, numbered about 17.3 million in 1971, or about 46% of the population, and is expected to increase to 19.6 million in 1976.[6] About 56% of the economically active population are unpaid family workers, which somewhat inflates the labor force participation rates among younger workers and among females. The average participation rate is about 80%.[7] The annual population growth rate is about 3.1%, the median age of the population is about 17 years, some 51% are in the age category 15–64, and average life expectancy at birth is 58.5 years.[8]

In the 1969 Labor Force Survey, those who were not actively seeking work were excluded from the definition of the unemployed, and in Bangkok–Thonburi, the unemployment rate was reported as 1.6%; in other municipalities it was 0.8%, and in rural areas, it was 0.1%. Because so many workers are in family enterprises (55.6%) or are self-employed (31.2%) in Thailand, consistent with Myrdal's argument, it is questionable whether measures of open unemployment are meaningful in this type of economy. Data on the employed labor force by economic sector for selected years are presented in Table 23.3.

Education

School attendance supposedly begins at age 7 and ideally continues to age 15, or through grade 7, but facilities to continue education beyond

[6] The 1960 census and 1969 Labor Force Survey defined the labor force as consisting of all employed and unemployed persons 11 years of age or over, and by this definition, the labor force comprised 66% of the population. Pertinent reasons for excluding persons under the age of 15 from the labor force definition in underdeveloped countries are presented by M. L. Gupta, "Patterns of Economic Activity in the Philippines and Some Methodological Issues Involved," *International Labor Review* (April 1970).

[7] Department of Labor, Ministry of Interior, *Year Book of Labor Statistics*, 1968.

[8] National Statistical Office, Office of the Prime Minister, *Report on the Survey of Population Change, 1964–67* (Bangkok: 1969), pp. 11–17, 25.

TABLE 23.3
EMPLOYMENT IN THAILAND, AGE 15 YEARS OR OLDER, BY MAJOR SECTORS IN SELECTED YEARS
[Thousands]

Sector	1947[a]	1960[b]	1969[c]	1971[d]	Estimated 1976	1981
A						
Agriculture, forestry, hunting and fishing	7,623.2	10,341.9	12,509.0	13,039.4	14,035.4	15,543.0
M	—	—	—	—	2,222.4	3,142.3
Mining and quarrying	4.8	20.4	39.3[e]	40.1	—	—
Manufacturing	195.9	454.8	830.0[e]	856.7	—	—
Construction	8.1	68.3	190.0[e]	190.0	—	—
Electricity, gas, water and sanitation	2.2	15.4	31.0[e]	39.4	—	—
Transport, storage and communication	65.9	164.1	272.0	314.9	—	—
S	—	—	—	—	3,934.9	5,442.5
Trade	707.0	744.4	1,224.7[e]	1,363.1	—	—
Services, finance, government, and miscellaneous	237.7	643.6	1,317.2[e]	1,424.7	—	—
Total	8,844.8	12,452.9	16,413.2	17,268.3	20,192.7	24,127.8

[a] 1947 Census of Population.

[b] 1960 Census of Population.

[c] 1969 Labor Force Survey, August.

[d] 1969 data adjusted by National Economic Development Board Estimated Growth Rates, 1969–1971.

[e] Adjusted for Seasonal Variation.

grade 4 were available to only one in five Thai children in 1971.[9] Of the some 30,000 public and private schools in 1967, not quite 10% offered education beyond grade 4. Because the rapid growth in the population of school age children has exceeded the construction of facilities, many schools operate two sessions per day and many classes have large enrollments, particularly in urban areas. Hence, compliance with the legal requirement

[9] National Economic Development Board, *Third National Economic and Social Development Plan 1976*, Chapter 14. It should be noted that in terms of human resource development, Thailand has been classified as a semiadvanced country along with such nations as Norway, Czechoslovakia, South Africa, and Mexico. See F. H. Harbison and C. A. Myers, *Education, Manpower and Economic Growth* (New York: McGraw-Hill Book Co., 1964), pp. 23–48.

TABLE 23.4
ESTIMATED INCREASES IN ENROLLMENTS AND TEACHER REQUIREMENTS SINCE 1971, BY EDUCATIONAL LEVELS

Level of Education	1971 Enrollment	Teacher–Student Ratio		1976			1981		
		Low[a]	High	Increase in Enrollments from 1971	Additional Teachers Required		Increase in Enrollments from 1971	Additional Teachers Required	
					Low	High		Low	High
Lower primary (1–4)	4,856.0	1:35	1:40	947,000	27,058	23,675	2,003,000	57,229	50,075
Upper primary (5–7)	863.0	1:25	1:40	531,000	21,240	13,275	1,500,000	60,000	37,500
Secondary, academic (8–12)	538.3	1:25	1:40	226,000	9,040	5,650	821,000	32,840	20,525
Secondary, vocational (8–13)	63.0	1:15	1:30	100,000	6,667	3,334	219,000	14,600	7,300
Teacher training (11–16)	65.4	1:10	1:40	33,100	3,310	828	85,300	8,530	2,133
Technical college (13–16)	11.8	1:10	1:30	7,800	780	260	15,600	1,560	520
University	47.5	1:10	1:30	16,200	1,620	540	32,400	3,240	1,080
Totals	—	—	—	1,861,000	69,715	47,562	4,676,300	177,999	119,133

[a] Specified by the National Economic Development Board.

of seven grades of education for Thai children will remain feasibly impossible in the next decade.

Students continuing their education beyond the primary grades may enter one of two secondary streams, either academic or vocational. Lower academic and prevocational secondary education encompasses grades 8 through 10, and similar courses are taught in each, but with differences in emphasis. However, only 2% of students in grades 8–10 are enrolled in the prevocational program and this program is to be discontinued. Upper secondary schools provide for either two years of precollege academic training or three years of vocational education. Many of the graduates from the lower secondary academic program enter into vocational training. Private secondary schools outnumbered public schools in 1967 two to one, and the ratio is only slightly smaller in terms of the number of students in each.

Higher education consists of a variety of public institutions. Teacher colleges offer programs leading to a certificate (one year),[10] diploma (two years), baccalaureate degree (four years), and the master's degree (five or more years). Technical institutes offer one-, two-, and three-year programs, and universities offer baccalaureate and master's degrees; the medical science institution offers doctoral training. Enrollment data for the educational system in Thailand are presented in Table 23.4, and flows through the educational system are presented in Chart 23.2.

The Model

The model by means of which manpower estimates can be derived can be formally specified.

DEFINITION OF TERMS The following symbols with their meaning are used in the model.

$Y_{i,t}$: Gross Domestic Product in sector i at time t in constant prices.

$$r_i = \left(\text{antilog} \left[\frac{\log Y_{i,t} - \log Y_{i,t-1}}{n} \right] - 1 \right):$$ average annual growth rate of Y_i in period of n years.

$N_{i,t}$: sector i employment in time t.

$$\lambda_{i,t} \equiv \left(\frac{Y_i}{N_i} \right):$$ output–labor ratio at time t.

---

[10] Although the program in teacher-training colleges leading to the certificate is a three-year one, entry into the program follows completion of lower secondary schools (grade 10).

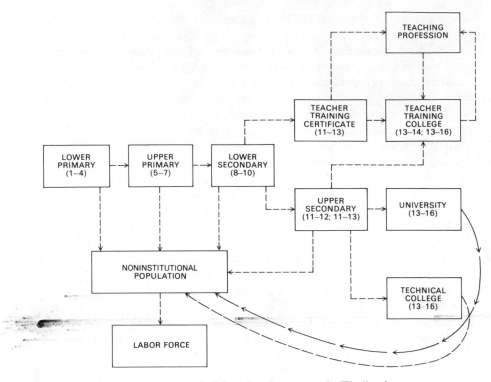

CHART 23.2. Educational structure in Thailand.

$s_i \equiv$ average, annual growth rate of $\lambda_{i,t}$ in period of n years

$$= \left(\text{antilog} \left[\frac{\log \lambda_{i,t} - \log \lambda_{i,t-n}}{n} \right] - 1 \right).$$

$dN_i = N_{i,t} - N_{i,t-n}$:   increment in sector employment in n number of years.

$\bar{N}_{i,f}$:   employment in sector i with f level of education.

$\pi_{if} = \dfrac{\bar{N}_{if}}{N_i}$:   ratio of sector employment by educational level to total sector employment.

$E_{g,v}$:   enrollment in grade g in year v.

$\#$:   age of entering grade 1.

γ: annual rate of increase in grade 1. Functionally related to γ are the lagged birth rate, the death rate in years, and repeaters of grade 1.

$E_{i,0}(1 + \gamma)^v$:   enrollment in grade 1 in year v.

$S_{f,v}$:   dropouts at level f in year v; $f = g - 1$.

$S'_{f,y}$:   total entrants into noninstitutional population, P_n, age 15 years or over, with f years of education in year y.

$y = v + [15 - (f + \#)]$, for $[15 - (f + \#)] > 0$.

$y = v$, for $[15 - (f + \#)] \leq 0$.

$S_{f,n}$:   total entrants into P_n with f years of education in n years' interval.

$L_{f,n}$:   entrants into labor force at f level of education in n years' interval.

L_I: labor force at I age interval.

$f_I = \dfrac{L_I}{P_{nI}}$:   labor force participation rate at I age interval.

δ_n: attrition rate from labor force in n years' interval.

$Z_{f,n}$:   net addition to labor force at f level of education in n interval.

$\overline{Z}_n$:   total net increment in labor force over n interval.

DEMAND   The equations by which demand for educated manpower is estimated are as follows:

$$Y_{i,t} = Y_{i,0}(1 + r_i)^t \tag{23.1.0}$$

$$N_{i,t} = \frac{Y_{i,t}}{\lambda_{i,t}} \tag{23.2.0}$$

$$\lambda_{i,t} = \lambda_{i,0}(1 + s_i)^t \tag{23.2.1}$$

$$dN = \sum^i dN_i \tag{23.2.2}$$

$$M_{f,n} = \sum^i \pi_{if} \cdot dN_i \tag{23.3.0}$$

Equation (23.1.0) relates real sector income to geometric trends. Equation (23.2.0) is a forecasting equation of sector employment and is derived from projected sector output–labor ratios, specified in the trend equation given by Equation (23.2.1), and from projected real sector income. The change in total employment over any given interval n is the change in sector employment in that interval summed over all sectors, and this is represented in Equation (23.2.2). Equation (23.3.0) states that the increment in employment of labor with educational level f over period n is equal to the sum over i sectors of the increment in employment in sector i at f level of education in the interval n. To estimate manpower demand, projected increases in GDP are converted into aggregate labor requirements, and these in turn are converted into projected increases in demand for manpower by educational attainments.

The average real growth rate in Thailand for the period 1961–1970 for eight sectors has been computed, and this rate is used to estimate sector GDP for 1976 and 1981 by means of the discrete compounding equation given in (Equation 23.1.2), with sector GDP in 1965 taken as the base.

Because an aggregate production function for the Thai economy from which labor inputs can be derived for each estimated output with given stocks of capital does not exist, output–labor ratios have been used to convert sector estimates into employment estimates.[11] Estimates of changes in the ratios were derived by projecting their 1960–1969 growth rates and, given the estimates of sector GDP and the corresponding output–labor ratios for 1976 and 1981, the manpower estimates by sector for those years were then derived. The educational frequency distribution for the employed labor force in each sector has first been calculated and this distribution has then been applied to estimated incremental employment. The frequency distributions were obtained by tabulating the placements of job applicants by the Employment Service Division of the Department of Labor in the 1962–1968 interval.[12]

These percentages are then applied to 1976 and 1981 estimates of

---

[11] Paul Trescott has developed a Cobb–Douglas production function for the nonagricultural sector of the Thai economy based upon 1949–1965 data, "Measurement of Thailand's Economic Growth, 1946–1966," *Economic Journal of Thailand*, Vol. 4, No. 1 (March 1971), p. 86. He found high collinearity between labor and capital, as independent variables, in his linear logarithm regression equation. Constraining the regression coefficients to equal one yields the linear homogeneous production function, $Y = 0.04640L^{0.2696}C^{0.7304}$, with $R^2 = 0.984$. He found, consistent with the high collinearity between labor and capital, that either of the variables, taken individually, yielded equations of equally good fit; i.e., $Y = 0.90743C^{0.855}$, $R^2 = 0.983$, and $Y = 5.42497L^{1.972}$, $R^2 = 0.987$ ($Y \equiv$ nonagricultural output; $L \equiv$ labor; $C \equiv$ capital). Hence, either capital–output or labor–output ratios appear to have historical validity in Thailand as estimates for either output, given the inputs, or as estimates for inputs, given the output.

[12] The 1969 Labor Force Survey classifies educational attainments of the labor force as follows:

manpower demand by the Kuznets sector,[13] and the number required at each educational level is summed across sectors in order to yield manpower demand by education.[14] These sums are presented in Table 23.5 as estimates for 1976 and 1981. Subtracting these sums from 1971 employment by educational level yields the increment in manpower at each educational level consistent with the estimated national output.

SUPPLY   The equations by means of which the supply of educated manpower is estimated are as follows:

$$E_{g,v} = z_g E_{g-1,v-1} \tag{23.4.0}$$

$$z_g = \sum_{v=0}^{m-1} \left(\frac{E_{g,v} - E_{g-1,v-1}}{E_{g-1,v-1}} \right) \Big/ m, \ g = 2 \ldots n. \tag{23.4.1}$$

$$S_{f,v} = (1 - z_g) E_{g-1,v-1} \tag{23.5.0}$$

$$S'_{f,y} = (1 - z_{f+1}) E_{f,y-1}; f + 1 = g \tag{23.5.1}$$

$$S_{f,n} = \sum_{y=1}^{n} S'_{f,y} \tag{23.6.0}$$

		Sector		
Level	*Percent of Total*	*A*	*M*	*S*
No education	18.5	18.8	12.3	19.5
Primary	76.9	80.6	74.4	57.0
Secondary	3.4	0.4	11.0	17.3
Higher	0.7	—	0.9	4.8
Other	0.5	0.2	1.4	1.3

This distribution is suspect for two reasons. First, it does not define the educational categories; for example, how are dropouts in the third, sixth, and ninth grades classified? Secondly, the data on secondary education are questionable. The 1960 census revealed the percent of the population with secondary education to have been 3.7%. An examination of secondary enrollment in the past 15 years makes it obvious that the number with secondary education in 1969 exceeds the number in 1960. The population in 1960 exceeds the labor force in 1969. Hence, it should be mathematically impossible for the percent of the labor force with a secondary education in 1969 to be less than that of the population in 1960. For these reasons, data from the Employment Service Division are taken to be more representative.

[13] See Simon Kuznets, *Modern Economic Growth: Rate Structure, and Spread* (New Haven: Yale University Press, 1966), p. 86.

[14] Implicit in this procedure are two assumptions: (1) that the distribution of placements by education in the 1962–1968 period accurately represents the educational distribution of employment in each sector; and (2) that this distribution will be valid for the years 1976 and 1981. Some bias may be expected in that the more highly educated may be less likely to utilize the facilities of the Employment Service Division.

$$L_{f,n} = F_I(S_{f,n}) \qquad\qquad (23.7.0)$$

$$Z_{f,n} = (1 - \delta_f)L_{f,n} \qquad\qquad (23.8.0)$$

$$\bar{Z}_n = \sum^{f} Z_{f,n} \qquad\qquad (23.9.0)$$

The level of enrollments in grade g depends upon the percentage z_g of those in the preceding grade in the preceding year continuing on to grade g. Equation (23.4.0) shows this, where the percentage is based upon the average percentage between succeeding grades of m-year period [Equation (23.4.1)]. Enrollment in grade 1 is a special case and is given in the definition of terms; hence, g varies from 2 to n, where n is the terminal year of education. The number who do not continue in school, the graduates or dropouts $(1 - z_g)$, enter into the noninstitutional population [Equation (23.5.0)]. After a lag, these dropouts or graduates become components of the non-institutional population age 15 or older from which the labor force is drawn [Equation (23.5.1)]. The total entrants into the noninstitutional population from all levels of education in any given interval are found by summing over the appropriate years in that interval [Equation (23.6.0)].

Not all of those in the noninstitutional population actually participate in the labor force. That proportion who do participate is revealed by the labor force participation rate, which varies with each age grouping; hence, the labor force at each educational level is determined by the appropriate labor force participation rate multiplied by the noninstitutional population of that age category. The general equation for all levels of education is given by Equation (23.7.0). The net additions to the labor force depend not only upon the number of entrants but also upon the number of those who exit from the labor force. This attrition rate, given by δ, for f levels of education, is subtracted from the rate of entrants to determine the net increments in the labor force by each educational level in the appropriate period [Equation (23.8.0)]. The sum of net increments in this period for all educational levels equals the total net increment in the labor force [Equation (23.9.0)].

Educated manpower is generated through a flow process as students progress through the Thai school system. By calculating enrollments, dropouts, and graduates, and knowing labor force participation rates by age, it is possible to estimate the educational distribution of annual entrants into the Thai labor force.

Drop-out rates for grades 1 through 13 were determined by computing average drop-out rates between 1964 and 1969 and applying these to projected enrollments, and these drop-out rates were adjusted for consistency with goals stated in the Third Five-Year Plan. In the period 1966–1969, the rate

TABLE 23.5

INCREASE IN EMPLOYMENT DEMAND FROM 1971 BY EDUCATIONAL LEVELS FOR 1976 AND 1981

[Thousands]

Education Level	1976				1981			
	A	M	S	Total	A	M	S	Total
Less than 1	76.69	28.91	44.74	150.34	192.78	62.94	103.53	359.25
1–4	800.78	539.88	552.90	1,893.56	2,012.89	1,175.53	1,279.57	4,467.99
5–7	40.84	21.10	71.12	133.06	102.65	45.93	164.59	313.17
8–10	66.73	119.54	273.01	459.28	167.74	260.28	631.82	1,059.84
11–13	4.98	41.41	102.09	148.48	12.52	90.16	236.27	338.95
Postsecondary	5.98	30.47	103.24	139.69	15.02	66.35	238.92	320.29
Totals	996.00	781.31	1,147.10	2,924.41	2,503.60	1,701.19	2,654.70	6,859.49

TABLE 23.6
INCREMENTS TO THE LABOR FORCE 15 YEARS AND OVER, SINCE 1971, BY EDUCATIONAL LEVEL
[Thousands]

Type of Increment	Primary				Secondary				Postsecondary	
	Lower		Upper		Lower		Upper			
	1976	1981	1976	1981	1976	1981	1976	1981	1976	1981
Entrants into noninstitutional population (15 years and over)	5,323.6	10,814.6	327.0	921.0	414.0	1,063.0	236.7	632.1	203.2	514.4
Labor force participation rate	80.8	80.8	80.8	80.8	80.8	80.8	87.4	87.4	87.4	87.4
Entrants into the labor force	4,301.5	8,738.2	264.2	744.2	334.5	858.9	206.9	552.5	177.6	449.6
Attrition, prorated proportionately	1,088.3	2,210.8	66.8	188.3	84.6	217.3	52.3	139.8	44.9	133.7
Gross increase in labor force	3,213.2	6,527.4	197.4	555.9	249.9	641.6	154.6	412.7	132.7	335.9
Adjusted attrition	−124.4	−329.7	33.4	94.2	42.3	108.7	26.2	69.9	22.5	56.9
Net increase in labor force	3,088.8	6,197.7	230.8	650.1	292.2	750.3	180.8	482.6	155.2	392.8

TABLE 23.7
ESTIMATED MANPOWER IMBALANCES BY EDUCATIONAL LEVELS FOR 1976 AND 1981
[Thousands]

Educational Level	1976			1981		
	Increase in Demand from 1971	Increase in Supply from 1971	Surplus (+) or Deficit (−)	Increase in Demand from 1971	Increase in Supply from 1971	Surplus (+) or Deficit (−)
Lower primary or less	2,043.9	3,088.8	+1,044.9	4,827.2	6,197.7	+1,370.5
Upper primary	133.1	230.8	+97.7	313.2	650.1	336.9
Lower secondary	459.3	292.2	−167.1	1,059.8	750.3	−309.5
Upper secondary	148.5	180.8	+32.3	339.0	482.6	+143.6
Postsecondary	139.7	155.2	+15.5	320.3	392.8	72.5
Total	2,924.4	3,947.8	1,023.3	6,859.5	8,473.5	1,614.0
Agriculture:						
Lower primary or less	877.5	—	—	2,205.7	—	—
Upper primary	40.8	—	—	102.7	—	—
Lower secondary	66.7	—	—	167.7	—	—
Upper secondary	5.0	—	—	12.5	—	—
Postsecondary	6.0	—	—	15.0	—	—
Total	996.0	—	—	2,503.6	—	—
Nonagriculture:						
Lower primary or less	1,166.4	—	—	2,621.6	—	—
Upper primary	92.2	—	—	210.5	—	—
Lower secondary	392.6	—	—	892.1	—	—
Upper secondary	143.5	—	—	326.4	—	—
Postsecondary	133.7	—	—	305.3	—	—
Total	1,928.4	—	—	4,355.9	—	—

of increase in enrollment in grade 1 had averaged 3.4%. This rate appeared reasonable and was continued.[15]

Because of the absence of enrollment data by year of progression through institutions of higher learning, the above technique could not be applied to postsecondary education. Based upon 1961–1971 total enrollment data, linear least-square regression trend equations have been derived, with adjustments for 1976 planned targets for postsecondary teacher training, technical institutions, and university graduates by year of training. These equations permit estimates of the number of dropouts or graduates of postsecondary institutions for relevant years. With these data and allowing for lags of dropouts younger than age 15, estimates have been made of the number of students expected to leave each educational level through graduation or as dropouts, and who enter the noninstitutional population.

To estimate additions to the labor force, the average labor force participation rate for ages 15–19 has been applied to entrants into the noninstitutional population from the lower secondary level. Since the proportion of the population over 19 enrolled in secondary and post-secondary schools is not large, participation rates for ages 19–24 have been used for these dropouts and graduates. Growth in the labor force is less than the number of new entrants because of normal attrition through retirements, deaths, illness, and temporary withdrawals. NEDB attrition estimates, adjusted for consistency with the magnitudes estimated in this model, are used and the attrition is first prorated proportionately to that of the educational distribution of entrants; this figure is then subtracted from the number of entrants to obtain an estimate of net supply. A correction is made, since new entrants into the labor force in a developing economy normally will have higher educational attainments than withdrawals.[16] The adjusted available supply by educational level for the periods 1971–1976 and 1971–1981 is presented in Table 23.6.

IMBALANCES

$$M_{f,n} - Z_{f,n} \gtreqless 0 \tag{23.10.0}$$

[15] The reported annual birth rate in Thailand is 42 per thousand. With an annual death rate of 11 per thousand, the annual population growth rate is estimated to be about 3.1%. Assuming that half of the death rate occurs among children under 7 years of age, and assuming that some of the children reaching 7 years of age do not enroll in school, the growth rate for first-grade enrollment of 3.4% appears reasonable.

[16] In a sense, this upgrading of the educational attainments of the labor force reflects its "modernization." For a discussion of the modernization process in the services sector in the Philippines and Taiwan, see A. S. Bhalla, "The Role of Services in Employment Expansion," *International Labor Review*, Vol. 101, No. 5 (May 1970), pp. 519–539. It is assumed for Thailand that the percentage of withdrawals at each educational level above the lower primary is only one-half that of the new entrants.

$$\sum^{f} (M_{f,n} - Z_{f,n}) \gtreqless 0 \qquad (23.10.1)$$

Equilibrium at the end of n period between the demand and supply of labor at each educational level occurs when Equation (23.10.0) has a value of zero. No educational structural unemployment exists when this condition holds. Shortages are revealed in the equation when its value is greater than zero, surpluses when the value is less than zero. The relationship between aggregate demand and supply of labor at the end of n period is shown in Equation (23.10.1). The value of the two equations need not have the same sign. For example, the number of workers demanded in the economy $\sum^{f} M_{f,n}$ may equal the number available $\sum^{f} Z_{f,n}$, but surpluses and shortages can exist at various levels of education. Similarly, aggregate demand for labor may be deficient, yet for given levels of education, shortages may occur. Adaptations in the model can be made among levels of education when data do not permit the use of flow estimates. A combination of flow estimates and projections from regression equations is possible.

Estimates for 1976 and 1981 of manpower demand and supply by educational level in Thailand are combined in Table 23.7. Even if GDP grows exponentially at the rates assumed in this study, surpluses of personnel at the terminal dates will exist at all but the lower secondary educational level,[17] and the aggregate increments in demand will be about 1 million and 1.6 million less than that of supply in 1976 and 1981, respectively.

Implications and Conclusions

Manpower

By 1976, therefore, unemployment looms as a serious problem in the Thai economy even if the average exponential growth rate is maintained. The aggregate increment in supply will exceed the aggregate increment in demand by over one million, with excesses of supply existing at all but the lower secondary levels of education. Thus, Thailand may follow the path of other less-developed countries such as India in having an excess supply of the well educated.

In order to achieve full employment in 1976 and 1981, Gross Domestic Product measured in 1962 prices must be, respectively, 191.8 and 288.9 billion baht. Given an over-all annual growth rate in output per worker of

[17] NEDB established in the Third Development Plan the objective of a real annual growth rate of 7.0%. We used an average growth rate of about 7.9%. On the basis of recent evidence, it appears that the Thai economy has performed in the last half of the 1960–1971 interval at a rate (7.2%) below our estimated growth rate. Although our exponential estimate for 1976 appears to be more realistic than NEDB's estimate, it still may be too high.

4.77%,[18] this implies a GDP annual growth rate of 8.7% until 1981.[19] Such a large rate of growth has not been assumed.

Let us define three output labor ratios at time t. Let

$$\lambda_1 = \frac{Y_1}{N_1}; \qquad \lambda_2 = \frac{Y_2}{L_1}; \qquad \lambda_3 = \frac{Y_1}{L_1};$$

where λ_1 is the planned output–labor ratio, λ_2 is the full-employment ratio, and λ_3 is the potential (realized) ratio; Y_1 is the projected real GDP at time t; Y_2 is the full employment GDP at time t; N_1 is projected labor demand; and L_1 is projected labor supply. Next, let s_1 and s_2 be the rates of growth of Y_1 and Y_2 respectively, from time $t - n$. Call s_1 the projected growth rate and s_2 the full-employment growth rate. Now, if N_1 is to equal L_1, when λ_1 equals λ_2, then s_1 must equal s_2, and therefore $\lambda_1 = \lambda_2 = \lambda_3$. However, if $s_1 < s_2$, as is our case for Thailand for 1976 and 1981 where $Y_1 < Y_2$, then $N_1 < L_1$. This implies that $\lambda_1 > \lambda_3$, or that our planned output–labor ratio exceeds our potential (or realized) output–labor ratio. Since our estimated GNP growth rate is below the full-employment growth rate, then the potential output–labor ratio in 1976 must be lower than the projected ratio. This does not imply a lowering of the real per capita product growth rate, however. This depends on the ratio of the labor force to the population, which we shall call L^*. If L^* increases, then it is possible for the growth rate of per capita income to remain constant as λ_3 declines. Since the growth rate of the labor force in Thailand in the decade of the 1970s has been predetermined by earlier population growth rates, and since the family planning program of NEDB in the Third Five-Year Plan calls for a reduction of the annual birth rate from 3.1 to 2.6%, it is expected that L^* will increase. Whether it actually increases, or increases sufficiently to maintain the per capita income growth rate, remains to be seen. The interesting conclusion from this is that it is at least theoretically possible to have increasing unemployment with no reduction in the rate of economic development, measured by the rate of growth of per capita income.

Education

Experience in Thailand has revealed that past planned economic targets could not be achieved because of critical bottlenecks resulting from

---

[18] The output–labor growth rate has been calculated from 1960–1969 data. In this interval the annual rate of growth of GDP has been about 7.9%. If the ratio of the labor force to population has been approximately constant, and given an annual increase in the population growth rate of about 3.1% during this interval, this would imply an annual increase in real per capita product of about 4.8%. The closeness of our over-all average annual growth rate of the output–labor ratio to this per capita product rate implies some validity to the estimate of the former.

[19] Such a growth rate in GDP is not unachievable. It was approximated in 1963 and exceeded in 1966, 1968, and 1969.

manpower demand and supply imbalances. To provide trained manpower in sufficient numbers requires the expansion of postprimary educational facilities, including more teachers who must be attracted either from other occupations or from an increase in the number of graduates from teacher-training institutions. Market incentives do not appear to be sufficient to induce qualified personnel to leave another occupation to enter teaching.[20] Because of relatively low pay and low status, it is difficult to attract and keep qualified faculty, even in the greater Bangkok area, and this is especially true for institutions of higher learning in which prospective teachers are trained.[21]

It is doubtful if a sufficient number of teachers will be trained. Based upon our estimates of enrollments at various educational levels in 1976 (see Table 23.4), the number of new teachers required can be determined from the desired student–teacher ratios established by NEDB. To these estimates must be added some 12,600 additional teachers that will be needed between 1971 and 1976 to replace those who leave teaching because of retirement, death, or other causes. In 1981, replacement demand over the decade can be expected to total 27,000 teachers. Based upon our trend projections, teacher colleges are expected to produce 121,300 graduates (or dropouts qualified to teach) in the interval 1972–1976, and 313,300 in the interval 1972–1981. These numbers will be supplemented by graduates or dropouts from Thai universities.[22] However, it has been estimated that as many as 50% of graduates from teaching institutions do not remain in teaching. If this proportion is applied to our projections of teacher demand based on the high ratio, no shortage of teachers will exist in either 1976 or 1981. However,

[20] The 1964 wage survey of the Department of Labor revealed that the monthly salary of teachers (731 Baht) is less than one-half of the average of similarly trained professional and technical personnel (1490 Baht). For a discussion of the impact of the failure of the Civil Service System to adjust its wages and salaries to changes in the labor market, see H. D. Evers and T. H. Silcock, "Elites and Selection," *Thailand: Social and Economic Studies in Development*, T. H. Silcock, ed. (Canberra: Australia National University Press, 1967), pp. 96–100. The consequences of a failure of government salaries to keep pace with the market are also explored in Bevars D. Mabry, "Government Consumption Expenditures and Economic Development: A Rose By Any Other Name," *Economic Journal of Thailand*, Vol. 2, No. 2 (Fall 1968), pp. 11–20.
[21] College-trained personnel are extremely reluctant to leave the Bangkok–Thonburi area. For example, it has been difficult to staff a technical institute in Nakorn Pathom, only about 50 kilometers from Bangkok and connected with it by one of the best highways in Thailand, and one of the ten largest cities in Thailand.
[22] Between 1972 and 1976, some 83.8 thousand students are expected to graduate or drop out from universities; for technical institutes, the number will be 53.1 thousand. Between 1972 and 1981, the numbers of graduates or dropouts should be 196.2 and 134.9 thousand, respectively. Some undoubtedly can be expected to enter the teaching profession, especially if our forecast of surplus postsecondary manpower is valid.

the low ratio implies a shortage of over 21,000 teachers in 1976 and of over 48,000 teachers in 1981.

Unless personnel policies are formulated to encourage trained teachers to remain or reenter the profession, Thailand's educational objectives, modest as they may be, cannot be achieved within the foreseeable future.[23] In view of the projected surplus of the upper primary component of the labor force and the shortage of the lower secondary component, it appears that Thailand could better use its limited educational resources by some reallocation from the upper primary level to the lower secondary level.

Discussion Questions

1. By means of Chart 23.1, show in the TCB model how varying rates of flows of teachers, students, foreign aid, or withdrawal rates can alter the rate of growth of output? What assumptions must be made with respect to the aggregate production function?
2. How can the input–output model be adapted to show varying levels of skilled labor as inputs? Of what use are employment multipliers in manpower planning? What are the limitations of input–output analysis in manpower planning? Are these limitations more important in the long run or short run?
3. What justification can be used for treating the labor force as being drawn from the noninstitutional population 11 years of age and older? From 15 years of age and older? Under what circumstances would you expect to find a significant difference between the two? No significant difference?
4. (a) Evaluate the use of projected output–labor ratios as a proxy for estimating future labor demand. What assumptions are implied with respect to the aggregate production function?
   (b) It has been suggested that output–labor ratio projections are merely a disguised form of projecting per capita income. Evaluate.
5. (a) Is it consistent to expect a growing output–labor ratio while the distribution of the educated labor force by economic sector remains constant? Discuss, using the concept of human capital as a contributor to production.

---

[23] In order to encourage more trained teachers to practice their profession, the Ministry of Education announced in September 1971 that a higher salary schedule would be adopted and that larger living allowances will be paid to teachers in rural schools. The problems facing Thailand in achieving her educational objectives are similar to those in Nigeria identified by Samuel Bowles, "A Planning Model for the Efficient Allocation of Resources in Education," *op. cit.*: Thailand cannot expand enrollments at existing student–teacher ratios if it cannot provide teachers, and if it cannot expand enrollments beyond the primary grades, it cannot obtain the human-resource base for training more teachers.

(b) Projections of the supply of educated manpower require estimates of withdrawal rates during each year of schooling, plus estimates of the number of entrants into the educational system each year.

    (i) Note how variations in entrance rates and withdrawal rates can affect the supply of educated manpower.

    (ii) Sometimes linear projections of graduates from each major level of education are used. Compare the two methods in terms of reliability.

6. In Thailand, observed labor force participation rates have declined, although the proportion of the population in school, above age 11, has not increased. How can this paradox be explained?

7. Although our estimates project a surplus of labor at all levels of education except at the lower secondary level—and an unusually large surplus at the primary levels—educational policy is directed to expansion of enrollment essentially at the upper primary level. How can this policy be defended?

8. Teachers in Thailand, given their level of education, are underpaid, and shortages of teachers exist. Contrast the Thai experience with that of teachers in the United States.

24

New Directions in
Labor Market Policy

We began this book by observing that the labor market has changed over the years. Not only have technological change and varying consumer tastes brought about changes in the demand for labor, but the labor force also is subject to influences that continuously alter its structure.[1] Participation rates by age, sex, and race have varied through the years, declining in some cases while rising in others. Old skills have become obsolete as new skills are required. The labor force has undergone significant quality changes as educational levels and degrees of training have been upgraded, not to mention the lengthened life expectancy and improved health of its members. Mobility patterns have changed, both with respect to the international flow of labor and on the domestic scene. We can expect this change to continue, and in this concluding chapter we shall note some, but by no means all, of the sources of change which will influence the character of the labor market in the years to come.

Growth and Jobs

During the 20th century, real per capita income in the United States has increased at almost twice the rate of that of the advanced countries of

---

[1] The Kalachek effect views the labor force as being composed of a stock of workers at any point of time, but flows into and out of the labor force will change its composition over time. Presumably, a long period of sustained prosperity, such as in the 1960s, would contain more members of the secondary labor force than in intermittent periods of prosperity, such as in the 1950s.

635

Western Europe. Per capita income, almost at par with that of these countries in the late 19th century, is now higher than in any of these countries, although in recent years the gap appears to be narrowing. Countries such as Germany, Sweden, the Netherlands, and Italy have experienced annual growth rates in real GNP in the two decades after 1950 of about 6%, and Japan's has averaged nearly 12%, whereas that of the United States has been closer to 4.5%. Whether the United States can maintain its position of having the world's highest standard of living (and some say that Sweden has surpassed us already) depends upon whether it can increase its rate of growth. Estimates to 1980 indicate an annual growth rate of real GNP of about 4.3%.[2] This assumes a productivity growth rate, measured in terms of output per man-hour, of about 3% a year. The civilian labor force is expected to grow at about 1.8% per year, with a 0.2% annual decline in average weekly hours worked. By 1975 the civilian labor force will number more than 90 million workers and GNP, measured in 1969 dollars, will amount to almost $1200 billion. By 1980, the civilian labor force will number about 98 million, and employment is projected to be 95 million, based upon a 3% unemployment rate. The increase in productivity, output per man-hour, influences not only the rate of growth of real GNP, but also the number of workers needed, given any level of GNP. Obviously, the more fully the labor force is employed and the more rapidly productivity increases, then the more rapid is the growth in GNP. The major problem that this country will face is to maintain a level of aggregate demand sufficient to absorb a growing labor force that also is becoming more productive.

As more and more of the labor force is employed in the service-producing sectors, where increases in productivity are more difficult to generate, greater increases in productivity in the goods-producing sectors will be required to maintain a given level of productivity growth. Yet, what will be the attitudes of labor leaders toward attempts to increase productivity? Some labor leaders have been reported as saying that they were not concerned about the problem of productivity. Because productivity improvements often bring about dislocations in the employed labor force, organized labor frequently views such gains as a major threat to job security. Consequently, as desirable and necessary as increases in productivity are to economic growth, it is by no means certain that these increases will be forthcoming. If they are not, not only may we not have a rising level of real per capita income, but our competitive position in world markets may be undermined and it may be even more difficult to maintain full employment with stability in our balance of payments.

[2] U.S. Department of Labor, Bureau of Labor Statistics, *The U.S. Economy in 1980*, Bulletin No. 1673, see Table A–15.

The Role of National Priorities

The disengagement from Vietnam has freed substantial amounts of man-power and made possible a potential for reallocation of resources. How large is this potential and how will these resources be used? In Table 24.1

TABLE 24.1
PERCENTAGE DISTRIBUTION OF GNP IN CURRENT PRICES, BY FUNCTION, 1955, 1966, AND 1969

	Percent of Total GNP, Current Prices		
Function	*1955*	*1966*	*1969*
Total GNP	100.0	100.0	100.0
Basic necessities	45.7	42.3	41.6
Education and manpower	3.7	5.7	6.3
Health	4.1	5.6	6.4
Transportation	10.6	9.9	10.0
General government	2.0	2.7	3.1
Defense	9.3	7.8	8.3
New housing	5.9	3.5	3.7
Business fixed investment	9.6	10.9	10.7
Net exports and inventory change	2.0	2.7	1.1
All other	7.1	9.0	8.8

Note: Detail will not necessarily add to totals because of rounding.

Sources: Department of Commerce and Council of Economic Advisers. *Economic Report of the President, 1971*, p. 99.

is presented the distribution of GNP, in percentages, by class of expenditures. It can be seen that purchases of basic necessities—food, clothing, rents—have declined since 1955, as have expenditures on defense, in which allocations to the Vietnam War effort were included. New housing also declined, a victim of the high interest rates of the late 1960s. Education and manpower expenditures increased, although on-the-job training costs are not counted as part of GNP. Health expenditures also increased sub-stantially, in part a response to Medicare, as did expenditures on general government, which includes police protection and natural resource develop-ment and preservation. If we spend our money on the basis of a relative ranking of importance, this list indicates what our priorities have been in the recent past. Hidden in these expenditures somewhere is the *War on*

Poverty, the announced goal of the Johnson administration. What other goals are concealed? What will be the nation's goals in the future? What are the manpower implications of major national goals?

When World War II demobilization took place, many veterans took advantage of the G.I. Bill of Rights in order to continue their education. This pattern was repeated after the Korean War. However, returning veterans from the Vietnam War have not availed themselves of this opportunity to the same degree. Why? Initial evidence suggests that the G.I. benefits are not as liberal, since tuition and opportunity costs both have increased. It may be that the population eligible for such benefits is not as educable as were the World War II and Korean veterans. But if the latter is true, perhaps the G.I. benefits should have been adapted to provide these latest veterans with the type of training for which they are best suited.

Indeed, if education and training are means to achieve a more equitable society in terms of economic opportunity, we can expect still greater increases in expenditures for these services. A teacher surplus has been predicted until 1980. Yet, if educational opportunities are expanded, it is difficult to see how such a surplus can persist. If society truly values quality education, a reduction in the student–teacher ratio would be one means to achieve this goal and this reduction would increase the demand for teachers. If day-care centers for children of working mothers are expanded, and if Head-Start programs are extended to all disadvantaged children, educational personnel will be needed in greater numbers. If the surplus of teachers continues to persist, perhaps expanded educational and economic opportunities for all are really not grass-root national objectives.

Medicare has provided health care at low cost to the aged. Extensions of the program have been proposed for the disabled, the poor, and indeed the whole population. From whence shall come the medical personnel to care for this extended group? It has been recommended that former medical corpsmen from the military be used as subprofessionals, but few have actually been employed in that capacity. Life science Ph.D.'s, having difficulty in finding university employment, have been accepted in medical schools for a two-year training program in clinical medicine leading to the M.D. degree. More such programs could quickly provide the nation with needed general practitioners. Foreign M.D.'s in residency at United States hospitals are persuaded by the high incomes of physicians to remain in the United States. New medical schools are being built, and health-care facilities are being reorganized to economize on the scarce time and space of primary treatment centers.

If pollution and destruction of natural resources are really threats to national survival, will more than lip service be paid to their control? It has already been proposed that polluters be required to pay an amount equal to the social costs incurred in remedying the harmful effects of their waste products. If these charges are greater than the cost of pollution control, then polluters will have an incentive to devise methods to reduce their rate of pollution. But where will the technical personnel be secured to establish pollution standards, to measure pollution, and to administer the charges? If the automobile is the major villain in air pollution, as it is in traffic congestion, will a system of mass transportation be substituted? If so, what will happen to the displaced automobile and parts workers, not to mention the chain of dealerships, repair shops, and service stations? What will happen to shopping centers, the American style of life? The manpower implications are enormous. Is the atmosphere really so important that we should consider banning the automobile, or at least the internal combustion engine?

If the national goal is to conquer poverty, then who will perform our menial jobs? Who will collect our garbage, dry clean our clothes, clean our streets, harvest our crops, or baby-sit our children? Is a society in which everyone is middle class really possible? Those who have visited Sweden say the answer is yes. But do we really want such a society? What will we do with our submarginal workers? What does Sweden, or the Soviet Union, do with them? How will we reward superior effort or talent? Will our incentive system disappear if we no longer pay according to the value productivity contribution of a worker?

Inflation and Unemployment

In appraising the effectiveness of the Employment Act of 1946 on its 25th anniversary, the Council of Economic Advisers has noted that the average unemployment rate for the past 25 years has been 4.6% with a maximum annual average of 6.8%, whereas in the 25-year period before the Great Depression, the average was 4.7%, with a maximum annual average of 11.7%. The Council concluded, "This suggests that we have not appreciably reduced the incidence of small departures from maximum employment but that we have reduced the incidence of large departures, which is just what one would expect aggregate economic policy would do."[3] In the next quarter-century, the CEA believes that control of inflation, not unemployment, will be its primary concern.

Actually, one might regard an economy which utilizes 94 or 95% of its manpower to be one which is operating with reasonable efficiency. What, then, is the great concern about a 5 or 6% unemployment rate? If this unemployment rate were distributed evenly among economic sectors, geographical regions, ages, and races, perhaps the anxiety would not be as

[3] *Economic Report of the President, 1971*, p. 21.

great. But the unemployment rate is not evenly distributed. In particular, young people and non-Whites experience extremely large and disproportionate amounts of unemployment, and some economic sectors, such as the durable goods-producing sectors, bear the brunt of any small increase in the level of unemployment. Removing these disproportionate burdens of unemployment may be one of the important objectives of policy in years to come.

The persistence of inflation in the 1969–1971 period in the face of restrictive monetary policy, a declining rate of growth,[4] and increasing unemployment have led economists to question whether deflationary monetary (and fiscal) policies are sufficient to correct the inflationary pressures. If persistent unemployment and stagnant economic growth are the consequences, perhaps other methods of control are necessary. Certainly, the inflationary tendencies in the 1969–1971 period have lasted longer than those in the 1956–1957 period. The Council of Economic Advisers attributes this increased lag of the economy to corrective policy as owing to the momentum generated in the boom period since 1965. Expectations of continued inflation were reflected in negotiated wage increases, in higher tax rates, interest charges, and quoted prices. The CEA does not rule out the possibility that economic concentration may have increased among corporations and unions, which could have lengthened the inflationary period. However, the CEA does not believe that such concentrations of power have caused the inflation.

As yet, the CEA has not indicated the contribution of the Vietnam War effort to the origin and persistence of inflation. Although income is generated from the production of war goods, as resources are devoted to this type of output, no corresponding quantities of goods are made available to absorb the spending originating from these incomes. The result is a shortage of goods in the private sector. Although this same condition occurred during the Korean War, that war did not continue as long on the one hand, and on the other hand some economic controls were utilized to ration shortages and hence to mitigate price increases. Perhaps neither momentum nor increased concentration of economic power is the true villian, but rather the uncontrolled, unrationed scarcities induced by diverting large quantities of resources to the war effort may be to blame.

As inflation persisted into 1971 the need for controls became more and more obvious. At first, the CEA announced a program of sounding an "inflation alert" when wage increases or price increases were higher than warranted. This, of course, amounted to a form of "jawboning," or the

---

[4] During the period from the third quarter of 1969 to the third quarter of 1971, real output declined by almost 0.5%. The value of output rose by 4.6%, caused by a rise in the price level of 5%.

imposition of admonitions to hold the line on price increases. A second policy was directed at the construction industry in which large wage contracts had been negotiated. In order to elicit cooperation from the affected unions, President Nixon suspended the Bacon–Davis Act, a prevailing wage law that transmitted union wage increases throughout the public construction sector. Finally, the wage–price freeze in August 1971 and the wage–price regulations of November 1971 were imposed to "break the back" of the inflationary psychology. All these policies were instituted during a period in which considerable slack prevailed in the economy. Such policies undoubtedly will become the subject of additional econometric research in order to measure their effectiveness.

Whether or not inflation is less subject to control by monetary and fiscal policy, or whether a greater amount of unemployment is required to bring inflation under control, remains to be determined. How will the American economy behave under peacetime conditions? Will the Phillips curve relationship between unemployment and price changes return to the position of the 1950s, or will it shift upward? Indeed, the question that remains to be answered, as the monetary school alleges, is whether the Phillips curve is only an illusion that disappears in the long run. How much will the micro approach to inflation and unemployment contribute to an understanding of these phenomena? Will a reduction in the barriers to job search and an improvement in the dissemination of labor market information reduce the amount of unemployment required to bring about price stability? These are questions which future researchers will have to answer for us.

Public Security

Public security can be regarded as being directed toward two sources of threats—external and internal. Changes in attitudes toward each can have manpower implications. Suppose the trend continues in the public's reaction against international involvements. As a part of this attitude, suppose the reaction against the industrial–military complex brings about a sharp reduction in defense expenditures. What would be the impact upon employment? Some indications of the dimensions of the employment reallocation required are suggested in Tables 24.2 and 24.3 in which employment is related to the expenditures of the Department of Defense. The reduction since 1968, which represented the Vietnam War peak, is a consequence of the winding down of the war. The effect on manufacturing employment is seen in Chart 24.1. Production for defense against real or imaginary foreign foes has become a significant part of our output. If Congress reduces the military-aid component of foreign assistance, brings back our troops from Western Europe, and curtails expenditures on the research and development

TABLE 24.2
EMPLOYMENT ATTRIBUTABLE TO DEPARTMENT OF DEFENSE
EXPENDITURES AND PERSONNEL REQUIREMENTS, 1965 AND
1968–1971
[Thousands; fiscal years]

Type of Employment	1965	1968	1969	1970	1971[a]
Total Department of Defense- generated employment	5,759	8,129	7,944	7,374	6,354
Public employment	3,657	4,555	4,644	4,474	4,054
Federal military	2,716	3,460	3,534	3,398	3,034
Federal civilian	928	1,075	1,090	1,056	1,000
State and local	13	20	20	20	20
Private employment	2,102	3,574	3,300	2,900[a]	2,300

[a] Estimate.

Source: Department of Labor. *Economic Report of the President,
1971*, p. 44.

TABLE 24.3
CIVILIAN EMPLOYMENT ATTRIBUTABLE TO DEFENSE
EXPENDITURES FOR SELECTED NARROW OCCUPATIONAL
CATEGORIES, FISCAL YEAR 1968

	Defense-Generated Employment	
Occupational Category	Number (thousands)	Percent of Total Employment in Group
Technical engineers[a]	244	20
Aeronautical engineers	45	59
Electrical engineers	69	22
Mechanical engineers	49	20
Physicists	9	38
Machinists	113	19
Pattern and modelmakers	10	25
Sheetmetal workers	39	25
Airplane mechanics	73	54

[a] Includes some groups not shown separately.

Source: Department of Labor. *Economic Report of the President,
1971*, p. 46.

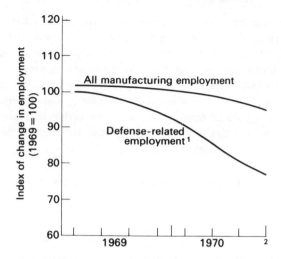

CHART 24.1. Sharp decline in defense-related employment has been a major factor in over-all decline in manufacturing employment.

[1] Represents employment in three industries most affected by defense cutbacks: ordnance and accessories, radio and TV communication equipment, and aircraft and parts.
[2] December data are preliminary.

Source: Department of Labor, *Manpower Report of the President, 1971*, p. 13.

of new weapons, what will happen to those sections of industry so effected? This kind of impact on jobs has already been observed in the aerospace industry. And what will happen to our balance of payments if the flow of obsolete military equipment, now exported to belligerents abroad, is lessened through reduced research and defense expenditures?

The change from conscription to a volunteer army will also have an effect on the labor force. Career uncertainties faced by youths will be altered, job rights of returning servicemen will be mitigated, and military turnover may be reduced. To the extent that enlistees choose the military service as a career, the external economies to the private economy associated with military training may be curtailed. Indeed, if the military services can retain their personnel, the scope of their training can be diminished, but the civilian sector may have to compensate for this reduction.

Internal security refers to the protection of the public from crime and disorder. If drug abuse becomes a national disaster, what type of personnel and how many will be required to detect and prosecute offenders, and rehabilitate victims? What are the barriers to employment of former addicts, and what types of manpower services can be provided to former prison inmates? If younger members of minority groups continue to face difficulties in obtaining reasonable employment opportunities, will they increasingly turn to illegal activities? Recent studies indicate that recourse to such activities has become so frequent that "it functions as an illegitimate third sector of the urban labor market, which must be taken account of in planning and operating work and training programs for disadvantaged youths."[5] Again, how much enforcement is necessary in order to make "crime not pay," and where will the manpower originate to provide the public this protection?

Changes in Labor Markets

Although most jobs are still found in the central cities, this dominance is weakening as industry and jobs expand more rapidly in the suburbs.[6] This tendency takes on increased importance as the United States becomes more urbanized. (See Chart 24.2.) How will this tendency affect employment opportunities in the ghettoes of the central cities? As population grows in these ghettoes from immigration from rural areas, by what process will these newly arrived migrants make occupational adjustments in urban areas? Will not the process of adjustment be impaired if job opportunities become stagnant in these areas? What are the best channels of communication in slum neighborhoods for communicating job information to job seekers? And what is the best method of transferring workers from areas of unemployment to areas of employment? Getting inner city residents to suburban jobs is a problem of no small magnitude as public transit systems decay. "There are records of journeys to work involving reverse commuting (inner city to suburbs in the morning, and the reverse in the late afternoon) in which disadvantaged workers spent up to 5 hours a day traveling by bus, with six transfers, to go to and from jobs paying $2 or less an hour."[7]

Today most rural residents are employed in nonfarm occupations, and although migration from farms continues at a decreasing rate, the rural population has not declined since 1940. This is depicted in Chart 24.3. As a proportion of the population, the percentage in rural areas has declined. Most rural emigrants are young adults, who are among the better educated. Those remaining, therefore, possess characteristics associated with those who are poor. Industries that locate in rural areas typically pay low wages, and hence the rural–urban wage differential tends to persist. To upgrade

---

[5] *Manpower Report of the President, 1971,* p. 97. Reference is made here to studies by Barry Bluestone, Daniel Fusfeld, and Stanley Friedlander. Friedlander had estimated that two out of every five adults in Harlem had some illegal income in 1966.

[6] *Ibid.,* see pp. 88–91.

[7] *Ibid.,* p. 96.

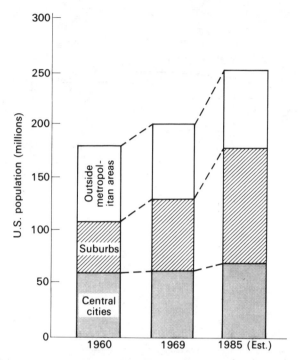

CHART 24.2. Population is increasingly concentrated in metropolitan areas, with fastest growth in the suburbs.

Source: Department of Labor, based on data from the Department of Commerce, *Manpower Report of the President, 1971*, p. 84.

opportunities for rural residents, either jobs must be brought to them, or else they must be transferred to areas where job opportunities abound. About one-half of all rural residents live within a 50-mile radius of a metropolitan city, and with the developing system of superhighways, the latter problem is not insurmountable. One of the big problems, however, will be to provide manpower services to these residents.

Employment characteristics of the labor force are changing. Service-producing sectors continue to expand while goods-producing sectors decline (see Chart 24.4); white-collar occupations grow more rapidly than blue-collar ones; and government employment becomes an increasing percentage of the employed labor force. We have already noted some of the implications of these changes on the productivity potential of the labor force. There are also implications with respect to the magnitude of fluctuations of unemployment levels. It may well be that changes in the structure of jobs have been

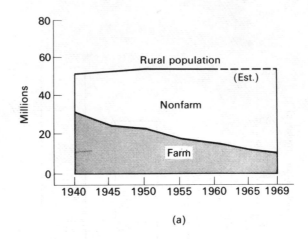

(a)

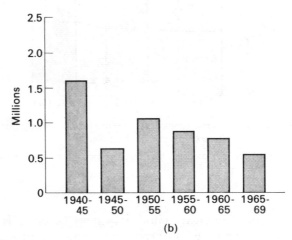

(b)

CHART 24.3. Rural nonfarm population grows and farm population declines as migration from farms continues. (a) Changes in composition of rural population. (b) Average annual net migration from farms.

Net change through migration and reclassification of residence from farm to nonfarm.

Source: Department of Labor, based on data from the Departments of Commerce and Agriculture, *Manpower Report of the President, 1971*, p. 114.

such that fewer jobs are subject to wide cyclical variations, and this may explain the reduction in the magnitude of unemployment variations, rather than aggregate contracyclical policies. Part-time jobs have increased and an expansion in these employment opportunities can increase the labor force participation of groups who are ordinarily not counted in the primary

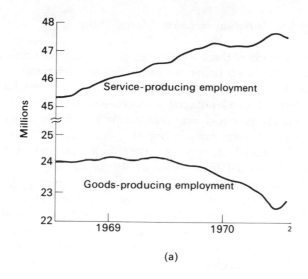

(a)

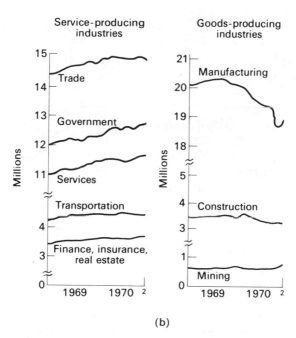

(b)

CHART 24.4. Employment continued to edge upward in service-producing industries in 1970 but declined substantially in goods-producing industries, with the drop concentrated in manufacturing. (a) Service-producing and goods-producing employment. (b) Breakdown by industry.

[1] Employment levels for all industries shown are based on seasonally adjusted payroll data.
[2] December data are preliminary.

Source: Department of Labor, *Manpower Report of the President, 1971*, p. 12.

labor force. How many of those who are employed only part time are really underemployed? We need better measurements of underemployment. We also need more local information on the actual and the potential supply of labor, particularly of disadvantaged workers. Analysis of movements into and out of the labor force and between occupations continues to be one of the high-priority manpower research topics.

Various institutional changes can alter the labor force. Expansion of postsecondary educational institutions at the junior college or technical institute level means that more and more youths are finding opportunities for additional training in the communities in which they reside. Undoubtedly, this will affect the labor-force participation rates of the age group of 20 to 24 years. Proposed increases in the minimum wage may create a new and larger class of the disadvantaged, those who cannot find jobs because of low productivity. Reductions in hours of work may stimulate the recreational industry even more, and impose new decisions on American laborers on how to use their increased leisure time. Perhaps moonlighting will expand. The movement of organized labor into public and professional employment will create new tensions on the American taxpayer and require him to pay more for public services. It may alter the quality of these services, for better or worse.

Manpower Programs

President Nixon began his 1971 Manpower Report to Congress by calling for greater decentralization of manpower programs. Funds would be disbursed to state and local governments on the basis of the area's proportionate number of workers, unemployed persons, and low-income adults, and wide discretion would be allowed the governments in determining how to use these funds. Prior to receiving the funds, objectives and proposed uses of the funds would be announced by states and localities. In view of the criticisms by competent manpower economists against the proliferation and lack of coordination among Manpower programs instituted during the 1960s, such a proposal seems to represent a step backward. However, Congress has been reluctant to release its hold on the purse strings, and revenue-sharing programs such as this one have not fared well before the legislature.

New programs have been established in the early 1970s. The Supplemental Training and Employment Program (STEP) has been designed for persons who have completed training programs, remain unemployed, and show promise of benefiting from further training. The Public Service Careers Program (PSC) was initiated to provide employment in federal, state, and local governments for disadvantaged members of the labor force.

The Concentrated Employment Program (CEP) has been designed to provide training and job information to people in slums and other pockets of poverty. The Work Incentive Program (WIN) is another project to bring recipients of welfare into the labor force. The Cooperative Area Manpower Planning System (CAMPS) has been established to coordinate the activities of all programs receiving federal funds. New types of centers have been set up under the Job Corps in order to provide social services and counseling, in order to reduce the drop-out rate from this program for disadvantaged youths. Computerized job banks have been established in over 100 metropolitan areas, and plans to expand job information services across interstate lines have been promulgated. As old programs are abandoned, new programs are instituted, with no guarantee that the new will yield any better results than those they have replaced.

In the meantime, research into manpower problems continues. Bit by bit, data are gathered which, when pieced together, may permit a comprehensive analysis of the nature and scope of training in business and industry. As more and more data become available, answers to such questions as the following may be possible:

1. What are the critical factors in employers' decisions to train or not to train?
2. What is the enrollment in, and completion ratio of, training programs by type, occupation, industry, and characteristics of trainees?
3. What is the minimum amount of remedial training required to overcome educational standards that serve as barriers to employment?
4. Why do manpower programs succeed or fail? How much coordination exists among manpower programs in a given area? Is the Employment Security Office the logical coordinating agency?
5. To what extent are programs developed from Manpower forecasts? Can forecasts be made for state and local areas?
6. Should private as well as public employment offices feed information on job vacancies into job banks? How much matching of applicants with openings is possible via computers?
7. What changes are needed in the system of public education to correct the problems of dropouts? How much preschool remedial training is required to prepare the disadvantaged for schooling, and how successful have these programs been?
8. What type of training or counseling is required to ease the transition of youths from school to work? Are Job Corps Centers and Neighborhood Youth Programs providing this training?

9. What proportion of the labor force has benefited from retraining? How much retraining will be required in the future and what facilities are being established to provide opportunities for replacing obsolete skills with new ones?
10. To what extent does upgrading occur within the internal labor market, and to what extent does it occur across such markets?

Studies are needed also to evaluate the effectiveness of manpower programs on reducing the inflation–unemployment tradeoff. One of the major goals of such programs is to improve the operation of the labor market by reducing structural unemployment. Similarly, how effective have these programs been in reducing the inequality of opportunity experienced by the disadvantaged? It is appropriate that these programs be evaluated on the basis of the degree of achievement of their stated goals.

Income Differentials and Social Justice

It is true that the United States has the highest per capita income in the world. Yet it is claimed that a greater proportion of citizens in Sweden enjoy a higher standard of living than in the United States. How can this be possible? If the claim is true, it undoubtedly results from the fact that the dispersion of income about the mean in Sweden is much less than that in the United States. In short, Sweden enjoys more income equality than does the United States. There are no slums in Sweden, and few are poverty stricken. Can the United States achieve this level of social justice, and does it really wish to do so?

We do know that the poor in this country have low incomes. In fact, that is how we define the poor. Poverty is a result of inadequate earnings and intermittent employment. To understand fully the sources of poverty, however, we need more and better data on the earnings of part-time and part-year workers. We also need to possess more data on the changes in income over the work-life cycle. How does poverty perpetuate itself? What is the effect of family incomes on a child's education? What are the probabilities of mental retardation or school dropouts for children from different income classes? How much does discrimination contribute to poverty, both directly and indirectly? In what forms and to what degree is discrimination present at different occupational levels? Do families, or can they, uplift themselves through their own engagement in unpaid work? What type of attitudes permit a family to raise its level of living by its own "bootstraps"? In a related vein, what is the internal rate of return to a recipient of welfare as compared with that of working?

Answers to these questions may enable the policy makers to plan programs more rationally to win the war on poverty and to enhance social justice in the United States, if by social justice we mean a more equitable sharing in the fruits of this country's production.

Discussion Questions

1. The 1980 estimate of labor force size at just under 100 million is based upon an unemployment rate of 3%. Suppose the "natural" rate of unemployment is 4.5%. Then what implications are associated with the 1980 projections?
2. Explain the obstacles to continued rapid rates of growth in productivity? What are the implications of these obstacles? Are they present in other countries also?
3. What are the most pressing national priorities? What are their manpower implications? Suppose defense and military expenditures are substantially reduced as the United States moves toward a more neutral international position. How might this affect the supply of and demand for labor?
4. Suppose an enlightened manpower policy succeeds in shifting the Phillips curve to the left. How might this affect national economic policy with respect to inflation, unemployment, and international trade?
5. Why is it that urban problems in European cities are not as pressing as those in the United States? How does the urban labor market affect these problems?
6. (a) Would a change in our educational system reduce manpower problems? Explain. Can we reduce poverty without manpower programs?
   (b) Are manpower programs consistent with the philosophy of our laissez-faire, capitalistic economic system?

Selected Bibliography and Suggested Readings

Books, Monographs, Reports

ACKLEY, GARDNER. *Macroeconomic Theory*. New York: The Macmillan Co., 1961.

ADELMAN, IRMA and THORBECKE, E., eds. *The Theory and Design of Economic Development*. Baltimore: Johns Hopkins Press, 1966.

ALLEN, R. G. D. *Mathematical Analysis for Economists*. London: Macmillan and Co., 1938.

ANDERSON, C. A. and BOWMAN, M. J., eds. *Education and Economic Development*. Chicago: Aldine Publishing Co., 1965.

BACKMAN, JULES; MEANS, GARDINER C.; and DONALD, W. J. *Administered Prices, Administered Wages and Inflation*. New York: National Industrial Conference Board, 1957.

BARLOW, ROBIN; BRAZER, H. E.; and MORGAN, J. N. *Economic Behavior of the Affluent*. Washington: The Brookings Institution, 1966.

BECKER, GARY. *Economics of Discrimination*. Chicago: University of Chicago Press, 1957.

BECKER, GARY. *Human Capital*. New York: Columbia University Press, 1964.

BLAUG, MARK, ed. *Economics of Education*, 2 vols. Baltimore: Penguin Books, 1968.

BLAUG, MARK, ed. *Economic Theory in Retrospect*. Homewood, Ill.: R. D. Irwin, Inc., 1962.

BOWEN, W. C. *The Wage-Price Issue*. Princeton: Princeton University Press, 1960.

BOWEN, W. C. and FINNEGAN, T. A. *The Economics of Labor Force Participation*. Princeton: Princeton University Press, 1969.

CARTTER, A. M. *Theory of Wages and Employment*. Homewood: R. D. Irwin, Inc., 1959.

CHAMBERLAIN, NEIL. *Collective Bargaining*. New York: McGraw-Hill Book Co., 1951.

CHAMBERLIN, E. H. *The Theory of Monopolistic Competition*. Cambridge, Mass.: Harvard University Press, 1933.

CROSS, J. C. *The Economics of Bargaining.* New York: Basic Books, 1969.

DE GRAZIA, S. *Of Time, Work and Leisure.* New York: The Twentieth Century Fund, 1962.

DELEHANTY, J. A. *Manpower Problems and Policies.* Scranton: International Textbook Co., 1970.

DENISON, E. F. *The Sources of Economic Growth in the United States and the Alternatives Before Us,* Supplementary Paper No. 13. New York: Committee for Economic Development, 1962.

DOERINGER, P. B. and PIORE, M. J. *Internal Labor Markets and Manpower Analysis.* Lexington, Mass.: D. C. Heath and Co., 1971.

DOLLARD, JOHN and MILLER, N. E. *Personality and Psychotherapy.* New York: McGraw-Hill Book Co., 1950.

DOUGLAS, PAUL. *Real Wages in the United States, 1890–1926.* Boston: Houghton Mifflin & Co., 1930.

DUNLOP, J. T. *Wage Determination Under Trade Unions.* New York: Macmillan Co., 1944.

Economic Report of the President, Selected Years. Washington, D.C.: Government Printing Office. Annual Publication.

FEI, JOHN and RANIS, GUSTAV. *Development of the Labor Surplus Economy.* Homewood: Richard D. Irwin, Inc., 1964.

FELLNER, WILLIAM and HALEY, B. F., eds. *Readings in the Theory of Income Distribution.* Philadelphia: The Blakiston Company, 1951.

FERGUSON, C. F. *The Neoclassical Theory of Production and Distribution.* Cambridge: University Press, 1969.

FINKEL, S. R. and TARASCIO, V. J. *Wage and Employment Theory.* New York: Ronald Press, 1971.

FOLTMAN, F. F. *White- and Blue-Collars in a Mill Shutdown.* Ithaca: School of Industrial and Labor Relations, Cornell University, 1969.

FRIEDMAN, MILTON. *Dollars and Deficits: Living with America's Economic Problems.* Englewood Cliffs: Prentice-Hall, Inc., 1968.

FRIEDMAN, MILTON. *A Theory of the Consumption Function.* Princeton: Princeton University Press, 1957.

FRIEDMAN, MILTON, ed. *Studies in the Quantity Theory of Money.* Chicago: University of Chicago Press, 1956.

FUCHS, V. R. *Differentials in Hourly Earnings by Region and City,* Occasional Paper No. 101. New York: National Bureau of Economic Research, 1967.

GALENSON, WALTER and PYATT, GEORGE. *The Quality of Labor and Economic Development in Certain Countries.* Geneva: International Labor Office, 1964.

GORDON, R. A. and GORDON, M. S., eds. *Prosperity and Unemployment.* New York: John Wiley and Sons, Inc., 1966.

HANNA, F. A. *State Income Differentials, 1919–1954.* Durham: Duke University Press, 1959.

HARBISON, F. H. and MYERS, C. A. *Education, Manpower and Economic Growth.* New York: McGraw-Hill Book Co., 1964.

HICKS, J. R. *The Theory of Wages,* 2nd ed. London: Macmillan and Co., 1963.

HICKS, J. R. *Value and Capital*, 2nd ed. Oxford: Clarendon Press, 1953.

HUNTER, L. C.; REID, G. L.; and BODDY, D. *Labour Problems of Technological Change.* London: George Allen and Unwin, Ltd., 1970.

KALACHEK, E. D. *The Determinants of Higher Unemployment Rates, 1958–60.* Cambridge: Unpublished Doctoral Dissertation, M.I.T., 1963.

KEYNES, J. M. *The General Theory of Employment, Interest, and Money.* New York: Harcourt, Brace and Co., 1936.

LESTER, R. A. *Manpower Planning in a Free Society.* Princeton: Princeton University Press, 1966.

LEVINSON, H. M. *Postwar Movements of Price and Wages in Manufacturing Industries,* Study Paper No. 21, Joint Economic Committee, Eighty-sixth Congress, 2nd sess. Washington, D.C.: Government Printing Office, 1960.

LEVINSON, H. M. *Unionism, Wage Trends and Income Distribution, 1914–1947.* Ann Arbor: Bureau of Business Research, 1951.

LEWIS, H. G. *Unionism and Relative Wages in the United States: An Empirical Inquiry.* Chicago: University of Chicago Press, 1963.

LINDER, S. B. *The Harried Leisure Class.* New York: Columbia University Press, 1970.

LONG, CLARENCE. *The Labor Force under Changing Income and Employment.* Princeton: Princeton University Press, 1958.

MABRY, B. D. *Labor Relations and Collective Bargaining.* New York: The Ronald Press, 1966.

MARSHALL, ALFRED. *Principles of Economics*, 8th ed. London: Macmillan and Co., 1961.

MORGAN, J. N.; DAVID, M. H.; COHEN, W. J.; and BRAZER, H. E. *Income and Welfare in the United States.* New York: McGraw-Hill Book Co., 1962.

NATIONAL BUREAU OF ECONOMIC RESEARCH. *Aspects of Labor Economics.* Princeton: Princeton University Press, 1962.

O.E.C.D. *Occupational and Educational Structures of the Labor Force and Levels of Economic Development.* 2 vols. Paris: Organization for Economic Cooperation and Development, 1971.

O.E.C.D. *Manpower Policy in the United Kingdom.* Paris: Organization for Economic Cooperation and Development, 1970.

OKUN, A. M. *The Battle Against Unemployment.* New York: W. W. Norton, 1965.

PATINKIN, DON. *Money, Interest, and Prices: An Intergration of Monetary and Value Theory,* 2nd ed. New York: Harper and Row, Inc., 1965.

PEN, JAN. *The Wage Rate Under Collective Bargaining.* Cambridge: Harvard University Press, 1959.

PERLMAN, RICHARD. *Labor Theory.* New York: John Wiley and Sons, Inc., 1969.

PERRY, G. L. *Unemployment, Money-Wage Rates and Inflation.* Cambridge: M.I.T. Press, 1966.

PHELPS, E. S., ed. *Microeconomic Foundations of Employment and Inflation Theory.* New York: W. W. Norton and Co., 1970.

PIGOU, A. C. *Economics of Welfare*, 4th ed. London: Macmillan and Co., 1962.

REPORT OF THE PRESIDENT'S COMMISSION ON INCOME MAINTENANCE PROGRAMS. *Background Papers.* Washington, D.C.: Government Printing Office, 1969.

REPORT OF THE PRESIDENT'S COMMISSION ON INCOME MAINTENANCE PROGRAMS. *Poverty Amid Plenty: the American Paradox.* Washington, D.C.: Government Printing Office, 1969.

REYNOLDS, L. L. *The Structure of Labor Markets.* New York: Harper and Bros., 1951.

REYNOLDS, L. L. and GREGORY, P. *Wages, Productivity, and Industrialization in Puerto Rico.* Homewood: R. D. Irwin, Inc., 1965.

ROBINSON, E. A. G. and VAIZEY, J. E., eds. *The Economics of Education.* New York: St. Martin's Press, 1966.

ROBINSON, JOAN. *Economics of Imperfect Competition.* London: Macmillan and Co., 1933.

ROSS, A. M., ed. *Employment Policy and the Labor Market.* Berkeley: University of California Press, 1965.

ROSS, A. M., ed. *Trade Union Wage Policy.* Berkeley: University of California Press, 1948.

SAMUELSON, P. A. *Foundations of Economic Analysis.* Cambridge: Harvard University Press, 1955.

SCHULTZ, C. L. *Recent Inflation in the United States*, Study Paper No. 1, Joint Economic Committee, U.S. Congress. Washington, D.C.: Government Printing Office, 1959.

SCHULTZ, G. P. and ALIBER, R. Z. *Guidelines, Informal Controls, and the Market Place.* Chicago: University of Chicago Press, 1969.

SCHUMPETER, J. A. *History of Economic Analysis.* New York: Oxford University Press, 1954.

SCOVILLE, J. G. *The Job Content of the U.S. Economy, 1940–70.* New York: The McGraw-Hill Book Co., 1969.

SIEGEL, SIDNEY and FOURAKER, L. E. *Bargaining and Group Decision Making: Experiments in Bilateral Monopoly.* New York: McGraw-Hill Book Co., 1960.

SMITH, ADAM. *The Wealth of Nations.* E. Cannan, ed. New York: The Modern Library, 1937.

SOLOW, R. M. *Price Expectations and the Behavior of the Price Level.* Manchester: University of Manchester Press, 1969.

STEVENS, CARL. *Strategy and Collective Bargaining Negotiations.* New York: McGraw-Hill Book Co., 1963.

STIGLER, GEORGE J. *Production and Distribution Theories.* New York: The Macmillan Co., 1946.

STIGLER, GEORGE J. *The Theory of Price,* 3rd ed. New York: Macmillan Co., 1966.

TABB, WILLIAM. *The Political Economy of the Black Ghetto.* New York: W. W. Norton, 1970.

TRIFFIN, ROBERT. *Monopolistic Competition and General Equilibrium Theory.* Cambridge: Harvard University Press, 1949.

U.S. DEPARTMENT OF LABOR. *Manpower Report of the President, 1969, 1971, 1972.* Washington, D.C.: Government Printing Office.

WOLFBEIN, SEYMOUR. *Employment, Unemployment, and Public Policy.* New York: Random House, Inc., 1965.

WRIGHT, D. M., ed. *The Impact of the Union.* New York: Harcourt, Brace, and World, Inc., 1951.

Articles

ALBRECHT, W. P., "The Relationship between Wage Change and Unemployment in Metropolitan and Industrial Labor Markets," *Yale Economic Essays* (Fall 1966), 279–341.

ALLEN, B. T., "Market Concentration and Wage Increases; U.S. Manufacturing, 1947–1964," *Industrial and Labor Relations Review*, Vol. 21, No. 3 (April 1968), 353–366.

ARROW, K. J., "The Economic Implications of Learning By Doing," *Review of Economic Studies* (June 1962).

ASHENFELTER, O. and MOONEY, J. D., "Some Evidence on Private Returns to Graduate Education," *Southern Economic Journal*, Vol. 35, No. 3 (January 1969).

BARLOW, ROBIN, "The Economic Effects of Malaria Eradication," *American Economic Review*, Vol. 56, No. 2 (May 1967).

BAYER, A. E. and ASTIN, H. S., "Sex Differences in Academic Rank and Salary Among Science Doctorates in Teaching," *Journal of Human Resources*, Vol. 3, No. 2 (Spring 1968).

BEAR, D. V. T., "Inferior Inputs and The Theory of the Firm," *Journal of Political Economy*, Vol. 73, No. 3 (June 1965), 287–289.

BELLI, PEDRO, "The Economic Consequences of Malnutrition: The Dismal Science Revisited," *Economic Development and Cultural Change*, Vol. 20, No. 1 (October 1971), 2–10.

BECKER, GARY, "Underinvestment in College Education," *American Economic Review*, Vol. 48, No. 2 (May 1960).

BECKER, GARY, "A Theory of the Allocation of Time," *The Economic Journal*, Vol. 75 (September 1965), 493–517.

BEHMAN, SARA, "Wage Changes, Institutions, and Relative Factor Prices in Manufacturing," *Review of Economic Studies*, Vol. 51, No. 3 (August 1969).

BEHMAN, SARA, "Wage-Determination in U.S. Manufacturing," *Quarterly Journal of Economics*, Vol. 82, No. 1 (February 1968), 117–142.

BENEWITZ, MAURICE and WEINTRAUB, R. E., "Employment Effects of a Local Minimum Wage," *Industrial and Labor Relations Review*, Vol. 17 (January 1964), 276–288.

BLACK, S. W. and RUSSELL, R. R., "Participation Functions and the Potential Labor Force," *Industrial and Labor Relations Review*, Vol. 24, No. 1 (October 1970).

BELL, F. W., "The Relation of the Region, Industrial Mix and Production Functions to Metropolitan Wage Levels," *Review of Economic Studies* (August 1967).

BLANDY, RICHARD, "Marshall on Human Capital," *Journal of Political Economy*, Vol. 75, No. 6 (December 1967), 874–875.

BLAUG, MARK, "The Rate of Return on Investment in Education in Great Britain," *The Manchester School* (September 1965), 205–261.

BOWLES, SAMUEL, "The Efficient Allocation of Resources in Education," *Quarterly Journal of Economics*, Vol. 81, No. 3 (August 1967).

BOWEN, W. G. and MASTERS, S. H., "Shifts in Composition of Demand and the Inflation Problem," *American Economic Review*, Vol. 54, No. 5 (December 1964), 975–984.

BREHM, C. T. and SAVING, T. R., "The Demand for General Assistance Payments," *American Economic Review*, Vol. 54, No. 5 (December 1964), 1002–1018.

BRONFENBRENNER, M. and HOLZMAN, F. H., "Survey of Inflation Theory," *American Economic Review*, Vol. 53, No. 4 (September 1963), 543–561.

BURNS, A. F., "Wages and Prices by Formula," *Harvard Business Review* (April 1965), 57–64.

BURROWS, PAUL, "Manpower Policy and the Structure of Unemployment," *Scottish Journal of Political Economy*, Vol. 15, No. 1 (February 1968), 77–83.

BUTLER, A. D. and DEMOPOULOS, G. D., "Labor Force Behavior in a Full Employment Economy," *Industrial and Labor Relations Review*, Vol. 24, No. 3 (April 1971), 375–388.

CARGILL, T. F., "An Empirical Investigation of the Wage-Lag Hypothesis," *American Economic Review*, Vol. 59, No. 5 (December 1969).

COELHO, P. R. R. and GHALI, M. A., "The End of the North-South Wage Differential," *American Economic Review*, Vol. 61, No. 5 (December 1971).

COHEN, M. S., "Married Women in the Labor Force: An Analysis of Participation Rates," *Monthly Labor Review*, Vol. 92, No. 10 (October 1969).

CORREA, HECTOR and CUMMINS, GAYLORD, "Contribution of Nutrition to Economic Growth," *The American Journal of Clinical Nutrition*, Vol. 23, No. 5 (May 1970), 560–565.

DEUTERMANN, WILLIAM, "Educational Attainments of Workers," *Monthly Labor Review*, Vol. 93, No. 10 (October 1970).

DOUTY, H. M., "Wage-Differentials: Forces and Counterforces," *Monthly Labor Review*, Vol. 91, No. 3 (March 1968), 74–81.

DERNBURG, T. F. and STRAND, K. T., "Hidden Unemployment, 1956–1962: A Quantitative Analysis by Age and Sex," *American Economic Review* (March 1966), 71–95.

DERNBURG, T. F. and STRAND, K. T., "Cyclical Variation in Labor Force Participation," *Review of Economic Studies*, Vol. 46 (November 1964), 378–391.

ECKSTEIN, OTTO, "Money Wage Determination Revisited," *Review of Economic Studies* (April 1968), 133–143.

ECKSTEIN, OTTO and WILSON, T. A., "The Determination of Money Wages in American Industry," *Quarterly Journal of Economics*, Vol. 76 (August 1962), 379–414.

EVANS, ROBERT, "Note on Wage Differentials, Excess Demand for Labor, and Inflation," *Review of Economic Studies*, Vol. 45 (February 1963), 95–98.

FABRICANT, R. A., "An Expectational Model of Migration," *Journal of Regional Science*, Vol. 10, No. 1 (April 1970), 13–24.

FALK, HUGH, "Effect of Private Pension Plans on Labor Mobility," *Monthly Labor Review*, Vol. 86, No. 3 (March 1963).

FELLNER, WILLIAM, "Prices and Wages Under Bilateral Monopoly," *Quarterly Journal of Economics*, Vol. 61, No. 3 (August 1947), 503–532.

FINEGAN, T. A., "Hours of Work in the United States: A Cross Sectional Analysis," *Journal of Political Economy*, Vol. 70, No. 5 (October 1962).

FRANCE, R. R., "Wages, Unemployment, and Prices in the United States, 1890–1932, 1947–1957," *Industrial and Labor Relations Review*, Vol. 15 (January 1962), 171–190.

FRIEDMAN, MILTON, "The Role of Monetary Policy," *American Economic Review*, Vol. 55, No. 1 (March 1968), 1–11.

GALLOWAY, L. E., "The Economics of the Right-to-Work Controversy," *Southern Economic Journal*, Vol. 32, No. 3 (January 1966), 310–316.

GALLOWAY, L. E., "Industry Variations in Geographic Labor Mobility Patterns," *Journal of Human Resources*, Vol. 2, No. 4 (Fall 1967).

GALLOWAY, L. E., "Labor Mobility, Resource Allocation, and Structural Unemployment," *American Economic Review*, Vol. 53, No. 4 (September 1963).

GALLOWAY, L. E., "The North–South Differential," *Review of Economic Studies*, Vol. 65 (August 1963).

GALLOWAY, L. E., "A Note on the Incidence of Hidden Unemployment in the United States," *Western Economic Journal*, Vol. 7, No. 1 (March 1969), 71–83.

GARBARINO, J. W., "A Theory of Interindustry Wage Structure Variation," *Quarterly Journal of Economics*, Vol. 64 (May 1950), 282–305.

GILMAN, H. J., "Economic Discrimination and Unemployment," *American Economic Review*, Vol. 55, No. 5 (December 1965), 1077–1096.

GITELMAN, H. M., "Occupational Mobility Within the Firm," *Industrial and Labor Relations Review*, Vol. 20, No. 1 (October 1966), 50–65.

GORDON, R. A., "Has Structural Unemployment Worsened?" *Industrial Relations*, Vol. 3 (May 1964), 53–77.

HANNA, F. A., "Contribution of Manufacturing Wages to Regional Differences in Per Capita Income," *Review of Economic Studies*, Vol. 33 (February 1951), 18–28.

HANSEN, W. H.; WEISBROD, B. A.; and SCANLON, W. J., "Schooling and Earnings of Low-Achievers," *American Economic Review*, Vol. 60, No. 3 (June 1970), 409–418.

HARNETT, D. L., "Bargaining and Negotiation in a Mixed-Motive Game: Price Leadership Bilateral Monopoly," *Southern Economic Journal*, Vol. 33, No. 4 (April 1967), 479–487.

HINES, A. G., "Trade Unions and Wage Inflation in the United Kingdom, 1893–1961," *Review of Economic Studies*, Vol. 31 (1964), 221–251.

HINES, A. G., "Unemployment and the Rate of Change of Money Wages in the United Kingdom, 1862–1963: A Reappraisal," *Review of Economic Studies* (February 1968), 60–67.

HOLT, C. C., "Improving the Labor Market Trade-Off Between Inflation and Unemployment," *American Economic Review*, Vol. 59, No. 2 (May 1969), 135–146.

HOLTZMAN, F. D., "Inflation: Cost-Push and Demand-Pull," *American Economic Review*, Vol. 50, No. 1 (March 1960), 20–42.

KALDOR, NICHOLAS, "Alternative Theories of Distribution," *Review of Economic Studies*, Vol. 23 (1955–1956), 83–100.

KALDOR, NICHOLAS, "Economic Growth and Problems of Inflation," *Economica* (November 1959), 293–295.

KANNINEN, TOIVO, "Occupational Wage Relationships in Manufacturing," *Monthly Labor Review*, Vol. 76 (November 1953), 1171–1178.

KASPER, HERSCHEL, "The Asking Price of Labor and the Duration of Unemployment," *Review of Economic Studies*, Vol. 49, No. 2 (May 1970).

KAUN, D. E., "Minimum Wages, Factor Substitution, and the Marginal Producer," *Quarterly Journal of Economics* (August 1965), 478–486.

KAUN, D. E., "Union–Nonunion Wage Differentials Revisited," *Journal of Political Economy*, Vol. 72, No. 4 (August 1964), 403–413.

KEAT, P. G., "Long-Run Changes in the Occupational Wage Structure, 1900–1956," *Journal of Political Economy*, Vol. 68 (December 1960), 584–600.

KENDRICK, J. W. and SATO, RYUZO, "Factor Prices, Productivity and Economic Growth," *American Economic Review*, Vol. 53, No. 5 (December 1963).

KIKER, B. F., "The Historical Roots of the Concept of Human Capital," *Journal of Political Economy*, Vol. 74, No. 5 (October 1966), 481–499.

KOZIARA, E. C. and KOZIARA, K. S., "Development of Relocation Allowances as Manpower Policy," *Industrial and Labor Relations Review*, Vol. 20, No. 1 (October 1969), 66–75.

KUH, EDWIN, "A Productivity Theory of Wage Levels—An Alternative to the Phillips Curve," *Review of Economic Studies* (October 1967).

LANDON, J. H., "The Association of Market Concentration on Wage Levels: An Intra-Industry Approach," *Industrial and Labor Relations Review*, Vol. 23, No. 2 (January 1970), 237–247.

LASSITER, R. L., "The Association of Income and Education for Males by Region, Race, and Age," *Southern Economic Journal*, Vol. 32, No. 1 (July 1964), 15–22.

LAVELLE, M. J., "Soviet Views on American Unemployment, 1953–1963," *Kyklos*, Vol. 21, No. 2 (1968), 313–325.

LEIBENSTEIN, HARVEY, "The Theory of Underemployment in Backward Economies," *Journal of Political Economy*, Vol. 65 (April 1957), 91–103.

LERNER, A. P., "On Generalizing the General Theory," *American Economic Review*, Vol. 50, No. 1 (March 1960), 121–143.

LESTER, R. A., "Benefits as a Preferred Form of Compensation," Vol. 33, No. 4 (April 1967).

LEVINSON, H. M., "Unionism, Concentration, and Wage Changes: Toward a Unified Theory," *Industrial and Labor Relations Review*, Vol. 20, No. 2 (January 1967), 198–205.

LEWIS, B. W., "Economics by Admonition," *American Economic Review*, Vol. 49 (May 1959), 384–398.

LINDAUER, J. H., "Effects of Selected Methods to Improve Unemployment Rates Used to Identify Depressed Areas," *Industrial and Labor Relations*, Vol. 20, No. 3 (April 1967), 433–440.

LIPSEY, R. G., "The Relationship between Unemployment and the Rate of Change of Money Wage Rates in the United Kingdom, 1862–1957: A Further Analysis," *Economica* (February 1960), 1–31.

LIPSEY, R. G. and STEUR, M. D., "The Relation Between Profits and Wage Rates," *Economica* (May 1961), 137–155.

LIPSKEY, D. B.; DROTNING, J. E.; and FOTTLER, M. D., "Some Correlates of Trainee Success in a Coupled On-the-Job Training Program," *Quarterly Review of Economics and Business*, Vol. 11, No. 2 (Summer 1971), 41–62.

LONG, CLARENCE, "The Illusion of Wage Rigidity: Long and Short Cycles in Wages and Labor," *Review of Economic Studies*, Vol. 4 (May 1960), 140–161.

LURIE, M. and RAYACK, E., "Racial Differences in Migration and Job Search: A Case Study," *Southern Economic Journal*, Vol. 33, No. 1 (July 1966).

MABRY, B. D., "An Analysis of Work and Other Constraints on Choices of Activities," *Western Economic Journal*, Vol. 8, No. 3 (September 1970), 213–225.

MABRY, B. D., "Income-Leisure Analysis and the Salaried Professional," *Industrial Relations*, Vol. 8, No. 2 (February 1969), 162–173.

MABRY, B. D., "The Pure Theory of Bargaining," *Industrial and Labor Relations Review*, Vol. 18, No. 4 (July 1965), 479–502.

McCAFFREE, K. M., "A Further Consideration of Wages, Unemployment, and Prices in the United States, 1948–1958," *Industrial and Labor Relations Review* (October 1963), 60–74.

McCALL, J. J., "Economics of Information and Job Search," *Quarterly Journal of Economics*, Vol. 84, No. 1 (February 1970).

MAHER, J. E., "Union, Nonunion Wage Differentials," *American Economic Review*, Vol. 46, No. 3 (June 1956), 336–352.

MIERNYK, W. H., "Experience Under the British Local Employment Acts of 1960 and 1963," *Industrial and Labor Relations Review*, Vol. 20, No. 1 (October 1966), 30–49.

MINCER, JACOB, "The Distribution of Labor Incomes: A Survey with Special Reference to the Human Capital Approach," *Journal of Economic Literature*, Vol. 8, No. 1 (March 1970), 1–26.

MINCER, JACOB, "On-the-Job Training: Costs, Returns, and Some Implications," *Journal of Political Economy*, Vol. 70, No. 5 (Supplement, October 1962), 50–79.

MISHAN, E. J., "The Demand for Labor in a Classical and Keynesian Framework," *Journal of Political Economy*, Vol. 72 (December 1964), 610–616.

MUSKIN, S. J., "Health as an Investment," *Journal of Political Economy*, Vol. 70, No. 5 (Supplement, October 1962), 149–157.

OBER, HARRY, "Occupational Wage Differentials, 1907–1947," *Monthly Labor Review*, Vol. 71 (August 1948), 127–134.

OI, WALTER, "Labor As a Quasi-Fixed Factor," *Journal of Political Economy*, Vol. 70, No. 6 (December 1962), 538–555.

OSHIMA, HARRY, "Food Consumption, Nutrition, and Economic Development," *Economic Development and Cultural Change*, Vol. 15, No. 4 (July 1967).

PALEN, J. J. and FAHEY, F. J., "Unemployment and Reemployment Success: An Analysis of the Studebaker Shutdown," *Industrial and Labor Relations Review*, Vol. 21, No. 2 (January 1968), 234–250.

PERLMAN, RICHARD, "Forces Widening Occupational Wage Differentials," *Review of Economic Studies*, Vol. 40 (May 1958), 107–109.

PERLMAN, RICHARD, "Observation on Overtime and Moonlighting," *Southern Economic Journal* (October 1966), 237–244.

PERRELLA, V. C., "Moonlighters: Their Motivations and Characteristics," *Monthly Labor Review*, Vol. 93, No. 8 (August 1970), 57–64.

PERRY, G. L., "Wages and the Guideposts," *American Economic Review*, Vol. 57 (September 1967), 897–904.

MOLONEY, J. F., "Some Effects of the Fair Labor Standards Act upon Southern Industry," *Southern Economic Journal*, Vol. 9 (July 1942), 5–23.

MOONEY, J. D., "Urban Poverty and Labor Force Participation Rates," *American Economic Review*, Vol. 57, No. 1 (March 1967).

MOORE, T. G., "The Effect of Minimum Wages on Teenage Unemployment Rates," *Journal of Political Economy*, Vol. 79, No. 4 (July–August 1971), 897–902.

MORGAN, J. N., "The Supply of Effort, the Measurement of Well-Being, and the Dynamics of Improvement," *American Economic Review*, Vol. 58, No. 2 (May 1968), 31–39.

MORGAN, J. N. and SMITH, J. D., "Measures of Economic Well-offness and their Correlates," *American Economic Review*, Vol. 59, No. 2 (May 1969). 45–62.

MORTON, W. A., "Trade Unionism, Full Employment, and Inflation," *American Economic Review*, Vol. 40, No. 1 (March 1950).

MOSSIN, JAN and BRONFENBRENNER, MARTIN, "The Shorter Workweek and the Labor Supply," *Southern Economic Journal* (January 1967), 322–331.

MOSES, L. N., "Income, Leisure and Wage Pressure," *The Economic Journal* (June 1962), 320–335.

MOSES, L. N. and WILLIAMSON, H. F., "Value of Time, Choice of Mode, and the Subsidy Issue in Urban Transportation," *Journal of Political Economy*, Vol. 71, No. 3 (June 1963), 247–264.

PHILLIPS, A. W., "The Relationship Between Unemployment and the Rate of Change of Money Wage Rates in the United Kingdom, 1861–1957," *Economica* (November 1958), 283–299.

PIERSON, GAIL, "The Effect of Union Strength on the U.S. Phillips Curve," *American Economic Review*, Vol. 58, No. 3 (June 1968), 456–467.

PRONAU, REUBEN, "Information and Frictional Unemployment," *American Economic Review*, Vol. 61, No. 3 (June 1971), 290–301.

RADER, T., "Normally, Factor Inputs Are Never Gross Substitutes," *Journal of Political Economy*, Vol. 75, No. 1 (February 1967), 39–40.

RAIMON, R. L., "Interstate Migration and Wage Theory," *Review of Economic Studies*, Vol. 44 (November 1962).

RAIMON, R. L. and STOIKOV, V., "The Effect of Blue-Collar Unionism on White-Collar Earnings," *Industrial and Labor Relations Review*, Vol. 22, No. 3 (April 1969), 358–374.

REDER, M. W., "The Theory of Occupational Wage Differentials," *American Economic Review*, Vol. 44, No. 5 (December 1955), 833–852.

REDER, M. W., "Unions and Wages: The Problem of Measurement," *Journal of Political Economy*, Vol. 73 (April 1965), 188–196.

REDER, M. W., "Wage Structure and Structural Unemployment," *Review of Economic Studies*, Vol. 31 (October 1964), 309–322.

REES, ALBERT, "Effect of Unions on Resource Allocation," *Journal of Law and Economics* (October 1963), 67–78.

REES, ALBERT, "Wage Determination in the Basic Steel Industry," *American Economic Review*, Vol. 40, No. 3 (June 1951), 389–404.

RICE, R. G., "Skill Earnings and the Growth of Wage Supplements," *American Economic Review*, Vol. 56, No. 2 (May 1966), 583–592.

ROSS, A. M. and GOLDNER, W., "Forces Affecting the Interindustry Wage Structure," *Quarterly Journal of Economics*, Vol. 64, No. 2 (May 1950).

ROTTENBERG, SIMON, "On Choice in Labor Markets," *Industrial and Labor Relations Review*, Vol. 9 (January 1956), 183–199.

ROWAN, RICHARD, "Negro Employment in Basic Steel," *Industrial and Labor Relations Review*, Vol. 23, No. 1 (October 1969), 29–39.

SABEN, SAMUEL, "Geographic Mobility and Employment Status, March 1962–March 1963," *Monthly Labor Review*, Vol. 87, No. 8 (August 1964), 873–881.

SAMUELSON, P. A. and SOLOW, R. M., "Analytical Aspects of Anti-Inflation Policy," *American Economic Review*, Vol. 50, No. 2 (May 1960).

SAVING, T. R., "Note on Factor Demand Elasticity," *Econometrica*, Vol. 31, No. 3 (July 1963), 556.

SCHULTZ, T. W., "Reflections on Investment in Man," *Journal of Political Economy*, Vol. 70, No. 5 (Supplement, October 1962), 1–8.

SCHULTZ, T. W., "Investment in Human Capital," *American Economic Review*, Vol. 49, No. 1 (March 1961).

SCOTT, L. C., "The Economic Effectiveness of On-the-Job-Training: The Experience of the Bureau of Indian Affairs in Oklahoma," *Industrial and Labor Relations Review*, Vol. 23, No. 2 (January 1970), 220–236.

SEVERN, A. K., "Upward Labor Mobility: Opportunity or Incentive," *Quarterly Journal of Economics*, Vol. 82 (February 1968), 143–151.

SHORROCKS, A. F., "Measuring the Imaginary: The Employment Effect of Imported Steel," *Industrial and Labor Relations Review*, Vol. 24, No. 2 (January 1971), 203–215.

SIEBERT, C. B. and ZAIDI, M. A., "The Short-run Wage-Price Mechanism in U.S. Manufacturing," *Western Economic Journal*, Vol. 9, No. 3 (September 1971), 278–287.

SIMLER, N. J., "Long-Term Unemployment, the Structural Hypothesis, and Public Policy," *American Economic Review*, Vol. 54, No. 6 (December 1964), 985–1001.

SIMLER, N. J., "Unionism and Labor's Share in Manufacturing Industries," *Review of Economic Studies*, Vol. 43, No. 3 (August 1961).

SIMLER, N. J. and TELLA, A., "Labor Reserves and the Phillips Curve," *Review of Economic Studies*, Vol. 50 (February 1968), 32–49.

SIMON, J. L. and GARDNER, D. M., "World Food Needs and 'New Proteins'," *Economic Development and Cultural Change*, Vol. 17, No. 4 (July 1969).

SJAASTAD, L. A., "The Costs and Returns of Human Migration," *Journal of Political Economy*, Vol. 70, No. 5 (Supplement, October 1962), 80–93.

SOLIE, R. J., "Employment Effects of Retraining the Unemployed," *Industrial and Labor Relations Review*, Vol. 21, No. 2 (January 1968), 21–25.

SOLOW, R. M., "A Policy for Full Employment," *Industrial Relations* (October 1963).

SRAFFA, PIERO, "The Laws of Return under Competitive Condition," *The Economic Journal*, Vol. 36 (1926), 535–550.

STEWART, C. T., "Wage Structure in an Expanding Labor Market: The Electronics Industry in San Jose," *Industrial and Labor Relations Review*, Vol. 21, No. 1 (October 1967), 73–91.

STIGLER, G. J., "Economics of Information," *Journal of Political Economy*, Vol. 69, No. 3 (June 1961), 213–225.

STIGLER, G. J., "Information in the Labor Market," *Journal of Political Economy*, Vol. 70, No. 5 (Supplement, October 1962), 94–105.

STOIKOV, VLADIMIR and RAIMON, R. L., "Determinants of Differences in the Quit Rate Among Industries," *American Economic Review*, Vol. 58, No. 5 (December 1968), 1284–1298.

TINBERGEN, JAN and CORREA, HECTOR, "Quantitative Adaptation of Education to Accelerated Growth," *Kyklos*, Vol. 15 (1962).

TAYLOR, C. E. and HALL, M. F., "Health, Population, and Economic Development," *Science*, Vol. 157 (August 1967), 653.

TAYLOR, DAVID, "Discrimination and Occupational Wage Differentials in Markets for Unskilled Labor," *Industrial and Labor Relations Review*, Vol. 21, No. 3 (April 1968), 375–390.

THROOP, A. W., "The Union-Nonunion Wage Differential and Cost-Push Inflation," *American Economic Review*, Vol. 58, No. 1 (March 1968), 79–99.

THUROW, LESTER and RAPPAPORT, C., "Law Enforcement and Cost-Benefit Analysis," *Public Finance/Financee Publiques*, Vol. 24, No. 1 (1969).

ULMAN, LLOYD, "Labor Mobility and the Industrial Wage Structure in the Postwar United States," *Quarterly Journal of Economics*, Vol. 79 (February 1965), 73–97.

VANDERKAMP, JOHN, "Wage and Price Determination: An Empirical Model for Canada," *Economica* (May 1966).

WEISBROD, B. A. and KARPOFF, P., "Monetary Returns to College Education, Student Ability and College Quality," *Review of Economic Studies*, Vol. 50, No. 4 (November 1968), 491–510.

WEISS, W., "Concentration and Labor Earnings," *American Economic Review*, Vol. 56, No. 1 (March 1966), 96–117.

WELCH, FINIS, "Labor Market Discrimination: An Interpretation of Income Differences in the Rural South," *Journal of Political Economy*, Vol. 75, No. 3 (June 1967), 222–242.

WETZEL, J. R., "Long Hours and Premium Pay," *Monthly Labor Review*, Vol. 88, No. 9 (September 1965).

WETZEL, J. R., "Overtime Hours and Premium Pay, May 1965," *Monthly Labor Review*, Vol. 89, No. 9 (September 1966), 973–977.

WILENSKY, H. L., "The Uneven Distribution of Leisure: The Impact of the Economic Growth of 'Free-Time,' " *Social Problems* (January 1961).

WILSON, GEORGE, "The Relationship Between Output and Employment," *Review of Economic Studies*, Vol. 42 (February 1960), 37–43.

WONNACOTT, R. J., "Wage Levels and Employment Structure in United States Regions: A Free Trade Precedent," *Journal of Political Economy*, Vol. 72 (August 1964), 414–419.

YOTOPOULOS, P. A., "The Wage-Productivity Theory of Under-Employment: A Refinement," *Review of Economic Studies*, Vol. 32 (January 1965), 59–65.

ZAIDI, M. A., "Structural Unemployment, Labor Market Efficiency, and the Intrafactor Allocation Mechanism in the United States and Canada," *Southern Economic Journal*, Vol. 35, No. 3 (January 1969).

Index